LORD DERBY

'KING OF LANCASHIRE'

BOOKS BY

RANDOLPH S. CHURCHILL

EDITED COLLECTIONS OF
SIR WINSTON CHURCHILL'S
SPEECHES

Arms and the Covenant

Into Battle

The Sinews of Peace

The Story of the Coronation

They Serve the Queen

Fifteen Famous English Homes

Churchill, His Life in Photographs

What I Said About the Press

The Rise and Fall of Sir Anthony Eden

Lord Derby: 'King of Lancashire'

Edward George Villiers Stanley

17th Earl of Derby

RANDOLPH S. CHURCHILL

LORD DERBY

'KING OF LANCASHIRE'

The Official Life of

Edward, Seventeenth Earl of Derby

1865 – 1948

HEINEMANN

LONDON MELBOURNE TORONTO

William Heinemann Ltd
LONDON MELBOURNE TORONTO
CAPE TOWN AUCKLAND
THE HAGUE

First published 1959

Printed in Great Britain by
Billing and Sons Limited
Guildford and London

Contents

1 Ancestry and Youth 1

2 Parliament and the Turf 37

3 The South African War 56

4 Financial Secretary to the War Office and Postmaster-General 69

5 The Inheritance 92

6 The Parliament Act 115

7 Lord Mayor of Liverpool 129

8 Tariff Reform and Food Taxes 146

9 The Derby Plan 184

10 Under-Secretary of State for War 209

11 The Fall of Mr Asquith 228

12 Secretary of State for War 242

13 Passchendaele 267

14 The Dismissal of Sir William Robertson 295

15 Derby Leaves the War Office 335

16 The Paris Embassy 353

17	Back to Lancashire	383
18	The Irish Settlement	402
19	Chanak	425
20	The Fall of the Coalition	438
21	The General Election of October 1922	459
22	Back at the War Office	483
23	The Advent of Mr. Baldwin	500
24	Mr. Baldwin's Tariff Election	522
25	Mr. Baldwin Retains the Leadership	542
26	King of Lancashire	567
27	Last Years	607
	Index	619

Illustrations

Edward George Villiers Stanley, 17th Earl of Derby *Frontispiece*

Letter from Queen Victoria *page* 13

Map of the Derby estates *page* 97

Lord Derby in fancy dress (*Topley of Ottawa*) *facing page* 30

Prince George and Lady Alice (*Lafayette*) 30

Derby House (*National Buildings Record*) 98

Crag Hall (*Airviews Ltd*) 98

Knowsley as it was (*Acropolis Ltd*) 103

Knowsley to-day (*Stewart Bale Ltd*) 103

A royal visit to Lancashire 107

King Edward VII, Queen Alexandra and the Stanley family 108

Lord Derby in 1912 (*Radio Times Hulton Picture Library*) 162

Lord Derby with his children 162

Lord Derby with King George V 242

On the platform with Mr. Lloyd George (*P.A.—Reuter Photos Ltd*) 242

At 10 Downing Street with Mr. Lloyd George 388

With Mr. Bonar Law in 1922
(*Radio Times Hulton Picture Library*) *facing page* 450

The political crisis of November 1923
(*Radio Times Hulton Picture Library*) 450

Leading in Sansovino (*Central Press Photos Ltd*) 570

Hyperion (*The British Racehorse*) 570

A group at Ascot (*Mirrorpic*) 578

Lord Derby in 1939 (*Radio Times Hulton Picture Library*) 607

Acknowledgements

THE author wishes first to acknowledge his indebtedness to Her Majesty the Queen who graciously gave permission for him to have access to the Royal Archives at Windsor. For guidance in the selection and use of this material the author is indebted to Sir Michael Adeane, Her Majesty's Private Secretary and Keeper of the Royal Archives, and to Sir Owen Morshead, until recently Librarian at Windsor Castle.

The great bulk of the material on which this book is based was made available by Lord Derby, to whom the author's thanks are due. When no source is given for information the reader should assume that it has been extracted from the Derby Papers.

Much valuable material was generously supplied by Lord Beaverbrook from his own records and also from the Lloyd George and the Bonar Law Papers.

The numerous friends who have read the book in whole or in part and to whom it is right to extend a special word of thanks are:

Mr. Robert Blake
Sir Malcolm Bullock, Bt.
Sir Herbert Creedy
The late Mr. Kenneth Lyon
Sir Harold Nicolson
Mr. Richard Stanley, M.P.

None of the above gentlemen is, however, in any way responsible for any of the statements of fact or opinion recorded in this book.

The author also desires to express his indebtedness to the following who in the five years of the book's preparation have successively assisted him in assembling and studying the material:

Mr. Alan Brien
Mr. Maurice Shock
Mr. Ivan Yates
Mr. Leonard Peach
Mr. Milo Cripps
Mr. Michael Molian.

A very special debt is due to the secretaries who have performed the laborious task of shorthand and typing required:

Miss Mary Lennon
Mrs. B. G. Verran
Miss Ruth George (now Mrs. John Keeble).

The following have kindly given permission to reproduce copyright material: The Controller of H.M. Stationery Office, Odhams Press Ltd. (*The Aftermath* by Sir Winston S. Churchill, K.G., O.M.), Sir Maurice Bonham Carter, K.C.B., K.C.V.O. (*Letters from Lord Asquith to a Friend*), Lt.-Col. G. I. Malcolm of Poltalloch (*Peace Conference Paris* 1918 by Sir Ian Malcolm, K.C.M.G.), Messrs. Cotterill & Cromb (*Sir James Sexton, Agitator* by James Sexton), Duff Cooper's literary executor (*Haig* and *Old Men Forget*), Beaverbrook Newspapers Ltd. (*War Memoirs* by David Lloyd George), Messrs. Ivor Nicholson & Watson Ltd. (*Lord Riddell's War Diary* and *War Memoirs* by David Lloyd George), *The Times* Publishing Company (*History of The Times*), Messrs. Eyre & Spottiswoode Ltd. (*The Private Papers of Sir Douglas Haig* and *The Unknown Prime Minister*, both by Robert Blake), Messrs. Cassell & Co. Ltd. (*Soldiers and Statesmen 1914–1918* by Sir William Robertson), Messrs. Macmillan & Co. Ltd. (*Life of Lord Kitchener* by Sir George Arthur), Messrs. Hamish Hamilton Ltd. (an essay by Evelyn Waugh from *Noblesse Oblige*, edited by Nancy Mitford), Messrs. Hutchinson & Co. Ltd. (*My Political Life* by Leopold Amery), Mrs. George Bambridge and Messrs. Methuen & Co. Ltd. ("The Islander" and "Gehazi" by Rudyard Kipling), Messrs. Rupert Hart-Davis Ltd. (*A Blessed Girl* by Lady Emily Lutyens), *The Liverpool Review*, Messrs. Longmans, Green & Co. Ltd. (*The Annual Register*), the *Daily Express*, the *Daily Herald*.

Preface

THE late Lord Derby seems to have written on an average throughout his adult life about forty letters a day. He daily received an equal number. Like most of his generation he attached great importance to his correspondence, and when he was called each morning at eight o'clock he avidly devoured his post-bag. If by any chance the post was late, he would be much perturbed. He usually took his breakfast in the dining-room at nine o'clock, and for an hour between 9.30 and 10.30 he would dictate letters to his secretary, Mr. Harrap. Then, if he were at Knowsley, he would be apt to drive out and keep appointments in the neighbourhood. At Derby House in London he would be occupied until noon with a series of callers; then before luncheon he would read and sign his letters.

Forty letters a day, 6 days a week, 52 weeks in the year makes 12,480. This multiplied by sixty—the years of his adult life—makes 748,800. Double the number to allow for the letters received, and we have a gross figure of 1,497,600.

Lord Derby was far from a pithy writer. Indeed he inclined to the diffuse. Many of his correspondents were even more long-winded than he was. Everything he received and everything he dictated to the admirable Mr. Harrap was kept and filed. The biographer's task of winnowing the grain from the chaff has been laborious; but the resultant harvest is substantial.

With the exception of the years 1900–1908, for which period the papers are lost, there exists—if it is not churlish for a biographer to say so—a vast excess of material. In reading this stupendous mass of documents, I early had to make the important decision whether to confine my story to matters in which Lord Derby was personally and actively concerned, or whether I should take advantage of the opportunity I had to record facts and comments on other people and other transactions which cast a new light on matters of general interest. After much thought I decided that the latter was the proper course. No doubt other people in future will have access to the Derby papers, but it is unlikely that anyone who was not writing about Lord Derby himself would be prepared to wade through this Sargasso Sea of correspondence.

I therefore thought it right, at the risk of swelling the book to a disproportionate bulk, to preserve for posterity nearly everything which I thought would be of more than transient value, even when the subject of my book was only indirectly involved as the confidant of famous people and the spectator of crucial events.

R. S. C.

Stour, East Bergholt,
Suffolk.
1 *October* 1959.

To

JOHN

Eighteenth Earl of Derby

this book about his grandfather

I

Ancestry and Youth

EDWARD GEORGE VILLIERS STANLEY, who was to become the seventeenth Earl of Derby in 1908, was born at Derby House, 23 St. James's Square, on 4 April 1865. His father, the Hon. Frederick Arthur Stanley, was the second son of Edward Geoffrey Stanley, fourteenth Earl of Derby, who was three times Prime Minister. His mother was Lady Constance Villiers, the eldest daughter of the Liberal politician George William Frederick Villiers, fourth Earl of Clarendon. At the time of his birth there seemed little prospect of his inheriting the family estates and titles. His father's elder brother was at that time unmarried; but he was only thirty-eight. In 1870, however, when young Edward Stanley was still a child of five, his uncle married Mary Catherine, daughter of the fifth Earl De La Warr and widow of James, second Marquess of Salisbury. She had married Lord Salisbury in 1847 when she was twenty-two and he was fifty-six. She had borne five children to him, but her second marriage, at the advanced age of forty-five, to the fifteenth Earl of Derby, as he had become the year before, gave little hope of issue; and plainly improved the worldly prospects of one who had been born the eldest son of a younger son.

Though young Edward's father now became, at the age of twenty-eight, his brother's heir presumptive he was far from being possessed of a large income: certainly not one commensurate with the size to which his family was to grow. Edward's birth was followed by that of seven more boys and two daughters. His father did not succeed as sixteenth Earl until April 1893, when he was fifty-two. Edward was then twenty-eight, had been married for four years and was himself the father of a child.

Edward's early years were therefore spent in circumstances which, though comfortable, were far removed from those which are the usual lot of those ultimately destined to inherit vast possessions. And when his time came to go to a public school, it was not to Eton, the family school for four generations, to which he and his brothers were sent but to the less expensive and less fashionable Wellington.

Edward's political heritage, however, was unrivalled, for no English family can show a longer record of public activity and public service than the Stanleys. None has exercised political power and influence for so many centuries. The great house of Cecil was still unknown when in 1485 Thomas, second Lord Stanley, Sovereign Lord of the Isle of Man, deserting Richard III in the middle of the Battle of Bosworth, decisively turned the tide of battle and set the crown upon the head of his stepson, Henry Tudor. The Stanleys had been rich and powerful for a hundred years before Bosworth, while the family can trace its origins to the first century after the Conquest.

The surname of the family derives from Stanley in Leek, Staffordshire. Round indicated in his *Studies of Peerage, Law and Family History* that the descent of the Stanley landed holdings reveals that the Earls of Derby were certainly sprung from the male line of Adam de Stanley, who was living in the time of Stephen (1135–54) and Henry II (1154–89). The name of Liulf de Audley, Adam's probable brother, would seem to indicate that the family was of native English descent, though no other evidence exists to prove this.

Even so, a gap exists in the pedigree of the family. The line can be traced to the son of Adam de Stanley, William, who received the grant of the area of Stanley from his kinsman Adam de Audley *circa* 1170–90. It then disappears for a hundred years until its reappearance in the person of Walter de Stanley, who held a free tenement in that area. There is still extant a charter of Henry de Audley dated 1223 which numbers among its witnesses a certain William 'de Stant', which *The Complete Peerage* accepts as an abbreviation of Stanley. This William, found in association with a member of the Audley family with whom the early Stanleys were intimately connected by both family relationship and tenurial holdings, is accepted by the College of Arms as providing the missing link in a possible line of descent connecting Adam and William with the later Walter de Stanley of 1270. The evidence for this is the 1223 charter and a manuscript pedigree of the early seventeenth century which indicated such a connection, though by descent lines only. The editor of *The Complete Peerage*, however, on the grounds of lack of documentary evidence, does not accept this and prefers to leave the precise descent as uncertain.

The family remains of local importance, with lands in Staffordshire and Cheshire, until it emerges on the national scene under John de Stanley in the reign of Richard II. This de Stanley, noted for his courage in personal combat, was knighted by King Edward III.

He it was who married the heiress, Isabel of Lathom, who brought great Lancashire estates into the family. Sir John Stanley was appointed Lord Deputy of Ireland by Richard II, but when Henry Duke of Lancaster revolted against King Richard, Stanley adhered to the Duke. Lancaster ascended the throne as Henry IV and reappointed Stanley Lord Deputy of Ireland. When Henry Percy, Earl of Northumberland, was attainted in 1406, Stanley was created Lord of the Isle of Man 'to be holden of the said King, his heirs, and successors, by homage, and service of two falcons, payable on the days of their coronation'.

Powerful and well-established as the Stanleys already were, their aggrandisement after Bosworth raised them far higher. Thomas second Lord Stanley was created Earl of Derby and was granted all the estates in the north forfeited by the Yorkists who had adhered to Richard III. Just as the Dukes of Devonshire have never owned any land in that county or the Dukes of Fife and the Marquesses of Exeter in the counties from which their titles derive, so the Earls of Derby have never owned any in Derbyshire. The title came from the hundred of West Derby in the county of Lancaster. In addition, seventy other distinct estates, belonging amongst others to Viscount Lovell, Sir Thomas Pilkington, Robert Hilton, Sir Thomas Broughton and James Harrington, were ceded to him. His brother, Sir

William Stanley, was also well rewarded and was appointed Lord Chamberlain of the King's Household. Ten years after Bosworth he was executed on a charge of conspiring to place Perkin Warbeck on the throne. Derby was fortunate that Tudor vengeance on him was limited to his being compelled to receive the King at Lathom within four months of his brother's execution. Kennitt's MSS. record a family tradition that Derby took the King on to the roof at Lathom to view the countryside:

> The Earl's fool was in company, who, observing the King draw near to the edge of the leads, not guarded with bannisters, stepped up to the Earl, and pointing down the precipice, said, 'Tom, remember Will'. The King understood the meaning, and made all haste down the stairs, and out of the house, and the fool long after seemed mightily concerned that his lord had not courage to take that opportunity of revenging himself for the death of his brother.

In succeeding generations the Stanleys were to be distinguished for their military prowess. It was Edward Stanley, a younger son of the first Earl, who commanded the English left wing at Flodden in 1513. His prompt and courageous leadership saved the day. He was awarded the Garter and raised to the peerage as Baron Monteagle. The creation only survived a few generations, but he is immortalised in the lines of Sir Walter Scott's 'Marmion':

> Charge, Chester, charge!
> On, Stanley, on!

Edward, third Earl of Derby, was the great-grandson of the first Earl. He succeeded in 1521, and lived in a style second only to that of the King. Camden, in his *Annals*, says: 'with Edward, Earl of Derby's death, the glory of hospitality seemed to fall asleep.' Howard Evans, in *Our Old Nobility*, writes:

> His household expenses are said to have amounted to £4,000 per annum. His political career was, however, most inglorious; under Edward VI he acted as a Commissioner for the advancement of the Reformation; under Mary he delivered Protestants to be burnt at the stake; under Elizabeth he hunted Catholics to the death. Thus he contrived to keep all he had and to acquire still more.

The editor of *The Complete Peerage* sourly remarks on this: 'The Stanley motto "Sans Changer" was as inappropriate to him as to his ancestor, the first Earl of Derby.'

The family continued to play a leading part in the life of the country. James, seventh Earl of Derby, who was beheaded at Bolton after being court-martialled by the Parliamentary Army after the battle of Worcester in 1651, was the most remarkable holder of the title since the first Earl. It was his wife, Charlotte de la Tremoille, daughter of the Duc de la Tremoille, who maintained the famous siege of Lathom House. James, Earl of Derby, was the staunchest of all the Royalists and he and his family suffered grievously for their devotion.

The eighth Earl, son of the seventh Earl, carried the third sword at the coronation of Charles II in 1661. Like so many cavaliers whose families had espoused the Royalist cause, he was disappointed that the King could not make a full restoration of all his properties. Henceforward for several generations the Stanleys remained quiescent in the North. The ninth Earl who died in 1702 was so mortified at the extent to which the family had come down in the world that in the words of a nineteenth century writer:

> Notwithstanding, however, his natural endowments and varied accomplishments, he was greatly opposed to taking any active part in the great affairs of the State, which, perhaps, may be attributed mainly to a consideration of the hard and unmerited sufferings of his grandfather, and the ingratitude experienced by his heroic grandmother and father, the remembrance of which, as Seacombe, his household steward, informs us, induced his lordship to prefer a country retirement, as he frequently declared upon many occasions, before any honour or preferments at Court; nor need there be any surprise at this choice on the part of the Earl, as the sad experience of his family had produced anything but agreeable results to their representative, who found the princely estates of his noble ancestors so disposed of, and allowed to be so disposed of by the reigning dynasty on whose behalf they had been sacrificed, that he was in possession of no estate in Lancashire, Cheshire, Westmorland, Cumberland, Warwickshire, York or Wales from which he could not see another of equal value lost by his grandfather for his loyalty to the Crown.

The family were, however, far from being paupers. The tenth Earl, between the years 1722 and 1732, engaged in much building at Knowsley, his principal seat. Now that the present Lord Derby has pulled down nearly all the ugly Victorian and Edwardian additions, the house is very much as it was left by him. The tenth Earl's sense of Royal ingratitude and injustice was, however, so lively that, eighty years after the execution of his ancestor, he caused to be inscribed above the colonnade with which he adorned the new south front, the words:

> James, Earl of Derby, Lord of Man and the Isles, grandson of James, Earl of Derby and Charlotte daughter of Claude, Duke de la Tremoille, whose husband, James, was beheaded at Bolton, XV October, MDCLI, for strenuously adhering to Charles II who refused a bill past [sic] unanimously by both Houses of Parliament for restoring to the family the estate lost by his loyalty to him, MDCCXXXII.

The seventh Lord Derby's character, courage and tragic end won for him the title 'The Great Lord Derby'. None of his descendants or successors challenged him in this appellation until the nineteenth century, when Edward Geoffrey, fourteenth Earl, embarked on a Parliamentary career of exceptional brilliance which led to him being three times Prime Minister. He could not boast the blood of the seventh Earl in his veins since the tenth Earl had died without issue in 1736. Most of the estates as well as the Lordship of the Isle of Man devolved on the heir-general, James, second Duke of Atholl, who was the grandson and heir of Amelia, Marchioness of Atholl, the only child whose issue then remained of the seventh Earl of Derby. The Earldom of Derby devolved upon a sixth cousin, Sir Edward Stanley, fifth Baronet of Bickerstaffe, who traced his descent directly from Sir James Stanley of Croxall, younger brother of the second Earl. Edward Geoffrey, fourteenth Earl of Derby, who was born in 1799, was the great-great-grandson of the eleventh Earl.

When, in 1822, he was returned to the House of Commons at the age of twenty-two for the rotten borough of Stockbridge, the family talent for politics had been dormant for one hundred and seventy years. The ingratitude of the Stuarts had led the Stanleys to abandon their instinctive Toryism. The ninth Earl had borne the second sword at the Coronation of James II in 1685. He had married in 1673 Elizabeth, sister of James, second Duke of Ormonde. Her mother was a daughter of the Countess of Ossory, who was the daughter of Henry de Nassau, Lord of Auverquerque in Holland. His Dutch connections and the family distaste for the Stuarts combined to make him one of the first of the English nobles to welcome the arrival of Dutch William. The eleventh, twelfth and thirteenth Earls, before they succeeded to the peerage, all sat in the House of Commons as Whigs and it was as a Whig that the future fourteenth Earl was returned to Parliament in 1822.

He was not a man with an exceptionally strong character but had a delightful and varied personality. Educated at Eton and Oxford, he followed the fashion of many Christ Church men of that period by not putting the examiners to the trouble of examining him for a degree. He won, however, the Chancellor's prize for Latin verse in 1819 with a poem on Syracuse. By contrast, according to Hiscock's *Christ Church Miscellany*, he took part in 1817 in a riotous party which culminated in the destruction of the statue of Mercury in Tom Quad, as a result of which the fountain in Oxford's most splendid quadrangle lacked a statue for more than a hundred years.

In later life he found time between racing and politics to translate Homer's *Iliad* into English blank verse. He had already been Prime Minister when he published this work in 1864, and this circumstance no doubt encouraged the public to buy five editions of it within the first seven months of its publication. The sixth edition was published in 1867.[1] His wide reading and facility for languages also enabled him to write and publish without ridicule, translations from Latin, French, German and Italian authors.

After serving first as Irish Secretary and later as Colonial Secretary

[1] In reply to an enquiry as to the view held today on Derby's Homer, the late Professor Gilbert Murray, to whom the author is indebted, wrote as follows:

'I think you can safely say that Lord Derby's translation of Homer was the most successful at the time when Pope had gone out of fashion and the prose translation of Andrew Lang and Leaf, and the verse of William Morris had not yet come in.'

in Lord Grey's administration from 1830 to 1834, he resigned, and after a time in the political wilderness became Colonial Secretary once more in Sir Robert Peel's Conservative administration in 1841. He broke with Peel on the issue of protection in 1845 and became the nominal leader of the Protectionist Tories in association with Mr. Disraeli and Lord George Bentinck. He served as Prime Minister three times but always for brief periods—for ten months in 1852, for eighteen months in 1858–9 and for nearly two years in 1866–8, when he resigned because of bad health. He died the following year. All his administrations suffered from the fact that he never had a clear majority in the House of Commons. His brilliant oratorical powers, combined with an attitude towards politics which was both rash and dilettante, earned him the title of 'The Rupert of Debate'.

Gladstone is quoted by his biographer, John Morley, as recording a conversation he had in 1838 with Samuel Rogers:

> He said, when Stanley came out in public life, and at the age of thirty, he was by far the cleverest young man of the day; and at sixty he would be the same, still by far the cleverest young man of the day.

Derby was really happier on the Turf than in the House of Commons, and though he never won the Derby his horses in his lifetime won stakes worth nearly £100,000 in days when prizes for racing were far smaller than they are today. In his diary of 10 April 1851, Greville has preserved us this sketch:

> It is worth while to be at Newmarket to see Stanley. A few weeks ago he was on the point of being Prime Minister, which only depended on himself. Then, he stood up in the House of Lords and delivered an oration full of gravity and dignity such as became the man who had just undertaken to form an Administration. . . . If any of his vociferous disciples and admirers, if some grave members of either House of Parliament or any distinguished foreigner who knew nothing of Lord Stanley but what he saw, heard or read of him could have suddenly found himself in the betting room at Newmarket on Tuesday evening and seen Stanley there, I think they would have been in a pretty state of astonishment. There he was in the midst of a crowd of blacklegs betting men and loose characters of every description in uproarious spirits, chaffing, rowing and shouting with laughter and

joking. His amusement was to lay Lord Glasgow a wager that he did not sneeze in a given time, for which purpose he (Lord G.) took pinch after pinch of snuff while Stanley jeered at him and quizzed him with such noise that he drew the whole mob around him to partake of the coarse merriment he excited. It really was a sight and a wonder to see any man playing such different parts so naturally and obey all his impulses in such a way utterly regardless of appearances and not caring what anybody might think of the minister and statesman as long as he could have his fun.

The great Lord Derby was succeeded by his eldest son, Edward Henry, fifteenth Earl of Derby, the uncle of the subject of this biography. In his youth the fifteenth Earl had been expelled from Eton, supposedly for kleptomania, and this fact, as we shall see, was later to have an important effect upon the upbringing of his nephew. After leaving Eton he completed his education at Rugby and Cambridge. At the age of twenty-eight, such were his abilities and the value of his family connections that Lord Palmerston invited him to join his Cabinet in 1855.

Among the Derby papers at Knowsley there is a bundle marked 'Papers of possible use for a biography of Lord Derby', and in it there is an ordinary exercise book in which, partly in pencil and partly in ink, he left a record in the third person of his official life. His account of these early days in politics is as follows:

Unpublished memorandum of Edward Henry, fifteenth Earl of Derby

. . . It was at this time that he received from Lord Palmerston the offer of a seat in the Cabinet to succeed Sir W. Molesworth as Secretary of State for the Colonies. Lord Stanley saw at once that he could not accept this offer without breaking family relations with his father. His own opinions and sympathies were in the main with the Liberal Party of that period and during the session of 1855 he had been on terms of friendship with Mr. Bright. Lord Stanley went at once to his father at Knowsley. Lord Derby did not seem to look upon the offer as a compliment and was perhaps rather vexed than pleased; treating the acceptance as quite impossible, and Lord Stanley wrote to Lord Palmerston declining. Lord Stanley was only twenty-eight. The offer was a flattering one; he would have been a member of a Cabinet with whose principles he in the main agreed, he felt disappointment whilst he did not wish to be on the other side of the house as against his father, but he would perhaps have felt less keenly had his father seemed to estimate what he had relinquished. . . .

The sacrifice of ambition and principle, which he made in the cause of filial piety, was not, however, to go unrewarded, for in his father's second administration in 1858 he served successively as Secretary of State for the Colonies, Secretary of the Board of Control, and Secretary of State for India. And in his father's third administration from July 1866 to February 1868 he served as Secretary of State for Foreign Affairs, an office which he was to hold again in 1878, when Mr. Disraeli succeeded Mr. Gladstone as Prime Minister.

He had long held Liberal rather than Tory views, as we have seen in the passage quoted above from his memorandum. He had had doubts about the propriety of joining his father's second administration, and in the same memorandum wrote: 'When Lord Derby formed his Government in 1858 it was uncertain for a few days if Lord Stanley could find himself sufficiently in unison with his father and his colleagues to take office. Sir W. Jolliffe, the Conservative Whip, said the public would expect it; that a large section in the country trusted Lord Stanley and would not be satisfied without it. Lord Stanley in the end accepted the office of Secretary of State for the Colonies.' If the fifteenth Earl's account can be credited, public opinion about political nepotism was very different in those days from what it is today.

In 1878 it seemed as if Britain might go to war with Russia to safeguard the position of Turkey. The Queen's patriotism became aroused, and in her collected letters there are innumerable protests to Mr. Disraeli about the weak attitude adopted by Lord Derby. He strove incessantly for a peaceful solution of the dispute, and after one abortive resignation, left the Government. Thereafter he joined the Liberals and for three years, from 1882 to 1885, served as Secretary of State for the Colonies in Mr. Gladstone's second administration. In 1886, however, he parted from Gladstone on the Home Rule issue and until 1891 led the newly formed Liberal Unionist Party in the House of Lords.

The fifteenth Lord Derby has probably been treated by history less well than he deserved. He was never happy in the Tory Party, and when he left it on the issue of sending the fleet to Gallipoli in 1878, and subsequently joined the Liberal Party, he was naturally an object of aversion not only to the Queen but to all those Tories who espoused Mr. Disraeli's conceptions of imperialism and foreign policy. His subsequent breach with Mr. Gladstone on the issue of Home Rule shows that he was a man of principle, but this did not commend him to the Liberals. He was far from achieving the wide and almost universal popularity which was later to be vouchsafed to his nephew, but his long and varied career in which he always 'kicked against the pricks' shows that he must have been a man of exceptional ability and one whose biography should one day be written. His liberal outlook and record, aided doubtless by the fact that his father had recently been Prime Minister, combined to prompt the Greeks, after the deposition of Otto I, to offer the Throne of Greece to Lord Stanley, as he then was. According to Lord Lytton's account in his life of his grandfather, Bulwer Lytton, Disraeli wrote to a friend at this time to say:

> The Greeks really want to make my friend Lord Stanley their King. This beats any novel, but he will not. Had I his youth, I would not hesitate, even with the Earldom of Derby in the distance. It is a dazzling adventure for the house of Stanley, but they are not an imaginative race, and I fancy they will prefer Knowsley to the Parthenon and Lancashire to the Attic Plains.

On his death few voices were raised in his praise, but a paper called *The Speaker*, on 29 April 1893, recorded:

> ... So he goes to the grave the victim of a great misconception on the part of all sections of his fellow-countrymen, and it is only those who knew him personally who can truly realise what it is that we have lost. Yet Liberals at all events ought not to forget that particular episode in his career which determined his ultimate fate. They at least should be able to realise that fact that in the Government of Lord Beaconsfield, when this country was being dragged by reckless and unscrupulous hands to the very verge of an unnecessary war which might have

left the British Empire in ruins, it was Lord Derby who, at the sacrifice of his own career, saved the nation from the doom which seemed to be impending over her.

The foregoing summary of the history of the Stanley family will have shown the political and social heritage to which the future seventeenth Earl was born. His grandfather was to become Prime Minister for the third time a few months later, in July 1866. Young Edward's uncle was also to join the Cabinet at the same time.

Though the Stanleys were out of office at the time of Edward's birth, the great Lord Derby happened to be staying at Windsor, and in the record book which the newly born child's mother, Lady Constance Stanley, kept for the benefit of her son there is preserved the following letter written on the day of his birth (it is reproduced in facsimile on page 13):

The Queen to Lord Derby

The Queen is most truly rejoiced to hear of dear Constance's safety and of the birth of Lord Derby's grandson—and she is pleased to think he should have heard of it here. She congratulates him on this happy event which she knows must give him and Lady Derby such pleasure and sincerely hopes that the Mother may go on as well as possible and Lord Derby derive much comfort and pleasure from his little grandson.

The Prince of Wales wrote and congratulated the father:

The Prince of Wales to Hon. Frederick Stanley

6 April 1865 — Marlborough House

My dear Stanley,

I only heard yesterday of the good news, and that you are now a father. Pray accept my most sincere congratulations on this happy event, and I trust that Lady Constance is going on as well as possible, and your little boy also. May I also ask you to congratulate Lord and Lady Derby on having a grandson.

I remain,

My dear Stanley,

Yours very sincerely,

Albert Edward

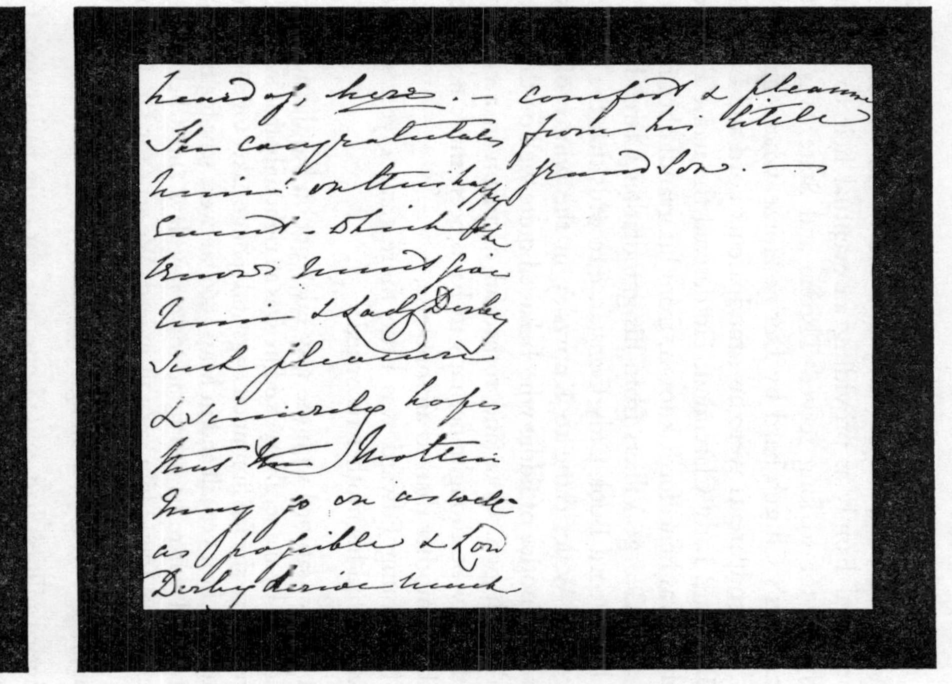

Windsor Castle.

April 4. 1865

The Queen is most truly rejoiced to hear of the Countess's safety & of the birth of Lord Derby's grand-son. — She is pleased to think he should have heard of, here. — She congratulates him on this happy event – which the Queen must give him & Lady Derby such pleasure & sincerely hopes that the Mother may go on as well as possible & Lord Derby derive much comfort & pleasure from his little grand son. —

The young man, whose entry into the world was so gratifying to the Royal Family as providing an eventual heir to the family which had for so long served Throne and State, was christened at St. James's Church hard by Derby House where he had been born. His godparents were his grandparents Lord and Lady Derby and Lord and Lady Clarendon. He derived the name Edward, by which he was henceforth known, from his grandfather Derby, and the names George Villiers from his grandfather Clarendon.[1]

In her Record Book Lady Constance records that the Prince and Princess of Wales came to Knowsley in the winter of 1865 and 'took great notice of Eddie who behaved quite well on the whole to them'. Such precocious and respectful decorum in a child of six months may be thought perhaps to have been more noticeable to the child's mother than to anyone else.

When young Edward was little more than a year old he fell gravely ill and his mother recorded:

> I was not satisfied with the way Eddy got on but the nurse he had, Anderson by name, always said he was all right only that he would not take milk so she fed him upon eggs and sponge cake. Of course in time that made him very ill and in May 1866 we were sent for from Strawberry Hill where he had gone for a few days and when we got to London we found him very ill indeed. We sent for Dr. Gream, Dr. Miller and Dr. Jenner. They gave us but little hope. However, thank God, he got well again though very slowly.

Edward's illness had caused concern not only to his own family but to the Queen.

The Queen to Lord Derby

Telegram 26 May 1866

I am truly rejoiced to hear of your little grandson's recovery.

Edward's father and mother, Captain Frederick and Lady Constance Stanley, as they were called at that time, continued to live at Derby House. Stanley had joined the Grenadier Guards in 1858. He resigned his commission and entered Parliament as the Member

[1] Villiers is the family name of the Earls of Clarendon.

for Preston in the year of Edward's birth. As a bachelor his grandfather had given him rooms at Derby House, and he lived there, while in London, for some time after he was married, and even after the birth of his eldest son. On his marriage in 1864 his grandfather had given him the choice of Witherslack, the family property in Westmorland, or Ballykisteen in Ireland. Stanley opted for Witherslack. This property of 1,600 acres lies in the wildest and most beautiful part of Westmorland. There was at that time only a very old farm-house on the property and it was decided to build a bigger house. This, however, was not done for some years, and during the early part of their marriage Stanley and his wife lived at the small house on the property later to be called Halecote. Meanwhile the present house at Witherslack was being built.

The young Stanleys soon acquired a house in Lowndes Square; but this proved too small for their growing family and sometime in 1872 they moved to a bigger house, 5 Portland Place. There the family were normally in residence from the end of January to the end of July, while the rest of the year was spent almost entirely at Witherslack.

Edward's birth in 1865 was to be followed at regular intervals by that of seven brothers and two sisters. They will crop up again in these pages, and for the convenience of the reader a brief account of their lives is given in an Appendix at the end of this chapter. Ten was a considerable number of children even by Victorian standards.

Lady Constance recorded on the birth of the twins: 'Eddy was much pleased with his twin brothers who were born on November 18 at The Grove. Eddy was delighted when he was told that he was the eldest of five, and not yet five years old!'

Young Edward does not seem to have shown as much respect for foreign Royalty as his mother would have us believe he had shown towards the Prince and Princess of Wales. She records that Edward was at Knowsley during the visit of the Queen of Holland in September 1867, when he was little over two years old. She writes. 'Eddy did not behave well to her and would say "Me don't like that nasty woman".' She added: 'He will call his grandfather "Derby".'

From the same record we learn that when he was three years old he was brought home one morning 'with a most awful cut on his arm; it bled so much we were frightened. Victor cut his eyelid open the same day and E. said "if Victor is not deaded I will give him all my toys".'

Lady Constance's sister, Lady Lathom, lived at nearby Lathom House. This property had come into the Stanley family in 1385 when John de Stanley[1] married Isabel de Lathom. It was acquired in 1725 by Sir Thomas Bootle of Melling, Chancellor to Frederick, Prince of Wales. The property was inherited by Bootle's niece, who married Richard Wilbraham-Bootle. Their son, in 1828, was created Baron Skelmersdale. His grandson, the second Baron Skelmersdale, was created Earl of Lathom in 1880. He had married in 1860 Lady Alice Villiers, younger sister of Lady Constance Stanley. Thus the ancient Stanley property which had been alienated for more than 130 years came once more through the marriages of Lord Clarendon's two daughters into close family association, and the Stanley children at Witherslack had cousins of the same age at Lathom. There was thus much coming and going at this time between Witherslack and Lathom, and also between both these houses and Knowsley.

In September 1872 Edward and all his brothers went with their governess Miss Hand on a short visit to the Isle of Man. While there they received the news of the birth of another brother.

In May 1874, shortly after Edward's birthday, he and his brother Victor were taken to the Foreign Office to see the dinner given in honour of the Emperor of Russia. Lady Constance wrote in Edward's book: '. . . you had a very good view of him and all the other royalties who were the Prince and Princess of Wales, the Duke and Duchess of Edinburgh, the Duke of Connaught, the Duke of Cambridge, the Grand Duke Vladimir. You also saw Mr. Disraeli, Mr. Gladstone, Lord Granville, Lord Salisbury.'

Another treat this summer was a ten day visit to Dieppe, his first to the Continent. A few days after his tenth birthday in 1875 Edward went to boarding school for the first time. The school selected, which all his brothers attended in succession, was Perceval House at Blackheath, just outside London. No records seem to

[1] Grandfather of the first Lord Stanley.

remain of his school days save that in his second term he had mumps. As usual the family went to Witherslack for the summer holidays. The new big house was nearly finished and this was the last summer they spent in the small house which it was now decided to call Halecote.

During the first ten years of their marriage Frederick and Constance were often separated for many months at a time. Frederick's parliamentary duties kept him much in London and Constance and the children were mostly at Witherslack or visiting the children's cousins at Lathom or their grandmother Clarendon at The Grove, near Watford in Hertfordshire. The young couple plainly pined at these separations and the few letters which survive show that both frequently felt lonely. Although Frederick seems to have enjoyed an income of some £7,000 a year at a time when surtax did not exist and income tax was as low as *2d.* in the £ (1875-7), his expenditure, enhanced by the large and growing family for which he was responsible, involved him in debts which caused his wife no little concern. We find Constance writing from Witherslack in 1873 about a bill owing in the neighbouring town of Kendal for £3 15*s.* 4*d.* She pays this on her husband's behalf 'as I do so fear you are getting a bad name in Kendal. I hope you won't be angry with me dearest'. A little later the same year she writes: 'Thanks so much for your dear letter of today and the financial talk which tells me as I see as well as you do (you make it quite clear) we have only got to live carefully and save when we can on unnecessary outgoings and in time outstanding bills will get paid . . .'

While Edward was having mumps at school his brother Arthur contracted scarlet fever at Witherslack. The three younger boys—Ferdinand, George and Algernon—were moved to London; but they developed it there. Meanwhile Constance, who had just borne her second daughter, Isobel, was ill with neuralgia at The Grove. The children were evidently in some danger and all these worries were aggravated by financial stress. On 17 October 1875, Constance wrote to Frederick:

> This is a dreadful day not hearing anything about all my darlings and I feel *so* low having been very bad with neuralgia. It is all over

now and when Baley comes to me I feel as if I should go mad. I am taking no end of port wine and quinine so I am in hopes it will go; it is the natural result of all we went through last week when of course every nerve was strained and the reaction must come. I thought of you so much my duck yesterday after we parted for I am sure your life is too terribly lonely and dull, but I feel we must only be so thankful that a worse misery was spared to us for how unhappy we were this time last week, and I feel things will brighten and we shall not be so long separated as we now think. Then as to expense darling I don't see how you can make out that this illness will cost £500. The doctors' bills can't be very heavy and even if you burnt everything in every room it would not amount to £100, so I hope and think you will find it is not so bad as it looks now. Oh! how nice it would be to have a real nice comfortable talk but as that can't be we must not long for it more than one can help. . . .

When he was thirteen Edward went to Wellington, as later did all his brothers save Victor who was destined for the Navy. He was enrolled in Kempthorne's House. The determining factor in sending Edward and his brothers to Wellington instead of to Eton, where all the Stanleys had gone for some generations, is not clear. Edward's father was to some extent financially dependent upon his elder brother, who had been expelled from Eton and had completed his public school education at Rugby. It may be that the latter had conceived some prejudice against Eton. If it was not to be Eton, Wellington was the natural choice. The fourteenth Lord Derby had been one of the founders of the College in 1856 and was its first Vice-President. On the death of the Prince Consort in 1862 he had been elected President. The fourteenth Earl was greatly interested in the welfare of this school which was intended to provide a good but economical education for the sons of Army officers. In 1865 he awarded a prize which is known as 'The Earl of Derby's Gift', and which was financed out of his profits from the publication of his translation of the *Iliad*. There is another prize at Wellington known as 'The Earl of Derby's French Prize', which was founded in 1871. It was probably established in memory of the fourteenth Earl, though this is uncertain.

Whatever the reasons which led to Edward and his brothers

going to Wellington, he seems for the most part to have been very happy there and all his life he maintained a close contact with the school. On his father's death in 1908 he succeeded him as Vice-President of the Governing Body and actively discharged the office until 1941.

In 1925 an opportunity arose for Wellington to acquire twenty two acres of grassland opposite the Wellington Hotel and just outside the College boundaries. This land had formerly been used as a polo field. He gave £1000 towards the purchase price and offered to advance the rest of the money free of interest until the balance could be collected. The land was duly bought and became the College's playing fields. It is now referred to as 'Derby Ground', or more usually just 'Derby'. A fine portrait of him by James Gunn hangs in the dining hall and worthily commemorates his long association with the school.

None of his school reports have come to light, but some account of his progress can be gleaned from the letters he wrote to his mother during his five years there:

Edward to his Mother

1878 Wellington College

MY DEAR MOTHER,

Thank you very much for your letter. I am awfully jolly here. I enclose a plan of my room. I find the work much harder in Greek and *French* than at Perceval House. I am higher than I expected to be. I am top in French and Arithmetic, 5th in Latin and 7th in Greek. There are 15 fellows in the class so I hope to get a remove. I have bought some pictures for my room at Crowthorne a village close to here. I have made friends with Locke, Seymour, Logan (in our House) and Watts. All are such jolly chaps. Cavins major is a jolly chap and is awful pals with Talbot but Cavins minor is rather a fool. I am very glad Arty did not suffer much. What a lucky dog. Vic is getting £2. He wrote and told me about it and about writing to implore you to let him have a gun. If you are writing to him will you please thank him for his letter and tell him I will write on Sunday as I have no other time and please note to address letters like this: Master Stanley, Revd. G. Kempthorne's. Old Kemp is a jolly chap. I have got hardly anything else to say except do please send me some stamps as I have not got any. I will write and ask you to come down (if you will) to see me. Charlie has been awfully jolly to me in every way. I have just had my bath. You are only allowed 12 minutes to have your bath dry yourself and come up to your room again. I hope Father is all right. The House got up a subscription the other night to buy papers. Every fellow went in. Here comes Kemp so goodbye with a lot of love to all at home.

I remain,
Your affecate,
EDDY

Edward to his Mother

1878 Wellington College

MY DEAREST MOTHER,

Thank you so much for your letter. I am only too delighted that Arty is coming up with me as it would have been awfully dull without anyone at all. Isn't it jolly, only a fortnight more to the end of term. We begin exams this week. I hope to do well as I know all my work very well. I think I have got one prize but I may get licked in the exams but I hardly think it is probable. I suppose Arty will be in London at 5 P.P.[1] on the 27th. We break up on that day but he only breaks up on the 28th but I suppose he won't lose any prizes by coming away a day sooner will he! Do you mind signing the piece of paper I enclose and send it back in your next letter? We are having beautiful weather here, warm and fine. What sort are you having? What a terrible explosion this must have been in Tottenham Court Road. Did you feel it at all at 5 P.P. or are you too far off? Will you let me know all about the trains etc. for the end of the term. I am longing for the end of the term. I think that I am homesick, for the first term everybody is. Here we are doing the same work over and over again. *Oh* I shall be *so* glad when the end comes. I think that my promotion is pretty certain as I shall have been in the first 5 for the last three weeks and have done much better since half-term. Please don't forget to send back that piece of paper. K. says I must have it. Has Father sold the yacht well? I hope he has. Has he got her for the rest of the season or not?

With very much love,
ever yr most affecate.
EDDY

[1] 5 Portland Place.

Edward to his Mother

1881

MY DEAREST MOTHER,

Thank you so much for your letter. About Latin I think that it is the best thing I can do to try and beat the difficulties and so as I will do my very best I think we can consider that settled, but about the leaving, it is all rot about the masters wanting me to pass from here. You say I shall be dull in London but it will be lovely [compared] to this place. You don't know what it is like in the winter. I hate it at this time of year. But I am getting rather sick of this place and if I began with a tutor I think it would give me quite a fresh start. Unless you or Father mind, I think far the best thing will be for me to leave at Easter. I had rather set my heart upon it as I can give most of my time to mathematics which is the thing I most want. I don't think that if I stay here I shall have the slightest chance of getting into Woolwich [Artillery School]. Almost all the fellows I have asked who are going to Woolwich are first going to a crammer. You see that mathematics count 4000 in the exam against 2000 for French, German and Latin, so it's long odds against me passing if I don't do a good exam in mathematics and I certainly don't think I should pass a good one from here. I am in the bottom Woolwich set and I am afraid I am nearly bottom of that. I hope you will decide for my leaving at Easter. I think I shall find plenty to do in London and I might go down on Saturday afternoons to Perceval House and play cricket there. I don't think they would mind. And then you know it is not I but Victor who is so miserable in London. I don't mind it half so much as he does. *Please* write soon and let me know what you have settled about my leaving. I am going to do my *very* best to learn Latin and I daresay I shall be able to learn quite enough to pass an exam. I asked Kempthorne if he had received Father's letter. He said he had and so I told him that you had told me that he was going to speak to me about leaving and all he said was that he would speak to me at another time but he has not said anything more about it so I don't think he cares much about it either way. With very much love.

Ever your most affec.

EDDY

(*Please* write soon)

Edward was not remarked upon for any athletic prowess at school and his academic achievements were equally undistinguished. The Rev. C. W. Trevelyan, M.C., who was an assistant master at Wellington for many years and who knew him well, has preserved the following recollection:

> Surprisingly enough, I have evidence that Derby *RAN*! When the present Talbot House came into use, Malim was ill, and he asked me to show Derby round the House on Speech Day. He had with him Major H. Milner, who held some position like Chief of his Household. They had been to Wellington together as boys, and were great friends. I knew Milner because he was A.D.C. to my General in the 55th Division. I took Derby and Milner into our Dining Hall and Common Room, and we held at that time the cup for the winner of the Big Kingsley and also an inter-House cup for which we competed annually with the Stanley (formerly Kempthorne's) Derby's old House. It all interested me, as I was able to establish as fact the fabulous record of Milner as a runner. Then Derby pointed to the inter-House cup, and said to Milner: 'Harry, I ran for that cup!' At that time he was enormous and puffing and blowing! and it was hard to picture him as a runner. I have no idea whether a picked team ran, or the whole house. Derby always spoke of himself as completely undistinguished at school.

The fact that Edward was a runner in his youth naturally surprised a later generation which was accustomed to his heavy girth and bulk. But in his youth he was of slender build and in the holidays at Witherslack his chief delight was his pack of beagles. In later life his sporting interests were largely confined to horse-racing. As a boy he had a small boat which he sailed on Lake Windermere. Edward and the other children led an ideal life at Witherslack, which even today is one of the most unspoiled parts of the county of Westmorland. All the family letters and records show that they were a happy family, and that the children were united in love and loyalty to their parents.

Edward's mother seems to have abandoned her record book in 1877. Later she handed it over to Edward, who kept it somewhat sparsely for a few years beginning in 1882. In February of that year he passed the Preliminary Examination for Sandhurst, and in May he was gazetted as a lieutenant in the militia in the 4th King's Royal Lancashire Regiment. At the end of 1884 he wrote:

Edward's Diary 1884

> So ends what was to me a very happy year. I was successful in my examination, I first began to go out to balls in London, and I went four times to Knowsley on each visit enjoying myself immensely. In fact there was not a single thing went wrong, except the deaths of Uncle Bob and Uncle Charles neither of whom I really knew. I only wish Vic had been home.

He added:

> This has been a great political year. The Reform Bill was carried in the H. of C. and thrown out by the H. of L. An autumn session was held and again the H. of C. passed the bill, and a compromise was made by which the Representation (New Seats) Bill was brought in and passed by the H. of C. and on this condition the H. of L. passed the Reform Bill.

He was only nineteen but his interest in politics had started to bud. At this time his uncle was Secretary of State for the Colonies in Mr. Gladstone's Government and his father, during Edward's school days, had been successively Financial Secretary to the War Office, Financial Secretary to the Treasury and from 1878 to 1880 Secretary of State for War. So, although he had embarked on a military career it was probably already clear to him that he would be likely through family associations and background to be drawn into the House of Commons himself. Edward at this time of his life was exceptionally thin and as a result had nearly failed the medical examination for the Army. In later life his younger brothers used to find much delight in chaffing him on this score.

In April 1885 Edward received his commission in the Grenadier Guards, a regiment with which his family had many connections. His father had served for seven years in the regiment, his great-uncle, Charles Stanley, who had rented Halecote when the new house at Witherslack was completed, had been a Lieutenant-

Colonel of the Grenadiers as was also his son, Charles Edward Stanley, Edward's first cousin once removed. Edward, like nearly all who have been members of that famous regiment, cherished the warmest sentiments for it throughout his life and the family association was to be continued by his eldest son, Edward, who served with the Grenadiers in the First World War and his grandson, John, the present holder of the title, who in the Second World War was awarded the Military Cross while fighting with the regiment on the beach-head at Anzio.

For the next few years his life was typical of a young subaltern in a Guards regiment. He was mostly stationed near London, and in the intervals between his military duties attended all the fashionable balls. He was also a keen play-goer and his journal for 1885 shows that in the month of April alone he went to the theatre nine times. He saw *The Mikado*, which he pronounced 'very good, pretty music, the best thing Sullivan and Gilbert have written'.

Later his battalion of the Grenadiers was posted to Ireland and he wrote to his mother an account of his arrival there:

Edward to his Mother

1886 Richmond Barracks, Dublin

My dearest Mother,

At last I have time to write you a longer letter. First let me ask you to send over my camp looking glass as soon as possible. We started from London on Tuesday and from the excitement it caused among the men and the crowds we might have been going on active service. We were all embarked on the *Assistance* by 3 o'clock but did not start till seven the next morning. You can have no idea of the discomfort we went through; we were packed like herrings in a barrel, three of us in a little cabin one above the other and so small that we had to get up and dress for dinner etc. one at a time. Wednesday was a lovely day, quite calm till about six o'clock when the wind began to get up and shifted round into a head wind. By the next morning it was very rough and about three o'clock in the afternoon I was fearfully ill and so continued for about 12 hours. Thursday night it was blowing a gale and we only made 10 knots in 8 hours. Everything that could be carried away was, and to add to the misery of the men (who were in holes not fit for dogs) we shipped three or four big seas so that on the troop deck there was at one time a couple of feet of water. They were wet through, blankets, clothing etc. all ruined and all this on account of the damned stinginess of the W.O., how we cursed them. Friday there was a long swell, but I was all right so did not mind it. We got in early on Saturday morning to find that the officials had not expected us till Monday on account of the roughness. Consequently the Scots Guards were still in our rooms, the men had no dinners, and we were all damned for imaginary faults by the various shirty officials. However here we are now comfortably settled in the most 'stinky' barracks in the United Kingdom. I went to see Princess E. on Tuesday and she asked me to come and dine which I did and very jolly she was. We are to have the state entry of the Lord-Lieutenant on Saturday. I hope it will go off all right but there are very great doubts. Please thank George for his letter, it is all right about the dogs. I ordered them to be sent away and Algy is the real possessor of them. Best love. Please don't forget the looking glass. My pony comes over next Monday.

Ever your very affec.,

EDDY

Edward only served for a few months in Ireland. While there he contracted typhoid fever and partly, no doubt, with the object of recovering from this illness, early in the new year he embarked on a voyage round the world. While on this voyage he wrote regular letters to his mother which he posted from convenient ports of call. He does not seem to have had any great adventures and his experiences were such as might have been encountered by any other young man at the time.

His route was Malta, Port Said, Suez, Colombo, Perth, Adelaide, Melbourne. In later life he was to find himself to an exceptional extent at ease with all sorts and conditions of his fellow men, and this voyage, no doubt, was a help in broadening his mind. At the outset he was naïvely surprised at the personalities of some of his fellow travellers, and we find him writing to his mother from Suez: 'Our new passengers are a terribly poor lot. You may judge the class they belong to, when I tell you that two of them are Sydney bookmakers.'

Edward broke his journey in Australia, where he spent a few weeks and was much attracted by the gay social and sporting life into which he was immediately plunged. He was soon to find on dry land confirmation of the hostile view he had already formed at sea of the Australian bookmakers; for we find him writing to his mother:

> Deerhurst has got into a row out here and has had to give up his A.D.C. and will have to go home. I won't go into details, but roughly he refused to pay a bookmaker, the latter struck him. D. then got him turned out of the betting club. Sutton (the bookmaker) summoned him for assault. D. issued a counter summons, and the result was Sutton got 14 days. This he has appealed against. Of course, D. had to resign. He thinks he has been hardly used by the Lochs.[1] This I don't think but I also think Government House is not quite a bed of roses for A.D.C.s.

Edward was impressed by the martial activities of his Australian hosts. A little later he writes: 'It is astonishing what a warlike people this is, almost everyone is a soldier. They can put 7000 men in the field in 24 hours and 15,000 in a week, pretty good for such a scattered population isn't it?'

From Australia Edward returned across the Pacific and the United States. With his head turned towards home, and feeling perhaps that he would almost outstrip any correspondence, we have no record of this part of his journey. He would have liked to have taken more time on his way home and applied for additional leave. This, however, was not granted, and in June 1887 after six months abroad he was back with his regiment in London.

Sometime in October 1888 Edward became engaged to Lady Alice Montagu, youngest daughter of the seventh Duke of Manchester. Edward was now twenty-three and his fiancée was twenty-six. Alice was the youngest of a family which consisted of two boys and three girls. Her mother was a German, Louisa Fredericka Augusta Countess Von Alten, daughter of Count Von Alten of

[1] Henry Brougham Loch, created first Baron Loch in 1895, was at this time Governor of Victoria.

Hanover. This beautiful and brilliant woman was destined to play a notable part in British politics for, two years after the death of the Duke of Manchester in 1890, she married the celebrated Whig politician the Marquess of Hartington, who a year later succeeded his father as eighth Duke of Devonshire. In consequence she became known as the 'double duchess'.

In the Victorian age brides were most carefully vetted by the intending bridegroom's family, and these preliminaries to the tying of the bridal knot must have been a grim ordeal for the young people concerned. In 1886 Edward's father had been appointed President of the Board of Trade and had been created Baron Stanley of Preston. In 1888 he had been appointed Governor-General of Canada. Thus it came about that Edward's parents, Lord and Lady Stanley, were in Ottawa at the time of Edward's engagement. The process of vetting was therefore undertaken by Edward's uncle and aunt, Lord and Lady Derby. Edward was not required to be present at the ordeal but his aunt reported to him:

Lady Derby to Edward

11 November 1888 Derby House

All right dearest Edward. Greatly pleased and we got on admirably. Uncle Stanley came up and I could see in a moment all would be well. He says genuinely: 'I am very much pleased—it will do. She is what she should be and I like her expression and her smile.' I assure you it would have done you good to see from behind a curtain how well the trial went off and the Duke was very pleasant and easy and natural and we talked of old days. I am *quite quite* satisfied.

It was far better than if you had been there and I told her she must come again with you at the end of the week. . . .

The marriage took place on 5 January 1889, at the Guards' Chapel, Wellington Barracks. The absence of the bridegroom's parents in Canada, though doubtless a disappointment to the young couple, bore biographical fruit as many friends and relations hastened to write long accounts to the absent parents. Of these the liveliest was that of Edward's brother Victor:

Victor to Lady Stanley

6 January 1889 Derby House

Dearest Mother,

At last I can write you a description of the ceremony which went off splendidly. Such a pretty wedding it was. I haven't had much experience of weddings myself but any amount of people told me that it was quite the prettiest they had ever seen. So it ought to be, in that very pretty chapel and the men of his company lining the aisle, and all that sort of thing. I must tell you that he gave a bachelor dinner the night before attended by nine grenadiers and the 'Naval Brigade' as they christened me at once, and it was a very warm night. I know we drank his health four times and didn't leave the dinner table till a quarter to twelve. To go on with the wedding, everyone was there—Tum,[1] Mrs. Tum, 5 little Tums, Princess Mary, Duke of Cambridge and a lot of others. I went down to the Church early so as to put our relations in their places which I did very satisfactorily, I think. Fish read the service so well, and both Eddy and Alice bellowed their answers out. The way Eddy brought out 'I will' made everyone in the Church start. It was a sort of 'Won't I.' The eight little bridesmaids looked *so nice* dressed after the picture of 'Cherry Ripe'. E.'s present to them was very handsome, a moonstone in a double heart of diamonds. At first there was a great crush at Stanhope Street to see the presents. They were beautiful and some of the things she got in the way of jewellery were lovely. Nunky's tiara was very fine and so much admired. It was such a pretty shape. Dudley gave a very handsome bracelet, but the thing they had most of was silver. There was a tremendous lot of that, and such handsome stuff too. The regiment's present was very pretty and that of the staff was admired as much as anything I saw. Altogether they have come as well out of it in the present line as they possibly could. Tum was very gracious to me, came up and asked if I was E.'s brother and talked to me for a long time. He told me to tell you how much he and everybody else wished you had been there, and so they did dear Mamma, on all sides and from everyone you heard 'Oh what a pity dear Constance isn't here'. That's nice, isn't it. Princess Mary came up behind me and patted me on the shoulder and asked me if I was going to continue the flirtation

[1] 'Tum' was the Stanley family's nickname for H.R.H. The Prince of Wales, later King Edward VII.

with her that we began at Wellington and the last thing she asked me before she went away was if I was going to telegraph to you and when I told her I was she said: 'Mind you say that we all thought of her.' I hope you got my telegram all right. I sent it as soon as I could and calculated it ought to have reached you about luncheon time. I forgot to tell you that I was a little disappointed in Alice's looks at the Church yesterday, though everyone said she looked so well. She certainly had a splendid figure and looks very fine but the time she looked really well and I admired her very much then, and that was in her travelling dress. Some red plush thing and a hat very much turned up on one side and very much down on the other, don't you know. They didn't go away till ½ past 5, for Holwood, so very few people stayed to see them off. Only about twenty, all the Royalties, the Hamiltons, Gosfords and one or two others. I did of course. On their arrival at Holwood they were to be met by a band, which has learnt 'Stanley for ever' for the occasion, and torches.

Before I forget it I must tell you a thing that has reached me. *Strictly private, of course.* A certain person was overheard asking Aunt A. who was the extraordinary being reading the service, on which Aunt A. turned round and snapped out: 'My son-in-law.' Can't you hear her. Aunt Emilia was very flourishing and so smart. And now I think this rambling account is about over. You will get heaps of better ones, but I can't help that. The Derbys have been everything that's nice about it, Aunt M. sends you her love and the normal regrets about your not having been there. Another present I forgot to mention which was very nice of them was a lamp from the Knowsley gamekeepers. Wasn't that nice! Something over 300 they had altogether between them.

(7th). Everyone I went to see yesterday and there were a good number, told me they were writing to you so the amount of letters and accounts of the wedding you will get will be enormous. However, I suppose everyone will be a bit different. A very nice letter came yesterday for Aunt Mary from E. saying that everything was perfect down there and they were as comfortable as possible. The other married couple the Monks have been lent Holywell, (I can't for the life of me remember if this is the right name) so they are only a mile away from one another. This makes E. very angry. . . .

The honeymoon was divided between his uncle's house at Holwood in Kent and his maternal grandfather's house, The Grove, which he had visited so often in his childhood. Six weeks after the wedding the young couple sailed for Canada, where for two years Edward served as his father's A.D.C. Stanley greatly enjoyed his time in Canada, particularly the summer months, which were passed in the Citadel at Quebec. In the winter they played ice hockey and in the summer they would go off for weeks at a time to the Cascopedia for fishing. In the summer of 1889 Edward accompanied his father on a six weeks' tour of the west by train, visiting Winnipeg, Calgary and Banff.

The young Stanleys returned to England early in 1891 and in February stayed at Sandringham with the Prince and Princess of Wales. From there Alice wrote an account of Sandringham life to Prince George (later King George V), who was at that time a Naval officer and was commanding the gunboat H.M.S. *Thrush* in foreign waters:

Lady Alice Stanley to Prince George[1]

February 1891 London

MY DEAR PRINCE GEORGE,

My letter to you has rather shared the fate of the letter we were always going to write from Quebec to Princess Victoria—i.e., always contemplated but never written. Somehow it is very difficult to find time to write a long letter. I wanted to tell you about Sandringham where we had great fun. The first day or two, it was so unlucky; Princess Victoria could not go out, or even dine downstairs as she had such a bad cough, and the Princess had what she called a 'furious eye' which necessitated a shade and great care. Later on in the week everyone was well and after three days shooting the men joined us at hockey and we had some splendid fun. You would have laughed to see some of them. Colonel Brabazon was as brave as a lion. He had skated three times before only; but quite undaunted he threw himself into the fray and had fall after fall. Always too falling on the same place in a sitting position. Colonel Vivian was also a skater of the same calibre but he must have something wrong with his balance as whenever he tried a step forward, he tottered, waved his stick round his head and fell heavily. Eddy got one terrible whack from someone just on his

[1] Royal Archives.

At a fancy dress party in Ottawa.

Lady Alice with Prince George (later King George V) at a ball given by the Duchess of Devonshire in 1897.

knee, so Sir Oscar Clayton comforted him by saying that something most important had burst and that Eddy would have to lay up for at least six weeks. However next day found him playing hockey and the knee has been well ever since. Arthur Sassoon was too amusing and always made the most inappropriate remarks. The Prince sent Lord Curzon and him out duck shooting one day, so when they got home he told Mrs. Arthur that the shooting was rot, but the luncheon good. She with accurate knowledge of her husband begged him not to say that to the Prince who had been so kind in sending him out; but alas in the evening he was heard to say 'Well, Sir, the shooting was *not* much, but the luncheon was *excellent*!!!' I suppose you heard of the famous bet that a young Mr. Charteris, son of Lady Margaret Charteris, made unwittingly, and it was snapped up by Bunny Leigh? Well, this same young man has wound up this year well by entering into a matrimonial alliance with a young lady of theatrical fame—Miss de Bere!! Lady Margaret was seated at tea with a friend one evening when a female was ushered in and announced herself as the lady's daughter-in-law. Imagine the tableau. The consequence is that the youth is disinherited and his younger brother comes into the money.

I have seen John Baring a few times. They say the New Bank that he is in is getting on very well indeed. So I hope there is some chance of his being better off before long.... You never saw anything so beautiful as the house in Charles Street is on the outside. They hope to be able to keep the house and live in a corner of it. We have invested in a mansion in Cumberland Place, but I am afraid it will not be ready to live in for two or three months. In the meantime we stay here in Stanhope Street with Mamma. I have got my two horses at Leighton and I go down to the Leo Rothschild's for a day or two each week. Eddy has not found out yet when he is wanted in Canada. Shall you go for the fishing? I wish I could get out this year again just for that....

Eddy wants me to send his love. In great haste.

Believe me,

Yours very sincerely,

ALICE STANLEY

At this time Edward found himself in financial difficulties, as his father had some years before. In later life he often used to tell his friends that he never gambled or bet on horses because in his youth he had got into a great betting scrape which had worried him more than any other episode in his life. It seems probable, though there is no direct documentary evidence, that his worries at this time arose from this cause.

Alice to Edward

4 October 1891 Wilverley Park, Lyndhurst

Many thanks for your letter and its contents. Of course it would be an awful relief to pay off all those beastly bills; but at the same time I do so loathe asking and begging and Nunky is not the sort of person to understand. If it was a very enormous sum it would be worth eating dirt to get it, but for this I don't know that we need do so. Charlie [Montagu, her brother] would lend us the money and we could pay it back by instalments, if you think we could do this instead of going to Nunky. Till you talked about paying off the bills I never realized what a relief it would be to get them off one's mind. I owe about £500 for the bills I have got and of course it is difficult to screw that out of £2700—and you with things to pay besides. However we will talk it over. . . .

Either Edward had not disclosed to his wife his full position or else it must have become aggravated in the next few months. In any case, recourse was made to Nunky:

Lady Stanley to Edward

10 December 1891 Government House, Ottawa

I do hope that all will go well with dear Alice this time, but I am sure the having to keep quiet will be a great trial to her. . . .

Dear old boy we are *so* very pleased to hear about Uncle Stanley's great kindness. He really is most generous to you and how right you were to go straight to him about your debts. I hope your mind is quite at ease for I know you hate to have unpaid bills. Now the next thing I hope for you is that you will be returned unopposed to Parliament. They seem to keep you pretty hard at work but the trouble is worth while.

The electric cars in Ottawa are an enormous success and though they were only started in July have already paid. They add to the dangers of driving very much as they come along at an awful pace and as for overhead the whole space as far as you can see is one network of wires. The great question is will they be able to run when the winter really comes. A heavy fall of snow and icicles form on the wires. The dangers will be great indeed. Father is now quite devoted to 'Dinah' a large black retriever that belongs to the Canada and that Victor asked to leave here because she could not stand the heat of the West Indies. He is quite a slave to her. Jessie is more beautiful than ever. Age has made her face more attractive and Isobel's puppy Tim is quite devoted to her and they play for everlasting together. . . . So the Duke of Clarence marries the Teck girl after all, and I suppose by this time he thinks himself in love with her. I wonder what Prince George says.[1] I hope he is really recovering well—poor little fellow he didn't look as if he could stand much pulling down by fever.

Now goodbye dearest Eddy. Much love to darling Alice from

Your most affectionate Mother,

C. Stanley

Lady Stanley's good wishes for 'dear Alice this time' were realised, and on 24 June 1892 Alice presented her husband with their first child, a daughter, who was christened Victoria Alice Louise.

Lady Stanley's aspirations for her son's political career were also soon to be realised. At the time when Edward returned to England it had been envisaged that he would go back to his father's staff after two or three months. He decided, however, that he would prefer to do some regimental soldiering and some correspondence passed between him and his father with a view to his resigning his appointment in Ottawa and joining the 3rd Battalion, Grenadier Guards when a vacancy could be found. Meanwhile an opportunity presented itself to nurse the Lancashire constituency of Westhoughton which was to become vacant at the next general election.

[1] In fact the Duke of Clarence died on 14 January 1892 before his proposed marriage, and Prince George himself married 'the Teck girl', Princess Mary. The Clarendon family were well-informed in court tittle-tattle, and this sentence would seem to imply that the future King George V did not merely take on his brother's fiancée as a family responsibility but already had a romantic interest in her during his brother's lifetime. Those who ought to know, while admitting there is nothing damaging to the memory of King George V in it, state, after due enquiry, that 'the intriguing hypothesis is in fact not true'.

While nursing his new constituency he also gained experience in public speaking by addressing meetings in other parts of Lancashire. A speech which he made in Bolton won him the commendation of his uncle:

Lord Derby to Mr. Edward Stanley

30 March 1891 Fairhill,
Tonbridge

DEAR NED,

I have been reading your speech in the Bolton paper, and can honestly congratulate you upon it. You chose your topics judiciously and handled them skilfully. You said nothing that would have been better let alone, and your treatment of the labour question showed tact. You were a little 'flabby' on the free trade question as connected with the colonies; but something must be forgiven to the son of a colonial governor. Altogether the speech is a success, and does you credit.

Ever yours affec.,
DERBY

You will probably receive this on All Fools' Day; but you need not consider it as a 'poisson d'Avril'. D.

His father concluded a letter dated 26 December 1891:

. . . Goodbye dear boy for the present. Let us have your news from time to time—especially I like to hear of your success in canvassing and in speaking. I should hope that you are safe—but the surest way of avoiding a contest is to work from the beginning up to the last moment, even when you are not opposed.

APPENDIX TO CHAPTER ONE

Victor.	b. 17 January 1867. m. 25 November 1896 Annie Bickerton, daughter of the Hon. C. E. Pooley, President of the Council of the British Columbia Cabinet. d. June 1934.	1880 Navy; 1882 Egyptian War; 1905–9 Captain and Naval Attaché Russia, Norway and Sweden; 1912–14 Commandant Royal Naval College, Dartmouth; 1926 retired with the rank of Admiral, after commanding the Reserve Fleet.
Katharine Mary.	b. 1868 d. October 1871.	
Arthur.	b. 18 November 1869. d. November 1947.	1892 Private Secretary to Mr. Balfour (First Lord of the Treasury); later Attaché, Diplomatic Service and Clerk in Foreign Office; 1898–1918 M.P. for Ormskirk Division S. Lancs.
Geoffrey.	b. 18 November 1869. d. 16 March 1871.	
Ferdinand Charles.	b. 28 January 1871. m. 15 February 1904 The Hon. Alexandra Frances Anne Fellowes, eldest daughter 2nd Baron de Ramsey. d. March 1935.	1898 Nile Expedition; 1899–1901 South African War, awarded the D.S.O.; Captain Grenadier Guards and extra A.D.C. to the Lord Lieutenant of Ireland; 1914–18 Brevet Lieut.-Colonel.
George Frederick.	b. 14 October 1872. m. 26 November 1903 Lady Beatrix Taylour, daughter of 3rd Marquess of Headfort. d. July 1938.	1893 entered R.H.A.; 1899–1900 South African War; 1904–9 Adj. Hon. Artillery Coy.; 1914–18 Lieut.-Colonel, R.H.A.; 1910–22 M.P. for Preston; 1924–9 M.P. for East Willesden; 1912–13 Parliamentary Private Secretary to the Leader of the Opposition (Bonar Law); 1913–14 Opposition Whip; 1916–17 Parliamentary Private Secretary to Secretary of State for War; 1919–21 Comptroller Royal Household; 1921 Financial Secretary to War Office and member Army Council; 1922–3 Under Secretary of State for Home Affairs;

		1924–9 Parliamentary Secretary to Minister of Pensions; 1929 Governor of Madras.
Algernon Francis.	b. 8 January 1874. m. 18 April 1918 Lady Mary Crichton, 3rd daughter 1st Duke of Westminster, widow Henry William, Viscount Crichton.	1899–1900 South African War; 1916 Colonel 2nd Life Guards; awarded the D.S.O.; 1923–7 Colonel Commandant 159th Infantry Brigade.
Isobel Constance Mary.	b. 20 September 1875. m. 10 December 1898 Lieut.-Gen. the Hon. Sir John Gathorne-Hardy, 2nd son 2nd Earl of Cranbrook.	1914–20 Woman of the Bedchamber to Queen Mary.
Frederick William.	b. 27 May 1878. m. 17 June 1905 Lady Alexandra Louise Acheson, eldest daughter 4th Earl of Gosford. d. 1942.	1899–1902 South African War; 1914–18 Captain 12th Hussars, awarded the D.S.O.; Brevet Lieut.-Colonel Reserve of Officers, late Lancashire Hussars Yeomanry.

II

Parliament and the Turf

IN 1886 Lord Salisbury, Lord Randolph Churchill and Mr. Joseph Chamberlain, fighting in unison on the Irish issue against Mr. Gladstone's Home Rule policy, had secured an overall majority in the House of Commons of 116. But in the ensuing years by-elections and defections had reduced that majority to 66; and it was without great confidence that the Conservatives and Liberal Unionists approached the general election of July 1892. Gladstone appears to have thought that he would obtain a majority of above a hundred. In the event it amounted to 40 and this included the Irish members.

Stanley fought a vigorous and successful campaign at Westhoughton against his Liberal opponent. The result was:

Mr. Edward Stanley	6,711
Mr. Lewis Haslam	4,871
Majority	1,840

Defeated at the polls, the Government decided, in accordance with the usage of that time, to take its defeat from the House of Commons. The Parliament was opened on August 4, not by the Queen, but by a Commission. For, as the Lord Chancellor explained, 'Her Majesty did not think fit to be personally present here this day'. The Queen's speech was read by the Lord Chancellor and, in view of the obviously impending demise of the administration, was of exceptional brevity. On the second day of the Commons debate on the Address, Mr. Asquith moved an amendment of 'no confidence' in the Government. On August 11 Stanley took the opportunity of making his maiden speech against Asquith's amendment. It was not a great oratorical performance, nor did it aim to be. It was a reasonable, modest, party speech from a young man of twenty-seven. He argued that the Liberals owed their victory not to their policy of Home Rule but to their proposal for an Eight Hours Bill.

Recognizing the inevitable defeat of the Government, he concluded his speech with these words:

> We have been called a beaten, captured, and conquered army. But we are not. If we were a captured army we should have to walk out without our arms and the stipulation that we fight no longer. On the contrary, we march out with all the honours of war, a compact body ready to follow our one Leader, and ready to follow him anywhere. We shall cross the floor not only prepared to hold our ground, but prepared to make counter-attacks. I prophesy it will not be long before we again recapture the seats.

Asquith's amendment was carried by 350 to 310. Salisbury resigned and Gladstone was entrusted with the formation of a new government. He was now eighty-two and the Queen, to spare him the rigour of a visit to Osborne, which would scarcely have given her more pleasure than him, was graciously pleased to signify her royal pleasure through her private secretary, Sir Henry Ponsonby.

Mr. Gladstone did not present his new Government to Parliament until it met again on 3 January 1893. Within a month he introduced a new Home Rule Bill. It was substantially the same as that of 1886, save that the Irish Members were to be permitted to speak and vote in the Imperial Parliament on certain issues. The Bill finally passed the House of Commons in September by a majority of 34 but was rejected by 419 to 41 in the House of Lords. The Irish problem was thereafter left in abeyance. Mr. Gladstone hinted that it would soon be solved, but practical considerations seemed indefinitely to defer such a solution. In March 1894 Gladstone, frustrated in his great enterprise of Home Rule, exhausted by his prodigious labours and wearying of his colleagues—though none of them would have dared admit wearying of him—laid down his labours and was succeeded by Lord Rosebery. Rosebery's brief ministry of fifteen months was unhappy and abortive and he succeeded in further dividing the Liberal Party. Indeed his short sway is principally remarkable for the fact that he succeeded, while Prime Minister, in winning the Derby twice, with Ladas II in 1894 and with Sir Visto in 1895. And this glittering and unique achievement scarcely commended him to the Nonconformist conscience on which Gladstone had taught the Liberal Party 'confidently to rely'.

Such in brief was the political background of the first parliament in which Stanley sat. He was regular in his attendance at the House and made many friends but not much mark. His interventions in debate were infrequent but he asked questions on matters which interested him from time to time. His main interest was the Army and he seems particularly to have been concerned with the drains in Her Majesty's Barracks, notably at Chelsea, Wellington, St. George's and Kensington Palace. He alleged that two officers, one in his own regiment, had died of typhoid fever, a result of the insanitary conditions which, he stated, were infinitely worse for the officers than they were for the men. He also intervened on the Swine Fever Bill. In 1893 he asked the Prime Minister whether in view of the fact that there had been no quorum the year before on Derby Day, it would not be advisable for the House not to sit on May 30. Mr. Gladstone replied that the House could not stand adjourned on that day, but that he would do his best 'to make a House on Derby Day'. Encouraged by his Tory friends, Stanley introduced a motion that 'this House on rising do adjourn till May 31'. A division was called and Stanley's motion was negatived by 281 to 169.

* * *

In April 1893 Stanley's uncle, the fifteenth Earl, died at Knowsley at the age of sixty-six. He was succeeded in the title and the ownership of the Derby estates by Stanley's father.

A glimpse of what life at Knowsley was like soon after the succession has been preserved for us in the letters which Lady Emily Lutyens wrote as a girl to her friend and confidant, the Reverend

Whitwell Elwin.[1] Her father, Robert Lytton, was the son of the novelist Bulwer Lytton, and her mother was the daughter of Edward Villiers, younger brother of the fourth Earl of Clarendon, and a first cousin of Stanley's mother, Lady Derby.

This young lady, whose father was successively Viceroy of India and Ambassador in Paris, had a critical eye for all around her. Just before going to stay at Knowsley, she took the occasion to express her disapproval of her sister, Lady Constance Lytton, later a militant suffragette, because she was writing for the newspapers: 'I don't think that even were I starving,' she wrote to the Reverend Mr. Elwin, 'and certainly not before, that I could descend so low as to write articles for a miserable paper.'

The next day, her correspondent replied:

The Reverend Whitwell Elwin to Lady Emily Lytton

4 October 1893 Booton Rectory

Betty[2] explains to me that Con is paid £2 2*s*. a column, and as her articles commonly fill two columns, this amounts to £4 4*s*. per week. It shows what a title is worth to such a paper. Of course the ordinary rate of payment is barely a fourth of what Con receives. The rest is paid to her title. With readers of the upper and middle classes a title prefixed to such an article would not enhance its value. Rather the reverse. It is otherwise when you drop lower. Fanny tells me that our servants take in three Society Papers, and they like to have their news and sentiments fresh from the Queen herself, or her associates. This explains the pay, which is to me a novel fact in modern literature. As titled contributors multiply the pay will diminish. The wisdom is to earn a fortune while golden harvests can be had.

Lady Emily's mother was now a widow in relatively modest circumstances, and as an ex-Vicereine and Ambassadress, a trifle jealous of her cousin, Lady Derby's, good fortune. Her daughter recorded all she saw with the alert eye and censorious pen of Victorian youth.

[1] *A Blessed Girl*, by Lady Emily Lutyens.

[2] Her sister, Lady Elizabeth, who married Mr. Gerald Balfour, younger brother of Arthur James Balfour, first Earl Balfour.

Lady Emily Lytton to the Reverend Whitwell Elwin

14 October 1893 Knowsley

This house is enormous and very rambling. There are something over 80 bedrooms, all very small. None of the house is pretty, though some very old, but it has been so patched and pulled about by different owners, especially the last Lord Derby, that it is really hideous. It is built of a dull red brick. The rooms are all small, with the exception of one dining-room which is enormous and a very fine room, only terribly modernised and spoilt. Inside it is very comfortable and nice. There is a fascinating library, a suite of little rooms lined with books and ending in a large odd-shaped room, something like the long room with books at Longleat.[1] The present owners abuse right and left what was done by the last Lord Derby, in a way which I think is very unkind and disagreeable considering that he was a brother. They have jumped into his shoes and can only abuse him. The only people in the house besides the family, which consists of the Derbys, Isobel, one son and a secretary, are Lady Emma Talbot, Lord Derby's sister, and her husband, neither of them at all lively. Cousin C.[2] has the family failing of abusing everybody in a very nasty way. Lord Derby is rather like a boy, very jovial and full of bad jokes, but I should say without much else.

14 October 1893 Knowsley

We drove to church this morning, it being some little way off. After church we were taken round the house and its ugliness was roundly abused. This afternoon we went to the stables, which are magnificent. An old coachman who has been here for years and is a great rogue, although a great character, showed us round with the most tremendous pride. They have over forty magnificent horses. The stables are kept spotlessly clean which they ought to be considering that they have twenty men to look after them. The gardens are large and ugly, and these require twenty-four gardeners. Thank goodness I am not obliged to live here. The luxury of a small home and a few servants can only be properly appreciated by coming to a house like this. The whole house and stables are lit with electric light, which is nice. On Tuesday we are going into Preston to hear Lord Salisbury speak, which will be something to tell you about.

[1] The home of the Marquess of Bath. [2] Lady Derby.

18 October 1893 Knowsley

All the gentlemen went last night to a dinner given by Mr. Birley, the chairman who is to preside over the meeting in Liverpool. I should think few of them felt inclined to a big dinner at 5 o'clock. We had a most excellent meal in an hotel, where the Lathom party also dined, only in a separate room, as Lady Derby was most anxious to be independent and have her own way. It is very comic the pride she takes in her new position and her delight in lording it over Lady Lathom, who is fearfully jealous. It is also comic the way Mother brings forward her glory in India and Paris, and each tries to outdo the other. Only with Mother it is also very pathetic, as it is a terrible trial to her to see Cousin C. in such a splendid position and to feel that hers from a worldly point of view has gone. She is wonderfully good over it, but I know she feels it very much. I was glad that yesterday she was also put well in front and shown great respect. The meeting in the evening was a wonderful sight. The huge hall was packed; they said there were 8,000 people in it, and thousands more tried to force their way in. Forty policemen were fighting with the crowd and kept them out with great difficulty. Though noisy at first they kept as still as possible during Lord Salisbury's speech, and were most appreciative, seeing every point. They gave him a most enthusiastic reception.

In every word you feel what a great man Lord Salisbury is. His speech was received with great enthusiasm. After his speech was done the meeting became dreadfully tedious. Mr. Hanbury's speech was popular, but, I thought, vulgar and commonplace. Lord Derby was received with immense enthusiasm, and one man shouted, 'Good boy, Fred'. He is very popular in Preston.

20 October 1893 Knowsley

I am much more at home here now. Yesterday, Isobel took me boating on the big water and we were very friendly together. Lady Alice Stanley, the eldest son's wife, is here now, and though I do not care much for her, she is so nice to me I quite like her for that. Then the last two evenings there have been big dinners, and I can get on much better talking to one person instead of joining in general conversation. Last night I sat by Gwenny, which was a treat. I have not seen much of her, but merely to know she is there is nice. We were going yesterday to see the watch-making at Prescot, which is a trade that has been revived there, only they feared there might be some disturbances from the miners, who are out of work, or anyhow there are so many people starving they thought it would not be right to go in smart carriages to see the town, and so it was given up. The misery must be fearful. About 100 miners were out yesterday with the shooters as beaters, and they seemed extremely cheerful and were capital men.

There was a large dinner-party last night with the Lord Mayor and his wife, and the Bishop and his daughter, and just before dinner out went the electric light. Happily there was gas in the passages, but it was a great nuisance. Everyone, though, enjoyed the joke, and the light came on again during dinner. These luxuries have their drawbacks.

* * *

At this time there was emerging upon the Liverpool political scene a figure who was destined to play an almost unique role in English political life and to become a lifelong friend and political associate of Stanley. Archibald Salvidge was born in 1863. He was the second son of a Liverpool brewer whose predecessors had been Somersetshire squires. Salvidge was educated at a local Wesleyan School and at the Liverpool Institute. He went to work in his youth for Bent's Brewery, the leading brewery firm on Merseyside. He had secured this situation, from which he ultimately rose to be managing director of the Company, by the purchase and good management of two public houses which he had succeeded in selling to Bent's Brewery at the time of his successful application for employment. Liberals, with their temperance and cocoa connections, have always made mock of the Tory Party's connection with beer and it is certainly true that at every level from the Guinnesses and Grettons down to the poorest tied-publican there has historically been an agreeable association between the purveyors of the national beverage and the Tory Party.

Salvidge believed in combining politics with business and while still in his youth became an active member of the Liverpool Conservative Working Men's Association. His political hero at this time was Lord Randolph Churchill, whose speeches about Tory democracy had fired his youthful imagination. In 1892, the year in which

Stanley was first returned to Parliament, Salvidge was elected chairman of the Liverpool Conservative Working Men's Association. He marked his accession to this office by taking a deputation to London to invite Lord Randolph Churchill to address a public meeting of the Association at the Liverpool Hippodrome. It was now six years since Lord Randolph had resigned in dramatic circumstances from Lord Salisbury's Government and he was no longer the man he had been. Nonetheless he still made a powerful appeal to working-class audiences and was more capable of attracting a crowd than any other politician of the day.

Successive extensions of the franchise during the nineteenth century had always alarmed the Tory Party. The Tories tended to assume that as more and more manual workers were given the vote Tory fortunes were bound to decline at the polls. Disraeli, and later Lord Randolph Churchill, had shown how the doctrine of Tory democracy could be effectively preached to the masses and how the newly enrolled electors could be led away from subversive and radical doctrines towards the support of Church and State. Salvidge was a disciple of these ideas and by propagating them in Liverpool he created a position of considerable power for himself. Stanley had a natural flair for politics and for easy association with Lancastrians of all classes. Salvidge had the better brain and the more acute intelligence; and over the years which lay ahead he was often able to guide Stanley's political footsteps. Their association was helpful to both and was on occasion to have important consequences. Part of Stanley's strength in later life was his knowledge of the thoughts and aspirations of the man in the street. This he acquired to a large extent from Salvidge. Stanley's contacts with the big world of London were useful to Salvidge, but while the latter always remained in close alliance with Stanley, he was to establish his own independent relations with national leaders such as Mr. Lloyd George, Lord Birkenhead and Mr. Winston Churchill.

* * *

In June 1895 Rosebery's Government was defeated on the question of the supply of cordite. The Queen, on Rosebery's advice, dissolved Parliament and the ensuing general election resulted in a Conservative and Liberal Unionist majority of 152. Stanley himself was returned unopposed for Westhoughton. Salisbury once more became Prime Minister.

In the new Government Stanley received his first political appointment, that of a junior Lord of the Treasury. He thus became one of the Government Whips. A Government Whip is precluded from taking part in debate, but his duties require a regular attendance at the House so that he may procure the attendance of other members of his own party to 'keep a House' and above all to ensure a majority on critical issues. Stanley's geniality and ability to get on easily with his fellow Members marked him out for the appointment. The Whips not only have the duty of seeing that the Government at all times have a majority available in the House; they are the main channels by which the party leader keeps himself informed of changing opinion among his supporters. In January 1914 the Radical Irish Nationalist T. P. O'Connor, M.P. for the Scotland Division of Liverpool, wrote in the *Pall Mall Magazine*:

> Lord Derby was quite content for some years to fill the office of a Whip while his party was in power. There are few people outside the House of Commons who can realize all the drudgery and even humiliation which this office involves. The Whip has to stand for hours at the exit door of the Inner Lobby; to bully or cajole every member of his party to remain in the House, or at least not to go away without securing a 'pair'. He has to keep out of the chamber itself, however interesting the debate may be there; he is bound to a silence almost as rigid as that of an anchorite; in short, he has the duties of an Upper Class servant. And every time I saw this heir to a great and historic name and to a vast fortune doing work almost menial, I saw in him the best object-lesson of the intensity with which to this day every class in England holds to the duty of playing a part in the political history of their country.

* * *

Soon after entering the House of Commons Stanley persuaded his father to take an interest in the Turf. The House of Stanley had long been interested in racing. It was Stanley's great-great-grandfather, the twelfth Earl of Derby, who in 1780 with a number of friends established the annual race on Epsom Downs which was to become, under his name, the most famous horse race in the world. Apart from Derby, the leading figure in establishing this race was Sir Thomas Charles Bunbury, Bt. According to a tradition which survives in the Bunbury family and which, though unsupported by any contemporary documentary evidence, is not challenged by the Stanley family today, it was an even money chance that the race might have been called the Bunbury. A member of the Bunbury family has written to the author as follows:

Mr. E. J. Bunbury to Mr. Randolph S. Churchill

> It has always been the traditional story in my family that Sir Thomas Charles Bunbury, Bt., and Lord Derby invented the Derby Race on Epsom Downs and that they dined together the night before the race (run on May 4th, 1780) and tossed up as to whether it would be called the Derby or the Bunbury. Derby won the toss and it was called the Derby. Bunbury won the race with his Diomed, a chestnut by Florizel out of a Spectator mare bred by Mr. Tanken, bought by Bunbury and named by him Diomed. Out of a field of 9 Diomed started favourite at 6 to 4 against. Diomed was subsequently sold to U.S.A. where he sired many famous American race horses—and to quote Brian Vesey-FitzGerald 'he served for ten years in America and exercised a tremendous influence on the thoroughbred in that country.'

Mr. E. J. Bunbury has a copy of the famous portrait of Diomed painted by Stubbs, the original of which hangs in the Jockey Club of America. It is amusing to think of a minor consequence which would have arisen if Sir Thomas Bunbury had won the toss and not Lord Derby. When Oscar Wilde came in 1895 to write *The Importance of Being Earnest*, the name Bunbury would have had a fame and precise application which would have precluded him from giving it to the fictitious and hypochondriacal friend of his co-hero Mr. Algernon Moncrieff. Bunbury would have passed into the language with an entirely different connotation and Wilde would have had to seek elsewhere for a nomenclature with equally comical overtones.

* * *

In 1779, the year before the Derby was established, Derby had founded a race for fillies, which was named the Oaks after the house on Banstead Downs which he had purchased from General Burgoyne, who is best known to history for having surrendered to the American Colonists at Saratoga. Burgoyne was a son-in-law of the eleventh Lord Derby, having, while stationed at Preston as a lieutenant in the 13th Light Dragoons, eloped with his daughter, Lady Charlotte Stanley. This elopement caused her father the keenest displeasure; according to the *Dictionary of National Biography*, he 'only gave her a small sum of money and declared he would never see her again'. With this money Burgoyne bought a captaincy in his regiment. Derby eventually acquiesced in his daughter's marriage, jobbed Burgoyne into Parliament for the family borough of Preston 'with free leave to say what he liked' and in his will left his daughter £25,000 and an annuity of £400. These sums should be multiplied at least tenfold if we are to understand them in modern values.

In Parliament Burgoyne principally concerned himself with Indian affairs and early sought to impeach Lord Clive. It is however to his credit that he was the first to propound the principle, later incorporated in the India Bills of Pitt and Fox, that the British Government should assume some control over the activities of the East India Company.

Rake, gambler, playwright, amateur actor, Burgoyne persevered in his military career and having served in two separate junior posts in the war against the American Colonies was eventually sent back to Canada in 1777 in supreme command of a force for which he had designed the plan of invading the Colony of New York from the north. With only half the forces which he had predicated to be necessary for victory, he advanced rapidly and enjoyed some early success. After a six-day siege, he captured Ticonderoga. For this success George III offered him the Order of the Bath. But the twelfth Lord Derby refused it on his brother-in-law's behalf. The American commander, General Schuyler, retreated. He was superseded by General Gates, who compelled Burgoyne to capitulate at Saratoga on 17 October 1777.

On his return, Burgoyne, who was under fire alike for his defeat and for his speedy return with General Washington's permission, deserted the Tories and sided with Fox. When the latter formed the notorious Fox-North coalition in 1782, Burgoyne was appointed Commander-in-Chief in Ireland. But, on the fall of Fox, he was dismissed. He occupied the remainder of his life writing plays, bringing the actress, Miss Elizabeth Farran, into his brother-in-law's life, impeaching Warren Hastings and begetting by Miss Susan Caulfield, a contemporary singer, four bastard children whom he left to be cared for at Knowsley. Of him Horace Walpole wrote: 'Burgoyne's battles and speeches will be forgotten; but his delicious comedy of the *Heiress* still continues to be the delight of the stage.' Values have changed since Horace Walpole expressed this opinion, and today Burgoyne is still best remembered on both sides of the Atlantic for his surrender at Saratoga.

* * *

Derby won the Oaks the first time it was run, in 1779, with a filly named Bridget; but he had to wait till 1787 to win the Derby with Sir Peter Teazle. Derby's wife, a daughter of the sixth Duke of Hamilton, deserted him for the Duke of Dorset. A few weeks after her death in 1797, Derby married Miss Elizabeth Farran, the actress with whom he had been brought together by Burgoyne.

The thirteenth Earl, a famous zoologist, was not interested in racing but the stable was revived by his son, the great Lord Derby, who, in the intervals of being Prime Minister three times, managed to spend a great deal of his time upon the racecourse. He never won the Derby, but was successful in the Oaks, the 2,000 Guineas and the 1,000 Guineas. He raced with particular success in the North. His horses were trained at Malton in Yorkshire by the celebrated John Scott, 'The Wizard of the North'. On his death the stable lapsed again.

Stanley's uncle, the fifteenth Earl, took no interest in sport, and the sixteenth Earl had no horses until his son persuaded him to buy a few in 1893. It was Stanley who prevailed upon the Hon. George Lambton, brother of the third Earl of Durham, to train the family horses. He explained to Lambton that he hoped to revive the old prestige of the Derby stable. Lambton, feeling that he lacked sufficient experience, was at first reluctant to accept, but Stanley over-persuaded him and thus was started a racing partnership which was to last for forty years and be one of the most memorable in the annals of the British Turf.

Lambton was one of the greatest trainers of the century. Stanley was as fortunate in the choice he made for his father of a stud groom. In 1894 he heard that the Dowager Duchess of Montrose was selling her bloodstock. He at once wrote to Griffiths, the Duchess's stud groom, asking whether he was available, as Lord Derby was considering restarting the stud farm at Knowsley and would like Griffiths to take charge of it. Griffiths accepted and his second son, Walter, continued to run the stud until 1953, a rare and wonderfully successful father-and-son combination extending over nearly sixty years. Stanley's first racehorse of his own, Greywell, was given him by his father. It won its first race at Liverpool, a course where he was to have innumerable victories during his career on the Turf. Some twenty years later, in the middle of the First World War, Derby, as he had then become, was to do for his son what his father had done for him. He presented his eldest son, Lord Stanley, with his first horse, Young Pegasus, which, like Greywell, also won its first race carrying his colours.

* * *

The first filly bought by Lord Stanley for himself was Hettie Sorrel, the third dam (i.e. great-grandmother) of Alycidon, the outstanding stayer bred in this country since the Second World War. And the first filly Lord Stanley bought for his father was Canterbury Pilgrim, who was destined to be the best filly of her year.[1] She won the Oaks and was the dam of Swynford, winner of the St. Leger, who, in the opinion of George Lambton, was the best of the many horses he trained at Stanley House, Hyperion not excepted.

[1] At the same Newmarket Sales where Stanley bought Canterbury Pilgrim he had bid to £4,000 for a previous lot, a colt named Rock Sand. It was knocked down to the next bidder for £4,100, a very large sum for a yearling in those days. Rock Sand won the Derby of 1903. If Stanley's purse had been a little longer his father might have won the Derby as well as the Oaks in the same year.

Canterbury Pilgrim won the Oaks of 1896. The only other classic success that fell to the sixteenth Lord Derby was the Oaks of 1906, won by Keystone II, who like Canterbury Pilgrim came from a mare of the Duchess of Montrose's blood. The sixteenth Earl had only these two classic victories to his name when he died in 1908.

In the next forty years his son was to win twenty classic races; among them the Derby three times—with Sansovino in 1924, with Hyperion in 1933, and with Watling Street in 1942, but this last victory was only in a war-time substitute at Newmarket. It was the Derby that he wished to win above all other races. He also won the Oaks twice, the St. Leger six times, the 1,000 Guineas seven times and the 2,000 Guineas twice. In addition he won nearly every famous weight-for-age race in the Calendar, and over twenty Liverpool Cups. In all he was to win 1,000 races on the Turf and about £845,000 in prize money.

A notable feature of the success of the Stanley stable was that, unlike many other racing stables, it was not founded on the purchase of scores of expensive yearlings. Almost all the most brilliant Stanley horses were bred at Stanley House in Newmarket. It was as an owner-breeder that Stanley was to be pre-eminent in the world during the first half of the twentieth century. He did not head the list of leading owners in England as often as did the Aga Khan, for the latter kept many more horses in training and raced on a much bigger scale. But Stanley was to be the leading breeder in more years than any other man; and in the last twenty-five years of his life a stallion of his breeding was the leading English stallion of the year more often than not.

An owner's many successes on the Turf may well be forgotten in a generation, but the seventeenth Earl of Derby will be remembered, as long as racing continues in this country, for two reasons. He won the Derby three times.[1] He also produced a number of brilliant

[1] Eleven other owners have won the Derby three or more times. The Aga Khan and the third Earl of Egremont won it five times. The first Duke of Westminster and Sir Joseph Hawley won it four times; those who share with Derby the distinction of having won it three times are the first Lord Grosvenor, the eighth Duke of Bedford, Sir F. Standish, the third Duke of Grafton, the fifth Earl of Jersey, Mr. Bowes and the fifth Earl of Rosebery.

stallions whose blood will enter into the pedigrees of racehorses in all parts of the world of racing for half a century to come.

In the Aga Khan's studs in Ireland there used in the thirties to be over a hundred brood mares. Derby's studs, like the late Lord Astor's, were much smaller. They were built up from small and modest purchases at a time when bloodstock was far less costly than it was to become in the next thirty or forty years; and Derby never made a capital investment in the Turf comparable to that made by owner-breeders such as the Aga Khan, Lord Woolavington, Lord Glanely and M. Marcel Boussac.

Nearly all Derby's greatest breeding triumphs stem back to eight brood mares. Five of these were purchased for his father during the first two years of their joint racing career. The first was a filly called Hettie Sorrel, which was the next horse purchased after Greywell. He bought her as a two-year-old from the future Lord Esher, also a patron of Lambton's stable. Hettie Sorrel had been sent to Lambton to train and was put in a selling race at the first July meeting at Newmarket in 1893. After being badly outpaced she struggled on well near the finish and was placed second. Her jockey on dismounting advised Lambton not to let anyone claim her as he felt sure she would do well in long-distance nurseries, and he was proved right. She proceeded to win five races off the reel, and since, as a racing commentator observed, she would have raced with a donkey and only just have pulled out enough to win by perhaps a neck or half a length, she kept on beating the handicapper. After her third victory, the future Lord Esher sold her to the future Lord Derby and this ex-selling-plater was to breed six winners, including the filly Marchetta, from whom stem Alycidon, Acropolis and Borealis, all top-class winners for Stanley House, and other big winners in My Babu and Sayani for outside stables.

When the Dowager Duchess of Montrose sold her stud, Stanley not only bought Canterbury Pilgrim at 1,800 guineas for his father, but also gave 600 guineas for a brood mare called Broad Corrie for himself. Both these animals were acquired on the advice of Griffiths. Broad Corrie, like Hettie Sorrel, was to prove a goldmine, for, through one of her daughters, Glasalt, descend the Oaks winner

Toboggan, the 1,000 Guineas winner Canyon, the 2,000 Guineas winner Colorado and the Eclipse Stakes winner Caerleon (own brother to Colorado), of whom we shall later hear more.

* * *

Canterbury Pilgrim was to prove an even more spectacularly successful purchase than Hettie Sorrel and Broad Corrie. As a yearling, Lambton thought her a rather small filly and as a two-year-old she was excitable in her work and had a bad mouth. When she tried, she showed speed for about three and a half furlongs, but in the five races she ran as a two-year-old she was only placed once. Lambton however did not despair of her. As she was highly strung and irritable she was given a quiet old gelding as her companion; his presence calmed her and made it possible to work her normally. Lambton's skill was to be rewarded. Canterbury Pilgrim improved out of all knowledge and as a three-year-old proceeded to win the Oaks and the Park Hill Stakes at Doncaster. At stud she was destined to breed seven winners, including Swynford, winner of the 1910 St. Leger and sire of Stanley House's first Derby winner, Sansovino. Two other fillies were bought within the first two years of the re-establishment of the stud farm at Knowsley; Lock and Key, who was full of the Duchess of Montrose's best blood, and Bridget. From the former came Keystone II; from the latter Tide-Way, winner of the 1,000 Guineas, and Sun Stream, winner of the 1,000 Guineas and the Oaks.

The three other notable brood mares which, with the above five, constituted the foundation of the stud were Anchora, Gondolette, and Ranaï. These three were all bought after Stanley had succeeded his father in 1908. Gondolette, like Hettie Sorrel, was a selling-plater at one time. Bred by the late Mr. Henry Waring of the Beenham Stud near Reading, she was sold as a yearling for only seventy-five guineas. After winning small races at Brighton and at Epsom, she was bought by Lord Westbury for 800 guineas, and won for him a selling race at Newmarket. At the end of the season the brewer Mr. Hall Walker (afterwards Lord Wavertree) bought her as a potential brood mare for his famous Tully Stud in Kildare. Several years later Hall Walker sent her up to the Newmarket Sales of 1912 in foal to King Edward VII's Derby winner Minoru. Derby bought her for 1,550 guineas, planning to inbreed to the great mare Pilgrimage with her. The foal she was carrying was the filly Serenissima, later to be the dam of the 1,000 Guineas and St. Leger winner Tranquil, and the grand-dam of the one and only Hyperion. This was a tremendous and unexpected piece of good fortune. But Derby and his advisers deserve credit for sound judgment; the result of the inbreeding experiment to Pilgrimage was Sansovino, who won the Derby in 1924.

Anchora was bought a few months before Gondolette. She was still in training and the winner of eight races. For her he gave 1,300 guineas; two years later she dropped a filly foal called Scapa Flow, who was to prove of no account on the racecourse but one of the greatest brood mares in the history of racing. So unregarded was Scapa Flow as a racemare that she was sent to run in the Norton Selling Handicap of five furlongs at Stockton as a three-year-old, and in this obscure race she finished second. Mr. Wallace Wyllie, a north-country owner-trainer, was inclined to claim her according to the rules for selling races at the value of the stake plus the price at which she was entered to be sold—£50. Unfortunately for him, he mentioned the fact to another north-country trainer John McGuigan, who, trying to be helpful, said he thought he might be able to buy Scapa Flow for Mr. Wyllie at less than the claiming price. When Lambton heard that Scapa Flow might be claimed, and lost to Derby, he quickly got a friend to put in a claim on the latter's behalf, and Scapa Flow was saved for the stud.

The foals of this humble selling-plater were destined to win more in stake money than had ever been won before by the offspring of any brood mare. Not only did Scapa Flow bear the St. Leger winner Fairway, the best three-year-old of his generation, but the Derby second, Pharos, the 1,000 Guineas winner Fair Isle, and five other winners. Her foals won over £85,000 in stake money.

The last of the great brood mares was Ranaï, which Lord Derby bought as a yearling filly in France at the Deauville Sales in 1926 at the instance of his daughter, Lady Victoria. She was to be the dam of ten winners, including the Derby winner Watling Street, and Garden Path, one of the few fillies to win the 2,000 Guineas. Of Derby's sixteen winners of one or more classic races all but one trace in direct female line to one of these eight brood mares.

* * *

Derby in one important particular followed the teaching of his forebear, the twelfth Earl, the founder of the Derby, namely that a certain amount of inbreeding was likely to bear good results. The twelfth Earl inbred too closely; the seventeenth Earl undoubtedly owed a considerable amount of his success to judicious inbreeding. His first Derby winner, Sansovino, was inbred to the great racemare Pilgrimage. She was one of the grandmothers of Sansovino's sire, Swynford, and also of Sansovino's dam, Gondolette. His second Derby winner, Hyperion, was also inbred, but not too closely, and in this case not to a mare but to a stallion. In layman's parlance, one of the great-grandfathers of Hyperion's sire, Gainsborough, was St. Simon, whilst St. Simon was one of the grandfathers of Hyperion's dam, Selene. The third Derby winner, Watling Street, was inbred to St. Simon in an exactly similar way. Five other of Derby's classic winners were also inbred. In technical language thirteen of his sixteen classic winners were inbred at either two or three generations, a clear proof of the value of inbreeding when skilfully used.

There was one other principle to which Derby also adhered in his breeding. He never sent his mares to purely sprinting stallions. He used stallions with a mixture of stamina and speed. All his racehorses, on their breeding, were broadly speaking capable of winning either the Derby or the Oaks, according to their sex. He steadfastly avoided stallions who begat only sprinters. His constant aim was to breed horses to win over the classic distance of one and a half miles —the distance of the Derby.

A large part of Derby's success in breeding and racing was due to three men, whom he had personally selected—his trainer, George Lambton, his stud manager, Walter Alston, and his stud groom,

John Griffiths. Lambton, in addition to being an outstanding trainer, was a fine judge of a horse and it was he who advised the Aga Khan when the latter started a stud. Derby not only found these three men; his infectious enthusiasm for the Turf welded them under his leadership into the most brilliant race-winning team of his generation.

III

The South African War

BETWEEN the Battle of Waterloo and the outbreak of the South African War in 1899, Britain had not fought a major war except in the Crimea. Frontier skirmishes and small punitive campaigns, except in the case of Kitchener's reconquest of the Sudan in 1898, scarcely involving more than a few hundred troops and a few gunboats, had sufficed in the Victorian Age to give a spice of martial and imperial glory to a society which, living in absolute security behind the overwhelming might of the Royal Navy, was profoundly pacific in its outlook. The increasingly prosperous and dominant mercantile society which dwelt in these islands would have been horrified if they had been told that by the turn of the century they would become involved in a war in which more than a quarter of a million men would be required to serve before victory and peace were to be achieved. Smug, self-righteous and sedate, they were now plunged into what, by the standards of the time, seemed a series of colossal military disasters; and the issues involved stirred up a host of critics and enemies abroad and deeply divided the nation on a moral basis at home.

The first European settlement in South Africa dates back to 1652, when the Dutch East India Company established a station at Cape Town. The revocation of the Edict of Nantes in 1685 caused an infusion of Huguenot refugees. The size and prosperity of the Colony soon created trouble with the natives; and the Dutch Court of Governors restricted immigration. When, in 1795, Holland fell under the sway of the French Revolutionary Government, Britain took possession of the Colony in the name of the Prince of Orange who was a refugee in England. At the Peace of Amiens in 1803 the

Colony was restored to the Dutch, but on the resumption of the Napoleonic War Britain fitted out an expedition and once more took possession of the Colony, which was formally ceded to her by the Dutch in 1814. No great enthusiasm for this acquisition was evinced by the British public, and to the Government the Colony was no more than a burden whose future was not seen to merit the tiresome attentions which its current problems demanded. A distant bureaucracy is even less palatable than a local one and Whitehall's failure to ratify such agreements as successive governors made with the natives, its delayed mismanagement of issues which called for prompt attention and its ignorance of and indifference towards the problems of a population who were British in law only, caused resentment and dissatisfaction. This dreary pattern is broken only by the British Government's action in 1834 in declaring slavery illegal which occasioned fury in the Colony.

Some twenty years after Britain's acquisition of the Colony the 'Great Trek' of Boers—or farmers—began. They travelled beyond the Orange and Vaal Rivers into hitherto barely explored parts of South Africa which later became known as the Orange Free State and the Transvaal. Others penetrated to the north-east into Natal through the passes of the Drakensberg, where there had been a British settlement since 1823. In 1842 Lord Stanley (afterwards fourteenth Earl of Derby and grandfather of the subject of this work), who was then Secretary for the Colonies, agreed somewhat reluctantly to proclaim Natal a British Colony. This was not popular with the Dutch and by the end of the year there were only about five hundred Dutch families left in the Colony.

The history of the next forty years in these new areas is that of vacillation in London and of local lawlessness. The Boers were beset by hostile native tribes and their own Government was not able adequately to defend them. The spirit of independence which had impelled them to march into the hinterland to be free of British control now found outlet in internal dissension. The Orange Free State was at loggerheads with the Transvaal and both, supposedly, detested the British. In 1848 Sir Harry Smith, Governor of the Cape, issued a proclamation annexing the Orange Free State; but when four years later the annexation was annulled, the Free State Boers protested vigorously. Lord Grey had declared: 'The ultimate abandonment of the Orange Sovereignty should be a settled point in our policy', but the inhabitants thought otherwise and sent two delegates to plead the cause of annexation in London.

Probably at any time up to the late seventies a federation of these states with the Cape Colony could have been achieved with little difficulty. This fortunate and peaceful outcome was precluded by the liberal policy of 'Little Englandism', based on the deliberate restriction of the dimensions and responsibilities of the British Empire.

In 1877 Disraeli's Government, using hardly more than a handful of police, annexed the Transvaal. It had been promised that the Boers should enjoy a liberal constitution with full legislative powers of their own; but the fulfilment of this promise was deferred on the pretext of the hostilities in which we were engaged against the Zulus. Gladstone in his Midlothian campaign in 1879 denounced the acquisition of the Transvaal because it was 'dishonourable to the character of our country'. This naturally gave rise to the hope among the Boers that if Gladstone won the election he would abandon Britain's sovereignty of the Transvaal. Gladstone won the election, but was no more scrupulous in meeting Boer expectations than had been Disraeli. The Boers revolted, and Britain, after two humiliating defeats at Laing's Neck and Majuba, entered into the Pretoria Convention of 1881 by which self-government was granted to the Boers under the sovereignty of the Queen.

In 1886 what was to prove the richest goldfield in the world was discovered at Witwatersrand. Adventurers from a score of countries poured into the Transvaal. Johannesburg was founded and the scale of immigration into the Transvaal can be judged by the fact that within ten years the city had a population of above 100,000, half of whom were Europeans. The impact of these avaricious prospectors upon the primitive, patriarchal, agrarian Boer government of President Kruger produced tension and unrest. Kruger and the Boers were determined to maintain their land-owning oligarchy and sought to do this by means of repressive legislation against the immigrants, or Uitlanders as they were called. Although many of the Uitlanders were soon among the richest members of the community, they were discriminated against and were denied any right of voting until they had been ten years in the country. Cecil Rhodes, Prime Minister of Cape Colony, in common with the rest of the British community, sympathised strongly with the Uitlanders and sought to exploit their grievances for the further extension of his wide imperial horizons. With his connivance there took place the Jameson Raid in 1896. This was an unofficial and abortive attempt by a few hundred men to seize control of the Transvaal by a commando raid. The whole enterprise miscarried grotesquely. Rhodes, who was deeply compromised in the affair, was compelled to resign and the position of the Uitlanders was worse than before. Finally in the spring of 1899 more than 21,000 of them signed a petition requesting Queen Victoria to intervene. The High Commissioner at the Cape, Sir Alfred Milner, entered into negotiations with Kruger in Bloemfontein, the capital of the Orange Free State. While these negotiations were in progress the British reinforced their military establishments in the Cape and war became ever more likely.

On 9 October 1899, the Boer leaders presented an ultimatum to Milner. British troops must be withdrawn from the borders of the Transvaal or the Boers would attack. After the long catalogue of humiliations already endured this was one which could not be accepted. The ultimatum was rejected and two days later the Boers invaded Cape Colony and Natal.

* * *

Stanley had resigned his commission in the Grenadier Guards in April 1895. When the Boer War broke out he had been a member of parliament for seven years and a Government Whip for four. He was a married man of thirty-four with three children and an interesting political career ahead of him, who could not have been criticised if he had stayed at home, particularly as everyone thought that this was going to be a very short and a very small war. Nonetheless he quit his post in the Government. With the honorary rank of colonel, he set sail for Cape Town, where he arrived before the end of the year to assume the duties of Chief Press Censor. It was doubtless his experience in the House of Commons and his knowledge of politics which were held to make him suitable for what is always a difficult and vulnerable post in time of war.

The campaign had opened badly for the British. Within the first few weeks Magersfontein and Kimberley in Cape Colony and Ladysmith in northern Natal had been invested by the Boers; and in the middle of December there was to be 'Black Week', when General Gatacre was repulsed at Stormberg; a serious reversal was sustained at Magersfontein by Lord Methuen and the Commander-in-Chief, Sir Redvers Buller, suffered casualties of over a thousand at Colenso.

Amongst other young Englishmen who had hurried off to the war in South Africa was Mr. Winston Churchill, who represented the *Morning Post*. He had just made his famous escape from Pretoria and he cabled to his paper at this time, pointing out that Britain was fighting 'a formidable and terrible adversary'. He went on: 'We must face the facts. The individual Boer, mounted in suitable country, is worth from three to five regular soldiers.' He concluded: 'There is plenty of work here for a quarter of a million men, and South Africa is well worth the cost in blood and money. More irregular corps are wanted. Are the gentlemen of England all fox-hunting?'

Another young Englishman in South Africa at this time was Rudyard Kipling. His feelings on the inefficient and dilettante way in which the war was being conducted found expression in his poem 'The Islanders', published two years later, which constitutes one of the most powerful arguments for compulsory National Service ever penned:

> Then were the judgments loosened; then was
> your shame revealed,
> At the hands of a little people, few but apt
> in the field.

Though the public at home still perhaps did not realise the size of the task with which Britain was confronted, the Government now began to display exceptional energy. After his repulse at Colenso, a mood of defeatism settled upon Buller and he telegraphed to London stating that it was impossible for him to relieve Ladysmith, and that he proposed to instruct Sir George White, who was shut up there, to fire off his ammunition and surrender. The message arrived on a Saturday when the English week-end was still known as 'Saturday to Monday' and was apt to find us just as much off our guard as 'week-ends' did in the days of Hitler. Balfour was the only member of the Cabinet in London. Without even consulting his uncle, the Prime Minister, Lord Salisbury, who was at Hatfield —and this would have been easy as Hatfield was one of the first houses in England to have a telephone installed—he telegraphed at once to Buller in the name of the Government: 'If you cannot relieve Ladysmith hand your command over to Sir Francis Clery and return home.' Such aristocratic and instantaneous acceptance of responsibility is, of course, now a thing of the past. Today we should probably have a Gallup poll.

Buller's telegram, coming on top of the news of 'Black Week', decided the Government to supersede Buller in the chief command and to place over him Britain's greatest soldier, Field-Marshal Lord Roberts of Kandahar, who was at that time Commander-in-Chief in Ireland. On the day that he was appointed to the command, he received the news that his son had been killed at Colenso. On the arrival of Roberts, Buller was to be reduced to the command of the forces in Natal.

Press censorship was an innovation at this time. Before the days of war correspondents and telegraphy, there was no need for censorship in the interests of military security and, until the days of mass armies and the popular Press, little need to worry about morale on the home front. This was the first war in which Britain had been engaged where any large number of correspondents was present in the field and it was plainly necessary to have a censorship on military grounds; though, before the days of Marconi, there must have been a considerable delay before anything published in England could have trickled back to the Boers. The censorship in South Africa, as in the First World War, seems to have been largely directed towards protecting the High Command from criticism. Stanley's censorship was lenient and gave satisfaction both to his military superiors and to the war correspondents—a double event which few military Press censors have achieved in subsequent wars.

In addition to Mr. Winston Churchill, there was his fellow Old Harrovian, Mr. Leopold Amery, representing *The Times*. Mr. Amery has left an amusing account in the first volume of his memoirs, *My Political Life*, of the immense pains he was at to circumvent the censorship, lenient though it was. In the middle of February 1900, Roberts had liberated Kimberley and was on his way, via Paardeberg, to the assault of Bloemfontein. Mr. Amery wrote:

> I conceived the idea of a journalistic scoop never yet effected in war, namely, telegraphing with my account a complete map of the field of battle itself. I did this by the simple method of making a map of 400 squares, indicating by the numbers the sinuous course of the Modder River, the position of sundry heights close by which affected the fighting, and the disposition of all the forces. Stanley (afterwards Lord Derby), the Chief Press Censor, had meanwhile arrived with Lord Roberts at headquarters, and was most helpful in sending special messages down the line to enable my cable to pass in spite of the fact that it appeared to be in cipher. Press messages could only go from Modder River at that moment, as the one field telegraph was fully occupied with military work. So I rode my message back myself, cantering nearly halfway to Modder River to meet my dispatch rider, and felt that I had done a big thing. I heard no more till I received three weeks later at Cape Town an irate letter from Moberly Bell[1] asking why I had wasted £1,000 and more on an unintelligible cipher message. Sorely perturbed, I tracked the message down as correctly transmitted all the way to London and apparently duly acknowledged by *The Times* office. But the acknowledgement of one section—the vital section containing the explanation of the cipher—was simply initialled and not stamped, as usual, with *The Times's* clock face. A messenger on his way from the Eastern Telegraph office had got drunk, lost the message, and forged the receipt! So much for the best-laid scoops of war correspondents.

[1] Manager of *The Times*.

Stanley seems to have discharged his difficult duties with good sense and tact and a number of letters survive from war correspondents testifying to this. The *Daily Mail* correspondent, before returning to England, wrote:

Mr. Julian Ralph to Lord Stanley

3 May 1900 *Cape Times,*
Cape Town

On the chance that I do not get well before the curtain falls I want to take this opportunity to assure you of my gratitude for your always just, equal and liberal relation towards all correspondents. If any of those who cause you trouble shall question your fairness I am sure all the reputable and responsible men of 'your corps' will be as eager as I to drown them in the truth.

For your unvarying kindness and friendliness to me I thank you most warmly.

A number of correspondents, with Stanley's encouragement, had organised a paper for the troops:

Mr. Julian Ralph to Lord Stanley

11 November 1900 70 Holland Road,
Kensington

Mr. Kipling and I wish to know whether you do not feel yourself by right of having been our 'managing editor', entitled to membership of our very small and exclusive little band of 'Friendlies', led by Lord Roberts and otherwise consisting of Kipling, Gwynne [of the *Morning Post*], Landon [of *The Times*] and myself. We should all be proud to hear that you insist upon remaining our censor and indulgent master 'so long as grass grows and water runs' as the lawyers phrase it. We have not yet ordered a badge (which costs £4 10. 0.) but will be glad to do so on hearing of your desire to continue to honour our company with yours. I am getting out a limited, numbered, edition de luxe of the *Friend* which will thus become a literary record and prize as well as a historic and journalistic monument. In it I mean to tell the whole history of the only paper ever managed by an army for an army in the field of war.

Mr. Winston Churchill was not so entirely happy in his relations with the military authorities as the others seem to have been. He had started the war as a jingo but, after the relief of Ladysmith, he had cabled to the *Morning Post* urging 'that a generous and forgiving policy be followed. . . . The wise and right course is to beat down all who resist, even the last man, but not to withhold forgiveness or friendship from any who wish to surrender.' This message was ill-received at home and at Army Headquarters in South Africa, and when he wished to join Lord Roberts's forces in front of Bloemfontein for the advance on Pretoria his application was disregarded. It appeared that Mr. Churchill's occasion of offence was not merely this dispatch but also another, in which he had criticised the sermon preached by an army chaplain. This criticism had caused indignation among leading churchmen in England and, as he has recorded: 'Several of the most eloquent divines, vacating their pulpits, had volunteered for the front and were at this moment swiftly journeying to South Africa to bring needed reinforcement to the well-meant exertions of the Army Chaplain Corps.' These strictures on an Army chaplain had also caused distress to Lord Roberts. In consequence, for several days Mr. Churchill languished disconsolately amid the Capuan delights of the Mount Nelson Hotel.

Lord Roberts's Chief of Staff, Lord Kitchener, was also hostile to Mr. Churchill because of what the latter had written about the Sudan campaign. However, Mr. Churchill had powerful friends at court in the shape of General Ian Hamilton and General Nicholson. Making use of them, and by-passing Stanley, he managed eventually to obtain a pass to Lord Roberts's headquarters.

Upon his arrival in Bloemfontein, he was treated with some coldness, but after he had made a personal reconnaissance of Johannesburg and returned to headquarters with news two days ahead of the Intelligence Branch, he was warmly welcomed by the Commander-in-Chief and his Staff. Later he was able to render Lord Roberts a small service. The Commander-in-Chief at this time had on his staff no fewer than three dukes, Norfolk, Marlborough and Westminster, and the aristocratic character of his *entourage* was being made mock of in Radical circles at home. For the advance on Pretoria he proposed to leave the Duke of Marlborough behind. Marlborough was deeply mortified at what he regarded as an affront, but was consoled when he was invited to join forces with his cousin, Mr. Churchill, for the advance. Roberts was appreciative of this solution.

* * *

Meanwhile the fortunes of the war had undergone a speedy transformation. The arrival of Roberts and Kitchener early in January 1900, together with numerous reinforcements which were pouring in from nearly every country in the Empire, enabled rapid advances to be made on all fronts. Kimberley was relieved by Roberts on February 15, the Boer leader Cronje surrendered at Paardeberg on the 27th and the following day the siege of Ladysmith was raised. Bloemfontein was captured on March 13 and on May 17 Mafeking was relieved after a stubborn defence under Colonel Robert Baden-Powell lasting two hundred and seventeen days. The gallant defence of this town by the man who was later to found the Boy Scout movement and its dramatic relief caused such uproarious rejoicing in London that the word 'mafficking' has passed into the language. Pretoria fell on June 4 and on September 11 President Kruger fled via Lourenço Marques to Holland. With the capture of Komati Poort on September 24, it seemed that the war, except for mopping up, was over. On September 25 the British Government, understandably anxious to exploit a successful war for which they had been so much criticised, dissolved Parliament and the famous Khaki Election was fought.

Stanley had not been left uninformed as to political developments in England and his wife and family were active in his interests. In September Lady Alice forwarded to him a letter which she had received from the Duke of Devonshire, who by virtue of his marriage in 1892 to her mother, the Duchess of Manchester, was her stepfather. He was at that time leader of the Liberal Unionists, who had broken with Gladstone on Home Rule, and Lord President of the Council in Salisbury's government.

The Duke of Devonshire to Lady Alice Stanley

31 August 1900 Devonshire House, Piccadilly

I should think that whenever a general election comes there will be *some* changes in the Govt., though I believe Ld. S. [Salisbury] is averse to making any, and then I hope that there may be an Under-Secretaryship or something of that sort for Eddy, but if nothing happens he had better go back to his Whip's work.

One of the few letters from Lady Alice at this time which seems to have been preserved gives news and gossip from home:

Lady Alice Stanley to Lord Stanley

9 September 1900 Witherslack

Eve's little boy was with them—he is tiny—as he is only a year less than *Edward*. I must say the *latter* is solid—he was weighed in the potato machine this morning—and turned the scale at 5st. 1 lb.—Victoria 3st. 9 lb. and Oliver 3st. 2lb. Both boys have got colds. Oliver started one yesterday and Howard followed. . . . It will amuse you to hear of the D. of Marlborough who is in Paris with Winston Churchill and accepted to dine one night with the G. D. Michael.[1] Just before the day came the D. of Marlborough wrote 'my dear Grand Duke, Winston Churchill has made other arrangements for me so I am sorry I cannot dine with you'. Poor Miche was terribly upset as much by the way he was addressed as by the scant courtesy of the excuse!

Stanley could not be back in time for the General Election, and in his absence his wife carried his banner and kept him informed. Polling in the different constituencies in those days was spread over several weeks. The poll in his constituency, Westhoughton, was on October 5 and Stanley, despite his absence, was returned to Westminster with a majority of 3,040. A few days later we find her cabling him:

[1] His Imperial Highness the Grand Duke Michael.

Lady Alice Stanley to Lord Stanley

23 October 1900

FRIENDS WORKING GOOD CHANCE IF VACANCY WIRE HEALTH—ALICE.

And again:

4 November 1900

MISERABLE DELAY, BRODRICK WAR, SELBORNE ADMIRALTY, RITCHIE HOME, LANSDOWNE FOREIGN—ALICE.

Finally, four days later came the good news of political promotion:

Lord Salisbury to Lord Stanley

8 November 1900

WILL YOU ACCEPT FINANCIAL SECRETARY TO WAR OFFICE—SALISBURY.

The war was to drag on for another eighteen months. The Boers now resorted to guerrilla tactics. These tactics were ultimately overcome by the creation of a widespread network of block-houses but it was not until 31 May 1902 that the peace treaty was signed in Pretoria. But since the war seemed to have been won after the flight of Kruger, Lord Roberts handed over command to his Chief of Staff Lord Kitchener and on 11 December 1900, sailed in H.M.S. *Canada* for England. Stanley's old friend St. John Brodrick, who, after the Khaki Election, had succeeded Lord Lansdowne as Secretary of State for War, was clamouring for Stanley's return, since he was greatly overworked. Stanley accordingly sailed with Roberts. Before they left Cape Town, Kitchener telegraphed to Stanley and other members of Roberts's staff who were going home, notably General Ian Hamilton, Colonel Cowan and Sir Henry Rawlinson:

11 December 1900

GOODBYE TO YOU ALL AND BEST OF WISHES DON'T FORGET THOSE YOU LEAVE BEHIND.

The journey was broken at Madeira where Christmas was celebrated. Stanley had now been away above a year. He received what must have been a welcome cable:

Lady Alice Stanley to Lord Stanley

24 December 1900 Knowsley,
Prescot

MERRY XMAS SHALL GO SOUTHAMPTON SECOND NOT TAKING CHILDREN LONDON AS NO PROCESSION WIRE IF YOU WANT VICTORIA ALL FLOURISHING AND LONGING FOR YOUR RETURN—ALICE.

IV

Financial Secretary to The War Office and Postmaster-General

ON his voyage back to England, Stanley received at Gibraltar a long letter awaiting him from his new chief:

Mr. St. John Brodrick to Lord Stanley

Confidential War Office

22 December 1900

MY DEAR EDDY,

I am most grateful to you for two excellent long letters. I am not going to attempt to reply because I am sending my schemes for 1901 by this mail to Ld. Roberts, and having been up half the night all the week I cannot make a long job of it.

I am very glad you will be home at last. In truth, though I fully realised your position, I think had you seen our difficulties here you would have started back a month earlier.

The press of work beats anything which I have seen here in ten years experience. We have a cooked up Army at home all serving on abnormal conditions, and therefore raising every species of question. We are carrying on a great war, and have had since you left [Capetown] to order large reinforcements. The telegrams from Kitchener, Milner and the Admiral all concur that the position in Cape Colony is very grave. Beach stood in the way till last night. But I went down to see Ld. Salisbury who promised if necessary to call a Cabinet and promised me support. This morning I managed to carry Beach and have put under orders 2 Cavalry Regts.; 800 Mounted Infantry; quickened the 10,000 Mounted Police; invited Australia to send all they can at 'Bushmens' rates and have put up the yeomanry to 5*s.*

besides giving a fillip to Militia and Vols. It has taken all day, but now at 1 a.m. I am taking up the 'day's' work! . . .

But I have had to do all your work—yours is one of the heaviest posts in the Govt. if you *do* work—Contracts, New Barrack Scheme, the £10,000,000 for Ordnance now rapidly growing &c., &c. . . .

The governing mind of Britain, no less than the British public, had been disturbed by the revelation of the British Army's inadequacy for war-like purposes in the early months of the South African War. St. John Brodrick was determined that a radical overhaul of the whole system should be instituted. It was decided that Lord Roberts should take over the job of Commander-in-Chief of the Imperial Forces, a post which had been royally encumbered by the martinetship of the Duke of Cambridge from 1856 to 1895. In 1895 the Duke of Cambridge had been succeeded as Commander-in-Chief by Lord Wolseley, who as Sir Garnet Wolseley had earned the confidence and affection of the British public by the tidy and prompt execution of the tasks entrusted to him in Burma, the Crimea, India and China; and, most notably of all, by his brilliant campaign against Arabi Pasha in 1882 when his forces promptly occupied Ismailia. His military successes came to be regarded as so inevitable that the phrase 'It's all Sir Garnet' came into the language as a hallmark of correctitude.[1]

As Adjutant-General Wolseley had struggled manfully to push forward the Army reforms which Gladstone's Secretary of State for War, Cardwell, had initiated in the late sixties; but he was unable to overcome the obduracy of the Duke of Cambridge. It needed the shock of the Boer War to create the climate of public opinion in which large-scale reform was politically possible.

Roberts on his way home from South Africa received at Madeira a long letter from Brodrick. In this letter Brodrick outlined his plan for regrouping the whole British Army on the basis of six army

[1] The author remembers the late Lord Norwich relating with gusto and satisfaction how a railway porter, during the Second World War, after stacking the suitcases neatly in the luggage rack said: 'It's all Sir Garnet.' Mr. Duff Cooper (as he then was) was so delighted by the survival of the phrase that he gave the porter five shillings, a considerable tip in those days.

corps, each nominally of three divisions. Three of these army corps were to consist entirely of professional soldiers, while the other three were to incorporate part-time Territorial units. Doubtless Brodrick and the Prime Minister, Lord Salisbury, were influenced in their choice of Stanley as Financial Secretary by the fact that he and Roberts were already friends who had worked harmoniously together.

Public and ministerial disquietude about the Army led to the setting up of a Royal Commission under the chairmanship of Lord Elgin and, later, of a committee under Lord Esher, which starting work on the basis of the abortive proposals of Lord Hartington's committee of 1891 recommended the abolition of the post of Commander-in-Chief, the creation of a Committee of Imperial Defence, the establishment of an Army Council which was to have functions comparable to those of the Board of Admiralty and, perhaps most important of all, the formation of an Army General Staff. These valuable reforms were not implemented until after both Brodrick and Stanley had left the War Office but both men played their parts in pushing forward this important work.

In its first report the Esher Committee put its finger on the nub of the strategical problem in this pregnant passage:

> The British Empire is pre-eminently a great naval, Indian and Colonial Power. There are, nevertheless, no means for co-ordinating defence problems, or for dealing with them as a whole. . . . We are driven to the conclusion that no measure of War Office reform will avail, unless it is associated with provision for obtaining and co-ordinating for the use of the Cabinet all the information and expert advice required for the shaping of national policy in war, and for determining the necessary preparations in peace. Such information and advice must necessarily embrace not only the sphere of the War Office but also the spheres of the Admiralty and of other offices of state.

The remedy proposed by the Committee was the creation of a Committee of Imperial Defence. The Prime Minister was to be its 'invariable President', with 'absolute discretion in the selection or variation of its members': and there was to be a small permanent secretariat, which would, among other things, provide continuity. The Conservative Prime Minister of the day, Mr. Arthur Balfour, accepted its recommendation and the Secretariat was established in Mr. Disraeli's old house in Whitehall Gardens on the opposite side of Whitehall from Downing Street.

Mr. St. John Brodrick's letter to Lord Stanley telling him how much work his new position would entail was in no way an over-statement. Nor did Stanley shirk his responsibilities. Brodrick had written: 'Yours is one of the heaviest posts in the Government if you *do* work.' Stanley's unremitting activity in the House of Commons must have reassured Brodrick that his appointment, due largely to the influence of family power and connections, was justified on grounds of assiduity and merit. The Financial Secretaryship was Stanley's first executive appointment and his success in attending to it singled him out for the advancement which he was to receive in 1903 when, as Postmaster-General, he achieved Cabinet rank.

While the Royal Commission under Lord Elgin's chairmanship was debating matters of supreme importance for the future of the British Army, and Lord Roberts, with Mr. Brodrick, was implementing as far as possible ideas of military administration acquired during a lifetime's experience in the field, it was only natural that the public, for whom the abstract and technical concepts of military organisation and method were difficult to comprehend, should express its own concern and dismay at the state of affairs by seizing on defects of a less radical but more readily intelligible nature; and in the House of Commons much more time was devoted to the detailed discussion of allegedly fraudulent contracts for the supply of victuals and horses to the Army in South Africa than was allotted to the discussion of the system itself under which such contracts were possible.

More than half a million horses had had to be bought by the Government for the Army in South Africa and there were constant allegations that too much had been paid and that contractors, agents and middlemen had made excessive profits. The Liberal opposition, particularly those who were opposed to the war, were zealous and meticulous in scrutinizing these accounts. Income Tax had been raised from 1*s.* to what most people then regarded as the astronomical level of 1*s.* 3*d.* and it was not until 1903 that it was reduced to 11*d.* Apart from the criticisms that were merely those of factious opposition there was very genuine disquietude throughout the country at what seemed the prodigal expenditure in which the country had become involved. Most of the extra money had been spent by the Army and Brodrick and Stanley had to bear the brunt of the criticisms. An Army Supplementary Estimate of £5,000,000, £2,000,000 for horses and £3,000,000 for fodder, which Brodrick had to introduce at this time, caused a particularly bitter debate. Stanley himself played no great part in the debate, but many friends wrote to sympathise with him for being involved with his colleagues in all this vexatious business:

Lady Wolverton to Lord Stanley

5 February 1902 Cannes

MY DEAR LORD STANLEY,

Thank you ever so much for your long letter cram full of gossip. You have the greatest genius for collecting it of any human being I ever knew!

We have quite settled down again into the regular life out here; gambling, golf and grand dukes! . . . We took ourselves off to Monte Carlo and gambled. F. and I with great success—and went to the Opera to hear Melba and a beautiful new tenor sing *La Bohème*. The tenor is a fresh discovery and they say he is only twenty-five, but Melba who is jealous of him says he is forty if he is a day! . . . It really is good news, de Wet's last guns having been captured. I really think the Boers are lunatics to hold out any longer—and *very* wicked into the bargain. . . . According to the *New York Herald* you seem to have had a rough and tumble in the House of Commons on Monday and Mr. Brodrick had to call other ministers to the rescue . . .

A new motor has come, and is a great success as far as the car goes but the carriage part is not quite right or as we wished it to be. Also the chauffeur is rather overwhelming at present—he worries me because he will go fifty miles an hour and aims at *all* the dogs and babies he can find! And he worries Freddie because he will not share! In fact we have got our hands very full with trying to tame him at this moment.

. . . Goodbye—take care the Liberals don't eat up all you poor War Office people. I think I shall write and advise my John to retire into the safety of private life.

Meat contracts continued to involve the Government in conflict and on one occasion there seems to have been a serious difference of opinion between Stanley and his chief as to his functions in this matter. Stanley disliked controversy of any kind and indeed was unsuited to it. He was also inclined to be touchy.

Mr. St. John Brodrick to Lord Stanley

Private War Office

13 February 1902

I am *very* sorry for your annoyance and still more that you should feel you are not trusted.

I can assure you this is as far from my wish or feeling as anything can be.

I asked that you should come to W.O. and have tried to show my sense of your value by giving you a free hand which no Under Sec. or Fin. Sec. has had in my sixteen years recollection.

To illustrate this I may say that while I submitted to Mr. Smith, Stanhope and Lansdowne every large contract, the meat contract is the first which I have gone into since we became partners.

But it is an invariable rule in the War Office, and I believe in all other offices, that a subject once before the head of the office is not dealt with or altered without his concurrence. This is no question of confidence, but different men cannot decide on the same thing.

This particular business was really a Cabinet question since Balfour and Chamberlain had spent hours over it with me.

My instinct about it may be all wrong and yours all right, but after all I am responsible and I cannot see any reason for giving, to the advantage of the syndicate, anything which may give us Parliamentary trouble.

It distresses me extremely that you should take this personally, but we have plenty of hard times before us, and we cannot afford a slip.

Remember, it would be different if you had ideal permanent officials to rely on, but some are overworked just now, and we are constantly being let down by the want of knowledge of others. I have perfectly hated today, but if you could realise that it is only ordinary procedure and not personal confidence which has been in question, I do not think we need give the past a moment's thought.

It does, however, appear in a letter from General Sir Ian Hamilton that Stanley's action in regard to this particular meat contract with which his chief had found fault was at least profitable to the Army. The second paragraph shows the great affection and respect which Hamilton entertained for Kitchener, a feeling which Stanley also had developed from his acquaintance with the latter during the South African War:

General Sir Ian Hamilton to Lord Stanley

Private
15 March 1902

Army Headquarters,
South Africa,
Pretoria

Your note of 21 February to hand. I do not see how anyone in this world can quarrel with your action in regard to the Meat Contract seeing that up to the present we have sold over £200,000 worth at a shilling a lb. which said £200,000 we shall now proceed to buy back at eightpence a lb. I think if you tell Sir Michael Hicks Beach this, it ought to cheer him up a little bit. . . .

With regard to the peace negotiations now coming on again you will, from my previous letters to you, be able pretty well to forecast my views. So long as Lord K. conducts the business personally he can talk these fellows over and make them agree to anything. The moment a pedantic civilian with an eyeglass and a cynical smile enters upon the scene then there will be inevitable breaking off of all attempts at negotiations. . . .

Before this reassuring reply arrived from South Africa to what must have been a letter begging for reassurance Stanley had had recourse to a threat which is repeated throughout his life in the monotone of a litany. If they did not value his services they would perhaps be better off without them. This time it is Lady Wolverton's turn again to do the reassuring:

Lady Wolverton to Lord Stanley

3 March 1902 Cannes

. . . I am sorry you have been so badgered and worried lately—it is bad luck too—being held responsible for contracts and arrangements which I suppose were made by your predecessors in office whilst you were thousands of miles away in S. Africa? Anyway you must try and keep your patience and temper with Mr. Brodrick as it would do your career a lot of harm if you really were to resign though I expect you have never actually contemplated doing such a thing—but only suggested it in a moment of fury! . . .

* * *

In September Lady Alice stayed for a week at Balmoral. She wrote to her husband every day and her letters cast light upon life in Scotland in the early Edwardian era.

Lady Alice Stanley to Lord Stanley

8 September 1902 Balmoral Castle

. . . It was so funny after they had had their tea, they all came out to stroll about—King, Queen, Duke and Duchess of York and all their children. Presently all their dogs were let out to them. The King's dog looked as if it was going dotty. It turned out that it had bitten a man and had probably got a good licking—it rushed about, the children after it, they were called not to go near, then a strange dog off the yacht still more frightened the King's dog and the yacht dog made tracks towards the Queen's little dogs!! It was altogether a scene of the wildest confusion and I only dreaded that Sol would leap out of my window and join the fray; but he didn't!!

11 September 1902

. . . I was forgetting to tell you of our dreadful amusement last night. We spent from 10 to 11 standing out of doors surrounded by dead stags and looking at gillies hopping about on the gravel. They were very sedate at first but as the bonfire got lower and the whiskey mounted higher they capered more energetically. The King had killed five of the stags, so he was in great spirits. Everyone else had got stags too, unlike the Mar drives . . .

12 September 1902

. . . I see that all the Royal Carriages are painted in the way that they propose painting your motor—do you think it matters? We shall have red upholstery and they have blue so perhaps the resemblance will not be so great[1]. . .

If you think it matters about the car you had better make them paint ours blue.

13 September 1902

. . . We are to have a cinematograph and neighbours this evening.

14 September 1902

. . . The cinematograph was not very good last night and it entailed a good deal of standing about afterwards which did not suit me very well, my indigestion of the last two days having culminated in severe pains! The Duke of Fife tho' was still more to be pitied as after driving 14 miles here he had to retire to bed instead of getting his dinner. I believe more from nervousness than anything else . . .

* * *

In September 1903 the Colonial Secretary, Joseph Chamberlain, resigned from the Government to popularise the cause of Tariff Reform to which he had long been addicted. Victorian England felt in her bones that her rise to industrial and mercantile pre-eminence was associated with the Free Trade cause, yet for some time an active group of Tories had been agitating for the institution of a protective tariff with a measure of preference for the Empire. In later life Stanley used to recall how in 1895 he accompanied Balfour to a meeting at the Free Trade Hall in Manchester to celebrate the Conservative victories at the polls and how Balfour said to him: 'I wonder how long it will be before this Free Trade Hall is packed with people clamouring for Protection.'

[1] The car eventually had red panels on a black foundation, to match the upholstery, which was crimson. It was a Siamese Phaeton with a canopy. It cost £460, had no 'front glass screen' but a special glazed frame at the back. It was designed to carry four passengers and a driver; its horsepower was 10. Lord Stanley disposed of it two years later to the Earl of Radnor. The author is indebted for these curiosities to the Wolseley Motor Company Limited whose filing system appears to be a model of correctitude.

Chamberlain and his associates were inspired by a broad and bold conception: it was the building of a wall of tariffs round the Empire. Reciprocal preferences between the individual dominions and colonies would place the Empire on a more solid and self-contained economic basis at a time when many long-established markets were being penetrated by the growing industrial and commercial power both of Germany and the United States. Imperial preference was integral to the Chamberlain conception. He wanted to introduce tariffs so that there could be imperial preference; protection of the home manufacturer was only incidental. But since at this time nearly all the industrial power of the Empire was concentrated in these small islands, scarcely any advantage could be derived by the colonies from imperial preference unless the general tariff structure included a tax on at least some articles of foodstuffs or raw materials.

It was on this issue that Chamberlain was to founder. The majority of the Tory Party, though they would have liked to include some food taxes in the tariff structure, realised that this would be most unpopular with the industrial masses whose relatively high prosperity had been made possible by cheap food. Hence the tariff proposals, which the Party brought forward from time to time, were limited to taxation on manufactured goods.

The exclusion of food taxes made the proposals less unacceptable to the general public; but the Liberals had little difficulty in persuading the electorate that it was food that the Tories really wanted to tax. And the fear of this was to hamstring the Party for many years. Thus the successive compromise policies achieved over the years inside the Party on this issue only resulted in the worst of all situations; the Tories became branded with a desire to tax the people's food while Chamberlain's imperial dream was scuppered. There were still to be many Tories in the years ahead who would press the Party to adopt a high tariff policy; but after the 1906 Election very few of them were prepared to swallow food taxes. Thus many enthusiasts for the Chamberlain policy, notably Lord Beaverbrook, became chagrined that that policy had lost its imperial content and was no longer of any aid either to Empire or British farmers. They felt that it could only serve the narrow interests of British industrialists who, caring little for the wide imperial projects of Chamberlain and his followers, nonetheless as the century progressed became increasingly attracted by the simple idea of protecting their own manufactures in the home market from the growing competition of an increasingly industrialised world.

* * *

When Chamberlain resigned from the Government he was persuaded by Balfour to keep his resignation secret for a few days. During this interval the three strong Free Traders in the Cabinet—Mr. Ritchie, the Chancellor of the Exchequer, Lord George Hamilton and Lord Balfour of Burleigh—wrongly concluded that Balfour intended to support Chamberlain on the protectionist issue. Accordingly they resigned. Balfour was glad to let them go as a balance to Chamberlain's resignation. Moreover he suspected that they were engaged in a plot to form a new government under the leadership of the Duke of Devonshire who in fiscal matters was of their opinion, but who in fact was far from being informed as to what was going on.

The political transaction by which Balfour rid his Government of the two extreme wings who were bedevilling the Party's future with their doctrinaire quarrel about tariffs was, at the time, a matter of perplexed controversy. And many objective observers believed that Balfour had been guilty of sharp practice and had disencumbered himself of Mr. Ritchie and his friends by methods of deception scarcely acceptable among political colleagues. In 1931 Mr. Winston Churchill published an article in the now defunct *Strand Magazine* about Mr. Balfour. This led Derby, as Stanley had now become, to write to Mr. Churchill a letter which constitutes an interesting footnote to the chronicles of these times:

Lord Derby to Mr. Winston Churchill

Private 27 March 1931

I am going to write to you on a political matter but of ancient date. I have read your article on Arthur Balfour in the *Strand Magazine* and there is an inaccuracy in it which, for your own private information, I am going to correct. You say that, at the Cabinet from which

Chamberlain broke away, Balfour took the Duke of Devonshire into his room and told him that Joe had resigned and that his resignation had been accepted. That is not quite right. What happened was this. That afternoon the Duke came away from the Cabinet certainly under the impression that Chamberlain had perhaps offered to resign in a half-hearted way and his offer had been refused. He and I went to Leo Rothschild's at Gunnersbury to dine. Whilst we were at dinner a Red Cabinet Box came down. Lord Hartington, as I always called him, turned to me and said 'I have left my Cabinet key in London, lend me yours.' Of course I had not got a Cabinet key and told him so. The box remained unopened and came back with us to London. The next morning I saw Arthur Balfour and he told me that Joe had resigned and he had accepted his resignation. At luncheon I met my brother-in-law Charlie Montagu, who of course was Lord Hartington's step-son, and he asked me to go and see him as he was very lonely, the Duchess was away and he had nobody to talk to.

I went to Devonshire House. Found him walking about his room. He said: 'Of course I have written to resign.' I asked him what he had given as his reason and he said that he could not remain in the same Cabinet as Joe Chamberlain. My answer was: 'But as Joe has resigned that is no excuse at all.' He jumped as if he had been shot and said: 'I know nothing about it.' It then struck me that the Red Box the night before had contained the information and so like him he had never opened the box and did it then and found, as I thought he might do, the letter from Balfour telling him that Joe had resigned and hoping that he would stay. He was then in a great fix because he had sent his letter of resignation to Balfour by hand. I volunteered to go down and see Balfour which I did. At first he would not see me and was rather annoyed at being interrupted as he told me he was writing a letter to the Duke saying how much he regretted his resignation etc. I told him he need not write the letter as the Duke was ready to withdraw the letter of resignation which had been written under a misapprehension. A. J. B. then asked me to go and get the Duke to come and see him. This I did. The Duke and I dined together in the evening and he told me then everything had been satisfactorily arranged.

Now with regard to the final resignation. Much of what you say is quite true. I was at Newmarket. He asked me to come in and see him after racing on the first day which I did. He then showed me a letter from Ritchie. You never saw such a letter in your life. He accused him of every crime under the sun—breach of faith, dishonesty, every sort of thing. It upset the old Duke very much indeed. As he said to me: 'To think I have gone all through my life and then at the end of it to have these sort of accusations levelled at my head.' He was really quite hysterical about it. The result however was that after Arthur Balfour had spoken at Sheffield he got hold of one sentence as you say and made that a peg on which to hang his resignation. Quite between you and me however the real person who made him resign was the Duchess, and I am certain she got both Ritchie and Balfour of Burleigh to write to him, though naturally she never anticipated Ritchie would write in such a strain. I am sure her idea was that Balfour must fall and that he, the Duke, would be sent for to form a Government.

* * *

The campaign to thrust Tariff Reform down the throats of the Tory Party had been given renewed emphasis by the Colonial Secretary, Joseph Chamberlain, in a speech which he had made to his constituents in Birmingham in May 1903. This speech had 'put the cat among the pigeons' and produced a division in the Tory Party which was to continue for twenty years. The repercussions in Liverpool had been immediate. Though it was usually Salvidge who was more prescient than Stanley, on this occasion the roles seem to have been reversed. Salvidge was at first attracted by Joseph Chamberlain's policy, which, though it could never have obtained the support of the majority of the nation, made a very widespread appeal to the patriotic instincts of many sections of the community. Stanley, from the outset, had a more acute and practical perception of this issue than Salvidge and realised that Tariff Reform with its potential undertones of food taxes would certainly be a vote loser. It took the electoral landslide of 1906 to confirm Stanley in this belief and to convert Salvidge to it as well. We shall see in a later chapter how, working together, they were able to impose their convictions upon the rest of the Tory Party.

Meanwhile the advancement of Salvidge in Liverpool politics and the increasing influence of the Liverpool Working Men's Association was causing resentment among the more old-fashioned members of the Party:

Mr. J. Morris to Lord Stanley

17 May 1903 160 Princes Road,
Liverpool

. . . If we are to remain under the hand of Mr. Salvidge there may be worse things in store than entire reorganisation. I know you will forgive me for speaking so plainly on this matter, I don't think I have said so much before to anyone. I have no ill will towards Salvidge, if anything it is the contrary, neither am I indifferent to the Church question, but the better class of Unionists will hold back so long as he rules or seems to rule. . . .

In June of the same year Salvidge was invited by Mr. Winston Churchill to a private dinner at the House of Commons. The other guests included Lord Hugh Cecil, Mr. Goschen and Sir Michael Hicks Beach. Salvidge accepted the invitation, but his son records in *Salvidge of Liverpool* that during the dinner a suggestion was made that each guest should in turn speak his mind about how best to stimulate opposition to Mr. Chamberlain's proposals.

'I am afraid,' said Salvidge, to the cold dismay of the company, 'that, with all respect, I had better give my views first. I have come here under some misapprehension as to the nature of the gathering. I look upon it as little short of a cave or plot against one of the leaders of our party—a leader who means more to the masses of the Industrial Midlands and North than all of us put together. I am sorry to make such a poor return for hospitality, but I think it would facilitate the business in hand if I now withdrew from this table.'

Prior to his resignation from the Government, Chamberlain had already agreed to address a public meeting at Liverpool for 27 October 1903. Salvidge had committed his Working Men's Association to unqualified support. The day is chiefly memorable on two accounts: Mr. F. E. Smith, the future Lord Birkenhead, made his first public speech in following Mr. Chamberlain, and Lord Stanley, the most important Conservative in the North of England, was absent from the platform, although his father and mother and a large party from Knowsley occupied seats upon it.

The departure from the Cabinet of so many important statesmen from both flanks of the Party left a void which could only be filled with new or innocuous figures from the centre. To placate the formidable 'Jo', Balfour advanced his son Austen, a political stripling of thirty-nine who had only been eleven years in the House of Commons, to the position of Chancellor of the Exchequer, relinquished by Ritchie. This left the Post Office open and among other consequential appointments Stanley entered the Cabinet as Postmaster-General.

In those days it was necessary for a Member of Parliament on joining the Cabinet to vacate his seat and to seek re-election. This dated back to a clause in the Act of Settlement in 1707 which was designed to prevent the Hanoverian dynasty when it should succeed Queen Anne from corrupting the Parliament with numerous jobs and pensions. In modern times it became a considerable political inconvenience. In 1919 this was amended so that re-election became unnecessary within nine months of a general election, and Parliament finally abolished the principle altogether in the Amending Act of 1926. Under the old law Stanley resigned his seat, but he was returned for Westhoughton without a contest.

Stanley's short tenure of the Post Office was not marked by any outstanding reforms or advances. Nonetheless, he pushed forward the work of the department in a sensible fashion. The Wireless Telegraph Act of 1904, from which the present broadcast licence system devolves, made it illegal for anyone to install or work wireless apparatus in the United Kingdom or in British ships in territorial waters without licences from the Postmaster-General. Stanley apparently received many applications for licences under the Act, but in his report for 1904/1905 said that great difficulty was being experienced in this matter because an insufficiency of technical knowledge made it impossible to control mutual interference between rival commercial stations. It was not until eighteen years later that Station 2LO began daily broadcasting from London, thus inaugurating the official wireless service now known as the B.B.C. On 2 February 1905, the Post Office and the National Telegraph Company concluded an agreement whereby there was to be intercommunication between the two services and the Post Office was to purchase the Company's entire system in 1911. Hull at the present time is the only city in England now running its own telephone service. In April 1905 the first official parcel post with the U.S.A. was instituted, which for a time worked concurrently with the American Express Company which hitherto had monopolised this service. Towards the end of Stanley's period as Postmaster-General, King Edward VII opened the new and present London General Post Office in King Edward Street, E.C.1.

* * *

Stanley's refusal to accept the recommendations on rates of pay for postal employees made by the Bradford Committee which had been set up by his predecessor, Austen Chamberlain, involved him in a most vexatious and uncharacteristic indiscretion which was to dog him for many years of his political life. Speaking on the Post Office Estimates in July 1905, he explained in reply to a number of interruptions how the Post Office employees were bombarding Members of Parliament, at a time when it was known there would soon be a general election, with letters of a minatory nature demanding increases of pay. Warming to his topic, according to *Hansard* of 6 July 1905:

> Lord Stanley said the demands made by employees generally before the Bradford Committee, with the pay of all the supervising classes raised in proportion, would have meant the payment from the Exchequer of no less than £2,500,000 a year. He was entitled to ask when was this to cease. Hon. Members knew better than he how they were being bombarded with applications from Post Office employees and other classes of Civil Servants for increases of wages. This had taken a form which was not illegal, but which he could not help thinking was an abuse of their rights, viz. the form of a political threat. They had circulated an appeal in which they expressed very clearly and very frankly their intention, and it was one of which the Committee would have to take note now or it would be much worse in the future. They said:
>
> 'Two thirds at least of one political party are in great fear of losing their seats. The swing of the pendulum is against them, and any Member who receives forty or fifty such letters will under present

circumstances have to consider very seriously whether on this question he can afford to go into the wrong lobby. This is taking advantage of the political situation.'

It was indeed, but it was abusing, as it seemed to him, their rights as voters. It was nothing more nor less than blackmail. It was nothing more nor less than asking Members to purchase votes for themselves at the general election at the expense of the public Exchequer. Both sides would have to make up their minds that some means should be devised by which there should not be this continual blood-sucking on the part of the public servants. How it was to be done was not for him to say, but he had suggested, and he still thought, that there would have to be some organisation outside Party politics altogether, and unconnected with and unmoved by Parliamentary and political considerations to whom such questions should be referred and by whom an impartial opinion should be given.

In a speech at Little Lever on 27 November 1905, Lord Stanley withdrew the term 'bloodsucker', adding, when confirming this in a letter of December 1 to the General Secretary of the Postal Telegraph Clerks' Association, that he did not withdraw the term 'blackmail', but applied it only to the writers of the circular; in the meantime the Association had vigorously attacked him for using these terms. Nevertheless, following the resignation of the Government in December 1905, *St. Martin's-le-Grand*, predecessor of the present *Post Office Magazine*, wrote in March 1906: 'We have parted with Lord Stanley with many regrets, and those especially who have personal dealings with him will remember him as a man whose thoughtfulness, courtesy, ease and charm of manner and approachableness helped considerably to oil the wheels of official life.'

Stanley's *gaffe* did not find him, however, entirely bereft of support. The Joint Permanent Secretary to the Treasury wrote:

Sir Edward Hamilton to Lord Stanley

Private — Treasury, S.W.
8 July 1905

I meant to have written yesterday to thank you for your courageous speech the night before. I do so now. It was capital, and it will have a good effect for a limited time.

My own belief is, that there are only two remedies for the present state of things. One is that every civil servant should be disfranchised; but I am afraid that that is an impossibility. The other is that Post Office employees etc. should have a member of their own; but the day for fancy franchises is over. One remedy is as unpractical as the other, I am afraid, and so I suppose we must be content with periodical speeches like yours, on which I congratulate you.

* * *

In December 1905 Balfour resigned and the King entrusted the formation of the new Liberal Government to Sir Henry Campbell-Bannerman. Dissensions over the tariff issue, successive resignations of important ministers and a steady procession of defeats at by-elections had led the Tory leaders to look with apprehension on the outcome of a general election which could not be postponed much longer. It was thought that the Liberals who were also considerably divided, particularly over their attitude to the Boer War, would find difficulty in forming a cohesive Government which could adequately present itself to the electorate. These expectations proved ill-founded and in the event Campbell-Bannerman succeeded in forming an administration which under his leadership and subsequently under that of Asquith has been regarded as the most talented of this century.

Campbell-Bannerman's Government was in a minority in the House of Commons. Consequently he at once obtained a dissolution from the King and a general election was held in January of 1906. The results proved catastrophic to the Conservatives. At the time of the dissolution, they had held 334 seats. They returned to Westminster after the election a depleted band of 157, of whom 109 were committed to Chamberlain's tariff policy, 32 followed Balfour's indecisive leadership and 11 were pledged to Free Trade. In the campaign, the Tories had not only been hampered by their partial espousal of tariffs, which the Liberals, of course, asserted would include food taxes; they were also assailed with the cry of Chinese slavery, arising out of the use of indentured Chinese labour on the Rand goldfields.

The Tory slaughter was particularly heavy in the north. In Manchester, where the Free Trade argument was advanced with especial vigour by Mr. Winston Churchill, six seats were at issue when Mr. Churchill woke up in the morning; one was Liberal Unionist, one Liberal and four were Conservative. When he went to bed that night, the four Conservative seats and the Liberal-Unionist seat had changed hands; and the city's representation consisted of four Liberals and two Socialists. Liverpool has traditionally been a more Conservative city than Manchester. Of its nine seats, seven of which were held by Conservatives, one by a Liberal Unionist and one by an Irish Nationalist (the famous T. P. O'Connor), two were lost to the Liberals.

Stanley was among the numerous Tories who went down to defeat, despite the fact that he declared himself to be a Free Trader. He fought a hard and vigorous campaign, but his defeat, though a shock to himself and his family, was not altogether a surprise, at least to the *Bolton Evening News* (a Liberal paper) which on polling day, January 18th, wrote:

> The political fate of Lord Stanley is in the balance today. The Westhoughton Division with an electorate of 18,173 is deciding the issue between his Lordship, who has represented the constituency since 1892, and Mr. W. T. Wilson, an operative carpenter and joiner, of Bolton, the representative of the Labour Party. Since the commencement of the campaign both candidates have addressed innumerable meetings in all parts of the Division, Lord Stanley coming in for some lively greetings and very considerable heckling. Mr. Wilson has not experienced anything like so much hostility if, indeed, there has really been any hostility to him. He has been subjected to a few sharp questions, but as time has advanced he has grown greatly in favour. . . . The certainty about Lord Stanley being again returned received its first shaking when a Blackrod[1] meeting declined to give him a vote of confidence, and the adverse voting at several other meetings has led to an extremely strong feeling that Toryism in Westhoughton is about to totter tonight. Lord Stanley has said a good deal about Post Office matters but the public soon became sated of that topic and have given

[1] A village in the Westhoughton Division.

him more than one uncomfortable quarter-hour on Chinese Labour. He has, however, iterated and re-iterated his belief in the necessity for this. As to Free Trade he has expressed approval provided powers of Retaliation be held ready for us if necessary.

When the votes were counted it was apparent that Stanley had had a catastrophic reverse. The figures were:

W. T. Wilson (Labour)	9,262
Lord Stanley (Conservative)	6,134
Majority	3,128

The majority of 3,040 which he had obtained at the Khaki Election despite his absence in South Africa had disappeared and his opponent won by a slightly larger margin. The electorate had increased during the intervening six years but a turnover of 6,000 votes in a total poll of only 15,000 was certainly a smack in the eye, particularly for a member of the Cabinet, who was also the personal standard-bearer of a family which had such wide hereditary influence in the county. Mr. Cyril Banks, who is today the Conservative Agent for the North-west Area, has forwarded to the author the following account from Mr. Frank Morris, Chairman of the Bolton Conservative Association:

Mr. Frank Morris to Mr. Cyril Banks

February 1957

I was only a youngster at the time of the 1906 Election, but I have a vivid recollection of the shock this result had on my parents and elders. This particular election has always been associated with the term 'bloodsucker' . . . and my early recollections are of stories that wherever Lord Stanley appeared he was greeted with this cry of 'bloodsuckers'.

The fact that the heir to the House of Derby was beaten by a working carpenter had a tremendous effect on this part of industrial Lancashire.

* * *

This was not the first time that the Stanleys had suffered a dunching electoral reverse. Twice before the family had been severely embarrassed in their own particular pocket borough of Preston. Stanley's grandfather, who was later to be three times Conservative Prime Minister, had started his political career as a Whig. In 1830, upon the resignation of the Duke of Wellington and the formation of a Whig government under Earl Grey, he was appointed Chief Secretary for Ireland. Earlier in the year there had been a general election at which Stanley retained the Preston seat which he had occupied since 1826. But in the by-election that now took place he was defeated by his Radical opponent Mr. Hunt.

So mortified were the Stanleys by this unexpected electoral reverse that in the words of a pious and respectful family chronicler, William Pollard,[1] the twelfth Earl of Derby, grandfather of the defeated candidate, who had been born in Preston, 'keenly felt the blow and in a short time after the close of the contest the windows of Patton House, in Church Street, the family mansion in Preston, were blocked up, and all the attendants withdrawn, giving to the otherwise noble building a desolate and dismal appearance; the races, also, which the family had warmly patronised, they no longer supported, which caused them to be discontinued, and generally the Stanleys withdrew themselves from all association with the town'.

The earlier dispute concerned Stanley's great-grandfather, the Lord Stanley who was to become the thirteenth Earl. Preston is one of the oldest boroughs in the country, having received a Royal Charter in the twelfth century from Henry II. And it was not for nothing that it was glad to call itself 'poor, proud Preston'. From 1768 to 1795 the Lord Derby of the day had been able to nominate both candidates for this double-barrelled constituency. However, in 1796, when the son of the twelfth Earl was put forward for one of the seats, Preston was feeling as proud as ever and less poor. John Horrocks, head of the rising firm of Lancashire mill-owners, Horrocks, Miller and Company (a firm which still exists as Horrockses, Crewsdon) wished to be a candidate and he received the backing of the Corporation. An exceptionally vigorous campaign was fought, the poll being kept open for eleven days. Stanley and Horrocks were both elected but Stanley's fellow Whig candidate

[1] *The Stanleys of Knowsley* by William Pollard (Frederick Warne & Co., 1869).

was defeated and one of the seats was irretrievably lost to the family interest. In 1812 Stanley ceased to sit for Preston but was returned to Parliament for Lancaster until the passage of the Reform Bill in 1832. In 1832 when Lord Grey's administration required greater numbers in the Lords he was called up in his father's life-time as Baron Stanley of Bickerstaffe. Thereafter he took no part in public life but devoted himself to zoology.

* * *

Stanley was chagrined at his spectacular defeat and toyed with the idea of abandoning his political career. But comfort came to him on speedy wings from his leader, Arthur Balfour, who had himself been defeated in Manchester, and from Austen Chamberlain:

Mr. Austen Chamberlain to Lord Stanley

26 January 1906 — Highbury,
Moor Green,
Birmingham

Dictated as I am still obliged to pass the day on the sofa.

Though there may be some difference of view between us, you and I are too good friends for me to pass by the loss of your seat without telling you how much I regret it. Whatever our differences amounted to they never prevented our working cordially together and I hope we shall remain equally good friends and allies in future.

I suppose that, in the great wave that swept over Lancashire, nothing could have saved your seat, and though I should like very much to tell you my view of the cause of our disaster and of how to retrieve it, I will not at this moment say anything that you might think controversial, but will only end, as I began, by expressing my genuine regret at the defeat of a friend and colleague.

Mr. Arthur Balfour to Lord Stanley

Private — Whittingehame,
27 January 1906 — Prestonkirk

A thousand thanks for your letter. But what nonsense you talk in it! *Why* are you not coming back to the House of Commons? I believe that, in spite of its drawbacks, you enjoyed political life more than you will ever enjoy any other; and you really must not take these rash decisions. A month abroad is all right—you have well earned it; but nothing palls so quickly as a holiday.

I never doubted that your defeat was due to *Labour*. And you probably had the same experience that I had, namely, that the constituency did not the least want to argue any question at all except Chinese Labour, which was a convenient peg upon which to hang their programme.

Stanley was to take Balfour's advice. In the spring of 1906 he made a tour of Italy, Malta and Sicily and enjoyed the rest which this provided. Lady Alice wrote to him advising him not to eat Italian oysters which she felt sure must be grown in drains. However, his defeat at the polls was not taken by all those with whom he had been in contact as an occasion for commiseration. Indeed a Post Office official seized the opportunity to practise an amusing revenge upon Stanley for his charge of 'blackmailers and bloodsuckers'. In those days of Morse telegraphy, the word T-I-M-E was sent out to every office in the country at 9.59 a.m. Then on receipt of the signal from Greenwich to the Central Telegraph Office, the letters T-E-N were sent out, thus giving the official time by which clocks were adjusted. On this occasion, instead of the signal TEN, the words 'STANLEY OUT' were transmitted and re-transmitted to all telegraph offices in the country.

V

The Inheritance

STANLEY'S father, the sixteenth Earl of Derby, died of heart failure at Holwood on 14 June 1908 at the age of sixty-seven. He had had a long career of public service. First elected to Parliament in 1865 for the family borough of Preston, he had sat in the House of Commons for more than twenty years until in his brother's lifetime he was called up to the House of Lords as Baron Stanley of Preston. His first ministerial appointment was that of Financial Secretary to the War Office, the post which his son subsequently occupied. Other offices he filled were those of Secretary of State for War, Secretary of State for the Colonies, President of the Board of Trade and Governor-General of Canada. It was in 1893 while he was serving in Canada that his brother died and he succeeded to the earldom. The responsibilities of his inheritance led him to resign the Governor-Generalship and to return to England before the completion of his term. He had, however, already been in Canada for five years and his memory is still preserved in Canada as a popular and successful Governor-General.

Among the letters of condolence which the new earl received was one from his father's old friend, King Edward:

H.M. The King to Lord Derby

15 June 1908 Buckingham Palace

MY DEAR EDDY,

Although I have written to your poor dear afflicted Mother I must write you a few lines to express my deepest sympathy with you—your Brothers & Sisters at the terrible loss you have sustained!

When the sad news reached me I cannot express how great the shock was & grief at the loss of one of my oldest & best friends. We were born in the same year. I had known him when he was a boy at Eton—& we served for a few months together in the Guards. Though the suddenness of the end was fearful, still for his sake it is perhaps best so—as he was spared a long & painful illness. It may truly be said 'In the midst of life we are in death!'

Your dear kind Father had I am sure not a single enemy in the world & he will be deeply regretted though never forgotten by all those who had the advantage of knowing him & appreciating his excellent qualities.

The breaking up of your happy home must be a great blow for you but fortunately you are all such a united Family that the traditions will ever remain the same.

I am,
Yours very sincerely,
EDWARD R.

The Prince of Wales wrote:

H.R.H. The Prince of Wales to Lord Derby

16 June 1908 Frogmore,
Windsor

MY DEAR EDDY,

I have known you for so many years and we are such old friends, that I cannot express what my feelings are at such a sad moment as this, I can only say that in your dear father, whom I have known since I was a child, I have lost a kind and valued friend. I think your family was the happiest and most united one I have ever seen, therefore I can well imagine what a terrible break up this means to you all and how irreparable your loss is. Everyone is mourning his loss and he will be greatly missed by his host of friends. Today at Ascot one heard nothing but kind and sympathetic expressions about your dear father. We are so glad to hear dear Lady Derby is bearing up so well; both the Princess and I beg to offer you and yours our deepest sympathy in your terrible sorrow.

On the day of his father's funeral Derby replied:

Lord Derby to H.R.H. the Prince of Wales

18 June 1908 Knowsley

SIR,

No friend could ever have written to another friend a kinder letter than Your Royal Highness has written to me, and I appreciate it most deeply.

I don't think anybody who was privileged to know my dear father could help loving him, so gentle, so kind to everyone, and so absolutely straight. I was on terms with him that I should think have never existed between father and a son. I think he trusted me absolutely and I have never had a secret from him. He was my dearest friend as well as my father and to have lost both in one dreadful minute is indeed hard to bear. I have had all the fun of life, thanks to him, without the responsibilities and the future must be very different from the past. My mother is too splendid for words, so brave, so resigned, but that is because she can look back upon forty-four years of married life unclouded in any way, without a moment of regret. They were as much in love with each other when he died as when they married. He had had a happy life and he died the death he had always wanted to die—talking to her with a smile on his lips.

Your Royal Highness so rightly talks of us as a united family. It was thanks to father and mother that we were so and it won't be Alice's and my fault if we do not profit by the example and do all we can to make mother, brothers and sister feel that though it can never be quite the same, the home is still there.

I know I shall be forgiven for writing in this somewhat unconventional style, but I do so appreciate the letter written by 'a friend to a friend' that I have ventured to answer it in the same way. I thank Your Royal Highness from the bottom of my heart and am Your Royal Highness's obedient servant.

STANLEY [sic]

* * *

Derby, as we must now call him, was forty-three years old when he succeeded to the splendid titles and magnificent possessions which his family had acquired and developed in the previous eight hundred years. He was the last of those great English territorial magnates who exercised an effective and pervasive political influence based on the ownership of land and the maintenance of an historic association with it. His acres were not exceptionally wide but they were of exceptional value. He inherited nearly seventy thousand acres; but at that time there were at least forty other magnates with more extensive properties. The Duke of Richmond and Gordon owned about a quarter of a million acres, the Duke of Buccleuch nearly half a million, while the Duke of Sutherland, the largest landowner in the kingdom, was the proprietor of something in excess of a million and a quarter. Most of the estates which were larger than Derby's were, in the main, agricultural; and those of almost Texan proportions had most of their land in the north of Scotland, a bleak and desolate region of barren moors and mountainous forests, maintained for purposes of sport. Derby's modest acreage had, however, risen immensely in value through the process of the Industrial Revolution. On what a hundred years before had been farmland now stood thriving factories and populous cities, furnishing a rent roll which afforded him one of the largest incomes in the kingdom. The gross rent roll of the Derby estates at this time, before expenditure on maintenance, amounted to little short of three hundred thousand pounds a year. Some two-thirds of this was re-invested in improvements but he received, from his landed properties alone, a net taxable income of around one hundred thousand pounds a year at a time when the standard rate of income tax was one shilling in the pound. It is doubtful whether there were in 1908 more than a handful of other landed proprietors enjoying greater incomes from ground and agricultural rents. Indeed, with the exceptions of the Duke of Westminster, the Duke of Bedford, the Duke of Portland, the Duke of Devonshire, the Duke of Sutherland, the Duke of Northumberland and the Marquess of Bute, no nobleman readily occurs to one who can have had a larger income in 1908 than the seventeenth Earl of Derby.

The principal Stanley estates at this time were as follows:

Knowsley. This included Knowsley Hall and domain and about 21,316 acres of agricultural property surrounding it and extending northwards to Bickerstaffe and Newburgh.[1] Large parts of this estate had been in the possession of the family since the Middle Ages.

[1] These properties were still in Derby's possession at the time of his death.

Burscough. About 4,225 acres of agricultural land at Burscough, north of Ormskirk. Lord Derby sold this estate in 1916. Part of this estate was apparently acquired on the Dissolution of the Monasteries.

Bispham. About 841 acres of agricultural land at Bispham, north-west of Ormskirk. The Manor is known to have been owned by the second Earl.[1]

Ormskirk. Property in the town; but there were also about 300 acres of agricultural land on the outskirts. Edward third Earl settled land at Ormskirk in 1569 and the Manor was granted by King James I in 1603.[1]

Preston. Property in the town. Part of it was apparently granted by Henry VII.[1]

The Fylde. About 10,446 acres of agricultural land to the east of Blackpool. Large parts of this estate had been in the possession of the family since the Middle Ages.[1]

Chipping and Thornley. About 5,786 acres of agricultural land to the north and north-east of Longridge. Thomas, second Earl of Derby owned the Manor of Thornley at his death in 1521.[1]

Cheshire Estates. The Crag estate near Macclesfield, comprising Crag Hall and about 9,614 acres of hill farms situated to the north-west of Macclesfield had been in the possession of the Earls of Derby for very many years and it would seem from the Calendar of Deeds that parts of it had been granted by King Henry VI and King Edward IV, when the Stanleys also became Stewards and Master Foresters of the Forest of Macclesfield. There was also Old Derby House, a medieval house in Watergate Street, Chester, which was a family residence during the Civil Wars and where the seventh Lord Derby slept on the night before his execution by the Commonwealth Army in 1651.

Liverpool Estates. Extensive residential and commercial property in the City of Liverpool and in the Kirkdale, Bootle and Walton on the Hill suburbs. Derby sold the Liverpool estates in 1928. Thomas, second Earl of Derby, owned the Manor of Liverpool at his death in 1521.

East Lancashire Estates. These estates were in the area between

[1] These properties were still in Derby's possession at the time of his death.

Kendal
WESTMORLAND
CUMBERLAND
Witherslack Hall
Witherslack Estate
NORTH RIDING
N
YORKSHIRE
WEST RIDING
Barrow in Furness
Morecambe
Lancaster
Shipton
Chipping & Thornley Estate
Colne Estate
The Fylde Estate
Clitheroe
Colne
Blackpool
Burnley
Preston
Accrington
Blackburn
Preston Estate
Darwen
LANCASHIRE
Southport
Chorley
Burscough Estate
Bispham Estate
Horwood
Breightmet
Rochdale
Bolton
Bury
Bury Estate
Breightmet Estate
Ormskirk Estate
Ormskirk
Unsworth
Whitefield
Oldham
Pilkington Estate
Prestwich
Crosby
Wigan
Kearsley
Cheetham Hill
Ashton-under-Lyne
Knowsley Estate
Broughton
Liverpool Estates
LIVERPOOL
Leigh
Eccles
MANCHESTER
Kirkdale
Walton
Salford
Hyde
Wallasey
St. Helens
DERBYSHIRE
Birkenhead
Widnes
Warrington
Stockport
Manchester Estate
Northwich
Macclesfield
CHESHIRE
Crag Estate
0 5 10 15 20 25 MILES
STAFFS
Lord Derby's estates
Limits of town estates
Built-up areas

Manchester and Bury and extended into Manchester, Colne, Pilkington and Breightmet. There were about 11,477 acres of agricultural land and very extensive town property. Derby sold the whole of these estates between 1919 and 1925. Parts of them had been granted to the family by King Henry VII.

Newmarket. The nucleus of this estate was bought by the sixteenth Earl of Derby between 1899 and 1904 and the seventeenth Earl extended it by further purchases in 1909, 1912 and 1921.[1]

Witherslack. This estate consisted of Witherslack Hall and about 1,621 acres. The manor was granted by Henry VII. Derby gave it to his son, Colonel Oliver Stanley, in 1923.

Holwood. This estate, consisting of Holwood House and about 620 acres, was purchased by Edward Henry, fifteenth Earl, in 1874. Derby gave the estate to his eldest son, Lord Stanley, in 1923. When Derby succeeded to the title the estate also included Cudham Court and lands at Tonbridge, which he sold by auction in 1909; and Keston Lodge and lands which he sold in 1923.

Coworth Park. This house near Sunningdale was bought by the sixteenth Earl in 1895. Derby's widow lived there until her death in July 1957.[1]

The Witley Park Estate, Surrey. This had been bought by the fifteenth Earl in 1876. Derby sold it in 1909.

The Fairhill House Estate, Kent. This had been bought by the fifteenth Earl in 1873. Derby sold it between 1909 and 1911.

Derby House. This comprised Derby House, 33 St. James's Square, and the Advowson of Badsworth in Yorkshire.

* * *

Shortly after he succeeded Derby disposed of the family house in St. James's Square and bought a more substantial mansion in Stratford Place which he named Derby House. This house, which later became the headquarters of the publishing firm, Messrs. Hutchinson & Company, is now the head office of Birfield Ltd., the light engineering firm.

Neither Derby nor his wife really lived at the new Derby

[1] These properties were still in Derby's possession at the time of his death.

Derby House, London.

Derby's shooting box at Crag.

House. It was mostly used for entertainment, either of a political or social character. In the thirties he used it so little that one of his factotums suggested that it was an extravagance to keep it going. Derby is said to have replied: 'Well, Lady Derby must have somewhere to change when she comes up from Coworth to go to the play.'

In 1937 Derby replying to Mr. Shane Leslie (now Sir Shane Leslie, Bart.) who was perpending a pamphlet on this house, which once belonged to his family, wrote:

Lord Derby to Mr. Shane Leslie

I bought this house from the Colebrookes, who had bought it from the Guthries, who in turn had bought it from Sir John Leslie. They, Colebrookes and Guthries, made many alterations in the house, but I have no record of them, except that the room that is now known as the French Drawing Room was panelled by them. When I took it I made still more extensive alterations.

On each side of the house there was a little colonnade, very shallow and only going up to the first floor. It was outside the room which is now my sitting room. I did away with that so as to get more light into the room.

Some years ago the vibration of the tube brought down part of the house, and it was found then that the stonework was really only veneer. It had to be replaced entirely by stone, and the balustrading which was crumbling away had to be replaced. But what was more curious, and much more expensive, was that the foundations had to be put in again for the old part of the house, as we found they were built on wooden piles.

As you know this house was in the old days the Lord Mayor of London's fishing cottage, and the Corporation of London were, until I was able to purchase the freehold, my landlords.

It is a curious position with regard to this house. There is a subway running down to Oxford Street. What the use of it was I do not know, but that and the roadway above it belong to me. I thought at one time I would exercise the right and try and exclude parking, but I found if I did that, as it was private property, the police could not help me, so I abandoned the idea.

Whilst still on the outside I may tell you of a thing which has always very much distressed me. At the entrance to Oxford Street you will see on the one side opposite the Bank some sort of sentry box. There was one on the other side, and when there were some alterations going on I begged Lilley & Skinner, who were the holders of the property, not to remove it. I got a charming letter back saying they realised what an attraction it was and they were not going to alter it. However, some years later, when the Managing Head had passed away, they did do away with it, and built the hideous erection which is now their shop. I have never forgiven them for that.

Now to go back to the house itself.

The big dining-room with the ballroom above it, and all that part of the house which on the ground floor is called the small dining-room and above the winter garden, were built by me, as were also the kitchens etc. underneath. In the old days they were the stables. I pulled them down and built that part of the house as you now see it. The kitchens were at the far end of the house. Where they got them in I cannot quite remember.

The dining-room was what is now my sitting-room, but I cut off that portion which makes the passage down to the big dining room. In my room, however, I was very careful to preserve exactly the ceiling.

The big dining-room ceiling, and indeed the room itself, was copied as far as it could be from a temporary building my ancestor (the man who started the Derby) put up in his house at Epsom, 'The Oaks', for his marriage with Lady Elizabeth Hamilton. The pictures in the ceiling, by a painter called Romanelli (I know nothing about him) were in that particular dining-room and ballroom.

I have of course altered the staircases, servants' rooms etc. How ever a big family got into this house I do not know.

You will see therefore that there are very few rooms which exist as they existed in your grandfather's time. The drawing room is the same, except that there is a door cut out into the ballroom, and the little front drawing room, which I think is the prettiest room in the house with its waggon roof ceiling, is just as it was.

The chimney pieces in my sitting room and in the big dining room are of course as they were. Some of the others I have put in. The little one in Lady Derby's dressing room came from Derby House, St. James's Square.

On Derby's letter Leslie at the time commented thus:

> The house belonged to Lady Anne Bentinck who was blind and had a hand railing for her round the garden. My father went to a party there about 1867. When she died my grandfather telegraphed to George Bentinck for remainder of lease (£11,000) but the further lease had to be bought later from Col. Diver for £8,000. The kitchens were out of doors and contained the only hot water tap from which all baths had to be supplied by housemaids going out of doors. The stables were beyond and beside 8 horses coachman Kirby kept chickens to supply my grandmother with fresh eggs. My mother sat on one in the sociable once.
>
> My grandfather would never change the sanitation. There was a man's lavatory under the stairs without a window. The lady's lavatory aired into the three servants rooms or dungeons. Upstairs there was a sink made to provide cold bilge water. The male servants slept in the servants' hall. There was a cess pool which Murray Guthrie paid to be covered over before he had bought the house. There was a pump and a well fallen in the garden. The cess pool horrified the surveyors who had never seen such a horror. It was built by Ld. Aldboro to entertain George IV as Regent.

* * *

Since the Civil Wars, Knowsley has been the chief seat of the Stanleys. When Derby inherited it, it was one of the four or five largest houses in the kingdom. The oldest surviving portion of the house dates from the thirteenth century. It first came into the possession of the Stanleys in the fourteenth century on the marriage of Sir John Stanley to Isabel, daughter and heiress of Sir Thomas Lathom.

Succeeding generations made alterations and additions; but by far the largest part of Knowsley as it existed in Derby's time had been built by the tenth Earl in the reign of George II. The twelfth Earl (he who founded the Derby) planned, then abandoned, a complete reconstruction. However, he added a dining-room of vast proportions that came near to being an embarrassment to his successors.

Creevey, staying with Lord Sefton at nearby Croxteth Hall, gives a good account of it shortly after its completion in 1822:

> We all dined at Knowsley last night. The new dining-room is opened: it is 53 feet by 37, and such a height that it destroys the effect of all the other apartments. . . . You enter it from a passage by two great Gothic church-like doors the whole height of the room. This entrance is in itself fatal to the effect. Ly. Derby (like herself), when I objected to the immensity of the doors, said: 'You've heard General Grosvenor's remark upon them have you not? He asked in his grave, pompous manner—"Pray are those great doors to be opened for every pat of butter that comes into the room?" ' At the opposite end of the room is an immense Gothic window, and the rest of the light is given by a skylight mountains high. There are two fireplaces; and the day we dined there, there were 36 wax candles over the table, 14 on it, and 10 great lamps on tall pedestals about the room; and yet those at the bottom of the table said it was quite petrifying in that neighbourhood, and the report here is that they have since been obliged to abandon it entirely from the cold. . . . My lord and my lady were all kindness to me, but only think of their neither knowing nor caring about Spain or France, nor whether war or peace between these two nations was at all in agitation!
>
> I must say I never saw a man or woman live more happily with nine grown up children. It is my lord [Derby] who is the great moving principle. . . . [1]

In this room during the month of September 1812 Lord Derby and his friends are said to have consumed 38 head of cattle, 75 sheep, 12 lambs, 6 calves, 4 buck, 400 fowls, 400 rabbits, 593 partridges, 21 turkeys, 14 geese and 2,688 eggs. In the same period they drank 2,940 gallons of beer, 527 bottles of wine and 36 bottles of spirits.

The twelfth Earl died in 1834 three years before the accession of Queen Victoria. His successors made extensive additions to the house in the infelicitous style of their period. When Derby inherited in 1908, Knowsley was an ill-assorted agglomeration of buildings. He sought to introduce some consistency and order. Derby was

[1] *The Creevey Papers*, Vol. II, p. 57.

Knowsley as it was in the time of the seventeenth Earl.

Knowsley as it is today.

responsible for a newly designed centre of the east front and for the terraces and walls which surround it. He re-sashed all the windows, thereby greatly improving the house's general appearance. To the main block he added a third storey and surmounted it with the family crest, the Eagle and Child, in Portland stone.

He also altered the level of the ground before the west front and formed terraces containing store-rooms across the length of it. His grandson, the present Earl, who succeeded him in 1948, has pulled down nearly half the house as it was at the time of his grandfather's death. As a result of these demolitions Knowsley has gained in handsomeness what it has lost in size; it is still a very large house.

* * *

Derby's income, as we have seen, was enormous: his style of living was correspondingly lavish. Household expenditure, an item in the estate accounts, which were drawn up annually for Derby by a Liverpool firm of chartered accountants, amounted even before the First World War to nearly fifty thousand pounds. With his vast fortune Derby had inherited the pleasant obligation and tradition of spending a large part of the income accruing from it. Circumstance enforced a lavishness which now has passed away; the benevolently feudal role which Derby played in local affairs, and which the entire county of Lancashire devotedly wished him to play, combined with the immensity of Knowsley in imposing a massive expenditure. A style of living, rich, ordered, comfortable, lacking both rash extravagance and any form of pretension was his by centuries of tradition; and when he came into his inheritance he proceeded to enjoy it with a firm conviction in the propriety of the social order which made this style possible. It was a style with which he was pre-eminently compatible and which struck neither Derby nor anyone else as anything but natural and ordained.

In the pantry at Knowsley there were fourteen servants: the butler and two under-butlers, a valet, a retired butler, a groom of the chambers, a second groom of the chambers, three footmen, two boys, an odd man and a Steward's Room footman. This last functionary was a servants' servant. The rigidly hierarchical structure of nineteenth-century society extended below stairs. There were two distinct classes. Either a servant ate in the Steward's Room or he ate in the Servants' Hall. The senior servants who were entitled by age, experience, and position to a certain deference from their inferiors were waited upon, as they ate, by the Steward's Room footman. Questions of precedence among servants were decided by the butler, who was in charge of the male staff, and the housekeeper, in charge of the female staff; visiting valets and ladies' maids were accorded the precedence, in their own categories, of their masters and mistresses. It was usual at the time of the Grand National when the King and Queen came to stay at Knowsley for forty to eat in the dining-room, sixty in the Steward's Room (a seemingly high proportion; but visiting valets and ladies' maids qualified ex-officio, and in borderline cases, where professional qualification seemed somewhat lacking, the rank of their employers would have prevailed) and sixty in the Servants' Hall.

The big dining-room table could accommodate up to forty-six people and on big occasions there were five separate services, each being conducted from a separate table, by a separate staff, and working concurrently with three wine services, these likewise conducted from separate serving tables and by separate staff. In the kitchen were two chefs, four or five kitchen maids, a scullery maid and a scullion. Under the housekeeper were eight housemaids, two basement maids, one lady's maid, whose status was of course enhanced by the proximity she enjoyed to her mistress, one linen maid and two maids of the stillroom.

These thirty-eight domestic servants were, in 1910, just outnumbered by the horticultural staff. Thirty-nine gardeners tended the great flower borders with which the house was surrounded, relentlessly weeded the lawns, and operated an enormous kitchen garden, the entire produce of which was consumed either at Knowsley or at Stanley House, Newmarket. Derby House in London was supplied by the gardens at Coworth.

The kindness with which these servants were treated was also a part of the Stanley tradition. When Derby's uncle died in 1893 he left £62,000 to be divided between his 727 servants, gardeners and the staff of the various branches of his estate office.

Talleyrand used to say that no one who had not lived before the French Revolution could know what was *la douceur de la vie*. In a changing world subsequent generations of the educated and governing classes in all European countries have tended to deliver comparably defeatist homilies to their children. Young men who went up to Oxford in the twenties were told by their fathers that University life would not be as spacious or agreeable as that which prevailed before 1914; and the same young men who had a riotous time at Oxford in the twenties and thirties are still telling their sons what a grey, drab, arduous, egalitarian life they will lead, compared to that which they themselves had in an earlier generation. The eighteenth century was the golden age of English oratory, statesmanship, literature and society. That was the age which Disraeli described as being 'for the few and the very few'. Since then a tremendous advance has been made in the material and social well-being of the wage-earning classes; and to some extent this has involved a decline in the standards of living of the rich and the very rich. And rightly so. But there has been no revolution; there has been no liquidation of the ancient aristocracy who, with an especial genius for survival, have successfully adapted themselves to the changing world in which they live. Thus it is that, despite Lloyd George, two world wars, six years of Socialist Government from 1945 to 1951, penal taxation, raised not for the purpose of discharging the obligations of government but with the naked desire to re-distribute the wealth of the country and produce an egalitarian society, a very large number of people still live in the houses of their ancestors and, on a smaller scale, discharge the responsibilities of which they feel themselves to be the legatees.

The country houses of England, great and small, are part of the heritage of the English people. They have long provided centres of initiative and organization for the social life, at all levels, of the counties in which they are situate. When a family which, for ten or more generations, has occupied the same house, is compelled, through high taxation, misfortune or folly, to sell the house and property to some public institution, such as the Coal Board or Electricity Authority, or a parvenu operator of a bucket-shop, there are few inhabitants of the county or parish who rejoice at the event or who regard it even as a symptom of social progress. This is a fact which the clever, town-bred Wykehamist members of the Labour Party have never understood. That is why, besotted with the alien, archaic opinions which two German Jews dreamt up in the British Museum in the middle of the last century, they are unlikely, except for some absurd momentary aberration of the electorate, to put their silly hands on the levers of British power for any lengthy period.

Derby, though he would not have rationalized these ideas into any coherent form of thought, was a natural, inevitable and highly successful aristocrat. He took it for granted that his employees, his tenants, his neighbours and, indeed, the entire population of the County Palatine, would expect him to live and behave as his ancestors had done in earlier centuries. He proceeded on this simple assumption amid the growing affection and approbation not only of the county but of the nation. However rich a man may be he cannot wear more than one suit of clothes at a time nor eat more than three or four square meals a day. If a very rich man spends his money helping his family, entertaining his friends and neighbours, looking after his properties in an enlightened way and devoting most of his time to the promotion of every good cause in his part of the world, his neighbours are, on the whole, unlikely to wish to evict him from the house in which he and his ancestors have lived for a thousand years and to replace him with some unknown *arriviste* bureaucrat.

The country houses of England, great and small, have given to the country its unique character and distinction. Even today in the vast progress of urbanization, they still survive on a reduced scale and still provide a hundred thousand centres for the preservation of the historic culture, civilization and freedom of the land. When all men are equal, none will be free. And it is the acceptance over the centuries of a graded order of society, in which all may rise and many may fall, which has fostered English civilization and preserved English liberty.

A house party at Knowsley attended by King Edward VII and Queen Alexandra shortly after Derby succeeded to the title.

The great Whig lords of the eighteenth century were men of exceptional talent and even genius. And at Chatsworth, Woburn and Althorp one can still admire the taste and sense of elegance which led the Cavendishes, the Russells and the Spencers, to name but three families, to adorn their houses with the finest paintings and sculptures of France, Italy and Greece. It must be regretfully recorded that the Stanleys, in all generations of which we have record, had little sense of elegance, style, fashion or taste. It was not that they had bad taste, but that they had no taste at all. Each generation accepted what it found and thought it very good. It did not occur to them to question what they inherited. Their instinctive tendency was to make it larger.

Thus it is that Knowsley, apart from a famous Rembrandt, depicting Belshazzar's Feast with the Writing on the Wall, and six fine seascapes by Vandevelde, can boast few works of art or furniture to compare with the glorious treasures at Chatsworth, Woburn and Althorp. Everything was good and very solid and it never occurred to anyone to talk about the contents of the house. They were taken for granted. Derby had as a neighbour the twenty-seventh Earl of Crawford and Balcarres who was a trustee of the National Gallery and a considerable judge of works of art. Sometime in the twenties he was invited to luncheon at Knowsley, and, noting the general ugliness of the furniture, felt moved to say to Derby, 'That's a very fine set of Charles II dining-room chairs'. Derby made no comment but after his guest had left he snorted and said, 'Damn cheek, that fellow noticing my chairs!' Neither he nor any of his ancestors had ever noticed them before. Evidently he thought it an impertinence and even rather common that a guest should draw attention to something which all his life he had taken for granted.

Knowsley in fact was nothing but a large, tasteless hotel. Someone said of Derby that he was a man who had eight houses and no home. Knowsley was the nearest thing he had to a home, but certainly in his later life, until his old age, he seldom in any year spent more than ten or eleven weeks there. He did not himself care for shooting, but the park nurtured an abundance of pheasants and he would often fill the house with relations and dependants and provide for them two shoots a day, one on one side of the house and one on the other. Christmas was usually spent at Knowsley and it was a family party. The other great event of the year was the Grand National when the King and Queen were often guests. Any well-known politician who was to speak in Liverpool or Manchester, Conservative, Liberal or Socialist, would be put up for the night but there was no social entertaining in the ordinary sense of the phrase. In whichever of his houses Derby found himself, he tended to be surrounded merely by relations and hangers-on. And the visitors' book at Knowsley disappointingly chronicles an almost exact repetition of the same visitors year after year.

Mr. Evelyn Waugh in his contribution to *Noblesse Oblige*, a social extravaganza promoted by Miss Nancy Mitford, says:

> Look back twenty-five years to the time when there was still a fairly firm aristocratic structure and the country was still divided into spheres of influence among hereditary magnates. My memory is that the grandees avoided one another unless they were closely related. They met on state occasions and on the race-course. They did not frequent one another's houses. You might find almost anyone in a ducal castle—convalescent, penurious cousins, advisory experts, sycophants, gigolos and plain blackmailers. The one thing you could be sure of not finding was a concourse of other dukes. English society, it seemed to me, was a complex of tribes, each with its chief and elders and witch-doctors and braves, each with its own dialect and deity, each strongly xenophobic.

Mr. Waugh has been for the last thirty years an acute observer of the English social scene and few would care to quarrel with his sapient diagnosis. Derby's son-in-law, Sir Malcolm Bullock, recalls how on one occasion in the thirties he arrived at Knowsley having spent the night before at Chatsworth with the Duke of Devonshire. 'I don't suppose you got much to eat or drink,' said Derby. On being reassured on this point, he said: 'Well, I'm sure you must have had a very dull time. It's always very dull at Chatsworth.' On another occasion one of his daughters-in-law wrote a bread-and-butter letter to him from Blenheim, and after the

The officer wearing the full dress of the Grenadier Guards is the host, Derby. Behind Derby, wearing a top hat, is his eldest son, the late Right Hon. Lord Stanley, M.P. Lady Derby (or Lady Alice as she was generally known) is on the King's left, with her younger son, the late Right Hon. Oliver Stanley, M.P., beside her.

normal compliments added: 'Blenheim is a veritable palace and Sunny [the ninth Duke of Marlborough] is a prince of hosts'. Derby read it out to Bullock at the breakfast table and then chucking the letter across the table, observed: 'Well, we needn't ask *her* for some time, need we?'

Except for his Mediterranean tour after the 1906 Election and his brief circumnavigation of the world in 1887, Derby was not in his youth much addicted to foreign travel. His roots were understandably at home. It may be that he heeded the advice of his collateral forebear, the seventh Lord Derby, who admonished his son, 'And if your sons are by curiosity and custom inclined to travel, suffer them not to pass the Alps; for there is nothing to be learned there but pride, vice, luxury and atheism, with a few useless words of no profit.'

* * *

In the years before the First World War, Derby had not yet attained that virtual immunity from criticism which later characterized his public existence. He had not yet become the arbiter of honour and integrity whose moral support far abler politicians were eager to purchase even at the price of listening on occasion to his counsel. His person and character never had been and never would be attacked in public, but his large holdings of town property were an obvious target for the Liberals who in Lloyd George's budget of 1909 had attempted to introduce a Land Tax, designed as a levy on the capital increment in urban land values brought about by progressive industrialisation. The tax was never introduced; the budget in which it was contained was defeated by the House of Lords, thus entailing the General Election of 1910. The tax, however, remained a tenet of the more radical and doctrinaire wing of the Liberal Party, more particularly at election time, since the figure of a wicked Tory landowner was a most convenient foil to the purity of their own beliefs. In November 1913 Lloyd George, then Chancellor of the Exchequer, speaking at Middlesbrough, was reported by *The Times* as having said:

> They had heard of Bootle? There was a street there with 87 houses to the acre. Stanley-street—that looked as if it had something to do with the landlords—had 51 to the acre, and in Knowsley-street—that also had something to do with the landlords—there were 52 to the acre. Under those conditions it was really almost impossible for people to preserve their own health and it was still more difficult to preserve the health and the lives of the little children. The first motto of their land campaign was 'Justice to the little children'.

Lloyd George was more moderate than the Baron de Forest, a naturalized Englishman who until 1899 had been Herr Maurice Arnold Bischoffsheim, one of the adopted sons of Baron Hirsch, the Austrian financier. The latter had made a great fortune out of Turkish Railways and had left about three million pounds sterling; his widow who survived him bequeathed a large portion of her own five million pound estate to the two adopted children. Baron de Forest had been educated at Eton and Christ Church and obtained in 1900 a Royal Licence to use his Austrian title in Great Britain. He embraced radicalism with a Moravian fervour and several million pounds. The Tories' second line of defence against the Land Taxes, after repudiating them as morally indefensible and generally repugnant, was to argue that there were in fact no great increments in value on which the tax could be levied. The Tories frequently quoted figures in support of this highly doubtful thesis. At Bootle in February 1914, Baron de Forest made an inflammatory speech on the great increment in value which had accrued to the Stanley property in the area. Derby answered him at a meeting of the Liverpool Conservative Working-men's Association. He first dealt with Lloyd George's accusations. The statistics quoted by Mr. Lloyd George, he said, were totally inaccurate and property development in the area had followed the normally accepted pattern of similar estates. He went on to deal with the Baron:

> You have heard of a land report and a rural section of it—that secret land enquiry which was to be so truthful and so unbiased. Part of it is written by a man you may have heard of; he is an alien, a gentleman owning no land in this country, who has come over here to tell us what landlords ought to do. He is a certain Baron de Forest. I have no

particular love for him, but in your presence I intend to do him a good turn and make him a most generous offer. He has written these words: 'The most conservative estimate (this is referring to Bootle, explained Lord Derby) of the annual income of the Derby estate from this property today may safely be put at not less than 100,000. The capital value, having regard to the undevelopment of the greater part of the area, cannot be put at less than between 3,000,000 and 4,000,000.' I am going to make him an offer. You have heard of the Scotch offer of the Duke of Sutherland, and when the price was quoted to Mr. Lloyd George he said, 'The price is too much.' I am going to be thoroughly quixotic, and I am going to say to this Baron de Forest: 'You have really quoted too much. I am only too anxious to add to my own prosperity incidentally, and at the same time to give you a chance of making for yourself and your party a large fortune. You say that it may be worth 4,000,000 and that it is certainly worth 3,000,000. Therefore, if I offered him the property for 3,000,000, you would see there is a possibility of his making a million. But I am going much further than that. He says it is certainly worth 3,000,000. I give him a firm offer here that if he puts down 1,500,000 he shall have it (loud applause and a Voice: 'Rub it in'). Gentlemen, there is nothing to 'rub in'; it is only for him to pay up (laughter and applause). I certainly do not make that offer at any loss to myself. I make him that firm offer, and I ask you, if he refuses it, to judge what confidence you can put in any figures that he quotes. Baron de Forest is not a man that one need pay much attention to, and I should not have paid this attention to him but for one thing, that in this very speech of Mr. Lloyd George's to which I have alluded he refers to this land enquiry and says it is on their figures and their statistics that he is basing his speech.

The *Daily Express*, in a note under the title of 'Bootle's Baby', observed:

So Baron de Forest, M.P., the people's friend, is willing to plank down a spare million and a half of money to buy Lord Derby's property in Bootle. That will be great news for the people. They will leap with joy. They will hang out banners and burn bonfires. They will be glad that Baron de Forest is so rich, and that he means to do so much for them. They will look forward to the new Bootle, freed from the exacting tyrannies of an English earl and refurbished by the democratic fervour of the kindly baron, who is wise enough to keep a few million idle for the undoing of the British aristocrat. And what would Baron de Forest do with Bootle if he bought it? Would he pull down the houses and use the land as a private park in which he might hunt the fox without let or hindrance? Would he put in force in his Bootle estate the methods obtaining on the little model estate of 30,000 acres which he holds in Moravia? . . . Oh, there may be glad times coming for Bootle, Baron, and the downtrodden masses who linger miserably in the Derby dungeons. And Lord Derby, too! How nice to be offered a million and a half, and to be taken—nearly—at his word. It is true that the bountiful baron himself estimated at three or four millions the worth of the property for which he now offers a million and a half. But your true Moravian landowner likes to see a profit on transactions in real estate. It is true also that Baron de Forest makes important reservations in his offer. On these negotiations might break down. Which would be beastly for Bootle.

* * *

This was not the first time that Derby had found himself at cross purposes with Baron de Forest, who was of a somewhat litigious nature. In 1911 de Forest had taken the unusual course of suing his own mother-in-law, Lady Gerard, and Major Harry Milner, the comptroller of Derby's household, for slander. Milner, who had been a great friend of Derby's at Wellington and who had earned Derby's affection by protecting him from being bullied by some of the older boys, had been working for Derby for some years. De Forest alleged that Milner had told Derby that de Forest had treated his wife with cruelty. The case against Milner came on first; and seldom can a case of so comparatively trivial a nature have procured the appearance in court of such a glittering array of learned counsel. De Forest was represented by Sir Edward Clarke, K.C., Mr. Astbury, K.C., Mr. Hemmerde, K.C., and Mr. F. E. Smith, K.C.; while Sir Edward Carson, K.C., and Mr. Duke, K.C., appeared for Major Milner.

Apart from his own client, de Forest, who testified at length about his relations with his wife but who had no direct evidence of the slanders which he alleged had been perpetrated by Lady Gerard and Major Milner, the only witness called by Sir Edward Clarke was Derby. And since Derby was most reluctant to go into the witness box in what promised to be a singularly distasteful case, de Forest's solicitors were put to the doubtful expedient of compelling Derby's appearance by subpœna. There are grave dangers inherent in founding an action for libel or slander exclusively on the testimony of a witness who is brought into the box against his will. For unless such a witness shows himself markedly hostile and gives evidence of an inherently and manifestly untrue character, it is not permissible for the plaintiff's counsel to subject him to cross-examination. Everything he says must be accepted. Sir Edward Clarke tried to persuade Mr. Justice Darling that he was entitled to treat Derby as a hostile witness. In his opening statement he had said that the accusations which Milner was supposed to have made to Derby about de Forest were to the effect that 'he assaulted his wife, treated her brutally, kicked her downstairs . . .' According to *The Times* report of 28 March 1911 the following exchanges took place when Sir Edward put Derby in the box:

Sir E. Clarke: What information, if any, did Mr. Milner give you as to the Baron's treatment of his wife? What did he say?

Mr. Justice Darling: You must *not* give your impression of a conversation. If you can remember, tell us as nearly as you can what was said.

Derby: I cannot remember the exact words which he used.

Sir E. Clarke: To the best of your recollection tell me.—To the best of my recollection he told me that he had travelled down with Baroness de Forest in the train, and that she had told him that the Baron had behaved disgracefully to her, but I do not remember any detailed account of what he had done.

Sir E. Clarke: Is that the best of your recollection?—That is the best of my recollection. I could not give any detailed account of what he said.

Sir E. Clarke: I shall ask to be allowed to put the words to the witness. We have subpœnaed him.

Mr. Justice Darling: On what ground?

Sir E. Clarke: On the ground that the witness is not giving his evidence in the way in which I am entitled to get it.

Sir E. Carson: The way in which you would like to get it. (Laughter.)

Mr. Justice Darling: You have to satisfy me that the witness is not doing his best to answer your questions truthfully.

Sir E. Clarke: I do not want to make that suggestion.

Mr. Justice Darling: I cannot allow you to cross-examine unless you satisfy me as to that, and I am not satisfied of it by a very long way.

Sir E. Clarke (to Derby): Does not your recollecting over the matter enable you to recall some phrases used by him in telling you that?—No, I do not remember any particular phrase in which he told me that Baron de Forest had ill-treated his wife.

Sir E. Clarke: You cannot recollect any particular phrase in which he told you so? —No, I cannot recollect.

Sir E. Clarke (to Judge): I submit that I am entitled to put to the witness the question 'Did he mention violence?'

Mr. Justice Darling: I do not think so. . . . If I thought that Lord Derby was not doing his best to remember and answer you freely I would allow you in a moment to put him to what would be cross-examination. But he must be treated just like any other witness, although he is a peer. (Laughter.)

Sir E. Clarke (to Derby): On the occasion of which you have spoken, where did the conversation take place?—At Knowsley.

Sir E. Clarke: Were there other persons present at the time?—No, I do not remember anybody else being there.

Derby's inability to charge his memory with any precise recollection of what Milner had said placed Sir Edward Clarke in considerable difficulty and a good deal before the usual hour he asked if there might be an adjournment for luncheon so that another witness could be brought into Court. However, when the court reassembled Sir Edward had to announce that the lady on whom he had been relying was not prepared to testify. In these circumstances the case abruptly collapsed and the suit was withdrawn. De Forest also abandoned his case against Lady Gerard.

VI

The Parliament Act

THE role that Derby had already played and which he was increasingly to play on the stage of national politics was almost entirely conditioned by the pre-eminent position which he was now building for himself in Lancashire. As a great Lancashire magnate he could speak in London with an authority which, since the Liberal victory of 1906, was becoming increasingly rare for men of his class. Conversely, the position which he had in London through his hereditary friendship with the Royal Family, through his racing and social activities, through his vast wealth, hospitality and genial social gifts contributed to the authority and prestige which he would anyhow have enjoyed in Lancashire. From the time that he came into his inheritance in 1908 he consciously or unconsciously became a two-way channel by which Lancashire opinion could transmit itself to the highest governing elements in London and by which the latter could seek to exert influence over Lancashire opinion of all classes and parties. He had not yet achieved or exploited this largely natural situation to the full extent. But the year 1911 is of particular interest in Derby's career as we can see him playing the game of politics on both sides of the table to exceptional advantage and laying the foundations both in London and Lancashire on which he was later to build a career and discharge local and national services in a way already falling into desuetude and which today has faded almost completely from the political landscape. At the end of 1911 Lord Derby, like so many of his ancestors, was elected Lord Mayor of Liverpool and earlier in the year, though the Unionist Party was in opposition and he was discharging no official role, we see him concerning himself actively, if to no great effect, in the violent political disputes which marked the passage of the Parliament Act.

The Liberal Government of Sir Henry Campbell-Bannerman and that of Mr. Asquith, which succeeded it in 1908 on the former's death, have long been regarded as the most brilliant and progressive administrations which Britain has ever had. They laid the foundations of that system of social security on which for the next forty years was to be erected the edifice now known as the Welfare State.

British Socialists today are apt to claim that all social legislation in Britain started with the Socialist Government of 1945. These extravagant assertions, which overlook the tremendous advances made by the Liberal Governments between 1906 and 1912 and by the Conservative Government between 1924 and 1929, are as wide of the mark as those of Liberals who think that all social progress began in 1906. In fact, the Germans under Bismarck in the eighties had pioneered schemes of social reform in the fields of education, workmen's compensation and old age pensions far in advance of anything else existing in the world and by 1914 incomparably superior even to the far-reaching legislation which Mr. Lloyd George and Mr. Winston Churchill under the leadership of Mr. Asquith had been able in a few years to introduce in Britain. These facts, however, were largely obscured or obliterated from British comprehension by First World War propaganda which, basing itself on the undeniable militarism of Prussia, was to close everyone's eyes to any German achievement. Thus is history falsified.

The Liberals, who came into power in 1906 after twenty years of almost unbroken Tory rule, were animated by strongly radical motives. Men like Asquith, Campbell-Bannerman, Haldane, Morley, Grey, Lloyd George, Churchill and Runciman, all to a greater or lesser degree, desired to better the lot of the working-classes of Britain which at that time was the most powerful and prosperous community the world had ever seen. The Boer War had let loose smaller yet comparable social pressures to those which exploded after 1918 and 1945. It was the good fortune of the period with which we are concerned that the pressures were less than in later times; and that the Liberal statesmen who were coping with them were for the most part of a higher intellectual calibre than the statesmen of 1918, who were too preoccupied with other matters to do more than tinker with the problems, and than those of 1945 who, history will perhaps record, bit off rather more than the country's economy could chew.

Be that as it may, the whole programme of well-thought-out progressive Bills concerned with education, plural voting, land valuation and other measures deemed of a progressive and useful character was vetoed by an overwhelming Conservative majority in the House of Lords. The Liberal Party, with their brilliant leadership and large majority in the Commons and country, naturally felt frustrated by this series of reverses. Lloyd George, the Chancellor of the Exchequer, sought means to end the veto which the Conservatives in the Lords were plainly abusing. For at least two centuries it had been the rule that finance was the prerogative of the House of Commons and that the Lords could not intrude into this domain. In order to provoke the Lords into using their veto in a field where both tradition and public opinion would not support them, Lloyd George deliberately, and artfully, introduced into his Budget of 1909 a proposal for a tax on 'unearned increments' on land.[1] The proposal was not in itself very far-reaching, but it touched on a point of principle which affected all the land- and property-owning classes of the country, both large and small. It was a red flag deliberately flaunted in the face of the Unionist Party. Thus was precipitated the issue of the Lords versus the People which culminated in the Parliament Act of 1911 whereby the authority of the Upper House was reduced from a power of veto to a power of delay.

The defeat of Mr. Lloyd George's 1909 Budget inevitably led to the General Election of January 1910. The Unionists had high hopes of defeating the Government, but though in the upshot they gained 116 seats, the Liberal Government still had a majority of two over their Tory opponents. This was a remarkable rebuff, but it left the Liberals still in the saddle. Thus it was that the issue of Home Rule for Ireland, which had been largely dormant since Mr. Gladstone's defeat in 1880, once more returned to hagride the British political

[1] This led the late Sir Edward Marsh, at one time private secretary to Sir Winston Churchill, to remark 'Earned increments are sweet, but those unearned are sweeter'.

scene. Mr. Asquith's Government was now dependent for its effective survival upon the support of the eighty Irish Nationalist members. The Irish leader, Mr. John Redmond, was able to drive a hard bargain, and henceforward the Liberal Government to a large extent became the prisoners of the Irish Nationalists. Thus Tory opposition to the Parliament Bill inevitably became intensified. For, once the Bill was put upon the Statute Book, the power of the Lords to sustain the union with Ireland would be lost for ever.

It was immediately manifest that the Lords were certain to reject the Bill, and during the summer an all-party conference sought means of ending the deadlock; but by early November the Conference broke down, mainly because of Mr. Asquith's inability to find a formula which would satisfy both the Tories and Mr. Redmond on the re-emergence of Home Rule for Ireland. It was in these circumstances that Mr. Asquith had recourse to his proposal for a mass creation of peers. There were examples in English history for the creation of peers in order to secure a majority in the Upper House for the Government of the day. The most notable was in 1711, when Queen Anne followed up her dismissal of the Duke of Marlborough by creating twelve Tory peers in order to ensure a Tory majority in the House of Lords for Harley's and Bolingbroke's policy of making a separate peace with France at the expense of our Dutch allies. But none of these examples could be held to be valid precedents for the creation of the four or five hundred peers which would be necessary to procure a Liberal majority in the House of Lords. This proposed swamping of the Upper House was to appear even to many objective people as an act of constitutional indecency. Nonetheless, there was certainly no theoretical constitutional limitation on the royal prerogative as to the number of peers that might be created; and unquestionably this part of the royal prerogative could be brought into play on the advice of the Prime Minister, whatever the Sovereign might feel, unless he were prepared to exercise his ultimate sanction under the Constitution of dismissing the Prime Minister.

The King was sorely troubled when, following the breakdown of the party talks, the Prime Minister asked for a guarantee that he might make the necessary creations. As Sir Harold Nicolson has made clear in his life of King George V, the King would have been within his constitutional rights in refusing to act on the Prime Minister's advice and in accepting his inevitable resignation, but he could only do this, without jeopardising the monarchical system, if he were certain that there was someone willing and able to form an alternative Government. Lord Knollys, an ardent Radical whom King George had inherited as his private secretary from his father, advised him that there was no one available for such a task. But as Sir Harold has revealed, Lord Knollys was guilty of duplicity. Knollys had himself informed King Edward a week before his death that Mr. Balfour was prepared to form an alternative Government 'in order to prevent the King being put in the position contemplated by the demand for the creation of peers'. King Edward omitted to inform his son of this vital information, and Lord Knollys not only withheld the information but volunteered an account which was the reverse of the truth. It was not till three years later that the Knollys letters and memoranda regarding this fact came into the hands of the King, who then dictated the following note: '. . . the knowledge of their contents would undoubtedly have had an important bearing and influence with regard to Mr. Asquith's request for guarantees on 16 November 1910.'[1] Balfour's position in the matter finds confirmation in a letter which his secretary wrote to Derby the following summer.

Mr. J. S. Sandars to Lord Derby

Confidential
3 August 1911

4 Carlton Gardens,
Pall Mall, S.W.

. . . The following may interest you:

The Chief had an opportunity of writing to Bigge the day before yesterday. In his letter he told Bigge that he had heard that it was

[1] Mr. Balfour certainly considered that Knollys had behaved extremely badly, not only to the King but also towards himself. Though in most respects a very easy-going man, once when asked by the late Lady Desborough whom he would like to meet or not to meet at a weekend at Taplow, he replied: 'My dear Ettie, I should enjoy meeting any man in England, except Lord Knollys: him I will not meet.' This anecdote was subsequently recounted by Lady Desborough to Sir Harold Nicolson, to whom the author is grateful for communicating it to him.

freely canvassed in Court and other circles that he had declined in the winter to assist the King by forming a Government of his own. He, in most direct language, then said to Bigge—(1) that he had never been asked to form a Government, and (2) that if he had been asked to form a Government, with full knowledge that he [the King] was being bullied to give guarantees in respect of a Bill which had not been discussed in Parliament, and seven months before its shape was definitely settled in Parliament, he would certainly have accepted office; and more particularly because he would then have known that the Bill was going to be employed to prevent the question of Home Rule being submitted to the constituencies. Bigge has replied to this letter by saying that the Chief's letter will have to be shown to the King, and don't you think there will be a little flutter in Royal circles at this very plain speaking. . . .?

It was in these circumstances that the second Election of 1910 was fought. The result of this Election was that the Government lost three seats and the Conservatives one: while the nascent Labour Party and the Irish Nationalists both gained two. The Tories and Liberals were in exact equipoise in the House. The indecisive nature of the contest made all politicians realise, among other things, that the deadly issues which divided the two parties could hardly be resolved by further recourse to the electorate. The country was more evenly divided than it was to be for another forty years. Only continuing stalemate could be expected from any further election.

* * *

One interesting feature of this election was the defeat of Mr. Bonar Law in North-west Manchester. Bonar Law had been returned for the safe constituency of Dulwich in a by-election in 1906 with a comfortable majority which he had doubled in the first election of 1910. Derby had not as yet developed the hostility towards Tariff Reform which was to animate so much of his political conduct in the years ahead. He conceived the idea that if the Tory Party were to fight the next election on a protectionist platform, a leading protectionist of the calibre of Bonar Law ought to fight a marginal seat in Lancashire:

Lord Derby to Mr. Bonar Law

Confidential Coworth

4 August 1910

DEAR BONAR LAW,

I cannot describe to you my feelings when Goulding told me that he thought you would be prepared to leave Dulwich and stand for Manchester: I cannot imagine a greater service to the Party. I will not call it a sacrifice because I feel perfectly certain that you would get in for N. West Manchester, but the effect that such a move on your part would have on the whole of the surrounding constituencies cannot be estimated—it would mean the gain of many seats—I do hope therefore that you will be prepared to help us as Goulding suggests—I shall not mention my own gratitude—but the gratitude of the whole of the Party would be beyond description—I don't ask you of course for a definite answer now—I feel you will want time to consider the position, and time also to consult your Dulwich friends, but I do hope—and beg, that your answer when it comes will be favourable.

I am leaving here tomorrow—so please answer to Derby House—Stratford Place.

Yours sincerely,

DERBY.

Bonar Law was somewhat sceptical as to the advantages of this project and Derby wrote again a week later stressing that he thought North-west Manchester would be 'an equally safe seat'. Balfour was also doubtful whether this would be a wise move:

Mr. Balfour to Lord Derby

10 October 1910

. . . Is North West Manchester an absolutely safe seat? Please remember what happened to Birrell (if I remember rightly) in that very constituency; he was pressed, I presume by the Party Whips, to contest the seat against poor Jim Ferguson: he was beaten; and he was out of Parliament for five years. It would really be a very serious thing for us in the House of Commons if any similar disaster happened to Bonar Law and I do not think we ought to sacrifice the Party in the House of Commons even to help so important a centre as Manchester . . .

Derby made his suggestion more attractive by guaranteeing an alternative seat in case anything went wrong in Manchester:

Lord Derby to Mr. E. Goulding

Confidential — Knowsley
10 October 1910

I have talked to my brother Arthur.[1] He is perfectly prepared to stand at the next Election and if Bonar Law was defeated to surrender his seat to him. I think it is a perfectly safe seat and I have written to Arthur Balfour to tell him how matters stand and have asked him whether he now sees his way to approve of Bonar Law's candidature for North West Manchester . . .

Fortified by these assurances Balfour encouraged Bonar Law to make the move: 'The electioneering authorities have, however, now convinced me that there will be no difficulty in finding you a new seat should things go against you in your new constituency and this being so I no longer hesitate . . . Of this I am sure, if you accept Derby's invitation you will both deserve and earn the gratitude of the whole Party.'[2]

In the event Bonar Law failed to carry North-west Manchester. He was narrowly defeated by 445 votes in a poll of nearly 11,000.

Lord Derby to Mr. Bonar Law

4 December 1910 — Knowsley

MY DEAR BONAR LAW,

I cannot tell you with what bitter disappointment I heard last night that after your gallant fight—you had failed to win N.W. Manchester—and it is almost with a feeling of guilt that I today write to condole with a man for whose appearance at Manchester I was responsible. I try to think of anything we left undone—but can only come to the conclusion that large as was your majority in the thinking and business part of the town—the majority in the foreign Jew quarter was too strong for us.

I know you will acquit me of blame in the matter—I did what I did for the best, & I think I can honestly say that I worked as hard as

[1] For many years Member of Parliament for Ormskirk. [2] Bonar Law Papers.

any man could to secure your success. Still I feel that I am the responsible person and as such I ask for your forgiveness—My brother is I know also writing to you.

* * *

When in the summer of 1911 it became known that the King had given his contingent guarantee to Mr. Asquith and it appeared that Mr. Asquith intended to exercise this power to any degree necessary to make it effective, the Unionists both in the Commons and the Lords were split. On the one hand there were those under the leadership of the aged Lord Halsbury who believed that the threat was a bluff and who were prepared to see the Upper House swamped with any number of new creations rather than acquiesce in a curtailment of their powers. This faction came to be known as the 'Ditchers', since they were prepared to 'die in the last ditch'. The 'Ditchers' comprised not only die-hard peers who resented any encroachment on their general authority, but also those who adhered to the Union with Ireland and who realised that once the Parliament Bill was carried their power to resist the repeal of the Union would disappear for ever.

Opposed to the 'Ditchers' were the 'Hedgers', under the leadership of Lord Lansdowne. Their view was that it was better to submit, since so vast an influx of new peers would be intolerable and would render illusory if not abortive such powers as might still remain to the Upper House after the inevitable passage of the Bill.

Derby started with the 'Ditchers', but like so many other 'Ditchers'—notably Lord Curzon—he ended up reluctantly in the camp of the 'Hedgers'. He, like Halsbury, believed that Asquith was bluffing and so advised the King early in July. Later the same month the following exchange took place between him and Mr. L. J. Maxse, editor of the *National Review*:

Mr. L. J. Maxse to Lord Derby

29 July 1911 National Review

DEAR LORD DERBY,

As a warm admirer of the great work you have been doing for Unionism in Lancashire during the last two or three years, may I be allowed to express my profound regret, which is shared by many other Unionists I have spoken to, that you contemplate throwing in your lot with that portion of the Peerage who have decided, for reasons which have never been divulged and never can be divulged because they are of so flimsy and contemptible a character, to allow this infamous Parliament Bill to go through by default sooner than that a single peer should be created. It is surely not surprising that your Lancashire friends are utterly bewildered by the action of those who have decided to follow Lord Lansdowne in his base surrender to Messrs. Asquith, Redmond and Patrick Ford. There is really no other way of putting it, because, just as the Prime Minister has 'toed the line' amid the universal contempt and derision of all decent citizens to the Leader of the Molly Maguires, so the Unionist Leaders are deliberately 'toeing the line' to the Prime Minister. You are perturbed at Lancashire anxieties as to whether you are actually going into the Demagogues' Lobby; but what is the great moral difference between allowing a Bill to go by default in order to stop a creation of peers, and actually voting for that Bill with the same object, which seems to be the sole object of the Unionist Mandarins.

To me, as an onlooker and outsider deeply attached to Unionist principles and with some experience of Unionist sentiment, the House of Lords seems to be committing suicide. It has no friends in the Radical ranks, except a few plutocrats who anticipate the divine moment when they may be in a position to purchase a peerage. What friends can the House of Lords expect to retain in the Unionist ranks on the Lansdowne House policy? How can our candidates be fairly asked to defend its actions, if it convicts itself at this grave crisis of being governed by craven counsels or snobbish considerations—save in so far as its honour is vindicated by the action of Lord Halsbury and the Stalwarts, which provides the one bright spot in the present political situation. Should the scuttlers prevail in their policy of helping the Demagogues to avoid the odium of a special creation of Radical peers in order that an outrageous measure may become the law of the land, how many years purchase do you give to a House of Lords which in cold blood sacrifices great national and constitutional interests solely in order to save itself from an infusion of outsiders, who would from every point of view strengthen the Upper House and weaken its enemies by depriving the latter of their one solid grievance —the overwhelming one-sidedness of the present House of Lords?

A golden opportunity is offered for real reform, which would at once discredit the Government and strengthen the House of Lords not only by a more rational distribution of Parties, which would immensely increase the authority of our Second Chamber, but likewise provide valuable allies in recovering the powers lost under the Parliament Bill. All these and many other fruits of the policy of courage are to be wantonly thrown away at the bidding of a timid Whig [Lansdowne] and a cynical philosopher [Balfour]. All we helpless onlookers can say is 'Heaven defend us from our friends. We can defend ourselves from our enemies.'

P.S.

I had no intention of writing anything for publication, but if you could write me an answer for publication I would gladly send both letters to the Press. I can assure you the public, by which I mean the Unionist public, are simply staggered by the performances of many Unionist peers and some Unionist newspapers.

Lord Derby to Mr. L. J. Maxse

Confidential

Derby House
31 July 1911

I have been away Saturday to Monday and have only just got your letter, first of all let me thank you for the very kind personal references you make to myself. You ask me whether I will write you an answer for publication to which my reply must be 'no', because my doing so would necessitate the publication of your letter and I venture to think that on reconsideration you will see that such a course is not calculated to do what I am sure you and I both wish, and that is to heal the wound in our Party as soon as possible. I think and others who agree with me would have cause to resent your calling those whom I follow 'a timid Whig and a cynical philosopher'. I can conscientiously say that in matters political I would sooner follow the advice of those you abuse than any other two men in England. I won't enter into a long argument with you as to the rights or wrongs of the case, sufficient to say that I should certainly have been with the Stalwarts if I thought I could have done any good by so doing, but as the action they take will neither defeat the Bill nor result in the insertion of our amendments but only on the contrary present the Government with a majority in the Upper House as well as in the Lower House, I can see no good to be gained by dying in the last ditch. Expediency therefore and loyalty to my Chief are the reasons why I am going to act as I propose to do.

The views so well expressed by Derby in the above letter became increasingly prevalent during these days, and when the vote was taken on August 11 in scenes of unbearable tension and with the thermometer standing at one time in the day at 100°, it was found that there were enough 'Hedgers' who abstained to ensure the Government a small majority. Against the Bill there voted 114. The Government succeeded in mustering, in addition to their own 81 supporters, 13 Bishops and 37 Unionists. Thus the Government's narrow victory depended not only on the abstention of the main body of 'Hedgers' but on 'Hedgers' who actually voted in the Government lobby. Derby, like his leader Lord Lansdowne, was among the large body of 'Hedgers' who abstained.

Ten days after the passage of the Bill, Derby was shooting grouse with the Duke of Devonshire at Bolton Abbey. The King was present and he confided to Derby his account of what had happened. Fortunately Derby immediately set down a record in his own hand of what the King had told him. The account which the King gave to Derby of these dramatic events, in particular of the pressure exerted on him by Asquith and Crewe, goes far beyond anything which has so far been published. It therefore is of exceptional and historic interest.

20 August 1911 — Derby House

At Bolton Abbey today (20.8.11) H.M. was good enough to tell me all that led up to his giving his guarantee with reference to the Veto Bill. Asquith went down to York Cottage last November and told the King he wanted an immediate dissolution, that he had arranged all dates, etc., and that he wanted to make the announcement at once so that it should all be over by Xmas. The King asked him why he wanted it, that Parliament was still very young and the Govt. had got a good majority. Asquith, who was in a very bullying mood, said that it was to pass the Veto Bill and as his side was ready and ours wasn't he wanted it at once, that it was no good sending the Veto resolution up to the House of Lords as they would only refuse to pass it, and much time would be lost. The King absolutely refused to give the dissolution until the resolution had been first submitted to the H. of L. This was before dinner. After dinner Asquith returned to the attack but the King still refused. The next morning Asquith, seeing the King meant what he said—gave way. The King said: 'Remember I only give you the dissolution, I give you no guarantee as to the creation of peers.' 'No', said Asquith, 'I quite understand that. I would not dream of asking you for that.'

The King afterwards went to London and here saw Asquith and Crewe. When they asked him for guarantees he complained that this was putting a pistol to his head and asked Asquith what he (A) would do if he refused. The answer was: 'I should immediately resign and at the next election should make the cry "The King and the Peers against the people."' He then appealed to Crewe, who said that he supported Asquith and that the whole Cabinet was united on the subject. He further urged that they were asking the King to do nothing unconstitutional. He begged to be allowed to see Arthur Balfour and Lansdowne but this was peremptorily refused. They bullied him for an hour and a half and he then told them that he would give guarantees if they got a majority and asked to be allowed to make this public. He said: 'I have been forced into this and I should like the country to know it.' They declined and said that this was a confidential pledge and must be kept so. In fact they bullied him and in his own language 'behaved disgracefully to me'.

Certain things he told me incidentally are of interest. 'They sent a cabinet memo to my father but I have no idea, nor would they tell me, what his answer was . . .' 'I had no idea of how my father would have dealt with the request, he never mentioned the subject to me at all . . .' 'I was given to understand that Balfour would have refused to form a Government—I know now that was not true.'

'Morley's words with reference to the creation of peers—which he read—on the final draft were written and submitted to me for my approval. I insisted they should be.'

'People must have been mad who thought I should only create enough peers to give a bare majority. I should have been forced to create 450, and as I told Asquith, I should never have held up my head again.'

'There was only one name I told him whatever happened I should refuse to accept—and that was de Forest.'

Though Asquith continued in the main to enjoy the King's esteem for him as a public servant and though Crewe remained a lifelong friend, there is little doubt that the King felt that he had been hardly used so early in his reign. He thought that excessive pressure had been put upon him and he is known to have expressed in later years the view that had he had the experience then that he acquired in the following twenty years he would have known that it was not constitutional for a Prime Minister to ask for guarantees which could only mature after a general election when he might be receiving the advice of a different Prime Minister.

VII

Lord Mayor of Liverpool

THE first member of the Derby family to be Lord Mayor of Liverpool was Sir Thomas Stanley, second son of the third Earl of Derby, who was chosen for the office in 1568. Since then, fourteen members of the family have been elected in four successive centuries as Chief Magistrate of this great commercial port and town which lay and still lies within its wide territorial influence.

During the nineteenth century, all of them took an intimate and continual interest in all the public affairs of the county despite their many other activities in national politics. The fourteenth Earl, who was known as the 'great Lord Derby', and was three times Prime Minister, was a shrewd man of business and took great interest in the cotton trade. In 1862 he was Chairman of the Central Relief Committee at Manchester during the cotton famine, brought about by the American Civil War, and it was due to his efforts that the relief movement was a success. His son, the fifteenth Earl, who was Foreign Secretary under Disraeli, was content in his later years to be Chairman of Quarter Sessions in Lancashire. His brother, who succeeded him as sixteenth Earl after having been Secretary of State for War and for the Colonies, as well as Governor-General of Canada, became in 1895 at the age of fifty-four, Lord Mayor of Liverpool. All three of them spoke with Lancashire accents and were widely popular among Lancashire people.

Edward, the seventeenth Earl, was to become even more popular in the county and was known through a great part of his life as 'The Uncrowned King of Lancashire'. In 1911 he became, like his father, Lord Mayor of Liverpool. He had already played a prominent part in the life of the city as Honorary Colonel of several Lancashire Territorial Force units and Chairman of the West Lancashire Territorial Force Association.

In 1908 he had been elected to the Chancellorship of Liverpool University and in January 1910 he became President of the Chamber of Commerce, an office he held continuously until 1943, and he remained for another five years an elected member of the Council. It was also in 1910 that he became President of the British Cotton Growers Association, further strengthening his connection with Liverpool, a port which owed the larger portion of its wealth to the importing and merchanting of cotton for the Lancashire textile industry during its great expansion in the nineteenth century. In the same year he was elected Chairman of the Liverpool Cathedral Building Fund and himself contributed £5,000 towards this object.

Commenting at the time of his death on his work for the Chamber of Commerce, the *Liverpool Trade Review* in February 1948 wrote:

> It might be thought by some that his interests in many directions and the claims upon his time and knowledge for the solution of problems of the highest importance would cause him to look upon the affairs of a Chamber of Commerce as being of little moment and himself a figure-head. Never could a greater mistake be made and those who were privileged to work with Lord Derby would give the lie to the thought in no uncertain manner. Punctilious in his attention to detail, Lord Derby never failed to preside over the Annual meetings of the Chamber and the successive Chairmen of the Chamber pay tribute to the fact that never was he found wanting when consulted on major issues, where his *entrée* to the highest councils of the nation was of inestimable value to the Chamber.[1]

[1] Among the matters which he took up on behalf of the Chamber of Commerce and for which he mobilised opinion not only in Lancashire but often in London as well, may be mentioned: recruiting from Liverpool business houses in the First World War; The Liverpool Merchants' Mobile Hospital; representation of Liverpool at the British Empire Exhibition; appeal for a Liverpool Chamber of Commerce Capital Fund; foundation of the Liverpool Junior Chamber of Commerce; visit of the Association of British Chambers of Commerce to Liverpool in 1927; proposed trunk road between Liverpool and North-west Lancashire; the Mersey Tunnel; formation of the Lancashire Industrial Development Council; formation of the Lancashire Chambers of Commerce Central Committee.

These were only a few of the local duties and responsibilities which Derby took on his shoulders and to which many more were to be added in the future. Derby was never a man to allow himself to be used as a mere figurehead. If he accepted the chairmanship or presidency of any enterprise he insisted on knowing exactly what was going on and lent much more than his name or even his presence, that was to become increasingly impressive, to the undertaking. The massive appearance he was already beginning to acquire and particularly his appearance in old age, by which he is best remembered today, might easily give people the idea that he was a lethargic or slow-moving person. On the contrary, he was a man of superabundant vitality and energy and his day was filled with ceaseless activity from dawn till dusk. 'He's a real live Lord,' said a Trade Union official at this time. Though a pleasure-loving man and one who enjoyed to an exceptional extent the company of his friends, he never allowed his social or sporting pleasures to interfere with his numerous public engagements.

He was elected Lord Mayor on 10 November 1911. It was not an easy year in Liverpool. There were many outbreaks of gang warfare by hooligans, whose religious slogans served as excuses for their brawling, and these led to intense feeling between the Roman Catholics and Protestants in the city. There were several large strikes and some industrial disasters. Derby was able to mitigate the religious dissension and also intervened successfully in one of the strikes. He was less tactful perhaps with the Liverpool City Council who did not always take kindly to the strict House of Commons rule of procedure which he enforced in the Chamber. The report of the first meeting contains many passages such as these:

Liverpool Daily Post and Mercury, 7 December 1911

Alderman Salvidge: I consider that this is so serious a matter that the Council ought not to dismiss it today without some consideration. Some steps should be taken to bring pressure upon the Government to consider it.

A Member: Is this in order?

The Lord Mayor: There can be no discussion whatever on this subject.

There has been a question asked and answered. A further question could be asked to elucidate anything in the answer that may not be clear, but there can be no discussion arising out of the question as originally asked (Hear, hear).

Alderman Maxwell, the chairman of the committee, asked the indulgence of the Council to take this matter immediately (cries of 'No'). It was a matter of serious importance to the Head Constable (No, no).

The Lord Mayor ruled that it would have to take its proper place in the opposed business.

Alderman Salvidge suggested that as a matter of courtesy Alderman Maxwell might be allowed to state his reasons for making this claim on the indulgence of the Council.

Alderman Maxwell said he was only anxious that no injustice should be done to the Head Constable.

Mr. Austin Harford: The Lord Mayor has already given his ruling.

The Lord Mayor: Order, please.

Alderman Salvidge: I submit that it is not a question of ruling, but—

The Lord Mayor (rapping sharply with his hammer): Order, please, order. . . . That is one of the things to which I must draw particular attention. I will not have these interruptions while I am in charge of the chamber (Hear, hear).

Alderman Salvidge, the local Conservative leader, with whom Derby had been acquainted for many years and who henceforward was to play an increasing role in his life, was one of the most remarkable men ever produced in the municipal life of England. Municipal politics in England, in contrast to those in the United States, are on the whole a pallid, drab and unimportant affair. The city budgets are much smaller, the patronage is relatively microscopic, the graft, with rare exceptions, infinitesimal, and the power through political control of even the largest cities to exercise an influence in national affairs virtually non-existent. Consequently the city boss has been almost unknown in this country. Indeed, with the exception of the notorious Schadhorst, who built the political machine in Birmingham in conjunction with Joseph Chamberlain in the seventies, Alderman Salvidge stands out pre-eminent in this sphere of English politics.

Salvidge, a man of exceptional industry and flair for politics and a brilliant electioneer, was also of outstanding personal integrity, and was more than once, through his influence and sagacity, to play an important part in national affairs. It was he who brought the then unknown Mr. F. E. Smith, later first Earl of Birkenhead, into politics; and for his outstanding loyalty and services to Mr. Lloyd George he was ultimately to be awarded the unique distinction for a politician who had never been at Westminster of receiving a privy councillorship.

Conservative politics in Liverpool were organised on an anti-Irish basis. The relatively high wages in Liverpool had attracted a vast influx of cheap labour from Ireland. They naturally tended to vote for the Liberal party which was promising Ireland Home Rule. The Conservative vote was therefore organised not only on defence of the Union, but also on a strident anti-Catholicism. The Liverpool Constitutional Association and the Conservative Working Men's Clubs in which Salvidge had made his name both barred Roman Catholics from membership, and the more extreme among the Protestants, who belonged to the Orange Societies, annually celebrated Dutch William's victory over the Irish at the Battle of the Boyne on 1 July 1690 by marching through the streets and with bonfires amid which effigies of the Pope of Rome were consumed.

No one had his finger so closely on the pulse of this great city as Salvidge, and Derby became more and more dependent upon him for gathering the information on which he was able to give advice to his political associates and leaders in London as to party prospects in the north. Derby and Salvidge proved a most effective political combination and we shall see in the next chapter how their joint ingenuity and influence were able to win for Lancashire a unique victory in the annals of the Unionist Party.

Derby plunged himself with zest into all the charitable, social and administrative activities incumbent upon the holder of his office. What others might regard as irksome civic duty he welcomed with enthusiasm and let slip no opportunity of implementing his firm belief that every occasion in whatever sphere of action and on whatever plane of life was an occasion where he, by virtue of his ancestry and position might give counsel to greater effect, mediate with better chance of promoting agreement, and if necessary dictate with less fear of opposition. The civic work he accomplished during this year bears witness to his efforts. He not only discharged the routine duties which are the lot of every Lord Mayor, he threw himself with enthusiasm into every aspect of the city's business and social life. The reason why he was so successful was that quite apart from a feeling of his inherited responsibilities for the welfare of Liverpool's citizens he had a genuine relish for this sort of work. The happy people in life are those whose work is their pleasure. Derby had the good fortune to find delight in discharging duties which most people would find burdensome if not positively distasteful. It was because he so obviously enjoyed his work that he was able to communicate so much pleasure to those among whom he moved.

The local newspapers had little cause for complaint during his term of office. Day after day the Lord Mayor performed some ceremony or presided over some meeting which endeared him increasingly to the citizens of Liverpool and enhanced the growing Derby legend. In the space of a few months we see Lord Derby co-ordinating the various boys' organisations so that under a partially centralised management there should be less waste of labour and no overlapping in finding the boys jobs on emergence from their tutelage; organising the fund for the survivors of the *Titanic* disaster, devoting his attention now to welfare of the poor and ill, now to promotion of a correct civic pride.

He addressed the marine cadets at the Florence Institute for Boys exhorting them to take full advantage of their opportunities in the world of affairs which they were to enter. He opened the Scotch Home Industries Bazaar and a new Home for Poor Girls, and he presented colours to the Fourth Battalion The King's (Liverpool) Regiment. His interest in childhood and youth is apparent from the records of the year. He gave a fancy dress ball in the Town Hall on 2 January 1912: 'Last night the Town Hall showed us again the fair and lovely scene of children at play, masquerading as kings and queens and princes and princesses, as great courtiers and court ladies, as minstrels, acrobats and butterflies, as fairies and gnomes and elves, as brigands and soldiers and monks and, most beautiful of all, as twilights and dawns and sunsets and rainbows and flowers of field and garden.' Such was the felicitous account in the *Liverpool Courier*. He also presided over a meeting to discuss the establishment of scholarships for 'necessitous students'. Some of these charitable occasions involved a personal contact of a sort that under the Welfare State has now gone out of fashion. At Christmas time Lord Derby distributed 'hot pots' to the needy of the city and was himself given one to sample. He took it and presented it to a cripple.[1]

There are humorous touches of the period which emerge from the newspapers. Derby presided at a meeting of the Church of England Temperance Society in January 1911 where the Bishop of Liverpool, referring to the activities of the 'suffragettes' who were claiming equal political rights with men, said that very much was heard about the rights of women; he would like to plead for a moment for the rights of men. His speech was carried by the *Courier* under the title 'Woman drunkards. Protection of Husbands'.

An annual function attended by all Lord Mayors was the consular banquet to which were invited all the numerous foreign consuls in the city. The *Courier* record is worthy of preservation since it is a good specimen of Derby's after-dinner style of speaking. The simple jests which on another man's lips would scarcely have provoked a smile, aided and transmuted by his exceptional bonhomie, charm and abundantly genial presence seem to have dissolved the company in laughter at almost every sentence.

> The Lord Mayor, who was very warmly received, said he naturally did not respond for Lord and Lady Derby. They were a most uninteresting couple, who liked to go to bed early, and to have their meals at regular hours (*laughter*). He left them out of the question, and would only venture to respond in the name of the Lord Mayor and the Lady Mayoress. In doing so he felt at a great disadvantage. Everyone of

[1] A note in the programme of the Christmas Hot Pot Fund Grand Matinée says: 'In the making up of the 10,000 Hot-Pots the following are required:

123,200 pounds of Potatoes.
54,648 pounds of Best Beef.
10,000 pounds of Onions.
625 pounds of Salt.
39 pounds of Pepper.'

them could probably speak five or six languages, whereas he could only speak one, and that indifferently (*laughter*). The chairman spoke about Charles V, and asked a question as to what he would have thought about the English language. But, though he asked the question, neither he nor anyone else had attempted to give the response. All he (his Lordship) could say was that it seemed to get them on pretty well over most of the world, and though it might not be the language of poetry, sometimes when they heard it down at the docks it was at all events forcible and to the point (*laughter*). The chairman referred to the great want in this city of a proper opera house, and he rather indicated that they were devoid of musical intelligence. He (Lord Derby) did not speak for himself, because he confessed that the only thing he liked was a brass band with a big drum—(*laughter*)—but as one who cared so much for music why, he asked, did they as an accompaniment to the toast of the Rulers of all nations have the tune of a cake walk? (*Laughter.*)

Mr. J. O. Bunster (Consul-General of Chile) proposed the toast of 'Our Guests'. The Earl of Derby, he observed, not only could have been the historical and actual King of Man, while an ancestor had been offered the Crown of Greece, but he was in truth the uncrowned King of Liverpool.

Lord Derby, in submitting the health of the Chairman, said the Consul-General for Chile had alluded to him as the uncrowned king (*laughter*). He spoke of his family having given up the crown of the Isle of Man. They did not give it up: they lost it unfortunately to a Scotsman—(*laughter*)—and the Scotsman sold it (*laughter*). There was another nationality to which he referred, but as a matter of fact that crown was never offered (*laughter*). His ancestor was asked whether, if it was offered, he would accept it, and like a fool he said no (*laughter*). He (his Lordship) thought he was wrong—he certainly felt how wrong he was when he saw what an excellent subject one would have had organising that record banquet that night (*laughter*, and *hear*, *hear*).

Mr. Percy Corkhill, who was the Lord Mayor's secretary during this time, recalls:

Lord Derby delighted in arranging banquets at the Town Hall and was in his element at such gatherings—full of humour and indulging in badinage. But like so many public men he disliked the wearisome after-dinner flow of what is meant for oratory. He introduced instead musical entertainment in the Council Chamber where so many dull debates had been carried out by tired aldermen and ambitious councillors. But alas, the experiment did not please certain of the public men who loved to pour out their repertoire of platitudes, and the experiment was reluctantly curtailed.

We have referred above to the religious disputes which were an unpleasant aspect of Liverpool life, more especially since they intruded themselves so markedly into local politics. As the Irish disputes became more bitter, passions were roused, and with a view to assuaging them one of Derby's first acts as Lord Mayor was to convene a meeting consisting of the Bishop of Liverpool (Dr. Chavasse), the Roman Catholic Archbishop (Dr. Whiteside), Mr. T. P. O'Connor, M.P., Colonel Kyffin-Taylor, M.P., Alderman Salvidge and a number of other local notables. This conference succeeded in making recommendations which though not of a very far-reaching character seemed to have done a good deal to reduce the local ill-feeling. The main recommendations were directed towards minimising the disputes which were apt to occur when the local factions held demonstrations. Derby was not content with the pious declarations achieved by the 'Peace Conference' as it came to be called, but made it his business to see that the spirit behind the conclusions was translated into action. When Alderman Salvidge, representing the Conservative working men, wished in August 1912 to stage a mass anti-Home Rule demonstration on St. George's Hall Plateau in the centre of the city, he persuaded Salvidge to alter the venue to Sheil Park where a demonstration was less likely to provoke a disturbance.

Because of this sensible action on his part he received the plaudits of the Conservative *Courier*, ever ready to be his spokesman or apologist, and also of the *Liverpool Post*, a powerful Liberal organ. By his skill in pacifying so effectively these local sectarian factions, Derby acquired a reputation which at the end of the war was to lead to his becoming involved in an attempt to settle the age-long dispute between Britain and Ireland.

The high esteem in which Derby was held by all sections and parties in the community combined with his exceptional ability for getting on with and bringing out the best in his fellow men, of whatever station, made him an ideal mediator and arbitrator in industrial disputes. During his term of office as Lord Mayor his arbitration in a strike in the wholesale furnishing trade was accepted, and later in the same year when a strike of 60,000 transport workers was threatened he persuaded the employers to make concessions which made a compromise solution possible.

Derby gained the lifelong esteem of both sides in these industrial troubles. A letter to Derby from Mr. Collins, Chairman of the National (Wholesale) Furniture Manufacturers Association, written immediately after Derby's successful intervention in the strike, shows the deep gratitude the commercial community of Liverpool entertained towards him:

Mr. Campbell Collins to Lord Derby

13 September 1912

My dear Lord Mayor,

My members desire me to convey to your Lordship the expression of their grateful appreciation of the wonderful tact, patience and ability displayed by you in settling the labour trouble in the Furniture Trade.

They are confident that without your intervention it would have been almost impossible to have effected a settlement so honourable and acceptable to both sides.

It may possibly interest your Lordship to know that the signed agreement now in your possession is the most comprehensive settlement that has ever been made in the history of our trade and in it there are embodied principles that we trust will be universally recognised wherever disputes occur in the Furniture Trade for some considerable time.

For myself, and also on behalf of my colleagues who sat with me at the actual Conference (and the whole of the members of the Liverpool Association), I desire to express my extreme gratification and sincerest thanks for your unfailing kindness and fine courtesy. The ease with which you grasped difficulties, many of a purely technical nature, and the valuable suggestions you made to solve such difficulties made our position and the settlement of the trouble possible.

I am sure by the enthusiastic manner you threw yourself into the conference, that the settlement of the difficulties will personally give you great pleasure—as I am sure it has given profound thankfulness to many whose living and comfort depended upon the resumption of work by the men interested.

Derby's relations with labour leaders were no less amicable. It was in 1907 at Kirkdale that the first straight fight between a Unionist and a Labour candidate took place. On this occasion Salvidge telegraphed the Tory Central Office: 'It is not sufficient to call the Socialists names. Send us arguments'. So little had the nascent Labour Party been considered as a serious political force that no preparation had been made to combat the strange doctrines which were promulgated by the Labour candidate. It is interesting to note that Kirkdale was won by the Tories after Salvidge had arranged the publication in leaflet form of extracts from a book by an acknowledged Socialist thinker which contained atheistic propaganda.

One of the most important Labour politicians active in Liverpool during these years was Sir James Sexton. He began work when he was eight. At nine he was earning *2s. 6d.* a week, working twelve-hour shifts in a glass factory. After an adventurous youth spent in the merchant marine and in Canada he returned to Liverpool and in 1881 suffered a serious injury to his face caused by defective tackle in the docks. He was unable to obtain compensation from his employers, and discovered subsequently that the fare of the taxi which conveyed him to hospital was to be deducted from his first pay packet in the job obtained for him after the injury.

In 1893 he became secretary of the National Union of Dock Workers, and in the same year he was active as a founder-member of the Independent Labour Party. In 1897 he exerted great influence in the passage of the Workmen's Compensation Act. His subsequent life was devoted to the service of the ideals of social justice and social welfare. Sexton, with whom Derby was to form a valuable friendship during the First World War when, under Derby's aegis, he organised the Liverpool Dockers' Battalion, left in his autobiography (*Sir James Sexton, Agitator*) this recollection of his boyhood contacts with Knowsley:

As a matter of fact, I visited his estate fairly frequently in my boyhood days, always in company with my father, who had acquired, during his nomadic life, some rather curious and heterodox views upon such matters as the Game Laws. He used to arouse me before dawn of a summer day—and right gladly I answered the call—and we would set off for Knowsley Park, which extended to the boundary of St. Helens. Our equipment was always the same—a pillow-slip and some funnels made out of sugar paper. The inside of the funnels was smeared with bird-lime, upon which currants had been sprinkled. These contrivances were inserted in holes in the ground.

Now, pheasants are exceedingly found of currants, and when they tried to extract the fruit they were securely bonneted by the funnels. The pillow-slip completed their discomfiture. They passed into our possession.

Years later, when I had reached man's estate and my mother was living with me in the evening of her life, Lord Derby frequently sent us a haunch of venison or a brace of pheasants. On one of these occasions, when writing to thank his lordship for his kindness, I acted upon the old lady's suggestion, and informed him we had previously enjoyed game from Knowsley acquired in another and less direct but more picturesque manner. Lord Derby narrated this to King George when I was at Knowsley, and His Majesty seemed greatly amused by the story.

* * *

On 22 June 1911, King George V was crowned. A magnificent procession accompanied Their Majesties from Buckingham Palace to the Abbey. Rajahs and Maharajahs of India, Princes from the Malay States, rulers and potentates, chiefs and sheiks from every corner of Africa, Asia and Australasia, Dominion Premiers, Governors of Crown Colonies, detachments of troops representing all branches of the services and the Indian Army, Crown Princes and Emissaries Extraordinary from all the great powers of Europe, Representatives and Dignitaries from all the countries of the new world, all bore testimony to the extent of the King Emperor's power and domains.

On the day after the Coronation Their Majesties reviewed at Spithead the most formidable naval armada ever assembled. There were 165 British warships, including eight dreadnoughts, twenty-four battleships and thirty-four cruisers, eighteen foreign warships represented the European and foreign navies, while many large British ocean liners proclaimed the mercantile hegemony of the United Kingdom.

On 27 June 1911, about a week after the Coronation, Derby and his wife gave a ball at Derby House. The social season of 1911 was the most brilliant London has ever witnessed, and the supper list of this ball at Derby House recalls a vanished world of brilliance and splendour.

Derby House

Supper *Tuesday* *27 June* 1911

The Earl of Derby.

H.I.H. The Crown Prince of Germany.

H.I.H. The Hereditary Prince Youssouf Effendi of Turkey.

H.I.H. The Grand Duke Boris of Russia.

H.I.H. The Archduke Karl Franz of Austria.

H.R.H. The Infante Don Fernando of Spain.

H.I.H. The Prince Higashi-Fushimi of Japan.

H.R.H. The Crown Prince of Greece.

H.R.H. The Crown Prince of Roumania.

H.R.H. The Prince Alexander of Servia.

H.R.H. The Crown Prince of Denmark.

The Countess of Derby.

H.R.H. The Crown Prince of Sweden.

H.R.H. The Crown Prince of Bulgaria.

H.R.H. The Grand Duke of Hesse.

H.R.H. The Grand Duke of Mecklenburg-Schwerin.

Mr. John Hayes Hammond.[1]

Vice-Admiral Fauques de Jonquières.

H.I.H. The Crown Princess of Germany.

H.I.H. The Princess Higashi-Fushimi of Japan.

H.R.H. The Crown Princess of Greece.

H.R.H. The Crown Princess of Roumania.

H.R.H. The Crown Princess of Sweden.

[1] The high precedence awarded to Mr. Hammond, an American mining engineer, is explained by the fact that he was the personal representative at the Coronation of President Taft.

H.R.H. The Grand Duchess of Hesse.
H.R.H. The Grand Duchess of Mecklenburg-Schwerin.
H.R.H. The Princess Royal.
H.R.H. The Duchess of Connaught.
H.R.H. The Princess Victoria Patricia of Connaught.
H.R.H. The Princess Alexander of Teck.
H.R.H. The Duchess of Coburg.
The Countess Benckendorff.
Mrs. Whitlaw Reid.
Madame de Villa Urrurtia.
Madame Kato.
H.R.H. The Duke of Connaught.
His Ex. The French Ambassador.
His Ex. The Russian Ambassador.
His Ex. The Austrian Ambassador.
His Ex. The United States Ambassador.
His Ex. The Spanish Ambassador.
His Ex. The Japanese Ambassador.
H.R.H. Prince Henry of Prussia.
H.R.H. Duke of Coburg.
H.R.H. Duke Albrecht of Württemberg.
H.R.H. Prince Rupprecht of Bavaria.
H.R.H. Prince John George of Saxony.
H.R.H. Prince Henry of the Netherlands.
H.R.H. Prince George of Greece.
H.I.H. The Grand Duke Michael Michaelovitch.
H.R.H. The Grand Duke of Mecklenburg-Strelitz.
H.R.H. The Duke George William of Brunswick Luneburg.
H.R.H. Prince Arthur of Connaught.
H.H. Prince Frederick Charles of Hesse.
H.H. Prince Alexander of Battenburg.
H.S.H. The Prince of Monaco.
H.R.H. The Princess of Saxe-Meiningen.
H.H. The Princess Frederick Charles of Hesse.
H.R.H. Princess John George of Saxony.
H.R.H. The Princess George of Greece.
H.S.D.H. Princess Louis of Battenburg.
H.H. The Princess Alexandra.
H.H. The Princess Maud.
H.H. The Duchess of Teck.
H.S.H. The Princess Louise of Battenburg.
Mrs. Hayes Hammond.
The Duchess of Marlborough.
The Duchess of Roxburghe.
The Duchess of Portland.
The Duchess of Manchester.
The Duchess of Sutherland.
The Duchess of Rutland.
The Duchess of Westminster.

The Marchioness of Salisbury.
The Marchioness of Londonderry.
The Marchioness of Lansdowne.
The Countess of Essex.
The Countess Torby.
H.S.H. The Prince Alexander of Teck.
The Duke of Fife.
Prince de Ligne.
H.H. Maharajah-Dhiraja Holkar of Indore.
H.H. Maharajah of Patiala.
H.H. The Maharajah of Bikanir.
H.H. Aga Khan.
H.S.H. Prince Pless.
His Ex. Monsieur Johannes Irgens.
H.S.H. Prince Schonburg.
General von Plessen.
Admiral von Usedom.

Admiral Togo.
General Nogi.
Prince Bielosselsky-Bielosersky.
H.E. Abdul-Hak Hamid Bey.
The Marchioness of Graham.
The Marchioness of Hamilton.
Madame Genadins.
The Countess of Shaftesbury.
The Countess of Granard.
The Countess of Chesterfield.
The Countess of Mar.
Madame Lalaing.
Madame Rehbinder.
The Countess of Lanesborough.
The Countess of Cadogan.
The Countess of Dudley.
Madame Herwignen.
The Countess of Granville.
The Countess of Crewe.
Madame Catargi.

* * *

Perhaps the most striking tribute to Lord Derby's period as Lord Mayor of Liverpool is to be found in the impression he made on those who were his political opponents. In an article in the *Pall Mall Magazine* (already quoted on p. 45) Mr. T. P. O'Connor, the Irish Nationalist M.P. for the Scotland Division of Liverpool, summed up in January 1914 Derby's achievements in that city under this challenging and surprising headline:

Will Lord Derby be Prime Minister?

'The present head of the Stanleys', says Mr. O'Connor, 'is typically Lancashire; with even a faint trace in his accent of the Lancashire brogue. He has a bluff manner and the brusque and jerky speech of the Lancashireman. If you did not know that he was a great noble, you might take him for the heir to some vast cotton-spinning business which had built gigantic mills and exported its goods by the million to all parts of the world. And he has also a good deal of the Lancashire doggedness underneath all his air of bonhomie and easy-goingness. He is always doing something; he is always moving somewhere; he is ever ready to take up any job, whether it be serious business or merely ceremonial. And he has enormous personal influence over men —at least in Lancashire.

'I saw a remarkable example of this at a curious conference in which he took a leading part and of which I was a member. For some years Liverpool had suffered under a fierce spirit of sectarianism unknown in any other part of the British Isles, except in one or two parts of Ireland. This spirit had resulted in violent collisions; in fierce party feeling which penetrated almost everywhere—even dividing men into different and quarrelling sections at their workshops; and incidentally adding a large sum yearly to the rates of the city.

'At last the good sense and Christian feeling of the city rose in revolt; and Colonel Kyffin-Taylor and myself resolved to make an attempt to bring the hideous scandal to an end. But we realised that one man above all others was inevitable and essential; and that was Lord Derby. He undertook to preside; and never did a man perform a difficult task more admirably. And indeed it was a difficult team he had to drive. In this strange gathering there were ecclesiastics of all the creeds; the Catholic Archbishop; the Protestant Bishop of Liverpool; the Rev. Mr. Rogers, a Nonconformist clergyman; Mr. Austin Harford, the leading Nationalist, confronted Grand Masters of Orange lodges; the Rev. George Wise, famous as a vehement controversialist, was cheek by jowl with a strong Catholic; and Mr. Archie Salvidge represented the working-class Unionist element.

'But Lord Derby had only to rise, and immediately everybody succumbed; he carried his point, and the lions and the lambs sat down together in peace and agreed unanimously on a report. It was impossible to say how Lord Derby did it; but he did it.

'It is for the Unionist Party', Mr. O'Connor proceeds, 'to choose its own leaders, of course; but Lord Derby has the good will, which is something, of even his political opponents. Strong in party spirit and party loyalty, he is quite free from personal rancour; he knows as many Liberals as Unionists, and when he was in the House of Commons he was the friend of nearly every Nationalist. Indeed, it is one of the little secrets of the place that he put money into some of their pockets by judicious tips on the great races. In appearance he remains a great, ruddy-cheeked, robust boy; the roundness is not broken by a single line of care or of rancour; and the eye, large, open and frank, retains a certain boyishness of look.

'He has the world all before him; for he is still quite young. He has a vast fortune; he has no passion for anything except politics, leaving out of account a slight love for the racecourse and the stable; and he can work hard, and at any job that comes to his hand.

'He once said with characteristic frankness that he had three ambitions: to be Lord Mayor of Liverpool, to win the Derby, and to be Prime Minister. All three ambitions may be gratified. In the present welter and even chaos of politics and of political personalities, it may be that he will prove to be the man who divides his party least.'

VIII

Tariff Reform and Food Taxes

EVER since the Liberal landslide of 1906, there had been mounting criticism inside the Tory Party of its leader, Mr. Arthur Balfour. Not only was he blamed for the defeat: it was also felt that his inability to make up his mind on the Tariff issue was prejudicial to the Party's fortunes. These stresses within the Party continued to be aggravated; criticism of Balfour daily increased. Derby's loyalty to Balfour had made him accept the tariff policy which the Party had embraced in 1905 and which had contributed to the electoral disaster of 1906. Now that there were indications that Balfour might be pushed out of the leadership of the Party Derby's political thoughts began to crystallise into the clearest and most consistent political policy of his lifetime, namely opposition to food taxes.

Derby was no economist and he seldom used any argument save that food taxes would lose votes. He believed that the Conservative Party had more important causes to defend and that these would be jeopardised if the agitation of the Food Taxers should rivet this burden round the Party's neck. The controversy in which Derby was now to engage and which will be recorded in this chapter afforded him the only great political victory of his lifetime; and at the end he emerged with greatly enhanced political influence, if not power. His time-honoured, hereditary role, aided and augmented by his increasing association with the life of Lancashire, was already achieving for him the leadership of the county on a foundation considerably broader and deeper than Party. His successful handling of this controversy was to consolidate his power and to extend his influence to Whitehall and Westminster. How his thought was moving at this time is well shown in the following letter:

Lord Derby to Mr. Walter Long

19 October 1911 Knowsley

I quite understand your not coming here though I should like to have had a talk with you as I am not at all happy about the state of our Party here—or indeed anywhere else. The promoters may profess loyalty as much as ever they like but this new Halsbury Club is undoubtedly an anti-Balfour one and indeed an anti-Lansdowne one too, and the very name is bound to keep to the differences that exist between the 'hedgers' and 'ditchers'. But while I am angry with them I am also very distressed about A. J. B.'s attitude. All these things have been done against him, all these evidences of disloyalty, and yet he makes absolutely no move. If he would only call the Party together and say all these things are evidences of opposition to his leadership and resign, he would find that the disloyal party, though doing most of the talking, have got very little real influence and they would have to yield. But as he allowed things to go on they will get more and more recruits and at the end it will be impossible for him to resist and he will be kicked out instead of kicking them out . . .

The labour unrest is due to the fact that the price of living has gone up in an immeasurably greater proportion than has been the rise of wages and yet here are we, to go through yet another election—the fourth, with our opponents able to taunt us with still further increasing the price of food . . . Bread is looked upon as the staple food and increase the price of that and you never can get away from the taunt that you are increasing the price of food. I have talked to many Tariff Reformers and however ardent supporters they may be of the policy you will find almost everyone of them agrees with me that if we could drop this part of our policy we should sweep the board with a tax on imported manufactured articles. And yet here we have an official announcement on behalf of practically the whole party signed by Austen Chamberlain and Duncannon again tying this millstone round our neck and saying that they will refuse to recognise any candidate who does not adhere to Joe's policy exactly as he first put it forward. I do not pretend to have much influence but I think I have got a little in Lancashire and unless a change is made in the direction

I mean to withdraw next year entirely from the Party and enter into a crusade on my own against the imposition of these taxes. I think you would probably find that with the exception of Hewins[1] I should get every Lancashire candidate to fall in with my views. This of course is all for your private eye but I am rather bitter at the present moment at seeing our real leader doing nothing whilst Chamberlain, F. E. Smith, Carson and Co. are apparently trying to lead our Party by a syndicate.

Meanwhile Derby had deduced that Balfour was thinking of throwing in his hand. He was much concerned at this prospect and some letters passed between them:

Lord Derby to Mr. Balfour[2]

Confidential — Stanley House,
25 October 1911 — Newmarket

I understand from Balcarres that he has repeated to you a statement I made at a meeting we held in Devonshire House on Tuesday—for fear you should think me guilty of a breach of confidence I am writing you this note to explain the circumstances. The meeting as you have now been told was held to consider the best way in which those of us who are absolutely loyal to you could show that loyalty—and make clear to the public—and the Party—our detestation of the policy of a few individuals. All sorts of schemes were discussed and I said that something must be done at once—because I was quite certain from something you had said the night before that you had resignation of the leadership in contemplation. You said nothing to me direct—but you let fall two phrases which gave me the impression. That is all I told him—and I hope you will believe I only said it with a view of emphasising the necessity for a move to be made at once by the loyalists—and if I was guilty of something I ought not to have done—it was an indiscretion with a motive you would appreciate.

I can't tell you how strongly I feel as to the infamous way a few noisy

[1] W. A. S. Hewins, 1865–1931, an ardent Tariff Reformer who unsuccessfully contested South-east Lancashire in the Unionist interest in 1910 and 1911. He later sat for Hereford and was Under-Secretary of State for the Colonies, 1917–19.

[2] Balfour Papers.

busybodies—and two newspaper men—have treated you. Sink or swim you may be always certain of my loyalty—you are the only leader I follow. There is only one thing to be said for your resignation —if that really is in your mind—and that is that you would have proof of how insignificant in both numbers and influence the rebels are—when you see the list of men who will *insist* on your retaining the leadership.

Mr. Balfour to Lord Derby

Private
28 October 1911

The Warren House,
Stanmore

... You must not blame Bal [Balcarres] for what seems to have been my mistake. I could not for the life of me remember *what* I had said at the Wolvertons' which occasioned your commentary to the meeting at Devonshire House. I opined that I had been grumbling (like other old gentlemen) at my advancing years and increasing infirmities; and that you had interpreted these observations in a very precise fashion. I now know that I was mistaken: for before getting your second letter, I dined again at the Wolvertons' and asked Lady W. exactly what I *had* said on Monday. She gave me exactly the same version as you have done: so that the accuracy of your recollections and the imperfection of mine are fully established. The matter is perhaps not worth pursuing further now: I need only say for the present that while I *do* hang very loosely to my present job I had not the least intention in what I casually said on Monday last of giving expression to any defined policy . . .

Lord Derby to Mr. Balfour [1]

29 October 1911

Knowsley

... Your letter has made me quite happy—I have forgiven Balcarres. All the more am I made happy by the fact that I was wrong, in what I thought were your intentions . . .

Mr. Balfour to Lord Derby

2 November 1911

Somehow we have been at cross purposes—partly because I have been too stupid, partly because you have been too clever. I never had

[1] Balfour Papers.

the least intention of saying anything at the Wolvertons' about giving up the lead and was quite unaware (as I wrote you) that I had ever done so, but your conjecture whether really justified by my language or only a case of brilliant intuition was quite correct although, till I had had the matter out with Lansdowne—I did not wish it known even by friends as close and colleagues as trusted as yourself. Had you been able to stay in London, or had I seen you at the beginning of this week I would have explained the matter.

My fundamental reason, which neither Bob Douglas nor Sandars think can be answered, is this: I am quite sure that I have not the physical vigour required for a new term of office. I have had a longer and heavier dose of continuous political office than any of my predecessors. Office, whether as Minister or a Leader of Opposition in the H. of C., means (as *I* conceive its duties) *more*, not *less*, labour as time goes on. Younger men *must* take on the job. If this be granted (and it is in my opinion unarguable) the only question is one of dates. *When* ought I to give up? I have thought deeply and long on the matter, and my answer is clear—*Now*. If I defer it till next session it will damage our fight on Home Rule. If I put it off till the session after we shall be approaching dangerously near the General Election (which *might* indeed happen in 1912). The present session is relatively uncontroversial. If my retirement causes difficulties for the moment—there will be time to get over them before the fighting session begins. I don't propose leaving the H. of C. or abandoning political life. I shall still be able to take a share in the mêlée, though I shall not lead it.

Please keep this to yourself for the moment.

Balfour's skilful if ironic flattery of Derby was very much in keeping with the silky urbanity with which he had so long handled his political colleagues. His reference to Derby's 'cleverness' recalls the epigram of Asquith's younger daughter, Elizabeth (Princess Antoine Bibesco): 'Lord Derby is sufficiently clever to pretend to be stupid, in order that people may think him honest.'

Derby was distressed to find that his intuition had not been at fault:

Lord Derby to Mr. Balfour

Confidential Knowsley

5 November 1911

My dear Arthur,

Thank you very much for your letter and for your confidence which naturally I shall keep, but at which I was aghast. I am afraid I cannot influence your decision but I do hope you will reconsider it. I quite understand the reasons which prompt you to resign, but I do not agree with Bob Douglas and Jack Sandars that they are unanswerable. You say that you have not the physical vigour required for a new term of office. That is a subject on which you alone can speak and you alone decide, but are we anywhere near to a term of office? I think not, but still in view of what you say about the increasing burdens of a leader in opposition I will accept the fact that you feel the time has come when you must consider resignation but what I don't agree about is your statement that *now* is the right time to do it and I will give you my reasons. If, as in your own case when Lord Salisbury resigned, there existed somebody whom everybody recognised as the fit successor I might agree with you but you know better than I do the jealousies that exist between our colleagues when it comes to merely a question of leading the opposition. Your resignation would inevitably lead to a split in the party and that just at a time when we wanted to be united in our opposition to Home Rule. And, what is more, that split would extend to our House, as I feel that Lansdowne will resign if you do and we shall have, not our Austen Chamberlain and Walter Long parties but our Selborne and Curzon factions. There is another matter which I think ought to weigh with you. Won't it rather look as if the rebels had got what they wanted and forced you to retire? I can quite understand your disgust at their tactics but do you realise what a very small, though noisy, body they are? Yesterday at Manchester we had our quarterly meeting of the Lancashire National Union; a quite spontaneous vote of confidence was passed in you. It was proposed by Holt (of Manchester) and seconded by Salvidge who made one of the strongest speeches I have ever heard him make and the resolution was passed absolutely unanimously, and really that reflects the feeling that exists in this part of the world with reference to your leadership.

Now may I make a proposition which I do hope you will consider? Appoint a second in command. It doesn't matter who it is—Austen

Chamberlain or Walter Long. The whole party would accept whichever you selected for that position, so long as he was under your leadership. If your choice turned out well he would gradually get the support of the whole party and then you would be in a position to hand over the leadership. But I expect if you go now before there is an obvious successor to you, you will not only see the party split in two, but you will find that scores of men will take no further part in politics. And that brings me to something which personally I shall feel most deeply. I owe you everything politically. You have always been the kindest of friends and most lenient of chiefs. I would do anything—and I hope I have shown I would do so—to support you, but my allegiance to you is a purely personal one and could not be transferred to another. I am not at heart an enthusiastic Tariff Reformer, indeed but for you I should have followed the Free Fooders and with your resignation of the leadership will go my own participation in politics in this country. This might have come whenever you resigned but I feel it the more now when my sole reason for any political work is to back you up and fight these cursed rebels and their dastardly attacks. I never can express myself well and therefore cannot make you understand what a real blow your decision has given me and (you may take it from me) scores who think like me. . . .

It had long been assumed that if and when Balfour resigned the leadership he would be succeeded by either Austen Chamberlain or Walter Long. But Sir Max Aitken, M.P., a brilliant political adventurer from Canada, had, as early as October, started to organise support for the almost unknown Bonar Law. In view of the fact that the National Union of the Conservative Party was due to meet at Leeds the following week it was necessary that a decision should be taken promptly if the tradition were to be preserved that Party leaders are chosen by the Party's Parliamentary supporters, as in the case when Disraeli resigned in 1880. There is no record of the Conservative Party choosing a leader of the whole Party when in opposition. There was a single apparent exception when Mr. Bonar Law became Prime Minister in 1922. But it was known that he was to be invited to be Prime Minister within a few hours, and it was at his own urgent wish that he was elected to the leadership of the Party before he was called upon to accept the King's commission to form a Government. Under the evolving traditions of the Tory Party a Party meeting to choose a leader is only summoned after a member of the Party has actually become Prime Minister. Disraeli resigned following the Conservative defeat in the General Election of 1880 and the leadership of the Party then fell into abeyance or commission, Lord Salisbury leading it in the House of Lords and Sir Stafford Northcote in the House of Commons. It was not until after the Election of 1885 when Lord Salisbury had been entrusted by Queen Victoria with the formation of a government that he was elected leader of the Party. Thus when Balfour resigned the leadership of the Party there was no need to call a full party meeting which would have included peers. Instead the Conservative Chief Whip, Balcarres, summoned a meeting of Conservative Members of the House of Commons to the Carlton Club for November 13, only five days after Balfour had vacated the leadership.

Long and Chamberlain were at this time on terms of enmity as well as of rivalry with each other. Balcarres and the Party managers were anxious to avoid a split. To this end Balcarres conducted a series of unofficial canvasses to discover which way members would vote, in the hope that the supporters of one of the two candidates would easily outnumber the other and that a unanimous vote could then be obtained at the meeting for him.

Mr. Robert McKenzie in his invaluable *British Political Parties* has altogether underestimated the nature of the struggle which took place in these few days. The full story is admirably set forth in Mr. Robert Blake's *Unknown Prime Minister*. Balcarres had made his plan without reckoning upon the machinations of Aitken who had complicated the already vexed situation by inducing Bonar Law to let it be known that he too would be a candidate. In addition, whenever the unofficial canvassing seemed to show that either Long or Chamberlain would prevail, Aitken contrived that the thirty or forty members whom he had whipped up for Bonar Law should show a preference for whichever of the leading contenders appeared to be lying second. These transatlantic tactics, reminiscent of the smoke-filled room of an American political convention, were novel, and proved successful. They brought about a stalemate in which it was ultimately possible to induce both Long and Chamberlain to stand down and for the dark horse, Bonar Law, to be unanimously elected at the Carlton Club meeting. Lord Lansdowne continued as the Tory leader in the Lords.

While Derby hastened to send a formal note of congratulation to Bonar Law on his succession to the leadership in the Commons it was significant that in what, on the face of it, was intended as a message of goodwill he should have instantly made plain his doubts about Tariff Reform and above all his opposition to food taxes:

Lord Derby to Mr. Bonar Law

Confidential — Knowsley

13 November 1911

I must write one line in hearty congratulation of your anticipated election today as successor to Arthur Balfour. I can imagine no better selection and I really think I, who saw you during the hardest fight of your life, am as good a judge as anybody. Anyhow you can rest assured that you will have the most loyal support from me in any way that I can possibly give it. Not only for friendship's sake but out of gratitude for the work you did for us in N.W. Manchester.

I am rather tied up here now owing to my having taken the office of Lord Mayor of Liverpool, but I am very anxious to see you. If therefore by any chance you are going up to Bootle [Law's constituency] to address a meeting, I wish you would come here for the night. I will tell you perfectly candidly that I am quite convinced that Tariff Reform as at present advocated will not do for us here and by hook or by crook we have got to make some such alteration as will prevent our opponents having the very taking cry that we are taxing the people's food and I am in hopes that you may see a way out of the difficulty.

P.S. If you want an M.P. secretary (honorary) I wish you would think of my brother George.

Mr. Bonar Law to Lord Derby

Personal — 14 November 1911

Many thanks for your letter, and for the very kind way in which you welcome me to my new position.

If you are in town, do come and see me. I think there is nothing for us but to go straight forward with the programme as it is, but I should like to speak to you about it. Until we have met I am sure you will say nothing to commit you in any way. I have to speak in Bootle on the 7th December, and if it is convenient to you I shall be delighted to stay at Knowsley, but I hope to see you before then.

It is very good of your brother to think of being willing to assist me. As it happens another Member has been helping me unofficially in the House, and I am afraid that he has claims to become my Parliamentary Private Secretary which I cannot overlook; but I shall make no decision about this for some weeks.

Lord Derby to Mr. Bonar Law

Confidential — Knowsley

16 November 1911

Many thanks for your letter. Certainly I shall not commit myself to anything except absolute loyalty to yourself before seeing you. But I feel somewhat strongly on this point knowing as I do that unless the difficulty is met in some way or other it is hopeless to think of our winning. I shall be only too delighted to see you here on the 7th. I hope you will come fairly early, have some dinner and I will send you in a motor to your meeting. We can have a talk either before or after. I am afraid this is my only chance of seeing you as now I am Lord Mayor of Liverpool I am tied down here to a degree you can hardly imagine.

It would be very good of you if you would think of my brother. Perhaps it would be possible for him to do any Parliamentary work connected with Lancashire. He knows a great many people here and making this his headquarters he could always go about anywhere for you.

Derby's private view of Bonar Law finds expression in a letter which he wrote to the King at this time on family matters:

Lord Derby to the King

16 November 1911 — Knowsley

. . . Your Majesty will have heard from many people of the election of Bonar Law to fill Arthur Balfour's place as leader. I won't use the word replace because that is quite impossible. I know him well and persuaded him to stand first for N.W. Manchester where he was beaten and afterwards for Bootle where he now sits as member. He is a curious mixture—never very gay, he has become even less so since the death of his wife to whom he was devoted, but still he has a great sense of humour. A first-class debater and a good, though not a rousing, platform speaker. A great master of figures which he can use to great advantage. He has all the qualities of a great leader except one, and that is he has no personal magnetism and can inspire no man to real enthusiasm. But his election has done good and our party is quite united in loyalty to him. Still I can't help feeling that six months from now when Balfour is taking, as he must do, *the* leading part in the fight against Home Rule, the party will want him back and wonder at their disloyalty to him and I hope be ashamed of themselves.

Alice went to see Princess Victoria yesterday and thought she looked extremely well.

May I wish Your Majesties a very happy and prosperous time in India and a safe return.

I am, Sir,
Your Majesty's humble and obedient subject,
DERBY

* * *

Derby's eldest son Edward was now seventeen years old. The Prince of Wales was the same age. Edward was at Eton, the Prince of Wales at the Royal Naval College at Dartmouth. King George had conceived the idea that the two boys should both go to Oxford together. In the letter, from which we have just quoted, Derby wrote:

Lord Derby to the King

16 November 1911 Knowsley

SIR,

First of all may I say that I trust your Majesties have had a happy and prosperous journey. I am afraid from all account the passage across the Bay was anything but pleasant.

Mr. Hansell has been to see me and tells me Your Majesty would like my eldest boy to go to the same college as H.R.H. The Prince of

Wales. I cannot say how pleased and honoured I am and how gladly I will consent to his going to whatever college is chosen.

There appear to be three in the running—Christ Church, New and Magdalen. New College I should not like as according to the Archbishop of York there is much trouble there,[1] and his is a judgment I would implicitly rely on. Christ Church is a large college apparently where all the *nouveaux riches* go and where the sole object seems to be to spend money and prove themselves men instead of being what they are—boys. Magdalen would appear to have none of these disadvantages, and if Your Majesty choose this college I can only most humbly say I should be very content. I had a long talk with Mr. Hansell on various subjects and never have I found a man who understood boys better. Absolutely straight, but very broad minded. I can imagine no man better able to guide rather than drive a boy, and moreover well able to put him on the right path at Magdalen where apparently he was. Of course when a boy goes to Oxford, he ceases to be a schoolboy and I can imagine nobody better than Mr. Hansell to look after him, see that he goes straight and yet not make him think he is still in leading strings. We also talked over tutors in France and Germany, but doubtless he will have written Your Majesty on the subject. May I again say how honoured I am by Your Majesty's wish and how much I hope that Edward may be as devoted to the Prince of Wales as I am to Your Majesty. . . .

The King to Lord Derby

Suez to Aden — H.M.S. *Medina*
24 November 1911 — At Sea

My dear Eddy,

Many thanks for your long letter and for all your good wishes for our visit to India.

I am so glad you had a satisfactory talk with Hansell and thought him sensible and broad-minded. I always think his judgment is good. He has also written to me on the subject of your conversation.

Although I do not propose to settle anything until my return home, I should think that Magdalen College without a doubt is the one I shall choose as it appears to have all the advantages and none of the

[1] Doubtless the Archbishop had heard of the incendiary activities two years before of Mr. Alfred Duff Cooper and his friends. See *Old Men Forget* by Duff Cooper.

disadvantages of the other two. Both the Queen and I are delighted that you are willing and ready for your son to go to the same college as ours and I only hope that my boy will get on with and be as fond of your boy as I am of you. I will also consider the question of tutors in France and Germany on my return, no doubt we shall be able to arrange something satisfactory to both of us.

Yes, I have heard and read a good deal about Bonar Law's election as leader of the Unionist party and from all accounts I think he will do well and that anyhow at the present moment, the whole party seems to wish to be loyal to him and support him in the uphill fight they have before them next year. I agree with you in thinking that before long the party will wish to have Arthur Balfour back again and will realise all that they have lost and I hope they will be ashamed of themselves for the disloyal way in which they treated him.

With the exception of a gale which we encountered in the Bay, when practically everybody was seasick, including most of the men, we have had beautiful weather and a smooth sea. We are now in the middle of the Red Sea, temperature 80° but rather damp and sticky, still it must sound nice to you shivering in England. The Khedive paid us a visit at Port Said. Kitchener, as I knew he would, has already created a most excellent impression in Egypt, the people in the East like a strong man.

With every good wish for Xmas and the New Year for you and Alice from the Queen and myself.

Believe me, my dear Eddy,
Your sincere friend,
GEORGE R.I.

Children often fail to embrace friendships which are planned for them by their parents and though the Prince of Wales and Lord Stanley spent two years at Magdalen together they did not in fact become intimate friends until they both joined the Grenadier Guards at the outbreak of the war in 1914. The Prince of Wales, during his Oxford days, had to endure the supervision of his former tutor Mr. Henry Hansell and it may well be that he resented the benevolent conspiracy of his father and Lord Derby to subject him in addition to what he may have regarded as the chaperonage of Lord Stanley.

Derby had been devoted to his father and mother. He enjoyed the happiest of relations with his children. He was later to be distressed to find how difficult were the relations between the King's sons and the King. The author is indebted to Sir Harold Nicolson for the following account:

> Derby was distressed by the way King George bullied his children, and he ventured one day at Knowsley when they were walking up and down the terrace, to raise the subject, justifying his remarks on the ground that he was the King's oldest friend. He said what delightful companions his own children had become for him when they grew up, and begged the King to realise that the royal children were on the verge of manhood and that he was missing very much in life by frightening them and continuing to treat them as if they were naughty schoolboys. Lord Derby told me that the King remained silent for some four minutes after this and then said: 'My father was frightened of his mother; I was frightened of my father, and I am damned well going to see to it that my children are frightened of me.'

* * *

The Tories had greatly improved their position at Westminster in the first of the two elections held in 1910. They had gained 116 seats and the triumphant Liberal Government of 1906 now only had a majority of two over their Tory opponents. Henceforward they had to depend increasingly on the Irish vote. Both the 1910 elections arose from the Government's necessity to carry the Parliament Act and so to curb the power of the Lords who had thrown out Lloyd George's Budget of 1909. The Parliament Act brought the Irish issue once more into the centre of the political arena with a bitterness never known before. For once the Parliament Act was on the statute book the power of the Lords to sustain the Union with Ireland would be lost for ever. Tariff Reform was therefore only a secondary issue in both elections, but the minority in the Tory Party which adhered to Joseph Chamberlain's principles was still powerful enough to insist in the first 1910 election on a strong tariff plank in the Party's programme. The Liberals naturally raised the cry 'your food will cost you more'. No one could tell how effective this propaganda had been in the first general election. There were many Conservatives, notably the Cecils and Lord Derby, who were convinced that much damage had been done. These fears worked upon the mind of Balfour who, in a famous speech at the Albert Hall at the end of November, only a few days before the poll at the second general election, announced that, if the Tories won, no tax on food would be introduced until the electorate had had the opportunity of expressing its view in a referendum conducted on this sole issue. The results of the second general election proved indecisive. Though many seats changed hands, the Tories and Liberals were in exact equipoise in the House. The indecisive nature of the contest made all politicians realise, among other things, that the deadly issues which divided the two parties could hardly be resolved by further recourse to the electorate.

No sooner was the election over than the Tariff Reformers sought to extricate themselves and the Party from the referendum pledge. Austen Chamberlain denounced the pledge both in public and in private. A speech which he made at this time revived all the apprehensions of the Free Trade element in the Party and Derby wrote in indignation to Balfour's confidential secretary:

Lord Derby to Mr. Jack Sandars[1]

15 December 1910 — Derby House

MY DEAR JACK,

What the devil is the meaning of Austen's speech? I hold A. J. B. has bound his party to submit Tariff Reform to a referendum—before it becomes law—that promise holds good for all time and not only as Austen says for *this* election.

I certainly consider I am absolutely so bound and I don't see how Bonar Law can get out of it either. Damn these Chamberlains—they are the curse of our party and of the country.

Lord Derby to Mr. Jack Sandars[1]

19 December 1910

Thank you so much for your letter. I do so entirely agree with what you say. I saw F. E. Smith today—we had luncheon together—

[1] Balfour Papers.

he is terribly distressed at the report of his speech, and wants A. J. B. to know that he does not at all approve of Austen and is absolutely loyal to him—you might let the Chief know this.

The one thing which must be prevented is A. J. B. giving any explanation of his pledge—at all events now—later it may be wise to lay down exactly what will be referred to the referendum—at Dartford he said it would be the T.R. budget—at Albert Hall he said T.R. *principles*—I can't help thinking the latter is the safest course. I also think that the referendum as a policy—what can and what can not be sent for decision should be now most carefully thought out by a small committee. We may be called upon at any time in the H. of L. to make some sort of further declaration to our own reform—but at the present moment when I suppose the Chief is bombarded with questions—I do hope that if he is obliged to give an answer that he will confine himself to simply stating that his pledge holds good not only for this but at any subsequent elections—we *can't* go back . . .

Yours ever,

D.

Nonetheless, as soon as Bonar Law had assumed the leadership of the Party at the end of 1911 the various factions in the Party sought to influence the new leader as to future policy on Tariff Reform. An election was bound to come sooner or later and it was vital for the Tory Party to have a programme which would win the day. Those Tories who regarded Home Rule as the paramount political issue naturally sought to retain the referendum which would largely keep the dear food question out of an election. The ardent protectionists, led by Austen Chamberlain, sought by every argument and device to secure its repudiation.

Those who wished to abandon the referendum had a strong case. Balfour, when giving the pledge, had made it contingent on a reciprocal pledge by the Liberal Government that they would not introduce Home Rule into Ireland without also holding a referendum. And the Liberals had refused to give such a pledge. It could be argued therefore that the Tory referendum had died a natural death. But the Free Trade wing of the Party cared nothing for such theoretical arguments. Derby was firmly convinced that food taxes were a millstone round the Party's neck and was determined that when next the Party fought there should still be the same or a similar guarantee to the electorate.

Lord Derby to Mr. Bonar Law

Strictly Confidential 14 March 1912

I am still a little disturbed as to whether or no we are right to adhere to the food taxes. I admit to the full that to drop them now would probably split the Party absolutely, although there is no doubt they are a dead weight round our necks. But when we come to introduce them, if we ever do so, I feel the danger of a split is just as great and I tell you perfectly candidly that I do not think that I should be able to support them. The question to my mind therefore is if one could suggest some means by which we could decently bury them and the only suggestion I myself can make is this, that you should say that if we came in preferential treatment of the Colonies should be taken quite apart from any taxation for Revenue purposes. That it should form the subject of an enquiry which should try and ascertain if there was no preferential treatment which would meet the case of the Colonies other than a tax on food. The treatment might vary according to the Colony. If there was then that would be adopted in preference to the food taxes but if food taxes had to be adopted it should be made a subject for the referendum. I honestly do not believe you will get the food taxes through the House of Commons however big our majority and if we split and went out we should be in the wilderness for 20 years. . . .

The issue came to a head at a meeting of the Shadow Cabinet held in April 1912. It was decided that food taxes should remain a plank in the Party programme and that the referendum should be abandoned. It was further decided to keep these decisions secret for the moment. Among the dissenting minority were Salisbury, Curzon, Londonderry and Derby. In June the Canadian Prime Minister, Sir Robert Borden, visited London. Bonar Law took the opportunity to find out what value Canada would attach to the imposition of food taxes under which the Empire would enjoy a preference. Satisfied on this point, Bonar Law and Lansdowne, without consulting the Shadow Cabinet, decided that the time had

Derby in 1912.

Derby with his three children: (left to right) Oliver, Victoria, Edward.

come for a public statement about the policy that had been secretly agreed upon in the spring.

This was the more necessary as the growing propaganda of the Food Taxers was provoking increasingly vociferous criticism from Tory Free Traders. Derby, though he had not yet pronounced himself publicly, was raising shrill cries of alarm in private; and we find the Conservative Chief Whip in the House of Commons reporting to his leader:

Lord Balcarres to Mr. Bonar Law

5 September 1912 Balcarres, Fife

... Extract from a letter just received from Lord Derby. 'I am coming out against the Food Taxes. I can't stand them any longer. If Tariff Reformers had had their way we should have lost North West Manchester. Tariff Reform hasn't gained the least ground in Lancashire.'

I am writing to him in emollient terms, but he is very strong on the subject, and he is a growing power in Lancashire. ...

The public announcement of the new policy was made by Lansdowne at the Albert Hall in November. It threw the Party into a convulsion. Bonar Law was snowed under by indignant letters from the Free Trade wing of the Party. He was, however, determined to press on and a month later, on December 16, speaking in Aitken's constituency at Ashton-under-Lyne, he reiterated with greater clarity Lansdowne's Albert Hall declaration.

He boldly stated that food taxes were essential to any system of imperial preference, and that an imperial conference would be summoned to consider the whole question of preferential trade as soon as the Unionists were returned to office. If the Dominions' representatives did not regard food duties as essential to preference, then food duties would not be imposed. But if food duties were considered necessary by the conference 'then I for one do not believe that the people of this country would not be ready to make that readjustment which is necessary to effect the purpose. It would not be fair,' he added, 'to submit the result of the negotiations with the

Dominions to a referendum.'[1] The speech was received with great enthusiasm which was fanned by the skilful Canadian propagandist tactics of Sir Max Aitken. A hundred torch-bearers escorted the speakers to the railway station.

Derby was naturally among those Tories who opposed this new policy. Mr. F. E. Smith, member for the Walton division of Liverpool, himself a Tariff Reformer but above all at this period an opponent of Home Rule, was among the first to detect the threat implicit to the Party in the incipient Lancashire revolt. He telegraphed:

Mr. F. E. Smith to Mr. Bonar Law

Lancashire serious. Chamberlain, you, I, Carson, and if possible Long should meet immediately. Salvidge joining D.

Mr. F. E. Smith to Mr. Bonar Law

18 December 1912 — Blenheim Palace

You must think of politics. Things in Lancashire are on the verge of a smash. I think Salvidge will support Derby. You, I, Austen, Carson and if he is well enough, Long ought *to meet at once*. Unless effective steps are taken a resolution will be passed at the Lancashire meeting that the food taxes recommended (if such be the case) at the Conference should not become law without an election. Such a resolution —though personally I have under existing circumstances much sympathy with it—is wholly inconsistent, it seems to me, with your position; it can be dealt with; possibly it can even be controlled but you must move. I am going to the adjourned meeting. Max Aitken should immediately intrigue with all the Lancashire members in favour of the only amendment which I think could be carried to the hostile resolution, viz.—that a deputation should wait upon you—I mean of course a private one . . . You know I am not an alarmist and have good nerves but unless the position is promptly dealt with we are going straight on the rocks.

At the same time he had already written to Derby:

[1] *The Strange Case of Andrew Bonar Law* by H. A. Taylor.

Mr. F. E. Smith to Lord Derby

17 December 1912 — 70 Eccleston Square

I know all our Lancashire difficulties but even so think it would be lamentable if you made the speech you indicate on Saturday. It will split the party from top to bottom and perhaps keep us out of power for twenty years.

I am not without sympathy with your disappointment after so much ungrudging work. But the only way in which *from your point of view* you can do good is to contend that any recommendation made by the Conference must in so far as it places fresh taxes on food be submitted to the people. Holding your views you are fully entitled to try and secure this safeguard but I very much hope you will not even say this in public. The truth is we are in a powder magazine, a casual spark may send us all to Hell in bitter dissension. Your hand is far too loyal, and your heart too deeply concerned with both the cause and your colleagues to be the instrument by which that spark is applied.

Why not write privately as a colleague to Austen telling him your impression of the Lancashire position? Don't commit yourself in public yet.

Widespread anxiety spread throughout the Tory Party as it became known that Derby intended to make a speech on December 21 at the meeting of the Lancashire Conservative Association which would constitute a serious threat to Bonar Law's leadership and which would be bound to split the Party from top to bottom. Everyone thought capable of influencing Derby was mobilised to urge restraint upon him.

None wrote more cogently than Lord Hugh Cecil who was an ardent Free Trader and had very nearly crossed the floor of the House of Commons on this issue with Mr. Winston Churchill in 1904.

Lord Hugh Cecil to Lord Derby

18 December 1912 — Carlton Club

MY DEAR EDDY,

Steel-Maitland has been talking to me about the present rather alarming situation. It is clear that the Party are in a very awkward position; and what is more important the Union, the Constitution and the Welsh Church are threatened with destruction as a consequence of another disastrous General Election. I need not tell you that I agree with what I am told are your views, and that I think the Albert Hall declaration is a most deplorable blunder. The only question is what is the best way of mending the broken crockery.

I have very little doubt that in the end the food taxes must be got rid of—I do not say permanently but as an issue at the next election. I don't believe we can win if we carry that overpowering weight. The problem is how to bury the Albert Hall declaration gracefully. I think we want time for this. Perhaps the Canadians will make it clear that they do not want us to tax food unless we think it right on our own interests. That may give us a way out. But at any rate our leaders must not make any more statements of policy for some reasonable time. Repeated modifications of policy have a ridiculous effect. For the moment it is most desirable that they should 'jouk and let the jaw gang by'.[1] Let us get back to Home Rule and Disestablishment and drop the infernal subject for the time.

This brings me to my point. I understand you are going to make a speech soon and that you contemplate declaring for some abandonment of the Albert Hall folly. Of course you are quite right on the merits. But just now a worse and more unpopular thing than even food taxes threatens us and that is public dissension. We must not get back to the situation of 1904 and 1905. Signs of our divisions must surely be kept hidden if we are to have any hope of winning. And we MUST win. Everything fiscal must be subordinated to getting the Govt. out. So I do suggest that it will not serve this object which I know you have as much at heart as any one, to reopen the miserable tariff discussion. I plead for a truce and a few weeks of Xmas and calm to get the matter quietly reconsidered.

I need not say that I am not against but strongly in favour of whatever can privately be done to get rid of our burden. Above all, Austen C. must really be induced to give up the position that if he does not get his own way he will split the Party. We can all of us split the Party: nothing is easier, but it is not the way to win the election or carry Tariff Reform for that matter.

[1] Scottish proverb meaning 'Stoop and let the rush of water pass by'. This proverb is quoted with a minor variant in Sir Walter Scott's *Rob Roy* (chap. XXV): 'Jonk and let the jaw gae by'.

Northcliffe had assailed Bonar Law's speech at Ashton-under-Lyne in both *The Times* and *Daily Mail*. Bonar Law's friends inspired Mr. H. A. Gwynne, brilliant and highly respected editor of the *Morning Post*, to repress Derby's ebullience:

Mr. H. A. Gwynne to Lord Derby

Private *The Morning Post*
18 December 1912

I do not think that I have ever addressed you on politics since I have known you, but I am going to do so now because I think a great crisis has arisen in our Party, and because I have heard that you are going to make a speech very shortly in which you do not mean to hide altogether your opinions about the pronouncements of Lansdowne and Bonar Law.

May I venture to put before you some considerations which I hope will have some little weight with you? The question of the referendum is one of tactics, not one of principle. The pronouncements may be right, or they may be wrong. I have my own views and I certainly had an alternative plan which, in my opinion, is as good, if not better than, that of Mr. Bonar Law; but I would no more think of taking up an attitude of hostility to our leaders on the question than I would of joining the Radical ranks, for the alternative before those who disagree with Bonar Law and Lansdowne is simply this: Are you prepared to split the Party from top to bottom or are you not? If you are—and I am perfectly certain that if you have made up your mind to this course, your resolution is absolutely honest and straight-forward—I have nothing more to say except to express regret. If you are not, then for the sake of the Party, for the sake of the Church, and for the sake of the Constitution, do not make public your criticisms. Make any representations you like to your leaders and put before them all the arguments you can possibly adduce to try to persuade them to your point of view. All that is legitimate and right. But if you speak out, and if your speaking out results in a split in the Party, do please consider what that means. It would result, in my opinion, in our wandering in the wilderness for twenty years, in our losing all that we wish for, and in a grave risk to our national safety. Surely the preservation of all these things is worth more than the pleasure or the duty of publicly criticising our official attitude?

Do you not agree with me that within the next year or two years, a totally different complexion may be put upon all this? It may be that Canada, Australia, New Zealand and South Africa will boldly say that they do not want any taxation of food, that they will be quite content with preference on the present duties, and some form of bounty on their shipping, and they will at once release Bonar Law from his promise. That being so, why rush into criticism when at the moment of an election the conditions which now obtain may be abolished? I know you will understand my motive in writing to you. I know the enormous influence you wield in Lancashire and in the Party, and therefore I thought it my duty as one who thinks that the Unionist Party is destined to regenerate the country, to make our Empire a real thing and successfully resist the encroachments of demagogues and destroyers, to put my view before you.

At the same time there were not lacking siren voices which suggested that Derby could combine his duty to Lancashire with the advancement of his own political career:

Mr. E. L. Oliver to Lord Derby

18 December 1912

The Waterhouse,
Bollington,
Macclesfield

. . . There seems to be a feeling that Lancashire has been ruled by Birmingham quite long enough. I know that you are 'not the man to split the party'. The party *is* split, but not by you, and it may be that patriotism and duty will compel you to raise your standard in favour of a moderate conservatism to which 60 to 70 per cent of the party will gladly devotedly and enthusiastically rally at once. . . .

I noted with extreme pleasure your remark last autumn, the day after you opened the Macclesfield Conservative Bazaar.

You said you had the ambition to win the Derby and be Prime Minister. You richly deserve the latter high honour.

If circumstances compel a change of leadership it is your Lordship who would be most welcome. . . .

Smith continued his pressure upon Derby and on the eve of the Lancashire Party meeting wrote again:

Mr. F. E. Smith to Lord Derby

Private | The Priory,
20 December 1912 | Dudley

I am so sorry that you adhere to your view. If the party doesn't support Law he is going to resign. Carson, Long, & Chamberlain support him. What will happen to the party in that contingency? We are done. For the moment unity is vital. Privately I do not in fact believe we shall fight the election with the food taxes against us but for the moment nothing can be done.

I feel so strongly the necessity of supporting Law that if opposition attacks him in Lancashire I shall go up and answer him as soon as a meeting can be arranged.

Arthur Balfour, himself the author of the referendum, was also roped in to bring pressure on Derby. Though he can scarcely fail to have smiled sardonically at the difficulties in which the Party found itself under its new leadership, he loyally came to the aid of his successor, though, as we shall see, his cogent advice to Derby, whether wilfully or not, arrived too late to have any influence on the course of events.

Mr. Balfour to Lord Derby [1]

Private | 20 December 1912

Mr. Steel-Maitland tells me that at your Quarterly Meeting to-morrow you are going to deal with the subject of food taxes. It is not for me to judge whether this is necessary or not, but unless it be really and absolutely necessary, I should venture with great diffidence to doubt its expediency.

We have gone through many periods of anxiety and trouble over this question, but none I think more serious than the present. I do not feel in a position to make any forecast of the issue, but I cannot help thinking that the very worst thing that could happen to us at this moment will be any public expression of opinion on the part of Leaders like yourself, which would give the impression of acute differences of opinion, and increase the anxiety which already prevails. It was Austen's original speech at the White City which did much to produce the present crisis; but the gravity of the crisis will only be

[1] Balfour Papers.

aggravated by other speeches of a different tenor, pointing in a different direction. If there are members of the Party who cannot see eye to eye with the Leaders on this subject the time may come, I suppose, when they will have publicly to express dissent. I earnestly hope it will *never* come; but I am sure the longer the fateful moment can be deferred the better.

Remember that *if Bonar Law goes the Party, as far as I can see, is doomed.* The most wary walking is necessary; and the whole diplomacy of those who entertain doubts with regard to recent declarations of policy should be devoted to allaying panic and smoothing down causes of friction. This diplomacy becomes difficult, if not impossible, if everybody makes platform professions of their own particular shade of opinion; and the danger, which is great anywhere and with any speaker, is doubly great when Lancashire is the place and the speaker is the head of our Lancashire organisation.

I feel that I am interfering in matters which are really no longer my business; but you and I have always talked over public matters in a manner so intimate and so friendly that I thought you would forgive me—and my anxiety is great.

On December 21 Derby was in the chair at the meeting in Manchester. In a brief opening address in which he asserted that there was no split in the Party, that any differences were not of principle but of method, he affirmed the loyalty of the whole meeting to Bonar Law and Lansdowne. He then called upon the Press to withdraw and took the meeting into secret session. The temper of the meeting was high and Derby had difficulty in restraining the delegates from carrying resolutions which would have made Bonar Law's position impossible. He only succeeded in doing so by suggesting that the conference should adjourn for three weeks until January 11. Derby was to arouse the suspicion in the minds of Bonar Law and the Party managers that so far from seeking to quieten the Lancashire agitation he was in fact exploiting it for all he was worth. This allegation seems to have been unfair. In fact, and certainly at this stage, Derby ran the risk of compromising his own position in Lancashire for the sake of Party harmony. Whatever his motives and conduct, Derby hastened to report fully to his leader:

Lord Derby to Mr. Bonar Law [1]

Confidential

Knowsley

21 December 1912

DEAR BONAR LAW,

I have only 5 minutes in which to write to you before the post goes, to tell you about the meeting today. You will probably hear of it from other sources and I think that they will probably give me credit for having loyally kept my word to you that I would say nothing which would in any way upset the party. But I must tell you that things are very critical. I would not let them come to a vote but if they had I have not the least doubt they would practically unanimously have passed a vote asking that the question of preferential treatment with the Colonies should be postponed and not be a subject for discussion at the next General Election. They were equally unanimous in saying that they did not know whether they could carry seats even if there were a referendum for food taxes, but that they were perfectly certain not to be able to carry them, but on the contrary to lose them, unless there were some such reference. Two candidates who were present said under the present circumstances they would not be able to stand. They were very desirous of coming to some definite conclusion but I have prevented that and suggested an adjournment which I wanted to be for some considerable time but they would not hear of one later than the 11th of January when I do not think we can possibly avoid some definite resolutions. I proposed for them to consider whether there was not some qualification of your statement which would meet the case and I think I could get a unanimous consent to a policy such as I suggested to you, namely that if we came into power our representatives should have full power to negotiate with the Colonies and endeavour to come to some agreement. If such agreement did not include food taxes it should become operative at once. If it did include food taxes that it should not become operative until after another General Election. The 11th will be a very critical day for our Party in Lancashire and I want to make a suggestion to you. You were good enough to say that you would attend a dinner of Lancashire Members in London. Instead of that if I had a luncheon on the 10th for the members and candidates and for a few of the influential political leaders of the county, could you possibly come up for it? I could have it at

[1] Bonar Law Papers.

1.15 and if you left London on the Friday by the 8 o'c. train you would be in plenty of time and of course I hope you would stay the night.

This is a very hurried note but if you could telegraph me whether you would do this I will set things in motion at once. But please believe me I have acted absolutely loyally to you today and have entirely subordinated my own opinions in the hope of being able to secure unanimity in our Party.

Derby now acknowledged Balfour's tardy letter of December 20.

Lord Derby to Mr. Balfour

22 December 1912

Very many thanks for your letter which must have crossed mine. I am so much obliged to you for giving me the advice that you did. It arrived after my meeting but luckily I had acted very much in the spirit which you advise.

But the matter is very serious, much more so even than I had expected. This county is perfectly determined not to go to the next Election if they can help it with the Food Taxes and at the meeting yesterday all the delegates (if I had not stopped it and got them to consent to an adjournment for 3 weeks) would have passed a resolution hostile to Bonar Law. What is to be done? I could not keep silent when I knew that, if the present policy is persevered with, it must mean a certain defeat at the next election and a great loss of seats in this county. The feeling roughly is this—We have been dictated to by Birmingham for several years past. We have fought three elections with the millstone of Tariff Reform tied round our necks and each time we have been defeated. We are going to cut ourselves away from it now. Surely we have paid enough tribute to the Birmingham gang? I know you are loyalty itself but could you not come back with a policy that did not include food taxes? If you did I believe the county would rally to you in a marvellous way and many of those who would come in are those who are now loudest in proclaiming their belief in Tariff Reform. What personally makes me so angry is that I get letters from London from people who tell me I am splitting the Party, as if it were not they who, by this cursed change of front, are splitting it from top to bottom. It really is so very disheartening. I have worked like a slave in Manchester and the district to try and get them right and had succeeded and now by one speech the whole of one's work has been destroyed and Manchester I feel perfectly certain will go solid against us at the next election. I am miserable at the outlook and do not see a single bright spot relieving the darkness. . . .

Bonar Law does not seem to have been any more impressed by Derby's protestations of loyalty than he was by his claim to have been of service at the Lancashire Conference, and in a cool reply rejected Derby's suggested good offices in arranging a meeting with leaders of Lancashire opinion:

Mr. Bonar Law to Lord Derby

24 December 1912 Edwardes Square,
Kensington

I got back last night too late either to write or telegraph you. I sent you a wire this morning saying that I could not attend the luncheon which you suggest.

I do not think it would be wise for me to attend the luncheon. You, of course, understand now how serious the position is. I believe that a way out might be found if things were allowed to rest for the present; but if resolutions were adopted by the Lancashire Association contrary to the declared policy of the Party it would, I expect, be necessary to summon a Party meeting, and, in my opinion, a complete split in the Party would result. It is, of course, as you know, an unheard of thing for one Provincial Division of the National Union to formulate the policy of the Party, but I am not personally going to take any steps to prevent it. If you are not able to prevent such action being taken, then things must take their course.

As Balcarres is a Lancashire Member I am sending your letter to him and copy of my reply, and when he returns to town I shall have a talk with him about the situation in Lancashire.

P.S. Though I am not willing to go to Lancashire, I should of course be glad to see half a dozen Lancashire representatives; and I could arrange to see them at the same time as I have the meeting with the Lancashire Members which I am having in any case.

Mr. Bonar Law to Lord Balcarres [1]

24 December 1912

I enclose letter from Derby (which you might return to me) and copy of my reply. I also enclose report [Steel-] Maitland has got of the meeting. This shows that Derby is the sole cause of all the trouble, as I suspected. In my opinion, the only chance of an outlet without a complete split is that there should be peace and quiet for a while, and I think the only way to deal with the Lancashire meeting is for you to go yourself accompanied by as many of the Lancashire Members as will support you, and tell them to ignore policy and simply pass a vote of confidence in the Party Leaders. If you agree with this we can settle details when we meet.

Balcarres with more information took a different view:

Lord Balcarres to Mr. Bonar Law [1]

[*Undated*]

Haigh Hall
Wigan

I have had a long talk with Derby, and coinciding with a similar discussion with my chairman I am left very low. The Xmas recess has not had the mollifying effect I had hoped. I will talk to you when we meet on Monday.

Meanwhile however I am glad to say that after an exhaustive discussion with Derby I have come to the conclusion that [Steel-] Maitland's comments were incomplete, and to a certain extent misleading—for Derby's attitude at the council meeting was largely dictated by the firm position taken up by the previous meeting of the executive committee. The evidence of disquiet is so substantial that there is (alas) no need to think he has stimulated it.

Meanwhile Derby was circulating around Lancashire a questionnaire designed to test opinion on the tariff issue. This was to arouse further suspicions in Bonar Law's already troubled mind:

[1] Bonar Law Papers.

Mr. Bonar Law to Lord Lansdowne

25 December 1912 Pembroke Lodge

Just let me give you all good wishes for you and yours.

The position has not I think greatly improved since I saw you. At first my speech at Ashton did I think do some good but the effect of it has been destroyed by two things; first Northcliffe with his papers and second I am sorry to say by Derby through the position he holds in Lancashire and the use he is making of it. They had their meeting on Saturday and Derby has written me implying that he was doing everything he could in the interest of unity but I receive other accounts which show that he . . . is I believe the chief cause of the discontent there. The meeting has been adjourned till the 11th Jany. and in the meantime I hear that he has been sending out to the different Associations asking answers to the following questions:

Do you think the abandonment of the referendum will do harm?

Do you think we could carry the election with food taxes?

Do you think that after the Colonial Conference it should be laid down that any agreement come to between the Mother Country and the Colonies should only become operative after a General Election?

All this from a man who was present when the division was taken and who promised loyally to accept it is pretty strong!

I have sent an account of this to Balcarres and have suggested to him that he must go, as a Lancashire Member, to the meeting on the 11th taking with him as many Members as will support him and get the meeting to say nothing about policy and simply to pass a vote of confidence in the Leaders. I think this can probably be done, but if any resolution should be passed hostile to our declaration then I think our position would be impossible and we should have to call a meeting of the party (either together or the two houses separately) and then I am afraid that we—at least that is my feeling—must resign.

I shall keep you posted as to what happens but there will be nothing to write I expect till the House meets on Monday.

After our conversation I think you and I will take the same view as to what our duty is and I shall of course do nothing decisive without consulting you beforehand.

In spite of the difficulties, I think it possible that if time were given a split might be avoided but if things are not allowed to remain as they are for the present then I see no way out.

Yours sincerely,
A. BONAR LAW

How far Bonar Law was justified in objecting to the questions in the document which Derby circulated is a nice point. Certainly they were what are called in legal circles 'leading questions' and they certainly resulted in answers which almost unanimously condemned food taxes. It may well be that this is what Derby wished and expected, but the current state of Lancashire opinion made it inevitable, however the questions had been framed, that the replies would have sustained the Free Trade cause.

Derby had been subjected to many-sided pressures; he himself took steps to press his own views in uncommitted and influential quarters. The acute and urgent state of this political crisis can be judged by the fact that this competitive campaign of letter writing proceeded all through the Christmas holidays. Bonar Law had written to Lansdowne on Christmas Day and Derby, in the intervals of celebrating his Christmas in the traditionally spacious Knowsley style in the midst of a large family gathering, also found time to write:

Lord Derby to Mr. Walter Long

25 December 1912 Knowsley

Many thanks for your letter. The position is very serious. As you know I warned the Shadow [Cabinet] what the effect of withdrawing the referendum pledge would be, and matters are really worse than I anticipated. There was absolute unanimity in the meeting. They are quite determined that they will not have Food Taxes—some of them, a majority I think, wanted to throw over Tariff Reform altogether. I wanted to adjourn for 6 weeks, but they would not do so for more than three weeks. On January 11 we shall pass a resolution calling on Bonar Law to give us some guarantee that there should be some appeal to the country before Food Taxes are imposed. It would be useless to try and stop them. Moreover I entirely agree with them. This matter cannot be hushed up, nor in my opinion is time of any value. If we had had this out after 1906 we should be in a much better position now.

I am not going to be browbeaten by the food taxers any more, they have persistently ignored the fact that Lancashire hates Tariff Reform, and have paid no respect to our wishes in this subject. They are going to learn that they have to. A split seems to me inevitable, unless the food taxers give way.

It is not a very cheerful Xmas—but I wish you (& our party!!) a happier New Year.

On Boxing Day Derby replied to Bonar Law's letter of December 24. Despite Bonar Law's somewhat chilly reply to Derby's various suggestions for helping his leader to gauge Lancashire opinion for himself, and though his good offices had been rejected, he continued to press facilities upon him:

Lord Derby to Mr. Bonar Law

26 December 1912 Knowsley

Thank you for your letter. I notice that you state you are going to have a meeting of Lancashire members. That was all I had in view when I suggested the luncheon here so my object is gained. I am sure good will come of it but may I suggest that you should also ask candidates and a few prominent men from the county. Chairmen of Divisions and such men as Holt and Woodhouse from Manchester with Petrie and Salvidge from Liverpool. If you would like my London house to meet in I should be very glad to put it at your disposal. Would you let me know about this as soon as possible as the room would have to be got ready. I can't help thinking from your letter that you misconstrue my action and think I am not behaving with perfect loyalty to you. I think that I must leave it to others to convince you to the contrary. My brothers Arthur and George are here. Balcarres is coming over tomorrow. I will tell them the whole position as it appears to me and ask them to report to you. I think it is better than writing at length to you.

If you will let me know when you propose to hold your meeting (whether at my house or not) I will postpone the National Union Meeting. I can do it on the grounds that it would not be advisable for it to be held before you have had your meeting.

Derby had taken umbrage at F. E. Smith's threat of coming up to Lancashire and holding a meeting at which he would answer Bonar

Law's critics. Smith sought to placate him and agreed to come and speak at the adjourned meeting in Manchester on the 11th:

Mr. F. E. Smith to Lord Derby

28 December 1912 Blenheim Palace

There is none in politics with whom I should be sorrier to reach cross purposes than yourself. Our principal field of operations lies and must lie in the same district and I have long watched with admiration your outstanding exertions in Lancashire. I can quite understand your feelings when you see ground painfully and laboriously won slipping away from you. Indeed I share these feelings and like you thought the Albert Hall announcement ill-judged and premature. Like you I think we should have used the two years before us for the legitimate purposes of an opposition while always privately attempting to discover some honourable means of diminishing our electioneering difficulties upon this particular question.

But we have to face two facts:

(1) The Albert Hall speech has been made.

(2) If there is serious disaffection in the party—and a Lancashire revolt would constitute such disaffection—Lansdowne and B. Law will resign and neither Chamberlain, Long nor Carson will take their places.

How this will help the party I simply cannot imagine. Surely the right course is to avoid all *public controversy* at all costs and try and swing the party into a tenable position by *private* influence legitimately exercised.

I really don't see why you should take offence at my last letter. I wrote it under extreme pressure after a day in the law courts and before my Dudley speech. After all you told me quite plainly that if I made a die-hard speech in Lancashire you would feel it your duty to reply. I don't take this as a threat but as a friendly indication of the extent of our difficulties and the risks involved in their public ventilation. But if in the very busy life I lead I expressed myself with undue curtness take no offence for none was intended. I will gladly come and express my views on the 11th if no reporters are present. I cannot if the discussion is public without defeating my own object.

In a letter at the end of the year to Mr. Edward Hulton, the newspaper proprietor, Derby expressed the fear that Bonar Law would either stick to his guns or retire 'either of which would be a disaster'. He wrote of his own proposal, which he had put to Bonar Law, that neither Tariff Reform nor reciprocal relations with the Colonies should be dropped but that if the Tories came into power there should be a conference with the Colonies and that thereafter if an arrangement could be made without food taxes it should be implemented immediately, but that if food taxes were proposed action should be deferred until after another general election. This proposal, which he described as a 'golden bridge', was in fact the policy which was shortly to be adopted.

As the new year started the deadlock seemed complete and despite all that everyone had done to alarm Derby with the dreadful consequences of the resignation of Bonar Law and Lansdowne he seems to have faced the situation with stoicism if not complacency:

Lord Derby to Lord Hugh Cecil

Confidential　　　　1 January 1913

Many thanks for your letter. Everything tends to confirm what I have always held and that is for the last year or so the whole Party has been led by the nose by the extreme Tariff Reformers, and unless we put our foot down we shall be led to certain defeat at the next election by the same gang. I am keeping quite quiet about things at the present moment because Bonar Law is going to see Lancashire Members on Thursday. I am to see him on Monday and it is possible that he will see more Lancashire representatives one day next week. I am afraid from what I hear this morning that he is immovable and sooner than yield will resign. I should be very sorry if this happened, especially as everybody tells me it would be fatal to the Party. Personally I confess I prefer followers without a leader rather than a leader without followers, because under the first condition a leader generally appears and if I saw at the present moment any man in the House of Commons who was likely to make even a decent leader I should not hesitate to come out strongly against food taxes in this county.

I am going to London on Friday. Would you care to have a talk with me? If so would you come to Derby House about 12 o'c., or I would meet you anywhere else if you wished. I should very much like to talk matters over with you.

Bonar Law received the Lancashire Members of Parliament on January 2. Derby's brother George, who was a Whip as well as a Lancashire Member, was well placed to give a balanced account of the meeting. He reported to Derby immediately:

Hon. George Stanley to Lord Derby

2 January 1913 House of Commons

Bonar Law told me to write and say that he did not think it necessary to see the candidates unless you thought it desirable.

He saw the Lancashire members this afternoon and pointed out the whole position which briefly is this:

He and Lord Lansdowne have publicly enunciated a policy which they thought had the support of the whole party—they have since realised that the majority of the party think the food taxes too heavy a burden to carry. To climb down under pressure is, of course, impossible and equally it is imperative that there should be no split in the party. If a resolution is carried at the meeting on the 11th condemning the food taxes, that must be regarded by both Bonar Law and Lansdowne as a vote of want of confidence and they both resign. Arty [Stanley] then asked whether, if a resolution of confidence in him and Lord Lansdowne and also another condemning the food taxes were passed, they would consider that as a vote of want of confidence. He said they would so regard it and must resign. That, of course, as everyone agreed, is unthinkable in the present state of affairs. The party would be split from top to bottom and the consequences would be disastrous. It seems therefore that the only possible way to do things is to discuss privately the question of the food taxes on the 11th and to pass publicly a vote of confidence in Bonar Law and Lord Lansdowne.

This is strictly between ourselves but I am as certain as I can be that he is working for some method of dropping the food taxes without abandoning the principle—*but the one way to make him and Lord Lansdowne cling to those taxes is to bring pressure to bear at this moment.* I have shown this to Balcarres and he agrees.

Meanwhile it was becoming apparent to the Party leaders in London that there were no means of quelling the Lancashire revolt. Moreover, an increasing number of Tory M.P.s, including many who were ardent Tariff Reformers, some of them even Food Taxers, were persuaded that quite apart from the inevitable split that was opening, food taxes were going to be altogether too great a burden at the next election. Save for the hard core of Tariff Reformers, which included Chamberlain, Amery and Aitken, the vast majority of the Party at Westminster cared infinitely more for saving the union with Ireland than for Tariff Reform. This view became widespread and active during the next few days as a result of a project conceived by Carson to memorialise Bonar Law and Lansdowne urging that the issue of food taxes should be deferred indefinitely and that, notwithstanding this, they should retain the leadership. It was felt that if a sufficient number of signatories could be mobilised it would be very difficult for Bonar Law and Lansdowne to carry out their threat of calling a Party meeting and offering their resignations. Derby was kept informed of these transactions by Gwynne of the *Morning Post*:

Mr. H. A. Gwynne to Lord Derby

Private *The Morning Post*

8 January 1913

I am sending you this letter to tell you what has happened. It may be stale news to you, but at the same time I think it is essential that you should know the facts and more especially how they strike a convinced Food Taxer like myself. As you know the position yesterday was that Bonar Law and Lansdowne stood to resign inasmuch as they had announced a policy which the party obviously did not endorse. You will agree, I am sure, that as honest and honourable men, they could no longer with any dignity carry on the functions of leaders of the party which had repudiated their policy solemnly declared and announced. This was the state of affairs up till yesterday and, as I ventured to tell you in a former letter of mine, it was but the natural consequence of the action of the Free Fooders. No way out seemed possible until late yesterday afternoon, when the feeling of the party was found to be very much opposed to the resignations of Bonar Law and Lansdowne and that a new situation had arisen.

There is no doubt whatever that the two leaders, if they had called a meeting of the party, could have carried it in face of the fact that a change in leadership would be so distasteful to them; but it would have been a Pyrrhic victory and, what is worse, it would not have prevented a recurrence of the same agitation. In these circumstances the party, practically of its own volition on the suggestion of one or two of the leaders, determined to write a letter to Bonar Law asking him to retain his position in spite of the fact that the party could not adopt food taxes. This letter will be signed by Food Taxers and Free Fooders and it will bear the signature of practically every man in the party.

To this unanimous demand of the party Bonar Law will be bound to yield, though his private convictions, I feel pretty certain, would be in favour of giving up the leadership and letting the party have a leader who would carry out their policy. Now the chief reason why I am writing to you is to ask you to use all your influence with all your friends to prevent a crowing over the party to which I belong. If we are to be assailed by articles and speeches which hurt us, the trouble is not over and it is possible that there may be a counter attack. But if moderation is shown and if people in your position will do something to soothe the feelings of men of my section of the party, I think that the incident will pass without very great harm. At the same time I want to tell you, as I told you yesterday, that I look upon the abolition of the Food Taxes as possibly the end of Preference altogether, and to me it is a subject of keen regret such as I have not felt for many years.

However, I do wish to put on record to you privately my humble appreciation of the high sense of honour and straightforwardness with which you carried on a most difficult situation. Victory has come to you, but I feel sure that you will be too generous to use it unworthily.

As soon as Derby heard the news of the projected 'memorial' he took the responsibility of postponing the Manchester meeting for another week, since it looked as if he was about to achieve all that he and the Lancashire Unionists had been pressing for. This indeed proved to be so. All except six Tory backbenchers, who included Aitken, Amery and Page-Croft, signed the letter. Bonar Law and Lansdowne, despite the humiliation of being forced to go back on their own policy and eat so many words, consented, in view of the near unanimity and loyal terms in which they were addressed, to remain at the head of the Party.

At the meeting of the Lancashire Tories, which was now held on January 18 in public, Derby nobly responded to Gwynne's appeal, welcomed the terms of the memorial and dwelt with satisfaction upon its acceptance by Bonar Law and Lansdowne. Referring to the previous meeting and the adjournment he had procured he said: 'We all left this room desiring to see a golden bridge over which the Party could march in safety. Gentlemen, I venture to say that golden bridge has been found and over it every single member of the Party can march without feeling he has sacrificed in any way the principles he has advocated for the last few years.'

Derby's victory in this controversy had been complete and it was celebrated a week later at a dinner at the Manchester Constitutional Club attended by two hundred leading Lancashire Tories organised and presided over by Alderman Salvidge. Throughout this controversy Derby displayed determination and self-confidence of a high degree and his conduct established him as the undisputed Tory spokesman of Lancashire. It also, however much this may have been resented by Bonar Law, added to his stature in national politics. One might have thought that this notable political venture would have tautened Derby's political fibre and that he would have played henceforward an increasingly dominant role in the political arena.

He was indeed in the future to hold high office for many years, but he never acted again either with the determination or with the self-confidence which he manifested on this occasion. It may be that he was nerved and steeled to this contest by his native Lancashire patriotism. He had been designated, he told the Manchester meeting, as their ambassador to the Tory leadership in London and though he did all he could to avoid aggravating the situation he had not the smallest doubt where his first and overwhelming duty lay—namely to those among whom he lived and who had named him their spokesman. The issues were clear and, as we can see by everything he wrote and said at the time, he never hesitated or compromised. In later years he was involved in controversies far more complex: these nearly always found him with divided loyalties. Thus, though he was to re-emerge and flourish for many years upon the high plateau of national politics and was to render eminent services to his party and his country, he will perhaps be judged in this political battle to have lived his finest hour.

IX

The Derby Plan

THE spacious, genial Victorian and Edwardian world in which Derby and his contemporaries had lived was now to be largely shattered by the grisly catastrophe of the First World War. During the first year of the war, Derby devoted all his energy and time to Army recruiting. He was chairman of the West Lancashire Territorial Association. This involved not only a great mass of administrative work but innumerable speeches at recruiting meetings. A typical speech is the following reported at Rainford in the *Northern Daily Mail*:

> I have only two sons. One is at the front. He has been home for a few days leave and went back to the front again on Thursday. My other boy is in the artillery, and when properly trained will go to the front. If I had twenty sons I should be ashamed if every one of them did not go to the front when his turn came.
>
> England is not going to be unprepared again and the moment that peace is signed you may make up your mind that England will have not national service, but conscription, and the only men who will have to be trained are the men who have stayed behind.
>
> When the war is over I intend, as far as I possibly can, to employ nobody except men who have taken their duty at the front. I go further than that, and say that, all things being equal, if two men come to me for a farm and one has been at the front there is no doubt which is going to get the farm.

These recruiting speeches aroused the anger of some Labour and trade union circles. The *Daily Herald* reacted violently to Derby's statement that the failure of voluntary recruiting would lead to conscription:

Lord Derby, in addition to being a great territorial magnate, is one of those persons who take life very seriously. For months past he has been preaching National Service. Now that the Government has taken the plunge, and we are all to be registered, he comes forward to assure us that, in spite of official assurances and denials, the National Register is the first step towards compulsory military service . . . What we don't quite understand is where his lordship proposes to come in under a scheme of National Service. We shall expect him to give up drawing unearned income and himself be willing to push a truck on the quays alongside the Mersey, stoke a furnace, or any other odd job that needs doing. We shall be glad to reckon him as a comrade and a worker, and a faithful adherent of equal pay as well as equal work for all. But we have not yet heard that those Liverpool ground-rents have been given up. After all, the Stanleys have a good deal left to fight for even in these hard times.

To begin with in Lancashire and elsewhere all went well. Indeed, the Army could scarcely cope with the eager press of volunteers which came forward, and, as happened at the outset of the Second World War, there were more men than weapons. However, by the summer of 1915, the first generous enthusiasm was dying down and the demands of the Army were daily increasing. Three letters which Derby wrote at this time give an idea both of the progress he had been making and the difficulties he was encountering in West Lancashire:

Lord Derby to Lord Kitchener

2 July 1915

I was obliged to telegraph to you today as this new order which forces recruits for the Territorials to sign to say they are willing when enlisted to transfer to any other Regiment, has simply murdered recruiting in this district. We cannot get a man. It really is heart-breaking to think that some d——d fool should send out this order without consulting anybody connected with the Territorial Forces. I am perfectly certain you would not have authorised it if you had known. It is so futile too. You have got the power once the men are in to transfer in cases of emergency. Why therefore allow the recruit to be choked off when he comes up for enlistment? I am afraid the harm has been done and although the instant withdrawal of this order may have some effect recruiting for the Territorial Force is dead for the next two months till the bad impression caused by it wears off.

There is another matter on which I have telegraphed to Sclater! We are having a very large rejection of men on medical grounds. Flat feet, bad teeth, etc. Many of these men would do perfectly well for Home Service Battalions. Why not allow us to recruit up our Home Service Territorials, who are now formed into composite Battalions, into full Battalions as I think we could easily do. If this were carried out it would double your force for Home Defence and in that way liberate a lot more Territorials for Foreign Service.

There is also another thing that is choking off recruiting and that is the way in which Dependents' Allowances have been paid. It is absolutely in a chaotic state, but it is hardly fair to say it is entirely the fault of the War Office. In the vast majority of cases it is the fault of the Pension Officer who is I daresay overwhelmed with work but still in many cases does not seem to make an effort to get things put straight. I wish you could get somebody to go into this matter as recruiting is in a very parlous state even in Lancashire at this moment.

Lord Derby to Sir George Arthur

Very Confidential 5 July 1915

I hear Carson is going to speak on Friday at the Guildhall and with myself will be the only speaker in addition to Lord Kitchener. I shall be very brief and really I think after Asquith's announcement today it is hardly worth while holding a meeting. Recruiting is dead as far as this part of the world is concerned. I have been today to see our 2nd line Territorial Units. They cannot get a single man. Captain Hollins, a very well known Preston man, son of Sir Frank Hollins, the biggest employer in Preston, tells me that during the last ten days he has been round trying to get men for his special Company in the Regulars. He has got altogether 25 and he had answers from 500 or 600 to the effect that they would only come when they were fetched. Now Asquith tells them that they never will be fetched. I confess it makes one despair as to the result of the War.

Lord Derby to Sir Henry Sclater

Confidential 13 August 1915

I am in receipt of your letter asking me to raise another Heavy Battery on a regular basis. Will you give me a little breathing space?

I daresay I shall be able to do it for you later but I do not think I can at the present moment. I think the demands on me at the present moment are rather more than I can meet. I have been told to bring my 2nd and 3rd line Territorial Artillery up to full strength. That will require 1,000 men. I have also got to raise a Territorial Pioneer Battalion, another 1,000 men. I have been asked to raise a Regular Pioneer Battalion but that I must defer till the Territorial one is raised and I have also heard from Colonel Malcolm Peake who wants me to raise a complete Brigade of Artillery. Give me time and I think I could manage it but if the raising of both the Brigade of Artillery and the Heavy Battery must be begun immediately I am afraid I must say 'No'. Have you asked Manchester to raise a Heavy Battery? I am on the Committee there and we are raising a regular Pioneer Battalion but if you would like me to approach it with a view to also raising a Heavy Battery I will gladly see what can be done.

* * *

On 5 October 1915, the Prime Minister, Mr. Asquith, appointed Lord Derby Director-General of Recruiting. Derby had for many years before the war devoted much of his time to the Territorial Army in Lancashire; he had also been an ardent supporter of Lord Roberts' campaign for compulsory National Service. However, Asquith and still more Kitchener managed to convince him that feeling was so divided in the country on the question of conscription that it would only be after all voluntary schemes had been tried and proved unsuccessful that conscription would be accepted. He determined to do everything possible to make the voluntary system a success.

Derby's selection for this important post in this critical last phase of the voluntary system was widely applauded. His selection was due to the energy and success he had shown as Chairman of the West Lancashire Territorial Association. The results he had procured were outstandingly superior to those achieved in other parts of the country and Lloyd George had dubbed him 'the most efficient recruiting sergeant in England'. For an objective and contemporary account of his work during the first year of the war we cannot do better than cite the *Manchester Guardian* for 7 October 1915:

The appointment of Lord Derby as Director-General of Recruiting has come as a surprise to many, but to Lancashire men it seems the most appropriate and fitting selection which Lord Kitchener could have made at the present juncture. Perhaps in the days to come, when the history of the war is written, it will be said that Lord Derby saved the voluntary system, for if only he can organise the whole country as he has organised West Lancashire in his capacity of chairman of the West Lancashire Territorial Association, and produce equally steady results, compulsion will probably be unnecessary in most areas.

His success as a recruiter dated from the early days of the war. The Territorial Division for which he was responsible was up to strength within a few days of mobilisation, and a very few days later he was devoting himself to the raising of a second line. Liverpool then received his attention, for he quickly raised a Brigade of 'Pals'. Next the County Palatine Artillery were raised, and, if numbers are significant, it appears that he enlisted double the number of men for whom he asked originally. He was the founder, too, of the Dockers' Battalion.

But recruiting in the first six months of the war was comparatively simple. The difficulties arose early in the summer, at the time when the War Office, for some inexplicable reason, slackened off in its recruiting efforts. Lord Derby grasped the situation promptly, and his first recruiting campaign in West Lancashire started during the first week in May. . . . No sooner was the first campaign completed than Lord Derby began to organise a second. This was devoted purely to industrial centres, and it has been publicly announced that the number of men obtained were within a few hundred of the thousands asked for to provide the essential reserves for the West Lancashire Territorial Division.

. . . Lord Derby is so much in touch with modern English life that he recognised that the trade union organisers possess an influence which may be unseen and unadvertised but is one of the most powerful factors in moulding public opinion. Therefore he appealed to the trade unionists for help four months ago—months before Labour Recruiting Rallies were dreamt of. Labour leaders like Stephen Walsh, Thomas Greenall, John McGurk, J. A. Seddon, and James Sexton gave him unfailing assistance, and by a few weighty words at private conferences inspired men in their organisations to enlist. But it was Lord Derby who said the right word at the right season which moved men of all parties to work for the nation's good.

Another characteristic which has helped him to be successful is his Lancashire out-spokenness. . . . The dullest man could understand such sentences as these, uttered at Skelmersdale on October 1:

'This Pioneer battalion is being raised from the miners and others of Lancashire, and I am appealing to the miners of Skelmersdale to help to gain a substantial addition to the ranks . . . I, who am responsible for obtaining officers for this battalion, beg you to accept my assurance that nobody will go into the ranks of the officers unless I am certain he is qualified as a leader of men. On this platform are two members of the battalion—Mr. Arthur Walsh, son of Mr. Stephen Walsh, and Mr. Tinker, who is learning his work from the very bottom by going through the ranks to learn from experience.'

In those few sentences are contained the whole secret of Lord Derby's success at recruiting. There is plain, even blunt speaking. He appeals to a definite class of a definite district. Every miner in Skelmersdale in the audience knew that the call was to him or to his sons. But Lord Derby showed that he knew also that the miners were suspicious of their possible officers. Without equivocation he then explained that he recognised their suspicions, and had taken care that those who joined should be led by qualified men. Driving home his point, he turned to two of the men whom he had selected, the one the son of an old political opponent, 'Stephen Walsh's lad'; the other Joe Tinker, the local miner's agent, formerly the strongest anti-militarist of the district, now a member of the Inns of Court O.T.C.

One of the many unsolved enigmas inherent in the character and career of Lord Kitchener has always been his opposition to compulsory military service. Lord Roberts had plodded from one end of the country to the other for ten years before the war urging the need for a compulsory system. Kitchener had not for forty years prior to the outbreak of the war spent a winter in England. His whole life had been passed in military service abroad. He seems to have expressed no opinion in the pre-war years; and when war came and as Secretary of State for War he found himself invested with unique powers he invariably threw his weight against what was ultimately accepted as an indispensable measure. His own devoted biographer, Sir George Arthur. writing in 1920 recorded:

Before the war, when questioned as to General Military Service, he always declined to commit himself—partly perhaps because he thought that his judgment, unless based on particular knowledge and pronounced *ex cathedra*, would possess but little practical utility. A prolonged absence from England had precluded the study of the subject in all its bearings, particularly with reference to the feelings of the working classes. He certainly had a latent fear lest economic conditions, no less than deep-rooted English tradition, might conflict sharply with any attempt to maintain a large Standing Army raised by Compulsion. When, on the declaration of war, the Recruiting question in all its complexities had to be squarely faced, the War Minister still disposed himself to treat General Service—whenever and however it might be required—not as a fixed policy, nor as a fundamental principle, but as meeting a simple military requirement of the hour.[1]

When the National Registration Act was passed in July 1915 there was considerable agitation in both the Liberal and Conservative Parties for varying forms of compulsion. Kitchener, who had obtained a pledge from Mr. Arthur Henderson, who represented the Labour Party in the Cabinet, that the Labour Party would never 'corporately oppose any legislative measure which the War Minister should pronounce indispensable to secure victory' was, according to his biographer, 'dismayed a few weeks later to hear a clamour, inspired by a patriotic "zeal not according to knowledge" for the enforcement of General Service'.

Mr. Robert Blake in his life of Bonar Law, coming fresh from the study of the documents of the period, tells us that 'Kitchener, for reasons not easy to understand, viewed conscription with a strange hostility'. Sir George Arthur says of Kitchener: 'He did not live to see the end, but he willed and fashioned the means'. This judgment cannot be accepted. It is to Kitchener's enduring fame that when at the outset of war nearly everyone, soldier and politician alike, thought that Britain's Continental contribution should be limited to ten divisions at the most he was planning an army of seventy divisions, and that despite enormous pressure he retained in Britain the key specialists round whom the vast Kitchener

[1] *Life of Lord Kitchener* by Sir George Arthur, Vol. III.

Armies were formed. However Kitchener on arrival at the War Office found that already on mobilisation nearly all the younger and abler staff officers had gone to France in the Expeditionary Force. For years they had seen that war was inevitable and had secured promises in advance of employment on their staffs from those who were likely to exercise command in the field. Kitchener was therefore compelled, perhaps not altogether against his inclination, to make do with 'dug-outs' who had served with him in his campaigns against the Mahdi in the Sudan. Moreover, he greatly underestimated the potential quality of the Territorial Army and, partly from pride at the considerable success achieved by the voluntary system in his name, he became the principal stumbling-block to conscription. How could Liberal politicians achieve this essential requirement of victory when they were constantly told by the greatest living British soldier that such a measure was unnecessary? More especially when Kitchener was regarded politically as a Conservative.

Those who, inside and outside the Cabinet, had been pressing for conscription felt that Derby's appointment as Director-General of Recruiting was merely a device for postponing an urgent and inevitable decision. They were an able and determined body of men and they did their best to coerce Derby to their point of view. Derby was easily swayed on many occasions in his life but this time he was sure what his duty was and nothing could shake him.

Six years later Derby had luncheon with Lloyd George and they discussed Lord Esher's recently published book on Kitchener and agreed in condemning it as 'a thoroughly mean book written by a man whom Kitchener trusted, who owed everything to Kitchener, and who seemed to go out of his way to pick out all that was detrimental to Kitchener in the administration of the War Office and nothing that was good'. The occasion moved Derby to make the following entry in his diary:

Diary

28 *August* 1921

. . . It may be as well to put down now, while I remember it, what happened about my taking up the Direction of Recruiting. Kitchener sent for me to go and see him, and he told me he wished me to take up the Direction of Recruiting. I told him that I thought voluntary recruiting had practically come to an end, and that we must have compulsory service. He answered saying that it would be my duty to prove to Labour that we had come to an end, and that he himself felt that compulsory service would be necessary, but he wished to put it off as far as possible. He used the same expression that Esher uses in his book, 'It is not the first, but the last million that will tell'. What he said he wanted was when we had tired out and exhausted the spirit of the Germans then to have compulsory service as a final push. He added one other thing and that was, 'What I am anxious for is that when it comes to peace we shall have the the biggest army in the field. It would never do for the French to have more than us'. He did not at that moment anticipate America coming in. I told him I would consider whether I would accept. He asked for an immediate answer. I told him I was going up to Knowsley, but that I would let him know in 48 hours. By the time I got to Knowsley I found two telegrams from him begging for an immediate response, and I determined that night to accept. I had to speak at Rossendale and went to London the next morning. I got a message from Lord Lansdowne asking me to come to Curzon's house in Carlton House Terrace. When I arrived I found Lansdowne, Curzon, F. E. Smith, Austen Chamberlain and Winston. They were perfectly furious about my appointment. They said it had been done without any knowledge whatsoever of the Cabinet, and as a matter of fact they had got Asquith in such a position that within the week he would have had to consent to compulsory service. They therefore begged me to withdraw my acceptance of the position. This I absolutely declined to do. I told them that naturally I did not know that the Cabinet had not been consulted, which they quite understood, and that I had given my promise to Kitchener and Asquith whom I had previously seen. If they chose to absolve me from acceptance I was quite ready, and indeed anxious, not to undertake the work. I said, however, I would see Asquith again and get from him an assurance that in the event of my campaign proving unsuccessful he would introduce compulsory service. I went to see Asquith who signed a paper which I considered satisfactory, and took it back to the meeting. They were not satisfied. I told them as far as I was concerned the matter was over. I had accepted; I had got a letter from Asquith which satisfied me that in the event of failure conscription would be imposed, and that if they wanted to take further action it was up to them to do so, but for my part, though I had always been for compulsory service, I meant to do my very best to make the voluntary system a success up to the very end, and they must not expect me to do anything which would play into their hands. There I left the matter and the rest of the story is well known.

* * *

The nation had gone to war with enthusiasm. Lloyd George had trembled on the brink of pacifism until the last hour. When he decided to throw aside his Little Englandism and his pacifism, none was more fervent than he. On 19 September 1914 he delivered his celebrated speech at the Queen's Hall in London and in his peroration uttered words which, coming from a radical pacifist little Welshman, thrilled the nation and the Empire:

> We have been living in a sheltered valley for generations. We have been too comfortable and too indulgent—many, perhaps, too selfish—and the stern hand of Fate has scourged us to an elevation where we can see the everlasting things that matter for a nation—the high peaks we had forgotten, of Honour, Duty, Patriotism, and, clad in glittering white, the great pinnacle of Sacrifice, pointing like a rugged finger to Heaven.

By the time Derby had become Director-General about 3,000,000 had volunteered. Some thirty-five divisions now stood along the fronts all over the world and another thirty-five divisions were in the process of forming. The severe fighting and casualties in the battle of Loos in September were only a foretaste of what was to come. It was established beyond doubt that the voluntary system could never supply the manpower to keep an army of seventy divisions at fighting strength. Asquith's coalition Cabinet had for some time been deeply split on this issue of conscription. In July a memorandum calling for conscription signed by Winston Churchill, Curzon, Austen Chamberlain, Selborne and others had been circulated in the Cabinet.

In mid-October, shortly before Derby's appointment, a group of nine ministers, including Lloyd George and Churchill, met at Curzon's house in Carlton House Terrace and determined to bring the matter to a head. This was substantially the same group of ministers who a few days later, as we have seen, had unsuccessfully waylaid Derby en route to Downing Street formally to accept Asquith's offer of the job of Director-General. It was to forestall the pressure of these ministers that Asquith and Kitchener had sent for Derby. Asquith and Kitchener must have known that however successful Derby might be in the short term, his endeavours could only be of a palliative character. But they sincerely thought that the country, or at least the rank and file of the Liberal Party, would never accept conscription until its need had been proved beyond the smallest doubt. This was the unenviable task to which Derby now lent his remarkable energies and the not inconsiderable prestige of his name.

The essence of the Derby Plan, as it came to be called, was that all men between the ages of eighteen and forty-one, whose names appeared on the recently compiled National Register, should be persuaded to attest their willingness to serve with the armed forces when called upon. They were placed in forty-six groups according to age, twenty-three for married men and twenty-three for bachelors. Asquith gave a pledge that the married men would not be called up until after all the unmarried men had been drawn into the armies. This pledge was given by the Prime Minister in the House of Commons on 2 November 1915:

> I am told by Lord Derby that there is some doubt among the married men who are now being asked to enlist as to whether they may not be called upon to serve, having enlisted, while younger and unmarried men are holding back and not doing their duty. Let them disabuse themselves of that notion at once. So far as I am concerned, I would certainly say that the obligation of the married men to enlist is an obligation which ought not to be enforced, and ought not to be held binding on them unless and until we can obtain, I hope by voluntary effort, but if it were needed, and as a last resort by other means, as I have stated, the unmarried men.

This rash and unthinking pledge was to bedevil the whole Derby Plan. About this time Derby discussed his problems with Lord Riddell who noted in his *War Diary*:

October 1915

Lord D. said he must keep faith with the married men, who were enlisting more freely than the young unmarried men. The married must not be called out unless the unmarried had enlisted in reasonable numbers. He hoped the P.M. would make this plain in his speech on Tuesday. (Lord D. had already written me to that effect.) We talked of the military situation, which Lord D. regards as very serious. He said that no man ever described his own character in a phrase better than Asquith—'Wait and see', I said, 'Mr. A. has wonderful judgment and great dexterity in a political crisis.' Lord D. agreed. I said, 'The whole situation revolves round Asquith and Kitchener—and particularly the latter'. Lord Derby replied, 'K's administration has been a complete muddle'. We talked of L. G.:—Lord D. said, 'He is a great man, but loses himself when he gets on his legs and says things which come home to roost in an unfortunate way'.

Lord D. considers it an amazing sign of weakness that at such a time the Cabinet, feeling as they do, should not have the courage to reform the military administration. They are frightened of the people who do not know the facts.[1]

Lord Derby to Lord Stamfordham[2]

Confidential — Derby House

20 November 1915

We had a terrible setback to recruiting this week. I really don't think Asquith is to blame—it is this d—d cross-questioning in the H. of C. However I trust and believe things will improve and we may do a big thing. We are averaging about 4,500 men a day actually joining and about 10,000 a day joining the groups. So far in my five weeks at the W.O. we have taken about 270,000 men under the two headings. Not so bad, but I hope to more than double that in the next fortnight. . .

* * *

When Derby took over the task of Director-General of Recruiting and launched his famous Derby Scheme voluntary recruiting had in fact virtually exhausted itself. The cream of the nation had responded to Kitchener's successive calls, had marched off to the

[1] *Lord Riddell's War Diary*, 1914–18. [2] Royal Archives.

wars and had been immolated in France and Flanders and at Gallipoli. Gestures of absurd and uneconomic quixotry such as the formation of public-school battalions had burnt up the potential officer class. Nearly all those who were likely to come forward through patriotism or a sense of adventure had already been prematurely consumed, and there only remained at home those who like the miners had, in many cases against their will, been rightly kept at home to dig the essential coal and others of varying ages and callings who for the most part would do their duty if the lot fell upon them and they were summoned, but who for a variety of personal and domestic reasons saw no particular need to hurl themselves into the battle. This was the difficult background of the situation against which Derby had to operate. It was aggravated by the natural animosity of the mothers, wives and sweethearts of those men who had gone of their own choosing to the front and who were now dead or about to die. They looked with a sour eye upon the contemporaries of their menfolk who had found some safe billet at home, where with wartime inflation they drew wages and salaries anything from five to ten times greater than those received by private soldiers and officers who were fighting in the Flanders mud. Many of these devoted relations, particularly the ladies, were accustomed to move around the larger cities of the British Isles presenting white feathers to anyone they saw in civilian clothes. Sometimes they were abashed to discover that the recipient of their favour was a holder of the Victoria Cross or the Distinguished Service Order who had been invalided out of the forces after having been shot to pieces in some bloody battle on the Marne, the Aisne or at Loos.

* * *

Derby shouldered his new job with his usual energy but from the first he found himself fatally handicapped by the fact that the married men, or at any rate the wives of the married men, placed no firm confidence in Asquith's pledge. As it became apparent that the unmarried men were coming forward sparsely and reluctantly and as casualties mounted in the Army, increasing agitation was set on foot which Derby had to meet as best he could by countersigning over and over again the Prime Minister's pledge. It must have been most distasteful and the speeches he was compelled to make in the hope of producing adequate reasons for a voluntary system were scarcely those that any man of patriotism and high spirit would wish to make when a nation was fighting for its life. For instance at Glasgow on November 19 the situation compelled him to speak as follows:

> The great thing is to keep faith. If Germany had kept faith to Belgium this war would not have existed—and it is for us as a nation that did keep faith as a nation to another nation to see that individuals and communities within the Empire keep faith with the Empire and with those who rule over its destinies. Now there is one matter in which during the last forty-eight hours there seems to be a little doubt and it is again a question of keeping faith. The question is—Is faith going to be kept with the married men who have attested and now, I hope, will attest in thousands—the pledge that they shall only be taken when the younger men have taken their part in the struggle? Ladies and gentlemen, I have made that pledge myself. Mr. Asquith has made it in the House of Commons and in the communication sent through me—his communication—to the newspapers, and I would as soon believe that he would break faith as I would believe it of myself. I pledge myself here, as I have done in Edinburgh, to keep faith with those who have acted on this pledge, and nothing will induce me to be a party, either directly or indirectly, with anything that can savour of shilly-shallying with that pledge. I don't believe for one moment there is any such intention. I am perfectly certain that faith will be kept, and I ask you to take it from me that as long as you see me in the office I now hold that faith will be kept. I am not going to deal with all that has gone on before. I only ask you to take my assurance, and I can give it with the utmost confidence because I am perfectly certain that it will be endorsed absolutely and without equivocation by the Prime Minister speaking on behalf of the Government as a whole.

This was scarcely the heroic language of a war leader or even of a recruiting sergeant which might have been expected at such a time. But since the Government still baulked at the necessary measure of conscription, and since Asquith had given his pledge Derby had to spend half his time reassuring people that they would not be called up instead of explaining why they should. And what was this illusory distinction made between married and unmarried men? A married man with children has a greater stake in the country than one who has not yet given these 'hostages to fortune'. He has fulfilled himself and performed a very important part of his duty to society. Looking back we can see that the very pledges that had to be given to a married man were not only a manifestation of the unrealistic crypto-pacifist philosophy which was an ingredient of the Liberal Party but also proved quite plainly that despite the mock heroics of the popular Press and the recruiting platform it was utterly impossible to get the men the Army needed except by compulsion. Britain's life and honour were at stake and it was certainly no service to either cause to advertise much longer the bankruptcy of the voluntary principle.

* * *

Since his unfortunate lapse at the Post Office many years before about bloodsuckers and blackmailers, Derby had acquired the trained politician's habit of voicing his criticisms with caution and choosing his words with care. However, the manifold difficulties and frustrations which confronted him at this time led him, when addressing the Stock Exchange, into the use of words for which he subsequently had to apologise. According to *The Times* of November 25, he went so far as to call Lord St. Davids a liar and Lord Ribblesdale, by implication, a traitor:[1]

> . . . I dislike to think that the House of Lords should be in need of a censor, but two speeches were made the other day in that House which, I think, ought to have been censored. There was one to which I can give the lie direct—the accusations against the Headquarters Staff. I have been there on many occasions myself, and I know that there is

[1] Lord St. Davids had suggested that the staff of G.H.Q. seldom visited the front and Lord Ribblesdale had declared that it was common knowledge that Sir Charles Monro, who had been sent out to the Dardanelles to report on the situation, had recommended the withdrawal of British troops from this theatre.

not a word of truth in what Lord St. Davids said. I will sum up his speech in a very few words—no gentleman would have said it, and no gentleman will believe it.

Lord Ribblesdale's speech to my mind was absolute—well, I will not say it. (A voice—'piffle'.) A man who gives information to the enemy goes by a very ugly name and it can be given just as much by a speech delivered in the House of Lords as it can be by the man who is risking his life to get information for a foreign country. . . .

Some member of Derby's audience was quick to retaliate, for a blistering letter simply signed 'A' appeared in the same issue of *The Times* that reported his speech:

Lord Derby may draw uproarious cheers from the Stock Exchange, but he will not help the campaign in which he is engaged if he catches the infection of his political surroundings and begins playing to the gallery. The part of the bluff Englishman who says what he thinks is very popular, but it may be overdone.

Many public moralists have already dealt faithfully with Lord St. Davids' unforgivable accusations and Lord Ribblesdale's regrettable indiscretion. Both of these sensations are by this time 'stale fish' and neither of them seems to have the slightest relevance to Lord Derby's object in visiting the City—or, indeed, any practical value whatsoever, except that of raising the temperature of his meeting.

Everyone who knows Lord Ribblesdale, however slightly, will resent Lord Derby's offensive imputation, for they will never believe for a single moment that when Lord Ribblesdale referred to a certain rumour as 'common knowledge' it had ever crossed his mind that what he was saying could conceivably help the enemy. Unfortunately, speakers do not always weigh all the possible effects of their impulsive utterances, and this applies quite as much to the Commons as to the Lords. Apparently it applies equally to those who address public meetings. . . .

The next day, Derby apologised in another letter to *The Times*:

I feel that the reproach levelled at me by 'A', on the subject of my criticisms of Lord Ribblesdale's statement in the House of Lords, is not without justification. I quite admit that the words can be held to be an accusation that he DELIBERATELY said something that would be of use to the enemy and I beg unreservedly to withdraw such words and to offer my sincere apologies to Lord Ribblesdale, who, as 'A' rightly says, has suffered much for the country.

I feel, however, very strongly on the subject of public statements on matters which ought to be kept secret in Parliament by responsible people which, if they appeared in the ordinary columns of the newspapers, would at once come under the ban of the Censor.

With regard to my remarks, of which 'A' questions the relevancy at a recruiting meeting, I would like to point out that under the voluntary system it is essential that the men who are asked to join should have confidence in those who are to be their leaders; and I ask whether this confidence is likely to be maintained when statements such as that of Lord St. Davids are made, and when the public see that dispatches which should be kept strictly private become 'matters of common knowledge' as Lord Ribblesdale put it, within a few days of their receipt.

The object of this letter, however, is not to repeat my argument, but to offer my apologies to Lord Ribblesdale and to express my sincere regret for having made remarks with regard to him which I can quite see are not justifiable and which I fear may have caused him pain.

DERBY

But beneath Derby's letter appeared the following:

There are three points which occurred to me in reading Lord Derby's attack on Lord Ribblesdale. Perhaps you will allow me to make them.

1. If Lord Lansdowne shared Lord Derby's, and the Government's indignation at Sir Charles Monro's (assumed) verdict being quoted in the House of Lords, why did Lord Lansdowne not only answer the charge, but answer it in the affirmative?

2. It is generally better in these cases not to inquire too closely into 'Who the traitor was', or 'we Englishmen' may find ourselves landed in unpleasantly high political altitudes. The regrettable incident will, one can only hope, teach all concerned, especially Lord Derby's colleagues, one great virtue—lack of which they already so much deplore in others—the virtue of 'discretion'.

3. Lord Ribblesdale has suffered very heavily in England's wars, his only remaining son dying of wounds in the Dardanelles, while it will

be remembered that his eldest son fell in the Somali Expedition. Sir, is this a usual form of treason?

L. D.

* * *

The Derby Plan had originally envisaged the closing of the lists by the end of November. In view of the generally inadequate results the closing date was postponed for a fortnight. And even then Derby was a victim of Asquith's procrastination:

Mr. Asquith to Lord Derby

14 December 1915

In view of the importance of knowing more of the figures, the Cabinet decided to put off the statement as to men till early next week. All the same I shall be grateful to you for any materials you can send me in advance. You will no doubt be judiciously vague and non-committal in reply to Strachie . . .[1]

When the figures were published they proved a keen disappointment to those who still hoped to cling to a purely voluntary system. Certainly, a very large proportion of the married men, thinking that they were unlikely to be sent for, had attested; but a good deal less than half the unmarried men had followed their example. Of 2,170,000 unmarried men who were not enlisted on 23 October, 1915 when the scheme started only 1,150,000 had enlisted, attested or been medically rejected. And so many of those who had attested were medically unfit or were starred (i.e. employed in reserved occupations) that Derby had ultimately to report that his scheme had only produced some 340,000. Of the approximately one million unmarried men between the ages of eighteen and forty-one who had not attested it was computed that after deducting those who were indispensable at home there were above 650,000 eligible men who had so far not come forward. This was certainly not a negligible number and it was now clear that the Government

[1] Lord Strachie had put a series of questions on the paper for December 15 asking for the precise figures of the men obtained under the Derby scheme.

would have to redeem its pledge to the married men by using compulsion on the unmarried.

The matter was urgent and the Cabinet met on Boxing Day. Kitchener had by now been won over to the imperative need of conscripting at least the unmarried men. Asquith and his colleagues were forced to bow to the merciless logic of the situation. Only Sir John Simon, the Home Secretary, stood firmly by his pedantic principles. He left the Cabinet on New Year's Day.

The Bill embodying the Government's tardy decision was now presented to Parliament with expedition. It provided that the unattested unmarried men who had no grounds for exemption should be treated in every respect as if they had voluntarily attested under the Derby Plan. It was brought before the House of Commons by the Prime Minister himself on January 5 and was carried by large majorities in both Houses before the end of the month. In commending the Bill to the House Asquith said that the number of recruits obtained by Derby was encouraging and that the figures would not in his view justify general conscription. For the benefit of the faddists among his supporters he produced the sophistical argument that to conscript all the unmarried men in the country could not really be regarded as conscription because the new measure had no other purpose but to redeem his pledge, the object of which had been to preserve the voluntary system.

Notwithstanding the easy passage of the Bill, Derby was still confronted with much agitation from the married men, largely fomented by the cheaper section of the Northcliffe Press. Though the married men's grievances were exaggerated and exploited by this section of the Press, in some cases merely to discredit the voluntary system so that universal conscription would be brought nearer, there was a very widespread feeling on varying grounds that the system was unfair.

Some claimed that they would never have attested had they believed that they would ever be called on to fight. But the arguments of these callow volunteers received short shrift. Others, however, who had come forward at the call of their country felt that grave injustice would be done if those who had been less patriotic were not required to serve. They were far from emulating the heroic spirit of King Henry V on the eve of Agincourt—'The fewer men the greater share of honour'. Equality of sacrifice was their cry. And Derby—who had always favoured universal service—was sympathetic to their complaint. Yet others urged that more single men should be combed out; and, again, that better financial provision should be made for those with family responsibilities. These last complaints were promptly dealt with.

The *Manchester Guardian* on March 25 went so far as to claim that many married men attested in order that the voluntary principle might be maintained—in other words, they volunteered that others might escape military service. Gallup polls were not taken in those days; so no record remains of the number of quixotic married men who may have drafted themselves into this particular category in order to afford a statistical basis for the archaic principles of the Prime Minister and Mr. C. P. Scott.

That considerable numbers of the married men were genuinely disturbed is shown by the success of a meeting organised on March 24 in the Free Trade Hall in Manchester by the recently organised Attested Married Men's Union. More than 3,000 married men, who were required to show their attestation cards at the doors, attended. As the *Manchester Daily Dispatch* commented the next day: 'Seldom if ever has the Free Trade Hall held such a large audience of men all of the same age and all held in the bonds of wedlock'. This demonstration was a challenge to Derby on his own doorstep, but though the challenge was put in a way which he must have felt to be personal and disagreeable to himself, it is clear that these married men were not potential shirkers but men who believed that universal compulsory service was essential. The *Daily Dispatch* report continues:

> The dramatic moment was reached when the resignation of Lord Derby was called for. The vast audience at once rose from their seats and cheered the suggestion.
>
> The meeting was presided over by Mr. F. Cunliffe, of Southport, one of the founders of the union. He read his speech from manuscript, and

made it known that he spoke with the authority of delegates representing 500,000 attested married men.

It may be summed up in the following points:

1. Military service for all.
2. Resignation of Lord Derby.
3. Invitation to Lord Derby to become president of the Attested Married Men's Union.

But of all the criticisms which were levelled at Derby and his plan those that touched him most nearly were the reflections on his personal honour. Continued play was made with the charge that his solemn pledge to the married men had been broken. Derby denied this—but while he held his office his defence was muted; he could not snap the curb on his tongue. But there were some who defended him. The *Spectator*, for instance, of March 25 wrote:

> . . . It is as odious as it is unjust to talk about Lord Derby having failed to keep his word or having 'shuffled' in his explanations. He never concealed, but rather emphasised, the fact that a good many unmarried men would have to be exempted in order to perform necessary work in mining, munitions and agriculture. The essential part of the pledge was the promise to apply compulsion if an insufficient number of unmarried men proved willing to offer themselves voluntarily. Compulsion was only to be applied if the men who failed to volunteer were not a negligible quantity. To describe those who, like ourselves, call attention to these plain facts as indulging in 'shuffling' is to use language so mendacious as to pass the bounds which even the most panic-stricken publicists might be expected to set to their perfervid imaginations.

The *Spectator* went on to call for compulsion for all, to 'spread the duty of national preservation evenly through all classes'. Its call was about to be heeded. Even the *Manchester Guardian* in the course of a reasoned defence of the voluntary system was constrained to admit in an oblique fashion that there might be circumstances of 'the gravest military need' which would justify the Government in introducing compulsion for unmarried men.

That need was at last being recognised by the highest military advisers; and the pressure both inside and outside the Cabinet continued to mount. On April 25 there was a debate in secret session in the House of Commons. The late Mr. Leopold Amery has preserved for us in the second volume of his memoirs an account of his own speech, an excerpt from which will show how high passions were mounting and how almost exclusively criticism was being focussed on Asquith:

> . . . Why must we always do things in the worst, the most huckstering way? Can we never rise to the dignity of a great occasion? . . . The real source of all this indecision is the Prime Minister. What we need at the head of things is a single will, expressing the will of the nation; a thinking, foreseeing, planning mind; a purpose ardent, masterful, inflexible, an enthusiasm drawing inspiration from the inexhaustible well-spring of the nation's patriotism, kindling the nation's spirit to flame by the contagion of its own utterance and example. Without such leadership you cannot win . . . The blood of our nearest and dearest is being shed like water. The nation says nothing. But do you think it is indifferent? What have these men died for? Just to show that they were as brave as our rulers have been foolish? That they have not hesitated to risk everything to gain a yard of ground, or to set an example to their fellows, while Ministers dare risk nothing for fear of their own shadows? . . . Is all their effort and sacrifice to end ignobly in some miserable stalemate peace? Will no one lift us out of this atmosphere of hesitation, of sluggish indecision, of ignoble and pettifogging compromise? . . .

Asquith could withstand the pressure and logic of events no longer. On May 3 he introduced into the House of Commons a Bill for universal national service which was carried through all its stages in both Houses before the end of the month. It was Asquith's perversity in this vital matter which more than anything else sapped the confidence of his own colleagues and of Parliament in his capacity as a war leader. Carson and other Tory dissidents were hot-tongued against Asquith; and Lloyd George, who had so nearly resigned from the Government on the declaration of war in August 1914, was certainly by now beginning to detect that the road to power lay over the political corpse of Asquith and that he could be borne along it on the shoulders of the Tory Party which was, with a few exceptions, determined to fight the war at all costs and through every sacrifice to a triumphant conclusion.

The introduction by Asquith of the Bill for total compulsion brought to an end the energetic yet largely stultified labours in which Derby had been involved for seven months. He was now free to snap the curb and to answer his many critics. On May 6 he addressed the Lancashire Division of the National Union of Conservative Associations. We may well close this unhappy and frustrating chapter with an extract from the account given in *The Times* on the following Monday, May 8:

> He said that his mouth was now unclosed for the first time for the last few months to refute the malicious lies that had been circulated about him. He was not there to make any apology. He was there to give an explanation and to let them know how much truth there was in the various accusations.
>
> The pledge which he gave was that if more than a negligible number of single men not required for munition work or national service were left over then there would either be compulsion for single men or the married men would be released from their pledges. At the end of the campaign it was obvious that many more than this negligible number remained. His estimate, 650,000, turned out to be accurate, rather less than more. On the strength of that the Government fulfilled their pledge.
>
> Difficulties, however, soon became apparent, due to the starring and badging which exempted men from military service. This starring and badging, it should be borne in mind, were not done by the War Office but by the Civil Departments of the Government, who said that the men who were starred and badged were indispensable. Long before certain quarters found out this defect, he found it out and did his best to remedy it, but when men were unwilling to serve and were temporarily protected in that attitude by the State, they were difficult to deal with. Half the men were in munition works, and though the State would get them eventually, the work was slow and it could only be brought about by such substitution of labour as would in no way diminish the supply of ammunition. No one recognised this more than Mr. Lloyd George, and they would have, he hoped, Mr. Lloyd

George's assistance in adopting more stringent measures than had been possible hitherto.

A second agitation—the one of the attested married men against the unattested married men—brought into being three different classes: (1) Those who were pressed to attest against their will on the ground that, if they did not, something worse would happen to them; (2) those who attested, hoping and believing that they would never have to fight—he had no sympathy for that crowd—and (3) those who were ready to serve, but whose financial obligations when they left their wives and children were such as they did not care to contemplate. . . .

'The fact is,' Lord Derby continued, 'we ought to have had universal compulsion in the first week of the war. Afterwards there was only one way of obtaining it, and that was by putting all the facts before the people and urging that military necessity demanded that there should be universal compulsion.

'I cannot tell you how I welcome the decision to enforce compulsion. It is the carrying out of a principle I advocated long before this war began. There seems to be a feeling—and I hope publicity will be given to what I am now saying—that because the Group System has been re-opened that shows a weakening with regard to compulsory service. Nothing of the kind. It is only for the time that the Bill is before the two Houses of Parliament to give men a chance, which I hope they will take, of joining voluntarily.'

Proceeding, Lord Derby said that his resignation had been clamoured for, and he knew that by resigning he might have attained popularity for the moment but if he had gained popularity in that way he should have lost his own self-respect. If he had resigned in March the military authorities were not prepared to say that he would have been accurate in declaring compulsion was a military necessity, and what would have been his position, a civilian in the War Office, if he had taken his stand without the backing of their figures? Then there were others who urged that compulsory service was part of the pledge. On that point his personal honour was attacked and he consulted many people on the point. All told him he would have been wrong to read universal compulsion into the pledge, and that to do so would be a gross breach of faith. Among those who told him he would not have been honest if he had tried to read universal compulsion into the pledge were Sir Edward Carson, Lord Milner and Mr. Stephen Walsh.

'I ask you,' Lord Derby continued, 'if I have been honest or dishonest. I have withstood clamour, I have withstood insults, because I knew I was doing right. If I had to go through these six months again I should do again what I have done, but I would have chosen better some of those who at one time called themselves my friends. I have come to you because though I have a certain amount of work still to do I am now back in the arena of political life. I have never, never been a servant of the Government, but I have been, I hope, a friend of Lord Kitchener.'

X

Under-Secretary of State for War

KITCHENER sailed on his Russian mission in the cruiser *Hampshire* from Scapa Flow on 5 June 1916. Off the Orkneys in bad weather the *Hampshire* struck a mine and foundered. Kitchener was not among the twelve who survived. In his lifetime he seemed larger than he was, and within a few weeks of his death he had become a legend. Cynical people, who knew that the Government wished to be rid of him, alleged that it was the Government who had procured his death. The simple-minded, and they were legion, refused to believe that he was dead and were convinced that he had been picked up by a German U-boat and was safe and well in a German prison camp. This belief arose in part from the fact that there were prisoners-of-war from the Hampshire Regiment in a German camp. Derby was much afflicted by Kitchener's death and at the time paid him a warm-hearted tribute in the House of Lords.

Many years later something moved Derby to put a recollection of this period on paper:

Diary

26 *September* 1938

I am dictating this many years after the incidents that I am now recording took place but they are absolutely fresh in my memory and I have notes recording them. Kitchener, I think perhaps in some ways, confided more in me than in most people. Certainly more than in George Arthur who is at present writing his life.

Some time before he went off on his fatal last journey I was talking to him about his future and he told me that he was not looking forward to any future. There was only one thing that he really hoped to live for and that was to be one of the English delegates when Peace was made. I asked him whether, saying that, he had any strong views that he would want to put forward and he said he had one very strong one, and that was, whatever happened, not to take away one country's territory and give it to another. It only meant a running sore and provocation for a war of revenge to get back the ground so lost. He was most emphatic about that and when I said to him 'Surely you would not include in that Alsace and Lorraine', he said 'Yes, I should. I think if you take Alsace and Lorraine away from Germany and give them to France there will be a war of revenge.' I must say he added one thing which has come very true, that he did not think the inhabitants of Alsace and Lorraine had any very strong patriotic feelings. When they were under Germany they shouted for France and if they were put under France they would shout for Germany.

I asked him then about the Colonies and he said Yes, there again, he would not take away Colonies from Germany. It afforded a safety valve for them. They must have somewhere to go and if they had Colonies they would go there peacefully and not want to engage in war for new territory.

I was having dinner alone with him when he told me this and it was the last time that I saw him about three or four days before he sailed in the *Hampshire*. He knew that the Government was getting him out of the way but he did not mean to leave without a struggle. He left me a private code by which I was to tell him anything that might be of value to him with regard to his return to England. I was not of course then in the Government. My recruiting was over.

There is a general idea that Kitchener was strongly for conscription. That is entirely contrary to facts. When I started recruiting he begged me to do all that I could to prevent having to put on conscription at that moment. He told me he was sure conscription would have to come but he wanted it only to come at the last stage of the war when we should be then left with the biggest army and therefore more likely to be listened to by our Allies than if our army were only comparatively small.

He had great faith in Asquith. He was devoted to him and liked him very much indeed just as much as he cordially disliked Lloyd George. They had absolutely nothing in common and even if he had not lost his life in the *Hampshire* I do not think it would have been possible for Kitchener to have served under him at the War Office [i.e. after Lloyd George had become Prime Minister].

A full month passed between Kitchener's death on June 5 and Asquith making a decision as to his successor at the War Office. During the interregnum Asquith himself assumed the management at the War Office as he had for a few months after the Curragh incident in 1914. Many names were canvassed. Long, Milner, Curzon, Bonar Law, Lloyd George and Derby were all spoken of as possible successors.

The generals mobilised all their forces to stave off what seemed to them the ghastly prospect that they would come under the tutelage of Lloyd George. The right wing of the Tory Party, with the exception of Carson, was also opposed to this project. On June 17 we find Walter Long, President of the Local Government Board, writing to Stamfordham[1] urging that Lloyd George's appointment would be 'disastrous' and reporting that the day before he had urged Asquith to take the Seals himself with Derby as his second in command. The same day Stamfordham telegraphed to the King:

Lord Stamfordham to the King

8.15 p.m. 17 June 1916

Have seen P.M. L. G. wants War Office but with former plenary powers restored, which is impossible as Robertson's present position would be compromised. Best solution is for P.M. to remain at War Office. Whole Army Council want this. Derby might be second in command.

L. G.'s proposals go beyond what a unanimous Cabinet would sanction. Some of them already kicking . . .

Lord Beaverbrook tells us in *Politicians and the War* that Derby told Bonar Law that he would be glad to serve under him at the War Office and that he would prefer to be Under-Secretary than to have the first place. Mr. Blake, in *The Unknown Prime Minister*, states, without giving any authority, that Derby when it was suggested to him that many of the soldiers would favour his appointment 'indicated at once that he did not aspire to such a lofty position'. Whatever may have been Derby's outward com-

[1] Royal Archives.

portment at this time, in his heart he greatly desired to be Secretary of State:

Lord Derby to Lord Charles Montagu

23 June 1916 Knowsley

Now about the War Office. Of course, it is the one office I have ever really wanted. I would do anything to have it now, but I will not myself ask for it. It is nonsense to say I might resign if I did not actually see eye to eye with Asquith. If I had wanted to do that, I could have carted him last January and last March on the subject of compulsory service. I don't think Mr. A. quite realises what it would have meant if I had asked for more powers for myself on the Air Committee. The only power I could have asked for would have been that I should be made a Cabinet Minister and therefore Minister of the Air—the only office which I think it would be fatal to create at the present moment. It was all right an *existing* Cabinet Minister taking it, together with his other work; that created no new office. Mr. A. does not perhaps know that I only resigned after A. J. B. had told me he would resist any further powers given to me—after that I had no alternative. I cannot think that because of this action on my part it is fair to say I might always resign if I did not see eye to eye with the P.M. I don't see eye to eye with him on the Irish Question, but I am going to fight his and L. G.'s battle for all I am worth here, unless *all* our Unionists leave the Cabinet which they would be mad to do.

I should like the office—like it very much—but I can't bring myself to ask for it. If however you could do anything to get my claim considered, the P.M. need have no fear of my loyalty, but I am quite ready to serve in the second place under him and I believe I could relieve him of an immense amount of office work, leaving him to deal with all questions of policy, etc. I should like that nearly as much as being chief, but as I have said, that is really the only ambition I have at all.

Derby had, as all politicans should, a healthy appetite for office but it was coupled with an undue propensity to resign. Though he felt it was his duty to himself, his family and his country to take part in the government of the country, whether in an exalted or a humble capacity, he had a distaste for the rough and tumble of party politics and a notion that he could always at any time honourably retire from national politics and devote himself to his county work in Lancashire. This was a strength and also a weakness in his character no less than in his situation.

Derby's honourable ambition for the War Office was not, however, to be fulfilled for another six months. Though Lloyd George's appointment as Secretary of State for War was not announced until July 6, a full month after the death of Kitchener, it had been decided in principle some days before that he should have the job. By a compact negotiated between Bonar Law and Lloyd George at Sir Max Aitken's house at Cherkley, Bonar Law had agreed to back Lloyd George for the job. When Bonar Law the next day advised Asquith to this effect, the Prime Minister said: 'I offer it to you.' Bonar Law indicated that a week before he would have accepted, but that now he was pledged to Lloyd George.[1] Asquith's reluctance to place his Minister of Munitions in this key position was understandable. Lloyd George had already shown himself a difficult, ambitious and thrusting colleague who would stop at nothing to seize the power which he was by now coming to believe must be placed in his hands if the war was to be won. On the day that Mrs. Asquith heard that Lloyd George was to go to the War Office, she wrote in her diary with masculine prescience: 'We are out. It is only a question of time when we shall have to leave Downing Street.'

Although it had in fact been settled at Cherkley on June 11 and at the Wharf (Asquith's country house) on June 12 that Lloyd George was to go to the War Office his appointment was not announced, as we have seen, until July 6. Indeed, on June 17, the very day when Derby was writing to his brother-in-law, Lloyd George refused the post in a formal letter to Asquith. This, however, was because he was trying to bargain for greater powers as Secretary

[1] Lord Beaverbrook's *Politicians and the War*, Vol. I. For a later account of these transactions see Mr. Robert Blake's *The Unknown Prime Minister*. This account is unhappily marred by an uncorroborated and disputed story of Asquith being surprised at a game of bridge with three ladies. Students of the period and connoisseurs of political controversy should note the discrepancies between the first and second editions of Mr. Blake's book and also the lengthy correspondence in *The Times* initiated by Lady Violet Bonham-Carter and extending over a period of several weeks in January and February 1956.

of State for War than had been left to Kitchener after the Kitchener-Robertson Agreement and after (largely through Lloyd George's own instrumentality) the Ordnance Department had been taken away from the War Office and incorporated in the Ministry of Munitions. Ultimately Lloyd George agreed to go to the War Office without any of the added powers for which he had bargained. Derby, who would have preferred to have served under Asquith or Bonar Law, was appointed his Under-Secretary.

Lord Derby to the King[1]

30 June 1916 — Coworth Park

Your Majesty will remember the matter on which Your Majesty spoke to me the other day. The Prime Minister yesterday asked me to undertake the office of Under-Secretary to Lloyd George in the War Office and as I told Your Majesty I should do if it were official, I accepted the post. The Prime Minister was good enough to accompany it with a request that I should join the Cabinet.[2] This I declined because though appreciating the honour, I felt it would appear as if I wanted political recognition, whereas my one and only object is to take a post where I can work for the Army and be of some use to it. I hope Your Majesty will approve of my conduct.

The King to Lord Derby

30 June 1916 — Royal Pavilion, Aldershot Camp

MY DEAR EDDY,

I am delighted to hear from your letter just received that the Prime Minister has asked you to become Under-Secretary to Lloyd George

[1] Royal Archives.

[2] Though the idea of an Under-Secretary being a member of the Cabinet seems absurd in these modern days of swollen administrations, this was not the first time that such a plan had been envisaged. On 4 March 1908, Asquith wrote to his wife: 'He [the King] had heard gossip that Winston was anxious to get into the Cabinet, keeping his present office as Under-Secretary. He was opposed to this and said that Queen Victoria had vetoed a similar proposal by Rosebery in favour of E. Grey when he was Under-Secretary for Foreign Affairs. I said that Winston had every claim to Cabinet rank and that he had behaved very well when twice passed over for Loulou [Harcourt] and McKenna, both of whom had inferior claims. The King agreed and was quite warm in his praise of Winston, but thought he must wait till some real Cabinet Office fell vacant.'

at the War Office and that you have accepted the post. Let me again tell you how much I appreciate the patriotic spirit which you have evinced on this occasion and indeed ever since the war began. Having great faith and confidence in your judgement and knowledge of the Army my misgivings are considerably relieved as to the future working of the War Office.

With regard to your declining a seat in the Cabinet, I feel that you are the best judge, at all events you have shown that you are thoroughly disinterested and require no favours. Of course, my dear Eddy, all your letters are treated by me as absolutely confidential . . .

Believe me,

Your sincere old friend,

George R.I.

Later that day, on the eve of the Battle of the Somme, Derby wrote to the King once more:

Lord Derby to the King[1]

30 June 1916 Coworth Park

I can never sufficiently thank Your Majesty for the more than kind letter I have just received. As Your Majesty knows, I have but one wish and that is to serve Your Majesty to the very best of my abilities. The reason I telegraphed to Your Majesty with regard to the confidence of the letter was that as I have particularly asked the Prime Minister not to announce the appointment till Tuesday he might have thought I ought not to have written to Your Majesty on the subject. I had a long talk with Mr. Lloyd George this afternoon and am sure we shall work well together. He has great energy and if he will only leave Robertson alone and not take too active a part in the appointments, there need be no trouble. There is one great thing in his favour—he is out to win the war.

With Your Majesty's permission I shall from time to time write to Your Majesty and also, if I may, ask for an audience. There are so many matters one can tell but cannot write!

This is a moment of great anxiety. I have three brothers (Ferdy, George and Bill) and they're in the division which will probably have the brunt of the attack to bear. Please God they will come through all right.

Again thanking Your Majesty most gratefully.

[1] Royal Archives.

When Lloyd George and Derby took over the War Office on 7 July 1916, there was deep and growing anxiety about the progress of the war. The Dardanelles had been evacuated at the beginning of January. The considerable Anglo-French commitments at Salonika had yielded no results and were to prove progressively costly and abortive. Throughout the spring and early summer, the French Army, division by division, had been flattened on the anvil of Verdun, and when the tremendous and long-prepared Anglo-French offensive on the Somme was opened on July 1, only eighteen French divisions were available instead of the thirty-nine which had been the basis on which this grandiose and bloody battle had been planned. Within a month of the opening of the battle, we find Robertson writing to Haig:

Sir William Robertson to Sir Douglas Haig[1]

29 July 1916

The powers that be are beginning to get a little uneasy in regard to the situation. The casualties are mounting up, and Ministers are wondering whether we are likely to get a proper return for them. I do my best to keep the general situation to the front, and to explain what may be the effect of our efforts, and to ask what alternative could be adopted. I also try to make them think in German of the present situation. But they will persist in asking me whether I think a loss of, say, 300,000 men will lead to really great results, because if not we ought to be content with something less than what we are now doing, and they constantly inquire why we are fighting and the French are not . . . In general what is bothering them is the probability that we may soon have to face a bill of between 200,000 and 300,000 casualties with no very great gains additional to the present. It is thought that the primary object—the relief of Verdun—has to some extent been achieved.

Meanwhile in the East, Brusiloff's offensive against the Austrians in Galicia, which had been launched early in June, was achieving a wonderful success, but it was to be the dying thrust of Czarist Russia. At the end of August, the Russians' spectacular but fleeting

[1] *Soldiers and Statesmen*, 1914–1918, Vol. I, by Sir William Robertson.

advance, aided by Allied promises, was to lure Roumania into a declaration of war against the Central Powers; but this too was to prove a false dawn. By the end of the year, the German armies under Falkenhayn and Mackensen in a lightning campaign had destroyed the Roumanian Army and had occupied three-quarters of the territory of this presumptuous Balkan power.

* * *

Kitchener, when he died, despite his popular fame, was discredited among those who knew what was going on. Lloyd George's star was in the ascendant and many discerning eyes, not least his own, already saw him as the leader and man of action for whom widening circles of the public were looking. The new Secretary of State, however, found himself heir to the limitations which had been placed upon his office when Kitchener had appointed Sir William Robertson to the post of C.I.G.S. at the end of December 1915. When Kitchener went to the War Office in August 1914 he found there as C.I.G.S. Sir Charles Douglas, a colourless and ailing soldier whom he dominated and completely overshadowed. Douglas died in October of that year. Sir James Wolfe-Murray, who had lately returned from South Africa, was next appointed to this post. He was timid and overawed. After a short period he was succeeded by Sir Archibald Murray, who had proved unequal to the strain of staff duties in France. Kitchener continued to keep everything in his own hands. It is extraordinary that Kitchener, who set such a high standard for his own work, should have been content to allow the supreme military position in the British Empire, that of Chief of the Imperial General Staff, to be filled by a series of worn-out mediocrities. It seems that he was so preoccupied with his own work that he had insufficient time to supervise that of his subordinates. Moreover, an unduly delicate desire not to offend the somewhat touchy susceptibilities of Sir John French, with whom he was not on the best of terms, made him reluctant to recall any of the abler soldiers from France.

When Sir William Robertson was recalled (to succeed Sir James Wolfe-Murray) from Sir John French's staff, where he had been serving as Chief of the General Staff, he insisted upon receiving a new charter. After lengthy discussions between the Secretary of State and the C.I.G.S. designate, the following formula was embodied in an Order in Council dated 27 January 1916:

> The Chief of the Imperial General Staff shall, in addition to performing such other duties as may from time to time be assigned to him under the Order in Council dated 10th August 1914, be responsible for issuing the orders of the Government in regard to Military operations.[1]

Already, prior to the Kitchener-Robertson concordat, the Secretary of State's powers had been progressively pruned in the field of munitions. In March 1915 Lloyd George, while still Chancellor of the Exchequer, had become Chairman of the Munitions Committee, and on the formation of the first Coalition Government in May 1915 a new department had been created and Lloyd George had become Minister of Munitions. The massive, unwieldy, pervasive powers with which Kitchener had started the war, the extent of which more than anything else had led to his stultification, had been largely whittled away by the time that Lloyd George laid his eager and industrious hands upon the machine of the War Office.

Lloyd George, who for many months had been a critic of the generals, and in particular of Haig and Robertson, was alert to the limitations which circumscribed his position. Robertson was equally aware of the enormous potential political power of his new chief compared with that of Kitchener. Lloyd George played his hand warily even before his appointment. After receiving a letter from Robertson describing the situation as it had obtained under the Kitchener-Robertson regime and as he assumed it would continue, he, according to Robertson,[1] 'acknowledged the value of the change made by the Order in Council, and said that no War Minister was likely, and certainly not himself, to wish to alter it during the war'. Lloyd George proceeded to argue, however, that Robertson had overlooked certain considerations, in particular that the Secretary of State was ultimately responsible to Parliament and the

[1] *Soldiers and Statesmen*, by Sir William Robertson.

country for all War Office matters. Lloyd George went on to express the opinion that there was no great difference between their two views and that he believed that an effective co-operation between them could be secured. Lloyd George concluded by saying: 'After acting with you for six months on the War Committee I feel no doubt that you and I could work in complete harmony for the common good.'

These facile and perhaps disingenuous hopes were not to be vindicated by events, any more than was Lloyd George's assurance to Robertson that no one, least of all himself, would wish to alter the relationship between the Secretary of State and the C.I.G.S. In fact as Prime Minister he did this very thing at the beginning of 1918 when he installed Milner and Henry Wilson in the War Office in the place of Derby and Robertson.

* * *

The next twenty months which Derby spent at the War Office as Under-Secretary and then as Secretary of State, were to be the most testing time of his life. Well-intentioned, impetuous and easy-going, neither his parts nor the powers he wielded would have enabled him to play a commanding role. A service he sought to render, and in which to a large extent he succeeded, was in acting as a buffer between the soldiers and the politicians. In this difficult role he was perforce at times all things to all men. His genial disposition, his talent for bringing opponents together, his distaste for forcing things to an issue were all of service in this useful task.

But the savage warfare between the 'frocks' and the 'brass hats', as Henry Wilson always called them, and the complicated political intrigues which luxuriated on both sides, usually found him without a compass. Often, when the crisis came, he would be disregarded by both sides and the matter would be settled over his head or behind his back. He always wished to do what was honourable but often his loyalties and obligations seemed so divided that whatever course he took would involve him in reproaches from both sides.

When Lloyd George came to the War Office he had a clear and definite policy of curbing the power of the generals and of imposing civilian strategy and authority upon them. It is one of the strangest facts of the First World War that, with all the power Lloyd George amassed and with all his preternatural ability to handle men, he was never able, either at the War Office or later as Prime Minister, to impose his will effectively upon the soldiers. He rose to power, not only because of his war-winning qualities and his native genius, but by elaborate intrigue and skilful manipulation of the Press which exerted at that time a political power far beyond anything which Fleet Street has enjoyed before or since.

Those who have lived as adults through the Second World War must be surprised by two glaring contrasts when they come to study the history of the First World War. Anyone of this generation must be appalled by the almost total lack of military security and by the fantastically greater powers then exercised by the newspaper proprietors. It would have been unthinkable in the Second World War for a Cabinet Minister to have written daily accounts of Cabinet proceedings to a young lady with whom he was in love, for generals to have maintained a daily and sometimes hourly telephone connection with editors in Fleet Street, or for fashionable hostesses to have bandied about at crowded luncheon tables the date of the next offensive. The widespread lack of security common to so many politicians and soldiers was the product of the extraordinary sense of self-assurance instinctive among the governing class of an island race which had not for a hundred years been put to the necessity of fighting a major war. One cannot but sympathise with Kitchener's reluctance to impart his secret plans to a Cabinet of more than twenty members, many of whom, to assist their intrigues against each other or from a desire to seem important, would unthinkingly violate their oaths as Privy Councillors a dozen times a week.

In the Second World War no newspaper proprietor had one-tenth of the power or authority of a member of the War Cabinet. In the First World War individual ministers and sometimes whole Governments were driven from office by a campaign of press agitation and backstairs intrigue. Part of this contrast arises from the wide differences in the character and personality which can readily be observed between the two Prime Ministers. Lloyd George had clambered up the greasy pole of power by every Welsh artifice of political and newspaper machination, and it was not to be supposed that his many enemies, civilian and military, were likely to deny themselves the use of similar methods in their own self-defence and in the advocacy of the causes and projects in which they believed. But there was another reason of a more fundamental character. Although Britain entered the First World War with an unrivalled Navy and a first-class if small professional Army, on the civilian front the country was wholly unprepared for the waging of a long and bloody war. Questions of manpower, national service, direction of labour, the employment of women in factories, air-raid precautions and rationing had scarcely been considered by the governing mind of Britain. Still less had any plans been concerted for coping with these and a hundred kindred problems.

Thus in the First World War there were always novel issues which affected the life and comfort of every family in the land which could be stridently and irresponsibly agitated by a handful of men, some of whom seemed to think that their most useful contribution to the war effort was the hourly recitation of the daily grievances of the people. Powerful ministers quailed under the insolences of Northcliffe and winced even under the clumsy assaults of his younger brother, Rothermere. In the Second World War there was fortunately available the corrective influence of the B.B.C. which, though it has not provoked any very great improvement in the tone of the popular Press, has succeeded in inculcating into the minds of many people a growing distrust for the more extravagant falsehoods of the baser sections of the Press.

Thus it was that few newspaper campaigns were set on foot against the Coalition Government in the Second World War. And those which were launched never broke the nerve of those responsible for the conduct of our affairs. The *Daily Express*'s campaign for a second front, aided though it was by the magisterial authority of its principal proprietor, Lord Beaverbrook, who had only just ceased to be a powerful minister, did not advance the date of D-Day by an hour. And even the campaign which sought to prevent the

British Government from saving Greek freedom from a Communist tyranny, and in which *The Times*, to its eternal infamy, was involved, came to nothing. Lord Astor of Hever Castle can comfort himself with the knowledge and reflection that the Hammer and Sickle are not yet flying over the Parthenon.

* * *

Within a few weeks of Derby becoming Lloyd George's lieutenant he was aware of a process which he and many others had to endure for the rest of the war. On 17 September 1916, Foch visited Haig at his headquarters. Foch recounted a conversation that he had had with Lloyd George a few days earlier when Lloyd George had had luncheon with him. Foch said that Lloyd George had asked his opinion as to the ability of the British war generals. He added that Lloyd George was sufficiently patriotic not to criticise the British Commander-in-Chief but that he did not speak with confidence of other British generals as a whole. Haig commented: 'Unless I had been told of this conversation personally by Gen. Foch, I would not have believed that a British Minister could have been so ungentlemanly as to go to a foreigner and put such questions regarding his own subordinates.'[1]

Foch also recounted this incident to Sir Henry Wilson who noted in his diary that Lloyd George told Foch 'he gave Haig all the guns and ammunition and men he could use and nothing happened. Foch said that Lloyd George was *très monté* against Haig, and he did not think Haig's seat was very secure.'

Lord Derby to the King[2]

Confidential | Derby House
29 September 1916

Your Majesty may have seen the article in the *Morning Post*—a very bitter attack on Lloyd George and hinting at the trouble in France in a manner which is unmistakeable. It is very mischievous but it clearly shows the story is now well known. Lloyd George is writing a letter

[1] *Haig*, Vol. I, by Duff Cooper. [2] Royal Archives.

to the *Morning Post*—it is a good letter, but I am afraid it will provoke a reply in which i's will be dotted and t's crossed. I wish he had left it alone, but I have to admit it was very difficult for him to do so, and in some ways it will do good, as it gives Lloyd George a chance of stating his confidence in the leadership of the Army and really that is the thing which matters, as any idea that D.H. was not being supported by him would be fatal. But what I fear is that names—including those of French generals will be mentioned.

Lloyd George absolutely denies (and Reading who was his interpreter confirms this) that he ever asked any French general what he thought of our generals, or that he in any way compared our forces with those of the French to the disadvantage of the former. We shall see how things develop but though I hope Lloyd George's letter will be the end of the row, I am very much afraid it may only be the beginning. But there is another matter I feel I must mention to Your Majesty in the strictest confidence and I would beg that it should never be known to *anybody* except Stamfordham that I have mentioned it to Your Majesty. Lloyd George sent for Robertson yesterday and said he wished him (and the Prime Minister agreed with him in saying so) to go on a visit to Russia and be away about six weeks. Robertson in confidence consulted me and I told him to absolutely refuse to go—this advice coincided with his own feelings, and he has now written to both Lloyd George and the P.M. to say that he will not go. It would be absolutely impossible for him to leave, and especially at this juncture. He and I standing together can I think prevent any wildcat scheme, but alone I feel I should fail. Moreover there would be no buffer between Lloyd George and Haig which is essential. All this may never come to Your Majesty's ears. The scheme may be nipped in the bud, but I felt that Your Majesty would wish me to mention it to Your Majesty.

I am doing all I can to keep the peace and make things go smoothly, but I feel as if I was sitting on a volcano. There is a terrible lot of ill-feeling about. I am sorry because Lloyd George is a *good* man for the post—he has lots of drive and pluck and fights the battles of the War Office very magnificently both in the Cabinet and the H. of Commons. Moreover most of his suggestions are very sound and if only they can be put forward in a proper manner, I feel their adoption would be of great advantage to the Army. But it is very wearying. As soon as one trouble is over another crops up. I am glad to say I have just got a letter from G.H.Q. which makes me feel happier as evidently all trace of resentment on the part of D. Haig has quite passed off and the incident is now treated as something to laugh at.

I am writing this late on Thursday night and am going midday tomorrow to Knowsley, returning here on Sunday. If Your Majesty wishes to see me, I could always come down to Windsor, but if Your Majesty is coming up next week, I might be allowed to come to see Your Majesty.

The same day, the King replied from Windsor:

The King to Lord Derby

29 September 1916 Windsor Castle

Dear Eddy,

Thanks for your letter just received. Of course it is quite right for you to tell me; it is just questions like this that I must know if I am to be of any use. I had seen the article in *Morning Post*, L. G.'s letter and the answer. We must only hope the matter will end there; no doubt the story is practically public property by now and I think I shall mention it to the Prime Minister in confidence when I see him next week as he must have heard of it by now. As to the second question you write about, that is absolutely impossible. I will certainly not allow R. to go to Russia. He is first of all much too valuable a man to run risks with like poor K. and then it would be impossible to get on without him especially at this critical moment of the war. I will not hear of it and I trust that it is nipped in the bud and that the question will never even be suggested to me. Hanbury-Williams [Chief of the British Military Mission in Russia] goes back next week; surely he will be able to do all that is necessary, as the Emperor treats him with absolute confidence and talks to him about everything. I shall be in London on Monday, come to luncheon that day at 1.30, you will be able to tell me more by then.

I shall of course keep all you tell me secret and have only mentioned it to S.

Believe me
always your sincere friend
George R.I.

* * *

It was a little naïve of Derby to suggest to the King that the word of Reading was good corroborative evidence of Lloyd George's denials. Reading was under deep obligation to Lloyd George. His involvement in the Marconi Scandal had been brazened out by his appointment in 1913 as Lord Chief Justice. This appointment had prompted Kipling to write and circulate his insufficiently known lines under the title 'Gehazi'. To a less politically corrupt world it is staggering that a Lord Chief Justice of England could have allowed such words to be printed without either suing for libel or hauling the scrivener before him for contempt of court. It is inconceivable to suppose that Lord Hewart or Lord Goddard could have sat on their Bench with supine inattention while the greatest contemporary poet in England was publicising this lampoon:

Gehazi

Whence comest thou, Gehazi,
So reverend to behold,
In scarlet and in ermines
And chain of England's gold?
'From following after Naaman
To tell him all is well,
Whereby my zeal hath made me
A Judge in Israel.'

Well done, well done, Gehazi!
Stretch forth thy ready hand.
Thou barely 'scaped from judgment,
Take oath to judge the land
Unswayed by gift of money
Or privy bribe, more base,
Of knowledge which is profit
In any market-place.

Search out and probe, Gehazi,
As thou of all canst try,
The truthful, well-weighed answer
That tells the blacker lie—

The loud, uneasy virtue,
The anger feigned at will,
To overbear a witness
And make the Court keep still.

Thou mirror of uprightness,
What ails thee at thy vows?
What means the risen whiteness
Of the skin between thy brows?
The boils that shine and burrow,
The sores that slough and bleed—
The leprosy of Naaman
On thee and all thy seed?
Stand up, stand up, Gehazi,
Draw close thy robe and go,
Gehazi, Judge in Israel,
A leper white as snow.

It has been said of Lloyd George that 'at his best he could charm a bird out of a tree'. We do not know what guiles Lloyd George may have practised upon Derby but they were plainly effective. Only six weeks later Derby had changed his view:

Lord Derby to Mr. Lloyd George[1]

Confidential — Knowsley
12 November 1916

My dear S. of S.,
. . . Now about Robertson. He has I am sure still got an idea that his being sent to Russia means his being removed. Very ridiculous as I have told him—and shall continue to tell him. I am certain he will not consent to go unless Joffre goes—and I think if the latter does not go it would not be good policy to force Robertson. I had a talk to Macready[2] on the subject and suggested to him if you spoke to him on the subject to propose that Kiggell[3] should go in his place—but Robertson will have

[1] Lloyd George Papers.
[2] Lt.-Gen. Sir Nevil Macready, Adjutant-General, 1916–18.
[3] Lt.-Gen. Sir Launcelot Kiggell, Chief of the General Staff in France, 1915–18. He died in February 1954, aged 92.

to understand that if Grey and Kiggell go with planning powers, he, Robertson, will have to accept whatever decisions they may come to . . .

Early in October Derby had paid a visit to the British Army in France as the guest of the Commander-in-Chief.

Sir Douglas Haig to Lord Derby

13 October 1916 General Headquarters,
British Armies in France

Many thanks for writing.

I am very sorry indeed to hear that you had to lay up with the cold and I feel I ought to have insisted on your remaining here till you were better.

It was a bad mistake to send French out here for few of us have forgotten that he told *lies* in his Despatches etc. etc. but I have written Wully [Robertson] to tell him that he may count on my most thorough support in his efforts to help the country to win.

You must stop him from quarrelling with L.G. because the country's business is certain to suffer whenever there is friction.

Come back again whenever you can, and hoping soon to hear that you are quite fit again.

XI

The Fall of Mr. Asquith

As the year came to a close, discontent with the progress of the war and criticism of its conduct by the Government became increasingly clamant. The War Committee of the Government consisted at this time of seven members—Asquith, Prime Minister; Lloyd George, Secretary of State for War; Bonar Law, Secretary of State for the Colonies; Balfour, First Lord of the Admiralty; McKenna, Chancellor of the Exchequer; Lord Curzon, Lord Privy Seal; and Edwin Montagu, Minister of Munitions. Lloyd George had for some time been urging that a more vigorous prosecution of the war required a smaller body, all of whose members should be free from departmental duties. On December 1 he put forward his demand in clear-cut terms in a memorandum to the Prime Minister. In particular he asked that the War Committee should consist of three persons, two of whom should be the First Lord of the Admiralty and the Secretary of State for War. These two ministers were to have deputies who would relieve them of all departmental work. One of the three was to be chairman; the Prime Minister was not to belong to the Committee but merely to have the power to refer any decision of the War Committee to a meeting of the whole Cabinet.

Unfortunately Derby was not keeping his diary at this time and he seems to have written few letters. Consequently we cannot tell at what precise moment he was drawn into Lloyd George's plan for reshaping the War Committee. In his *War Memoirs* Lloyd George, after quoting the memorandum summarised above and stating that it was drawn up after conferring with Bonar Law, Carson and Aitken, added, 'I showed it to Lord Derby who fully approved of its terms'. Asquith in principle accepted Lloyd George's proposals but insisted that the Prime Minister must be chairman of the Committee and that it would be impossible to relegate him 'to the position of an arbiter in the background or a referee to the Cabinet'.

This was on the Friday. On the Sunday afternoon Bonar Law saw Asquith and told him of the outcome of a conclave of Tory Ministers at his house that morning. These Ministers, who included Curzon, Austen Chamberlain, Lord Robert Cecil and Walter Long, had been outraged by an article which had appeared in that day's issue of *Reynolds News*, which put Lloyd George's demands in detail and indicated that if he did not get his way he would resign and would campaign actively in the country in furtherance of his views. The article in *Reynolds* also stated that Bonar Law would probably resign with Lloyd George, that Derby was inclined that way and that Lloyd George also had the support of Carson. The Tory Ministers assumed that Lloyd George had inspired this article and were naturally indignant at such tactics.

That the newspapers had been well informed is shown by a letter written by Curzon to Lansdowne on the Sunday: '... Lloyd George, as the papers of yesterday and today will have shown you, has attempted to force the situation by announcing his own resignation, which is apparently to appear in the Press tomorrow. Derby is to resign with him, and Bonar Law has been so far implicated that his name appears with theirs in the papers, and he told us he meant to resign this afternoon.'[1]

The same Sunday Derby drafted in his own handwriting a letter to Haig. It is not clear whether the letter was completed and sent but the uncompleted draft shows what his view was on this critical day: '. . . *Pour-parlers* are still going on but unless he gets what he wants Ll. G. is going and I shall certainly go with him. We can't go on as we are. We shall be short of men next spring and yet there are plenty of men to be got but every day's delay will make it more difficult.'

The Tory Ministers at their Sunday morning meeting agreed upon the following resolution:

[1] Lord Curzon expressed himself with less than his usual clarity. He obviously must have meant to write: '. . . he told us this afternoon he meant to resign'.

We share the view expressed to you by Mr. Bonar Law some time ago that the Government cannot continue as it is.

It is evident that a change must be made, and, in our opinion, the publicity given to the intention of Mr. Lloyd George makes reconstruction from within no longer possible.

We therefore urge the Prime Minister to tender the resignation of the Government.

If he feels unable to take that step, we authorise Mr. Bonar Law to tender our resignations.

The intention of all the Tory Ministers, save Bonar Law, was to strengthen Asquith's hand against Lloyd George, but the resolution was of an ambiguous character. When a few hours later Bonar Law saw Asquith he did not read him the terms of the resolution and Asquith formed the view that his Tory colleagues were all as hostile to him on this issue as was Bonar Law, and wished to drive him from office. Both Lord Beaverbrook, who knew Bonar Law better than anyone else, and Mr. Robert Blake, the latter's biographer, repudiate the idea that Bonar Law would deliberately have deceived Asquith in this matter. Be this as it may, Asquith, either through a faulty explanation on the part of Bonar Law or through his own failure to comprehend what Bonar Law was telling him, was utterly misled; and an hour later when he received Lloyd George he conceded practically all that Lloyd George was asking for. The only matter which was not determined when they parted concerned the personnel of the committee. Late that night Edwin Montagu, with whom Asquith had dinner and who had a foot in both the Asquith and the Lloyd George camps, persuaded Asquith to issue a statement that: 'The Prime Minister, with a view to the most active prosecution of the war, has decided to advise His Majesty the King to consent to a reconstruction of the Government.' This amounted to a public recognition that the political crisis which had been agitated by the Press for the previous three days had been settled and that Lloyd George and Asquith were now in agreement.

Asquith wrote to a correspondent on the Sunday night: 'The "crisis" shows every sign of following its many predecessors to an early and unhonoured grave.' It was in fact about to reach its climax. For on the Monday the situation was to be transmogrified by three events. Of the Liberal ministers only Montagu, Crewe and Reading were informed about the plot which had been contrived by Lloyd George, Bonar Law, Carson and Aitken. It was not till the Monday morning when important Liberal ministers such as Grey, McKenna, Runciman and Harcourt read in the papers that the Ministry in which they served was about to be reconstructed that they suspected what was afoot. They immediately called on Asquith at Downing Street and when they learnt the terms which Lloyd George had extorted from him they were outraged. They thought it inconceivable that Lloyd George could form a Government commanding a majority in the House of Commons without the support of themselves and Asquith; and they strongly urged Asquith to repudiate his agreement with Lloyd George and to extrude him from the Government.

Shortly afterwards, Curzon and Robert Cecil called upon Asquith and made plain to him that their resolution of the day before was intended as a weapon which might destroy not him but Lloyd George by putting the latter in a position, through the resignation of Asquith, where it would be revealed that he was incapable of forming an alternative Government.

The precise reaction of Asquith to these views is still a matter of dispute but it seems clear that he must have been influenced by what his important Liberal colleagues told him. Accordingly, when Montagu came to see him a little later as an emissary of Lloyd George and suggested that the agreement reached the afternoon before should be ratified in writing, he failed to procure the Prime Minister's compliance.

The third event was not only important in itself; it afforded a handy device for the Prime Minister to rupture his agreement with Lloyd George. *The Times* of Monday, December 4, carried a leading article in which Lloyd George's proposals for a small war council were described with accuracy. Asquith had been told by Montagu that on the previous day he had seen Northcliffe in Lloyd George's ante-room at the War Office and Asquith naturally concluded that Lloyd George had inspired *The Times* leader and provided the information on which it was based. Mr. Blake in *The Unknown Prime Minister* makes considerable play with the fact that this was not the channel used, and that the information published was furnished to the editor, Mr. Geoffrey Dawson, by Carson. But all the extremely accurate information which was leaked to the Press and which appeared in the Aitken-controlled *Daily Express* and in the *Daily Chronicle* on the Saturday, in Sir Henry Dalziel's *Reynolds News* on the Sunday and in *The Times* on Monday could only have derived in the first instance from Lloyd George, since only he and Asquith were privy to the conversations and correspondence which had passed. In any event *The Times* revealed no more than had been in *Reynolds News* the day before, but in those days, as now, a statement of fact in *The Times* commanded wider attention in political circles than one in *Reynolds*. It matters not whose political lips whispered into whose journalistic ears or what the precise channels were which first leaked and then flooded to the Press; it was neither Asquith's habit nor interest to make known the threats to which he was being subjected and to which at one time he had bowed. Whether Aitken and Carson were authorised by Lloyd George to ventilate the matter in print is neither here nor there since neither of them could have supplied the information if it had not first been made available to them by Lloyd George; and of course we can see that the Press campaign was a necessary part of the plan of action which started out with the limited intention of making Lloyd George Chairman of the War Committee but which, owing to Asquith's mistaken judgment of the forces at work, ended in Lloyd George's arrival at 10 Downing Street.

Sir Max Aitken, who had a greater flair for Press manipulation than Lloyd George, Bonar Law and Carson combined, was in daily, often hourly, contact with Lloyd George. The latter may not have wished to know the exact details of how the Press campaign was being organised but he must have been a much less percipient man than one has supposed if he had not realised where the Press was getting its information. And if he had thought that it was harmful to his interests he would have had no difficulty in controlling it.

Aitken's role in the destruction of the Asquith Government was not, however, confined to the sphere of public relations. He was the indispensable catalyst who wrought changes in the conduct and actions of other public men and in their relationships with each other without which the conspiracy would have 'lost the name of action'. He was indeed the key figure in the whole of this conspiracy against Asquith. Lloyd George could never have effectively voiced his demands, valid though they were for the efficient conduct of the war, unless he had had the support of Carson and above all of Bonar Law. It was Aitken who had succeeded in bringing the three men together and in procuring their agreement in a course of action which resulted, whatever its intention, in destroying the Government. For a man of thirty-seven, who had been born in Canada and who had only lived in England for six or seven years, this was indeed an unique political coup.

Mr. Blake, in a curious passage, argues that Asquith was not the sort of man to take an important political action merely on the basis of a newspaper article and that he only used *The Times* article as an excuse. Mr. Blake writes:

> Asquith had already gone a very long way towards committing himself to Lloyd George, and it was not easy to find a good excuse to break off negotiations. Now it was precisely this excuse which *The Times* article provided. The Unionists had condemned Lloyd George for trafficking with the press. It was too late to use the article in *Reynolds News*, for Asquith had already, as it were, condoned that but *The Times* article seemed another striking example of Lloyd George's alleged press intrigues. Doubtless Asquith genuinely believed that Lloyd George had inspired *The Times* leader. 'Nonetheless,' as Beaverbrook writes, 'it wrongs Asquith to suppose him capable of changing his whole policy at the crucial moment of his life because of a leading article in a newspaper. Such a theory denies him the qualities of clarity of intellect, of a sense of relative proportion, even of personal dignity, which friend and foe alike have allowed him.' In other words, *The Times* article may well have been an excellent excuse for action which Asquith desired to take on other grounds.

Both Mr. Blake and Lord Beaverbrook seem to have overlooked an important factor which must have been operative in Asquith's mind. It is doubtless true that the assurances he received from his Liberal colleagues and the explanations he received from his Tory colleagues on the Monday morning may have emboldened him to tear up his agreement with Lloyd George of the day before. But it cannot be accepted that the publicity in the Press was a mere excuse on Asquith's part. How could he have with any sense of dignity carried out the necessary reforms in his administration when it had been openly proclaimed that he was acting under threats? He could perhaps have shrugged off the stories in the *Daily Express*, *Daily Chronicle* and *Reynolds News*. But when these were all confirmed in the august columns of *The Times*, the only newspaper which he himself read and to which he believed that Lloyd George had leaked directly, his position may well have seemed to him intolerable. To have carried through the arrangements arrived at on the Sunday afternoon would now be to admit to the world that Lloyd George and not Asquith was the master of the Government. Asquith's change of strategy on the Monday was clearly due to the more accurate appreciation he had now received of the political line-up. In this sense *The Times* article was, as suggested above, a handy device to break off the parleys now that the enemy seemed to be weakened. But who could doubt that even Asquith's Roman phlegm and fortitude must have been penetrated by a sense of outrage that a colleague should behave so dishonourably? And, whether or not he himself had time to look so far ahead in these crucial moments, who can suppose that Asquith would not have been reduced in a very few weeks to a state of public *chaperonage* if he had stood by Sunday's bargain in the light of Monday's Press?

The reader must assess these circumstances and arguments for himself since Asquith never publicly revealed which factors were dominant in his mind, and the accounts given by his biographers are in many respects unsatisfactory. Be this as it may Asquith decided on the Monday morning to fight it out:

Mr. Asquith to Mr. Lloyd George

Such productions as the first leading article in today's *Times*, showing the infinite possibilities for misunderstanding and misrepresentation of such an arrangement as we considered yesterday, make me at least doubtful as to its feasibility. Unless the impression is at once corrected that I am being relegated to the position of an irresponsible spectator of the war, I cannot possibly go on.

The suggested arrangement was to the following effect: The Prime Minister to have supreme and effective control of war policy.

The agenda of the War Committee will be submitted to him; its chairman will report to him daily; he can direct it to consider particular topics or proposals; and all its conclusions will be subject to his approval or veto. He can, of course, at his own discretion attend meetings of the Committee.

All day Lloyd George sought to make contact with Asquith, but the latter successfully evaded these approaches. It must have been very hard for Lloyd George to assess where the balance of power lay at this moment and he temporised by writing a letter of a conciliatory tone:

Mr. Lloyd George to the Prime Minister

4 December 1916 War Office

MY DEAR PRIME MINISTER,

I have not seen *The Times* article. But I hope you will not attach undue importance to these effusions. I have had these misrepresentations to put up with for months. Northcliffe frankly wants a smash. Derby and I do not. Northcliffe would like to make this and any other rearrangement under your Premiership impossible. Derby and I attach great importance to your retaining your present position—effectively. I cannot restrain or, I fear, influence Northcliffe. I fully accept in letter and in spirit your summary of the suggested arrangement—subject, of course, to personnel.

Ever sincerely,
D. LLOYD GEORGE

Lord Beaverbrook in his *Politicians and the War* comments on Derby's position at this time:

Derby's name was introduced into the letter with his consent and approval. Lloyd George's intention was no doubt to make a display of Conservative support which might be useful, particularly as practically all the other potentates of that party were ranged on the side of Asquith.

Bonar Law had at one time considered inviting Derby to the Sunday meeting of Tory Ministers at his house so that he would have at least one ally. Derby's standing in the Party would fully have warranted his attendance but since, as a junior minister, he lacked the technical status of the other ministers it was in the end thought wiser for him not to come. However, as we have seen, Lloyd George took an early opportunity of letting Asquith see that he had some Tory support, and that inside the War Office, for the reforms for which he was pressing.

Late on the Monday Asquith wrote once more to Lloyd George and this time he banged the door on any possible accommodation. He not only insisted on even sharper definition of the Prime Minister's powers over the new War Committee but also that the choice of personnel was his and his alone. Lloyd George did not receive this letter till the Tuesday morning, and when he did he instantly thought that resignation was his only weapon. In the course of a long and highly propagandist letter, plainly intended for publication, he wrote: 'As all delay is fatal in war, I place my office without further parley at your disposal.'

* * *

There is no doubt that Derby was fully involved with Lloyd George. He had called on Stamfordham on the Monday, and in the Royal Archives there is a memorandum of the crisis recorded by Lord Errington which states that on the Monday 'Lord Derby whom Lord Stamfordham also saw had apparently succumbed to Mr. Lloyd George's influence'. However, Derby was most anxious that the Prime Minister, for whom he entertained the highest personal regard, should not think he was party to an intrigue and the same day he wrote to him in this sense:

Lord Derby to the Prime Minister

Confidential — War Office

4 December 1916

A certain portion of the Press has given undue prominence to my views in the present crisis. It is quite true that I have been in Lloyd George's confidence and have entirely agreed with the representations he has made to you, but there is nothing I should dislike more than that you should think that my action was due in any way to disloyalty to yourself personally. You have always shown me the greatest kindness and consideration which I should ill requite by any intrigue against yourself. My sole object is to endeavour to get that administration which is most likely to secure prompt decision and take effective action for the conduct of this war, and you may rest assured that either in Office or out of Office I should always support those men and those measures which are most likely to conduce to this end.

I am glad to think that the whole trouble seems likely to be satisfactorily solved in a manner which will enable Lloyd George and those who, like myself, are in agreement with him to act in hearty co-operation with yourself.

Moreover on the decisive day of the crisis, Tuesday, December 5, Derby, Lloyd George, Bonar Law and Carson had breakfast at Derby House, and over the breakfast table there was a lively discussion as to what action should be taken. From Derby House Lloyd George drove to the War Office. It was on his arrival there that he found the letter which Asquith had written the night before and which prompted his letter of resignation. Derby also felt that Asquith's overnight letter had altered the situation and that he was bound to follow Lloyd George's lead:

Lord Derby to the Prime Minister

War Office

My dear Prime Minister,

Lloyd George has shown me a copy of his letter to you tendering his resignation. Whilst he has naturally had more opportunity than I have of judging the effects of the Cabinet's indecision, my own experience during the last few months has made very apparent to me the perilous state which such indecision has had on the conduct of the war—notably in the provision of an adequate number of men for the Army.

I feel therefore it is quite impossible for me not to associate myself with Ll. George and would ask you to accept my resignation at the same time as his.

I take this course with sincere regret. Firstly because I hold an Office to which I am much attached and secondly because I am very reluctant to add in any way to your difficulties having regard to the great kindness and consideration which you personally have always shown me.

While all this letter writing was in process at the War Office, Mr. Geoffrey Dawson, Editor of *The Times*, arrived by appointment to see Derby at 12.30. In the *History of The Times*, Vol. IV, Part 1, is recorded Dawson's account of his visit:

Next day the Editor was due to keep an appointment with Derby at the War Office. He duly arrived at 12.30 on the morning of the 5th [December].

'I was surprised' [reads Dawson's contemporary note] 'to find him in a thoroughly flabby state of mind. After committing himself during the last day or two to thoroughgoing support of Lloyd George, and if necessary to resignation with him, he was now full of every kind of qualification. He thought Asquith the one and only mouthpiece of the nation, had great doubts about the value of Bonar Law, told me mysteriously that Jellicoe would not on any account part with A. J. B. at the Admiralty, was nervously anxious lest L. G. should be over-"boomed", or his own position emphasised.'

The Editor was so impressed with Derby's condition of hopelessness that he asked to see Lloyd George, who had just announced his arrival in the office. Ten minutes later they met. Dawson writes in his note that 'I found him "pale, but determined", very much in earnest and quite clear about his own course. He told me that Asquith, who had agreed in principle to all his proposals on Sunday had this morning gone back, not merely on the details, but on the whole principle of the thing. That being so, he had no alternative but to back his opinion by resignation, and when I came in he was actually finishing a letter to this effect—a very good one, which he allowed me to read before sending it over to Downing Street by hand.

Derby had stood staunchly by the arrangements which he had made with Lloyd George. He had allowed his name to be used in Lloyd George's correspondence with the Prime Minister and he had himself proffered his own resignation. Once these letters had been dispatched events rolled inexorably forward. Derby all his life hated seeing things carried to extremes and it appears that on reflection he still felt that some settlement could be reached between Asquith and Lloyd George, for Lord Beaverbrook has recorded in his *Politicians and the War*:

> Lord Derby had made one last effort to avert the crash. He had visited the Prime Minister and implored him not to resign, but rather to come to an accommodation with Lloyd George. Asquith declined to enter into any argument. His mind, he said, was made up, and the motor which was to take him to Buckingham Palace with his resignation waited at the door.

* * *

After Asquith resigned, the King first called upon Bonar Law to form a Government, but when Bonar Law found that Asquith was not prepared to serve under him he remitted his commission to the King, who thereupon entrusted it to Lloyd George. It was not immediately certain whether Lloyd George could rally sufficient support but after Bonar Law had visited Balfour and had, on Lloyd George's behalf, procured his acceptance of the Foreign Office, everything and everybody fell into place quite easily.

One matter remains unresolved. Lloyd George had told Asquith some days before, during the negotiations about the reconstitution of the War Committee, that it would be necessary for Balfour to leave the Admiralty. Balfour knew this and on December 5 had written to Asquith resigning the Admiralty on the grounds that he would be an obstacle to the formation of the new War Committee. He adhered to this decision despite a letter from Asquith conjuring him to remain in his office.

Why should Balfour, who knew that Lloyd George wished to have him dismissed from the Admiralty, have been the first Tory Minister to accept office in the new Lloyd George Government?

And why should Lloyd George have supposed that Balfour would come along so readily? The answers to these questions are still to seek. Lloyd George had no personal hostility to Balfour but in the original plan which he had proposed to Asquith he had to find a place in the new War Committee for Carson, to whom he was deeply beholden. He meant to be the chairman and Bonar Law had to be included. It seemed very difficult to exclude the office of the First Lord from the Committee. It followed that Balfour must leave the Admiralty to make way for Carson.

In the light of Balfour's suave acceptance of the Foreign Office on the Wednesday from the man who he knew was seeking to expel him on the Monday, who can doubt that some prior arrangement had been reached? We cannot tell. But everything we know about the character of Balfour would disincline us to believe that, despite his indisposition, which might well have been of a diplomatic character, he was not informed from hour to hour about the complicated political manœuvres and transactions which were afoot. Everyone must judge for himself.

When Asquith heard of Balfour's adhesion to Lloyd George he was, on the basis of his information, rightly astounded. Lloyd George had the support of Bonar Law, Carson and Balfour. Asquith must have known his Curzon well enough to be sure that he would be padding hot foot in their tracks, and that all his other Tory colleagues would now find no difficulty in abandoning him and mounting the shiny and vigorously propelled political band-wagon which was rolling into Downing Street.

Asquith was not pulled down and Lloyd George set up without a good deal of rough work, as these pages have shown. Derby was always sensitive about such matters and speaking to the Aldwych Club on Thursday, December 7, the day after Lloyd George had taken office and as the Lloyd George Government was in the process of being formed, said:

> . . . I entered the Government in a subordinate position some months ago. I went to the War Office, an office with which I had previously been connected, with which for many months prior to that time I had been in intimate relation, and an office in which I have spent a very

happy time. I had hoped that by going there I could have kept myself free from politics, and have been of some service in the only office in which I could feel I could be of any use. I now find myself involved, certainly without my own seeking, in a political crisis, when all sorts of accusations are bandied about as to intrigues and disloyalty. I hope you will believe me when I say that I never will be disloyal and I never will enter into an intrigue. I know of no intrigue and, you may rest assured, I would not have been in one if I had known of it . . .[1]

In the Derby papers there is an undated document headed 'An Appreciation of the Political Situation' by Wedgwood. It is clear that this document was the work of Mr. Josiah Clement Wedgwood who represented Newcastle-under-Lyme first as Liberal and later as Labour Member from 1906 to 1942. The first and last paragraphs are worthy of quotation:

Whether Mr. Bonar Law, or Mr. Lloyd George, or Lord Derby are entrusted with the formation of the Ministry, it may now be taken for granted that the following will not join them (out of a feeling of loyalty to Mr. Asquith)—Grey, McKenna, Runciman, Harcourt, Crewe, Tennant, Buckmaster, Pease . . .

On account of the idea that Mr. Lloyd George has intrigued, and that Mr. Bonar Law represents the Conservative Party machine I would strongly urge that Lord Derby form the administration.

In the new administration Derby succeeded Lloyd George as Secretary of State for War. He had not played a leading role in the manœuvres which had brought about the change of Government, but his support of Lloyd George had been a substantial factor in bringing matters to a head. Lloyd George's fierce ambitions required at this time the ballast of Derby's prestige which was certainly a potent if imponderable element in the solution of the crisis. We have seen that to be Secretary of State for War was a genuine ambition of his, and no one was surprised at his appointment either on grounds of merit or on grounds of the services he had, partly unconsciously, rendered to Lloyd George in the political crisis. Indeed if he had been a more ambitious man it is not impossible that he could have fulfilled Wedgwood's expectations.

[1] *Daily Telegraph*, 8 December 1916.

XII

Secretary of State for War

LLOYD GEORGE accepted the King's Commission on December 7. Three days later he had formed his Government. Since Chatham, no British War Minister had had the power which was now vested in Lloyd George's hands. The new Prime Minister sensibly abandoned the plan he had been urging on Asquith of a small War Committee of three, operating under the final arbitrament of the Prime Minister and the Cabinet, and set up instead a War Cabinet of five whose decisions were to be mandatory over the whole administration. There had been twenty-one ministers in Asquith's Cabinet, the largest number in this century. Lloyd George replaced it with the smallest Cabinet which Britain has ever had since the system of Cabinet Government was established by Sir Robert Walpole in the early part of the eighteenth century. The War Cabinet consisted of Lloyd George, Prime Minister; Bonar Law, Leader of the House of Commons; Curzon, Lord President of the Council and Leader of the House of Lords; and Milner and Arthur Henderson, without Portfolio.

Except for Lloyd George, this was not, on paper, a particularly impressive quintet. Milner was a man of exceptional ability and enjoyed a preternatural prestige in the limited but active circles which found their inspiration in Printing House Square and the Cliveden and Round Table sets, but politically he mounted very few guns. Lloyd George had originally intended that Carson should be in the War Cabinet without Portfolio and that Milner should go to the Admiralty. There was no doubt that Carson's gifts were far more suited to the War Cabinet than to an administrative role like the Admiralty. Lloyd George, against his better judgment, switched

Derby with King George V at a war-time military inspection in Hyde Park.

Derby with the Prime Minister, Mr. David Lloyd George, on a visit to the Liverpool Docks.

the two men at the last moment as a result of hostility expressed by Carson's Conservative colleagues.

Curzon was included as a representative of the more old-fashioned section of the Tory Party which had been distressed by the intrigues of Aitken and Bonar Law. The unity of the Tory Party required a placation of these magnificoes. Curzon's political guns were of the largest calibre but, as he was subsequently to discover, they were mounted on a foundation of cardboard.

Arthur Henderson, as Paymaster-General with a seat in the Cabinet, had already been advising the Asquith Government on labour relations. Lloyd George, by bringing him right into the centre of the management of the war, greatly broadened the national base of his administration and insured himself against many potential troubles in industry.

Derby was present in Lloyd George's room when Lloyd George received not only the Parliamentary leaders of the Labour Party but also the representatives of the trade union movement. Doubtless Lloyd George realised what a useful and significant talisman Derby was with the trade union leaders. Among the trade unionists present at this meeting was Mr. Ernest Bevin, at that time a little-known adjutant of Mr. Ben Tillett, the leader of the Dock, Wharf, Riverside and General Workers Union. Bevin was opposed to Labour joining the new Government. However a deputation of Parliamentary and trade union leaders subsequently authorised Henderson to join the War Cabinet. Those who care for the continuity of English public life will reflect with satisfaction that nearly a quarter of a century later when England was in even greater jeopardy the same Ernest Bevin, who had by then become the most powerful trade union leader in the land, was brought into the War Cabinet of Winston Churchill by an equally imaginative gesture.

Bonar Law was a member of the War Cabinet, but his duties at the Treasury and the House of Commons made daily attendance impossible. Nevertheless he attended at all important occasions and, as leader of the Conservative Party, which was the largest party in the House of Commons and which, unlike the Liberal Party, was not split, he was without question, next to Lloyd George, the most powerful member of the Government.

Aitken, who had been promised the Board of Trade, was, like Carson, the victim of Tory hostility. He, to his lasting chagrin, was fobbed off with a peerage and under letters patent of 2 January 1917, became Baron Beaverbrook of Beaverbrook, in the Province of New Brunswick, in the Dominion of Canada and of Cherkley, Surrey. This was a spectacular advancement for an almost unknown Canadian at the age of thirty-seven, but considering the part he had played in the crisis it was a trumpery recompense. And even this he was not to receive without opposition from the Palace and from Derby. Derby had long held the view which, with a few exceptions, he successfully sustained throughout his life, that all patronage in Lancashire should pass through his hands and he complained that so junior a Lancashire Member of Parliament should be elevated to the peerage ahead of other party stalwarts of far longer standing. He probably was unaware of the unique and even transcendental services which Aitken had rendered to Lloyd George behind the scenes. At one moment Derby's intervention led to the offer of the peerage being withdrawn, but when it was found that a safe seat was needed for Sir Albert Stanley, who was appointed President of the Board of Trade instead of Beaverbrook, both Derby and the Palace were overborne and Aitken had to go upstairs. Derby's reward was the War Office, which, as we have seen in his letter to his brother-in-law, Lord Charles Montagu (see p. 212), was the one office he 'had ever really wanted'. Among those who wrote to congratulate Derby on his appointment was the Commander-in-Chief:

Sir Douglas Haig to Lord Derby

Personal
10 December 1916

General Headquarters,
British Armies in France

Very many thanks for writing. I reply at once to congratulate you with all my heart on your appointment as S. of S. and I also congratulate the Army and the Country on having *you* there at this time of crisis.

As you know I'll do my utmost to play up and help you in any way I can. Come over and stay whenever you can. I trust that you feel that *everyone* welcomes you in this Army whenever you come among us.

As regards our needs: '*men*', as you know, is causing us anxiety. Time is passing so quickly that I feel, unless someone ruthless and relentless is appointed to drag them away from Departs. etc. *at once* we shall find ourselves short in July!

I do sincerely trust there is no idea of sending more troops to Salonika. Sound strategy really indicates that that theatre should be reduced to a minimum and every Division and gun be brought to France for the coming summer.

We can employ every British and French Division in France with decisive results. Hoping to see you soon.

* * *

Lloyd George now had the power; he had fashioned in his small War Cabinet the war-winning instrument and he also had a fairly clear view of what he wished to do. Nonetheless, he found himself to a large extent the prisoner of previous commitments. A month before he became Prime Minister he had attended a meeting in Paris of Allied statesmen and generals. He had pressed for a united Allied strategy which would control action on all fronts and in particular would make available British and French reinforcements to the Italians so that an early and effective blow could be struck against Austria. With his necessarily limited authority he had not been able to make his view prevail. Contrary to his wishes, the generals had met in military conclave at Chantilly and had, before the statesmen had had a chance to meet and impose a general directive upon them, reached their own conclusions. Joffre and Haig had agreed to a joint Allied offensive on the Somme for the first half of February. The soldiers had also agreed to the principle of setting up some form of joint Anglo-French-Italian military supervising staff. Simultaneously the British, French and Italian Prime Ministers had agreed that there should be regular meetings of the three Allied Prime Ministers to plan the conduct of the war on a united basis. These were solid gains for Lloyd George and as soon as he became Prime Minister he sought to exploit them.

The first meeting of the Allied Prime Ministers took place in Rome early in January 1917. At this conference Lloyd George urged reinforcements for the Italian front, notably with three or four hundred heavy guns. The British and French military representatives opposed this suggested diversion from the Western front and the Italians evinced no marked enthusiasm for these reinforcements which would involve them in an offensive which they judged to be inopportune. Thwarted in his plan to animate and activate the Italian front and realising that he was compelled to fight in France or not at all, Lloyd George left Rome on the look-out for some method of procuring a unified direction of the war at least in the West.

On his way back to London his train halted at the Gare du Nord and the newly appointed French Commander-in-Chief, General Nivelle, who had replaced General Joffre a few days before, was brought to see him. This remarkable and gifted man, who had an English mother and the consequent advantage of speaking fluent English, made an instantaneous impression upon the British Prime Minister. Lloyd George was to prove tireless in seeking to procure unity of command and was to coin the aphorism 'it is not that one general is better than another, but that one general is better than two'. There is no doubt also that Lloyd George and some other leading English statesmen thought that the French school of generalship was superior to the British. In addition Lloyd George wished to stop the senseless carnage resulting from prolonged offensives and thought that this would be easier if all the armies were under a single command.

Nivelle captivated Lloyd George with his idea of a spectacularly rapid offensive which, if it did not procure a break-through, could be easily called off instead of getting bogged down, like the battles on the Somme, in almost endless slaughter. The details of Nivelle's new plan, which involved the French Army making the main assault while the British would only be committed to an earlier but limited diversionary thrust, had already been communicated to the War Cabinet; and Lloyd George, resilient as always, decided to throw himself wholeheartedly behind the project.

Nivelle was invited to London and brought before the War

Cabinet, on whom his magnetic charm worked almost as effectively as it had on the Prime Minister in the Gare du Nord. On January 15 in London, Haig, Robertson and Nivelle all signed a memorandum committing the British and French Armies to a co-ordinated attack which was to be unleashed not later than April 1. Thus the Nivelle Plan involved a two months' postponement in the original plan as drawn up by General Joffre. The British generals would probably not have agreed so easily to the new arrangement if they had known that Lloyd George was already resolving plans which he had even communicated to Nivelle, for placing the British Army under French command for the new offensive.

These plans were discussed by the Cabinet on February 24. Although they directly concerned both the War Office and the Army, Derby was not invited to be present; and Robertson was specifically told that there was no need for him to attend. In these circumstances Lloyd George procured the Cabinet's assent for Haig and the British Army to be placed under the operational control of Nivelle in the forthcoming offensive. Two days later Lloyd George, accompanied by Robertson, set out for Calais where they were to meet Haig and to confer with Briand, the French Prime Minister, General Lyautey, Minister of War, and General Nivelle. Ostensibly the purpose of the Conference was to discuss the transportation problems of the Allied Armies and, though Lloyd George had a long conversation on the journey over with Robertson, he did not take the opportunity to divulge to him the true purpose of their mission.

When the statesmen and generals assembled they quickly and even perfunctorily disposed of the nominal occasion for their meeting. According to Robertson the Prime Minister then proceeded to make some observations about the impending battle and asked General Nivelle 'whether anything further could be done to render British co-operation more effective'. Nivelle promptly produced a detailed, written plan for an Allied G.H.Q. in France, with a French Generalissimo and a British Chief of Staff, to which headquarters the Allied Armies of the Western Front were thenceforward to be subordinated. A British Commander-in-Chief was to be retained but he was to have no operational function. Lloyd George immediately gave the plan his blessing, subject only to details which could be worked out later. Haig and Robertson had been placed by their Prime Minister in a most odious position.

British officers and civil servants do not like to challenge the opinions of their political chiefs in front of foreigners. And it is seldom that they are deliberately placed in a position where they must do so or acquiesce in proposals with which they utterly disagree. Lloyd George had behind the backs of Derby and Robertson talked the Cabinet into going half-way along the road which he wished to travel to a unified command. Now by confronting Haig and Robertson in open council with our French Allies with what seemed a cut-and-dried plan he doubtless hoped to take advantage of a soldierly reluctance to oppose their own Prime Minister. Thereafter he would have had little difficulty in gaining the approval of the Cabinet for a *fait accompli* which would have gone far beyond what they had authorised, but which bore the imprimatur of the French civil and military leaders and of Haig and Robertson themselves. Haig and Robertson, however, though they avoided a wordy altercation with the Prime Minister in front of the French leaders, registered their protests and the Conference then broke up so that the two delegations could confer among themselves. It was only then for the first time that Lloyd George informed Robertson of the decision he had obtained from the Cabinet two days before. Confronted with the decision of the War Cabinet, Haig and Robertson could do no more than insist on Nivelle's plan being reduced from a permanent conception to the limited plan authorised by the Cabinet.

Out-manœuvred by Lloyd George and led by him into an ambush with their allies, they felt constrained the next day to put their initials to a revised document which gave Nivelle full powers of command for the April battle.

* * *

The decisions of the Calais Conference, and still more the subterfuges and stratagems by which they had been brought about, enraged both Derby and the soldiers:

Sir William Robertson to Sir Douglas Haig

28 February 1917

His [Lloyd George's] story at the War Cabinet this morning gave quite a wrong impression. He accused the French of putting forward a monstrous proposal, and yet you and I know that he was at the bottom of it. I believe he equally misled the Cabinet last Saturday. Derby is telling Balfour the whole truth. The former talked of resigning last night. He was furious and disgusted. He spoke up like a man for you this morning and insisted on a letter of confidence and explanation being sent to you. This will come in a day or two. Meanwhile I pray you and Nivelle may hit it off. These things always happen in war. But they are worse now than ever. Still I can't believe that a man such as he can remain for long head of any government. Surely some honesty and truth are required.

Derby thought it essential that the British Commander-in-Chief should be assured that he had not forfeited the confidence of the British Government. Accordingly he persuaded the Cabinet on February 28 to draw up a memorandum outlining their views on the situation obtaining after the Calais Conference. This he was authorised to forward to Haig with a formal letter:

Lord Derby to Sir Douglas Haig

Secret

War Office
2 March 1917

I have great pleasure in forwarding to you the following extract from the War Cabinet Minutes of a Meeting held on 28th ultimo:

13. The War Cabinet decided that:

'The Secretary of State for War should inform Field-Marshal Sir Douglas Haig that the arrangement made at the Calais Conference of the 27th instant regarding the relations to exist between him and General Nivelle during the forthcoming operations had for its object merely the securing of a clearly defined unity of control, and one which the French Government understood and definitely accepted.

'It was in no sense an aspersion on the ability and qualifications of Sir Douglas Haig, in whom the War Cabinet continue to entertain full confidence.'

I desire to add on behalf of myself and my colleagues on the Army Council that you may continue to rely with the utmost confidence on our whole-hearted and unswerving support in the execution of the great and responsible task which has been entrusted to you.

Sir Douglas Haig to Lord Derby

Saturday night, 3 March 1917 General Headquarters,
British Armies in France

. . . I don't think 'the Nivelle Battle' is at all likely to come off, so the War Cabinet agreement then falls to the ground. Our main object (after providing for our army's safety) then should be quietly and unobtrusively to show the French that we mean to be masters of our own army! N. seems *already* to have abandoned his battle plan! And I am *already* taking steps to protect my left.

You would have been aghast if you had been at the Conference and heard L. G. giving over to the French our vital interests in the matter of transportation. After all that England has done (mostly at L.G.'s bidding) in the matter of munitions, we are not to be allowed to reap the benefit and get the ammunition to the front because (with L.G.'s concurrence) the French refuse to give us more than a certain number of trains a day! In fact we are to be 'rationed' in this matter by the French and given what they think is right and proper!! . . .

The commotion created by the Calais Conference is shown by the fact that Derby felt the need of offering further reassurances to the Commander-in-Chief:

Lord Derby to Sir Douglas Haig[1]

3 March 1917 War Office

I have not troubled you with letters because I have known that Robertson has kept you fully informed of what goes on here, just the same as he has told me of what went on at Calais. I wrote briefly to Philip [Sassoon] and got his answer, and in it there is one phrase which I must just mention. He says—'I gather from your letter that you are as much in the dark as Robertson over the *coup de théâtre* which has been prepared'.

[1] *The Private Papers of Douglas Haig* by Robert Blake.

That is perfectly true. And it is perfectly certain that, if I had known there was to be any proposal to put you and our army under the full control of the French, I should most vigorously have protested.

It may be as well to let you know exactly what occurred as far as I know it. Mr. Lloyd George told us at the War Cabinet that, although an agreement had been arrived at at the Conference in London, there was nothing to which both our own representatives and those of the French had put their hand in a formal signature, and it was very advisable, in view of possible recriminations afterwards, to get those signatures. I therefore was under the impression that this was the sole object of the Conference so far as the fresh offensive was concerned, but that the matter of transportation was also going to be discussed. You can therefore judge of my surprise when I heard of what took place at Calais.

The proposal of the French was a preposterous one. As to who was the real originator, I should not like to say. I know that both Robertson and you think that its source was England, but, from what I have heard, I am not quite certain that it was not the politicians (not the soldiers) of France who were the primary instigators. I quite believe that neither Lyautey nor Nivelle knew of it until just before the meeting, and I also believe their assurances given, I think to Robertson and you, that they neither originated it nor desired it.

Of course the proposal was an impossible one, and could not have been accepted by anybody. I am not sure, however, that I like the new proposal much better. It all turns on the interpretation given to the word 'conform'. If that word means the carrying out 'by agreement' the general plans agreed upon, altering them as circumstances may require, well and good, because I am certain that your one wish has been loyally to carry out the wishes of the Cabinet in this matter and that, even if not in complete agreement, you would subordinate your views to Nivelle's, so long as they did not jeopardise your force, or any part of it.

But if 'conform' to orders means to obey orders given, then it seems to me that the necessity for agreement goes by the board, and that you and the British Army come directly under French control, with the power to move our troops how and where they like. . . .

When the Prime Minister related what had occurred at Calais, I pointed out that, not only the action of the French, but his own action on behalf of the War Cabinet might readily be interpreted by you as showing want of confidence in you as the head of the Army in France. I was assured that nothing was further from that intention, and the Cabinet at once passed a resolution—which I have sent you under another cover—expressing their confidence; and I venture to add an expression of that confidence which the Army Council and myself have always had in you, and always will have. . . .

The consensus of latter-day opinion is that Lloyd George was right to press for a unified command and it may be that the methods he employed to achieve this end were the only ones open to him in the situation of limited power in which he found himself. But his tortuous machinations left in their trail a whirlpool of misunderstanding and ill-feeling into which many others were inexorably sucked. Not only did Lloyd George's actions inflame the existing suspicions of Haig and Robertson, they provoked ill-will between the high commands and general staffs of the two allied armies. And naturally enough it was not long before accounts of the Calais Conference had begun to seep down to subordinate commands:

Sir Henry Rawlinson to Lord Derby

5 March 1917

. . . The story of the Calais Conference makes me feel anxious lest the politicians should commit some really serious mistake. It is monstrous that you and Wully [Robertson] should have known nothing of it until the day and I tremble to think of the result on the army out here had they brought off their coup and just at the opening of the most vitally important campaign in our history . . .

Further correspondence at this time confirms Robertson's view expressed in his letter, quoted above, to Haig of February 28:

Lord Derby to Lord Stamfordham [1]

Confidential — Derby House
4 March 1917

I saw Ll. G.—he admits it was wrong not to liaise either Robertson or me at last Saturday's meeting. I am going to write a protest which

[1] Royal Archives.

he will give me an answer to. I am going to see Robertson with reference to the employment of the troops in French areas. Ll. G. says what was decided was that the reserves of either nation might be used in the Mons area if considered necessary by Nivelle. He told me what I had not realised that this attack being Nivelle's plan we were co-operating in the manner now arranged, but that when it was over, whether it failed or succeeded, the arrangement ends, and the old system returns.

I wish I could make up my mind what was the right thing to do; on the one hand Haig may go; on the other Ll. G., and I don't think H.M. quite realises what the effect of the latter going would be—a General Election—his certain return to power—and a blow to the Monarchy from which it would never recover. I shall rely on you for advice and for once in my life be very free from impulse!

Lord Stamfordham to Lord Derby [1]

Private — Buckingham Palace
5 March 1917

I feel very sorry for you in the difficult position created for you by what the Prime Minister I am glad to think admits was a mistake—of course a change of such momentous importance in the conduct of the war ought not to have been even discussed without either you or the C.I.G.S. being present.

It is the old story of a thing—right or wrong in itself—being done in the wrong way. In my humble opinion you can only now register a protest and continue 'as you were': but if I may say so, it behoves all of us to be extremely watchful: for we are living under an order of things very different to that to which we have been accustomed!

I had a long talk with Curzon yesterday afternoon and he convinced me on the paramount importance of insuring that under no circumstances can the French, in case this coming action fails, be able to say that the failure is due to us. Apparently the Government think Nivelle the better man and that as we must secure an undivided command Nivelle ought for *this occasion only* to be supreme.

The question of moving units from Haig's Command to Nivelle's, Curzon felt was a Soldier's one but he could conceive that such transfers might be necessary: but he urged, and I think soundly, that between

[1] Royal Archives.

now and the commencement of the 'move' all these points could be threshed out especially if an able Liaison Officer were appointed to Nivelle's Staff.

Both he and Milner who has been here this morning consider that Robertson hasn't a leg to stand on in signing the agreement and then objecting to it.

Have you received the letter Nivelle wrote to Haig? Don't worry. Good will come out of this explosion. There must be no resignations: but as I repeat it is necessary to keep cool and be 'on guard'!

Lord Derby to Sir Douglas Haig

7 March 1917

. . . Robertson will be coming out to Italy and is certain to see you on his way. He will tell you better than any letter can tell you what has passed. I have been thinking most seriously of my own position with regard to the latest development. He will tell you why I have decided on the course I have taken of remaining in my present post. . . .

. . . I can't tell you how much I sympathise with you in the position in which you were placed at Calais—a position which I find myself in at the present moment—accept or refuse and by that means bring down as you assuredly would have done, the French alliance. You chose the lesser of two courses. Robertson is in a terrible state about things—it has quite ruined his nerves, and for the moment he has not quite got his usual sound judgement. For instance instead of putting your letter (stating that you proposed to make certain representations before Nivelle) in its entirety before the War C., he sent a summary, which did not in the least convey your meaning. Luckily I had the original and got matters straight. Don't let him know I have told you this. I am glad he is going away for a week; it will give him a bit of a rest. He is *absolutely* loyal to you, and I rely very much on his judgement.

How I hate all this intrigue. I wish I could stop it, and I could but only by pulling the house down about our ears. I don't see how we can go back on the agreement—for the *present* offensive—without infuriating the French and risking the alliance.

On Monday, 12 March 1917, Haig recorded in his diary:

At 9.30 a.m. I went to Derby House and had a long talk with Lord Derby, S. of S. for War. He looked more pulled down with worry over the Calais Conference than even Robertson did last night! He condoled with me, said Government had treated me disgracefully. I assured him that although I realised that fact, I felt no ill-will against any of them. That I wanted nothing more in the way of reward and that if the Government had anyone else whom they wished to put in my place, let them do it at once—and I would try and retire gracefully without causing the Government of the country any trouble or loss of prestige. He (like the King) assured me that the last thing they wanted was that I should retire. I told him that I had no objection to appointing Sir H. Wilson to be head of our British Mission at French G.Q.G.[1]—provided the duties of the appointment were first clearly settled, and in accordance with the needs of G.H.Q.[2]

Having worked under Lloyd George at the War Office, Derby had a lively appreciation of the tactics which the Prime Minister was likely to use to gain his ends. Shortly after becoming Secretary of State for War and nearly three months before the Calais Conference he had shrewdly foreseen and had attempted to forestall behaviour of this sort:

Lord Derby to the Prime Minister

Confidential — War Office
31 December 1916

With a view to regularising my position as regards the War Committee—I have asked Col. Hankey to send all orders requiring the attendance of War Office Officials at the War Committee—through me—in order that I may—if I so desire—see them before they attend—and if necessary attend myself. I trust this has your approval. It does not of course apply to Robertson's attendance. There is however a request I would make to you and that is that when proposals affecting the army are made I should be warned to attend the War Committee not for the purpose of discussion but in order that I may hear the whys and wherefores of any proposal before a decision is reached. I would particularly ask this when you contemplate making proposals to our allies which will involve great changes.

Believe me, I do not put this request forward with the intention of

[1] Grand Quartier Général.

[2] *The Private Papers of Douglas Haig* by Robert Blake.

forcing myself on the War Committee. I only do it in order that I may be better able to carry out any decisions the War Committee may come to.

Now that his worst fears had been fulfilled he wrote again. He doubtless felt that he owed it to himself no less than to his office to register a formal protest and to seek to safeguard his position for the future:

Lord Derby to the Prime Minister

Confidential 6 March 1917

It was understood, when you were good enough to offer me the post of Secretary of State for War, that I should not be a member of the War Cabinet, but that it should be a part of Sir William Robertson's duty to be present at all meetings where military matters were discussed in order to give the benefit of his advice and to take instructions of a military character.

I was at the same time informed that I could attend all meetings affecting my office. I considered, and still consider, that this was an excellent arrangement, as it enabled me to get on with the work of the Office and at the same time gave the Cabinet the benefit of a soldier's rather than a civilian's advice on military matters.

I think, however, that this carried with it the natural corollary that no War Cabinet should be held at which important decisions with regard to military matters were arrived at without the representative of the War Office being present.

On Saturday, the 24th February, a War Cabinet was held at which a momentous decision affecting the conduct of the war in France was reached, but to which no representative of the War Office was summoned. As this decision has been already acted upon, I see no use in arguing the merits of the matter, but I earnestly hope that steps will be taken which will prevent a recurrence of such procedure.

The Prime Minister delayed more than ten days before sending a considered answer:

The Prime Minister to Lord Derby

15 March 1917 10 Downing Street

I have been so hard pressed the last few days that I have had no time to reply to the letters you wrote me about the relations of the Secretary of State for War with the War Cabinet. I know that you prefer complete frankness, and I will therefore put before you the position exactly as it strikes me.

As you are aware, the new Cabinet was formed on the principle of bringing together a small number of men with no departmental obligations to direct the affairs of the Empire during the war. The only exception was Bonar Law, who as the Leader of the Unionist Party and the Leader of the House of Commons was in a very special position. The experience of the past had proved that this body must first of all be a small one, and secondly that those who constituted it must be able to devote the whole of their time to the consideration of the various problems that came before it. The country undoubtedly were pleased with the departure and approved of these two principles, and it is essential we should adhere to the basis of the new arrangement. The experience of the past proved that when Ministers with great Departmental obligations attended the War Cabinet, they were bound either to neglect their Departments or to neglect the general work of the Cabinet. At the Ministry of Munitions I found it almost impossible to attend the War Committee whilst I was running the Department, and a very large number of meetings I never attended at all. On the other hand, when I was Minister for War I had to delegate functions ordinarily discharged by the Secretary of State to the Under-Secretary. You therefore were practically joint Secretary of State with me.

You and Sir Edward Carson [the First Lord of the Admiralty] seem to me to be exactly in the same position in reference to the Cabinet. Your Departments are ordinarily represented at the Cabinet by your Chief Experts, the attendance of the two civilian Chiefs being confined either to occasions of an administrative character or to those on which the War Cabinet specially invite their attendance. I am anxious that we should not fall into the same slipshod methods as characterised the late War Committee. That was started as a small body, but as the result of pressure one Minister after another was added to it, so that a Committee of five ultimately developed into an unwieldy body of ten.

Mr. Balfour representing the Foreign Office attends almost regularly inasmuch as, apart from his unique position as the most experienced and distinguished of our imperial statesmen, most of the questions we discuss directly affect his Department. But if the Admiralty and the War Office are habitually represented by civilian heads whenever war questions are discussed, it would be impossible to rule out the Minister of Munitions who is also most intimately associated with all these questions: and Asquith for that reason placed the Minister of Munitions on the Committee.

I would not press the point that there is a danger of the Ministry ceasing to be a Coalition, as I should be the only Liberal in the War Cabinet. In a small body that does not matter as much, but the moment the Cabinet becomes a body of seven or eight, then as soon as the fact becomes realised that there is only one Liberal in it, out of seven or eight, that fact I am convinced would be a source of great weakness to the Government. Our critics are constantly taunting us with the fact that we have ceased to be a Coalition and that we are really a Unionist Administration. Up to the present they have not succeeded in establishing that contention in the minds of the majority of Liberals. Neil Primrose tells me that we can depend upon the support of anything between 150 and 100 Liberals and Labour men, and that there are only about fifty or sixty Liberals and Labour men who are out-and-out opponents of the Government. This gives the Government real strength and entitles it to claim the character of a National Government and not merely a party Government—a most important factor in the conduct of a great war which will strain the resources of the nation to the utmost and where the nation will have to be called upon ere we win to make sacrifices little thought of at the present moment. No mere party Government will ever succeed in ensuring the necessary unity for carrying us through those conditions.

As I understand your point of view, you are anxious that there should be no question discussed by the War Cabinet vitally affecting the Army at which the War Office is not represented either by you or by the Chief of the Staff; in that I entirely concur. Beyond that I hope you will not press the claims of the War Office. You know there is no member of the Administration I should be better pleased to see at our Council Table than yourself, as I always know that you take a patriotic and fair and sensible view of the questions that come before us.

As you know, the Colonial Secretary is also pressing his claims for attendance at our Cabinet meetings, as he contends that he represents practically the whole of our great Colonial Empire. The Indian Secretary might also put forward his claim. But I am apprehensive that the whole of the new system of Government by a small Cabinet of men freed from Departmental cares will go by the board unless we rigidly adhere to the principle which was accepted by all those who joined the Government.

I have spoken to Bonar Law about this, and he quite agrees.

This letter is a fine specimen of Lloyd George's dialectical evasiveness. By ascribing to Derby pretensions which Derby had never made, he affects to have administered a just rebuke to a pushing subordinate. He never once refers to the point at issue, namely that neither Derby nor Robertson were called to the Cabinet meeting of February 24. In the end, however, he grudgingly, without appearing to do so, concedes the point of principle which Derby had been concerned to make. Derby appears to have been content with this and wasted no more time in argument with this slippery controversialist.

Though at home much rumpled plumage had been smoothed, misunderstanding and bickering continued between the two High Commands in France:

Sir William Robertson to Lord Derby

7 March 1917 War Office

That fellow Nivelle is a fraud.

You remember Haig asked to discuss the changed situation with him. Instead of agreeing he has apparently written to his Govt. (I have not yet got a copy of the letter) to effect that Haig is trying to back out of the Calais agreement.

Fact is, the French want to get hold of our armies; they know Haig opposes this, and is in disfavour with LL.G.; they are exploiting the circumstances to get rid of Haig.

I hope to see you in the morning not later than 11. As sooner before as you like.

P.S. The matter is to be discussed tomorrow by W.C. [War Cabinet].

* * *

Derby was inclined throughout his life to give as much attention to small matters as to great and this lack of a balanced sense of proportion must be considered one of his defects. His *bête noire* in public life was Curzon (who, curiously enough, suffered from a similar failing) and he never let slip an opportunity of opposing or thwarting him. Curzon was prone to abuse the facilities which important ministers had in war-time in the matter of motor-cars and which were of particular value in the First World War when petrol rationing was even more strict than in the Second. Derby had two opportunities in the war of embarrassing Curzon in this matter and he made the most of both of them. A later generation which is accustomed to Government cars being made available, even in times of economic stringency, to junior ministers may think that Derby's attitude was somewhat petty. They must remember, however, that in earlier days hardly any ministers had cars provided for them in time of peace, and during the First World War only the most important ministers enjoyed such facilities. The first opportunity for Derby to harass Curzon arose in the spring of 1917:

Lord Derby to Mr. Bonar Law

Personal and Confidential — War Office

5 March 1917

I am sorry for going away, but I really could not stand hearing George Curzon talk, and I did not want to enter into incriminations. As a matter of fact he behaved disgracefully about the car, and it is undoubtedly his own fault that there is any trouble. There was a car placed at the disposal of the Air Board, but when I was Chairman I never once used it. When Curzon came to the Air Board he calmly took it for himself. He talks about it being for general use, but I should doubt a single soul having been in it except himself and his guests. He motors them down to Hackwood and uses the car for sending to the Station for his Saturday-to-Monday parties, and I should like to ask him whether it is not true on the occasion of his Dance the other night the car came backwards and forwards to London three times. I am sure that he would never deny that Lady Curzon invariably uses it, and he himself admitted to me that although he was ill in bed he had sent for the car in order to send a note down to Mrs. Harry Cust. Now this is a scandalous abuse of a Government car and needless to say makes everybody talk. He was to say the least of it incorrect as to what happened about the car in the beginning. I am going to try and find his letter, but he wrote to me, if I remember rightly, to say that the Prime Minister had authorised him to have a car. It now turns out that he telephoned to the Prime Minister to know whether he could have one and got no answer. He then told me he meant to keep the Air Board car. I told him that was entirely a matter of agreement between him and the Air Board, but a second car would have to be supplied and it did not make the least difference which it went to, upon which he telephoned to Cowdray (Cowdray told me this himself) to say that I had agreed, with the Prime Minister's consent, to his keeping his present car. It is very amusing his saying that his health can only be kept going by being able to go to Trent every Saturday to Monday. He has only had Trent since he married.

I am going to try and get out for you the amount of petrol that he has consumed in this car since he has had it, and I think it will be surprising. Of course, he kept on quoting me and it is quite true that both in peace time as well as in war, there is a car which is supposed to be the Secretary of State's, and I do have the same car, but if that is wanted for any military duty I should go without, and it probably will be wanted as we have to supply cars for all our Colonial Conference visitors. The real truth is he is just what he *says* he is not. He is one of the meanest men that I know. He was a tenant of mine at one time and I have good reason for knowing it.

Again in January 1918 Derby detected Curzon in a particularly flagrant abuse. This time instead of reporting the matter to Bonar Law he approached Curzon direct:

Lord Derby to Lord Curzon

Private and Personal — 15 January 1918

I write to you in strict confidence and as a friend with regard to the question of your car. A matter in connection with it has come up to me in the ordinary course of business.

Official cars are, as you know, only meant for the use of the Minister in question and under general circumstances, I think, for use in London, though to take a car down for Saturday to Monday is quite permissible as at any time the Minister might have to come up on a Sunday for business and not be able to find a train; but your car was absent with you from the 21st December and had not returned on the 9th January.

and your Driver had to telegraph to London for permission for more petrol. Naturally in connection with this he was called upon to give a return of how that petrol had been expended, and his return I enclose. You will, I am sure, see that, probably quite inadvertently, your official car has been used contrary to the general regulations which have been laid down for these cars to the effect that they shall only be used by the Minister himself, and if a question were asked in either House of Parliament, and you know people are on the look out to ask such questions, it would be a somewhat difficult one to answer.

I hope, therefore, again I say as an old friend, you won't mind my begging you to adhere strictly to the regulations which, of course, would not preclude your taking Lady Curzon down if you went away for a Saturday to Monday, but do preclude the car being used by anybody except when you, yourself, are present in it and on official duty.

Report by Pte. S. A. Johnson

8 January 1918

In answer to your letter of December 30 I beg to state:

I left London for Basingstoke on December 21 1917. I had a car load of luggage, no passengers.

December 22 left Basingstoke for Montacute with more luggage, no passengers.

December 22 same day went from Montacute to Yeovil Station to meet Lord and Lady Curzon and three of their family, back to Montacute.

December 23, went to Yeovil Station, picked up Lord Curzon's two daughters and maid, also two lady friends, took to Montacute, then returned to Yeovil for luggage.

December 24, drove Lady Curzon and two ladies, whom I did not know, to Yeovil for shopping.

December 25, drove Lord and Lady Curzon and two friends to Ham Hill, Stoke, and back to Montacute.

December 26. Not ordered out.

December 27, went to Yeovil Station. Left Lord Curzon and valet, returned to Montacute, later met Messenger from London, returned to Montacute.

December 28, took Lady Curzon to Yeovil to make calls.

December 29. Not ordered.

December 30, went to Yeovil with despatches and made calls.

December 31, took manservant to Yeovil Station and brought back luggage.

January 1, went to Yeovil for letters and parcels, later returned to Yeovil for Lord Curzon who arrived from London.

January 2, went into Yeovil with two ladies for train, back to Montacute.

January 3, Yeovil and back to Montacute with manservant.

January 4. Not ordered.

January 5. To Yeovil and back twice, with five passengers, three ladies, two men and luggage, then on to Basingstoke.

January 6. Left Basingstoke for London.

Lord Curzon to Lord Derby

16 January 1918

Your protest about the car is quite reasonable and I have no objection whatever to raise.

But I will tell you how it came about. I had no intention of going to Montacute for Xmas. It is much too far away. I was going to Hackwood and was not even going to take the car (of which, I may say in passing, that I have made no further use for months than to drive me to and from Downing St. or in the streets of London and which Lady Curzon never enters at all). But two days before Xmas my child's Governess at Hackwood suddenly developed measles, the whole house had to be shut up and I had to take my wife and family at the last moment to the only other open country house that I possess, Montacute. This is five miles from Yeovil. I am sorry to say that I have no carriage or motor there and that the local ones have ceased to ply.

In these circs. I could not have moved from the station to the house, nor out of the house, nor could my family have subsisted from day to day but for the motor. I daresay that my servants used it illegitimately without my knowledge and if so that was wrong. But without it I should not have had an Xmas holiday at all. The circs. were really quite exceptional and are not likely to recur.

Further, I was suddenly summoned to London for a Cabinet meeting in the middle of my short holiday. Without the motor there I should not have been able to come. A special messenger came down from London and without the motor he could not either have reached Montacute or returned. It is a mistake to say that the car had not returned on Jan. 9. We returned on Jan. 6.

Lord Derby to Lord Curzon

Private 17 January 1918

Very many thanks for your letter. I was sure you would not mind my bringing the facts about your motor to your notice, and your explanation is one which is so excellent that I can safely tell the people concerned that the incident is absolutely closed. You will understand my position in such a matter as this is rather a difficult one, as I know there are a number of people who are on the lookout, both in Parliament and out, to throw stones.

I am so sorry you are seedy, and hope you will soon be yourself again.

I am afraid I have been an absentee from the House of Lords, but there really has been nothing in which I thought the Government could be in danger, and I have had a great deal to do.

* * *

Meanwhile the battle beckoned imperiously. Controversies must be ended and the ranks closed. The mounting ill-will between the two Allied High Commands was so serious that the Prime Minister thought it necessary to invite the French War Minister, General Lyautey, to a further conference in London to settle the precise interpretation of what had been agreed at Calais. At this Conference, which was held on March 12, and at which the British representatives were Robertson and Haig, a solution was found to the principal difficulties which had been agitating the two High Commands, namely the method by which Nivelle was to transmit his orders to Haig. It was settled that Haig should send a British Military Mission headed by Sir Henry Wilson to Nivelle's Headquarters and that Wilson should be the channel through which these orders were to be transmitted.

Even Derby, who twelve days before had been encouraging Haig to resist Wilson's appointment, was beginning to think that Haig was being intransigent. He realised how vital it was that prejudices and animosities should be overcome, and three days later we find him drafting a letter of outstanding and tactful good sense which deserves to be preserved (even though it seems that in view of his forthcoming visit to General Headquarters the letter was not dispatched):

Lord Derby to Sir Douglas Haig

15 March 1917 War Office

I want to tell you by letter, what I shall repeat personally to you on Sunday, how extremely glad I am that the Conference went off in the way it did. There can be no doubt, after the way the Prime Minister spoke of you at the meeting, that the French will clearly understand you have the confidence of the Government of this country, and I know, from things which I have since heard indirectly, that they are letting this be known.

I am hopeful, too, that Henry Wilson will help you. I had a long talk with him, and I am convinced that he has only one idea in his head, and that is to serve you faithfully. He sees all the dangers very clearly, and I believe I told you, as he told me, that the only thing he fears is that stories of intrigues on his part may be brought to your ears which are just as false as the stories of the Calais Conference.[1] I have assured him that you are much too broad-minded to listen to tittle-tattle, and I therefore hope that nothing will disturb in any way the good relationship which must exist between you and him.

Now I want to go a little further. The Prime Minister was strictly right when he said that no agreement will ever work unless there is good-will on both sides. Both you and Nivelle have given your word that this good-will shall exist, and, knowing as you do my confidence in you, you will readily believe me when I say that I know you will carry your promise out. But I do wish that you would try to get, not your personal staff, but the General Staff of G.H.Q. to adopt the same attitude. As you may imagine, many things filter back to me from numerous sources, and I cannot conceal from myself the fact that many of those in high places (and I will expressly mention two men—Kiggell and Butler) have got a feeling of dislike for the French, which they do not hesitate to express. I admire men who do not hide their feelings in ordinary circumstances, but these are no ordinary times. If we are to win the war, we must work in thorough harmony with the French. This harmony will not be forthcoming unless both

[1] As the greatest natural intriguer among all the Allied and enemy soldiers and politicians, Wilson had just cause for his fears.

Staffs conceal any feelings with regard to each other which they may have, and which are not complimentary. I am sure a word from you would do it, and if you could let them all know that this mutual promise from the Cs.-in-C. has been made, will be kept, and will be entirely nullified unless the respective Staffs take the same line, then I am sure, whatever their feelings, their loyalty to you will make them carry out your instructions.

I am very anxious about the position all over the world, and any failure in our joint offensive will undoubtedly be put down by the French to our want of cordial co-operation. It is therefore most desirable that no handle should be given to such an excuse.

XIII

Passchendaele

MARCH 1917 marked the beginning of the Russian Revolution. In April the United States of America declared war on the Central Powers. By a blessed coincidence, as one great ally dropped out of the war, another, even more formidable, was drawn reluctantly but inevitably into the Allied camp. However, the consequences of these two tremendous events did not become operative for some time. Russia continued to fight and even to mount offensives for several months. While the entry of the United States, as in the Second World War, provided a guarantee of ultimate victory, for some time it proved an actual embarrassment. Munitions on order for the Allies in the United States were diverted for the provision of the mighty new armies of the great republic.

Meanwhile, General Nivelle had launched in April his long prepared and deliberately publicised offensive, originally planned by Joffre for February. By then the German High Command had transferred from the Somme to the sector which Nivelle was planning to attack the whole of their First Army; and sixty-six German divisions now stood where two months before there had only been twenty-one. On the front of twenty-five miles on the River Aisne, where Nivelle planned to make the break-through, which he boasted would annihilate the German Army in forty-eight hours, there were forty-three German divisions instead of ten.

Nivelle's offensive seemed to open well. Haig in the Battle of Arras secured the Vimy Ridge. The French in the first four days of the battle captured 21,000 prisoners and 183 guns, but their own casualties were above 100,000. Within four days Nivelle recognised his failure and greatly modified his plan. Although the French losses were considerably less than in the battles fought by Joffre on the Somme, the French Army soon became demoralised and mutinies were reported in sixteen separate Army Corps. On May 15 Nivelle was dismissed and Pétain was appointed Commander-in-Chief. Details of the mutinies were suppressed with astonishing effectiveness, but they bit deeply into the mind of Haig, and coupled with Jellicoe's alarmist view of the U-boat menace, reported to him on April 28 by Robertson, convinced him that a continuation of the offensive by the British Army was essential. Robertson had written to Haig:

> The situation at sea is very serious indeed. It has never been so bad as at present, and Jellicoe almost daily announces it to be hopeless. There may soon be a serious shortage of food in this country, and this has to be taken into consideration in regard to all theatres of war. For us to stop fighting now would seem to be a confession of failure and would allow the enemy to do as he likes.[1]

The British Army had had a more limited and less ambitious task than that of the French Army and had achieved everything that was expected of it. Derby sent his compliments to the Commander-in-Chief:

Lord Derby to Sir Douglas Haig

18 April 1917

> I have been very remiss about writing, but I am sure you will forgive me. First of all, many very hearty congratulations on your success. It does one a lot of good to be always able to say to the War Cabinet 'I told you so'. I really think at last they believe what fools they made of themselves at the Calais Conference.

And again:

Lord Derby to Sir Douglas Haig

Private

Derby House

26 April 1917

> . . . For many reasons I was very anxious to see you, the chief being that I wanted to congratulate you not only on your success at Arras,

[1] *Haig*, Vol. II, by Duff Cooper.

but on the complete vindication of your plans, and how right you were, and how wrong the French were. I am afraid the French Government will not be as pliable as ours was. If they were, you ought to be put in Supreme Command over the combined forces.

I am very anxious as to the attitude the French Government may adopt now that Nivelle's attack has not done all they expected, and am much afraid they will supersede him with Pétain and take up a defensive attitude, waiting for the Americans who will not be ready till next year, if then. I should be so much obliged if you could from time to time dictate me a line to say what your views of the situation are, and what attitude you think the Government here should take. If I know your views from time to time, it makes it easier to adopt the proper line with the War Cabinet. Perhaps you could depute Philip [Sassoon] to send them to me, as I know how busy you are.

I shall try to come out next week, but really after this experience, one dare not make one's plans a day—much less a week—ahead. Can't you find me a permanent place on your staff? I am sick of this country, with its pessimism and absolute want of patriotism. Remember me to all friends.

Manpower continued to be the chief preoccupation of the War Office at home. Haig's costly offensives and the still more costly projects he had in mind put a tremendous pressure on the War Office for larger drafts. At the same time the mounting success of the U-boat campaign led the Government to demand increased agricultural production, which policy could only be achieved by keeping more men upon the land. In January the Prime Minister, who only committed himself to paper in the most vital matters, had written:

The Prime Minister to Lord Derby

22 January 1917 10 Downing Street

I am receiving representations from every quarter about the calling up of the 30,000 men from Agriculture. The country is frightened, and rightly so, as to food supplies, and the submarine menace is becoming more and more formidable. The situation has been aggravated by the new raider development of the German fleet. I am convinced that under the circumstances you ought to go slow over the calling up of these 30,000 men during the next two or three months, until Prothero is satisfied that they can be dispensed with in the production of food for the 1917 harvest.

I agree it is hard on the Army, but unless we are able to increase the food supplies in this country we shall be beaten by starvation.

In March a Bill was introduced into Parliament tightening up the medical grounds under which men of military age could secure exemption. At the beginning of the war when there was no shortage of manpower in the Army many men were invalided out of the services because of trivial wounds and ailments which would not have been an obstacle to their conscription two years later. One of the objects of the Bill was to draft many thousands of such men back to the colours.

Lord Derby to the Prime Minister

Confidential — War Office

1 April 1917

The question of recruiting is so serious, that I feel I need make no apology for bringing it before your attention, especially in view of the line taken by the House of Commons with regard to the Bill for Medical Re-examination.

Let me state the figures briefly. In the first quarter of the year we required 350,000 'A' men. Towards that 350,000 we have got 202,000 in round numbers of which 60,000 are boys under nineteen and who cannot be immediately employed. We are therefore short by 210,000 men of the proper quota.

To be perfectly fair, I must state that the original number was based on the assumption that the offensive would be taken much earlier than it has been, and, owing to the losses having been correspondingly small, there is not the same demand for immediate drafts there would otherwise have been. But still, the fact remains that there is a very large deficiency which, as far as I can see under present circumstances, there is no chance of our being able to make good, and this deficiency will become an ever-increasing amount.

The objections by the Members of the House of Commons to the medical re-examination, as far as they are apparent, come under two categories: (1) The objection to calling up men for re-examination who have been invalided out of the service for wounds; and (2) the need for men in agriculture.

With regard to (1), although I think it is a sentimental objection, I have a certain amount of sympathy with it, and I have no wish to see impressed into the service men who have really suffered wounds, which, while they would prevent them from undertaking active service in the field, might allow of their being employed in other categories. But there is not the least doubt that at the beginning of the war when the need for men was not so obvious as it is now, many men were discharged—especially in the Territorial Force—whom we should not dream at the present moment of discharging. I do not hesitate to say that there are many thousands of these wounded who would be perfectly capable of again taking their places in the ranks, and very valuable many of them would be, as they are old and trained soldiers.

With regard to (2), nobody recognises more than I do the necessity for the cultivation of the land for food, but I think you can carry this too far, and I do not hesitate to say that, with the assistance the Army has given by returning men and by lending men, far from agriculture being under-staffed at the present moment, it is over-staffed. To give you only two instances, both in Sussex and North Wales, the Military Representatives and the Agricultural Representatives have agreed that there is a surplus of labour, and I believe the same thing exists in many parts of Scotland. Men at the present moment claim to be engaged in agriculture, and the Agricultural Department is claiming them as indispensable, whom I do not think you or any member of the War Cabinet would wish to protect for one minute. I give you two examples.

There is one man who is a shoemaker. He is claimed as indispensable by the Board of Agriculture not on the ground that he is indispensable for agriculture, but on the ground that, if he were taken, farm labourers would not be able to get their boots mended. The second case is that of a man who cultivates no land, but who is a game and poultry dealer, who again is supposed to be indispensable to our food supply. And these are only two of many cases; agriculture at the present moment is one of the biggest funk-holes that we have in this country.

But there are other influences at work in the House of Commons with regard to this Bill, and they are best expressed in a remark made by Winston Churchill to General Geddes to the effect that he would not help him to get men in order to send them to be murdered in France. . . .

There were also the increasing claims of the munition factories which were not only supplying the needs of the British Armies but to an ever-increasing extent those of the Allies. Moreover Lloyd George, from the time the United States entered the war, deliberately starved the British Army of manpower. The failure of Nivelle's offensive meant the ruin of Lloyd George's conception of a unified Allied command which might have restrained Haig from his unimaginative and bloody onslaughts. Tireless in his search for expedients to gain his way, Lloyd George increasingly throughout 1917 threw his influence against the demands of the Army:

Lord Derby to the Prime Minister

26 May 1917

I hope I was not very absent-minded last night, but between you and me I had somewhat of a shock. You may remember I went out of the room just to see my boy [Edward] for a minute, and he then told me he was engaged to be married, which of course I rather expected to be possible, but which came rather as a surprise at that moment. It is to Sybil[1] Cadogan, a most delightful girl. Please treat this at present as confidential. It is only in case you may have thought that I was not very clear-headed.

I think last night we at all events cleared the air about several matters, and I hope that my suggestion for a certain post may be of use to you. The more I think of it, the more suitable I think it would be. . . .

I know you think that sometimes I take too much the soldier view rather than the civilian. I want to emphasize to you that though I shall do that to the best of my ability when fighting this particularly, you may rely on my absolute loyalty to support whatever decision the War Cabinet arrive at in this matter. I am sure you will feel that it would be as wrong for me not to put up as good a fight as I possibly can to get men, as it would undoubtedly be wrong for me to remain in the Government and not support it in any decision they may arrive at. I wish we could get a move on in the States with regard to the sending of men. That would relieve us of much of our difficulty. . . .

[1] Though Lady Stanley was christened Sybil she has always been known as Portia.

Lord Derby to Sir Douglas Haig

27 May 1917

. . . I am sorry to say I found the War Cabinet in a very disagreeable state of mind. I had put up a memorandum saying how far short we were of the 500,000 asked for by Robertson and what measures I proposed should be taken. My proposals were turned down absolutely. Ll. George and Robertson dined alone with me on Friday. We discussed the question, but Ll. G. was very insistent that we could take no other measures to secure the men, that shipping, agriculture, etc., demanded all our resources, and ended up by saying that he considered as far as men were concerned that we were down to bedrock and 'must be content with the scrapings'. When we told him what this would mean from the point of view of shortage, he told us it could not be helped. He brought forward his old argument of reducing divisions to nine battns. making the other three battns. into reserve, and making good the loss of rifles by increased machine-guns and heavy guns. He further added that we must very much limit our attacks and wait till the Americans came in. In other words, we are to do exactly what he urged me to tell the French they were *not* to do. We may get some sort of modification of this but I am not sanguine. The Government is really scared at the last strike, and with the general condition of the country, and really I sympathise with them. The state of affairs is very bad, and there is no doubt the Russian revolution has created an unrest that is revolutionary and dangerous. The House of Commons too is in a very nasty mood. They are always professing a desire to find men for the Army but attack and ruin every proposal we make. I tell you all this in confidence, and will keep you fully informed. Things may turn out better than they at present look, but I think it right to warn you that it is more than probable that your shortage of men may be very large by the end of July.

Controversy about manpower for the Army was very bitter, and a verbal brush which Derby had with the Prime Minister led him once more to think of resigning. In the course of a long letter he wrote:

Lord Derby to Mr. Lloyd George

14 June 1917 War Office

I confess that I rather lost my temper this morning, and I cannot help thinking I had some cause to do so. I will put it to you perfectly

> straight—if you are not satisfied that I am doing all I can sufficient with the consistency of the service to get 'A' men out of this country, you should put somebody else in, in whom you have more confidence. . . .
>
> In conclusion I would like to repeat what I said at the beginning, that as apparently it is the desire of the War Cabinet to appoint a Committee to tell me how I am to run this Office, it would be much better that I should place my resignation in your hands.

Not for the first or the last time, Derby's threat of resignation was not carried into effect.

* * *

We must now interrupt this account of Derby's grinding and vexatious toil at the War Office for a minor political and family interlude. At the end of May a vacancy occurred in the Abercromby Division of Liverpool owing to the elevation to the peerage as Lord Gisborough of Colonel Chaloner, Mr. Walter Long's half-brother. At various times in Derby's life a large number of members of his family contested and often won Conservative seats in Lancashire in the Tory interest.

Derby was fond of boasting that he never exercised any influence to secure the nomination either of his friends or of his relations. This indeed was true. There was no need for him to do so. There was hardly a Conservative Association in Lancashire or Cheshire which, confronted with the necessity of finding a candidate, did not instinctively wonder whether there was any member of the Stanley family available to carry their banner. And they naturally wrote to Derby as head of this numerous, influential and respected family to enquire whether he had a relation available and if not whether he could suggest the next best thing.

Derby's eldest son Edward was now twenty-two years old and had been serving as an officer in the Grenadier Guards since the outbreak of war. There were no cut-and-dried rules as to officers standing for Parliament, but certainly in the Brigade of Guards there would be a natural prejudice against such a proposal. The story of the Abercromby by-election is of interest from this point of view and also because owing to Derby's being Secretary of State for War it led, considerably to Derby's embarrassment, to many vexed issues being fought out around the person of his own dearly loved son and on the doorstep of Knowsley.

The story is of further interest as illustrating the political influence of the Stanley family in Lancashire and of the way in which well-connected individuals could, in those days, gain entry to Parliament:

Lord Derby to Lord Stanley

12 June 1917

Portia will have warned you by telephone today that you may get a letter from me which is a little disturbing, but I hope that by tomorrow morning I can send you a telegram which will put matters in a different light.

The Liverpool people, the vacant Seat, had a name in front of them which they declined to entertain and Salvidge put your name forward instead. It met with universal acceptance and they have unanimously settled, that is to say the Selection Committee, to put your name forward to the General Council as a candidate. I should not have the least hesitation in advising you to accept, were it not that you have given Arty a sort of pledge to succeed him in the representation of Ormskirk. I am going to get hold of him this afternoon and talk to him about it because, as I don't think there will be an election till at least six months or a year after the war, Oliver, who is very keen to go into Parliament, might possibly be accepted as Arty's successor. I think both should be safe Seats, and there is no sentiment about either of them as they are neither family Seats, Arty having been the first of the family to sit for Ormskirk.

If, therefore, he agrees that it would not be a breach of faith to him and to the Constituency, I shall telegraph you advising you to accept. There need be no question of your attending any meetings, and I think I should stipulate that if there was a contest you would not stand, or, at all events, that you would not attend any meetings on the ground that, whilst the war is on, it does not become a serving soldier to make speeches. I should make an election address, which I will help you to draw up, and I should stand on that, and you may expect a telegram from me tomorrow morning.

How what was legitimately expected in war-time to be an uncontested election became a bitter fight which attracted the attention of the whole country has been admirably preserved in the contemporary account recorded by Sir Archibald Salvidge:

Salvidge Diary

May 1917

F. E. asked whether it had occurred to me that Lord Stanley would be an ideal candidate. He is a most gallant young soldier who has been twice wounded, and the local organisation would no doubt jump at him. He would be a great help to us in Liverpool. F. E. had not the least idea whether he would stand, but suggested that, if I approved, I should approach Lord Derby without letting it appear to come from F. E., as it would be much more of a compliment to young Stanley if the suggestion emanated locally.

Having ascertained that there would be sufficient support on the Divisional Council, I obtained the consent of both Lord Stanley and his father and the adoption was made. At that time it seemed possible, by putting forward a popular name, either to frighten off or gain the support of, the other political parties, thus filling the vacancy with an unopposed return without distracting people from their war-work by the raising of political clamour. So far good. But now it is known that the son of the War Minister is to be opposed by a one-legged ex-private, backed by Hogge [Mr. J. M. Hogge, M.P., a leading Liberal interested in the Soldiers' and Sailors' Federation], it looks as though I have made a false move and brought round the Stanley family the full force of the present discontents.

It is not as though either Lord Derby or Lord Stanley was particularly keen on the idea. At first, for instance, the latter's Commanding Officer refused the permission necessary before a regular soldier can stand for Parliament. Derby is not the sort to use his Cabinet rank to bring official pressure to bear, but luckily this C.O. is a family friend, so Derby had him round to his house and used the perfectly legitimate personal touch. After arguing with the stern soldier for hours, and explaining the pros and cons of the political situation, the required consent was forthcoming; but only on condition that no interference with military duties is entailed.

It was made quite clear to me that Lord Stanley cannot be at

Knowsley till ten days after the election. Feeling fairly confident there would be no contest, I agreed to manage the thing without the candidate making an appearance from start to finish. At present Lord Stanley is on a difficult Staff course at Cambridge. He is putting in a crowded few weeks, what with his exam., a candidature for Parliament, ending up on July 17 with his wedding and probably going back to France at the end of the month. Derby is now far from happy about the election. He says the opposition of the discharged soldiers is much more serious than I realise. There is going to be a tremendous row about it in Parliament. He contends he has been badly let down by the Medical Boards, which have gone far beyond what the War Office intended. But that is a story we cannot go into on an election platform. Derby fears the Opposition's policy will be to fight him through his son, and Lord Stanley not unnaturally feels he is in a somewhat false position. The military authorities are making it plain that they consider it bad for discipline for him to have the grouses of every war-weary Tommy centring round him. It has even been hinted to me from London that we had better withdraw Lord Stanley and find another candidate. Derby says he is largely to blame as he ought to have refused my suggestion point-blank at the beginning.

But anyhow we are in for it now and I have declined to countenance withdrawal; I have urged that Lord Stanley be allowed to appear for at least one meeting and have received a flat negative. But I. J. Macpherson [the Under-Secretary for War] is coming. Derby does not want to come himself if we can possibly help it, and I do not think he should. F. E. as the chief Law Officer of the Crown, has been advised to keep out of it. There are complete answers to most of the contentions of the Discharged Soldiers Society and Macpherson knows all the snags. He is a Liberal and a most effective speaker. If we win this election I shall feel it has killed all the lies that are going about and completely vindicate Lord Derby's administration at the War Office. If we lose, I fear I must admit I have been the means of doing a grave disservice to the Government, and therefore to the country, in the midst of what is so far the most critical year of the war.

July 1917. As we won Abercromby by a handsome majority[1] Lord Derby's popularity is unbounded. Considering the issues the election was fought on, and that his son was the candidate, it is tantamount to

[1] The figures were: Lord Stanley (Coalition), 2,224; Mr. F. B. Hughes (Independent), 794.

a huge vote of confidence in the War Minister. But the contest had many anxious moments. Macpherson was magnificent. At meeting after meeting he replied to strings of questions about pensions, allowances, medical examinations and so on, fired at him by the ex-service men. He never once lost his temper and always satisfied them. There was much ugly heckling, but it seldom came from the genuine Service element. Our poor wounded soldier opponent was only a cat's-paw. He was soon the centre of an amazing crowd of mixed elements made up of shell-shocked men who have fought, men who have not fought at all and never intend to, cranks, 'conchies', naturalised aliens and heaven knows what. I got a handbill out showing that the twenty signatures on his nomination papers included the names Lazarus, Isaac, Fineberg, Chishelsky, Kesler, Pochinsky, Neurick, Myer and Skulnick. That did it. The ex-soldier support of our opponent largely melted away then, and left us only the revolutionaries to cope with.

Tom [afterwards Sir Thomas] White was a great help over the handbill. He is a born electioneer who is making himself very useful to me and I shall do all I can for him. Lady Derby [Lord Stanley's mother], Lady Victoria [his sister] and Miss Cadogan [his fiancée] put in an appearance and pleased our workers immensely. Oliver Stanley [Lord Stanley's brother] happened to arrive on leave from the Front and came to one of the meetings merely as a spectator. A fellow in the audience challenged him with attending a political gathering in uniform. Young Oliver confessed his oversight so charmingly that the ex-service men cheered him. Yet at some of the meetings there was a nasty, strident, undisciplined note amongst the opposition that in a lifetime of British politics I have not heard before. It made one think of the disturbing things that are beginning to leak through about Russia. If this hysteria spreads, politics after the war are going to be dangerous. The Government announcement, made two days before the poll, that a Committee had been appointed to inquire into the whole working of the Review of Exemptions Act had a wonderfully good effect. The election has served to ventilate all genuine grievances....

* * *

This summer the Prime Minister was seeking a method of bringing Mr. Churchill back into the Government. Derby like nearly all the rest of the Tory Party and many Liberals was deeply distressed at this project; we find him writing to Haig:

Lord Derby to Sir Douglas Haig

8 June 1917

. . . There is rather bitter political controversy at the present moment in this country over the subject of the possible appointment of Winston Churchill to the Chairmanship of the Air Board. Personally I think his inclusion in any Government means its eventual downfall but the Prime Minister does not hold these views and personally I do not much mind his inclusion as long as he does not in any way interfere with the War and I hope that such conditions will be imposed upon him as will prevent that.

The same day he wrote to the Prime Minister:

Lord Derby to the Prime Minister

Confidential

Derby House,
8 June 1917

I much appreciated my talk with you this afternoon and I know you do not resent one saying exactly what one thinks. As to whether Winston Churchill will strengthen your Government or the reverse we must agree to differ as I do not think either could convince the other. I am really anxious to serve you and your Government and therefore feel you will forgive me if I put before you somewhat bluntly the position as it concerns me as head of the War Office.

If Winston Churchill is only to be a second Lord Cowdray I do not mind if he will only do his work half as well. Lord Cowdray has done a real amount of good for the Air Service and has worked most cordially with the War Office without in any way attempting to interfere with the administration of that office.

While I regret Winston Churchill's inclusion in the Government—if he be included—as being a source of weakness I feel that it would not affect the War Office if it was clearly understood:

(1) that he was not a member of the War Cabinet and did not attend any meetings unless specially summoned for business connected with the Board;

(2) that his duties as Chairman of the Board were the same as those

of Lord Cowdray and that he had nothing to do with either personnel, tactics or the nomination of the War Office representatives on the Board; and

(3) that he received no War Office telegrams other than those which were in any way connected with his particular department.

I gathered from you this afternoon that the conditions I have named were certainly those on which you would understand that he should enter the Government and that being so as far as my own office is concerned I personally can offer no objection, though I am bound to say I think there is a big 'if' in the question and that is *if* Winston Churchill will ever consent to occupy a comparatively minor position and do his own work without interfering with other people's. Perhaps you would let me know on Monday when I see you if I am right in my statement as to what your views on the position are.

Opposition to the proposed appointment was so widespread that the Prime Minister felt compelled to abandon it for the time being. When six weeks later there were rumours in the papers of a considerable reconstruction of the Government, and that in this process an important post would be found for Churchill, Derby sought an interview with the Prime Minister in order to express his hostility.

Derby's private secretary, Mr. H. J. Creedy,[1] made a note of what passed between them, which must have been based upon what Derby told him on his return to the War Office from 10 Downing Street:

Secret | War Office
17 July 1917

Lord Derby said he wished to speak quite frankly; he had seen the appointments in the paper for the first time that morning and thought that, in view of the misgivings he felt, he ought to tender his resignation.

The Prime Minister expressed his complete satisfaction with Lord Derby's conduct of the administration of the War Office and begged him not to consider such a step. He thought he had left it to Mr. Bonar Law to inform his Unionist colleagues of the new appointments. His own wish had been to send Mr. Churchill to the Air Board and Lord

[1] Later Sir Herbert Creedy.

Cowdray to the Ministry of Munitions, but had found the difficulties insurmountable. Mr. Churchill would be in precisely the same position as Dr. Addison except that his powers would be somewhat more limited as the new Minister of Reconstruction would take with him some of his old duties. Mr. Churchill would not be permitted to interfere with the War Office, as it would be his duty to supply that for which the War Office asked him, and the assurances given when it was in contemplation to make him President of the Air Board, would hold good now that he was at the Ministry of Munitions.

Mr. Lloyd George added that in matters of this kind he must exercise the prerogative of the Prime Minister to appoint those whom he thought likely to help him. He was in great need of men to go round the country in the next three months to expound the policy of the Government, and, if denied their assistance, he would much sooner resign himself now.

Lord Derby repeated that he thought a great mistake had been made which would do the Prime Minister much harm, but, so long as Mr. Churchill refrained from all interference with regard to the conduct of the war and confined himself to the business of his Department, he (Lord Derby) would not press his resignation.

Mr. Churchill was appointed to the Ministry of Munitions on July 17. Derby was quick to adjust himself to the new situation. In a ten-page typewritten letter to Sir Philip Sassoon dated July 22, which, however, on reconsideration he did not send, he wrote:

Lord Derby to Sir Philip Sassoon

. . . Now, as to things political. Strictly between ourselves, Lloyd George made a *coup de main* when he appointed Geddes, Winston Churchill and Montagu. I never knew a word about it until I saw it in the paper and was furious at being kept in ignorance, but you can judge of my surprise when I found that the War Cabinet had never been told! Lloyd George had acted on a prerogative, which is undoubtedly his, to make any appointment he likes without consulting his colleagues, though I believe they did know about Carson leaving the Admiralty. The latter, however, did not know that Geddes was going to succeed till he was informed the evening before.

Myself I do not think the appointments are so very bad. Winston

Churchill is the great danger, because I cannot believe in his being content to simply run his own show and I am sure he will have a try to have a finger in the Admiralty and War Office pies. We have an assurance that he will not do so, and I do not think that Geddes or I would stand for it for one moment, but I feel convinced he will try it on. The appointment of Montagu, a Jew, to the India Office has made, as far as I can judge, an uneasy feeling both in India and here, but I, personally, have a very high opinion of his capability and I expect he will do well. There is no doubt that the appointment of Winston and Montagu is a very clever move on Lloyd George's part. He has removed from Asquith his two most powerful lieutenants and he has provided for himself two first-class platform speakers and it will be platform speakers we shall require to steady the country which is at present very much rattled by that distinguished body the House of Commons. . . .

and the following day he wrote in a similar sense to the Prime Minister:

Lord Derby to the Prime Minister

Confidential — War Office

25 July 1917

. . . Other matters here are going smoothly. The majority for the Government the other night was very good. I saw Freddy Guest yesterday. He volunteered to me that the loyalty of the Unionists was above reproach; they were very sore about Winston but notwithstanding that they rallied to a man. The real truth is this, that when the Government put down their feet the whole party will rally to them. What puts them off their loyalty is any sign of weakness. . . .

Within a very few weeks Derby was finding that his worst misgivings about Mr. Churchill were coming true.

* * *

At this time Sir Eric Geddes, First Lord of the Admiralty, was nettled by Mr. Churchill's attempts to obtain some surplus guns from the Navy for the use of the Army. Derby heard of this and realised that Geddes might prove a useful ally in his unceasing campaign against Churchill. Indeed, he skilfully sought to employ

Geddes as a stalking-horse. This controversy scarcely rippled the waters of the political pond, but to Derby it seemed of the first importance and he set the full story down in a memorandum which he preserved among his papers:

Very Confidential 18 August 1917

Record of what has passed in the last few days in regard to Mr. Winston Churchill

On Wednesday the 15th a War Cabinet was held in my room at the War Office[1] at which there was a discussion on guns for Russia. In the opinion both of the C.I.G.S. and myself Mr. Winston Churchill out-stepped his province by giving his views and voting[2] on the policy to be pursued.

Directly after the meeting the C.I.G.S. and I agreed that although it was a small matter in itself the principle was a great one and could not be allowed to go unchallenged. We therefore decided to write a joint letter to the Prime Minister drawing his attention to the fact that there had been such interference and saying we felt perfectly certain after bringing it to his attention that he would protect us from being again put in the very false position we had been in the morning.

There was a War Cabinet in the afternoon which I did not attend but C.I.G.S. on his return told me that the question had arisen with regard to the giving up by the Navy of some guns for the use of the Army and that a Committee was to be formed to go into the matter. I left the matter there but the next morning I sent for General Furse to explain what had gone on as I knew that he had personally spoken to Sir Eric Geddes the day before asking him to enquire into the matter. General Furse told me that he was very much surprised when Mr. Winston Churchill brought the matter forward, especially as there was nobody from the Admiralty present, and he told me he was so afraid that Sir Eric Geddes would think that he (Furse) had behaved badly in bringing the matter forward before the War Cabinet, in view of the fact that he had spoken to him privately the day before and had been promised every possible assistance.

[1] Derby's recollection was imperfect. The meeting in question was held at 10 Downing Street.

[2] Votes in Cabinet are extremely rare. It is most improbable that a vote was actually taken, for this is not a practice at Cabinet meetings.

Almost immediately afterwards Sir Eric Geddes came over to see me and told me that he thought he had cause for complaint at our having brought this matter up at the War Cabinet. In fact, what General Furse had feared was realised. I sent for General Furse who then explained the circumstances and Sir Eric Geddes was quite satisfied. I must mention here that the letter sent by C.I.G.S. and myself was signed by me late on Wednesday night and I left it myself at York House for C.I.G.S. to sign. This he did and sent it up early on Thursday morning before proceeding to France.

Sir Eric Geddes told me that he resented the idea of a Committee and that he was going to remonstrate about it. He also told me at the time that he had grave cause to complain of Mr. Winston Churchill's interference in naval matters and that he proposed to make a remonstrance to the Prime Minister. I saw Sir Eric Geddes late on Friday when he showed me a letter he had written to the Prime Minister making the protest and he then told me of his interview with the Prime Minister in which the Prime Minister told him that the letter was an unjustifiable one and Mr. Winston Churchill had a perfect right to interfere and make the suggestions that he had done.

On asking Sir Eric Geddes what he intended to do he told me he intended to resign but that he would think it over till the next morning.

Saturday morning. He came over to see me and showed me a letter in which he tendered his resignation. After consultation he went over to see Mr. Bonar Law as leader of his party in the House of Commons, in the same way as I had previously consulted Lord Curzon as my leader in the House of Lords. I suggested an alteration in Sir Eric Geddes's letter which would give a loophole for the Prime Minister and which words Sir Eric Geddes inserted.

I then told Sir Eric Geddes what I thought my position was, as follows: if he received an assurance that Mr. Winston Churchill would not be allowed to interfere, then naturally that protection would be given to the War Office representatives. If on the other hand the Prime Minister accepted his resignation refusing to give the assurance, then I should write another letter to the Prime Minister. The first letter I had written did not invite a reply and I had no reason to complain that one had not been sent. It was just meant to show what the C.I.G.S.'s and my feelings were on the subject and as a warning that if it happened again we should have to consider our position. My next letter however would be to ask for distinct assurances that we should not have any interference and if the Prime Minister did not give us these assurances, and if he refused them to Sir Eric Geddes there was no reason why he should give them to me, I should pursue exactly the same course as Sir Eric Geddes and ask to be relieved at once of my post.

* * *

Derby was always searching for visible means of showing his confidence in Haig. He had been largely instrumental in obtaining a field-marshal's baton for him in the New Year Honours and he now wished that Haig's successful conduct of the Battle of Arras should be marked by the award of a peerage to the Commander-in-Chief.

Sir Douglas Haig to Lord Derby

Personal
24 June 1917

Eastcott,
Kingston Hill,
Surrey

As desired by you, I now reply *in writing* to the question which you were good enough to ask me this morning.

I feel that you have done me a very great honour by offering to recommend me for a Peerage. And, since I know you, I have thought most carefully over the matter. I value, more than I can say, your great kindness in wishing to put my name forward for so high a distinction. I am also fully alive to the great debt which I owe to my subordinates of all ranks in the Forces in France for all our successes, and I realise that in honouring me, their Commander, you are in a way honouring the whole army. Still I feel it is best for me to remain as I am, for the personal reasons which I mentioned to you this morning.[1]

With renewed thanks for your kindness in thinking of the desirability of rewarding me *at all*.

Derby's compliments and assurances to Haig did not, however, induce in him any strong conviction that the British Government was wholeheartedly behind his impending battle, for five weeks later we find him on the eve of Passchendaele writing in almost querulous terms:

[1] Haig, although well off, did not feel rich enough to sustain a peerage. When, in 1919, he accepted an earldom, it was coupled with a grant of £100,000. See *The Private Papers of Douglas Haig*, by Robert Blake.

Sir Douglas Haig to Lord Derby

Personal 29 July 1917

. . . What are the facts?

Less than a week ago (and after a desperate fight to gain supremacy in the Artillery contest that had been raging for a fortnight), I am told my plan has been approved. This approval is sandwiched between paras. indicating not only a readiness to stop my offensive on the first possible excuse, but that guns and personnel, with a liberal supply of amn. had already been sent to Italy. Plans too are to be prepared for sending more troops to that theatre.

How different to the wholehearted, almost unthinking support given by our Government to the Frenchman [Nivelle] last January.

Never a word have I received that the Govt. is really *determined* to concentrate all possible resources at this the decisive point, at the decisive moment. For instance, 18 pounder guns might have been collected from somewhere to keep my army up to establishment. Drafts are another item causing anxiety, and others which my official correspondence has brought to your notice.

It is this lack of 'hustle' on the part of the War Cabinet in essentials to success which really worries me, and makes me anxious for the future.

Forgive me writing in this strain in reply to your charming letter, but I feel it my duty to tell you what ought to be done to ensure success at (according to my opinion) this, the crisis of the war.

As we have seen, the failure of the Nivelle offensive had led to that general's dismissal and his replacement as French Commander-in-Chief by General Pétain. The British Army ceased to be under French command and Sir Henry Wilson returned from French Headquarters and was temporarily relegated to Eastern Command in Britain. Pétain had made a great reputation for himself at Verdun, but he was regarded as essentially a strategist of the defensive school. The French armies, under his firm but careful handling, were nursing themselves back to strength after the mutinies in May. It was bound to be many months before the French could be expected to mount a large-scale offensive.

Meanwhile Haig had long, in deadly secrecy, been maturing a grandiose conception of attack. Haig's plan envisaged a break-through to the North Sea with the first objective the Passchendaele and Messines Ridges, the second Ostend and the third Bruges. It was not until June that he laid his plans before the War Cabinet; but he and Robertson had been preparing them for more than six months. Since the beginning of the year he had been building up reserves of men, artillery and munitions for what was to be the biggest and the most costly punch ever struck by the British Army.

No wonder that he resented being put under Nivelle's command at the time of the Battle of Arras. All his carefully and secretly garnered reserves might have been thrown into a battle which he thought was being fought in the wrong place. No wonder too that he preferred Nivelle's actual plans to those of Joffre since they involved a considerably smaller British commitment. Thus, while the French Army was licking its wounds and was condemned to a defensive role, Haig, with the laurels of Arras on his brow and with British armies under his command whose strength, equipment and morale had never been higher, was ardently determined to exploit his limited success on the Vimy Ridge with a further and far more dramatic advance.

On the last day of July, to the accompaniment of a prodigious cannonade of gas and high-explosive shells, the British Fifth Army hurled itself against the enemy. Throughout August, September, October and November the fighting continued with intense severity and immense loss of life, the British casualties, since they were attacking, being greatly in excess of those of the enemy. British casualties in these four months of fighting amounted to the appalling figure of 350,000. In return there was little to show for it but a sea of disputed mud.

Though Lloyd George was to spend the rest of the war attempting to prevent Haig from launching offensives, he had on this occasion been an enthusiastic supporter of the battle. Early in May he had attended a conference in Paris. There he had actually preached to the French the merits of a war of attrition and urged them to co-operate with Haig in an all-out offensive which would leave the enemy no breathing-space. Lloyd George's mood at this time was affected by two things—he was committed to the merits of offensive warfare by his championing of the Nivelle Plan; and the Battle of Arras showed that considerable results could be gained without undue casualties. Moreover the mounting toll of the U-boats had engendered in almost all the leading British war leaders acceptance of Lord Fisher's slogan 'the Army must win the war before the Navy loses it'.

By October, however, the Prime Minister was appalled by the ill-return for such costly casualties and he cast about him for some means of bringing the battle to a halt. He summoned Sir Henry Wilson and Lord French as independent military advisers to the War Cabinet. Mr. Churchill tells us in his *World Crisis*:

> In formally consulting outside advisers the Prime Minister obviously courted the resignation of the Chief of the General Staff. It was not forthcoming. The Cabinet were not prepared to demand it; and nothing but mutual distrust resulted.

Lloyd George must by now have been beginning to suspect that in any dispute he might have with the generals Derby would side with them. And in his attempts to bring the battle to a close he does not appear to have consulted Derby. He worked as always through devious channels. Derby still had unlimited faith in Haig and his plan of attack. When the fighting for Passchendaele had been proceeding for two months he wrote:

Lord Derby to Sir Douglas Haig

Confidential 28 September 1917

MY DEAR HAIG,

Although I think you already know it, I write to tell you of my complete and absolute confidence in you. Robertson has told me of the worry that has been caused you in various ways, but I beg you to believe that he and I are prepared to back you in every way, and I should like you to feel that this additional worry is one you can shift to our shoulders. We will bear it for you. The best of luck to you. Believe me

Ever your very sincere friend and admirer,

DERBY

I feel that in expressing our confidence in you, Robertson and I are expressing the views of the country generally.

Lloyd George would still have liked, instead of fighting in the mud of Passchendaele, to send reinforcements and above all heavy guns from the Western front to assist the Italians in a stroke against the Austro-Hungarian armies.

When everything had been consumed at a prodigious rate in the fighting in Flanders, a heavy price had to be paid for the neglect of the Balkan Front. On October 24 the Austrian armies, stiffened by six German divisions, attacked on the Isonzo Front and in the ensuing disaster of Caporetto the Italian Army suffered casualties, most of them prisoners, amounting to above 800,000.

The reinforcements which Haig had begrudged a few months before now had to be sent to prevent Italy being knocked out of the war. Five British divisions under General Plumer and five French divisions under General Fayolle together with 300,000 rifles, 4,000 machine guns, 300 field guns, nearly 400 medium guns and howitzers and 40 heavy pieces, all complete with ammunition, were within a few days entrained for the Piave Front, where the Italian army was rallying.

The immediate consequence of the Caporetto disaster was the Conference of Rapallo. As a result of this conference General Cadorna was dismissed and replaced by General Diaz and a Supreme War Council was established. In its conception the Supreme War Council was intended to be a political body consisting of the Prime Ministers of Great Britain, France and Italy, each accompanied by one other minister of Cabinet rank. It was intended that this body should work out a unified strategy and give strategic directions to the Allied Armies and Navies. The Allied statesmen were, however, to be assisted and advised by high-ranking military and naval personalities.

The Supreme War Council held its first meeting on November 8 at Rapallo, and it was decided that its permanent headquarters should be situated at Versailles. Lord Milner was appointed to assist Mr. Lloyd George, and Sir Henry Wilson, who had been languishing in Eastern Command, was appointed as principal military adviser.

The French and Italian military representatives were General Foch and General Cadorna. At Calais Lloyd George had clipped

Haig's wings by subordinating him to Nivelle. He eagerly exploited the disaster at Caporetto and the resulting Rapallo Conference to set up a military hierarchy which would be superior in authority to Robertson and the General Staff and from which the British War Cabinet could receive advice of a more palatable character. We shall see in the next chapter how the skilful intrigues of the Prime Minister and his new henchman, Sir Henry Wilson, were to culminate successfully in driving Sir William Robertson from the War Office.

* * *

On 12 November 1917 Lloyd George took the opportunity at a public luncheon in Paris, where he stopped on his way back from Rapallo, to express doubts as to whether the war policy of the Allies was being conducted on the correct principles. He proceeded to voice his disappointment at the achievements of the British Army. 'We have won great victories. When I look at the appalling casualty lists I sometimes wish it had not been necessary to win so many.'

This attack by the Prime Minister on the British High Command roused much resentment. Carson, who was a member of the War Cabinet, said publicly a few days later:

> I have met in the course of my work as a member of H.M. Government three great men—I say that advisedly—Field-Marshal Haig, Sir William Robertson and Sir J. Jellicoe. They have my absolute confidence, and it is really difficult to understand the different trends of thought which have appeared in the last fortnight in relation to these men, who morning, noon and night go through anxieties which words cannot picture, who are burdened with orders and commands which involve hundreds of thousands of lives, and who see themselves held up from time to time to the odium of their countrymen as though in some way they were betraying their country, if not by their corruption at least by their incompetence.[1]

On Wednesday 14 November 1917 Haig recorded in his dairy:

[1] *Haig* by Duff Cooper.

I returned to Bavincourt about 5 p.m. A letter from Lord Derby (S. of S. for War) re Lloyd George's speech last Monday. 'I feel that it is a speech which you will possibly think reflects on you and your men. I want you to allow me to again express my entire confidence in you—and I shall probably have to show that confidence in an outward and visible way. You will understand what I mean.' I have not read L.G.'s speech, but from Reuter's summary of it, I gather that it is more likely to hearten the enemy and discourage the Italians than any other language![1]

Though Robertson had returned from Rapallo fully committed to the establishment of a new supreme council at Versailles he was still determined to dispute with the War Cabinet the question of the relative status of himself and the British representative at Versailles, Sir Henry Wilson. Robertson realised that Lloyd George would now try to settle everything at Versailles and would seek to rely for military advice on Wilson rather than himself. He was determined that it should be established that Wilson was subordinate to the War Office and could only advise the Supreme War Council after consultation with Whitehall. On his return to London in advance of the Prime Minister he quickly secured the adhesion of the War Council and of Derby to a determined opposition to what Lloyd George clearly had in mind. There followed an exchange of correspondence between Derby and the Prime Minister in which a compromise was gradually beaten out:

The Prime Minister to Lord Derby

26 November 1917 10 Downing Street

I am very glad to have your letter, and I appreciate greatly your efforts to make the new Inter-Allied War Council a really workable scheme. It must be a reality and not a sham. All the pressure from the Allied countries is towards increasing the powers of the Council rather than towards diminishing them. France and America are anxious to make it executive; M. Clemenceau would like a Generalissimo. The Rapallo scheme is therefore the very minimum the Cabinet can accept.

[1] *The Private Papers of Douglas Haig* by Robert Blake.

With the points you set out in your letter I am in substantial agreement but so much will depend on the practical working of the new machinery that I consider it would be a mistake to lay too much emphasis on details at the beginning. It is clear that while Sir Henry Wilson acts as one of the co-advisers to the War Council the C.I.G.S. remains the official adviser of the War Cabinet, and the latter will therefore continue to advise the Cabinet on all recommendations of the Council before they are finally adopted by the Cabinet. He will also accompany the Prime Minister to the meetings of the Council. Whether any particular matter is first mooted at the Council or at the War Cabinet is really an unimportant detail, so long as it is clear that the C.I.G.S. will have his say and the War Cabinet the final decision. In fact, if the C.I.G.S. accompanies the Prime Minister to the meetings of the Council, he will have his say in both places, and the question of where the matter is initiated becomes immaterial.

Lord Derby to the Prime Minister

Confidential — 28 November 1917

Thank you very much indeed for your letter of November 26. I have circulated a copy of it to each member of the Army Council with the following note which expresses my opinion:

> The Army Council will remember that I sent a letter to Mr. Lloyd George on the subject of the Inter-Allied Staff and have just received his answer. I do not propose to call an Army Council together to consider the letter, but think that every Member will wish to see it, and I should be glad if they would return their copy to me with such remarks as they may think necessary upon it. For myself, I may say that I consider the answer satisfactory in that it gives to C.I.G.S., and through him the Army Council, the final word before any decision is taken. There will undoubtedly be certain difficulties of administration, but given good will on both sides I have no doubt they will be overcome.

I sincerely hope you will impress upon Henry Wilson that there must be give and take and that he must not try to put himself into a position of greater authority than is contemplated in your letter. Personally I feel that he will not do so, and he cannot go wrong if, in any advice he gives, it is clearly understood that it is the advice of the Inter-Allied Staff as a whole. . . .

In November Derby was deeply affected by the death on active service in Palestine of his son-in-law Neil Primrose. This brilliant young man, the younger son of the great Lord Rosebery, had married Derby's daughter, Victoria, two years before. He had been a Liberal Member of Parliament for Wisbech since 1910, and had thrown up a most promising career as a junior minister in the Government in order to join the Bucks Yeomanry. In reply to a letter of condolence from Esher, Derby wrote:

Lord Derby to Lord Esher

Confidential

Derby House
25 November 1917

MY DEAR REGGIE,

I am afraid I have been most remiss in answering your last few letters, and I am all the more ashamed as they were most interesting and instructive. The last ten days are the worst I have ever been through, and my dear Neil's death coming on top of it all, has for the moment completely knocked me out, and made me feel at war with all my fellow creatures. He was one of the most lovable men I have ever come across, and one cannot but feel the glory of his death, an example to many men of his age who ought to be fighting, but let Parliament or other shield save them from doing so. . . .

I am very tired of things, and should like to resign and have done with it all. I nearly did so this week, but a talk with the P.M. made me much happier about things, and though I do not flatter myself my going would bring down the Government, it would have made things very unpleasant for them, and I do not want to do that. After all Ll. G. is to my mind the only possible P.M. I really like the man, sometimes his method infuriates me, but what I feel about him, he is all out to win the war and generally he is right in what he does. For the rest of the Cabinet, I have very little respect, except perhaps for Smuts, . . . and Carson whom I trust completely. Milner is intolerable, I should like to put him in the ranks for six months and teach him what soldiers are like, that perhaps would stop his continual sneering at soldiers as if they were all damned fools. If he only knew how the country generally, and the Labour Party in particular, hate and distrust him, he might learn a little wisdom. I believe he is to remain in Paris with Wilson; I very much distrust the combination.

I am low about my position, I feel I have let the army down by not resigning as a protest against this Inter-Allied Staff, but if it were not for the various personalities interested in the matter, I should really approve of it, and I don't quite see what good I should have done by resigning. I could not have stopped the Allied Staff being formed, even if I had wanted to, and I did get, by staying, the very necessary safeguard that Wully should attend all these conferences when the P.M. is present, as the constitutional military adviser of the British Government. The danger of a 'bust up' is over for the time, but I shall dread the future as it is sure to come up again. Wully and Henry Wilson being what they are, and the P.M. being what he is, all the same he is the *only* possible P.M. and he has more virtues than faults.

Derby's apprehensions about these clashing personalities were soon to be justified.

XIV

The Dismissal of Sir William Robertson

WE have seen how throughout 1917 Lloyd George had been carefully setting the stage to curb the power and procure the resignations of both Haig and Robertson. The creation of the Supreme War Council at Versailles provided the Prime Minister with an instrument with which he was able to achieve at least half his purpose. Derby's conduct in these transactions has often been criticised and it is right that the whole affair be laid in detail before the reader. There is a wealth of hitherto unpublished material available both in the Derby papers and in the Royal Archives which enables Derby's part in these events to be chronicled with considerable exactitude.

Of Lloyd George's secret machinations there can be no doubt. M. Paul Painlevé, the French War Minister, has described his meeting with Lloyd George at Boulogne on 28 September 1917 where they secretly agreed that unity of command on the war front could be procured in two stages.[1] The first stage was planned to be the creation of the Supreme War Council which would in fact be controlled by Foch with his long-time friend Sir Henry Wilson as British Representative, while in the second stage, when British public opinion had been suitably converted to the idea, Foch was to be officially appointed to the Supreme Command of both the Allied armies.

At the end of November the British Fifth Army launched the celebrated battle of Cambrai where, for the first time, several hundred tanks were used in a terrain suited to their capabilities and

[1] *Comment J'ai Nommé Foch et Pétain* by Paul Painlevé.

according to a plan which gave the tank a pre-eminent instead of only a co-operative role on the battlefield. The success of this stroke was fantastic. In the course of one day the whole German trench system was penetrated on a front of six miles and 10,000 prisoners and 200 guns were captured with only 1,500 British casualties. The British High Command was as much surprised by the success of this operation as was the German; and no effective plan had been made to exploit a success which had not been anticipated. This surprise stroke had been made upon a part of the German line which was not heavily defended but was served by good railway communications. Within a few days the Germans assembled reinforcements and, using for the first time tactics of infiltration, succeeded in recapturing all that the British tanks had gained.

The British High Command had been very prompt to claim the glory of their victory and their triumphant communiqués caused the church bells in Britain to be pealed from one end of the land to the other. When, however, Haig failed to exploit the initial gain and the German counter-stroke had fully restored the *status quo* British G.H.Q. were slow to admit the fact that the tables had been turned. This led to a marked diminution in public confidence in Haig. Meanwhile Derby renewed his pressure on Haig to get rid of his Director of Military Intelligence, Charteris. Derby had for a long time felt that Charteris's reports had been over-optimistic. He was not looking for a scapegoat but he did not wish to see Haig brought down out of an excess of loyalty to a subordinate who, at the time, was widely considered to have misled not only the Commander-in-Chief and the Government but also, through his rosy communiqués, the public, as to the true state of the war in France.[1]

Sir Douglas Haig to Lord Derby

December 1917

. . . I cannot agree that Charteris should be made 'whipping-boy' for the charge of undue optimism brought against myself.

His duty is to collect, collate and place before me all evidence

[1] In fact, as is revealed by Charteris's diaries, Haig when in London often exaggerated Charteris's already over-sanguine prognostics.

obtainable in regard to the enemy. He has unusually high qualifications for that duty and I am quite satisfied with the manner in which he has performed it since I have been in command. The responsibility for the judgment formed on the evidence obtained and for the views put forward to the War Cabinet rests on me and not on him; and if the War Cabinet are not satisfied with the views put forward by me it is I, and not Charteris, who must answer for those views . . .

Lloyd George was still busy converting his principal colleagues to the necessity for removing both Haig and Robertson. He had moreover convinced himself, or allowed himself to be convinced, of an implausible piece of gossip: that Robertson had prompted General Allenby (who had been instructed to capture Jerusalem) to ask for reinforcements on a scale which could manifestly not be supplied so that it would be easy to send none at all—thereby making more manpower available for Haig to stoke into future Passchendaeles. It was one of Lloyd George's defects as a war leader that he assumed that everyone with whom he did business had as tortuous a mind as his own, even if they had not been born in Wales. On December 11 he had a talk with Derby which seems to have gone some way in convincing the latter of the need for a change:

Lord Derby to the Prime Minister

Strictly Confidential

Derby House
11 December 1917

Our talk this afternoon has considerably disturbed me and while I would not ask you to look upon this as a carefully thought out letter I want to put down what on the spur of the moment occurs to me with regard to what you said.

In the first place if you are really thinking of making a complete change in the Supreme Command both at home and abroad, it is not the least use my going out and having a very unpleasant interview with Sir Douglas Haig with regard to the dismissal of what is after all only a subordinate officer. As it at present stands I must go out on Thursday but if you are really determined to make the big change I would not go if you would invent the excuse for me that you particularly wanted me at meetings on Thursday and Friday mornings. I leave this entirely to you but unless I hear from you to the contrary I shall go.

Now as regards the change of Haig and Robertson. I will deal with the former first. I do not think that the Cambrai affair is one on which you ought to hang so momentous a decision as the removal of a Commander-in-Chief. You may remember that the day before you went to Paris you told me that you had more confidence in Haig than you ever had before and if you had that confidence, and I believe you had, it would not be fair to remove him simply because a part of his line broke when the main attack for which he was chiefly prepared was successfully repulsed. I agree with you that it somewhat shakes one's confidence in anybody when you see the complete change of view that takes place between his letter of October 29 and those which he wrote subsequently but I ascribe, as I know you do, the first letter to the influence of Charteris whom it would be my mission to dismiss if I went out on Thursday. Therefore to dismiss Haig simply because of the Cambrai affair would to my mind be extremely unjust and I feel that I could not be a party to it.

Let us take however the other suggestion that it should not be a case of dismissal but rather a promotion and that he should be made Generalissimo of all the British Forces. There are certain difficulties in doing that which would have to be overcome, the principal one being the finding of a suitable Commander-in-Chief for the Western Front. Plumer is sound but certainly I think does not have that imagination for which you are looking. Birdwood to my mind would be absolutely out of the question. Monro would be the best man you could get and personally I look upon Rawlinson as a first-class soldier. I think Haig's successor, if the change is made, should lie between Monro and Rawlinson.

Now as to Haig's position if he is made Generalissimo. I am going into the question as to what the duties and powers of the Commander-in-Chief of old days were, but things have changed very much and I doubt whether the rules applicable then would apply now. The first question I would ask is what would be his relationship to the War Cabinet? Would he be the Chief Military Adviser to the War Cabinet? If so it is a most important post and one which anybody should hesitate before refusing. If on the other hand the advice to the War Cabinet is to be given by some other individual than the Generalissimo he is nothing more than an Inspector General, an inferior post which I do not think you could possibly ask Haig to accept. It would be much better to dismiss him altogether rather than to ask him to take a sinecure post. . . .

I confess that what you told me with regard to your suspicions today has shaken my confidence but I cannot believe that he (Robertson) would deliberately ask Allenby to send in a false telegram in order to deceive the Government. I agree with you that read in the light of subsequent events Allenby's telegram asking for the enormous increase in force in order to do what he has done with the existing forces seems ridiculous but that his former proposal should be put forward with a deliberate attempt to deceive the Government and that at the instance of Robertson, is almost beyond belief.

Though this letter shows Derby somewhat weakening in his support of Robertson and Haig, he clearly still thought that Haig might be saved if only he would dispense with Charteris. Accordingly he continued his pressure on Haig:

Lord Derby to Sir Douglas Haig

Strictly Personal and Confidential 12 December 1917

. . . I want to preface my remarks with a repetition of what I think you know already, namely, that I have and always shall have implicit confidence in you, and anything I may write is written from the point of view of a friend and not of an adverse critic. There are two kinds of friends. There is a friend who always tells you everything which he thinks you would like to hear, and there is a friend who tells you things which he thinks you should hear, even if they are not always pleasant. I look upon the latter as being the true friend, and it is from that point of view that I mean to write to you today.

First of all I will deal with the Charteris question. In the note I sent you yesterday I told you that I did not think that you could look upon me as wishing to make Charteris a whipping boy for the Cambrai affair. I have mentioned to you on more than one occasion that he was doing you an infinity of harm by his optimism and by what I consider his inaccurate information, and I have begged you to make a change. You tell me that you invariably make an allowance for the optimism of Charteris. That may be so, but I cannot think that you make sufficient allowance, and the best proof I have of that is your letter of October 8. That letter is clearly based on wrong information, and for that, although signed by you, I cannot hold you responsible. In view, not only of subsequent events, but of subsequent letters to you, I am sure you would never have put it forward if you had had proper information as to the enemy's reserves and possible reinforcements from the Russian Front.

It appears to me that too often the opinions, not only of the public but even of your subordinates and of the Army as a whole are not put before you. If they had been you would have realised that my view of Charteris as a public danger is shared by practically the whole of the Army, and I feel that if they do not put forward disagreeable facts to you, it is my duty to do so, however unpleasant it may be. I am afraid it is quite impossible for me to allow Charteris to remain as your Intelligence Officer, and much as I dislike giving you any instruction which I know is repugnant to you, I look upon you as a national asset and I cannot allow your loyalty to a subordinate to affect your position. I must, therefore, ask you to make a change within the next month, and shall be glad to hear either of your suggestions as to who should take his place or failing that, that I should make suggestions to you.

So much for Charteris. . . .

Yet another matter. The public are asking this—What lines have you got in the rear of our present one to which you can fall back? They have heard of this wonderful Hindenburg line with its extraordinary dugouts, etc. All this information has been used, and rightly used, to show what extraordinary courage is required on the part of our troops to take it. All people are asking if we have got anything of the same kind behind our line, and if not, why not. We hear of concrete pill-boxes—huge dugouts immune from artillery fire, etc., and they feel we ought to have the same, and I should be glad of your assurances that such lines exist. . . .

Lord Derby to the Prime Minister

13 December 1917

Enclosed is a copy of a letter I have written to Sir Douglas Haig, with which I hope you are in agreement. I have shown it to C.I.G.S., and as all the points I have mentioned are those which he thinks Haig himself must deal with in the manner I suggest, he is going over to France on Saturday morning as he has other matters he wishes to discuss with Haig. I have given him my letter. He is going to speak to Haig first and tell him what I have suggested should be carried out, and in the event of Haig refusing, he is going to hand him my letter as an order. As long as we get the thing done, it does not much matter what way we set about it, and I think this method that I suggest is the best one. There will be a rumpus, but I think everything will come all right.

I don't want to do anything to rattle Haig more than I can help at the present moment as there is no doubt he has been very much upset by the Cambrai affair. He certainly is a brave man, and that goes a long way with me. As soon as he heard of the trouble he was in the thick of the fighting himself.

The Prime Minister to Lord Derby

13 December 1917 — 10 Downing Street

Just read your letter. A fine straight letter that does you credit. It will do no end of good. The morale of the Army must be restored at all costs.

* * *

Shortly before Christmas Haig yielded to the many and long-standing pressures upon him. Though he still refused to dismiss Gough from the command of the Fifth Army—a course which Derby had also been pressing upon him—he grudgingly called for the resignation of Charteris who was replaced by General Sir Herbert Lawrence.

Immediately after Christmas the War Cabinet decided that Robertson must be replaced as C.I.G.S. In the Derby papers there is the following draft of a letter dealing with this; it is not clear whether it was despatched:

Lord Derby to the Prime Minister

Draft — War Office

27 December 1917

What you have told me with regard to the decision of the War Cabinet to make a fresh appointment to the post of C.I.G.S. naturally leads me to consider my own position.

> I accepted the office of S. of S. for War fully understanding that Sir William Robertson, as C.I.G.S., would be the principal military adviser of the War Cabinet to whom he would have the right of direct access on matters of a General Staff character and from whom he would take orders direct on such matters. In war this arrangement has obvious merits, and I had, and have, no wish to question the special position of the C.I.G.S.
>
> But, as in a general sense I am held to be responsible for all the work of the War Office I cannot dissociate myself from the consequences which flow from the resolve of the War Cabinet. Sir William Robertson is the senior military member of the War Cabinet and as such has rendered me loyal and devoted service. If, therefore, the War Cabinet wish to change their principal military adviser, I feel strongly that I ought not to appear to take advantage of any technicality; it is, as I conceive it, my clear duty as the Minister in charge of the War Office, and because, not being a member of the War Cabinet, I was not a party to their decision, to place my resignation in your hands and to ask you to submit it to the King for His Majesty's gracious acceptance.
>
> It is due to the great service over which I have had the honour to preside for twelve months, to my colleagues on the War Cabinet, and to yourself that I should see that, when, as head of His Majesty's Government, you are considering so vital a change in the administration of the Army, you should not be fettered in the advice you tender to the King by my retention of the seals of the War Department.

If Derby did not send this letter of resignation it is certain that he must have spoken in this sense to the Prime Minister. And on this occasion his threatened resignation was, if only temporarily, more effective than this gesture had proved and was to prove on numerous other occasions.

Haig left France on 29 December 1917, and on Tuesday 1 January 1918 he recorded in his diary in London:

> Lord Derby called to see me at 9.45 a.m. He first told me of Lloyd George's decision to change Robertson. This was only abandoned when Derby told him that he (D.) would also resign if either R. or myself were moved. The Prime Minister apparently was afraid of a Cabinet crisis and that his Government would be forced to go. With reference to the P.M.'s desire to change the C.I.G.S. it is interesting

to note that Sir Henry Wilson writes me *today*. 'I was wired for Sunday but return [to Paris?] tomorrow.' Doubtless L. G. intended him to succeed Robertson . . .[1]

Though as recently as September the British generals had been calling publicly for a continuance of the offensive, by the end of the year their mood had changed. The final collapse of Russia had enabled the Germans to move vast masses of men and munitions from the Eastern front and the possibility was dawning on the military mind that by the spring the Germans might have a superiority on the Western front even greater than that with which they had started the war. Consequently their continued clamour for fresh drafts to make good the losses of Passchendaele were animated by fear of a huge German offensive and not by a desire to launch a new offensive of their own. The Minister of Munitions, Churchill, on this occasion assessed the military situation in the same terms as did the soldiers and he was tireless in pressing Lloyd George to reinforce the Army. The Prime Minister, however, remained unconvinced that the generals had had a genuine change of heart and, while he was prepared to issue draconian decrees for calling up the last half million men capable of carrying a rifle, he was determined to keep them in England lest the arrival of such large reinforcements in France should tempt G.H.Q. to another costly offensive which would leave the country's reservoir of manpower drained utterly dry.

Consequently at this time Lloyd George sought to prove that the intelligence reports which spoke of massive troop movements to the West were exaggerated, and to argue that a German offensive was improbable and that if the existing British armies were properly disposed any such offensive could easily be held. Duff Cooper, in his life of Haig, describes the ingenious dilemma on which the Prime Minister sought to impale the Commander-in-Chief and which the latter was unable successfully to retort.

. . . Some members of the Cabinet, it appears, asked him whether, if he were Commander-in-Chief of the German Army, he would con-

[1] *The Private Papers of Douglas Haig* by Robert Blake.

sider that the chances of success were sufficient to justify him in incurring the losses which an attack on the Western Front must produce. It was a difficult question for Haig to answer, because it was his genuine opinion that if the Germans attacked in the spring, as it appeared that they would, and if the Allies could withstand their attack, as he believed that they could, then the Germans would be defeated in the autumn. He could therefore hardly admit that if he were in command of the German Army he would pursue a policy that would lead to the defeat of that Army in the same year. A skilful dialectician would have had little difficulty in extricating himself from the dilemma, but Haig was not a skilful dialectician and according to Robertson he said something to the effect that 'if the Germans were wise, they would think twice before making the attempt, because if they failed their position would be critical'. The politicians immediately pounced upon the statement and to Robertson's horror he saw Haig being manœuvred into the position of expressing doubts as to the probability of a German offensive.

'When coming away from the meeting,' writes Robertson, 'I remarked to the Field-Marshal that it would now be quite impossible for the War Office to secure for him the drafts which he required, since the War Cabinet would conclude from what he had told them that no serious attack need be apprehended, and consequently there was no urgency with respect to drafts. He denied having said anything that would bear that interpretation, and I could only reply that I was afraid the War Cabinet would think differently. Lord Derby, who was present, took the same view as myself, and we mutually hoped that the written statement which the Field-Marshal had been asked to send to the War Cabinet on the following day would help to restore matters to their true perspective.'

But the paper in which he stressed the importance of bringing and keeping his divisions up to strength was of no avail. When it came before the War Cabinet the Prime Minister tossed it contemptuously aside with the remark that it was inconsistent with what the Field-Marshal had said verbally. Haig had, in effect, been tricked into giving the opinion which the Cabinet wanted to hear, and even on such a vital matter they would not allow him to correct a false impression, nor would they take into account the written expression of his considered opinion. . . .[1]

[1] *Haig* by Duff Cooper.

An extract from Haig's diary at this time shows how Lloyd George even on a gay social occasion sought to shake Haig in his conviction that a heavy German offensive was to be feared:

Wednesday 9 January 1918

Doris and the children and I took a walk before lunch. D. and I then motored to London. I dropped her at Prince's Gate for lunch, and went to 10 Downing Street, where I lunched with the P.M. [Mr. Lloyd George]. We had a very cheery party. Conversation turned to the length of the war and some betting took place. Derby bet the P.M. 100 cigars to 100 cigarettes that war would be over by next New Year. L.G. disagreed. I said I thought the war would be over because of the internal state of Germany. Reports indicate that she was degenerating so fast that even if she won, there would not be the men to exploit and develop the industries of the country after the war. I also emphasised the critical nature of the coming four months on the Western Front if Germany did not make peace. Germany having only one million men as Reserves for this year's fighting, I doubted whether they would risk them in an attempt to 'break through'. If the Germans did attack it would be a gambler's throw. All seemed to depend on the struggle now going on in Germany between the Military and Civil parties. If the Military party won, they would certainly attack and try and deliver a knock-out blow against the Western Front. We must be prepared for this. The Prime Minister by cunning argument tried to get me to commit myself to an opinion that there would be 'no German offensive', that the 'German Army was done', but I refused to agree to his suggestions.[1]

Lloyd George was now fully resolved to bring matters to a conclusion with Robertson. He was seeking not only the downfall of the C.I.G.S. but hoped that his labours would result in procuring the object for which he had striven for nearly two years, that of a unified Allied command. Although Lloyd George had thought it prudent to tell the House of Commons on November 19 that he was 'personally utterly opposed to the suggestion' of the creation of a Generalissimo, 'for reasons into which it would not be desirable to enter' and that 'such a system would not work as it would only

[1] *The Private Papers of Douglas Haig* by Robert Blake.

produce real friction . . . not only friction between the Armies but friction between the nations and governments', early in the New Year he set in motion the measures which were designed to carry out his compact with Painlevé for which he had worked so tirelessly.[1] The occasion he selected was the meeting of the Supreme Allied Council at Versailles on February 1; the issue, the control of the Inter-Allied Reserve, which he and Clemenceau before the meeting took place had already decided should be set up. Robertson accompanied Lloyd George to the meeting; he reported to Derby:

Sir William Robertson to Lord Derby

Secret 2 February 1918

We had our final meeting this morning. The most important questions discussed at the Conference were Palestine, taking over the line, and the formation of Inter-Allied General Reserves. The extension of the line has been left more or less to be settled between Haig and Pétain. . . .

. . . As to the question of Inter-Allied Reserves you will find the whole case in the Papers enclosed. Of course it never was a question of reserves. The real question was one of command, and for all practical purposes we now have a French Generalissimo.[2] I do not know how or by whom powers are to be delegated to an officer, not on the Army Council and not directly under you, to issue orders to a Commander-in-Chief of about two million men. However, all this is alluded to in the Papers and I cannot help thinking that there is much trouble in store. It is folly, moreover, to imagine that anyone can issue orders about what is called General Reserves and stop there. The officer to issue orders about reserves must issue orders about many other things as well. It is folly to suppose it could be otherwise. The point is every officer must be under a civilian. Are you prepared to be Wilson's Minister and yet have no control over him? Who is to answer for the British Army and the future 'Cambrais'? The system is impossible, in my opinion. The P.M. got me out of it by saying I could not be spared from London, but surely I could find time to do on a part of one front what Ludendorff does on two fronts.

[1] See p. 295.

[2] This was, of course, a palpable exaggeration on Robertson's part.

P.S. (In the train) Forgive me for saying so, but the matter is a very serious one for *you*. The Army, the Army Council, the C.I.G.S. and Cs-in-Chief, will look to you, their Minister, to see that they are not placed in an impossible, unfair and unpractical position.

That Derby was alive to what was going on and that he fully recognised his own responsibilities in the matter is shown by the following:

Lord Derby to Sir Douglas Haig

30 January 1918

. . . We are going to be steadily attacked and between ourselves I feel the reason is that there is a certain gang who want to get rid of Robertson, not you, and they think that I stand in the way of their doing so, which is quite true. I do stand in their way and I mean to as long as I have the confidence in him that I now have, and I see no reason whatever for changing my view of his work . . .

At the Versailles meeting, which had been attended by the Prime Minister and Milner as well as by Robertson, it had been settled that an international reserve should be formed and that this reserve should be placed under the command of a committee consisting of the Military Representatives of all the Allied nations. In the case of France, however, General Foch was to take the place of General Weygand and was to become the president of the committee. The superior status of Foch as a Chief of Staff, though it did not warrant Robertson's allegation that 'for all practical purposes we now have a generalissimo', undoubtedly marked a tentative step in this direction. If there ever should be a generalissimo Foch was plainly designated for the job. Though Robertson had agreed in Paris to this arrangement and had, indeed, according to a memorandum which Derby drew up at the time, 'strongly advocated it', he succeeded on his return in inducing Derby to raise some doubts and difficulties about the constitutional position ensuing from the new arrangement.

At the Cabinet meeting where Lloyd George reported the decisions of the Versailles Conference, both Derby and Robertson were present. According to the account given by Lloyd George in his *War Memoirs* Derby stated that he had not yet had sufficient time to study the reports of the Conference and must therefore reserve judgment. The Prime Minister was obviously nearing the end of his patience in this matter and pointed out that as the matter had been decided unanimously by the Allied Representatives and by himself and Lord Milner, who had been endowed by the War Cabinet with full authority to deal with this question on their behalf, he trusted that the matter would be considered by the Army Council in a most helpful spirit and that there would be no delay in preparing the necessary Order in Council, if such were required, to give effect to their decision.

The need for a new Order in Council arose from the powers which had been given to Robertson when he first became C.I.G.S. Under the Order in Council issued at that time the C.I.G.S. had the sole right of issuing orders for operations subject, of course, to the over-riding direction of the Cabinet. The intention of the Paris Conference was that the new committee at Versailles should issue orders direct to the British divisions which were to be allocated to the reserve army. This would obviously be improper under the existing Order in Council. In Derby's memorandum it is stated that Robertson 'willingly agreed' to the rescinding of the old Order:

Lord Derby to Sir Douglas Haig

7 February 1918

There is a very acute crisis here with regard to the new Versailles agreement, and the Army Council met yesterday and unanimously passed the enclosed resolutions.

For my own part, I think that the conditions as they stand are contrary to the constitution and will require very great alteration before they can be made even workable; but the object of my letter is not to go into detail with you now, but to tell you of an interview I had with the Prime Minister this morning, and which has, to a certain extent, if his account be accurate, still further added to my perplexity on the subject.

The Prime Minister came to breakfast with me this morning, and he emphasised his determination to support you through thick and thin.

I asked him if he thought that this Versailles agreement was helping you, and whether you had agreed to it and were satisfied with the way it would work. He assured me that you had accepted it and, to use his own words, that he and you had met with greater cordiality than perhaps you had ever met before, and he gave me to understand that, although there were certain things which would have to be adjusted as to the giving of the orders to you, you agreed to the main principle. I told him I had not heard from you on the subject, but that I was surprised to hear his statement. He then went on to talk about Robertson, and, between you and me, whatever happens I think he is quite determined to get rid of him, and herein comes the difficulty of my position. If it is really so that you agree with the principles, provided the question of the conveyance of orders is settled, then I should be justified in remaining in office, because it would then be only a question of Robertson opposing a scheme to which you had given your assent. If, on the other hand, you are in agreement with Robertson, and Robertson is got rid of because he won't agree to it, then, naturally, I should have to go too.

The Prime Minister then put to me a question which you alone can answer. He asked whether it would be possible for you to come over and talk to him in the strictest confidence, and by confidence he means, seeing him and probably me as well, and speaking fully on the subject without feeling it your duty to report what took place to Robertson or to anybody else. I see the great advantage that might come of this, but, at the same time, I could not ask you to do it if you thought that by doing so you were acting in any way disloyally to Robertson. If you decide that you cannot come over, and as I say I hope you may find it possible to do so, perhaps you would kindly let me have at the earliest possible opportunity a statement which I could discuss with the Prime Minister, giving your views on the Versailles agreement.

Sir Douglas Haig to Lord Derby

Personal and Secret 8 February 1918

With reference to your letter of February 7th, I hope to reach London tomorrow afternoon about 3.30, and will call on arrival and see you and Robertson. I consider general reserve desirable but do not concur in system set up for commanding it. Most important that I should see you.

On February 16, when the crisis had finally been resolved with the dismissal of Robertson, Derby set down his own recollections of these events in a lengthy memorandum which has importance as a contemporary account and from which it will be necessary to quote as the story unfolds:

Lord Derby's Memorandum

16 February 1918

Sir Douglas Haig came over that afternoon (9 February 1918). I met him at the station and took him straight to Downing Street discussing with him the proposal on the way. He was of opinion that as far as his accepting orders from Versailles was concerned that the proposals were perfectly all right and he could legally accept them. When we got to Downing Street we met the Prime Minister and Mr. Macpherson. The Prime Minister then said that he had had a brain wave to the effect that as Sir William Robertson evidently thought that Versailles was going to have a great deal of power that he should have the option of taking that place in preference to that of C.I.G.S. In that case Sir Henry Wilson should become C.I.G.S. Sir Douglas Haig naturally declined to express any opinion on this, simply contenting himself with saying that as far as he was concerned as to his relations with Versailles he was quite satisfied. I was also quite ready to see Sir William Robertson accept Versailles as I felt that it was a post, not only of great importance at the present, but that as the Americans came into the field more and more work of co-ordination would have to be done there and I do not think it was in any way derogatory to Sir William Robertson to offer him the place. It was felt however it would be perfectly impossible to call him Deputy C.I.G.S. and therefore the words British Military Representative were substituted.

The Prime Minister to Lord Milner[1]

9 February 1918

I have had an afternoon of it with Haig and Derby. Haig was quite reasonable. He did not quite like Henry Wilson coming here, and thought the Army might be very shocked; but he said that was a matter for the Government. In fact, his attitude was perfectly correct. Derby, Haig and Macpherson thought that to make Robertson Deputy

[1] *War Memoirs* by Lloyd George.

would be to humiliate him, and they thought it quite unnecessary in view of the fact that Wilson was made the Chief Adviser of the Government. Subject to that, the document was signed by Derby, and he is to see the King later on about it.

Wully is to be told tomorrow by Macpherson, who is motoring over to Eastbourne to communicate the news to him. Derby is delighted with our change of plans; and as we had only the choice of three or four doubtful second bests, I am firmly convinced that this is the best of them.

* * *

Meanwhile, Robertson and those who were of his way of thinking at G.H.Q. had recourse to the Press to ventilate their grievances and to mobilise Parliamentary and public opinion against the arrangements agreed upon at Versailles. On February 8 the *Morning Post* carried a story from its military correspondent in Paris which stated:

> The decisions of the recent Inter-Allied War Council regarding the control of British troops in the field are reported to be of such strange character that Parliament should demand the fullest details and a Parliamentary Committee should examine them at once and take the opinions of our General Staff and of our Commanders in the field concerning the new arrangements.[1]

The author of this calculated and inspired indiscretion was Colonel Charles Repington who had been the military correspondent of *The Times* since 1905 but had, after quarrelling with the editor, Mr. Geoffrey Dawson, transferred a few weeks before to the *Morning Post*. Repington had started life as a professional soldier and was one of that brilliant group of officers, which included French, Henry Wilson and Haig, who had all served in the South African War and had come home convinced of the inevitability of a German war and dedicated to the task of fashioning a British Army

[1] Repington followed up his original story with a signed article which appeared in the *Morning Post* on February 11 in which he disclosed in much greater detail the Allied plan for a strategic reserve. On February 21 he and the editor of the *Morning Post* were both convicted under the Defence of the Realm Act for revealing military secrets and were each fined £100.

indoctrinated with the new lessons about fire power which had been learnt in South Africa, and fit to take its place as a major factor in a Continental war.

Derby, like Churchill, had served in the South African War and both of them were on friendly terms with all these men. While most of his friends continued their careers in the Army, Repington sharpened his pen and campaigned in the Press for all the new military ideas which were burgeoning in the pre-war years. When war came he constituted himself the mouthpiece of the High Command and General Staff and it was he who with Northcliffe's backing had exposed the scandal of the lack of shells in May 1915. Repington's connections included politicians in both parties and much of fashionable society. His diaries are among the most fascinating and informative of the period.

Repington had made himself a unique reputation on *The Times* but his outspoken methods usually commended themselves more to Lord Northcliffe than they did to the editor, Mr. Geoffrey Dawson. Eventually Dawson persuaded Northcliffe to dispense with Repington's services. The terms in which the historian of *The Times* records the services and departure of its military correspondent are worthy of preservation as a particularly fine specimen of the aura of smug superiority towards its staff which has long prevailed in Printing House Square:

> The editor, Steed, and the office generally were in constant disagreement with Repington about his articles. The censor's hand lay heavily enough on them; but the Press Bureau was concerned only with what should not be revealed to the enemy. Dawson had the more delicate task of preserving the paper's reputation for good sense and consistency; and submitted the Military Correspondent's articles to frequent and drastic revision. These rectifications, and the editorial insistence on anonymity which Repington was all too ready to abandon, led in the end to the latter's resignation from the paper in January 1918.
>
> The revision of the articles Repington wrote as Military Correspondent had been needed not only to make them consistent in some degree with one another, but above all to keep them in conformity with the leading articles in which the paper's policy for war was laid down.

The History adds a footnote which is a journalistic collector's piece:

> He transferred at once to the *Morning Post*, with which he had previously concerted terms advantageous to himself and arranged the syndicating of his articles in a chain of American newspapers. There he spent the rest of the war industriously destroying the reputation for intelligence which Dawson had preserved for him by judicious deletions while he worked with *The Times*. After Dawson's resignation, Repington vainly asked Northcliffe if he might return.

The naked admission that the news columns of *The Times* were, under the direction of Mr. Geoffrey Dawson, tailored to suit the opinions of the leading articles, instead, as one might have supposed in a serious newspaper, of the editor addressing his critical faculties to the news reports of his correspondents is altogether delightful and fully in keeping with the policy which Dawson relentlessly pursued down to the termination of his editorship. And what are we to think of the sanctimonious excuse for the 'judicious deletions' on the grounds that they were partly intended to preserve the correspondent's 'reputation for intelligence'? Or of the scarcely veiled suggestion that there was something indecent in Repington concerting 'terms advantageous to himself'? Would the pundits of Printing House Square have been less shocked if Repington's terms with the *Morning Post* had been *disadvantageous* to himself? As for the idea that Americans should be allowed to read what an Englishman had written, this naturally seemed to *The Times* the abomination of abominations.

The rumours which were already circulating at G.H.Q., in Paris and in London that Lloyd George was once more to attempt a trial of strength with the generals inevitably tended to bring about a coalescence of the Government's critics from both wings of the political stage. Repington noted in his diary for Saturday, February 9:

> Met Gwynne at the Bath Club. We compared notes and experiences. After I had told him what I had learned, he told me that there was a big row on here, and that he hoped the Army Council were all going to stand firm. Asquith has stated that he will speak on the debate on the

Address next Tuesday, and Gwynne and I agreed that I should write and expose the Paris proceedings either Monday or Tuesday. Gwynne is going to see Derby and try to hearten him up, and is all for fighting this matter out.

No evidence exists as to whether or not Gwynne succeeded in seeing Derby. In any case it is clear that Derby was not drawn into these political manœuvres. Indeed he is specifically exculpated from any such charge by Lloyd George in his *War Memoirs*:

> As a proof that Lord Derby was not implicated in these intrigues, I have a note taken at the time which showed that he denounced the article in question as clearly of a most mischievous character. He believed that it had been written from Paris, and said that it was clear that Colonel Repington had become acquainted with information of a secret and confidential character which had now been made public by the editor of the *Morning Post.*

* * *

Repington's revelations in the *Morning Post* were taken up by other newspapers, notably the *Globe*. Lloyd George was by this time determined to be rid of Robertson, even if this should involve the resignation of Haig and Derby as well. It was obvious that his political enemies meant to exploit the growing crisis to the maximum. Lloyd George decided to drive ahead. While he was animating Derby to have Repington prosecuted he drew up a nine-point plan setting out how the new Versailles Agreement was to work. He quickly procured the acquiescence not only of Derby but of Haig. Little evidence exists as to the wiles and inducements by which Lloyd George obtained Haig's agreement, but from this moment forward, though the crisis appeared to rage, Lloyd George had really won. If Robertson did not comply he would be isolated and Lloyd George, who had been prepared to face the resignation of two military chieftains, now only had to cope with that of one. Derby was still an uncertain factor, but so long as his resignation, which seemed likely, was not accompanied by those of both Haig and Robertson the situation was unlikely to prove destructive of the Government:

Lord Derby to Sir William Robertson

11 February 1918 War Office

This is the agreement arrived at between myself and the P.M. and to which Sir Douglas Haig assented. I propose to put it before the Army Council this afternoon with the exception of the last paragraph and ask their consent to it. I hope you will give me your support.

9 February 1918 10 Downing Street

1. The C.I.G.S. to hold office under the same conditions and with the same powers as every Chief of the Staff up to the appointment of Sir William Robertson.
2. The C.I.G.S. to continue to be the supreme military adviser of the Government.
3. The Military Representative at Versailles to be a Member of the Army Council.
4. The Military Representative at Versailles to be in constant communication and consultation with the C.I.G.S., but to be absolutely free and unfettered in the advice which he gives as a member of the Board of Military Representatives sitting at Versailles.
5. When that advice is formulated it is to be submitted to the C.I.G.S. for the purpose of advising the Cabinet thereon.
6. When it is necessary to summon a Supreme Council, either to decide upon a plan of operations or to settle differences that may have arisen between the various Commanders-in-Chief, or between any one or more of the Commanders-in-Chief and Versailles, or for any other purpose, the C.I.G.S. to accompany the Ministers delegated to attend the Council for the purpose of advising them as to the decisions to be taken, after hearing what the Military Representatives and the Commanders-in-Chief have to say from their respective points of view.
7. As prompt decisions may have to be taken as to the sending of reserves to one part or other of the battle front, and time lost in referring to London may be fatal, full powers must be given to the Military Repesentative in accordance with principles already settled to give the necessary orders in respect of Divisions included in the General Reserve.
8. The C.I.G.S., even when not accompanied by a Minister, to have

the right to go to France to consult in person with any one or all of the Military Representatives of the Supreme Council.

9. The Military Representative at Versailles to be Sir William Robertson and the C.I.G.S. to be Sir Henry Wilson.

D. LLOYD GEORGE

Lord Derby's Memorandum

. . . In the afternoon [February 11] we had a meeting of the Army Council where a resolution was unanimously passed that the Government proposals met the Constitutional difficulty. The Military members however suggested that the C.I.G.S. should also be our representative at Versailles. . . .

I reported this to the Prime Minister who said that the proposal that the Chiefs of the Staffs should be the Executive Committee had been proposed at Versailles and had been turned down. Incidentally I may mention here that although I have asked to see the *procès-verbal* of the meeting I have not hitherto been accorded the privilege and therefore I am completely in the dark as to what really took place there . . .

Lord Derby to Sir William Robertson

Confidential and Personal — War Office

11 February 1918

I brought the A.C. resolution before the W.C. but was informed that it had been definitely decided that the two posts of C.I.G.S. and Mil. Representative at Versailles could not be combined.

I earnestly trust you will see your way to accept the position offered to you as I feel convinced that more and more responsibility must fall on the man occupying it, and seeing that Gen. Foch has been specially selected as France's representative, it would I am sure appeal to the British public that you should be the representative safeguarding our interests.

Sir William Robertson to Lord Derby

11 February 1918 — War Office

Here is my reply. I greatly regret it is as it is. But the matter is too serious to play with. You may be sure I have reached my conclusion with sorrow. It is an unpleasant ending to a pleasant association. Personally, I imagine it means the end of my military career, after over 40 years hardish work, and it lands me once more into poverty. But these considerations must be ignored.

P.S. I would like to clear out *at once*. It is awkward for me and useless to the Army my hanging on.

Sir William Robertson to Lord Derby

Secret

War Office
11 February 1918

You have informed me this morning that the War Cabinet have decided to appoint General Sir H. Wilson as C.I.G.S., and to appoint me, with my present position as Army Councillor, British Military Representative to the Supreme War Council, vice General Wilson.

With respect to the first decision you informed me that the reason for removing me from my appointment is because the Prime Minister cannot 'get on' with me. For this I can only express my deep regret, because I have always tried to serve him loyally and to tell the truth fearlessly. Will you please say when I am to hand over my duties to General Wilson.

With respect to the second decision you will remember that at a meeting on the 6th instant the four Military Members present advised you that, in order to give effect to the intention of the Supreme War Council with respect to the formation and control of the Allied General Reserves, the Army Councillor holding the appointment of C.I.G.S., who is fully acquainted with the resources and needs of the British Military forces, is the proper officer to be delegated as British Military Representative on the Executive Committee at Versailles. After careful consideration I am convinced that there would be no difficulty in making such arrangements as would permit of the British C.I.G.S. carrying out the duty without interference with essential duties at home.

I am still unable to see any other practical and workable system, for the reasons given in the various Papers submitted to yourself and to the Prime Minister during the last fortnight, as well as for those put forward by Army Councillors at the meetings recently held. I need not further refer to them except to say that it is impossible in practice to separate action in connection with General Reserves from action concerning innumerable other matters which go to make up 'military operations'; and that the decision of the War Cabinet leaves, as before, the issue of orders affecting military operations in the hands of two different authorities—one the C.I.G.S. and the other the British Military Representative at Versailles. The fact of my remaining an Army Councillor does not in my judgment remove this defect.

It seems to me absolutely necessary that the General Staff officer who is to give orders regarding the reserves in question must be in constant and direct touch with the various departments of the War Office—the Great Headquarters of the Imperial Military Forces—and be directly served by, and in close touch with, the Intelligence Branch of the General Staff. Only the C.I.G.S., residing normally at the War Office, can be in this position, and for an officer who is not in that position to attempt to interfere with the employment and location of Reserve troops under the British Commanders-in-Chief in France, Italy, and the Balkans, upon the right use of which final victory depends, would inevitably lead to confusion and perhaps to disaster. So strongly am I convinced of this that I am compelled to say that I cannot undertake the very great responsibility involved. . . .

Lord Derby to Sir William Robertson

Very Secret 11 February 1918

It is with the greatest regret that I received your letter and I still will not take 'No' for an answer and hope that tomorrow morning may find you ready to reconsider your refusal to accept the post now offered to you.

You must allow me however to demur to that sentence in which you say that I informed you that the reason for removing you from your appointment was because the Prime Minister could not get on with you. I never gave that as a reason.

If that has been the reason for what you call your removal from your appointment I certainly should not have acted as an agent in conveying that decision to you as under those circumstances I should certainly have felt it my duty to resign. The reason for making the change is an entirely different one. As you know at the last Versailles Conference certain resolutions were unanimously accepted by the Ministers representing the various nations and these have now got to be put into effect. They differed from the previous resolutions in that they gave executive power to the military representatives, thus largely increasing their duties and their responsibilities. To show how this was appreciated by the French it is only necessary to bring to your notice the fact that General Foch was at once substituted for General Weygand as the French Military Representative. It became obvious that our Government must also reconsider our position.

I have always pointed out to you (and publicly) that the Government are perfectly justified in making any changes that they may think proper with regard to their Military Advisers and the Secretary of State's duty is either to carry them out if he thinks them proper decisions or to resign if he considers that they are contrary to the safety and welfare of the troops for whom under the Constitution he is responsible. The Government suggested to me that just as the French had put on their Chief of Staff, and the Americans had put on their Senior Officer, so should we put you on as our representative, in view of the fact that decisions might have to be taken at a moment's notice, and it was very desirable that if they were, they should be taken by a man in whom the Army had such complete confidence as yourself.

If I had thought this was derogatory to you I should not have assented, but I do not so consider it. On the contrary, I think it is placing you in a position where your knowledge can be put to even greater use than in your present position. You have never failed to impress upon me in conversation, and on myself and others at Army Council meetings, that much power had been taken away from the Army Council and put in the hands of the Military Representative at Versailles, and now when I ask you to take that place you tell me that you are not prepared to accept it. You contend that it would be possible for the C.I.G.S. to combine the two posts of C.I.G.S. at home and Military Representative in Paris. The Cabinet have considered this and they have come to the conclusion that it would not be possible, and I agree with them. When the Committee at Versailles was purely advisory it might have been done, though even then I do not think it would have been advisable. Now that it is executive I think it is absolutely impossible. C.I.G.S. living in London cannot possibly give a decision, delay in the giving of which might be fatal in France.

Again may I beg you to reconsider your decision. You are being offered no inferior post. On the contrary, you are being asked to take one which I think entails even more responsibility than your present one, and where your influence and the weight that you can bring to bear on this Committee will be invaluable in upholding the views and contentions with regard to the Reserve which Sir Douglas Haig may put forward.

You and I have been on such friendly terms that I should feel miserable if I thought I was doing anything that would mean that your services would be lost to the nation. I look upon it as indispensable that they should be retained and I ask therefore that whatever your personal feelings may be, you will as a soldier accept the position and by so doing I feel convinced you will be doing a great national service.

Sir William Robertson to Lord Derby

Secret War Office

15 February 1918

Secretary of State

You have asked me whether I would regard the Prime Minister's undated Note (prepared I understand on the 9th instant) as a workable arrangement—so far as concerns the control of the Inter-Allied Reserves —if I remain as C.I.G.S. and do not go to Versailles as Permanent British Military Representative.

In the first place I desire to repeat my earnest desire to serve His Majesty's Government to the best of my power, and to carry out such instructions as they may issue so far as that can possibly be done.

With regard to para 1 of the Note I have no remarks to make. The matter is one for His Majesty's Government.

With regard to the control of the Inter-Allied Reserves, there is no doubt that such Reserves are necessary, and I pointed the necessity out to the Prime Minister in my Note of 30th January, before the meeting of the Supreme Council. The only question still at issue is how this control can be exercised. This is in my judgment primarily a military question and I have never varied in the advice which I have given, namely, that the control should be exercised by the C.I.G.S., and in this I am supported by the Military Members of the Army Council. I stated in my Note to you of the 11th instant that for any officer other than the C.I.G.S. 'to attempt to interfere with the employment and location of Reserve troops under the British Commanders-in-Chief in France, Italy, and the Balkans, upon the right use of which final victory depends, would inevitably lead to confusion and perhaps to disaster'. After further consideration I am more strongly convinced than ever of the truth of this.

There need be no difficulty in the C.I.G.S. being represented on the Executive body, in his absence, by a Deputy who would keep him fully informed of the work of the Executive, warn him when his presence was required, and act for him in case of necessity. Nothing in this arrangement need in any way affect the position or duties of the British Military Representative to the Supreme War Council. The Deputy, if desired, could be made an Army Councillor, as in the case of the present D.C.I.G.S. at the War Office, and he could further, if desired, be British Military Representative on the Supreme War Council.

Events were moving faster and more decisively than either Robertson or Derby apprehended, as can be seen from Derby's own account:

Lord Derby's Memorandum

. . . I then returned to the original proposal of the Prime Minister which made Sir Henry Wilson a Deputy Chief of the Staff and our permanent member at Versailles, thus giving the power to Sir William Robertson to attend the Executive as the British Representative . . . I took this proposal to the Prime Minister on the 13th. It would I think have been acceded to by Sir William Robertson but the Prime Minister would not have it saying that such a proposal had already been turned down by the Versailles Conference, a fact which I did not understand as he had himself proposed it in the first instance. However he was perfectly determined that the amended memorandum must be the one on which any negotiations should take place . . .

In his desire to gain his ends the Prime Minister flirted with many possible solutions, but it is to be doubted whether he ever seriously entertained the idea which Derby describes as his 'original proposal' of giving Robertson as C.I.G.S. the power to attend the Versailles Executive as the British representative. This would have struck at the root of Lloyd George's main conception of Versailles which, as we have seen, was to provide the British Government with military advice independent of that provided by the War Office. It is not altogether surprising that Derby should have been misled by Robertson into making this last-minute and altogether unacceptable proposal since, as he records in his Memorandum dictated on

February 16, he had not even by then succeeded in seeing the verbatim report of the Versailles Conference. Whether this concealment of documents happened by design or accident it no doubt considerably advantaged the Prime Minister in his manœuvres.

The impatience of the Prime Minister in this matter and the pressure to which Derby was being subjected are shown by the following letter which was probably despatched between Derby's meeting with Lloyd George and the subsequent meeting of the War Cabinet:

Lord Derby to the Prime Minister

13 February 1918 War Office

I am afraid that I could not agree to the statement proposed. Is there any necessity to give an answer tonight? I am still hopeful that I may find a satisfactory conclusion but I can't do it at the point of a bayonet.

Lord Derby's Memorandum

. . . The matter came before the War Cabinet [on February 13] and there was a very sharp division of opinion as to what action should be taken. I suggested that Sir William Robertson should be asked to continue his work as C.I.G.S. under the same conditions as had been laid down by the Prime Minister. Lord Milner, Mr. Barnes and Mr. Bonar Law were against this and were of the opinion that as Sir William Robertson had refused Versailles his employment should cease. Lord Curzon and Mr. Balfour supported me and it was left for the Prime Minister to give the deciding vote. He took time to consider this and the next morning he invited Lord Milner and myself to breakfast. Lord Milner and I were absolutely opposed to each other and it was quite evident that whilst I wanted to keep Sir William Robertson and was indifferent to the fate of Sir Henry Wilson a precisely opposite view was taken by Lord Milner.

Later in the day the Prime Minister saw me and told me that his casting vote was given in my favour and the offer was to be made to Sir William Robertson. I told Sir William Robertson what had happened and later after consideration he came to me and told me he did not think he could accept, his position being that while he would be ready to serve in either place he could not do so because he thought the scheme was radically wrong and was likely to lead to disaster. I communicated this fact to the Cabinet, they settled that it was a question of his taking it or leaving it, Lord Curzon, Mr. Balfour and myself still being very averse to doing anything which would deprive us of Sir William Robertson's service . . .

The fullest account of the activities of these two crowded days is to be found in Stamfordham's diary which is carefully preserved in the Royal Archives. Stamfordham was in an unrivalled position to record an objective account of these events. He was at the centre of affairs, he repeatedly saw the leading figures to the dispute and it was his lifelong habit to keep a faithful chronicle of all business which concerned the King:

Memorandum of Lord Stamfordham

3.15 p.m., 13 February 1918 Buckingham Palace

I expressed the King's surprise to learn from the Minutes of the Cabinet that Sir William Robertson was no longer Chief of the Imperial General Staff, but that he was to be succeeded by Sir Henry Wilson, and it was suggested that Sir William Robertson should go to Paris as a Member of the Executive Committee of the Supreme War Council.

The Prime Minister when he saw the King on the 4th February never mentioned any idea of this change, indeed he told His Majesty that everything had gone smoothly in Paris the previous week, and that the agreements come to by the Supreme War Council were unanimous, and it was only on the 12th inst. that the King chanced to send for Lord Derby, who then told him of the contemplated new arrangement.

The Prime Minister replied that as Lord Derby told him that he was going to see the King on the 12th he (the Prime Minister) asked him to tell the King everything, and to show him a copy of the conditions which Lord Derby had agreed to and signed, governing the two appointments of C.I.G.S. and Member of the Executive Committee respectively. I said that I had not heard of this document, but the Prime Minister said that he knew Lord Derby had it in his pocket and more than once Mr. Lloyd George said 'Are you sure the King did not see it?' I could only answer that of course I could not be sure as I was not present at the interview, but that His Majesty had not mentioned anything about the document in question. The Prime Minister sent for the original and I brought away a copy. I told him that the King strongly deprecated the idea of Robertson being removed from the office of C.I.G.S., that his loss in that capacity would be an incalculable one to the Army, would be resented in the country, rejoiced in by the enemy, and I thought would damage the Government, and the King considered that Sir William Robertson had enjoyed the absolute confidence of the Army—Officers and Men. The Prime Minister said that he did not share the King's extremely favourable opinion of Sir William Robertson, who had never fought at the Front, had hardly ever visited the trenches, and was not known by the rank and file, and their confidence in him could not be compared to that which they reposed in Sir Herbert Plumer, and Mr. Lloyd George said that the opinions I relied on must be manufactured for the King. The previous week in Paris Robertson never raised any objections to the proposal, but, just as on the occasion of Rapallo, he waited until his return to London to make these known far and wide.

The Prime Minister said that Robertson had been offered either Paris or to remain as C.I.G.S., he declined either and wished to dictate to everyone, whereas the Prime Minister repeated what he said on the 22nd January, that Robertson had displayed no capacity as a strategist, and asked where anyone could put their finger on the map and say that this or that is due to Robertson's advice. In fact his forecasts had generally been wrong.

I pointed out that Robertson was only asking to be in a position similar to that of General Foch, who is both C.G.S. and Member of the Executive Committee in France. The Prime Minister replied that there was no analogy. For Foch is on the spot in Paris whereas Sir William Robertson would be in London, while it might be necessary to give orders to the Reserves at a moment's notice in cases of emergency.

Afterwards on returning to Buckingham Palace I rang up Lord Derby and told him of my conversation with the Prime Minister, the former said that Robertson was unreasonable in his demands, swollen headed, and that he (Lord Derby) was so tired of the whole question that he sometimes thought he would be better without Robertson, but himself felt ready to resign.

Later on Lord Derby and Sir William Robertson met in my room, and the whole question was threshed out and examined from all sides. Sir William Robertson gave me a copy of his written opinion as to the suggested plan, which to him had spelt disaster. Lord Derby did not agree, and reminded Sir William Robertson that Sir Douglas Haig had approved of the conditions and thought that they were workable. However, Lord Derby said that he should back up Sir William Robertson. But he knew that if the Prime Minister agreed to Sir W. R.'s terms, namely, that he should be both C.I.G.S. in London, and Member of the Executive Committee, with a Deputy to act for him in his absence, Lord Milner and Mr. Barnes would resign: if on the other hand Sir William Robertson were to resign, Lord Curzon, and he (Lord Derby) would leave the Government, and if this resulted in the fall of the Government there was a serious danger of its fate being attributed to the work of the Army and might be a very disagreeable cry with which to go to the country.

I begged Sir William Robertson in the King's name not to relinquish his post as C.I.G.S., but to record his disapproval of the system, his belief that it was unworkable, and might even cost us the War, but for the sake of the King, the Army and the Country, to remain on and do his best to carry out the new arrangement. He undertook to think it over, and said that he had to go with Lord Derby to breakfast with the Prime Minister in the morning. During this discussion Sir W. R. said with considerable warmth that the truth was the Prime Minister hated him.

I reported what had happened to the King at about 8.15 p.m.

14 *February* 1918

At 8.30 a.m. I sent a note to Sir William Robertson saying that I trusted that after sleeping over the matter he had decided to give effect to the King's wishes. Later on I heard that he had not breakfasted with the Prime Minister, but was to attend the Cabinet and lay before them his views.

Soon after 3.30 p.m. I called at 10 Downing Street, and found that the Cabinet had decided that Sir William Robertson must make up his mind to take either of the two appointments suggested, but he was to see Mr. Balfour about four o'clock.

I went to the War Office and saw Mr. Balfour and Lord Derby, immediately after the former had left Sir William Robertson, upon whom he said he had failed to make any impression, or to divert him from the attitude he had taken up.

I discussed Sir William Robertson's objections to the scheme, which Mr. Balfour thought were exaggerated, and would not hold water. He did not seem to recognise as much as I did the serious view which Sir W. R. took as to the results of the proposed arrangement, and indeed said that Sir William Robertson had not put the case as strongly as I had put it: I replied that I was merely repeating what Sir W. R. had said the previous evening, and I appealed to Lord Derby and asked him to show Mr. Balfour a copy of the paper which Sir William Robertson had given me, but Lord Derby replied that Sir W. R. had modified his views of the previous evening. I said that Sir William Robertson maintained that one man only could give orders to the Army, and that was the C.I.G.S., whereas by this plan there would be *two*, namely, the C.I.G.S. and the member of the Executive Committee.

Later on I saw Lord Derby, who said I was mistaken in thinking that he said Sir William Robertson had changed his views. I told him that Sir William Robertson would not give way or continue to be C.I.G.S. while disapproving of the scheme. Lord Derby said '*He believed it would work* and so did Sir Douglas Haig'. I said I thought there was nothing more to do. Lord Derby asked me to tell Sir William Robertson of the change in the opinion of Lord Curzon and Mr. Balfour, who now no longer supported him, and also to say that Sir H. Plumer would be telegraphed to and offered the appointment of C.I.G.S.

I accordingly wrote to Sir William Robertson, from whom in the meantime I had received a note confirming what he had said in conversation.

Balfour had been inclined to join with Derby in seeking at almost any cost to retain Robertson's services. Robertson, however, made an impression of undue obduracy on Balfour when the latter visited him on the morning of the 14th. Thereafter they had come to the parting of the ways.

Lord Derby to Sir William Robertson

Confidential and Personal — 14 February 1918

I am afraid that I must at last take your 'No' as being a final decision, but I need not tell you with what deep regret I do so. You have been a faithful friend and adviser to me ever since I have been in office, and it is a great blow to think that in this matter we cannot bring our views sufficiently into harmony to enable you to stay on.

I admire extremely the courage which prompts you to adhere to your decision, even though the grounds on which you arrive at it are not those which I can endorse, and I only hope that you part from me with the same regret that I part from you.

After hearing your statement this morning, the Cabinet were quite unanimous in holding to the conditions laid down, though one and all still hoped that you would re-consider your decision. The Cabinet have decided to offer your post to Sir Herbert Plumer, on the same conditions as those offered to you, and, in the event of his accepting, I am authorised to offer you the Command in Italy, which I hope you will accept, so as to keep unbroken your service to the country.

Pending an answer from Sir Herbert Plumer, I would ask you to carry on your duties as C.I.G.S., and I feel sure that, with your habitual wish to do your duty, you will not refuse me in this request.

I hope I may see you again here, so that we may part with a handshake of mutual regret.

Sir Douglas Haig's Diary[1]

Monday 18 *February* 1918

I next visited the War Office. I met Lord Derby on the main staircase. He told me that he had placed his resignation in the hands of the War Cabinet, and they could either accept it or not as they deemed right. I said I was very pleased to hear that he had decided to remain on.

The King, like Derby, laboured to the end to bring about a reconciliation between the Prime Minister and Robertson which would permit of the latter's services being retained in some important sphere. But by now matters had gone too far:

Lord Stamfordham's Diary

16 *February* 1918

The King saw the Prime Minister. Before doing so Mr. Lloyd George told me that the question of Sir William Robertson had now reached a point that if His Majesty insisted upon his (Sir W. R.) remaining in office on the terms he laid down the Government could not carry on, and the King would have to find other Ministers. The Government *must* govern, whereas this was practically military dictation.

[1] *Haig* by Duff Cooper.

I assured the Prime Minister that His Majesty had no idea of making any such insistence. That since I saw him (Mr. Lloyd George) on the 13th February, I had by the King's instructions done all in my power to induce Sir William Robertson to remain as C.I.G.S. even though he might consider that the Government's scheme was so dangerous as even risking our loss of the War. But Sir William Robertson said he could not do so, therefore the King regarded the matter as settled, and considered that Sir William Robertson had practically ceased to be C.I.G.S.

The King then saw the Prime Minister, and in discussing the question, stated that in his opinion Sir William Robertson's resignation would be a serious loss to the Army for both Officers and Men had the fullest confidence in him. This however the Prime Minister would not admit. He reminded the King that the scheme was agreed to in Paris when Sir William Robertson never raised a word of objection. Sir Douglas Haig, who after all was the person most concerned, accepted it, and Lord Derby thought it workable; so that the opposition really only came from Sir William Robertson, and Mr. Lloyd George thought that the personal dislike of Sir William Robertson to Sir Henry Wilson was a powerful influence in the case.

The Prime Minister quoted General Smuts as having no opinion of Sir William Robertson as a strategist, and his (Gen. S.'s) last words before leaving for Egypt were to the effect that we should never get on with the War so long as Sir William Robertson remained C.I.G.S.

Mr. Lloyd George asked His Majesty's permission to repeat the offer to Sir William Robertson either to go to Paris as Representative of the Executive, or to remain C.I.G.S. If he refused both, to appoint Sir Henry Wilson, C.I.G.S., but without the powers specially granted to Sir William Robertson when he took office. The Prime Minister also asked for permission to consult Sir Douglas Haig, who arrives this evening, as to who should go to Paris.

On Saturday the 16th Haig, summoned by Derby, arrived in London. The events of the next thirty-six hours are not covered by anything which Derby wrote and we must therefore rely upon the accounts given by Haig in his diary and by Lloyd George in his *War Memoirs*,

Sir Douglas Haig's Diary

Saturday 16 *February* 1918

The S. of S. for War [Lord Derby] met me at the station and motored with me to Kingston Hill. He told me that Robertson had declined to serve either as C.I.G.S. on the new conditions or to be Military Representative at Versailles, so Sir H. Wilson had been appointed C.I.G.S. He would call for me at 11.30 a.m. tomorrow and take me to see the P.M. I found Doris looking very fit and well. How petty all this squabbling in high places is compared with the great problem of beating Germany, and the present anxiety of Commanders in France.

By now Derby was urgently considering his own position. Robertson, in his letter to him of February 2nd, had clearly indicated that he considered that Derby's fortunes were involved with his. Derby felt this most keenly, but he also had a duty to Haig who since his return to London seemed strangely satisfied with the way events were shaping. Moreover, Derby thought that the new Versailles Agreement was a practicable affair and was on the record for this opinion. He only wished to do what was right and honourable but in this extremely vexed and complicated situation he found himself at sea without a compass or a chart. He was the victim of divided loyalties and uncertain duty. In his predicament he sought out his old friend the King:

Lord Stamfordham's Diary

Saturday 16 *February* 1918

Later in the day the King saw Lord Derby, who said that he felt there was nothing left for him to do but to resign, though he several times appealed to His Majesty to advise him as to the proper course he should follow. Lord Derby explained that although he personally thought that the Government's scheme was workable, on the other hand two high authorities—namely Sir William Robertson and Sir Herbert Plumer—both held opposite opinions, and in these circumstances he (Lord Derby) felt that he could not carry out the scheme, especially with Sir Henry Wilson as C.I.G.S.

The King told Lord Derby that after hearing his statement there seemed no alternative but his resignation.

Subsequently I saw Lord Derby who told me that he should resign, and that an announcement to that effect would be in Monday's morning newspapers, and that he would make his statement in the House of Lords on Tuesday.

Lord Derby admitted that his case was a weak one, for while supporting the Government's scheme he felt unable to carry it out. Lord Derby added that in his statement he should quote the opinion of Sir William Robertson and Sir Herbert Plumer, although Mr. Bonar Law said that he ought *not* to refer to the latter as the communication made to Sir Herbert Plumer was entirely confidential.

The next day Haig noted in his diary:

Sunday 17 *February* 1918

. . . Sir William Robertson came to see me at 9.30 a.m. He told me his story. He did not consider that Derby had been quite straight, and he thought that H. Wilson as C.I.G.S. would get the country into difficulties. I told R. that I had never been asked whether I approved the new scheme of higher control, but only whether I was satisfied with the proposed arrangements for giving me orders.

. . . At 10 o'clock Sir Philip Sassoon came to see me. He and Doris and I took a walk in the Park, and at 11.30 Lord Derby called and motored me to Lloyd George's house at Walton Heath.

The P.M.'s house reminds me of summer lodgings at the seaside—a sort of maid-of-all-work opened the door to us.

L. G. had been ill, and was resting upstairs when we arrived. He came down and saw Derby and myself together. In the course of our talk, I made it quite clear to the P.M. that I had never approved of any of the arrangements now under discussion. When asked, I had stated my reasons for disagreeing, but once the Cabinet had given its decision, I had loyally done my best to make the system run. I had only one object in view, viz., to beat the Germans. L. G. said that was so and warmly thanked me. L.G. left the room for a moment, and Derby said I had put my position quite clearly to the P.M. If the latter made any mis-statement regarding me in the House of Commons on this subject, he was prepared to get up in the House of Lords and deny it flatly . . .

Lloyd George in Volume V of his *War Memoirs*, published after Duff Cooper's life of Haig had led him to take a less favourable view of Derby than he had previously entertained, wrote of the same day's events:

> Haig and Derby came over on Sunday, the 17th February, to see me at my cottage at Walton Heath. We discussed the whole position for hours. Haig put up no fight for Robertson. He clearly did not approve of his defiance of a decision come to by the Government. I thought it right to inform him that Derby had placed his resignation in my hands. I was under the impression that he had a great regard and respect for his civilian chief. I was anxious to find out at once whether that would affect his attitude. I was surprised to discover that, so far from the news disturbing him, he sniffed it aside with an expression of contempt. He had a poor opinion of Derby's stalwartness, and did not hesitate to show it. Haig himself had no intention of resigning and gave no indication that he was not prepared to accept the Versailles decision . . .
>
> When Haig left me, Derby remained behind to place his resignation in my hands for the third time during the past 24 hours. This time he insisted that it was irrevocable. He explained that he did not do so because of any disagreement with the line taken by the Cabinet, but out of loyalty to the men with whom he had worked at the War Office. And he told me his decision was final. As soon, therefore, as he left I got on the telephone to Bonar Law and we agreed that the vacant Secretaryship of State should be offered—subject to the King's consent—to Austen Chamberlain. He was out of town at the time, but he motored to London at Bonar Law's request. Before, however, he reached Downing Street, Ian Macpherson, the Under-Secretary for the War Office, called at 11 Downing Street to inform Bonar Law that he had succeeded in persuading Derby to withdraw his resignation! The following day Bonar Law reported the appointment of Henry Wilson to the Cabinet and it was approved by them without a single protest . . .

From Walton Heath Haig returned to Kingston and Derby a little later to London. In the evening Derby drove down to Kingston and Haig recorded:

Sir Douglas Haig's Diary

Sunday 17 *February* 1918

About 6.30 p.m. Lord Derby came from London to see me. He looked tired and harassed. He did not know whether to resign or stay on as S. of S. for War. I told him that in the interests of the Army there should be no change, and that he should remain on. He said he would accept my advice. If he left, Lord Northcliffe would probably succeed him. This would be fatal to the Army and the Empire.

In an addendum to his diary entry for Saturday, February 16, Stamfordham wrote:

I heard nothing more until the evening of Sunday, February 17, when the Prime Minister's Private Secretary told me by telephone that Sir Douglas Haig (who had arrived on Saturday evening) had had a satisfactory talk with the Prime Minister and had also seen Sir Henry Wilson. Lord Derby had also seen the Prime Minister and would *not* resign.

The following day Stamfordham recorded:

Lord Derby himself told me by telephone that although he had sent in his resignation it was now practically withdrawn. Sir Douglas Haig had strongly urged him not to leave the War Office, so that his letter resigning remained in the hands of the War Cabinet to make use of or not as they thought fit. Lord Derby also asked for the King's approval of Sir William Robertson being appointed to the Eastern Command which His Majesty was very glad to do, and Sir William Robertson has accepted this position.

Lord Derby to Mr. Bonar Law[1]

I thought very carefully over what you said to me, and discussed the question of my resignation with Weir and Macpherson—and then went to see Haig. As the result of these conversations I did not put the notice in the papers, and am prepared, if you and my colleagues wish, to withdraw my resignation. You may rest assured I should loyally work and defend the scheme, but I shall quite understand it, if you think that it had better be run by somebody else.

[1] Bonar Law Papers.

I shall await your answer here and shall carry on till I do so.

I know you told Macpherson last night that you could speak in the name of the Cabinet in asking me to remain—or rather in allowing me to withdraw my resignation, but I think I had better have that from you in writing after consultation with the P.M. as he may not agree.

Mr. Bonar Law to Lord Derby

Private — 11 Downing Street
18 February 1918

I submitted your letter to the Cabinet and as I told you verbally I am very glad to express the pleasure felt by all your colleagues in the fact that you have thought it right to retain your post.

Personally, as I told you, I feel sure that your decision is the right one.

Lord Curzon to Lord Derby

10 Downing Street
18 February 1918

I need hardly say that the War Cabinet were unanimously of opinion that your resignation should not be accepted and that you may with perfect propriety and greatly to the public advantage continue to occupy your post.

I think it would be a good thing if you were rather careful to prepare what you say in reply to Crewe tomorrow and to let me see it in advance. I will write tonight and put up Crewe at the commencement of public business.

This chapter may fittingly conclude with an extract from the dignified defence of the Government which Derby gave in the House of Lords on February 19 when the matter of Robertson's dismissal was raised by Lord Crewe:

> . . . I had been carefully through this scheme. I had been through it with military advisers and with civilian advisers, and I had come to the conclusion that it was a perfectly workable scheme. I have always expressed—and I still express—the greatest possible confidence in Sir William Robertson, in his judgment as a strategist; and the high opinion which I have always held of him is enhanced by the courage that he has shown in adhering to the decision at which he arrived. But here

was where, if I may say so, my personal difficulty came in. A scheme proposed and accepted by the whole of the Allies could be upset only by the whole of the Allies. I approved of that scheme. I believed then—and I believe now—that it is a perfectly workable scheme; and the only alternative that was put in front of me was Sir William Robertson's position of 'accept my terms or lose my services'. A complaint has been made that some delay has occurred in settling this matter. I plead guilty to being the cause of that delay because I did all that I possibly could to get Sir William Robertson to accept a scheme which, as I have said, I considered perfectly workable. He did not see his way to do this. Now, it seems to me that it then became a question of principle against personality. In the very last speech that I made in a public place I praised Sir William Robertson in every way. I then emphasised one fact—and I emphasise it now—that, whoever the soldier be, the civil authority has to be, and must always remain, supreme; and if the civil authority, acting, as they did in this case, in uniformity with the Inter-Allied Conference, says that a certain thing is to be, then in my opinion no soldier ought to be able to put the alternative either of keeping his services or of reversing the decision arrived at. In the end, therefore, I held to my scheme. I held that I was right, and I hold that I am right now. And when the Government appointed—as they did appoint—Sir Henry Wilson to be Chief of the General Staff, and Sir Henry Rawlinson to be our representative at Versailles, I accepted it because I believed, and shall continue to believe—and I know that in this respect I have Sir Douglas Haig's own opinion—that, given good will (as it will be given), although there may be difficulties ahead, it is a workable scheme, and we are all determined to make it work.

But meanwhile I felt that my strong advocacy of Sir William Robertson had put me into a somewhat ambiguous position, and I placed myself unreservedly in the hands of the Prime Minister by asking him whether he would accept my resignation. He has asked me not to resign. I believe that my colleagues agree with that. I am staying, but through no love of office. Nobody would like to be in office now if he could help it. But, having set my hand to a paper, and having agreed to a scheme, which I still think is a good and a workable scheme, I have to make good by seeing that scheme through. I believe that I can make good . . .

XV

Derby Leaves the War Office

DERBY did not long survive Robertson at the War Office. In Volume II of his *Haig*, published in 1936, Mr. Duff Cooper printed a number of extracts from Haig's Diaries which showed the support which the Commander-in-Chief had quite properly received from the Secretary of State for War. These revelations outraged Lloyd George who was, at that time, engaged in writing the sixth volume of his *War Memoirs*, and he was stung by Mr. Duff Cooper's account of the part played by Lord Derby into expressing a revised opinion of Derby:

> But there is still one revelation in his story which I cannot pass over without comment. I do so with genuine regret, but the prominence given by Mr. Duff Cooper to Lord Derby's secret activities forces me to do so. Had he not thought fit to give publicity to these clandestine conversations I should not have alluded to them. Until these extracts from the Haig Diaries were published I never, as a fact, understood the extent to which Lord Derby as War Minister had encouraged Haig's and Robertson's resistance to the Cabinet policy of unity of command, and also to its efforts to avert or abate the tragic carnage of the Passchendaele campaign. Had Lord Derby exerted his conspicuous diplomatic gifts to promote these legitimate aims of the War Cabinet, the wasteful delays which occurred in achieving unity would have been avoided, Passchendaele might never have been fought, and the battle of the 21st March might have ended in a smashing triumph and not a defeat. But when so influential a personage as Lord Derby, holding such a key position as that of Secretary of State for War, by letter and talk expressed sympathy with Haig's and Robertson's stubborn opposition to the Cabinet's policy, they naturally thought they could rely upon him to help them to thwart it and at any rate to prevent any

serious mishap occurring to themselves if they committed their fortunes to a thwarting intrigue.

I regret being forced by Mr. Duff Cooper's disclosures to allude to the part Lord Derby played in these intrigues. Lord Derby has attractive qualities which make him an effective mediator. I was conscious that he was not as helpful as he might have been in reconciling the Generals to the policy of the Cabinet, but I had no idea that he was actually encouraging their opposition by expressing sympathy with their attitude. The events of the 21st March decided me that he was not an ideal War Minister. He was not at his best in a crisis. In an emergency leaders who sweat despondency are a source of weakness. I then made up my mind that the Ministry of War in the supreme trial of a tremendous struggle was not the role for which he was best fitted, and that he would render greater service to his country in a position where it would not be obvious that his bluffness was only bluff. As Ambassador in Paris he was a success. He was popular with both French and English alike. His beguiling geniality and forthrightness of manner concealed valuable powers of observation which were really serviceable to those who had to transact business amid the rapid and baffling fluctuations of French politics.[1]

In fact Lloyd George was contemplating long before March 21 easing Derby out of the War Office and sending him to Paris:

Lord Derby to the Prime Minister [2]

Confidential and Personal — Derby House

18 January 1918

My dear P.M.,

With reference to the question of a new Ambassador for Paris which you and I discussed at luncheon the other day and whom you wished to appoint with special powers. I think before the man we had in mind would take it, his powers would have to be clearly defined.

I do not know what powers have been given to Lord Reading but I presume that they are largely in excess of those which are given to the ordinary Ambassador. Would they equally apply in the case of Paris? Your answer will probably be 'No' because there is a great difference between Washington and Paris and to that I agree. But the real question is this. Would the Ambassador in Paris be more or less of a

[1] *War Memoirs* by Lloyd George.

[2] Lloyd George Papers.

colleague of members of the War Cabinet or would he be simply the mouthpiece of that body?

I am sure that what the person in question would first of all consider would be whether or not his acceptance of the post was in the National interest and I am quite sure that he would subordinate all questions of a personal character, which might make him inclined to refuse, if he thought he could be of any real use and assistance: but there is one thing I am convinced of and that is that he would never give up, except to a limited extent, his independence and it is on that question that the difficulty might arise.

A man in office is not only entitled, but it is his duty, to resign if he thinks that the Government to which he belongs is doing something which he disapproves of and which in his opinion is detrimental to the best interests of the nation.[1] I am naturally only referring to big questions, but would the same liberty be given to him as an Ambassador as would be given to anybody who was in a Government Department at home? . . .

On the other hand I do see that great advantage will be gained by having somebody in Paris who would be in close touch with you and your War Cabinet and who knows what I may call the train of thought there and knowing this would be able to transact business with the French Government which now you have to get done either yourself or by a member of your Government going personally to Paris.

I think also that he probably would be more able to get in personal touch with all political sections in Paris than Bertie has been able to do and by entertaining be able to bring the British Embassy in Paris more, what I may call, 'into the picture' than it is at the present moment.

I only put down these heads because I should like to have another talk with you on the subject because I think the man in question is likely to accept provided he is able to keep his independence—at all events to a limited extent, and is not called upon to be simply a mouthpiece of the Government and gagged on all these questions on which I know he holds a very strong opinion.

The person who was being considered to replace Lord Bertie in Paris was in fact Derby himself. Presumably he wrote, in what

[1] Derby's desire to preserve his right to threaten resignation was one of the most persistent threads in his public life.

seems, on the face of it, a somewhat coy fashion, because he did not wish either his own office or the Prime Minister's secretaries to know of the proposal. Any doubt is removed by the following:

Lord Derby to Mr. Balfour

Confidential 24 January 1918

I have been thinking very seriously over the talk you and I had with the Prime Minister yesterday. You are my oldest political friend and the only political leader I have ever recognised. I hope therefore you will not mind if I write to you my feelings on this particular subject and ask you to lay them before the Prime Minister and discuss the question with him.

I have consulted with Alice whose advice, as I told you both, was one which would weigh very much with me in coming to a decision as to what answer I should give to the extremely flattering offer made by the Prime Minister with I gather your consent. I am glad to say we are both of the same mind. Just at present when my administration of the War Office is being attacked it is not the time to leave it. I feel, and she agrees with me in feeling the same thing, that I should not be acting either courageously or honourably by accepting the position of Ambassador at Paris whilst the present attack is going on. I recognise that the attack is less directed against me than against Sir Douglas Haig and Sir William Robertson and the complaint is less what I have done wrong than that I will not do what they consider right, namely change certainly one and perhaps both of these high commands. They being soldiers are debarred from speaking and stating their cases and I am the only mouthpiece through which their defence can come and to desert them at the present moment would not be a policy I could accept. At the same time I am extremely anxious to do anything which may be, rightly or wrongly, considered of advantage to this Country and before declining the offer I would like to ask you, is it imperative that the answer should be given at once? You must give Bertie some notice and if he was told he must be prepared to go in a month's time I should be prepared then, not only to give my answer but if I accept to go at 24 hours' notice. Between now and then I shall have the opportunity of defending my administration of the War Office and stating my confidence in those with whom I am working and if I was empowered by the War Cabinet to state publicly that they had confidence in Sir Douglas Haig and Sir William Robertson my difficulties would be to a very great extent met and my answer would be accelerated.

I hope this letter, however badly expressed, will make you understand my position which to sum up is this:

(1) I desire to do anything that the Government thinks may be of value to the Nation and I much appreciate the honour which is offered me.

(2) I would accept the position although I frankly say it would mean making a great break for me; but

(3) I cannot go until I have either defended, not my own self or my personal administration of the War Office, but those who have placed confidence in me and in whom I have confidence and who are now the subject of this bitter attack.

The same day Derby wrote to Haig telling him of Lloyd George's suggestion and saying that he had only one idea, namely to assist the Army, and that he was not prepared to go at the present moment unless he could get a definite statement that he was not merely being sent in order to close his mouth and also that changes in the higher command would not be made as soon as he had gone. He added:

Lord Derby to Sir Douglas Haig

24 January 1918

I think I shall get this assurance but I want to ask you your candid opinion as to whether I should be able in Paris to be of more help to you than Bertie has been. I have got to give my decision almost at once and I should like to have your views on the subject. I do not say that I should abide by them and you may be perfectly certain of this that while this attack on the administration generally is going on I shall not quit my post until I have defended it in public and quieted as I hope the storm that is now raging.

Nothing on earth will make me desert my post if those I have confidence in are likely to suffer thereby.

There is a card in the Derby papers headed 10 Downing Street which Derby must have passed to Robertson at a Cabinet Meeting and on the back of which Robertson scribbled his reply:

Ll. G. has mentioned to me about my going to Paris—I should hate to leave the War Office. What do you think about it?
Honestly I think it would be a real disadvantage to Army and War if you leave War Office. We should all hate it. But this is no argument I fear. We must think of another.

This exchange is likely to have taken place at the first Cabinet attended by both Derby and Robertson subsequent to the matter having been broached to Derby by the Prime Minister. It is plain, however, that nothing was settled at this time, for at the end of January we find Derby writing a long routine letter to Lloyd George on a variety of War Office topics which concludes:

Lord Derby to the Prime Minister

30 January 1918

... There is every sort of wild rumour about that you and I have hopelessly quarrelled, and I hope I put a stop to that yesterday[1]; and I shall not believe we have quarrelled till you tell me so. I think, however, we are very likely to quarrel next Thursday because I have been asked by the Whips to give a breakfast for Rhondda,[2] and I fear the result will be that I shall either give too little for my guests to appreciate the breakfast, or too much for Rhondda's tender susceptibilities.

Though nothing had been decided, Lloyd George must have obtained an assurance from Derby that he would be willing to accept the Paris Embassy. Stamfordham noted in his diary on February 16 that Lloyd George had told the King that he intended to transfer Derby from the War Office to Paris. Moreover, this project was being widely discussed in London society for some time before Robertson's dismissal on February 15. On February 11 Repington noted in his diary:

Lunched with Lady X., and had a good talk to her about Derby, telling her that he was the appointed victim of the Downing Street

[1] He had made a speech at the Aldwych Club in which he had pooh-poohed any suggestion of a split in the Government.

[2] The Food Minister.

Camarilla, when Robertson was moved, and that if the Army Council did not stick together he would regret it. I said that Milner was to succeed him, and that if Derby went with the whole Army Council over a matter of principle he would stand on high, whereas if he let R. be sacrificed and stayed on, he would be put out in a fortnight amidst general derision. She is to speak to him this evening.

The reader who has persevered with the account in this and the previous chapter will be able to form his own deductions as to how and why Derby left the War Office and went to the Embassy in Paris. At the end of 1917 Lloyd George had made up his mind to dismiss both Haig and Robertson. He knew that this might involve the defeat of his own Government; but he was determined to take the risk. He knew that if he dismissed Haig and Robertson simultaneously Derby would certainly resign. To diminish this last possibility he dangled the Paris Embassy in front of Derby early in the new year. When, however, he found that Haig was prepared to conform to the Versailles decision and seemed unconcerned as to the fate of both Robertson and Derby, Lloyd George took a new look at the situation.

So long as Haig remained it did not matter to him politically whether Derby resigned or not. But even when he was sure that Haig would stay, it would still have been inconvenient if Derby had gone at the same time as Robertson. This inconvenience was obviated by the delay in appointing Derby to Paris. It is clear that Derby had already agreed in principle that he would go there, and we see him in his letter of January 24 to Haig canvassing support for the idea that he would actually be of more service to the Army at the Paris Embassy than he would be at the War Office. Although it was not until many years later that Lloyd George discovered that Derby was far more a servant of the soldiers than he was of the Prime Minister, he had already concluded that he needed in the War Office, even after he had disposed of Robertson, a Secretary of State who would be more serviceable to his will.

When Lloyd George was planning to dismiss Haig as well as Robertson it was essential to his plan to get Derby to go quietly. When Haig conformed to the Versailles plan and it was only necessary to dismiss Robertson, Lloyd George had no more need to worry about Derby. As, however, Lloyd George still hoped at a future date to dispense with Haig, and as he had got rid of Robertson without a serious political crisis, it seemed convenient to him to shunt Derby off to Paris.

All these considerations which had been forming in the Prime Minister's mind about Derby were doubtless reinforced by the immense German eruption of the Twenty-first of March. While Lloyd George had been tirelessly seeking to supersede his Commander-in-Chief and the Chief of the Imperial General Staff, the Germans equally tirelessly had been preparing what was to be the greatest single assault battle of the war. This had been long expected but its scale took everyone by surprise. The Germans attacked with thirty-seven divisions and 6,000 guns on a front of forty miles from the River Sensee to the Oise. They had thirty more divisions in close support. Opposed to them were seventeen British divisions and 2,500 guns with five divisions in support. On two ten-mile sectors of the front the Germans had an assaulting division for every thousand yards of ground and a superiority of four to one.

This attack shattered General Gough's Fifth Army, and though Haig had identified sixty-five German divisions in the line against him, Pétain claimed that the main blow was still to come on the French Army in Champagne. On March 24, when the Germans were still advancing rapidly, he told Haig that if the German advance continued he would have to withdraw his troops which were gathering at Montdidier to Beauvais in order to cover Paris. This would certainly have split the British from the French armies. This agonising crisis at length brought the unity of command for which Lloyd George had fought. Haig himself, when it was proposed that Foch should have control of all the forces in front of Amiens, asserted that this would not do and that Foch must be given command of all the French and British armies 'from the Alps to the North Sea'. This was agreed to on March 26. The line was restored and the unity of the Allied armies was preserved. Said Ludendorff: 'It was an established fact that the enemy's resistance was beyond our strength. . . . The battle was over by April 4.'

At one moment it had seemed as though the Germans might break through to the sea, and all in high positions passed days and nights of feverish anxiety and activity. Lloyd George, by denying Haig the reinforcements for which he had asked, in fear that they would be used for a new offensive, may be held partly responsible for the well-nigh catastrophic event.

Be that as it may, the danger of catastrophe had now been warded off and he was henceforward determined to be master in his own house. Unity of command had been established; Robertson had been got rid of; clearly this was the moment to install a man in the War Office who would do his bidding. He had carefully erected a silver, if not a golden bridge, which Derby could tread to Paris; and he has assured us that it was the event of the Twenty-first of March which determined him to make Derby do so.

It is clear from a letter from Stamfordham to Lloyd George's Secretary, Davies (a copy of which is in the Royal Archives), that as late as April 16, when it had been decided that Derby was to go to Paris, Lloyd George was contemplating taking over the War Office himself. And Stamfordham conveyed to the Prime Minister the King's anxiety as to whether 'he felt it possible to add to his present almost overwhelming work and responsibility, those of administering the War Office in this supreme moment . . .'

The next day Davies replied confirming that Lloyd George was still contemplating this action but adding 'he thinks there is great force in His Majesty's objections and he is considering alternative proposals for submission to the King. The best alternative in his opinion is Lord Milner, who is now in France but who I understand is returning to London this afternoon . . .' Milner was in fact appointed a few days later.

Derby, as we have seen, had had a miserable time during the previous three months. He was tortured by divided loyalties and obligations. He would have liked to have resigned when Robertson was dismissed but was genuinely impeded both by his acceptance of the new plan and by his instinctive and continuous desire not to 'rock the boat'. A more decisive man than he might have procured an agreement with Haig and Robertson which would have been acceptable to the soldiers or alternatively have created with them a situation which would have brought the Government down. Derby never played for such stakes. He genuinely thought that Lloyd George was the man to win the war. Although many people often flattered him with the idea that he was fit to take the first place he did not think so himself. If he had believed that he himself was the man to win the war, and had been prepared to make the necessary combination to procure himself the first place, this was his moment. The combination of lack of self-confidence and an honourable desire to keep the show together precluded this and involved him in a loss of prestige which even his wonderful success in Paris could not altogether efface.

* * *

Derby had started life as a professional soldier. He had served in the South African War where the military had for the most part enjoyed a free hand in the planning of military operations. He was on terms of personal friendship with a considerable number of the officers who had now risen to high command in the British Army. It was natural, therefore, that one of his temperament should incline to the military rather than to the civilian outlook in the ferocious conflict between the 'Brass Hats' and the 'Frocks'. His war-time years at the War Office had not been happy ones. He had allowed himself to be drawn into Lloyd George's successful intrigue against Asquith which had made Lloyd George Prime Minister and himself Secretary of State for War. During his sixteen months in charge of the War Office he had laboured to protect Robertson and Haig, and above all the latter, from the Prime Minister's machinations, but it was all to be in vain. As so often happens to the man who seeks to mediate between two contending factions, unless he be in every way the superior of both, he will in the end receive gratitude from neither. He will be the object of the suspicions and disdain of both. Repington, who was deeply in the confidence of G.H.Q., and was its unofficial mouthpiece, took the view that Derby had a greater loyalty to the Prime Minister than he had to the soldiers. And he wrote in the *Morning Post* on 26 April 1918:

Lord Derby's administration of the War Office has not been the success that it might have been had his character been stronger. He was popular with Army people and understood them, for he had been one of them. Everything within the War Office worked smoothly under him, and he did his work industriously to the best of his ability. But the harshness of the times demanded that Lord Derby should play a greater and more distinguished part in the war, and that the personal loyalty which he displayed towards Lord Kitchener first, and then towards Mr. Lloyd George, should have been merged in the greater loyalty which he owed to the country. Here, history will say, Lord Derby failed.

The recommendations of the General Staff and of the Adjutant-General's branch with regard to the need of men for our armies in France went to the War Cabinet, we must assume, in the form of Army Council letters or memoranda. They will, no doubt, when judicially investigated, do honour to the prescience and perspicacity of this body. Lord Derby was head of the Army Council. If the War Cabinet disregarded the advice, entreaties, and almost imprecations of the Army Council, it devolved upon Lord Derby to take the appropriate action. To send in strong papers and then to do nothing when the War Cabinet did not attend to them was obviously a futile course. The soldiers could not protest against any decision relating to policy. The War Secretary could protest. He could do more. He could resign and explain his reasons to Parliament. Lord Derby must have known all through the year 1917, and up to the date of the German attack this year, the dangers involved in the cowardice and procrastination of the War Cabinet. Yet he took no effective measures to meet these dangers, and he never informed the country how matters stood.

When the intrigue, begun by the Downing Street Press, against Sir William Robertson reached maturity, Lord Derby offered to resign, but did not do so because Mr. Lloyd George asked him not to do so. Either the Prime Minister was right, in which case Lord Derby should not have offered to resign, or Sir William Robertson was right, in which case Lord Derby should have persisted in his resignation. If he did not know that his dismissal and replacement by Lord Milner had been the subject of current gossip for weeks before he knew less than everyone else knew in London who was in touch with affairs. Easily led astray by the Prime Minister, Lord Derby conducted Sir William Robertson to the scaffold, and was then placed under the guillotine himself. Then, no one wept. He might have fallen, as Robertson fell, with honour and with credit amidst the sympathy of his fellow-citizens. He chose another course. Let us hope that in the new sphere to which he has been translated he will serve his country better.

The reader must judge for himself the value of these criticisms of Derby's desire to help the soldiers in fighting the war. Of his prolonged and unselfish efforts to protect them from Lloyd George there can be no doubt. If a decisive issue had arisen in which Derby, Haig and Robertson could all have stood together it would be easier to arrive at a just verdict. If Derby had been a decisive man of action he could have procured such a situation. As it was, he protested too much without gaining his point; and though the whole bent of his loyalty was towards Haig, the latter was scarcely more appreciative of Derby's efforts than was Robertson. How Derby saw it in immediate retrospect is shown by a letter he wrote shortly after his arrival in Paris:

Lord Derby to Mr. Edward Hulton

Private and Confidential 15 May 1918

. . . Of course the more I think of it the more I feel that for my own peace of mind and popularity it would have been better for me to have gone when Robertson went, but I should have been wrong to do so. I had never promised, as far as I remember, loyalty to Robertson alone; I had promised it to him and Haig. When there came a split between the two, which I had never anticipated, I had to choose to whom I should show loyalty. I chose Haig because I thought that Robertson was wrong—as did Haig—in going when he did. Of course the *Morning Post* articles have done me a lot of harm in the Army, and if ever you get an opportunity of putting forward the case of the loyalty I gave to Haig rather than to Robertson, you would be doing me good service. At the same time I do wish they could use Robertson in some way at the present moment. There is no doubt he gives the soundest advice, and although I admit he is not very elastic, it is advice such as his that we much require at the present moment. But at the same time you clearly understand I do not advocate his superseding Henry Wilson. It is only that I recognise, owing to personalities, how very difficult it is to bring these two together; but still I think at a moment of crisis like this an effort should be made to do so.

* * *

Haig had taken the dismissal of Robertson with considerable detachment. It seems plain that while in London he had received assurances from the Prime Minister as to his own future which made him feel that whatever happened at the War Office his authority and tenure as Commander-in-Chief were no longer threatened. He seemed equally unperturbed when Derby was moved from the War Office to the Paris Embassy. He contented himself with a telegram[1]: 'We shall miss you very much at the War Office but feel convinced you will be of great assistance to the Army in your new post.' Derby had shown outstanding loyalty to Haig and had repeatedly expressed his confidence in him and his determination to resign if Haig were to be threatened in his post. Moreover, Derby, as his correspondence has abundantly shown, had a genuine admiration and affection for Haig. He had been instrumental in getting him a field-marshal's baton, he had been prepared to recommend him for a peerage and Haig thought him responsible for the rare distinction of the Order of the Thistle which the King had bestowed on him in July 1917.

Sir Douglas Haig to Lord Derby

5 July 1917 General Headquarters,
British Armies in France

The King presented me with 'The Thistle' this afternoon on his arrival in France!

Nothing could have pleased me more than to be given this very ancient and exalted decoration.

I know how much I owe to you in this matter of rewarding me for such services as I have been able to render in this time of crisis, so I write to tell you how delighted I am, and at the same time to thank you for recommending me and for the friendship which you have at all times shewn me.

[1] *Haig*, Volume II, by Duff Cooper.

To what extent Haig truly reciprocated Derby's friendship is open to question. At one time he seems to have thought that Derby should be Prime Minister:

Sir Douglas Haig to Lord Derby

21 March 1916 General Headquarters,
British Army in the Field

. . . Forgive me if I urge on you once again the necessity of *you* taking on yourself the complete control of the Government as long as war lasts. The situation is too serious to continue this 'Wait and See' policy. . . .

As against this there is a good deal of evidence which reveals Haig in an unattractive light in his attitude towards someone who, whatever his limitations, had sought to help him to the limit of his abilities. Thus on 19 May 1917, we find Haig recording in his diary:

I spoke to Lord Derby (S. of S. for War) for at least an hour. He havers a good deal now, but is a nice gentlemanly fellow. I can't think how he can get through his work if he wastes so much time talking on matters of secondary importance.

And on 14 January 1918, Haig wrote to his wife:

I am still corresponding with Derby over Trenchard. D. is a very weak-minded fellow I am afraid, and, like the feather pillow, bears the marks of the last person who has sat on him! I hear he is called in London 'genial Judas'![1]

Yet three months later, just after Derby had left the War Office, we find Haig writing to his wife:

Sir Douglas Haig to Lady Haig[1]

22 April 1918

Lord Derby gave me the enclosed to send to you for his 'godson'. I believe it is £100 which he wants you to invest for the young man. I

[1] *Private Papers of Douglas Haig* by R. Blake.

told Derby that I felt ashamed at his giving such a large present: I personally would have preferred a spoon or cup or something small, but he said it was his *rule* to give £100 to every one of his godsons—so I accepted it with grateful thanks.

Derby left for Paris yesterday. He looked a different man! In such good spirits and eating well.

* * *

By the middle of April Derby, after much heart searching, realised that he had been manœuvred into a position where his easiest course was to accept the offer of the Paris Embassy. He keenly felt the criticisms which had been directed against him. Though he admired the new C.I.G.S., Sir Henry Wilson, he was suspicious of his methods and he must have welcomed the prospect of relief from the ceaseless intrigues of Whitehall and Downing Street. However, in accepting the Prime Minister's offer, he was careful to stipulate that he should receive powers considerably in excess of those of his predecessor, Lord Bertie:

Lord Derby to the Prime Minister

Very Confidential — War Office

16 April 1918

I feel in view of your request to me today, and Arthur Balfour's support of your suggestion, that I have no alternative left but to accept the post you offer me in Paris. Whatever may have been the result of my tenure of my present office, whether for good or ill, it has been, though a difficult, a very happy time for me, and I venture to think that I have secured the confidence of the Office.

To go to Paris at any time means the breaking of many ties in my public life both here, but more especially in Lancashire, but this is not a time to consider one's personal feelings, and if in your opinion and that of the Secretary of State for Foreign Affairs, I can do better service for you in Paris than I am doing here, I do not hesitate to obey the order.

I want, however, to have it made perfectly clear that I am endowed with further powers than those given to an Ambassador under ordinary circumstances, and I would ask that the same powers be entrusted to me as are given to Lord Reading in Washington.

I must stipulate to be kept very fully informed, not only on the diplomatic but on the military situation, and to have the right, if necessary, to return to this country and represent in person my views to the War Cabinet.

The ways of diplomacy are strange to me, and in my wildest moments I have never looked upon myself as a diplomat, but it may be that, in my new capacity, I shall be in a position to render service to the Army with which, both in peace and in war, my whole life has been bound up.

There are certain matters of a personal character which I must settle before I leave, but these need not take long: and there are the Seals of Office to be given up, and taken over by my successor; but all that I think I can conclude by Saturday morning. After that I shall be at the disposal of the Secretary of State for Foreign Affairs and could leave immediately.

I think it would be as well that the War Cabinet should lay down some definite instructions for me as to what duties they wish me to perform; and for the rest, I must ask that you should leave it to me to exercise my discretion, and to have at all events such confidence in me as to realise that I shall do all in my power to assist this country in this grave crisis.

The Prime Minister was very ready to agree to these wider powers which in effect did not amount to very much. In consequence, two days later he brought the matter before the War Cabinet who agreed to the arrangement.

One small hitch occurred before Derby's appointment to Paris could be officially announced. Lloyd George had little regard for protocol, particularly in war time. We have seen how Palace plumage was ruffled at changes in the Government being announced without the King being officially consulted. The Prime Minister's office had been able to show that on that occasion the Palace complaint lacked substance since Lloyd George had already adumbrated these changes to the King a month before. In a letter already quoted we find the Palace being a little sticky about Derby's appointment:

Lord Stamfordham to Mr. J. T. Davies[1]

16 April 1918 Windsor Castle

. . . As to the appointment of Lord Derby to the Embassy in Paris, as I have told you by telephone, His Majesty cannot give his approval until he knows that the proposed change has been submitted to, and approved by, the French Government.

The King assumes that the Prime Minister has carefully considered the wisdom and expediency of changing his representative in Paris at this critical moment in the War, and replacing a diplomatist of Lord Bertie's vast experience, one who thoroughly understands the French language and diplomacy, besides being a personal friend of Monsieur Clemenceau, by Lord Derby, who will, without any special equipment, make his debut in a new profession in this, the most important position in the diplomatic world . . .

Davies, in reply, stated that the necessity for a change at the Embassy in Paris had been on the Prime Minister's mind for some time and had become imperative in view of the fact that there was 'no one of very high standing in Paris at the moment in touch with Monsieur Clemenceau who understands thoroughly the military situation'. Davies added that Derby's appointment carried the approval of all his colleagues in the War Cabinet, notably that of Mr. Balfour. He went on:

Of course there was no intention of announcing the appointments before the President of the Republic gave his consent to the change, and the moment Mr. Lloyd George was assured that Lord Derby was prepared to accept his new post, if offered, he asked me to telephone you at once to inform you of what he proposed to do. I dare say it was a little premature to think that it would be possible to make the announcements today, for Mr. Lloyd George had perhaps overlooked the fact that the communications which would have to be sent to Paris—to Lord Bertie himself, and to the President of the Republic—would take some time, but he was anxious that the appointments should be announced at the earliest possible time lest any rumours of the proposed changes should reach the newspapers.[1]

[1] Royal Archives.

It was announced on April 18 that 'The King has been pleased to approve the appointment of the Earl of Derby as His Majesty's Ambassador Extraordinary and Plenipotentiary on a special mission to the Government of the French Republic in succession to Lord Bertie'. Two days later he was received in audience and surrendered his seals as Secretary of State for War. He left for Paris almost at once.

XVI

The Paris Embassy

DERBY'S two and a half years' tenure of the Paris Embassy was to be the most successful and happy period of his official life. Though he did not know France well and scarcely spoke any French he quickly found himself at home in the most beautiful and agreeable of all cities in the world. The work was varied, interesting and voluminous and Derby addressed himself to it with his usual superabundant energy and vitality. Despite various brushes with his Government at home, mostly on minor matters, he was to find his duties very much to his liking. The French Government and people for their part saw in Derby their *beau idéal* of the English *milord*. He was perfectly cast for this role; he looked the part and played it with verve and gusto. Lady Derby did not at first accompany him to Paris. She thought that the fact that her mother had been a German and had been born the Countess Von Alten might possibly in wartime Paris be an embarrassment to her husband's embassy. In fact her fears proved groundless. Although half German she did not speak the language, while her command of French was remarkable. She read a great deal of modern French literature and was happy in intellectual society where her friends included M. Jean Cocteau and the Etienne de Beaumonts. She was a regular visitor to the artistic and literary salons, particularly those of Madame de Chevigné and Princesse Lucien Murat. She was a keen theatre-goer and during her time in Paris saw almost every notable production. She and her husband entertained a very wide circle of friends and acquaintances at the Embassy at functions large and small, but she was always very happy to escape from the Embassy and have luncheon or dinner in a restaurant with her daughter, Victoria. Derby's social and diplomatic work in the official world took all his time, but in any case he was never much attracted by the pleasures of the mind. In consequence Lady Derby's life in the literary and artistic worlds of Paris usefully supplemented her husband's. When she ultimately came to Paris she was an immediate success and proved a considerable help to her husband. Meanwhile their daughter, Victoria, frequently came to Paris, where she temporarily acted as her father's hostess.

The previous ambassador, Lord Bertie, had been ill for some time, and Derby, with his usual consideration, did all he could to ease his lot. He had insisted on having the same nominal powers which Lord Reading exercised in Washington. These the Prime Minister had readily accorded him. Derby's great friend and political leader, Mr. Balfour, was still Foreign Secretary and Derby corresponded freely with him. In addition, however, perhaps to underline the extra status he had and his nominal authority over the numerous British missions established in Paris, he reported on many matters direct to Mr. Lloyd George:

Lord Derby to the Prime Minister

Private and Personal — British Embassy,
26 April 1918 — Paris

Here I am—but at present am not what C.I.G.S. calls 'functioning'—as my credentials have not arrived. I gather there is some hitch over the wording owing to the inclusion of my being head of the mission which, of course, is essential though naturally I shall not interfere with them. I am living with Sackville-West at Versailles so keep in close touch with them. I don't know when I shall get into this place. Bertie is very ill—much worse than he thinks—and there has just been a great consultation but they will not decide till Saturday whether he is to be operated on or not. I am afraid from what they say that if he leaves here at all alive it can only be for an operation which will leave him a permanent invalid. I am beginning to feel my way and I hope by entertaining on a small scale to get to know people. It is early times to give you any impressions as to what I think of the position here. I have an uneasy feeling that the French are rather inclined to pity us and at the same time to think we are not doing all we can in the way of manpower. Clemenceau wants me to talk the matter over with him. I think I know my figures fairly well. I ought to be considering all the attacks made on Home Forces by the Cabinet!! He (C) also says we have too many men behind the lines. Again I think he is wrong. Q.M.G. will tell you how many of our B motordrivers cracked up during the retreat. I have just heard it reported that Kemmel has been taken. I don't like that—hope it is not true.

I am not very happy here yet, but am gradually getting reconciled to exile. Any amount of food here and still many pretty women tho' most have bolted, but there are enough to make life tolerable. With regard to my position in reference to the Mission, please see the report of War Cabinet.

Derby's friend, Lord Esher, who had spent most of the war in Paris, ostensibly representing the Red Cross but in fact performing liaison and political intelligence work first for Kitchener and later for Asquith, was eager to help Derby in finding his way about Paris. Esher was a curious, enigmatic character, part courtier, part diplomat, part politician who moved discreetly behind the scenes in Paris and London. He was exceptionally well connected and was a man of intelligence and common sense. However, he preferred the shadows of negotiation and intrigue to the limelight and ardours of executive office; and though his letters, many of which have been published by his son, are among the most fascinating documents of the period, the public will have to wait until 1981 in order to be made privy to his secret diaries, which he deposited under seal in the British Museum. Esher's family are proud of his aversion to playing any active public role, and in one volume of his memoirs there is a fascinating list of the numerous eminent positions ranging from Viceroy of India to Secretary of State for War which he was offered, and which he refused.

Shortly after Derby arrived in Paris, he received a letter from Esher informing him in pemmicanised fashion, as if he were marking a race-card, of the 'form' of the people with whom he would be coming in contact.

Embassy

Grahame	Excellent capacity and much culture.
Eric Phipps	Typically pleasant. Son of 'Constantine'.
Joseph Addison	Brilliant but combative.
Leroy Lewis	A certain winner if ridden in a snaffle.
Rest of staff	Selling platers.

Governing Blokes

Clemenceau	Masterful—at a dangerous age. Life behind him instead of before him. 'Capable de tout.'
Pichon	Would never get half round the course at Aintree.
Jules Cambon	Old and foxy.
Pams	Rich and consequently honest.
The rest	Political hacks.

The Socialists

A. Thomas	Clever, ambitious—with a past.
Cachin	Clever, ambitious—with a future.
Sembach	Talented, learned and shifty.
The rest	Wind bags.

Ex-Ministers

Briand	Brilliant but luxurious.
Ribot	Old and futile.
Painlevé	Vain and vacillating—intelligent.
F. Bouillin	Charlatan and waster.
Viviani	F. E. Smith grown older.

Soldiers

Joffre	Buddha.
Foch	Cyrano de Bergerac.
Pétain	Wully [Robertson] with a dash of Rawly [Rawlinson].
Others	Sabretache.

By the time that Derby arrived in Paris more than a month had passed since the German assault of the Twenty-first of March. Though it came perilously near to success it was to prove, like the Rundstedt offensive of December 1944, a final German fling. Thereafter, the Germans, in 1918 as in 1944, were incapable of any major effort. This, however, was not immediately perceptible. Derby arrived in Paris at a time when, although unity of command had at last been achieved, relations between the British and French Allies were under severe stress. The governing minds of both countries had received an unexpected shock and the mood in the highest political and military circles was to gather and conserve their strength; await the arrival of the huge armies and vast output of munitions which were on the way across the Atlantic; and defer until the spring of 1919 the decisive Allied campaign.

Derby, fresh from the frenetic atmosphere of war-time London, was fully posted on all that had been going on at many levels and was well placed to win the confidence and esteem of those to whom he was accredited. Except to a small group of politicians in London, his transference from the War Office to Paris seemed like a promotion rather than a rebuff; and most people loyally co-operated in encouraging acceptance of this idea.

Derby early in his embassy established a most happy and intimate relationship with the French Prime Minister, Clemenceau. He soon acquired that most priceless asset for an ambassador, easy access to the man at the top. Indeed, reading the documents at this time it would seem that the British Ambassador seldom found it necessary to address himself to the Foreign Minister, Pichon, at the Quai d'Orsay, but was able, save on routine matters, to address himself directly to the Prime Minister at the Hôtel Matignon. Derby, though he never acquired more than a Ritz Hotel knowledge of the French language, soon gained an intimate understanding of the inner workings of French politics, which in wartime no less than in peace are of an exceptional complexity and usually incomprehensible to any foreigner. His rapidly acquired understanding of French politics and his intimacy with Clemenceau were greatly aided by the friendship he formed with a remarkable woman,

Madame Hennessy, wife of one of the principal proprietors of the famous Cognac firm and political Egeria of the French Prime Minister.

Esher continued to give Derby the benefit of his knowledge and experience of French politics:

Lord Esher to Lord Derby

22 April 1918 | 2 Tilney Street, Mayfair W.

Presently, when you are more settled, there are one or two people I should like you to see on the quiet.

In France, the most powerful forces are not on the surface of the waters. There are submarines everywhere. You should get to know about these. Only one or two men can give you a real insight into French politics.

I have a friend who is past master, and who will explain to you all the personalities that count. Before long I shall suggest you seeing him.

Mind you put aside all *prejudice*, whether against politicians or personalities! English or French—whether Franklin Bouillin or Jefferson Cohn.

It was this 'unambassadorial' frame of mind that so weakened Bertie as to render him useless. He let himself be swayed by his private curiosities, by his dislikes and likings. A man is not paid £10,000 a year by the State for self-indulgence!

Old Lord Clarendon once said 'An Ambassador has no right to private feelings.' It was a true point of view.

I am sure that you will be an unqualified success in Paris, and that you will quite possibly save a situation that is badly compromised. I told H. W. [Henry Wilson] yesterday *not* to accept Foch's refusal to have a British Etat Major, if H. W. desires to carry public opinion here along with Foch. When the pinch comes and big decisions have to be taken, he will command no confidence here unless he has a mixed staff.

You should get F. Maurice over to Versailles, and organize Versailles as Foch's Etat Major. That is the proper sequence of what has been accomplished. At present Foch is *not* General in Chief except in name.

Either you want 'Unity of Command' or you do not. But to have it in name, and not in fact, is simply no solution at all. Far better to to have it in fact and *not* in name! Short of a miracle you cannot beat the Boche. But you can prevent him from beating us. Not, however, if we muddle the next three months! Geoffrey Dawson lunches here today.

The *M. Post* today proposes *Cave* as P. M. Gwynne has no sense of humour.

The reader must already have noticed how changeable Lord Derby's opinion could be on men and events. He was never very sure of his own judgment—he was apt to be easily swayed by the opinions of the numerous and varied people he met in the course of his official life. Many more cases of this will have to be alluded to in future chapters, if his personality is to be fully understood. This tendency to blow hot and then cold is well illustrated by his attitude towards two staff officers serving in Paris at this time.

It was not long before Derby found himself obliged to consider the problem of the functions of the Military Attaché and whether the officer who held the position at the time, Colonel Leroy Lewis, should continue to discharge them. The question of the Military Attaché's functions, and the related question of the control and organisation of the various British Military Missions in Paris, constituted a minor but abiding source of irritation to Derby throughout his embassy.

Colonel Herman Leroy Lewis was born in 1860 and had served in the South African War with distinction. Derby's attitude towards the Military Attaché whom he inherited was to vary, as indeed were those of many other people concerned in these events. For instance, he wrote to the Secretary of State for War about a year after he had taken over the British Embassy:

Lord Derby to Mr. Winston Churchill

7 May 1919

. . . I suffered in the early part of my time here through having as Military Attaché, Leroy Lewis, who though he had my confidence was detested and distrusted in French political and military circles. I will not repeat the history of my being officially asked to have him removed but it is an experience that I do not wish to see repeated . . .

Derby, as we have seen, relied greatly on Esher's opinions and nearly a year before Derby went to Paris Esher, in the course of a letter, had written to him at the War Office as follows:

Lord Esher to Lord Derby

9 May 1917 Paris

A new ambassadorial phase is the refusal of F. Bertie to see or speak to Leroy Lewis.

The French ministers are scandalised, especially little Painlevé, who cannot comprehend any obstacles being allowed to the prosecution of the war.

As you are aware, Leroy Lewis, whatever his shortcomings, has worked without intermission for the good of the country and has established considerable authority here for himself.

He—alone—possesses the entrée to every bureau official or non-official where the business of the war progresses.

Neither the Ambassador nor any member of the Embassy can tell the P.M. or you or A. J. B. anything that is worth hearing. None of the official staff of the Embassy has set foot in the Chamber of Deputies since the war began.

They are not personally acquainted with any of the owners or directors of the great French newspapers.

They live in a small circumscribed area that is supposed to be 'smart' and is indescribably ignorant, and pitiably ineffective. Had it not been that poor old Fitz[1] put his finger accidentally upon an 'homme d'affaires' like Leroy Lewis and made him Military Attaché the Government and our country would be unrepresented here . . .

However, very early in Derby's embassy Esher seems to have changed his views of Leroy Lewis:

Lord Esher to Lord Derby

30 April 1918 Roman Camp,
Callander, N.B.

. . . I hear that you are getting rid of Leroy and and taking on Spiers.

The latter is a clever young fellow, with a good deal of charm.

[1] Lieut.-Col. Oswald Fitzgerald, C.M.G., Personal Military Secretary to Lord Kitchener, with whom he was drowned in 1916.

He is an ambitious youth, and small blame to him. He has not, of course, an experienced judgment.

I think Leroy has accomplished all the good work he is likely to do in Paris, as I told him long ago. It would be unfair, in view of his services, were he to remain unemployed, so you might get him a job in connection with propaganda or munitions. Either he would do excellently with . . .

Derby replied:

Lord Derby to Lord Esher

Confidential
9 May 1918

British Embassy,
Paris

. . . With regard to Leroy Lewis I certainly have not made up my mind to make a change. He is most useful and no new man could have the knowledge he has, but of course from a purely military point of view, and from the point of view of helping me to endeavour to co-ordinate the 57 missions that there are in this city, he is perhaps not as good as some regular soldier, and what I want, if possible, is to so arrange matters as to make use of him in the particular sphere to which he is accustomed, and Spiers in his sphere . . .

While Leroy Lewis seems to have had, at any rate at the outset, admirable relations with the French General Staff, few members of the British Embassy seem to have worked happily with him. Thus we find during a brief visit Derby paid to London in July 1918 his Counsellor, Sir George Grahame, complaining of Lewis's conduct to the Permanent Under Secretary at the Foreign Office, Lord Hardinge of Penshurst:

Lord Hardinge to Lord Derby

Private

Foreign Office
25 July 1918

You will remember that I spoke to you before you left in regard to the relations between the Embassy and Leroy Lewis. I have since received from George Grahame a formal complaint as to the way in which Leroy Lewis has failed to keep him informed during your absence. The particular incident to which Grahame calls attention is connected with the appointment of a French representative on the Inter-Allied Committee respecting Propaganda in enemy countries. It appears that Commandant Chaix had been in communication on the subject with the Military Attaché and that the Quai d'Orsay, concluding, as was natural, that Leroy Lewis would have informed the Embassy of what had passed, did not consider it necessary themselves to keep Grahame *au courant;* the result has been of course that Grahame has been unable to answer enquiries on the subject and has been obliged to refer to the Quai d'Orsay which has placed him in a somewhat awkward position.

Grahame adds in his letter to me that after Leroy Lewis's departure for England, he enquired of Major Roberts, who acts as the former's substitute, whether he had received any instructions as to furnishing the Embassy with military news. Major Roberts replied that he had received no such instructions and Grahame pointed out to him the necessity of the Embassy being kept informed. Major Roberts has since brought to Grahame several times a day a number of bulletins and has also told him verbally any news of importance which has reached him. This has been sufficient to indicate the extent to which Leroy Lewis has been withholding information.

I feel sure that you will agree with me that this system can only lead to duplication and misunderstandings, and that you will yourself explain to Leroy Lewis that it is his duty, in your absence, to keep the temporary Head of the Mission fully informed of any important news which may reach him.

The extraordinary confusion in which the various agencies of the British Forces in France had become involved at this time is well shown by Derby's answer. It shows a discrepancy between what he was later to report to the Secretary of State for War and indicates that at least at this stage he was intending to make the confusion more confounded:

Lord Derby to Lord Hardinge

Confidential 27 July 1918

Thank you for your letter with regard to the relationship between Leroy Lewis and Grahame. I have had a talk to the latter on the subject and I think all is smoothed over now. The real truth is this. If I had thought Leroy Lewis's Military knowledge of what was going on in the Military world was worth having I would have told him to give the information to Grahame but as a matter of fact I never speak to him on that subject at all. I get all my information direct from Spiers' Mission which of course is not under me as Ambassador but under me as head of the Military Missions. This Mission therefore would not naturally give the intelligence to anybody except myself. I will see however that next time Leroy Lewis does give any news he may get to Grahame for what it is worth.

The Commandant Chaix business is a little different and again I explained matters to Grahame. Leroy Lewis got the paper. He brought it over to London and gave it to me personally. I ought by rights to have sent it at once to the Foreign Office but there was other information I wanted to get before I could really understand what was desired and I kept it till I got back here. The matter has now gone in in the form of a Despatch to the Foreign Office.

Leroy Lewis eventually retired in September 1918. By now Derby had formed a more favourable opinion of his work and sought to smooth his departure:

Lord Derby to Mr. Herbert Creedy[1]

Confidential and Personal 22 June 1918

. . . The Military Attaché's work is not really military work at all and what there is to be done, Leroy Lewis does extremely well. I was as you know prejudiced against him. People here do not like him but there is no doubt that at his particular job he is first rate and he has helped me most loyally . . . I must tell you something in strict confidence with regard to Leroy Lewis. He was I think disappointed with his C.M.G. though I must say I do not think he has any reason to be. I congratulated him and he took it rather half-heartedly and said he really did not care about it. I asked him then what he wanted, a K.B.E., a Knighthood, a Baronetcy, or what, and his answer was 'My dear Sir, I do not want any reward. I refused a Peerage 20 years ago.' It amuses me because I am perfectly certain that he never did and would jump at it if it was offered now . . .

The discordance and inefficiency created by the overlapping of the

[1] Private Secretary to Secretaries of State for War 1913–1920.

Military Missions found reflection in another awkward personal question. This time the personality concerned was Brigadier-General E. L. Spiers, the head of the British Military Mission to Marshal Foch. This officer, who was born in Paris and whose family in the male line had lived much of their lives in France for three generations, had the advantage of speaking French almost better than English. He joined the Kildare Militia in Ireland in 1903. He later transferred to the 8th and subsequently to the 11th Hussars and made a notable career for himself in the First World War. His keen intelligence and his powers of observation, his brilliant dexterity with his pen and his bilinguality ordained him for a role of liaison officer. He rose rapidly through various echelons to the foremost liaison job between the British and French Commands. His experiences and observations are admirably recorded in his book *Liaison, 1914*, one of the most fascinating of all books on the 1914–1918 War. He managed to get on terms of intimacy with a great number of French officers of all ranks and at one time established an extremely valuable connection between himself and the French Prime Minister, Clemenceau. Coupled, however, with his flair for making intimate friendships was a capacity, not unusual in people of strong personality, for exciting bitter, if unjustified, animosities. And his relations with Clemenceau, Foch and Derby appear to have been subject to sharp fluctuations and marked revisions of opinion.

At this time Spiers was a man of thirty-one. He had rendered notable services to the Anglo-French alliance and had made himself one of the most fiercely discussed wartime personalities, not only in the army but in the highest diplomatic and political circles. On 18 August 1918, he changed his name to Spears and henceforward we shall write of him as such.[1]

Derby's opinion of Spears seems to have varied as much as did his opinion of Leroy Lewis. Thus we find him writing to the C.I.G.S., Sir Henry Wilson, in September 1918: 'I like him very much indeed.' But fifteen months later he writes again to Wilson, in January 1920: 'I really cannot stand his being here any longer.' When Leroy Lewis left Paris it was intended that Lieutenant-General Sir David Hender-

[1] See the *London Gazette*, 3 September 1918.

son should replace him. But Derby wished that Henderson should combine both jobs and be Military Attaché as well as head of the Military Mission with Spears subordinate to him. Spears strongly resisted this proposal and said he would brook no interference from Henderson, and argued that he should have both jobs under Henderson, who as Counsellor at the Embassy would rank immediately below the Ambassador:

Lord Derby to General Sir Henry Wilson

Confidential 13 September 1918

I had a talk with Spiers[1] yesterday and after making due allowance for his being rather sore I think he is inclined to be unreasonable. He said it would be impossible for him to have any interference with his work and if Henderson interfered he would be obliged to resign. I had to tell him that that would not be a question for him to decide and I think on the whole he will settle down. He is however very anxious to be made Military Attaché and to combine the two offices under Henderson. I discussed the question afterwards with the latter and we both agree that it would not be possible to do that and I should propose to leave the Military Attaché's post unfilled for the present moment and let Roberts act, put David Henderson in giving him some title (he is thinking what title will be the most appropriate) and let him have his three branches, Military Attaché, Mission and Central Area Control.

With regard to his relationship to Spiers it was decided that he should talk to Spiers. He says he is perfectly willing not to interfere in any way with Spiers's letters to you and Duncannon[2] as long as Spiers tells him everything of a purely military character that goes into those letters as he feels that as long as you see the information it is all right as you would communicate with him and keep him informed of anything Spiers was saying.

With regard to letters to D.M.I. [Director of Military Intelligence] he also sees no objection to the same course being pursued but he is going to have a talk with Spiers and I think, thanks to his tact, it will be satisfactorily arranged, but I hope that you will support me in not allowing Spiers to be dictatorial in the matter. He is very young—only

[1] Derby had evidently not read the *London Gazette*.

[2] Sir Henry Wilson's private secretary at the War Office.

thirty-one, very clever, does extraordinarily good work with which I do not want to interfere in the least, but it would never do for a man of thirty-one and who is really only a junior Captain and who has got extraordinary rapid promotion, to be allowed to dictate whether he will hold or resign an office simply because a senior officer is put over him and he thinks his position is thereby impaired. It won't be impaired and nobody will think it is unless he goes talking about it and I have told him that.

I saw Clemenceau this morning and told him the proposal. He is delighted with it. He thinks it will work admirably and he will be prepared to give the fullest information to David Henderson or myself as the case may be . . .

I think the scheme will work all right provided you are quite firm about Spiers but I know there will be an agitation on his behalf as he is a great friend of Winston and Winston will try and influence the Prime Minister.

In the end this tiresome squabble was settled by a compromise which was an innovation. Henderson, instead of being appointed Military Attaché, was given the more exalted and unique rank of Military Counsellor, ranking immediately after the Ambassador. The post of Military Attaché was not filled, and Spears, while nominally under Henderson, preserved a wide measure of autonomy. This arrangement worked after a fashion until the spring of 1919 when Henderson indicated his desire to be released from Paris in order to take up another appointment. The Secretary of State for War, Mr. Winston Churchill, tried to persuade Derby to accept Spears in his place. In a letter to the Secretary of State already quoted on page 359 Derby strongly resisted this proposal:

Lord Derby to Mr. Winston Churchill

Strictly Confidential and Personal 7 May 1919

. . . He [Henderson] also told me that you were anxious to appoint Spears to the post of Military Attaché and that you begged that I would not be very obstinate in opposing him. I am afraid I cannot give way on this point. I like Spears personally very much indeed but I think he is quite unsuitable as a Military Attaché (who must have, if he is to be of any use, not only the confidence of the Ambassador but also of those with whom he works).

Now Spears is to a great extent in exactly the same position [as Leroy Lewis had been]. He is intensely disliked in French military circles. It is quite true that when Painlevé was Minister for War, Spears being a personal friend of his, secured more recognition than he would otherwise have had, but when Painlevé went the opposition to him became very marked.

Of course in Paris as you know the position a man may hold in social circles is of far more consequence than it is in London and here again Spears fails lamentably. He is most unpopular, unjustly as I think. At the same time the fact remains.[1]

Of course I have had some experience of his work at the Head of the Mission as it was under me and is I believe still nominally, and personally I did not find that his information was either particularly good or particularly accurate. This however is a matter on which I am not as qualified to advise you as your military advisers in the War Office.

I repeat I am not in the least prejudiced against Spears. On the contrary I like him personally very much but I should be failing in my duty if I did not let you know now, how impossible it would be for me to acquiesce in his appointment as Military Attaché.

Evidently there was a considerable tussle on this issue and Derby sought to enlist the help of the C.I.G.S.:

Lord Derby to General Sir Henry Wilson

Confidential and Personal 28 May 1919

I had a little talk to the P.M. and Winston about the Spears affair and apparently it had been left that the P.M. shall discuss the question with you. I feel therefore that with your very different views on the subject Winston's wishes will not now prevail, especially as A. J. B. is equally against Spears. It was rather amusing yesterday. Winston handed a cutting from French's[2] articles on the subject of Spears to L. G. Neither of them had their glasses so I had to read it to the P.M., which naturally I did

[1] This was far too sweeping and indiscriminate a judgment on Derby's part. Spears certainly had his critics and even his enemies, but he also had a wide and varied circle of friends, who greatly admired his abilities and charm.

[2] Sir John French, later Lord Ypres.

without any comment whatever. I must say French does slobber people. He attributes every virtue to Spears and there is only one which he really possesses and that is bravery. He undoubtedly is brave but to say that he is tactful and popular with both French and English Staffs seems to me the absolute limit of inaccuracy.

I think if the P.M. does not send to you to talk to you about Spears the best thing would be for you to ask to see him. We really must get the matter settled and Winston's proposal that the Mission should go on and that I should be left here without a Military Attaché at all seems to me a monstrous and insulting proposal which I very much resent.

Derby eventually prevailed; and the job of Military Attaché, which had been in abeyance, was finally filled by Major-General Charles John Sackville-West, now the fourth Lord Sackville. Sackville-West had been British Military representative to the Allied War Council at Versailles, and it was at his house that Derby had stayed during his early weeks in Paris.

Meanwhile the Spears mission continued its activities and relations continued to deteriorate between the Embassy and Spears.

Lord Derby to Sir Henry Wilson

Confidential and Personal 8 January 1920

. . . to return to the eternal subject of Spears & Co. I really cannot stand his being here any longer. He really usurps a position—I do not think intentionally—which makes that of Sackville-West impossible. To give you an instance. I got a telegram to ask me to arrange for official cars from Clemenceau for the Prime Minister. I got Sackville-West to go down and see Mordacq, which he did, only to find that Spears had been telegraphed to to make the same arrangements. Sackville-West says it makes him look such a fool. However incidentally I will tell you that they were not prepared to give the cars to Spears but did to Sackville-West. Really the thing must end. I am quite good friends with Spears. I know that he wants to resign to take up civil life and I know the French want to get rid of him.[1] Do therefore just send a telegram that ends the Mission. It is no use whatever only an unneces-

[1] This is clearly an exaggeration on the part of Lord Derby.

sary expense. I feel very bitter against Winston over all this. He asked me as a personal favour to do what I could not to make Spears' position in Society here difficult when he ceased to be head of the Mission and he gave me to understand that the Mission should come to an end. I did what I should never have done otherwise. I accepted an invitation for us both to dine there so as to try and put the Spears right in the eyes of the social world and the only return I get is that this is allowed to drag on. I shall not forget it and some day, sooner or later, I will pay back Winston.

Eventually a compromise was put forward by the Secretary of State for War:

Mr. Winston Churchill to Lord Derby

11 April 1920 War Office

I propose to you the following arrangement, which will I hope meet the situation fully:—

The Spears Mission should become an autonomous department of the office of the Military Attaché. General Spears' communications to the War Office would be forwarded through the Military Attaché, who would also communicate to you anything which might be of interest to you. It would, of course, be understood that Sackville-West would not interfere with the interior management of Spears' Mission and would transmit to the War Office or to me all communications emanating from it.

Sackville-West's heavy duties at Versailles, in addition to his work as Attaché and the general complication of affairs at the present time, fully justify this elaboration of the Military Attaché's Department as a temporary measure. Sackville-West, as Military Attaché, reports to the General Staff on everything connected with the French Army, and Spears will report through him to the General Staff or to me on intelligence matters affecting other countries as collected by his Mission. The whole would be under your general authority, in the same way as the Ministry of Munitions Mission and other similar bodies were grouped under you with my full agreement during the war. Such an arrangement, worked with goodwill, would I am sure conduce greatly to the public interest.

Derby replied a few days later:

Lord Derby to Mr. Winston Churchill

Confidential 17 April 1920

I have thought very carefully over your suggestion with regard to Spears, as I realise you wish to put an end to a system which is extremely distasteful to me; but I fear the suggestion you make is not one that I can accept. You and I have always been good personal friends and strongly as I feel in this matter I for one won't let it interfere with our personal friendship. I feel as I say, very strongly in the matter, and I must write very plainly and bluntly to you.

In the first place, with regard to military information Spears would only be a fifth wheel to a coach. The proper channel for conveying military information to the Home Government is through the Military Attaché, and I am perfectly certain that apart from the Minister of War, the soldiers would be far more ready to give information to Sackville-West than they are to Spears. I consulted Henry Wilson, who was here, on this point, and he tells me that as far as he is concerned Spears is of no use whatever to him; that he has received an enormous number of letters from him and not one of them was of any information which required action on his part, or which was of any military value.[1] From a military point of view therefore it would appear as if Spears' Mission is no longer required; but as you yourself told me the other day it is not for the purpose of obtaining military information for you that you wish to keep Spears, but for the political information, and you say he gives you a lot of information which you do not get from any other source. But is it to you that other political information should go? I was always under the impression that it was the Government generally who got the information, and that ought to be sent to them through the Foreign Office or by private letters from the Ambassador. You apparently are not satisfied with this and wish to have an Embassy of your own. Well, that must be for you to settle with the Government. If they are not satisfied with the information I give they have only got to say so. I will be perfectly ready to make way for somebody else. But if they are satisfied then I do object most strongly to a rival body being set up, and whose political information may be as useless as apparently its military information is; and I think that you may find it difficult to justify this anomalous body being kept on at the expense of some £5,000 a year to the country . . .

[1] This is a palpable exaggeration on the part of Henry Wilson or a misunderstanding on the part of Lord Derby.

Though he deployed these arguments which were inconsistent with his earlier opinions, Derby was unable to get those whose business it was to decide to accept his view. Spears remained in an independent role and his Mission was not wound up until a good deal later in the year, about the time that Derby left the Embassy.

* * *

For the first eighteen months of Derby's tenure of the Paris Embassy his chief had been Mr. Balfour, the man whom of all British statesmen he most respected. His relations with the Foreign Office had consequently been happy. In October 1919 Balfour left the Foreign Office and was succeeded by Lord Curzon with whom, as we have already seen, Derby was inclined, often with some justice, to quarrel. Henceforward, though his Embassy prospered, numerous tiresome incidents arose between him and the Foreign Secretary. The author is indebted to Sir Malcolm Bullock for some interesting reminiscences of this period. Bullock, a young officer in the Scots Guards, had been wounded and he was seconded shortly after Derby's arrival in Paris to act as Military Secretary. His work at the Embassy brought him closely in touch with the Ambassador and his family, and in 1919 he was to marry Derby's only daughter, Victoria, whose first husband, Neil Primrose, had died on active service in 1917. Bullock recalls how early in his service at the Embassy Derby handed him a letter addressed to the Foreign Secretary which began as follows: 'My dear Curzon, I have always known you to be a cad. I now know that you are a liar.' Derby instructed Bullock to see that the letter was enclosed in that night's bag to London. Unaware of his new chief's impetuous nature, which often led him into imprudent epistolary outbursts which he regretted in the morning, and doubtful where his duty lay in the matter, he sought the advice of the Minister, Sir George Grahame. 'Just leave it there in that tray,' Grahame replied. 'He will probably have forgotten about it in the morning.' Derby, however, had not forgotten and in the morning sent for Bullock and asked him whether the letter had caught the bag. Bullock replied that it had been just too late. 'Just as well, perhaps,' said Derby. 'Let me have another look at it.'

On being shown it he said: 'Hmm, perhaps it is a bit too strong. I think I will have another go. Ring for the shorthand writer.' Derby then dictated a new letter beginning: 'My dear George, You and I have known each other too long to quarrel over so small a matter.'

Even in Paris Derby was glad to be informed of 'dear George's activities:

Lady Desborough to Lord Derby

28 June 1918 Taplow Court,
Berkshire

I got your delightful letter (you were *never* meant to answer!) and when you say write sometimes I simply can't help taking you at your word at once to tell you of G. N. C.'s [Curzon's] stupendous banquet on Wed. evening. You'll have perhaps already heard all about it but oh it was so amazing. He first asked sixty men—Premiers, poets, painters, philosophers, politicians—men only, all well and good; but *then* he asked ten women with the result that all the husbands were acutely affronted and in any case what were we among so many. You'd have laughed so at the startled looks of the married men, even those who *least* wished for their wives' presence, as they came into the room—Lloyd George, the Archbishop of Canterbury, etc. The Archbishop was not put near Countess Duggan [Lady Curzon, formerly Mrs. Duggan] or indeed by any woman at all, but sat looking much surprised between two men—Lloyd George, making rather heavy weather of his hostess, and Barrie the novelist on his other side. I had a lucky draw, between A. J. B. and John Morley, the latter looking as if he had been buried for twenty years, but A. J. B. with his magic galvanised the dear old dry bones into life, and they had an admirable talk across me of old House of Commons days—the Eighties, the G.O.M., Bradlaugh, all the giants of those days, and even kindled Lord Bryce into joining in, who was sitting like an old mummied monkey on A. J. B.'s other side. But the net result of the evening was that everyone seemed angry, and as Arthur said it appeared strange to take the trouble to have a dinner for sixty people in these difficult days in order to offend thirty of them.

There were seven tables, I think, in the ballroom, covered with roses; buckets of cream, all the most pre-war conditions. Our hostess was so nice I thought, quite natural and quiet and quiescent, well dressed in white with no jewels, beautifully done hair, but what an odd doll-like look a middle-aged face gets when it is so well massaged as not to show a single line? I really don't know that it isn't better to let time ravage and be hang to it. The war has had an odd external effect on L. G., his *face* has grown so big! Like a large round flat pale disc—I hadn't seen him for years. In fact, not having been to any party of any kind for three years, you can imagine the bewildering effect of this one—I felt like a person in a Cinematograph show.

George [Curzon] talked to me a little after dinner—in an intimidated voice I asked him about the wives, he said cheerfully 'My dear, on these occasions it is best to disregard peoples' feelings entirely.'

St. John [Lord Midleton] was in a towering rage saying, 'This is the first time for twenty years that I have been asked into the man's house' so I said 'Why did you come?' He said 'I had the greatest difficulty in persuading myself to do so.' If his object was to add to the general hilarity it failed. Did I tell you of his cri-de-coeur the other day? 'Oh Ettie, how I do hate dear darling Margot' . . .

Though Derby, as we have seen, bickered with Curzon all his life, his innate generosity led him after Curzon's death to take a sapient and magnanimous view of the dead statesman:

Lord Derby to Mr. Stanley Baldwin

Private 20 March 1925

. . . I have just heard that poor George Curzon has died. I was not surprised to get the news as I have the same doctor as he had and he told me forty-eight hours ago there was very little hope for him. I do not think I ever knew a man who was such a mixture of strong contradictions. He could be the most charming companion and at the same time a Chief who had no feelings of any sort or kind for his subordinates. He had a brilliant brain and yet he used to devote much of his time to insignificant work. I have known him longer than almost any other man. He made his first political speech when he was staying with my uncle at Knowsley at a big luncheon given for the coming of age of a cousin of mine and, so characteristic of George, made a brilliant Conservative speech abusing the Liberal party into whose Government my uncle who was his host had just entered.

* * *

At this time Derby was to be justly incensed by a *cause célèbre* which involved the name of his dead son-in-law, Neil Primrose. The military reverses which the Allied cause had sustained in the spring of 1918 and the general war-weariness from which the nation was suffering induced a mood of credulity and suspicion in the public mind, which unscrupulous people were able to exploit. In an atmosphere already charged with concern and alarm, it was very easy to persuade large sections of the public that the ill-progress of the war was due to treason rather than to mismanagement. People with German-sounding names whose families had been resident in Britain for several generations were subjected to all sorts of indignities and even persecution, and those who associated with them often themselves became the targets of the hysteria which was generated. Among those who stirred up these emotions and sought to make political capital by doing so was the Independent Member of Parliament for East Hertfordshire, Mr. Noel Pemberton Billing. Pemberton Billing ran a newspaper called *The Vigilante* in which he denounced great numbers of well-known people, accusing many of them not only of treason but also of sodomy.

Billing was finally prosecuted for criminal libel by Miss Maud Allan, a famous dancer. In his newspaper *The Vigilante* he had attacked her for accepting to play the title role in *Salome*, by Oscar Wilde, which had not been previously produced in England (it was banned by the Lord Chamberlain) and was to be given its first performance in a theatre club. Billing had written that *Salome* was lewd and perverted and that Miss Allan was about to encourage the very vices which were endangering the security of the English people. Most of those who would buy tickets, he had continued, were the very same whose names were in the Black Book, a dossier of some 47,000 English sexual aberrants, from every stratum of society, who were known as such to the German Secret Service, and whose loyalties were therefore suspect. Billing alleged that the Black Book was in the hands of Prince William of Wied, a German who had become King of Albania.

Mr. Hume-Williams, K.C., Miss Allan's Counsel in the action which began on 19 May 1918, under Mr. Justice Darling, introduced the subject of the Black Book into his opening speech for the prosecution. Billing conducted his own defence and Mr. Justice Darling allowed him for this reason more latitude than usual. The trial, however, from beginning to end, was a disorderly concatenation of innuendo, abuse and slander, all under the cloak of privilege and all from the defendant. The judge, a witty, soft-mannered lawyer, was unable to restrain Billing, who accused the judge himself of being in the Black Book and indicated besides many prominent politicians. A Mrs. Eileen Villiers Stuart testified that she had been shown the Black Book by Neil Primrose and Evelyn de Rothschild. Primrose and Rothschild had both been killed in the war and could therefore neither confirm nor refute this testimony.

Mr. Justice Darling summed up amid scenes of the wildest disorder during which he was interrupted not only by Pemberton Billing but by Lord Alfred Douglas who was outraged that the judge in his state of discomposure referred to him as the author of *Salome* which he described as 'sadist writing'. Lord Alfred in fact was only the translator of the play which Oscar Wilde had written in French. He shouted out: 'You've no right to say that I wrote it. You lie. You're a liar, a damned liar. If you say it outside the court I will prosecute you.' This unprecedented mode of address to one of His Majesty's judges was greeted with tumultuous applause in court, taking advantage of which Lord Alfred left the court before he could be ordered out. A little later a knock was heard on the door and Lord Alfred Douglas returned to recover his hat. Several members of the public were meanwhile ejected and it was in an atmosphere of hilarious farce that the learned judge concluded his summing up. The jury were out for an hour and a half and then returned with a verdict of acquittal for Billing.

Both Derby and his daughter Victoria were naturally incensed that the name of her late husband, to whom they were both devoted, should have been dragged into these scandalous proceedings—all the more so since they had no effective means of retaliation.

* * *

From the beginning of 1919 the ordinary routine work of the

Embassy was overladen with the work of the Peace Conference and the Embassy became an hotel and restaurant for the visiting ministers and a post office for despatches. The Prime Minister arrived in Paris on January 11 and took up his headquarters at the Hotel Majestic. The Conference opened on January 17. In addition to the Prime Minister, the British delegates were the Foreign Secretary, Mr. Balfour; the Lord Privy Seal and leader of the Conservative Party, Mr. Bonar Law; and Mr. G. N. Barnes. The Prime Ministers of Canada, Australia, New Zealand, South Africa and Newfoundland also attended. France was principally represented by Messrs. Clemenceau and Pichon; Italy by Signor Orlando and Baron Sonnino; and Japan by the Marquess Saionji and Baron Makino. The United States magnified and dignified, even if they did not smooth, the work to be done by the presence of their illustrious President, Woodrow Wilson. At the time it was the fashion to decry the immense delays attendant upon the making of peace. In fact the heads of the treaty with Germany were signed six months later on 28 June 1919. It certainly does not lie with a later generation which fourteen years after the Second World War has proved incapable of making any treaty at all, to reproach the peacemakers of Versailles, at least in this respect.

After the treaty had been signed various protocols had to be negotiated. The heads of delegations dropped out and Britain was for the time being represented by the Foreign Secretary, Mr. Balfour. Derby was not at this stage involved at all in the negotiations, as is shown by a letter he wrote many years later to the then incumbent of the Paris Embassy:

Lord Derby to Lord Tyrrell

Private — 23 January 1932

. . . I cannot think what I could have said at Cambridge that would make you think that I considered Paris was a rest cure; although as a matter of fact it was most of the time I was in Paris owing to the Peace Conference. We had at least three ambassadors there in the persons of Lloyd George, Milner and Balfour—and occasionally Bonar Law—in addition to another ambassador Charlie Hardinge, who had the onerous duty of issuing permits for people to dine at the Hotel Majestic.

'Charlie Hardinge' was Lord Hardinge of Penshurst, a professional diplomatist of great distinction, who had been Permanent Under-Secretary of State for Foreign Affairs since 1906, with the exception of the years 1910 to 1916 when he was Viceroy of India. He accompanied the British delegation to Paris for the Peace Conference and devised for himself the post of Superintending Ambassador, a designation to which Derby not surprisingly objected. His objection moved Sir Ian Malcolm (Mr. Balfour's private secretary at the Conference) to write the following lines:

A DIPLOMATIC INCIDENT

Who chaperones typists and watches their morals;
Who orders our motors and shares our meals;
Who changes our furniture, settles our quarrels
And patiently listens to all our appeals?
'Tis *HE!* whom Delhi and far Calcutta,
Paris and Petrograd, all adore.
HE! whose cognomen 'twere treason to utter;
Our Superintending Ambassador.

Who is it, conscious of superiority,
Pens a despatch to the Quai d'Orsay,
Quite overlooking the Seat of Authority
Down in the Faubourg St. Honoré?
'Tis HE! the Dictator of our Delegation
Whom Plenipotentiaries bow before:
HE! who invented the designation
Of 'Superintending Ambassador.'

Who is it needs this Superintendence
During his exile in gay 'Paree'?
Clerks aren't noted for independence,
It *must* be Derby or A. J. B.
Who, persistently disregarding
HIS commandments whose word is our Law,
Prove the case for appointing Hardinge
Superintending Ambassador.

It is hardly necessary to add that this effusion does less than justice to Lord Hardinge's brilliant work at the Conference.

* * *

During the summer of 1919 Derby had not been at all well:

Lord Derby to Lord Stamfordham[1]

Confidential
14 July 1919

British Embassy,
Paris

. . . I am going to London tomorrow Tuesday morning and am going to see Dawson and Rigby the surgeon. I have really been very bad, very much worse than my friends think and though in myself I feel quite well again now, apart from an attack of gout, the French surgeons here want me to have another operation. I expect it will be necessary but I do not want to have it without Dawson's advice. Really my illness was an extraordinary thing—an acute attack of blood poisoning. I was perfectly all right at Dinner. About 2 o'c in the morning I had a temperature of about 103. I got it down and came over here but it went up again and when they cut into me, which they did in two places both about 5 inches deep, they found a large number of abscesses which all apparently had developed in about 48 hours and the worst of it is they cannot at the present moment tell me what the reason is. If all goes well I am going to come back here in about a fortnight's time.

In the event Derby was too optimistic about his general state of health and he found in London that he must have another operation. He passed his convalescence on the Riviera and it was three months before he was able to resume his duties in Paris. Much had happened in his absence. He found that the Peace Conference had more or less broken up. Balfour had gone home and in his place the British Government was represented by Sir Eyre Crowe, Assistant Under-Secretary of State at the Foreign Office, who for the purpose had been made Minister Plenipotentiary. The British Government wished to dignify his status at the Peace Conference by appointing him Ambassador to the Conference as well as Minister Plenipotentiary. Derby resisted this on the grounds that it would be absurd to

[1] Royal Archives.

have two ambassadors in the same city. He gained this point and thereafter co-operated in every way with Crowe. He did more. When Lloyd George became displeased with Crowe on the grounds that he was being unduly anti-German in negotiations and went so far as to talk of recalling him, Derby, who was in London at the time, joined forces with Curzon, the Foreign Secretary, in strongly defending Crowe's work at the Conference.

Though numerous instances are recorded in these pages of Derby's brushes with Curzon and though there obviously was a latent antipathy between the two men, it is only necessary to read the despatches and correspondence which passed between them to see that these were minor episodes and where the transaction of important public business was concerned they nearly always saw eye to eye and co-operated smoothly and effectively. Both men showed a proper appreciation of each other's functions and business was discharged efficiently and with dignity.

Early in 1920 the subsidiary work of the Peace Conference was wound up. Lloyd George and a powerful delegation came to Paris to sign the final protocols and the task of implementing and supervising the carrying out of the Treaty already negotiated was remitted to the Conference of Ambassadors which had been set up for this purpose. The Conference met about twice a week and Derby was kept busy with discussions on all sorts of minor troublesome matters such as the delivery of German cruisers to France and Italy, the control of railway waggons, the handling of German war criminals and how German assaults on allied missions in Germany should be dealt with. The Conference laboured for many months and at length, having dealt more or less satisfactorily with all the problems, it was wound up in November:

Lord Curzon to Lord Derby

19 November 1920 Foreign Office

MY LORD,

I have received Your Excellency's despatch, No. 3302 of the 11th instant, in which you review the work of the Conference of Ambassadors and discuss the question whether it is desirable or possible to terminate the labours of that body in the immediate future.

2. I concur in the views expressed by you on that question.

3. I take this opportunity to express to you the cordial thanks of His Majesty's Government for the great service rendered by you as British representative on the Conference, and for the able and unflinching manner in which, under circumstances often of no small difficulty, you have duly maintained, not merely the honour, but the primacy of Great Britain.

The winding up of the Ambassadors' Conference was followed shortly by Derby's own departure from the Paris Embassy. When two months previously Lord Hardinge was designated by the King to be the new Ambassador, Derby sought the formal *agrément* of the President of the Republic. The President of the Council, Monsieur Millerand,[1] in his letter conveying the Government's acquiescence in the new appointment added the following words:

Monsieur Millerand to Lord Derby

le 8 Septembre 1920 Paris

... J'ai à coeur d'ajouter que la pensée de votre prochain départ inspire au Gouvernement de la République les plus vifs regrets. Par l'élévation de votre caractère, par l'autorité de vos conseils, par l'estime et la confiance que vous avez su vous acquérir parmi nous, vous avez rendu à la cause de l'Alliance franco-brittannique des services très précieux. Nous garderons de votre mission un souvenir aussi durable que sympathique . . .

On November 16 Derby gave a farewell dinner at the Embassy. Among the sixty guests were Monsieur Millerand, the new President of the Republic, Monsieur Leygues, President of the Council, and Marshal Foch. On November 21 Derby left Paris by train. Leygues came himself to the Gare du Nord where an unusually large crowd was gathered. Lord and Lady Derby's carriage was filled

[1] The President of the Republic, Monsieur Deschanel, who had succeeded Poincaré in January 1920 (beating Clemenceau in the fight for the succession) had been incapacitated since May, having fallen from his train while travelling by night. He resigned his office in the middle of September and was succeeded by Millerand.

with flowers. The French and English Press were unanimous in according the retiring Ambassador the highest praise for the charm and skill with which he had discharged his functions, and the Paris correspondent of *The Times* wrote:

> . . . Paris has known many British Ambassadors. We have had the courtly Lord Lyons, the literary Lord Lytton, the diplomatic Monson, the bluff, shrewd and cynical Lord Bertie. Now Lord Derby makes way for Lord Hardinge.
>
> The retiring Ambassador, when he first came to Paris, declared that so far as he could see, the only reasons why he had been offered the post were that he did not speak French and was not a diplomatist. Lord Derby has demolished whatever truth there may have been in this joke. He does now speak French, and he has become a diplomatist—and one who will be affectionately remembered in France for many years to come. Rank, fortune, and knowledge of affairs are the foundation upon which his success has been built; and that success has been cemented by a shrewd uprightness of character and a solid determination to be more than a mere mouthpiece of a Foreign Office or the reflex of the passing whims of a politician . . .

Of the many French tributes, that in the *Echo de Paris* perhaps described most happily the particular quality which Derby's personality and position had imparted to his embassy:

> . . . Lord Derby a tenu chez nous le rôle qu'il appartient à un ambassadeur d'Angleterre de tenir en régime d'Entente Cordiale. Il n'a pas été seulement le conseiller de son gouvernement: ses avis ont été souvent utilisés par nos propres dirigeants. C'est dire qu'entre lui et les porte-parole français la conversation ne demeurait pas officielle et pompeuse, mais se transformait aisément en une conversation d'ami à ami où les plus vives controverses étaient envisagées d'un point de vue commun et où intervenait, de part et d'autre, une grande liberté de jugement. Seul un ambassadeur sûr de la confiance qu'il inspire et de celle qu'on lui accorde, indépendant et fort vis-à-vis de ses ministres, peut prendre et soutenir pareille attitude. Au succès de Lord Derby Londres et Paris doivent peut-être que les affaires de Francfort, de la Pologne, de la Haute-Silésie et des réparations n'aient pas pris plus fâcheuse tournure . . .

When the official farewells were over Lord and Lady Derby entered the train. Just as it was about to leave there was a sudden movement in the crowd:

> . . . Une ou deux minutes avant le départ du train, un remous. Le maréchal et la maréchale Foch fendent l'élégante assistance et arrivent au marchepied, où descend rapidement lord Derby, tandis qu'à la portière la comtesse de Derby s'entretient avec la femme du glorieux soldat.
>
> Comme j'aurais été peiné de manquer votre départ, fait le maréchal, que l'ambassadeur a pris par l'épaule.
>
> 'Vous emportez quelque chose de nous, vous savez!' . . .

XVII

Back to Lancashire

WE have seen how, prior to the war, Derby had already built up for himself a great position in Lancashire and as early as 1912, when he defeated the whole official leadership of the Tory Party over food taxes, had become the county's effective leader and spokesman. But for more than five years now, since October 1915, when he came to London as Director-General of Recruiting, he had inevitably been cut off from Lancashire. While he had been at the War Office he had been able to make occasional brief visits to Knowsley, but during his service in Paris this was seldom possible. He continued to take a great interest in Lancashire affairs and his correspondence shows how eager he was to maintain such contact as he could with all the numerous institutions with which he had been associated. His experiences in national and international politics, particularly the former, had not been entirely happy and he felt an immense sense of comfort at being once more back in an atmosphere which was so congenial to him. He had far from abandoned the idea of playing a further rôle in national politics, but he was wise enough to see that he would be fortified in any future political rôle by regaining and re-asserting for himself his pre-eminent position in Lancashire.

Soon after Derby's return from Paris, the Prime Minister sent for him and offered him the Colonial Office which was shortly to be vacated by Milner. Derby took two days to think it over and then refused this important office, which of course carried with it a seat in the Cabinet.

Lord Derby to Mr. Lloyd George

15 December 1920

I need not tell you how honoured I was by your kind offer made to me on Monday, and how much I appreciate your wish that I should again serve with you in the Government. The Colonial Office is one which would particularly appeal to me if only for hereditary reasons, as my grandfather, uncle and father all held the post at some time or other,[1] and if the offer had come in six months' or a year's time I should have most gratefully accepted. But after very careful consideration I feel that I must decline. In the first place the doctors tell me (and I have seen mine since I saw you) that during these next six months I must take a cure which would mean three weeks' absence from England in February and again in July. But a stronger reason even for refusing is the fact that I feel there is so much I can do and ought to do in Lancashire. I resigned Paris for the purpose of coming here to take up the work, both political and otherwise, that I was doing before the war, and I feel that I ought to stick to it. Moreover, I cannot help feeling that in a way I may be of more use to you and your Government outside than I could be inside. Politics are in a funny state at the present moment, and I hope that any influence I may have in Lancashire will be better employed outside than inside the Government.

Writing the next day to Bonar Law, he repeated his reasons but made his willingness to join the Government at a later date a good deal more definite. 'If in a year's time,' he wrote, 'he [Mr. Lloyd George] is good enough to offer me to again join the Government you may be quite sure I should be only too glad to do so. It was a tempting offer for many reasons and I hesitated some time before I said No.'

Derby's first public action on returning to England was to advocate a definite alliance between Britain and France. He used the occasion of a luncheon given in his honour by the Manchester Chamber of Commerce on 2 December 1920 to champion this cause in which he had come to believe during his two and a half years at the Paris Embassy. According to *The Times* of December 3:

[1] His younger son Oliver was also destined to hold this office; and his elder son, Edward, was to be Dominions Secretary.

after remarking that he had left many friends in France whose friendship would be lifelong, he said the subject of a closer relationship between the two countries was very near to his heart. There was a certain amount of idle talk of the two countries being able to stand one without the other. It was quite possible that it was so; but even if that were possible, was it good for England, was it good for France, and was it good for the peace of the world? To which he would answer a very definite 'No'. There were some who said, 'Let us return to ten years ago. A hundred years ago we fought military aggression, retired behind our seas, and devoted ourselves simply and solely to our own business.'... 'Nineteen hundred and twenty is not 1815,' he went on. 'We have got commitments all over the world at the present moment, and even despite the seas which divide us, we are as interested in European questions as any one nation on the Continent. We have got to play our part and shoulder our responsibilities, and so far this country has never shirked responsibility. Let us see whether we cannot lessen the burden by joining ourselves in the closest friendship and alliance, and I personally say in *alliance*, with the great country we fought side by side with in the past war.

'There are those who say the time is not ripe for an alliance with France. I am not going to argue, but I am going to advocate it through thick and thin, because, in my humble opinion, if we had had an alliance with France, instead of merely an understanding, the war would not have taken place. If Germany had known we were going to come in on the side of France, she would not have taken aggressive action. War might have been postponed . . . Such an alliance would have proved a security against world-wide war, and we are justified in believing that such an alliance would prevent another such world-wide disaster.

'In order to bring the two countries to an alliance it is essential that we should do everything possible to bring, not only the Governments, but the peoples closer together, and to avoid as far as possible in the future any misunderstanding. Differences of opinion there always will be. At the present moment, with what knowledge I have got of the relationship between France and England, there is no difference of opinion that I know of that could not be perfectly overcome, granted two things—patience and good will. The strip of twenty-two miles of sea divides two peoples different in language, methods and customs, but it does not divide them in one thing, and that is their inborn love of peace. That love of peace would overwhelm any other feeling existing in either nation, I have had the opportunity of coming into contact with all conditions of men in France, and I have formed the conclusion that great as is the love of peace in England, it is equally great, if not greater, in France. . . .'

His first speech on domestic politics was made at a dinner given in his honour by the Liverpool Conservative Club on December 14. He admitted that after two and a half years abroad he felt somewhat in the dark, and after referring to the question of the fusion of the Conservative and Liberal Parties and suggesting that there were hundreds of thousands of electors who even if they would not join the Conservative Party, were ready to co-operate, concluded, according to the *Liverpool Courier*:

> If they could not enter the gates, I say let us co-operate. But let us keep our own organisation intact and strong. Let us keep to the principles we had before the war. Principles do not alter. During the last seven years we have all been tried in the furnace, and all we thought was gold was not gold, and we have had to make modifications in our policy, but at the same time I believe the sound policy of Conservatism was not only a sound policy in the past; it is the sound policy for the future. I say to the Conservative Party welcome those who will come into the ranks, advance to meet them, but remain a Conservative Party. I was a Conservative in the past, I am a Conservative, and, please God, I will die a Conservative.

The fusion of the two parties under Lloyd George's leadership had been much discussed behind the scenes ever since the end of the war, and there was considerable support in both parties for the project. Even the Tory Party's Chairman, Sir George Younger, who was later to play an important part in the destruction of the Coalition, was at one time the supporter of this policy. In a 'Private and Confidential' letter dated 15 October 1919 and circulated to some leading Conservatives who had enquired what the Party's policy was, after stating that: 'the very nature of the subjects which have already been dealt with, or are still in front of us, are the best reasons for the belief that this work can be more wisely and safely carried out by a Coalition than by any single party'; he concluded: 'I have always personally entertained the hope that the present Coalition would form the foundation of a permanently fused party.'

Back at Knowsley, he was quick to take up once more the threads of Lancashire political life. He reported his first impressions to Bonar Law:

Lord Derby to Mr. Bonar Law

18 December 1920

We had the first meeting since my return of the Lancashire Branch of the National Unionist Association, today. It was most satisfactory. They welcomed me, and I made a short speech composed of generalities, and preached loyalty to the Coalition. After that the reporters were cleared out of the room, and we had a resolution moved by a man from Manchester, advocating the breaking up of the Coalition, the statement of a purely Unionist Policy, advocating an immediate election. He did not even get a supporter, though somebody supported it *pro forma* so as to have a discussion. We really had a very good debate and the utmost loyalty was expressed to you. I had rather taken the wind out of the proposer's sails by what I had said in my opening remark, and the proposition fell very flat. I do not think you need have any fear of there being any break in the Coalition in Lancashire, but I am sure it is not advisable for many reasons to try and get Fusion. I found out that the feeling was against it, so I spoke against any attempt at Fusion, but strongly advocated Co-operation as soon as we possibly could without expecting the Liberals to come actually into our ranks. This found general favour. . . .

Derby continued to take the political temperature of Lancashire and writing a few days later to the Prime Minister's Parliamentary Private Secretary, Sir Philip Sassoon, he reported:

Lord Derby to Sir Philip Sassoon

23 December 1920

I have been doing a lot of work of different kinds up here, and I find there is a good bit to do politically. Lloyd George is very popular, but what I think strikes one even more than his popularity is the extreme loyalty of the Unionist Party to Bonar Law, and as long as Lloyd George and Bonar Law stick together I do not think we need have any fear with regard to the support of the Unionist Party in Lancashire. I have had to make two or three political speeches and I have dinned in the subject of loyalty.

But Salvidge, ever a devoted supporter of the Coalition, evidently thought that Derby was drifting away. He wrote to Derby at the end of January in this sense.

Salvidge had not been alone in thinking that Derby contemplated some new political departure. When on 28 January 1921 Derby was entertained to dinner by the Manchester Constitutional Club, the *Manchester Guardian*, reporting the speech under the heading 'LORD DERBY—NO INTENTION TO FORM A NEW PARTY', observed:

> His Lordship's speech was looked forward to with no little interest because of rumours which for some time have associated his name with a movement within the Conservative Party which is considered to indicate dissatisfaction with the Coalition Government.

The report went on:

> Lord Derby stated his position almost at the outset. He had been credited, he said, with two ambitions: to be Prime Minister and to win the Derby. 'I have one of those ambitions left. You can guess which.' He had been offered a position in the Government and had refused it for one reason only: because he felt a call to take up his work in Lancashire. He admitted that at first he thought the Coalition Government a mistake, but he had been obliged to acknowledge that he was wrong. What he wanted to see now was not two parties trying to run a government, but one party with a common policy based on the experience of the last few years. 'Believe me,' he said with emphasis, 'nothing is farther from my mind than to attempt to set up a party of my own.'

Finally Derby laughed the whole matter off by concluding:

Derby and Mr. Lloyd George on their way into the garden at 10 Downing Street.

If I did attempt to do so I know what that party would be. It would be a party which would have complete confidence in its leader, the leader would have complete confidence in it and its following, and it would be a party of one.

Derby's Lancashire activities had evidently been interpreted in London as showing some restiveness against the Government. For at the end of January, in a letter to the Prime Minister, he wrote:

Lord Derby to Mr. Lloyd George

31 January 1921

One line of hearty congratulations to you on having settled the Indemnity question. I was over in Paris last week and I told all my friends there that if there was one man more likely than any other French politician to come to an agreement with you it would be Briand and I am glad that my prophecy has been justified.

I am sure you will never for one minute have believed the various reports that I was trying to break up the Party and I hope what I said at Manchester will knock the rumour finally on the head. As you know I do not agree with your Turkish policy and I want to see a treaty with France, but there our differences end. There are however things in connection with the Party that I should very much like to talk to you about as I think very little would considerably improve matters. On the other hand if things are allowed to drift you may get a Conservative cave.

Within a few months of his return to Lancashire Lord Derby had become the focal point of Lancashire politics and the Conservative leaders, both municipal and parliamentary, were turning to him for guidance and leadership. Recognising that his motives might be misunderstood in London, he was careful to keep Bonar Law informed of his activities:

Lord Derby to Mr. Bonar Law

10 March 1921

. . . When I came back to England I was approached by many Lancashire and Cheshire Members of Parliament who were discon-

> tented with the present position. It was very clear to me that they did not wish to be disloyal to the Coalition—far from it. But what they felt was that their views were not made known to you except by speeches and amendments in the House of Commons. I, for my part, felt that this was a very undesirable position. It subjects Members who vote against you to a charge of disloyalty, which I think is unmerited; and I therefore agreed to call a meeting of the M.P.s of the Lancashire Branch of the National Union, in order that we should try and arrange some method by which you could be informed what public opinion was in Unionist Lancashire on the general principles of a Bill, before, and not after that Bill was introduced. . . .

Derby, no doubt correctly, guessed that his renewed activities in Lancashire might be resented by the Government. We have already seen in the chapter on the Parliament Act how Derby had originally started his political career by acting as a two-way channel between Lancashire and London, by transmitting London opinion to Lancashire and Lancashire opinion to London. The authorities in London found it very useful when they could use Derby's influence to head off political discontent in the north but they were naturally less gratified at the reverse process. And it was an idea unlikely to commend itself to the Government in London that Derby should mobilize all the Government supporters in Lancashire so that their united and particularist view could be effectively brought to bear, apparently, in Derby's view, on all legislation brought before Parliament. We do not know what the precise reaction was to these activities, for on 17 March 1921 Bonar Law, Lord Privy Seal and Leader of the House of Commons, resigned from the Government on the grounds of ill-health. He retained his seat in Parliament but resigned the leadership of the Party in the House of Commons. Austen Chamberlain was immediately elected leader in his place at a meeting of Conservative members of the House of Commons held at the Carlton Club.

Bonar Law's resignation involved a major reconstruction of the Government. Chamberlain, who had been Chancellor of the Exchequer, took Bonar Law's sinecure as Lord Privy Seal and also took over from him as Leader of the House. Horne replaced Chamberlain at the Treasury and the Financial Secretary of the Treasury, the almost unknown Mr. Stanley Baldwin, entered the Cabinet for the first time as President of the Board of Trade. Lloyd George took advantage of the re-shuffle to replace Lord Ypres as Viceroy of Ireland with Lord Edmund Talbot who was promoted to the peerage with the title of Viscount FitzAlan.

Though the Coalition was to last until October of the following year, it was sensibly weakened by Bonar Law's departure. Chamberlain was unable to acquire the same command over his followers as Bonar Law had exercised; and Bonar Law, though he later in the year was sufficiently restored to health to give his endorsement to the Irish settlement, did not share with the other Conservative leaders the full responsibility for what was such a grievous blow at many of the principles and prejudices of the right wing element in the Party. In consequence, he had by the turn of the year become a potential focus round which Tory dissidents could rally, and his progressive apparent recovery of health increasingly gave to the disaffected the possibility of an alternative and purely Conservative Government.

Derby appreciated what Bonar Law's departure would mean to the Prime Minister.

Lord Derby to Mr. Lloyd George

21 March 1921

I want to write one line of sincere sympathy with you. I know that Bonar having gone will mean not only a political but a real personal loss to you. You have paid many tributes to his loyalty, and knowing as I do what the relationship between you has been I think I may say that no tributes were ever more justly earned.

I fear you will find the position with Austen Chamberlain as leader of the House somewhat different to what it has been in the past, and I venture to urge on you again the absolute necessity of working for fusion of the two parties. It is to my mind essential.

Derby hastened to congratulate Chamberlain on being chosen to succeed Bonar Law.

Lord Derby to Mr. Austen Chamberlain

24 March 1921

First of all may I congratulate you on your selection as leader of our Party in succession to Bonar Law. You and I have been old friends and colleagues for many years and I venture to hope that although outside the Government I may still be of some assistance to you and if any occasion arises when I can be so I hope you will not hesitate to call upon me for such assistance.

Perhaps you are aware that Lancashire Unionist Members have agreed to meet once a week to discuss the political situation, not with any view of intriguing against the Government but on the contrary to assist them. I cannot do better to show you what the position is than to enclose you, as I now do, a copy of the letter I wrote to Bonar Law on the subject. The letter accompanied some resolutions with regard to the Anti-Dumping Bill, passed by the Lancashire Unionist Members, and I also enclose a copy of these resolutions in the hope that they may be of use to you in showing you the general trend of opinion in political Lancashire.

* * *

The great event of the year at Knowsley had, for many years, been the party for the Grand National. The war and Derby's tenure of the Paris Embassy had caused a seven-year gap in this agreeable function. This year it was revived, and King George and Queen Mary were the guests of honour. Derby liked doing everything himself, down to the smallest detail, in all that affected the conduct of his house, his travel and his hospitality. His eye for detail is well shown by his meticulous instructions to his son-in-law, Captain Bullock:

Lord Derby to Captain Malcolm Bullock

11 March 1921 Knowsley

Just one line to confirm the arrangements made. Four packets have been sent to you. For you; Wallace and Miss Becher; d'Audiffret Pasquiers; and the Saint Sauveurs. Each packet contains instructions (and I send you two or three extra copies of that) in regard to luggage and trains; a packet of labels—everything that comes by the luggage on the 11.45 must have one of those on; and a ticket for each person admitting to the platform for the Royal Train. In addition I send you half a dozen similar tickets in case anybody leaves theirs behind.

I think everything is quite clear. There will be two whole carriages reserved for people coming. They will be in the rear of the King's Saloon. If anybody has come without luncheon it would be possible for them to get a little cold meat, or they could have luncheon after the King has had his. There is not room in the Refreshment Car for other people besides the Royal Party.

I rely on you to see that all the French people get their packets. Wallace and Miss Becher and the d'Audiffret Pasquiers are going to the Ritz so you could deliver them there in case they do not dine with you. They are coming by the 9.45 train from Paris on Tuesday.

Trep.[1] is too idiotic for words. I told him not to send off these packets but to give them to me to send. He has just told me with pride that he has sent them off to you to-night! I only hope they will arrive—please see that they are all right, because he is quite capable of having omitted something—you might telephone me Tuesday night to say if all is right.

Love to Victoria.

And again three days later:

Lord Derby to Captain Malcolm Bullock

14 March 1921 Knowsley

Many thanks for your telegram. I hope all now will go right. If you can get to the Station a little early on Wednesday so as to see that all the guests and especially the French people are all right I should be very much obliged.

On arrival at Huyton you come in the opposite platform to which the train usually comes in—i.e. it comes in on the far side from here. Be careful about getting out because the train is so long that it may not be able to draw up and after the King and Queen have got out it may be necessary to draw it up further before you can get out. However, I am trying to arrange that the whole train shall be brought in.

[1] Short for 'Trepoff', nickname of Major Marcus Hervey Milner, D.S.O., an old friend from Wellington days who had recently become Derby's Comptroller at Knowsley. The real Trepoff had been Minister of Ways and Communications to the Tsar Nicholas II.

I send you a list of people who are supposed to be coming by the train. Will you tick them off and if any do not come send me a telegram? The Stationmaster would do it for you.

I send you a list of how people will go in the cars from the Station. I shall be there with Trepoff and Edward. I will look after the King and Queen if you would not mind helping the other two to look after other people. You will see I have put Victoria in with the d'Audiffret Pasquiers and B. Pembroke and I daresay she would take them under her wing. You might take the St. Sauveurs, Wallace and Becher.

I am sending Charlie a list also and asking him to look after the people for his car.

I also send you a list of how in all probability we shall go in to Dinner. It is subject to modification and if Victoria sees anything that she thinks not right I wish you would telegraph to me.

It is very good of you to have all these people to Dinner as you will be able to explain things to them. They must be on the platform at least 10 minutes before the train is due to start.

Very rough weather here. The glass is going up and of course the best thing we can hope for is that it should blow hard because it makes it so clear.

I presume you and Victoria are still going to the flat [in Paris] on the 22nd. If you are *not*, send me a wire to say when you do go.

Love to Victoria.

In addition to the King and Queen, the party included the Prince of Wales and Princess Mary. The other guests were the Hon. Hugh C. Wallace, Lord and Lady Pembroke and Montgomery, the Hon. and Mrs. George Lambton, the Marquis and Marquise de Saint Sauveur, the Comte and Comtesse d' Audiffret Pasquier, Mr. H. P. Lane, the Hon. Frederick Cripps, Lord Marcus Beresford, Colonel Eric Mackenzie, Lady Ampthill, Lord Charles Montagu, the Hon. Alexander Hardinge, Lady Mar and Kellie, Lord and Lady Airlie, Lord Apsley, Mrs. Sassoon, Baroness de Rothschild, Mr. Bryan Godfrey-Faussett and General Ferdinand Stanley.

To entertain his guests Derby had procured the services of George Carpentier and his sparring partner who gave a display of boxing in the riding school. The French Press was delighted and had articles headed 'les deux Georges'. Some members of the British public, however, were shocked that Queen Mary and above all Princess Mary, at the tender age of twenty-four, should have been exposed to so degrading a spectacle as a bout of fisticuffs; and Derby received a number of angry letters.

On the evening of the Grand National a film of the race was shown and it was thought wonderful that it was technically feasible to show it only a few hours after the race. At the end of the day's racing when the Royal party were leaving Derby's box Lord Pembroke had clowned around and bowed and lifted his hat to the crowd. This comical episode was recorded by the camera and appeared on the film. Derby and Lady Pembroke seemed upset by Pembroke's antics but Queen Mary thought it was very funny. After the film of the National a rather dull nature film was screened. In the course of this film a duck laid an egg. Derby's Comptroller, Harry Milner, had been told to vet it before dinner. He thought the egg-laying was unsuitable for Princess Mary and he had it blacked out. The King asked for an explanation of the gap in the film and greatly enjoyed Milner's discomfiture in explaining his work as an unofficial censor.

Four months later the Prince of Wales paid a five-day visit to south and west Lancashire. Derby was the Prince's host at Knowsley and accompanied him throughout his visit, which was one of the most successful of the numerous industrial tours which were such a happy feature of the Prince's activities at this time. Derby and the Prince were both extremely energetic men and they always believed in being very thorough in everything they did. Nonetheless even their energy must have had a considerable strain placed upon it for in these five days they visited Ormskirk, Southport, Formby, Great Crosby, Waterloo, Litherland, Bootle, Liverpool, Aston-under-Lyne, Oldham, Middleton, Bury, Bolton, Atherton, Hindley, Abram, Ashton-in-Makerfield, St. Helens, Manchester, Salford, Eccles, Irlam, Prescot, Fleetwood, Clevelys, Blackpool, St. Annes, Lytham, Kirkham, Mowbreck, Hale, Preston, Leyland, Chorley and Wigan. In Manchester more than 100,000 children turned out to welcome the Prince; in Salford the Prince visited the Metropolitan Vickers works and the birthplace of Mr. Lloyd George; at

Old Trafford a halt was made to witness a cricket match in progress between Lancashire and Australia; in Liverpool they visited the Cotton Exchange and in Bootle the dye works of Messrs. Johnson. Enormous and wildly enthusiastic crowds greeted the Prince throughout the whole of his arduous tour. The only misadventure was at Blackpool when a woman admirer threw a rose at the Prince who pricked his finger as he caught it.

Derby's friendship with the Royal Family naturally enhanced his own prestige in Lancashire. So often the host to royalty, he was able to bring many people into their lives whom otherwise they would not have met, with great advantage to all concerned. In his memoirs —*Sir James Sexton, Agitator*—James Sexton, the dockers' leader, whom we have come across before, records one such occasion in 1922:

> On another occasion Lord Derby invited me to his box at the Grand National meeting when he was entertaining the King and the Prince of Wales. His Majesty asked me what horse I had backed, and when I said Shaun Spadah, the previous year's winner, he inquired: 'Who gave you that tip?' I told him I had got it from the Prince of Wales. The King laughed and said: 'Why, he's the worst tipster I know. Take my tip, and back Master Robert. I don't bet myself, but the owner is staying at Knowsley, and the whole party is backing it.'
>
> That would have been good enough for the most cautious backer in the world, so I hastened down to Tattersall's, where I was told I could have thirty to one against Master Robert. I tendered a ten shilling note to the bookie. He curtly told me to go and buy cigarettes with it; they didn't deal in ten shilling notes in that ring, he said.
>
> The Prince was coming down the steps as I returned, somewhat crestfallen, to the stand. He asked me if I had taken his father's advice. He was immensely tickled by my description of what had happened in the ring, but offered to add my stake to his own, and so, helped by the King and his heir, I converted my ten shilling note into fifteen pounds.

* * *

Derby had received very little encouragement for the project of an Anglo-French alliance which he had made the theme of his first important speech in England after he had resigned from the Embassy in Paris. He was not a man who often interfered with policy, still less one who conceived policies of his own. When he did, however, he pursued them with determination even though he had little backing. In June he reopened the matter in a letter to the Prime Minister:

Lord Derby to Mr. Lloyd George

10 June 1921

I hope you will forgive me approaching you directly on a subject which I have very much at heart and which I have as you know strongly advocated both publicly and privately, namely a Defensive Alliance with France.

I feel that the time has come when I have the right to ask from the Government some expression of opinion on this subject.

I cannot in the short space of a letter enter into the arguments which can be employed in support of such an Alliance, nor deal with those, such as the ridiculous idea that France is involved in a militarist policy, which have been adduced by some against an Alliance. I would however ask you to allow me to state quite briefly the principal reason why I so strongly advocate this Alliance. Living as I do in the greatest commercial district of England I am extremely anxious to see good commercial relationships existing between our country and Germany, but I feel that just as I would like to see Germany re-established as a commercial nation, so must the French nation feel that if she is so re-established that there may be danger of her again reconstructing her army and navy and attempting a war of revenge. England and France are therefore bound to look at the resurrection of Germany from two different points of view, and the question is how can these views be so reconciled as to give us the commercial intercourse with Germany which we desire and at the same time safeguard France from military aggression. France within the lifetime of many men has seen her country twice overrun by German hordes. She has lived for fifty years with the sword of a German Damocles hanging over her head, and quite rightly she is determined that this is not a state that she can allow any longer to exist. In my humble opinion a Defensive Alliance between France and ourselves, only to come into operation in case of unprovoked attack by Germany on France in circumstances similar to those of 1914, would give the security that the latter nation asks for. In other words I wish France to know that by a written engagement we shall stand side by side with her in such an event as we did in 1914. Then our support was problematical. I wish to make it a certainty. The Alliance would be only against Germany, and would come into operation only in the event of an unprovoked attack by that country on France or ourselves.

I believe such an Alliance would have a double effect. I believe not only would it give France security, but it would show to Germany the impossibility of any further aggression on her part and would be more likely to make her decide on abandoning for ever her aggressive policy of the past. It would, I am sure, smooth over many of the difficulties which now exist between the policies of our two countries, France and England. We should be partners, and as partners we should have a right in either case to warn the other, if it was thought that the policy that was being pursued was not conducive to peace. This right does not at present exist.

I may be wrong, but I cannot help feeling that if America sees England and France joined by such an alliance, that country would be more likely than it seems to be now, to give both of us at all events their moral support.

The project plainly did not commend itself to Lloyd George, and he avoided the issue:

Mr. Lloyd George to Lord Derby

13 June 1921

I received your letter on a possible arrangement with France, but you must let me have a little more time to consider it. It is a question of policy on which there is a good deal of difference of opinion. I rather hold the middle view. I certainly would not object to Gt. Britain alone giving the guarantee which in conjunction with the United States she was prepared to extend to France, but I should not like to say so without having a Cabinet decision on the subject, as you will realise that on a matter of such moment the Cabinet ought to be consulted before any decision is arrived at.

* * *

After the war the Liverpool City Corporation found it necessary to expand the water facilities of the city. The area was becoming so built up that no conveniently adjacent site was available, save in the park at Knowsley. In January 1921 Derby, prompt to serve the interests of the city, presented 45½ acres of the park in Knowsley to the Corporation on a 999 years' lease at 1*s.* per year. The ground was worth £6,500. Derby always had an eye for detail and he further caused his agent to inform the Corporation that it need not erect an expensive fence around the reservoir but that iron railings would suffice. He additionally suggested that out of work ex-servicemen should be employed on the unskilled work in the undertaking.

* * *

Ever since the American Civil War had cut off the supplies of American cotton and had plunged Lancashire in unemployment and poverty there had been concern about the Cotton Industry's supplies of the raw material which came exclusively from overseas. To decrease Lancashire's dependence on the United States the British Cotton Growing Association was founded in 1902. This Association investigated conditions in almost every country in the Empire where cotton growing might prove feasible. Some useful work was done, but at the end of the war it was decided that a stronger body with wider functions and more adequate financial resources was necessary to cope with the task. Thus was incorporated in November 1921 the Empire Cotton Growing Corporation. It received a grant from the Government of nearly £1,000,000 and in addition received the income arising from a voluntary levy applied by the spinners of Great Britain on all cotton spun in this country. Derby was invited to be the President of the new Corporation, a post which he held until 1945 when declining health forced him to reduce his activities. However on his resignation he was invited to become Patron of the Corporation and continued as such until his death.

He threw himself into this new task with his accustomed energy, and in the following year he headed a deputation to Lord Balfour, then Foreign Secretary, to impress upon the Government the need for the early completion of the dam on the Blue Nile and of the Gezira Irrigation Scheme in the Sudan. The deputation clearly made a strong impression upon Balfour, for the construction of the dam which had been temporarily suspended was at once resumed. The great plantations which have been developed in the Sudan since then and which have provided Lancashire with valuable supplies of long staple cotton stem from these decisions.

Derby always impressed upon his associates in the Corporation the need for experimentation and research. The Corporation did not itself produce cotton, but provided the technical research and advice to help primary producers in all parts of the world. It was largely as a result of the Corporation's activities that the amount of cotton being annually imported into this country from the Empire grew from an average of 117,000 bales just after the war to more than 600,000 in 1951, the principal sources of supply being the Sudan, Uganda, Nigeria and Tanganyika. In 1951, also, Empire production reached the record figure of one million bales.[1]

* * *

In April 1922 Derby's mother died at the age of eighty-one. There had always been a most loving and intimate relationship between mother and son. Derby's mother had been so stricken by her husband's death in 1908 and so touched by the sympathy her children had shown that she felt moved within a month to write letters to them which were to be opened after her death:

Constance Lady Derby to Lord Derby

July 1908 Holwood

My Darling Eddy,

Please make all arrangements for my funeral the same as Father's. No flowers, no memorial services.

You have been the best and dearest of sons to me, and have done all in your power to make the terrible change in my life as easy as possible I leave you very little because you have everything and long may you live to enjoy the position and to be a worthy successor to Father whose real and only object in life was to do what was right and just. Bless you my darling and again thank you for what you have been to your most affectionate mother.

[1] The present Lord Derby has continued his grandfather's work as Chairman of the Cotton Corporation. While visiting Nigeria in 1957 on behalf of the Corporation, he contracted a tropical disease and was seriously ill for some months.

To darling Alice who has been as a daughter to me—I leave one or two things I love best in the hopes that she will love them for my sake.

Constance Lady Derby to all her children

July 1908

All my darlings:

How can I ever thank you enough for all you have been to me. And when you read this know that I have blessed you every hour of my life. Forgive all my many faults and think of me as having tried to walk in Father's footsteps and now going (I hope) to where he is—into the terrible mystery of the unknown world.

We find her writing to her son on the fiftieth anniversary of her wedding:

Constance Lady Derby to Lord Derby

31 May 1914 Holwood

My darling Eddy,

I am more touched than I say. How too dear of you all to have thought of this day. The love of all my darlings makes me really happy and so thankful—I have fifty years to look back to, forty-four the happiest any one could have had—, and now all of you make me really happy by your love.

Bless you and much, much love to you all and many, many grateful thanks from your old and very affectionate mother.

Give my extra love to darling Alice who from the first has been a real daughter to *us both*.

XVIII

The Irish Settlement

IN December 1920 the Royal Assent was given to the Government of Ireland Act. This conceded a wide measure of self-government to Ireland. The Act contained a clause by which the six northern counties of Ulster were permitted to opt out and have their own constitution and a parliament in Belfast. The Ulstermen by a large majority availed themselves of this option, while the leaders of Sinn Fein—'Ourselves Alone'—who had supplanted the old Nationalist Party as the effective political force in the South, refused to have anything to do with the constitution and themselves elected instead a rival parliament and Government which sought to gain its ends by a widespread campaign of arson and murder.

A large British army, a reinforced constabulary, and a special force which came to be known as the 'Black and Tans' were put into action against the rebels. The latter often used methods of counter-terrorism as odious and effective as those of the Irish Republican Army and the Irish Republican Brotherhood, the two secret societies through which the Sinn Fein operated. By the end of 1920 the British Government had done a great deal to restore some measure of order to Ireland; this prompted the hope that with perseverance the rebellion might be crushed.

Indeed Mr. Lloyd George went so far as to say at the Mansion House on 9 November 1920: 'We have murder by the throat.' Though by the end of 1920 the situation had ceased to deteriorate, bloodshed and violence were still the order of the day. During the first six months of 1921 nearly 100 British soldiers and about 220 British police lost their lives in Southern Ireland, and perhaps nearly as many casualties were incurred by the rebels. It was obvious that the state of anarchy could not be allowed to continue indefinitely.

By the spring of 1921 the British Government had accumulated and trained the forces which would perhaps have been sufficient to crush the rebellion; but by the time the power was available, the conscience of the British people, doubtless pricked by adverse publicity all over the world, began to assert itself. The reciprocal massacres perpetrated by both sides, often on innocent people, were evoking a mood in both islands which, behind masks of utter determination, gave grounds for serious people to think that a truce might be arranged and that if once that could be achieved, there might be a possibility of a final settlement of this seemingly intractable problem:

Mr. Edward Saunderson to Lord Derby

13 March 1921 — 99 Great Portland St.

I am sorry for bothering you but in the present state of politics over here with trust absolutely a minus quantity it is essential that some hand should appear which would restore a healthy atmosphere. Welsh juggling will never solve the Irish question.

You know well Arthur Balfour absolutely agreed with me at Whittinghame in the Autumn that the Irish will trust no one except a gentleman (and they are right). It is no use discussing what led up to the present wretched situation once there or analysing the different elements which made the present movement deeper than previous troubles.

It is better to face the situation as a doctor who is called in and finds his patient harassed by mischievous germs. . . .

The boycott of Ulster goods you read about is all humbug—only done for Sinn Fein propaganda.

Vide the following.

A man in Belfast, a friend of mine, who made an immense amount of money during the war, told me he intended to see what he could do to help the sleepy south. He is now the backbone of the meat packing place in Drogheda. He has bought the coal business of Dublin, Cork and Limerick, he has improved the existing facilities and is liked by all sides. Last week he bought a big milling and general business in Tralee, the centre of trouble.

If he, a shrewd business man of Belfast, does this, it is surely a sign of the lines to run on. You have the confidence of all classes in Ireland and what is far more important you command the confidence of the world.

I know how very busy you are but if you could spare a little time I feel quite convinced you can rescue Ireland from the pit she is blindly digging for herself.

Please forgive the scrawl. I nearly pegged out last week from food poisoning but as we say in Ireland I have it bet.

What a delightful pair Oliver and Maureen make. I hope he is all right again.

Derby replied:

Lord Derby to Mr. Edward Saunderson

Private 14 March 1921

Many thanks for your letter. Sorry to hear you have been ill but hope now you are on the high road to recovery. I am very unhappy like you about the state of Ireland. One cannot see what is going to be the outcome. It is quite impossible to go on under the present conditions. At the same time if Sinn Feiners go on with their murder programme I see no other policy except that of retaliation, and the worst of that is that even when the conflict has died down it will leave very bitter and lasting ill-feeling. . . .

Derby must have been discussing Irish affairs with a number of people at this time for already on March 23 we find Mr. Wickham Steed, Editor of *The Times*, writing to its principal proprietor Lord Northcliffe:

Mr. Wickham Steed to Lord Northcliffe [1]

23 March 1921

You will be glad to know that—barring some tremendous outbreak at Easter—things are really shaping more favourably in regard to Ireland. I had a long talk with Austen this afternoon, really for the purpose of finding out his attitude towards a settlement and how much he knew of what four at least of his colleagues had been doing. He knew very little, but his attitude is distinctly satisfactory. Derby also

[1] *History of The Times*, Vol. IV (part II).

is moving in a cunning underhand sort of way, doubtless in the hope of taking the wind out of L.G.'s sails by promoting a settlement.

Lancashire, with its large Irish population in Liverpool, had special links with Ireland and it was two Liverpool M.P.s, Sir James Reynolds and Colonel John Shute (both Roman Catholics), who in the middle of March conceived the idea of sending a mission to Dublin to seek out Mr. de Valera and test what hopes there were of opening formal negotiations. Derby, who had returned six months before from Paris, seemed to be the most outstanding unofficial personality available for this delicate and possibly dangerous task.

This period in Derby's life is exceptionally well documented and the story from which everyone, even Father Hughes, emerges with credit tells itself convincingly in the correspondence:

Lord Derby to Sir James Reynolds

Very Confidential 24 March 1921

You will remember that you and Shute both spoke to me with regard to the possibility of my being able to do something towards the amelioration of the terrible state of things in Ireland. I have thought very carefully over your suggestion as needless to say there is nothing I would not do to try and bring about some sort of understanding but the question that must first be decided is—at whose instigation should I offer myself as an intermediary? It would not do for it to come as a suggestion from the Government even if they were willing to do so. It would not do for it to come through Cardinal Bourne or an English Catholic Agency. The only real way would be for it to come through Cardinal Logue and if it came through him the question is what form should it take? To see him alone would be of some advantage but it probably would not result in anything very definite and to arrive at something definite you have got to get at the more active spirit of the Sinn Fein movement and to do this there is only one man to see and that is de Valera. Now I am not in the Government though naturally I am in fairly close touch with the members of it. I could go over with no distinct promises from the Government. I could only go over to Ireland to see Sinn Fein leaders and to learn from them exactly what their views were and to see how far I could bring them into conformity with Unionist views. That would have to be clearly understood but if these conditions were accepted I am at your disposal. To put it briefly if Cardinal Logue asks me to go to Ireland to see Valera with an absolutely unbiassed mind, simply with a view of hearing his views and then seeing, after consultation with the Government, whether I could not put forward some proposal which would be acceptable I am ready to go. You must let me know as soon as you can whether anything in this direction can be done, as naturally I have got a lot of engagements which I should have to cancel but cancel them I would for such an important matter.

Reynolds replied the next day:

Sir James Reynolds to Lord Derby

25 March 1921 Liverpool

It is strange that your view about our going direct to Cardinal Logue and not through Cardinal Bourne is what we determined upon. The plan is to send Father Hughes on Easter Monday to Ireland to interview Cardinal Logue. We had conceived the idea that if Cardinal Logue welcomed the proposal that we should then get Sir A. Salvidge to put the scheme of your acting as mediator before the Government to get their approval.

What will now be done in view of your letter will be simply for Father Hughes to report to you on his return. I will send him your letter so that he will have your wishes clearly before him.

I never remember the position being so ripe for conciliation on the part of the Hierarchy. I feel confident that if you had the good will of Cardinal Logue and the Hierarchy it will assure success, but what made me feel that the Government should be with you was to obtain for you a free hand over Lord Lieutenant and Macready. Either could queer the pitch if they were jealous of your interruption. These matters are however for you to decide. Once the invitation from Cardinal Logue is received you will have got a grip of things. I am sure you will get a good reception and we could not employ a better intermediary than Father Hughes as he had not only pre-conceived the idea himself but is conversant with your success in Liverpool amidst warring elements.

As a result of these conversations and correspondence Father Hughes, a Liverpool parish priest of Irish descent, well regarded by the Hierarchy in Liverpool and also in contact with leading ecclesiastics in the Irish Church, crossed over to Ireland to see Cardinal Logue. This was the first of the four visits to Ireland which Father Hughes undertook in this matter.

Reynolds reported to Derby:

Sir James Reynolds to Lord Derby

31 March 1921 Liverpool

Father Hughes has returned and I am delighted to say that the Cardinal is willing. His letter enclosed. Meanwhile steps are being taken to find out if a welcome would equally be extended from the other side. I shall know next week. I have informed Salvidge of what has transpired. No further steps will be taken unless at your suggestion.

Cardinal Logue to Father Hughes

30 March 1921 Ara Coeli,
Armagh

Like the great body of the people in Ireland I am most anxious for peace and to see an end put to the terrible state of things which now exist in this country. Hence I shall most willingly do anything I can to assist in bringing about peace. I think the scheme which you mention offers a fair chance of effecting it and I shall be prepared to give every assistance in promoting it.

Father Hughes visited Ireland for the second time on April 11 to concert the final arrangements for Derby's visit. He saw both the Cardinal and the Secretary of the Dail Cabinet. In the Derby papers there are two documents, both on Derby House writing-paper which summarise the practical arrangements which were to cover Derby's visit. It seems that they defined the arrangements which Father Hughes had made in Ireland. The choice of the code-names 'Administrator' for Mr. de Valera and 'Mr. Edwards' in place of the original 'N.N.' for Derby was that of Father Hughes, who is himself sometimes referred to in the documents as 'J.H.' The first document explains de Valera's position, the second Derby's.

1. The Administrator has perfect confidence in N.N.'s honour and will himself take precautions against any possible interference by Government officials.

2. The Administrator takes full responsibility for his own safety and guarantees the safety of N.N.
3. The Administrator will meet N.N. if he comes to the Gresham Hotel, Dublin, and is not concerned as to arrangements which N.N. will make as to coming to Ireland. (J.H.—avoiding Press publicity, requisite permissions, etc., etc.)
4. The Administrator will make arrangements for the interview in such a manner that it will not be known to the newspapers or to Government Officials of any kind.
5. Notice of day and hour of arrival can be sent to address in Fr. H's hands.
6. Administrator suggests that the use of an incognito at the hotel would be useful. (J.H.—I suggested 'Mr. Edwards'.)

Cardinal Logue can be at home to meet N.N. on any day next week and will await a letter or telegram fixing time of arrival. He has two spare bedrooms which he will gladly place at N.N.'s service and trusts that N.N. will be satisfied with whatever poor hospitality he can offer. He particularly desires that N.N. should come to Armagh before going to Dublin.

Notes on Conditions, &c.

1. Person indicated is in no way acting as agent of Government but he feels that in order to secure success it is essential that the good will of the Government be secured and that the matter of trip be mentioned in strict confidence to P.M. and Sir Hamar Greenwood (Chief Secretary for Ireland).
2. He agrees.
3. Whilst the individual concerned is perfectly prepared to give his word of honour not to disclose either how or where he and the Administrator meet, he wishes to point out that he is fairly well known and that the fact of his going over will most certainly be mentioned in newspapers, and he would probably be followed by Government detectives who would be able to ascertain with whom he meets and where he meets them with the result that, without any information of any sort being given by him, the place of meeting might be invaded by Government officials. . . .

   In order that there should be no misunderstanding the individual wishes it to be clearly understood that he will come with no executive authority, that his sole wish is to secure some agreement but he would have to submit any suggestions made by the Administrator to the Government.

4. With regard to the question of secrecy as to how the meeting was brought about he thinks that in order to prevent wild conjectures it would be advisable for him, if the matter becomes known, to say that the meeting was at the instance of Liverpool friends of his who had enlisted his services as Chairman to settle the sectarian differences in that City in 1910 and who thought that his having a conversation with Cardinal Logue might be of advantage.

   He again emphatically states that while pledging himself as far as he is personally concerned to complete and absolute secrecy he cannot guarantee that his visit will not become well known. This he is sure must be obvious, but, as it might be a question affecting his personal honour, he feels bound to impress the fact on the Administrator.

   He would like before going to have a confidential talk with P.M. with a view of ascertaining the Government position but if it was thought that such conversation would in any way bias his judgement he would without hesitation forego such a talk.

Everything now being concerted, Derby and Father Hughes sailed to Belfast on April 18 and on their way to Dublin called on Cardinal Logue at Armagh. It seems strange that Armagh with a population of less than ten thousand should have been for so many centuries the ecclesiastical metropolis and seat of the Roman Catholic Primates of all Ireland and for two hundred years the seat of the Protestant Primate as well. The name Armagh derives from Queen Macha of the Golden Hair who held sway in these parts one hundred years before the arrival of Saint Patrick, by whom Armagh, with more plausibility than many other Irish cities and towns, claims to have been founded.

Derby, in his disguise as Mr. Edwards, and Father Hughes arrived at the Gresham Hotel in Dublin at about 6 p.m. on the evening of April 21. Derby was taken by a devious route to the house of Mr. James O'Mara, T.D., at 43 Fitzwilliam Place, where he was received by Mr. de Valera. Derby left no account of the talks but Mr. de

Valera was good enough to supply the following account to the author:

> As regards what transpired at the actual meeting: when Lord Derby arrived at the meeting-place, we had tea together and discussed the political situation. He was evidently endeavouring to find out how far we were prepared to go to meet the British position; I believe that the talks that he had had, immediately before seeing me, with some representatives of nationalist opinion in the North of Ireland had the same object in view. I made our position clear: that the Republic had been declared and that it would have to be accepted as a basic fact. My recollection is that he stressed the difficulties from the British point of view, but I pointed out that the position of the Republic was fundamental.

After the talks Derby was brought back to the Gresham Hotel just before the Curfew began at 9.30 p.m. He returned the next day to London, where he reported to the Prime Minister. As a result of his talk with Lloyd George, Derby sent a reply by Father Hughes. For security's sake he did not sign it.

Lord Derby to Mr. Eamon de Valera

> As authorised by you I have given the Prime Minister a verbal statement of your position as explained to me. Mr. Lloyd George is speaking on the Irish question on Thursday and desires me to put following question to you. 'Is he entitled to say that those controlling the Irish movement will not consent to meet him or any representative of the Government unless the principle of complete independence is first conceded?' Mr. Lloyd George had previous information of your attitude and would have stated it but I am first asking you for your authority for it to be said for fear that to do so on the strength of my interview with you may appear to you as being a breach of confidence on my part. Mr. Lloyd George will not mention the source of information unless you would desire him to do so.
>
> Will you please give me your authority (or the reverse) by bearer?

Furnished with this reply Father Hughes set off for the fourth time to Dublin. On the previous visit he had not been allowed to accompany Derby into the presence of the rebel chief and doubtless he expected this exciting experience would be vouchsafed to him now that he was on his own. Outraged at discovering that he was regarded in no way as a plenipotentiary but only as a messenger and also that de Valera's answer reached him too late for him to catch the night packet to Holyhead, Father Hughes took up his pen:

Father Hughes to Mr. Eamon de Valera

26 April 1921. 8 p.m. Dublin

A letter addressed to Lord Derby has reached my hands at 7.50 which makes it impossible for me to catch the evening boat to Holyhead and so to hand your letter personally to Lord Derby in time for his meeting. The only method of getting any message into his hands now is to telegraph if possible to the address given by me to your Secretary a message which can then be telephoned to Lord Derby about 10 a.m.

May I add that I deeply regret that through what seems to me unmerited distrust you have not allowed me to meet you personally and thus obtain the necessary explanations much more speedily and certainly much more clearly than when they come through your Secretary. Under these circumstances I feel that I can no longer usefully serve the interest of the Irish people in Ireland and in England by continuing to act as an intermediary with an enormous amount of trouble and waste of time and apparently with no recognition of the goodwill shown thereby.

De Valera's reply to the unsigned note was as follows:

Mr. de Valera to Mr. Lloyd George

26 April 1921

Before I reply to the unsigned note, I would like to ask the British Premier a question: Will he not consent to meet me or any representative of the Government of Ireland unless the principle of complete independence be first surrendered by us?

The technique of replying to an awkward question by posing another was one which the Irish, like the ancient Greeks and the late Doctor C. E. M. Joad of the B.B.C. Brains Trust, had brought to a fine art. Later in the year when the Irish delegation were thrashing out the terms of the settlement ultimately arrived at, Lloyd George at a critical moment artfully put forward in writing the question: 'Do you concede the foreshores and harbours of Ireland?' An affirmative answer to this question would have conceded all that England required in the way of her vital defence and a negative answer at that stage of the negotiations would have entitled Lloyd George to break them off. Irish subtlety aided by the New Brunswick guile of Lord Beaverbrook produced the following counter question: 'What is Ireland?' These two episodes underlined the truth that when posed with a seemingly inescapable dilemma there is nearly always a method of dealing with it.

The fact that de Valera's reply arrived too late for Father Hughes to sail that night to Liverpool may have been partly the fault of Father Hughes. He had spent the morning arguing with the secretary of the Dail (the Republican Parliament) as to whether he could not present the letter in person to de Valera, and it was only in the afternoon that he eventually handed the letter over to de Valera's representative. This is made plain by Mr. de Valera in a letter to the author:

Mr. Eamon de Valera to Mr. Randolph S. Churchill

15 February 1954 — Department of the Taoiseach, Dublin

... Fr. Hughes wanted to accompany Lord Derby on the journey to our meeting-place on the 21st April, 1921, but he was not permitted to do so. Again, when he returned to Dublin with Lord Derby's unsigned note for me, he was insisting on delivering it to me personally but was informed that he would have to hand it over to the Secretary to the Cabinet, for me. It was not until the afternoon of the 26th April that he finally handed over the note to the Secretary to the Cabinet, and, in the circumstances of the times, to have received my reply that evening should have been a matter for satisfaction, rather than for complaint, on his part. He was clearly annoyed because he was not allowed to see me—and there was, of course, no purpose whatever in my seeing him; apart from anything else, I was obliged at the time, for obvious reasons, to restrict rigidly the number of my callers. . . .

Whoever was at fault, the late arrival of de Valera's answer placed Father Hughes in a ticklish plight. Derby's unsigned note had made it plain that the answer was needed in London the following morning so that the Prime Minister could make a statement in the House. The only way the information could be passed to Derby was by telegraph at eight o'clock the following morning. In these circumstances Hughes took it upon himself in the presence of the Secretary of the Dail and of another witness to open de Valera's letter and to draft a telegram to Derby which was despatched the following morning. This telegram read:

> Before replying unsigned note ask your rector is surrender principle complete independence condition of meeting.

It will be noticed that the text of this telegram compresses into an accurate paraphrase the text of de Valera's letter except for the substitution of code words in the interest of security. Both Derby and de Valera were subsequently to censure Father Hughes for his presumption in this matter. Neither of them at the time appreciated the full facts, for it seems that Father Hughes behaved on this occasion both honourably and sensibly.

De Valera's rebuke was contained in his answer the next morning to the letter of complaint which he had received from Father Hughes and which has been quoted.

Mr. Eamon de Valera to the Reverend James Hughes

27 April 1921 — Dublin

You surely must appreciate that it is not by hole and corner methods, nor by unofficial intermediaries to the *n*th degree removed, that questions affecting the fate of our nation should be dealt with.

I sent you, for Lord Derby, a signed reply to an unsigned note, which I presume was from him. I understand you opened that note. If you did so by Lord Derby's authority in order to communicate rapidly with him, you should have sent the contents as it was.

These are not matters of courtesy—they are matters of serious business.

On his return to Liverpool Father Hughes replied:

Father Hughes to Mr. de Valera

28 April 1921 Liverpool

Your letter which reached me at 5 p.m. yesterday seems to suggest a breach of confidence in opening your letter to Lord Derby when, through what seems to me the gross negligence and glaring unpunctuality of your representative it was delivered into my hands three hours later than I was given to anticipate so that it became impossible to carry it unopened to Lord Derby. I hesitated to open it and did so only in the presence of your representative and one of your strong sympathisers. The distinct mention of the British Government and the Premier seemed to me to gravely endanger the likelihood of its reaching Lord Derby unread. Last night was the third sleepless night that I was forced to pass in order to bring this letter to your hands. And the only thanks I received is your petulant remark about 'hole and corner methods and intermediaries to the *n*th degree.' This seems to me unworthy of you and perhaps you may feel on further reflection that even intermediaries to the *n*th degree may sometimes like the mouse in the fable succeed in gnawing through the bonds which are holding down a lion nation. Please do not answer this but try to believe that I have had no other motive than love of the Irish people and of the land in which I was born.

The same day he reported to Derby:

Father Hughes to Lord Derby

28 April 1921 Liverpool

My dear Lord,

I am very sorry that in spite of most strenuous efforts, as explained in the letters sent to you today by the afternoon train, I was not able to get a clear and definite answer to your letter even though I lost an extra day in the attempt. However, I tried to turn that day to some good account by procuring an interview in Mountjoy Prison with Griffiths, the brains of the Sinn Fein movement, and with Professor McNeill, its scholar. Of this interview I am ready to give you a full verbal account when you are next in Liverpool.

This letter with its carefree disclosure of a visit to Mountjoy Prison was, as we shall see, to exacerbate Derby's displeasure at the extracurricular activities in which Father Hughes, with the best intentions, had thought it right to indulge. Though nothing concrete emerged from Derby's visit it enabled Lloyd George to go a little further than he had before in indicating the Government's preparedness to enter into negotiations. Speaking in the House of Commons on April 28 he said that the Government were still willing at any time to meet any representative Irishmen not under suspicion of murder to discuss any problem of Irish Government without laying down any preliminary conditions.

Meanwhile Derby seems to have got the impression from de Valera's answer to his unsigned note that possibly the Irish leader was offended by this lack of formality. Accordingly he wrote:

Lord Derby to Mr. Eamon de Valera

28 April 1921 — Derby House

I am in receipt of your letter. I must apologise for my apparent discourtesy in not having signed my note to you. I did not do so under the impression that you did not desire my name mentioned.

I have also to apologise for the action of my messenger in opening your letter. He had no authority whatever to do so and as a matter of fact although you answer my question by asking another it was really a sufficient answer. Needless to say it is not one to which I can give you any reply but I was able to catch Mr. Lloyd George, who is to speak on the Irish question this afternoon, and he left me with the impression that he meant to make a public statement which in itself would give you the information you ask.

Derby was by this time vexed at Father Hughes's conduct and wrote to one of his sponsors:

Lord Derby to Colonel Shute, M.P.

Confidential — 29 April 1921

I am in receipt of your letter. I have also received one from Colonel Reynolds and one from Father Hughes himself. I should not again have mentioned the fact of Father Hughes having opened *my* letter were it not for the fact that he now discloses what I think is even a worse indiscretion. I was under the impression that he was kind enough to come with me just to put me in touch with people and nothing more, instead of which he appears to have taken upon himself the role of mediator and I can conceive nothing more calculated to nullify any good that might have come from my visit than his action on his last visit to Ireland. To have opened the letter to me was I think indefensible. All he had got to do was to telegraph saying it would be late getting to London. I should have understood that but I do not understand opening a communication which he must have known was of the most private character. Then to go and see Arthur Griffiths makes at once the Sinn Fein people think that we are most anxious to make advances to them. He had no authority to do so. He can speak for nobody and the only thing he has done is to make a complete mess of the whole thing. I honestly confess that I am more angry than I can say about it. I am writing a letter to him and will send you a copy.

* * *

Derby's visit to Dublin, as he had foreseen was likely, had now become public property. *The Times* correspondent in Dublin reported it as early as April 24. The idea that someone of Derby's bulk and well-known appearance could successfully disguise himself naturally gave rise to much jocose comment. It was freely alleged that he had worn dark or horn-rimmed spectacles to camouflage himself. Such devices could only have invited the attention of the curious, who were many. In fact, as Derby subsequently explained, he only took 'reading' glasses with him on his voyage; and these he took because he thought he might wish to read. The *Daily Express* of 25 April 1921 carried the following:

A Pair of Spectacles

Last Saturday week Lord Derby made a speech declaring that he knew his Lloyd George, and could work with him in perfect harmony. His lordship's face was then bare and his mind still innocent. On Sunday he went to Chequers. On Monday he is reported in Dublin, slightly disguised by a pair of spectacles. What influence the Premier must have with the ex-Ambassador in Paris! But he should have been more prudent in selecting his emissary's disguise. Has he never seen Sir John Hare in 'A Pair of Spectacles', or forgotten how the unsuspicious old gentleman turned into a doubter of all men as soon as he put them on? Mr. Lloyd George has put a pair of spectacles on Lord Derby. Will they show him such a rose-coloured picture of the Premier as he saw last week?

The sombre tragedy of Sinn Fein has been relieved before now by a few touches of comedy. Men have gone out to commit a murder and stayed to take a cup of tea. This atmosphere at once of the secret and the ludicrous has apparently infected the Premier. How else account for the picture of Lord Derby, of all men, masquerading as Mr. Edwards at an Irish commercial hotel?

And the *Liverpool Courier* five days later:

Why Lord Derby Laughed

A humorous story has just come to light apropos of Lord Derby's visit to Ireland as 'Mr. Edwards'. Walking down a Dublin street with Father Hughes, the Liverpool priest who was his companion, Lord Derby was introduced as 'Mr. Edwards' to another priest. The conversation turned on fruit-growing.

Lord Derby, whose interest in agriculture is well known,[1] asked his new acquaintance about the prospects for fruit growing in the Dublin neighbourhood. The priest replied that the conditions were very good indeed, especially for apples.

'What is the best kind of apple you are growing about here?' inquired Lord Derby.

'The very best is the "Lord Derby"' (a well-known class of apple), replied the priest. 'Of course, it is big and ugly, and it never gets ripe. Still it is a downright good apple for all that.'

Lord Derby and Father Hughes had a hearty laugh. The Irish priest doubtless laughed later when he learned who 'Mr. Edwards' was.

This publicity was distasteful to Derby. Replying to Father Hughes's letter of April 28 he wrote:

[1] The *Liverpool Courier* was misinformed. Derby often used to observe: 'I hate art and agriculture.'

Lord Derby to Father Hughes

Private 30 April 1921

I am in receipt of your letter and want in the first instance to thank you most sincerely for the trouble you took with regard to my letter. I quite understand the difficulty in which you were placed though I regret that you should have opened the letter as I am afraid that it has made the Administrator suspicious and I candidly confess I think there was some justice in his letter to you although it was couched in rather offensive language. But I cannot help protesting against your visit to Mr. Griffiths. From being the bearer of a letter which you kindly undertook to deliver you became a mediator and the impression undoubtedly will get abroad that you were sent with a mission. . . . You were good enough to accompany me to Ireland and in strict confidence I confided to you all that passed at our interview. . . . To see Mr. Griffiths gives the impression that I have entrusted you with work which should have been done only by me. I must tell you quite frankly that I consider this action of yours on the occasion of your last visit to Ireland may have nullified any good that I could have done and I do not propose to take any further action now in the matter.

Father Hughes, replying to Lord Derby on May 3, gave a lengthy but manly and satisfactory account of his activities. He began: 'It is good to get a rap on the knuckles occasionally even when one does not feel guilty, so I take it in that spirit.' He went on to deal seriatim with the charges Lord Derby had levelled against him. He defended his opening of de Valera's letter on the grounds of necessity. 'There are occasions when a subaltern separated from his C.O. in the battle line has to decide rapidly on his own responsibility what he thinks his chief would wish him to do.' Under the heading 'Letter Carrier, Mediator or Precursor' Father Hughes wrote: 'One of the busiest priests in Liverpool with charge of a large parish and a large public hospital could hardly imagine that he was asked to put himself under considerable obligation to other clergy . . . simply to perform the function of a letter carrier which could be done quite as well by a junior clerk or through the registered post.' Father Hughes argued that his preliminary conversation had been of the utmost benefit to Lord Derby; this, among other reasons, because it was possible for him to expound the great services Lord Derby had already rendered in the settlement of religious strife in Liverpool. Father Hughes suggested that de Valera had kept him waiting for a reply to the unsigned note because de Valera had been unable to consult his colleagues in the matter. It was a logical step for Father Hughes to interview the political prisoners in order to establish their reaction. Talking of Arthur Griffiths, Father Hughes wrote: 'He is a much more powerful man in the Sinn Fein movement, of which he is recognised as the controlling brain, than his nominal chief. I endeavoured, and I think I succeeded in my endeavour, to get him to recognise your sincerity of purpose.' Father Hughes ended his letter with an exhortation to Lord Derby: 'Your interview with the Administrator has for the moment left you despondent. . . . Take then your courage in both hands though some may doubt and some may sneer or criticise or blame. . . .'

To this letter Father Hughes appended a meticulous statement of account covering cash disbursements for tickets and the incidental expenses of his four visits to Dublin. These amounted to £31 4*s.* 7*d.* Father Hughes explained that he had already received £16 from Lord Derby and £23 12*s.* 0*d.* from Sir J. Reynolds to cover such expenses and that therefore there remained a surplus of £8 7*s.* 5*d.* He wondered to whom he should repay this. Father Hughes's punctilio in presenting such a detailed statement is, as we shall see from Derby's reply, matched by the latter's delicate generosity.

Derby was plainly impressed by Father Hughes's explanation:

Lord Derby to Father Hughes

Confidential and Personal 5 May 1921

Many thanks for your letter and I greatly appreciate the spirit in which you took my last letter. I quite see your point of view and I will not refer to the question again though it may be necessary for me to ask you to convey another letter to the Administrator or to get a question put to him as to whether he has seen Lloyd George's statement that he would meet him absolutely unreservedly and unconditionally and what answer he proposes to give to it. Please however do nothing in this matter till you hear from me again.

With regard to my own position I cannot quite make up my mind what to do. Theoretically the best thing would be for me to put forward whatever conditions are to my mind the best way of settling this question but on the other hand if these proposals are going to be immediately turned down by the Government and perhaps by my own Party I should only have done more harm than good. I am therefore gradually feeling my way but I hope I may be able to come out with some declaration within the course of the next month. Personally I do not think that any good would come of making such a declaration before the elections in Ireland have been held but this is a matter on which I am not quite certain at the present moment. . . .

. . . With regard to what you are kind enough to say about myself you may be quite sure that I shall try and do whatever is right but in this matter one has to take not only one's private opinions but also what is likely to be the political effect of any statement.

I see that your total expenses were £31 4*s*. 7*d*. on account of which I have paid you £16. I therefore owe you £15 4*s*. 7*d*. and so enclose you a cheque for £30 4*s*. 7*d*. the balance being for the two objects to which you know I wish to make an anonymous donation.

In some quarters there was a tendency to belittle the advantage of Derby's meeting with de Valera. The dark glasses and the indiscretions of Father Hughes offered rich material for cartoonists and satirists. Yet in the light of fuller knowledge than was available then it is clear that Derby's *démarche* was most serviceable as a first step in establishing a contact with the Irish leaders which was to lead to settlement at the end of the year. It is certain that Derby went with the full knowledge and encouragement of Lloyd George, though it was essential to any success he might achieve that this should, at least at the outset, be concealed.

Writing to the author, in a letter already quoted, Mr. de Valera gave his estimate of Derby's mission:

Mr. Eamon de Valera to Mr. Randolph S. Churchill

15 February 1954 — Department of the Taoiseach,
Dublin

. . . My view was that Lord Derby's visit was useful as the first important contact between the British and ourselves and that—as you put it—it was a breaking of the ice. I regarded it at the time from this twofold aspect: firstly, as a reconnaissance operation on the part of the British Government, with the object of getting a close-up view of the situation here; and, secondly, as an indication that the British Government wished to bring the existing position to an end and that they desired to make peace if satisfactory terms could be arranged. . . .

Derby's visit was followed by further acts of reconnaissance and gestures of conciliation. In May the Ulster leader Sir James Craig had secret talks with Mr. de Valera, who was still in hiding. On June 22 the King opening the Ulster Parliament spoke words which were deliberately intended to appeal to both Irish factions. His words touched the hearts and sympathies of many on both sides of the border, and when two days later the Prime Minister invited Sir James Craig and Mr. de Valera to a conference in London they both accepted and it was agreed that there should be a truce during the London talks, which began on July 14. The negotiations were not to reach their successful conclusion for five months and their progress was threatened in November by the annual meeting of the National Union of the Conservative and Unionist Associations at which Colonel John Gretton, M.P., was to move a resolution recording the conference's condemnation of the 'long continued ascendancy of crime and rebellion in Ireland' and resolved 'that no settlement of the Irish question would be acceptable which did not absolutely respect the position required by Ulster.'

If this resolution were to have been carried all hope of a successful outcome of the London talks would have disappeared and the Coalition Government would have been destroyed. The Coalition was based upon the support of the Tory Party, and though resolutions of the Annual Party Conference are not in themselves mandatory upon the Party leadership, a hostile vote at this time would have been decisive. Consequently much manœuvring preceded the Party Conference. It was fortunate for Lloyd George and his colleagues as well as for the outcome of the Anglo-Irish talks that the Tories were meeting in Liverpool, for though passions on the Irish issue might ride higher there than almost anywhere else in England, Lloyd George was to have the support on Merseyside in this issue of the political skill of Salvidge and the immense prestige of Derby. These were to prove a more than effective counterbalance to the ancient Protestant prejudices of the city. Salvidge for thirty years of his political life had preached the cause of the Union with Ireland and the sanctity of Ulster's claim that she should never be put under a Dublin parliament. Salvidge, however, was a staunch Coalitionist and he was not prepared to see the Diehards carry a resolution in Liverpool at a time when negotiations were still going on in London. While reaffirming his loyalty to Ulster and making it plain that if Ulster were to reject any proposed settlement Liverpool would stand staunchly by her, he announced before the Conference met in Liverpool that he would oppose the resolution proposed by Gretton and supported by the Diehards.

Derby was in favour of a settlement, but did not see how this could be brought about without a serious party split and this now, as always, he laboured to avoid. Derby's view at this time is shown in a letter to the Chairman of the Tory Party:

Lord Derby to Sir George Younger

5 November 1921

I myself shall stick to Lloyd George as long as he does not use any compulsion with regard to Ulster though I do not like this sort of purchasing of loyalty from the Sinn Feiners. . . . My fear is Lloyd George will see that this is the only solution and being bound by his pledge not to use compulsion with Ulster will resign. We shall then be up against the proposition that Ulster stands in the way of a settlement and Bonar Law may possibly come out again to lead those who think that it is better the negotiations should break down than that Ulster should be compelled to make any sacrifice. I should not agree with Ulster but at the same time seeing what our pledges are I personally should have no alternative except to go with that Party, though with reluctance. I suppose the next week will see something more definite but I anticipate by the time our meeting takes place we shall be having a most troublous time.

Derby, ever the peacemaker, invited representatives of both factions in the Party to stay with him at Knowsley before the Liverpool Conference. Two members of the Cabinet were present—Mr. Austen Chamberlain, the Lord Privy Seal and Party leader in the Commons, and Sir Laming Worthington-Evans, Secretary of State for War. Also invited was the Duke of Northumberland, the principal proprietor of the *Morning Post* and the most extreme of all the Diehards. To support the moderate balancing view which Derby took there were Lord Chaplin and Lord Midleton, the leader of the Southern Irish Unionists. For out and out settlement there were Lord and Lady Astor.

When the Conference met, Salvidge moved an amendment to Gretton's resolution. This amendment, while calling for certain safeguards, gave its blessing to the Anglo-Irish negotiations in London. Derby wound up the discussion with an artful and cogent speech in which he said: 'You have got to say here and now that you approve of the Conference being held and that you hope good may come of it.' He went on: 'I am not going to be stampeded into making a decision until I know what the whole proposition is and what is more I am not going then to be stampeded until I have made up my own mind as to what is right and what is wrong. That is the feeling in which I would ask you to support the amendment.' The Diehards were evidently at a considerable disadvantage for Derby felt no need to woo his audience. Towards the end of his speech he observed: 'I appeal to you not to make a decision on matters of which you know absolutely nothing.' With 1,900 delegates present Salvidge's amendment was carried with only some 70 Diehards dissenting. The threat to the Anglo-Irish Conference in London and to the Government, which had seemed very real at one time, was skilfully averted.

Derby wrote the next day to the Prime Minister:

Lord Derby to Mr. Lloyd George

18 November 1921

Our meeting is over and you will hear accounts of it from Austen Chamberlain and Worthington-Evans. On the whole I think it was a great success and there was not the least doubt that the result was to give you full authority to continue negotiations. But at the same time there was a good lot of underlying feeling which will become perhaps more apparent after the meeting than it was actually there. . . .

. . . With regard to the Coalition there is no doubt there is a distinct feeling against Coalition. I always thought, as you know, that you ought to have tried for an amalgamation of the Party eighteen months ago. It would have been carried then. We should probably have lost some of your people and a certain number of ours, but by now we should have been a consolidated party instead of which there is a growing feeling in our party against the Coalition. It all depends on what policy you are going to put forward whether we remain united. Here in Liverpool in municipal matters there was a distinct programme and Conservative and Liberal Coalitionists worked wholeheartedly together. I agree that can be done elsewhere but it requires some policy as a standard to which all can rally. Once you put a policy forward we shall soon see what support you would get for it, but to go into the next Election asking Liberals to vote for you, and Chamberlain asking Unionists to vote for him, must spell disaster.

To sum up, my feeling is one of satisfaction that it went well on the surface. On the other hand I cannot help feeling that there is a good bit of disquiet under the surface and that any false move that could be construed into a breach of faith on the Irish question would mean a complete swing of the pendulum to the opposite side. . . .

With this difficulty out of the way the London talks proceeded in their exhausting agony and eventually, on December 6, the Irish delegates capitulated to Lloyd George's ultimatum and signed an agreement by which the Irish Free State was to be brought into being. This, of course, was not the end of the story. Mr. de Valera, after his first visit to London, had refused to be a part of the Irish delegation. He repudiated what his envoys had accepted and peace was not to come to the Free State until after a civil war between the Irish factions, which was marked by as much ferocity and stained with as much bloodshed as the fight which had just been concluded between the Irish and the British.

Though not in office nor holding any official position Derby had played a courageous role in these events and his reputation both in Lancashire and in London was augmented by the turn of the year.

XIX

Chanak

EVENTS were now to take a turn in the Levant and India which as a minor consequence led to Derby being invited to rejoin Lloyd George's Coalition Government. To put these events in their proper setting a brief digression is required.

Under the terms of the Treaty of Sèvres which had been signed in August 1920 it had been agreed that amongst other things the whole area surrounding the Sea of Marmora which controlled the entry from the eastern Mediterranean through the Black Sea should be internationalised. In addition the British and French were to receive mandates over wide areas of the Ottoman Empire. Britain was to receive a mandate over Palestine and Iraq, while France was to have a mandate over Syria. These crushing terms could never have been imposed, even on the Sultan's decadent court, had it not been for the activities of the Greeks under M. Venizelos. Mr. Lloyd George had conceived an immense admiration for this extraordinary man in whom he detected qualities of oratory and war-like genius resembling his own, just as he affected to observe in his fellow Celts a resemblance to the people of Greece.

In the summer of 1919 the Greeks had occupied Smyrna, invaded Eastern Thrace and occupied Adrianople. Smyrna under the treaty was to be administered by Greece for five years and thereafter was to decide its own fate by plebiscite. This treaty was negotiated by the Allies with the Sultan's Government but the Sultan had little authority and many suspected that the real power in Turkey lay with Mustapha Kemal, the Turkish war-lord who had emerged during the war.

The Treaty of Sèvres had never been ratified and in February 1921 a conference met in London with a view to modifying some of the terms which had been imposed at Sèvres. This did not suit the Greeks. Already in 1920 they had started invading the interior of Asia Minor from Smyrna and in the summer of 1921 with the collusion and indeed the encouragement of Lloyd George they had thrust their armies forward in the direction of Ankara. Meanwhile the Triple Alliance had fallen apart and earlier in the year, in March, the Russians had concluded a treaty with Mustapha Kemal as a consequence of which they supplied him with arms. And later in the year, in October, the French reached a similar agreement with the Turks.

During the winter of 1921–2 the Greeks were entrenched in the interior of Anatolia; Kemal sagaciously refrained from attacking them and Greek morale declined. The pro-Greek policy of the British Prime Minister was undoubtedly an aberration. It was wholly contrary to British foreign policy which had traditionally been pro-Turk, not only in order to resist the expansion of Russia but also to avoid giving offence to the sixty to seventy million Moslems throughout Asia and Africa who were subjects of the King. It was calculated to alienate many of Lloyd George's Tory supporters who had long been nurtured in the faith that 'the Turk is a gentleman'. Nonetheless Lloyd George succeeded in seducing to the reversal of British foreign policy two of the leading Tories in his Cabinet, Balfour and Curzon. Strangely enough it was left to a Minister who was a Liberal and a Jew to fight the cause of Islam inside the British Cabinet. Edwin Samuel Montagu was Secretary of State for India; from 1919 onwards he consistently opposed Lloyd George's pro-Greek policy and later pressed for revisions of the Treaty of Sèvres which would satisfy Moslem opinion in India, and rally Turkey to opposition to Bolshevik Russia. Montagu received no satisfaction from his colleagues and eventually on 4 March 1922 he published a message from the Viceroy of India, Lord Reading, suggesting amendments to the Treaty of Sèvres. Reading, in the name of the Government of India and in sympathy with Moslem aspirations, recommended that Constantinople, Turkish Thrace, Smyrna and the Holy Places should be restored to the Sultan. Montagu published this message without submitting it to the Cabinet or, indeed, to any of his colleagues. His dismissal followed five days later.

At the time of Montagu's dismissal, Derby was on the Riviera. He recorded:

Diary

Cannes, Friday 10 March 1922

Received a telephone message to say that the Consul at Nice had a most important message for me which he would not give over the telephone. He came out to the golf course at Cannes and brought me the P.M.'s telegram offering me the India Office. My reply was I could not give an answer until I had had an opportunity of discussing the question with either him or Chamberlain.

The next day, Derby wrote to the Prime Minister from the Grand Hotel in Cannes:

Lord Derby to Mr. Lloyd George

Confidential — 11 March 1922

My DEAR P.M.,

The offer which you have honoured me with was brought to me on the golf course here yesterday afternoon. It was, of course, quite impossible to give you a definite answer. I must talk the matter over with you. At present we only know Montagu has resigned, and the French papers add that he resigned because the Government absolutely refused to entertain the suggestions of the Indian Government. If so that would render my acceptance of the post almost impossible, as I am, in the main in accord with the Indian Government on the subject of the Turkish Treaty. I was naturally only coming home on the 17th, but have telegraphed to you that if you want me earlier I will try and get places, but I don't know if I shall succeed as they are very hard to get at this time of year at a moment's notice.

Though it is very kind of you to offer me the post I think you are wrong to do so, as I believe I can be of much more use to you outside than inside the Cabinet, and I fear that Curzon's and my ideas of foreign policy are so very different that it will make co-operation with him very difficult.

The question of the 'places' was evidently resolved, for Derby left Cannes on the night of Monday March 13.

Diary

Northcliffe met me Tuesday morning in Paris and came to the Flat and had a long discussion with me. He was a different Northcliffe to what I had ever known.[1] Very moderate in his views; no abuse of the Government and discussing Indian matters with great clearness having evidently a very intimate knowledge of all that was going on. He said that while he would be sorry to see me join the Government in what he thought was a dying condition he at the same time would support me with his papers now that he had heard my views on the Indian situation and especially on the Turkish Treaty.

London, Wednesday 15 March 1922

Went down to see Austen Chamberlain and had a very frank discussion with him on the subject of my acceptance or the reverse of the India Office.

He frankly based his contention that I should accept on the fact that it would strengthen the Government at the present moment. That I had always loyally supported the Government and holding the position that I did in Lancashire it seemed only natural that I should be the first person to be asked to take what was a most important office.

I pointed out my reasons for doubting whether my acceptance would be of the use that he thought. The instant I joined the Government I became an interested party and my claims for support of that party would be much lessened. At the present moment, when I wanted to see the Conservative Party kept together and at a moment when a split between us and the Prime Minister might come at any moment, it was surely advisable that they should have somebody outside with a certain amount of authority who had not been tarred with a Government brush. . . .

I pointed out to him also differences that existed between Curzon's policy and my own and he then gave me to understand what I have always suspected and that was that Curzon has no weight whatsoever with Lloyd George in Foreign Affairs. That the management of

[1] This was one of Northcliffe's last recorded lucid moments. Three months later he was certified as insane. He died on 14 August 1922.

Foreign Affairs is practically in the P.M.'s hands. On that ground therefore I felt that I ought to refuse.

But when it came to a discussion on the policy to be adopted with regard to India I could not find out that they had any settled policy whatsoever and that one would really have to make a new policy with the pitch already queered and with no certainty that one would be supported by some of the Cabinet. The more we discussed it the more I think Chamberlain saw that my going in, though solving the present difficulty might in the long run and perhaps in a comparatively short time lead to other difficulties which might mean either my own or other resignations and then affairs would be even worse than they are at the present moment.

Derby then went to see Balfour who gave him almost the same advice as he had already received from Chamberlain.

Diary

He [Balfour] then told me in strict confidence that he was being pressed to take a Peerage and that he would be very much guided by my advice in the matter. I strongly advised him to take it as giving him a much greater opportunity than he could ever have in the House of Commons of helping our Party. I pointed out to him that we had got no leader of the Conservative Party in the House of Lords except Lord Lansdowne whose successor had never been appointed. That Curzon was the Leader of the Coalition in the House of Lords but not the leader of our Party in itself. He said that the distinction had never struck him but he seemed quite prepared to consider the proposition of his becoming our leader and he said that probably now that he had discussed it with me he would accept the Peerage.

Seven weeks later Balfour accepted this advice and went to the Lords as Earl of Balfour.

After seeing Chamberlain and Balfour, Derby wrote his formal refusal to the Prime Minister:

Lord Derby to Mr. Lloyd George

Private 15 March 1922

I got back late last night and today have seen both Chamberlain and Arthur Balfour. I have explained to them the whole of my feelings with regard to your offer of the Indian Secretaryship and my reasons for asking leave to decline and I think I can safely say that they are both in agreement with me in doing so.

At the same time I want you to let me thank you most sincerely for the honour you have done me in making me the offer. I appreciate it very much indeed and I beg that you will believe that in refusing it I have not done so out of any want of loyalty to you and your Government and I shall hope to continue to give you the same support outside—support which I think will be much more effective than if I were actually in your Government.

I hope you are better. When you come back to London I should very much like to see you and have a talk with you.

Diary

London, Thursday 16 March 1922

. . . When I came back I found Victor Cavendish [The Duke of Devonshire] here. He has been offered India and like me has refused. He showed me his letter which was practically word for word what I had said in talking to Austen Chamberlain. He tells me of a new intrigue that is going on—Bob Cecil and Steel-Maitland but we agreed that with two such shifty people there was no chance of its being a success though there were some very good fellows at a meeting they had,—curiously enough in Henry Bentinck's house who has kicked over every trace and now wants to get back if he can into a decent party. Victor I think hit the nail on the head when he said that probably we had less fault to find with the actual Government work as the way in which they did it and the complete want of unity of command. He is strongly for the Irish Bill and means to support it in every way. . . .

The refusal of the India Office by both Derby and Devonshire was most damaging to the prestige of the Government. 'The Coalition,' wrote *The Times*, 'is dying before our eyes.' With his third invitation, Lloyd George was more successful and Lord Peel was induced to take over the office vacated by Montagu.

On March 17 Derby gave a personal explanation in public to the Junior Carlton Club of his reasons for declining the offer of the India Office. In this speech, while admitting that he had certain points of difference on foreign policy with the Government, he indignantly repudiated the suggestion that he had refused to go aboard what was thought to be 'a sinking ship'.

His old friend St. John Brodrick (by now Lord Midleton), under whom he had served twenty years before at the War Office, was among those who welcomed his conduct:

Lord Midleton to Lord Derby

Secret — 34 Portland Place
18 March 1922

May I say how judicious I think your speech last night? I think your decision and Victor's have together sounded the death-knell of this Government as it is, and my feeling is that it is absolutely necessary that it should now come to an end and that the work of reconstruction be taken up by a fresh man. I have had one or two meetings with Ministers lately, amongst others, Horne. I was shocked to find how utterly worn out he was and how hysterical.

There is no doubt that Derby relished the political independence which had come to him after quitting the Paris Embassy. Shrewd party politicians were already peering ahead to the inevitable time when the Coalition would fall, party government would be resumed and the Conservative Party would almost certainly be called upon to govern once more by itself. Derby was certainly flattered by Lloyd George's invitation to join the Coalition but he plainly did not mean lightly to abandon either his independence or the growing influence and stature which that independence was bringing him. In the eyes of the Diehards nearly all the Tory leaders were tainted with the Irish Settlement. Only Bonar Law (and few could judge whether his health would ever permit him to return to active politics) and Derby were free and uncommitted. Both men at this time were loyal in general to the Coalition but both had one eye cocked to the weather and the eyes of the professional politicians were cocked on them. Thus in *The Unknown Prime Minister* we find that skilled intriguer Mr. J. C. C. Davidson, a loyal henchman of Mr. Baldwin's, writing on 13 January 1922 to Bonar Law who was in the South of France:

Mr. J. C. C. Davidson to Mr. Bonar Law

Derby in the Lords and you as leader and P.M. in the House of Commons has been mooted pretty widely. Naturally it is what I should like though I don't know whether D. is to be trusted. Birkenhead doesn't cut any ice with the public in the same way as D.

I hope the election will be postponed but if it comes the Tories must go separately to the Country. . . .

A speech which Derby made two months later at a dinner at the Constitutional Club was not to find as much favour with the Foreign Secretary, Lord Curzon, his old enemy, as his previous speech had found with Lord Midleton. Derby took the opportunity of underlining the differences between himself and the Government. In particular he criticised the Prime Minister's habit of attending international conferences himself and also spoke up in a manly fashion for the Anglo-French Alliance and for the French right under the Treaty of Versailles, which he described as 'holy', to exact reparations from Germany. We may be sure that it was the second point rather than the first which stirred Curzon's pedantic and ineffective rebuke:

Lord Curzon to Lord Derby

30 May 1922 Hackwood

I have been reading your speech, in most respects an excellent one, in the *Morning Post*.

I own, if you ask me, that I am not in favour of ex-Ambassadors going about and making speeches about Foreign Policy, however sound the views they profess, because I think it is a bad precedent. I am sure Lord Salisbury would have been much disturbed had Lord Lyons or Philip Currie or Lord Ampthill after their retirement from an Embassy continued to make public speeches about Foreign Policy in connection with the country where they had represented us; and I daresay if you were at the F.O. and Charlie Hardinge after returning from Paris were to do the same you would not altogether welcome it. I recognise of course that you are in rather an exceptional position because of your high state in this country; and in the present case any protest from me might seem both uncalled for and ungenerous because of your kindly references to myself and the general wisdom of your speech. But all the same I often wonder if it is quite right, and if, in the inverse position, you would think it right also. Another point is that you may give with all your authority an unfair impression, from an inevitable ignorance of the facts. . . .

I have written all this to you in confidence because it bears out what I have in my mind, viz. that there is some risk in even a man of your position and of your approved friendliness and unchallenged authority, making Foreign Affairs speeches without the fullest knowledge of the facts.

As to your views about the F.O. and No. 10, as you know I am in the warmest agreement and I greatly appreciate your courage and friendliness in making them. But it has been very difficult to recover a position which was thrown away in Paris in 1918.

Lord Derby to Lord Curzon

Confidential 1 June 1922

Very many thanks for your letter. I was glad to get it although I am sorry to see it is still written in pencil [indicating that Curzon was still indisposed].

Now for the contents of it. I am glad that on the whole you approved of what I said, although you question the desirability of an ex-Ambassador speaking on foreign politics in connection with the country where he had represented this country. I am afraid I cannot agree with you; nor can I see that there is any analogy between what is right for me and what would have been right for Philip Currie, Ampthill or Charlie Hardinge when he retires. The positions are entirely different. In the cases of the three men you have mentioned, their career was a diplomatic and not a political one. Mine is the reverse. I have spent the whole of my life in politics and I certainly cannot subscribe to the idea that because I interrupted that political life for 2½ years to go on a special mission to France which embraced the position of Ambassador but also embraced other matters as well, I should be debarred from taking part in any question of foreign politics in which France was concerned, and which as a matter of fact would practically amount to my not speaking on foreign politics at all. I cannot think that if the same rule was applied to you and you were told that you must not speak on the subject of India because you have been Viceroy, but that you would have the same opinion as I have. I might also add that your unfortunate illness has compelled me to make speeches in the country rather than in the House of Lords.

Now with regard to another point you mention—that I give an 'unfair impression from an inevitable ignorance of the facts'. Whose fault is it that I am ignorant? I have made a rule which I have studiously kept, that when I am in Paris I will not go and see any of the Ministers, who I may say would be only too ready to see me. I am not sure that for the future I shall keep to that rule, and I certainly shall not unless His Majesty's Government is more prepared to give the information which I seek than they have been ready to do up to the present moment.

I do not at the present moment mean to make another speech in the country on Anglo-French relations, but now that Arthur Balfour represents the Foreign Office in the House of Lords I intend with others to raise the whole question of relationship with France. I should, as I have said, have done so before if you had been able to be in your place, but in your absence I should have been answered by somebody who could not possibly have been conversant with the details and only have given some set reply.

I felt sure you would approve of what I said about Foreign Policy leaving Downing Street and going back to the Foreign Office. The present position is quite intolerable, and you must have felt it so many a time. I still feel that if you have the proper backing, as you would have in our House at all events, the old position of the Foreign Office could be regained.

I hope you are really getting better, but I equally hope that you are giving yourself a complete rest and not attempting to do any work until you are really restored to health.

* * *

At the end of 1920 King Alexander of the Hellenes, who had succeeded his father, the pro-German King Constantine, when the latter was deposed in 1917, was bitten by a pet monkey and died. Venizelos, who had been responsible for expelling King Constantine, wished to put in King Alexander's place Prince Paul, another son of Constantine's. But Prince Paul refused to accept the throne until a plebiscite showed that Greece preferred him to both his father and his elder brother Crown Prince George. Venizelos allowed these matters to go forward to a plebiscite and to everyone's astonishment Greece showed a marked preference for the return of King Constantine. Venizelos went into exile and Constantine ruled again.

By the summer of 1922 Constantine and his Prime Minister, Gounaris, realised that the Greek forces in Asia Minor were threatened by the newly awakening military activities of Mustapha Kemal. They decided that the best way to restore the situation was to withdraw two divisions from Asia Minor and put them into Thrace with a view to attacking Constantinople. However, the British, French and Italian Governments, whose forces were still on both sides of the Marmora and its approaches to the Dardanelles, refused to allow the attack on Constantinople. The nemesis of all these presumptuous and vacillating excursions on the part of Lloyd George and the Greeks was to be worthy of a classical tragedy.

In August Kemal realised that his hour had come. He struck at the weakened Greek army in Asia Minor but he did not concern himself with the subsequent outrageous slaughter of soldiers and civilians in Smyrna. He turned his main army about and approached the Allied zone on the southern shores of the Marmora. His victory over the Greeks had been made possible by Russian and French arms and the French chose this moment to announce that they intended to withdraw their contingents from the British flank. The British Commander, General Sir Charles Harington, found himself in a position of great danger and the British Government took decisive steps to retrieve the odious situation which, largely through Lloyd George's folly, had arisen.

Sir Winston Churchill, who played a notable part in saving the day, has recorded in *The Aftermath* how these grisly issues presented themselves at least to himself, Mr. Lloyd George and Lord Birkenhead:

> Were we really going to be chased out of Constantinople to our ships, leaving the Sultan, his Ministers, and every person who had followed our instructions in carrying out the conditions of the Armistice, to be punished as traitors to their country? Were the three Great Nations, with the screams of Smyrna in their ears, really to scuttle at the approach of armed men? Would they abandon the city on which they had laid their hands, for which they had assumed so direct a responsibility, to a ruthless vengeance, and still worse to a blind anarchy? But if this was not to be, something more was needed than bluff and blather; unless everything was to clatter down, someone must stand firm.

On September 15 the British Government appealed to the Dominion Governments to send contingents to hold the line. This appeal, which was drafted by Mr. Churchill, unfortunately became public in the form of a communiqué before the cypher telegrams reached the Dominion Prime Ministers; they were in consequence offended. Only New Zealand promised to send a contingent. Canada declined to be involved. For some days the situation at Chanak seemed instinct with disaster, but on September 29 the Cabinet authorised General Harington, who by now had been reinforced and had a powerful British Fleet behind him, to give the Turks an ultimatum to withdraw from the Allied zone which they had punctured at one or two points. Harington, on October 11, was able to reach an agreement with the Turks whereby the Turks agreed to respect the neutral zone. The Greeks were to vacate Eastern Thrace; but the Turks were not to occupy it until a final peace settlement.

It was to be claimed at the General Election held later in the year, and has often been claimed since, that the wise, cool judgment of Sir Charles Harington prevented Britain becoming involved in a war into which she was being thrust by her bellicose politicians. Certainly it was Chanak which was to bring the Government down. Yet the last action of the Coalition Government in its dying days was perhaps the most useful service it rendered the nation and the Allied cause in all these postwar years.[1] The Chanak affair was settled peacefully and with honour, and though General Harington did not find it necessary to use the ultimatum with which he had

[1] The Tory politicians who wished to destroy the Government were more concerned about Chanak than was the general public; but, for another view, see *Empire in the Air* by Viscount Templewood: 'I never remember so universal a protest against a government's policy.' Lord Templewood had forgotten the Hoare-Laval agreement, condoning Mussolini's attack on Abyssinia in 1935, which forced his own resignation from the Government when his policy was repudiated by all his colleagues. By contrast all Mr. Lloyd George's colleagues remained faithful to him at the time of Chanak; and the reader may perhaps reflect that, whereas British action at Chanak stopped a small war, Sir Samuel Hoare's transaction with M. Laval was one of the melancholy milestones marking the road down which Mr. Ramsay MacDonald, Lord Baldwin, Mr. Chamberlain, and, to a lesser extent, Sir Samuel himself, conducted Britain into the greatest war the world has ever known.

been armed it must have been a useful reserve weapon in his negotiations with the Turks. Often successful military action is paralysed by lack of support from the politicians at home. The commander in the field who feels assured of the support of his Government can often achieve more than one who has constantly to be looking over his shoulder in fear of an order which may discourage, arrest, or even discountenance his military operation.

XX

The Fall of the Coalition

LLOYD GEORGE'S Coalition was now slithering and lurching to its downfall, though this was not perceived by many of its leading members. Lloyd George depended for his majority upon the Tory Party which had swallowed the Irish settlement a year before with a heavy heart and had been suffering ever since from an acute bout of indigestion. It has been said that all governments are born to die; and of none is it more true than of a coalition forged on the anvil of war. Its inherent brittleness soon betrays it in the soft self-indulgent years of peace.

Many of the Tory members who were elected in 1918 were ill-instructed either in politics or in the true interests of their country; and some of them were more adept at exploiting for their own personal gain the opportunities which arose in war than they were at making any practical contribution to the national need. Mr. Baldwin said of them that they seemed to him the hard-faced men who had done well out of the war. They were to show that they meant to do as well out of the peace. The more respectable old-fashioned members of the Party were still licking their sores over Ireland. The majority of the newcomers, who cared as little for Ireland as they did for any other part of the Kingdom or Empire and many of whom were seeking opportunities of purchasing honours for which they had not contended on the field of battle, as well as sources of further peace-time enrichment, represented the most squalid and acquisitive segment of the community which was to make itself so prominent a quarter of a century later at the time of Munich. Though the Tory Party has never been so shot through with pacifism as the Labour Party there is nearly always an element in it which will respond to the cry of 'Peace at any price'.

It was this unlettered, base amalgam of self-made self-seekers who now at a critical moment in the country's destiny had the power, if conjoined with those Tories who were still bitter about the Irish Settlement, to bring the Coalition toppling down.

It is very hard to bring down a Prime Minister who is in the saddle, and it is essential for the purpose that there should be an alternative leader outside the Government, since an intrigue from within, with the rare exception of Lloyd George's intrigue against Asquith, is seldom successful. But as this chapter will show there was available, in the person of Bonar Law, who had left the Government sixteen months before on the grounds of ill-health, an alternative leader in the wings. A keen-eyed, cunning and audacious political manipulator, long-versed in the destruction of Governments and capable of assessing all these factors and co-ordinating and animating the varied, dull, inert, slumbering passions of the Tory back-benchers, was at hand to breathe action into the inadequate, doubting, self-questioning Bonar Law. Towards the end of September Beaverbrook, after a visit to Lord Wargrave's house, where he had met Birkenhead and Churchill, reported to his ostensible political leader, Bonar Law, 'These men mean war'.

The Times of October 7 carried a letter from Bonar Law in which he asserted:

> . . . When the Greek forces were annihilated in Asia Minor and driven into the sea at Smyrna, it seems to me certain that, unless a decisive warning had been issued, the Turkish forces flushed with victory would have attempted to enter Constantinople and cross into Thrace. . . .
>
> It would certainly have involved Thrace in horrors similar to those that have occurred in Anatolia, and the probability—indeed, I think it is a certainty—of the renewal of war throughout the Balkans.
>
> It was therefore undoubtedly right that the British Government should endeavour to prevent these misfortunes. It is not, however, right that the burden of taking action should fall on the British Empire alone . . .
>
> We cannot alone act as the policemen of the world. The financial and social condition of this country makes that impossible. It seems to me, therefore, that our duty is to say plainly to our French Allies that

the position in Constantinople and the Straits is as essential a part of the Peace Settlement as the arrangement with Germany, and that if they are not prepared to support us there, we shall not be able to bear the burden alone. . . .

While Bonar Law endorsed the Government's firm and successful action at Chanak, he questioned the policy by which such a dangerous situation had arisen. And his reference to Britain's inability to police the world alone proved to be the rallying-cry for all pacifists, isolationists and malcontents. The sting in the tail was to prove mortal to the Government.

Derby, like many other Conservatives, had for some time been increasingly distrustful of Mr. Lloyd George's Government. We have seen how in March of this year he had refused the Prime Minister's invitation to become Secretary of State for India on the grounds of his differences over foreign policy. By September his opinions had crystallised; this is clearly brought out by his correspondence with Mr. Austen Chamberlain:

Lord Derby to Mr. Austen Chamberlain

Strictly Confidential and Personal 1 September 1922

. . . The more I see and hear from people the more convinced I am that the Coalition as constituted at the present moment cannot go on. It certainly cannot survive a general election. There is no doubt that the vast sentiment of the electors favours Salisbury and his new party; not because they look upon them as being heaven-born politicians who will set the world right, but because they represent something to which they can attach themselves in opposition to the present Coalition. At the present moment I do not think many have so attached themselves, and the names that one sees as Salisbury's followers are the names of men, who, whatever Government was formed, would place themselves in opposition; but if no steps are taken to collect a party round you and our duly recognised Conservative leaders they will undoubtedly secure the adherence of many Unionists, myself included.[1]

[1] In *The Unknown Prime Minister* Mr. Blake states: 'He [Derby] now wrote to Chamberlain declaring that he could no longer support the Coalition and intended to join "Salisbury and his new party".' The text of the letter above makes it plain that Derby, so far from declaring a settled intention, was merely uttering a conditional threat.

I know how difficult it is to make a break, and the only break that can be made, without creating a real split in the party, would be Lloyd George resigning in a friendly spirit on the grounds that he was tired or any other such excuse that he liked to make. Then I think a Coalition with a Conservative at its head would succeed. We can easily persuade our people, at all events in Lancashire, to vote for a Liberal Coalitionist. You cannot get them to vote for a Liberal supporter of Lloyd George. I think you will note the difference. On the other hand, I think the Liberal Coalitionists as a whole would support our people, and there is no doubt we should get many of the old Liberals, who would willingly join us if it was not for Lloyd George.

For my own part, the Foreign Policy of the Government will prevent me from further supporting them. I am not alluding solely to the difference between ourselves and France, which by the way I look upon as being more a personal difference between Lloyd George and Poincaré than a difference between the two countries. . . . But affairs in the East—our dangers in Egypt, India, Mesopotamia and Palestine—are to my mind attributable, to a very large extent, to the policy that H.M. Government has displayed towards Turkey. That policy has always seemed to me fraught with disaster, and the blow has now fallen, and Lloyd George's eulogistic speech of the Greek Army is now shown, not only to have been foolish but extremely mischievous,[1] and probably his very active support of the Greeks has led to these Turkish attacks which to my mind are going to end in an overwhelming victory. This could, I am sure, have been avoided if the Government had only recognised that Mustapha Kemal was the real ruler of Turkey, and that the Government really created by the Allies in Constantinople was powerless and has never represented the Turkish nation. It is all very well to call Mustapha Kemal a rebel; but transpose England and Turkey; such a man would not have been looked upon as a rebel, but as a true patriot fighting for his country, and determined not to see it divided up and given to that wretched Greek nation which is incapable either of fighting for or of administrating a great Empire.

[1] Mr. Lloyd George speaking on the Adjournment in the House of Commons on August 4, after stating that the Turks had done the worst disservice any country could have done to the cause of the Allies in 1914, added: 'I do not know of any Army that would have gone so far as the Greeks have gone. It was a very daring and very dangerous military experience. They showed a military superiority in every pitched battle.'—*Hansard*.

He may have, and probably has, many faults, but, as I say, he represents patriotic Turkish opinion. George Curzon went over to Paris (I think it was in March), and at a Conference with the French did do valuable service; but what has come of his efforts? Nothing. I suppose the proposals were rejected because instead of recognising Mustapha Kemal we treated him as a rebel and refused to deal with him. All that I put down to the very baneful pro-Greek influence of Lloyd George....

I hope you do not mind my telling you this. I have luckily not got to speak on politics for another seven weeks; then I shall have to, and I am afraid, unless things are very much altered between now and then, I shall have to give up my hitherto loyal support of the Coalition.

I have told nobody of my intention, and I beg you to treat this letter as strictly confidential and personal to yourself; but you are the duly elected leader of our party,[1] and I do not wish to do anything which could in any way be considered to be acting behind your back. As I have said, do not trouble to answer this now. I shall be coming to London in the beginning of October, and will, if I may, come and have a talk with you.

After some further exchanges Derby wrote again:

Lord Derby to Mr. Austen Chamberlain

Confidential — 9 October 1922

I have been thinking very carefully over it and have come to the conclusion that it will be better for me not to speak with regard to the future of our party on October 21st. I put down some notes of what I should have said if I had spoken, and I feel that if I had said what I intended it might make your position at the General Meeting of the Association even more difficult than it is at the present moment. I think therefore the best course for me at our meeting on the 21st is to announce that I shall say nothing at that moment but that after you have made your pronouncement I should propose to call a special meeting to consider the position. That meeting could of course be deferred for a month or so. I hope this meets with your approval.

[1] Derby was technically incorrect. Austen Chamberlain was only the leader of the Conservative Party in the House of Commons. The Party as a whole had had no leader since the resignation of Mr. Balfour in 1911.

On the other hand, I shall have to speak with regard to Anglo-French Relations and I intend to speak out very openly on the way the French have behaved to us. Again I hope this will have your approval, as no member of the Government could of course say much on the subject and I do not think it ought to be left entirely to the newspapers. I should put everything so to speak interrogatively. Ask them did you do that, and if there is any particular point that you would wish me to bring out I should be glad if you would let me know. I should ask them:

(1) Did they enter into a private arrangement with Mustapha Kemal without informing us either that they were going to do so or after they had done it, that they had done so and what the terms were?
(2) Did they supply the Turks with arms?
(3) Did they assure us that notwithstanding any agreement they might have they held to the preservation of the neutral zones?
(4) If so did they without any previous intimation withdraw their troops from Chanak?

Lastly, after agreeing to a note to be sent on September 23, did they without any previous intimation to us authorise their representative at Mudania to alter these terms?

P.S.:

Since dictating above I have seen Woodhouse and several of the leading Manchester Conservatives. They confirm in every respect what you know to be my view of the position. There is no feeling against Liberal Coalitionists but there is intensely bitter feeling against Lloyd George, and unless there is some distinct understanding that in the event of our being returned with a big majority, the major part of whom are Conservative, he will not be the Prime Minister, there will be a complete break-away. Woodhouse tells me at the Manchester Annual Meeting the other day a lot of people supported him out of sheer loyalty, but while the voting showed (roughly) 300 to 100 in favour of the Coalition, or rather in favour of working co-operation with the Liberals, there were over 200 abstentions.

I shall be in London tomorrow week (Wednesday 18th) and if you would like to see me I would be very glad to come and have a talk to you. We could then decide whether I should say anything or not.

Mr. Austen Chamberlain to Lord Derby

Private and Personal 11 Downing Street.
11 October 1922

I hope we can arrange a meeting next week and I would defer till then an answer to your letter of the 9th received today. I am speaking in Birmingham on Friday, and the Prime Minister at Manchester on Saturday, and we shall both deal with the Near Eastern policy. What we say may affect the line that you take, or at any rate the form in which you would express your thoughts, and I think, therefore, that a further interchange of views between us will be more useful after the speeches. So let us meet on the 18th.

On September 21, Lord Grey, the Liberal Foreign Secretary who had so valiantly helped to carry Britain into war in 1914, had written to *The Times*:

On Saturday, our Government announced to the world a whole scheme of action, apparently without consultation with France. This was a terrible mistake. The reply of France has been the withdrawal of the French forces from Chanak . . . If what the Government contemplates is separate action in the Near East, we may be heading for disaster.

Two days later Lord Salisbury, the leader of the Conservative diehards, also wrote to *The Times* supporting Grey's plea for common action with France, and on September 30 a number of Conservative members wrote to *The Times* demanding the summoning of Parliament.

Derby was alarmed by what was going on at Chanak. He wrote to Bonar Law:

Lord Derby to Mr. Bonar Law

Confidential 22 September 1922

What on earth is going to happen? Surely this Government is not going to commit the crime of making war on the Turks—all because of L.G.'s insane love of the Greeks. I look upon his speech in August as the direct cause of half our trouble. How can you expect the Turks to negotiate with a Government at whose head is a man who could make such a speech?

Are you going to take any action? I wonder if you are coming to

Scotland. If so we might meet here (where I should be delighted to see you) or elsewhere—or if you would like to see me I could come down to London; but stop the war we must, if we can.

Bonar Law replied:

Mr. Bonar Law to Lord Derby

Personal 24 Onslow Gardens, S.W.7
25 September 1922

The Turkish business is, I think, over. There is a great deal to be *said* about that but nothing which it is worth while to *write*. The centre of gravity politically will, I think, rest in the National Union meeting in November.

I do not myself know what I ought to do then, but I hope that before it comes the right path will be plainer than it is now. I should like very much to have a talk with you and indeed I think we ought to meet before the time for decision comes, but I have no prospect of going to Scotland and it certainly would be very unnecessary for you to come south at present. I suppose, however, that you will be back before very long and I shall gladly arrange to see you whenever you come.

The Chanak affair clearly brought Derby into much closer relations with Bonar Law. On October 9 Derby wrote:

Lord Derby to Mr. Bonar Law

Confidential 9 October 1922

I was very glad to see that you acted up to the intention you had half expressed to me, of writing a letter to the papers and I think it has done a great deal of good, and I hope the crisis is now passed, though there must remain a lot of gunpowder about for some time to come.

With regard to the speech that I was thinking of making on the future of our party on October 21st, after thinking over the matter very carefully I have come to the conclusion that anything I could say would only hamper Austen Chamberlain and make his position more difficult at the general meeting. I have therefore decided not to speak but to call a special meeting of the Lancashire Branch of the National Union after the General Meeting and then discuss the position.

Bonar Law replied:

Mr. Bonar Law to Lord Derby

11 October 1922 24 Onslow Gardens, S.W.7

Thank you very much for your letter. I hear all sorts of rumours about an immediate election and everything of that kind, but nothing definite. I can hardly believe it possible that Austen would sanction an election just before the National Union meeting without first having a meeting of the Party in some form, and I am sure it would be a great mistake for him to do so.

Derby at once sought to use his influence with Chamberlain on this point:

Lord Derby to Mr. Austen Chamberlain

Confidential and Personal 13 October 1922

. . . Everything appears to be in rather a dreadful state, but there is one thing I do hope, and that is that there will be no question of rushing a General Election before our meeting of the National Union. I somehow am hopeful that we might be able then to come to some arrangement. I have had talks in Liverpool and Manchester with prominent men of our party. They all agree with what I have always told you that there is no feeling against the Coalition as a whole. It is against a Coalition being led by a Liberal after the Election if the Conservatives happen to be in a larger majority. I know this is equivalent to saying to Lloyd George he must go, but surely there would be a great difference between saying to him he must go now, and [saying] the Party as a whole must after the Election be at liberty to choose its own leader. If you had an election now I am convinced there would be a break away of the Party which I think even you can hardly realise.

A few days later Salvidge, who was still staunchly loyal to Lloyd George and the Coalition, sought to discourage Derby from any action against the Government:

Sir Archibald Salvidge to Lord Derby

Private Constitutional Association,
16 October 1922 Liverpool

Since our conversation at Knowsley last Sunday week I have been keeping a careful look-out in every direction that I might collect opinions from various sources and I am bound to say that I cannot find that discontent against the P.M. and the Coalition that you have found in other quarters. I was very careful to watch the effect of Chamberlain's speech for really this was the test as he boldly declared for the Coalition, and I was astonished to find not one single criticism or adverse view. Of course, I don't for a moment suggest that there is absolute unanimity, for here the Irish question would always make itself heard. Unless I am very much mistaken, if the representatives of all our organisations in Liverpool were called together, I believe there would be an overwhelming vote in favour of maintaining the Coalition. That raises the difficulty I put to you in our conversation at Knowsley: that if the Coalition or even a working understanding is to be maintained, how can it be done if the P.M. is thrown over? It would be illogical and impracticable.

I see a section of the Press is trying to rush you into a definite hostility. I don't presume to advise you, but I feel certain that caution at the moment is advisable and I am bound to say that an expression of opinion on the lines indicated to me would not meet with general acceptance or anything like it. These are my own frank views. I have not heard from anyone in London on the subject at all. I shall probably go to the Executive there on Wednesday, which as you know is called for the purpose of settling the Agenda for the Conference. If you are there I should like to have a word with you.

Without the return to active politics of Bonar Law, the meeting of the Conservative Party at the Carlton Club on October 19 would never have decided to insist upon the withdrawal of the Party from the Coalition Government. Bonar Law had resigned his office of Lord Privy Seal, Leader of the House and the leadership of his party in the Commons in March 1921 on the grounds of his ill-health. The motives and pressures which induced him to re-enter politics in so decisive a fashion, involving not only a challenge to Lloyd George, the Prime Minister under whom he had served and with whom he had no outward quarrel, but also to Austen Chamberlain who had replaced him as party leader in the Commons, and to whom he was under especial obligations, have never been fully plumbed.

It is evident that his decision was not a sudden one. Already on

September 25 we have seen him writing to Derby, 'The centre of gravity politically, I think, rests in the National Union Meeting in November'; and again on October 11 he had expressed to Derby the hope that Chamberlain would not anticipate a meeting of the National Union by agreeing with Lloyd George to an election. Moreover, there had been for some time other forces at work which sought either to bring Bonar Law back into the Government or else to use him as the instrument of the Government's downfall.

Although Bonar Law had been gradually steeling himself to the task of destroying the Government, he was often a prey to doubts, particularly because he was uncertain whether his health and expectation of life justified him in the action to which he was being urged by many of his friends and associates. Sir Archibald Salvidge visited him at his home in Onslow Gardens the night before the Carlton Club meeting. He recorded in his diary that Bonar Law 'spoke in the saddest and most gentle way', but told him that he had 'finally and definitely made up his mind to go to the Carlton Club meeting the next day, speak in favour of ending the Coalition, and indicate his willingness to resume the leadership and form an independent Conservative Government'. Salvidge told him that whatever he did would be decisive, but argued against a resumption of a purely party Government. 'How could it be called a United Conservative Government when—excepting himself—all the best Conservative brains were to be replaced by silly little Diehards?'

While they were talking, 'A man-servant entered and whispered something to Bonar'. When he had withdrawn, Salvidge made his final appeal. He reminded Bonar Law 'of the day in Downing Street, just after the war, when he told me of the tremendous gratitude the nation owed Lloyd George . . . "We must never let the little man go. His way and ours lie side by side in the future." . . . Bonar flushed deeply and made no attempt to hide how much the reminder had gone home.' When Bonar Law asserted that Lloyd George had failed to 'secure the adherence of the Conservative wing of the Coalition' and that 'our party must be kept together', Salvidge replied that Lloyd George had 'the unswerving support of every one of his Conservative colleagues in the Cabinet'. 'Bonar', recorded

Salvidge, 'puffed at his pipe for a few moments. At last he said, almost regretfully, without the slightest note of triumph in his voice, "I may as well tell you that Lord Curzon is here. He is waiting in another room." It was an absolute bombshell. So the much-vaunted loyalty of the Cabinet towards Lloyd George was a myth! Already the Coalition's Foreign Minister had a foot in the other camp! There was no more to be said and I rose to go.'

Salvidge had, in fact, chanced upon what was Curzon's second visit to Bonar Law that day. Curzon had visited Bonar Law in the morning and had, according to his earlier biographer, Mr. H. A. Taylor (*The Strange Case of Andrew Bonar Law*), found him 'depressed and worried by the appeals which were being made to him to thrust himself once more into the forefront of public life. . . . So distasteful was the prospect that Lord Curzon left him seriously thinking of resigning his seat in the House of Commons and retiring finally from public life.' By the time Curzon saw Bonar Law again, 'all had changed'. Plainly Salvidge's arguments had had no effect upon him, and Curzon recorded that he had resolved or been persuaded to assume the lead. He even outlined to Curzon what he proposed to say at the meeting.

Salvidge went from Onslow Gardens to Downing Street, where he found a number of the inner Cabinet assembled. 'I felt embarrassed and wretched. My news amounted to an announcement of the fall of Lloyd George's Government, and he must have guessed from my face that I was the bearer of bad tidings. Yet he was showing the same buoyant spirit that had carried the country through the darkest hours of the war.' When Salvidge recounted what he had heard, Lloyd George and his colleagues had already been apprised that Bonar Law would go to the Carlton Club meeting the next day, but his news of Curzon's defection produced a gasp of consternation all round. Someone said: 'So our punctilious Proconsul has ratted, has he?'

The news seems to have been accepted with resignation, and by Lloyd George with that gayness of spirit which served him so well throughout the tremendous and poignant crises of his life. Only Balfour was outraged. 'He banged the table with his fist and shouted, 'I say fight them, fight them! This thing is wrong. The Conservative Party has always acted on the advice of its leaders. Is the lead of Law and Curzon to count as everything, and the advice of the rest of us as nothing? This is a revolt and it should be crushed.' A little later Birkenhead came in from a public dinner, resplendent in full dress and decorations, and Salvidge had to retell his tale for him. Birkenhead 'sat with his hands thrust deep into his trousers pockets and his long legs stuck out. "I have always wanted to make a trip round the world," he said. "I think I've got a thousand pounds. I'll be able to go now. The Coalition will not survive tomorrow."'

Bonar Law was the key to the political crisis, and he had many visitors that evening. Derby was another who called. He sustained a different impression from Salvidge's. Either Bonar Law was in one of his moods of doubt or Derby's close friendship with Lloyd George and Birkenhead inclined him to treat this visitor with greater reserve than some others. The most effective visitor Bonar Law received that night was Beaverbrook who, thus far in the crisis, had kept away from Onslow Gardens. Some time around 7.30 p.m. he called, and it was as a result of their discussion that Bonar Law authorised him to issue to the Press Association an announcement that Bonar Law would attend the Carlton Club meeting in the morning. Beaverbrook telephoned this vital political fact to the Press Association from 'The Vineyard', a house he then occupied at Putney, between 8 and 9 p.m. It was instantly transmitted to all the newspapers. Even after this decisive action Bonar Law still seems to have vacillated, as is shown by a conversation which he had, certainly later that evening, with the Editor of *The Times*, Wickham Steed, and which is recounted in *The Times History*.

> Just after *The Times* went to press that night Bonar Law telephoned to the office to ask if there was anything new. The Editor told him that the only important news was the announcement that *The Times* would publish in the morning, to the effect that Bonar Law would attend the Carlton Club meeting and oppose the Government. 'But I have not yet decided to go,' answered Bonar Law. The Editor again pressed him to attend, and by upsetting the Coalition give the country a chance of

Derby with Mr. Bonar Law at the Tory Party meeting in the Hotel Cecil in October 1922 which elected the latter as Leader of the Party.

Derby leaving 10 Downing Street with the Duke of Devonshire during the political crisis of November 1923.

returning to straightforward party government. Were he to do this, the Editor promised the backing of *The Times*. It was a question of healthy party government, and the Editor said he would say the same if Asquith were in Bonar Law's position. The Editor was supported by his close colleagues, who also believed that the Coalition had outlived its usefulness and the country needed a strong Conservative and a strong Liberal Party. He thought from the tone of Bonar Law's final remarks that he was likely to attend, and retained the note to that effect in the commentary on the crisis for the first column of the bill page.[1]

Diary

Thursday 19 October 1922

Arty and Edward came to luncheon and directly afterwards we got news from the Carlton by telephone that Chamberlain had been defeated by an overwhelming majority. I confess I was very much surprised at the size of the majority, and what surprised me more was to hear from George [Stanley] who came up afterwards that Bonar Law had taken a very definite line. When I had left him the night before both George Younger and I were under the impression that he might not even attend the meeting; in fact when we got there we found he had already written a letter in which he resigned his seat, so that he should not have to take any part. We were both rather disgusted with what seemed to us his cowardice. However, all's well that ends well, and he apparently made a strong speech. Arthur Balfour seems to have been well received but he made a bad speech. Chamberlain equally, but from his point of view a good speech. The special object of resentment at the meeting seems to have been Birkenhead.

It is a delusion to suppose that the Carlton Club meeting was forced upon Austen Chamberlain and the Coalition Conservatives by the Diehards. As already shown, Bonar Law had for some weeks looked to a meeting of the National Union to achieve whatever he had in mind at that time. Austen Chamberlain and the Tory supporters of the Coalition sought to anticipate what they feared might be a large and difficult assembly which they could not control by a meeting consisting of Conservative members of Parliament and those peers who were members of the Government. Such a meeting

[1] *The Times*' jargon for main news page.

would be less exposed to the passionate oratory of the Diehards; and it was easier to fix a convenient date.

October 19 had been selected by Austen Chamberlain and Lloyd George's Tory friends because the day before there was to be a critical by-election at Newport, Monmouthshire. At the Coupon Election in 1918 the figures had been:

Coalition Liberal . . .	14,080
Labour	10,234
Independent . . .	647
Majority for Coalition Liberal	3,846

It was hoped by the Government forces that this by-election would show a popular support for the Coalition which would impress the meeting at the Carlton Club. However, the result announced in the morning papers of October 19 showed a strong anti-Coalition feeling:

Conservative . . .	13,515
Labour	11,425
Liberal	8,841
Majority for Conservative .	2,090

The Liberal candidate, who under the pact between the two parties had received Government support, including letters from Lloyd George and Chamberlain, was at the bottom of the poll. The supporters of the Coalition went to the Carlton Club therefore with two pieces of bad news, neither of which most of them had known until that morning—the by-election had been lost and Bonar Law would be there.

The prime mover and principal agent in the plan to bring down the Coalition Government was, however, Beaverbrook. As we have seen, he had played a leading part behind the scenes in the election of Bonar Law in 1911 as leader of the Conservative Party upon the resignation of Arthur Balfour. He had been active in the formation of the first Coalition under Asquith and he had probably done more than anyone else except Lloyd George to pull Asquith down and to set up Lloyd George in his place. Anyone who has read the chronicles of these times and has had the opportunity to discuss them with the leading figures cannot doubt that the decisive responsibility in persuading Bonar Law to come to the Carlton Club and announce his return to public life was Beaverbrook's. Though an unnatural modesty has led him to minimise his own rôle and the full degree of his influence over his ailing friend, his account must be considered to carry great authority.

In the afternoon Derby attended the meeting of the Executive of the National Union. It was decided in view of the cataclysmic event in the morning to postpone the calling of a special conference of the National Union for which the Diehards had been clamouring. When the meeting was over, Derby consulted with Leslie Wilson, the Chief Whip, and the Party Chairman, Sir George Younger, as to who was to be called to the special meeting next day at which a delegation would be selected to invite Bonar Law to allow his name to go forward as leader of the Party. That night Derby went once more to Onslow Gardens, and had a much fuller and freer conversation with Bonar Law than he had had the night before.

Diary

Thursday 19 October 1922

Dined in the evening with Maureen and Oliver. Only the Blandfords there; and I left at 9.30 to go and see Bonar Law. I found him an entirely different man from the night before, and quite full of fight. But he told me in confidence, though I think he will tell the meeting,[1] that whatever happens, he will only accept the leadership for a year and that at the end of a year's time he is to be allowed to go, without there being any attempt to persuade him to stay on. He says he thinks his health will last out for a year, but no longer. I told him that suited me very well, because I hated coming into office at all, and I should certainly go out with him on a reconstruction; so that I have only got to look forward to one year's penal servitude. He then began talking

[1] In his *Unknown Prime Minister* Mr. Blake makes it plain that Bonar Law was only deflected from this intention by his political friends who realised what an electoral liability such a statement would be.

about offices, and said that he wished to see me, perhaps on Sunday or Monday, with reference to it. He knew that I should like the Foreign Office, but said (and I quite agree with him) that as Curzon remained with him it would be impossible not to leave him there; and I think it very advisable he should be there because he gets on well with the French and has done particularly well in the negotiations lately. I told him that really what I should like would be to be Lord President of the Council, which would leave me free from office work, and I shall press him to give me that, though he told me he thought I should have to take one of the working offices, by which I presume he means perhaps the War Office, or the Colonial or India Office. In some ways I should like to go back to the War Office, though not particularly at the present time, and I do not think they could leave George [Stanley] there with me at the head, and he is so fond of his office there and his work that I should not like to be the cause of his displacement.

Bonar Law told me he was trying to get McKenna to be Chancellor of the Exchequer, but would not know till tomorrow whether he would accept or not. Of course McKenna would have to call himself a Conservative, but he did not think he would offer much objection to doing that. Bonar Law then said something which disquieted me, because he said there may be a point of difference between him and me on the question of tariffs. This looks as if he was still thinking of putting on a tariff. I told him perfectly frankly if he did he and I should part company. He said he only meant a tariff for revenue purposes, and it might be possible by that means to do two things which would be popular (1) give some aid to agriculture, and (2) to reduce the tax on beer. I said, 'What about income tax?' and he said, 'I fear there is no chance of being able to do much in that direction this year, as our finances are certainly worse than they were in March.' I do not believe this is quite the case; he is always so pessimistic about things.

I then told him I meant to go to Manchester unless he had any objection, just to explain my own personal position and to say something about Lloyd George, and at the same time to appeal that there should be no bitterness or vendetta against the Liberal Coalitionists. He quite agreed to this, telling me to be careful what I said, and it must only apply in those cases where the constituencies themselves, through their organisations, had settled to support the Liberal Coalitionists. The idea is to have a party meeting on Monday to get his Government settled, and approved by the King on Tuesday, and announce it with the dissolution on Wednesday. He thinks by that means we should get the dissolution over, and if we return to power we should then be able to confirm the Irish Constitution which has to be confirmed by December 6th. He told me Lloyd George had been to see him, and had been really very nice.

Friday 20 October 1922

Went to the meeting of a certain number of people, ex-Ministers, etc., to arrange about a deputation to ask Bonar Law to allow his name to be put forward at the meeting of the Party on Monday. We had a sort of desultory conversation, as Bonar Law wanted to know the views of those present on certain topics. I am glad to say that he declared quite definitely that he would support the Irish Treaty, at the same time quite rightly he said we should help to compensate the Unionists in the South for their losses. I pointed out, and it was accepted by those present, that it would never do for us to say England would compensate for all the losses. That would simply mean that the Free State Government would have no more interest in the matter, and the burden of compensation must be left on them although we might say we would confer with them as to the best way of dealing with the question.

Then there was rather a disturbing incident. He gave it to be understood his views on Tariff Reform were unchanged and of course if he is going to bring that up he is going to split the Party again at the beginning. However, Amery smoothed matters down by saying he only meant Trade within the Empire and a tariff if necessary for the purposes of Revenue in order to reduce certain home taxation. That is something I do not think anybody would object to and might be popular.

It was then decided that Salisbury and Amery should be the deputation and I as President for the year of the National Union should be associated with them. We went down and had a short talk—quite satisfactory—but all the same although he was excited and therefore more energetic than he had been, his health did not seem to me so particularly good.

Went by night train to Knowsley.

Before leaving, he wrote to Bonar Law:

Lord Derby to Mr. Bonar Law

20 October 1922

You may have thought I was chaffing when I said that I did not want office, but I was perfectly honest when I said so. You will have many applicants and I can assure you that the fact of not being given a post will not alter in any way the loyalty with which I will serve you. Do not think, on the other hand, that I am funking responsibility. Far from it. I only want you to feel you are absolutely at liberty to employ me, or leave me out as you may think fit.

But if you do think I can best serve you by taking office do let it be in one of those offices which are not in the limelight, Lord President or Lord Privy Seal. I say this with a reason. If I am of any value to you it is because of my friends in Lancashire, and to enable me to keep in close touch with them it is essential I should not be too much tied to London by office duties. Again, in such a position I could assist, or indeed deputise for Curzon in those negotiations which must take place, with French and Turks, with both of whom I am conceited enough to think I have a certain amount of influence. Further, if we are returned after a general election I should hold any office you may appoint me to at your disposal, if you find that any of our Unionist friends who are now separated from us, could be induced to take office under your leadership.

It seems that Derby, having first expressed a preference for one of the sinecure offices in the Cabinet, was soon persuaded to accept an executive function. Some misunderstanding however arose between him and Bonar Law as to whether his preference was for the Colonial Office or the War Office:

Mr Bonar Law to Lord Derby

23 October 1922 — 24 Onslow Gardens, S.W.7

Certainly! I thought from our telephone conversation this morning that you preferred the Colonial Office to any other. Now that I know you prefer the W.O., I think you may assume that it will be your new post.

Diary

Monday 23 October 1922

Wrote to Bonar Law and told him that I did not in the least want to press him to give me the Colonial Office and that if he would like me to go to the War Office, which I knew well, I would willingly change and go there. Answer back that he had thought I particularly wanted the Colonial Office that is why he had given it to me, but that he would certainly be for my going to the War Office.

Tuesday 24 October 1922

Alice not well and could not go to Newmarket.

Telephone message from Bonar Law to say he wanted to see me. I found him very much disturbed, first of all about the press. Rothermere had been to him and after having told him he would support him he now says that he will attack him unless he is at once given an Earldom. Bonar told him to go to the Devil and quite rightly so, and said if he earned it by good work it might be possible hereafter to give it to him but under no circumstances would he give it as a bribe for present support.

Wednesday 25 October 1922

Went round to see Winston who I did not find looking so well as he had done when I last saw him, and although he says his temperature is normal he admits that he has had a tremendous shock and that he finds himself quite incapable of doing any business. He is interesting about things. Says that with regard to the Government that he and his colleagues feel there are only two men against whom they have got no bitterness and who were perfectly right to join. They were Devonshire and myself. With regard to the others he has a certain amount of bitterness but it is apparently concentrated, as far as the Lords are concerned on Curzon, and on Leslie Wilson the Whip who he says was intriguing the whole time against Austen Chamberlain. He is of course very upset at the position and then he talked of general policy. At the end I asked him whether he remembered a conversation he and I had when we two walked back together, I to Cumberland Place and he to Mount Street, the evening that he had crossed the Floor of the House, and when after I asked him whether he had really considered whether he was right he had told me that Dilke had also asked him that and told him that he must remember that he could cross the Floor of the House once but not twice.[1] He said he perfectly remembered that but he said as a matter of fact 'I nearly did cross it twice or rather I nearly

[1] Dilke was wrong.

changed parties again.' I asked him what he meant and he told me if it had not been for the break he was on the point of joining the Conservative Party as he was more in accord with our general views than he was with those of the Liberals. I wonder whether that is really true. We talked a long time and then Arthur Balfour came in. He was very nice to me and yet I could feel somehow that he has got a great deal of bitterness about the situation, and indeed his speech the other night was for a man of his temperament perhaps the most disagreeable of all.

Went down to see Bonar Law to discuss with him his Election Address. Present there—George Curzon, Amery, Douglas Hogg, and Cave. We cut it about a great deal. It was not very well drafted and I do not wonder at that, and there were things in it which we all agreed could well be omitted. Bonar at the end said what was quite true, that everybody would think it was a very weak Address but so it must be. There can be no really definite policy to put forward except to endeavour to restore confidence and that you could really put in one sentence. After the meeting I had a little private breeze with Curzon who took upon himself to rather lecture me as to my conversations in Paris with various people. He said that I must remember now that I could not talk to any of these people. I told him that I knew perfectly well I must be careful what I said but that before I was in office I was at perfect liberty to say what I liked and even now in office I adhered to my right to discuss with any of my friends in Paris politics that concerned the two countries. I can see that he and I are not going to see eye to eye on many things.

In the evening dined at Claridges with Edward and Oliver.

Derby neatly summarised what many thought of this political crisis in a letter to his old American friend Mr. Wallace:

... It is impossible at the present moment to foretell the outcome of all this trouble but there has been a growing feeling against Lloyd George which except as regards his foreign policy I have not myself shared, but he brought us the other day to the brink of war and as somebody said of him 'we cannot afford to keep him any longer. It is too expensive'....

XXI

The General Election of October 1922

THE composition of Mr. Bonar Law's new Cabinet was announced on October 24. Of all the Conservatives who had held Cabinet office under Mr. Lloyd George, only Mr. Baldwin, Lord Curzon, Lord Peel and Sir Arthur Griffith-Boscawen were willing to be included. Mr. Austen Chamberlain, Lord Balfour, Lord Birkenhead, Sir Laming Worthington-Evans and Sir Robert Horne remained faithful to their pledges to Mr. Lloyd George. Mr. Baldwin, President of the Board of Trade in the recent administration, had given no pledge. The late Lord Birkenhead used to recall that no one bothered to seek an assurance from Baldwin since he was regarded as the 'Idiot Boy' of the Cabinet. With his deadly thrust at the Carlton Club—'Mr. Lloyd George has already destroyed his own party; let us leave him before he destroys ours'—he had done more than anyone, except Mr. Bonar Law and Lord Beaverbrook, to bring down the Coalition. His reward was the Treasury, which Mr. Reginald McKenna had refused. Despite his obscurity, this cannot in the circumstances be deemed to have been excessive. Lord Curzon's scruples were soon overcome by the plea that his services at the Foreign Office were indispensable. His engagements to his colleagues were almost always vulnerable to an appeal to his patriotism, particularly when this was accompanied by the promise of high office.

The abstention of so many powerful Tory chieftains, coupled with the departure of all the able Liberal Ministers, left a void which had to be filled by promotions, with backbenchers and from the House of Lords. Apart from Derby, Mr. Bonar Law's principal recruits from the upper House were Lord Salisbury, who became

Lord President of the Council, and the Duke of Devonshire, who went to the Colonial Office. We have seen how, earlier in the summer, Derby had declined Lloyd George's offer of the India Office. His instinct had served him true. At the time of Lloyd George's invitation, the Coalition was already discredited and dissolving. Derby may well have reflected that, though it is proverbially regarded as heroic to remain on board a sinking ship, there are no precepts or precedents even in the annals of Don Quixote which suggest that anyone should embark in such circumstances. He may well have assumed that it was only his name of which Lloyd George wished to make use. By holding himself in reserve, he was able to render an important service alike to the Conservative Party and to the nation. The Conservative Party was deeply divided, and it was essential that those of its leaders who had taken the responsibility of forming a Government should acquire the confidence of the rank and file in the country. Most of the politicians, Liberal and Tory alike, whose names had become household words in the war had departed. New forces had to be mobilised. At this time, in popular esteem in the Conservative Party, the name of Derby probably counted for more than that of either Devonshire or Salisbury; and each of the three for a great deal more than that of Curzon.

Further reinforcement had to be sought in the House of Lords. Lord Cave went to the Woolsack, and Lord Novar, who still called himself a Liberal, became Secretary of State for Scotland. Lord Peel remained at the India Office.

The difficulties in which the leading members of the Government found themselves at this time are well illustrated by an anecdote which is still told by two sons-in-law of the Duke of Devonshire. One evening while the Government was being formed Derby went round to Devonshire House. This was only a few months before this splendid building in Piccadilly, with its galaxy of memories of political confabulations extending over two centuries, was to be pulled down and replaced by Lord Rootes's glittering automible emporium. Devonshire expressed concern about the Government's lack of adequate representation in the Commons, and in particular as to who would be the Government's principal spokesman, Baldwin being at this time utterly unversed in Parliamentary technique. Someone said:

'Let's get some clever lawyer.'

'I know the very man,' said Derby. 'Someone was telling me about him the other day, a fellow called Pig'.

'The only Pig I know,' said Devonshire, 'is James Pigge in Surtees.'

Thus did that able lawyer, Sir Douglas Hogg, who at that time was probably the leading Silk at the Bar and who was destined as the first Viscount Hailsham to sit on the Woolsack, first come to the attention of the magnificoes of the Tory Party.

The *Daily Herald* commented a few days later:

> When we examine these titled Ministers, however, what do we find? Do we find that they are men of great experience; have they been the architects of their own careers; have they won through to the top after struggles and hard-won successes? Or are they men who would never have been heard of if they had not happened to be born either titled or rich?
>
> Without any wish to be unkind, we may say that is certainly the case with the Duke of Devonshire, Lord Salisbury, Lord Peel and Lord Novar. Lord Cave is a lawyer of repute; he made his own name. Lord Curzon and Lord Derby would both have reached some kind of distinction whatever they had been born to. One might have been a headmaster, the other would have made an energetic shop steward. The other four peers in the Cabinet have nothing but their names to recommend them.

After resurrecting Derby's unfortunate references of nearly twenty years before to Post Office officials as 'blackmailers' and 'bloodsuckers', and speculating that 'if Lord Derby had ever been obliged to support a family on a few pounds a week, he could not have shown this callousness, this utter lack of comradeship', the *Herald* concluded:

> Lord Derby is the dictator of Lancashire Toryism. He owes his eminence first to the wealth which, as hereditary receiver of ground rents in the cotton towns, he has automatically garnered from other

> people's labours; secondly, to inheritance of a name made famous by two 19th-century statesmen; and thirdly to a personality in which bluff heartiness of manner and appearance are combined with Mr. Lloyd George's knack of bringing discordant people into agreement. His visit to Dublin 18 months ago, as 'Mr. Edwards', in tortoiseshell spectacles, was a quaint incident in the furtive attempts then being made towards Irish reconciliation.

Meanwhile, Derby having re-entered the political arena had already flung himself into the long fight with vigour. His first duty plainly was to rally Lancashire. By chance he was already committed to a public speech, and he thus fired the opening shot before the campaign proper had opened. On October 21, three days before the composition of the Government was announced and prior to its having been decided what office he was to hold, he took the chair at a meeting in Manchester of the Lancashire Division of the National Unionist Association. While making his position clear, he said nothing to exacerbate feelings between the now warring members of the defunct Coalition.

Derby was no orator but on this occasion he made a speech which by its magnanimity, timing and direction proved of national importance. It was widely reported, *The Times* allotting it more than a column of direct quotes. Derby was gratified by the initial reaction to his speech:

Lord Derby to Sir Archibald Salvidge

23 October 1922

All letters that I have had, and all people that I have seen approved of what I said on Saturday, and I hope it will do good. I am sure it was the line you would have wished me to take, and I thank you for your support of me under very difficult circumstances.

I dare say I shall have a lot of difficulties in Lancashire in trying to stop the hot-heads from running impossible candidates, but I hope to succeed; and I am not sure that the best thing I can do will not be to speak at Bolton, where by an agreement a Conservative and Liberal Coalitionist are standing together. That I think might emphasise the honesty of my appeal for moderation. . . .

Salvidge agreed but reported a grievance against the *Daily Express*:

Sir Archibald Salvidge to Lord Derby

Private 24 October 1922

MY LORD,

Many thanks for your letter. I also hear on all sides the greatest praise for the able and tactful manner in which you dealt with the situation at Manchester and I appreciate very much your kind allusion to the support I gave you.

I was surprised to read in today's London *Daily Express* a leading article attacking me. I enclose a copy. I consider it very unfair. Within a few hours of the Carlton Club decision I gave an interview to the *Evening Standard* and stated unequivocally that I accepted it. The attitude of the *Daily Express* is not helpful in the difficult task of promoting unity.

The reference to my connection with the Beer trade is ridiculous. Both Younger and Gretton are in the same position. The members of the brewing trade have been at variance, as in most trades, over the political controversy. The reason for the attack, I think I can tell you when I see you.

As far as Liverpool is concerned I do not mind because no one believes it and I am confident the line I have taken meets with overwhelming support of the whole party.

The article of which Salvidge complained had appeared that morning in the *Daily Express* under the heading:

BEER AND CONSERVATISM

Now that the general election is upon us constitutents ought to press their candidates hard on the subject of the excessive price of beer. For the last two years consumers of light beer have been paying a penny a pint more than the 1920 price—and the difference has gone straight into the pocket of the brewers. This was made possible purely by the fiscal folly of Mr. Austen Chamberlain as Chancellor of the Exchequer. But the Conservative Party is now free of Mr. Chamberlain and his finance, and it is also free of Sir Archibald Salvidge, who is a brewer as well as a politician. Sir Archibald, who has always tried to wobble off on the winning side in internal party differences, has succeeded in wobbling off on the wrong one. At the meeting of the executive of the National Union he adopted a strong pro-Coalition and anti-Conservative attitude, and was hopelessly defeated. We shall not begrudge him a Lloyd George honour, but we desire that the Conservative Party should have done, once and for all, with the kind of influence and activity he represents. That party now has a chance to make a clean start in this matter, and it should take it. The electors ought to see to it that candidates pledge themselves to alter the existing taxation on beer so as to reduce without fail the price of beer by a penny a pint on the lighter varieties, and, if possible, by a penny a pint all round.

The motive for the *Daily Express* attack upon Salvidge is made plain in his diary. On the eve of the Carlton Club meeting Salvidge had separately recounted to both Birkenhead and Bonar Law that a rumour was circulating to the effect that 'much of the demand for a change of Government had been engineered by Lord Beaverbrook because, though he had till recently been a Coalition supporter, he had failed to exercise over the present Cabinet the influence he desired on behalf of certain oil interests in the East'. Birkenhead mischievously repeated this the following night at dinner to Beaverbrook without making it plain that Salvidge did not believe this fabrication himself, and was only passing it on as a sample of what people were saying. Since Beaverbrook had no oil interests, he was understandably annoyed. Apart from any personal feelings, Beaverbrook was naturally hostile to Salvidge whom, as a loyal Tory supporter of the Coalition, he regarded as a spy from the other camp.

Derby wrote to comfort Salvidge:

Lord Derby to Sir Archibald Salvidge

Confidential 25 October 1922

Many thanks for your letter. I quite agree with you that the article in the *Daily Express* is very unfair and between ourselves I have written privately to Blumenfeld the Editor on the subject telling him of your coming to support me last Saturday, of your moving the vote of confidence in me and of your promise to loyally support the Party and the action they have taken. I do not see that any man could do more.

I think between ourselves Oliver is now sorry he is not standing for Wavertree, though probably that is just because of the excitement of the Election. I suppose it would be too late for him to come forward there especially in view of Harold Smith's[1] attitude. It would be looked upon as a direct challenge to F. E. which is the last thing I want to do although I think that he is evidently going to be one of the late Government who will say bitter things. . . .

Derby did not have long to wait to see his prophecy about Birkenhead fulfilled:

Diary

Wednesday 1 November 1922

In the evening saw an attack on me by Birkenhead who has probably deliberately said that I appealed to Liberal Coalitionists to assist Unionists, whereas exactly the contrary is the case.

Thursday 2 November 1922

Was the guest of the Rotary Club. Made them a very short speech. Non-political, but even people like Max Muspratt and Liberals came up to me and told me what they thought of F. E.'s attack.

I walked back to the office with Salvidge who is perfectly furious about it. He says far from doing me harm it has done me a great deal of good. He advises my not writing to the papers but to mention it in my next speech. He himself was going to give an interview on the subject, and he told me as one of the instances of the effect it has had that Harold Smith was to be adopted tonight as the candidate for Wavertree but they had decided not to have him—they have got another man in reserve—unless he will publicly disclaim his brother's statement and Salvidge says he is going to insist that F. E. when he comes down here to speak shall withdraw what he said. I do not know that he will succeed in doing this. He told me that the Women's vote was the one which helped them most yesterday in their Municipal Elections.

Harold Smith succeeded in being adopted for Wavertree, but only after making a marked obeisance to Derby. In his speech at the adoption meeting, he described himself as a whole-hearted supporter

[1] Lord Birkenhead's brother.

of Bonar Law and added that he was in full agreement with Derby's Manchester speech.

The *Liverpool Courier* of November 3 reported him in part as saying:

I read Lord Derby's speech twice. It was an admirable pronouncement. It was the moderate speech of a patriotic man who realised the situation to the full. He regretted the break-up of the Coalition, and regretted any action within our party which rendered it not only unnecessary but difficult for us to co-operate with any National Liberals in the future.

It was a very wise, very moderate and very excellent speech from the great leader of the Unionists in the county of Lancaster. . . .

Throughout the election Derby corresponded freely with Sir George Younger, the Party chairman, who was organising the campaign:

Sir George Younger to Lord Derby

1 November 1922 — Unionist Central Office

. . . Everything is going well so far as I can judge, and Bonar, I think, is now ready to put some ginger into his speeches, beginning with a moderate dose tomorrow and with a larger one at Leeds on Saturday. He really must put some go into the thing and buck up his supporters. I think he is feeling rather annoyed and hurt by some of the offensive things that have been said by L. G. and F. E. He is in the humour to take a pretty strong line.

I hope all is going well in Liverpool and that Salvidge is putting his back into the fight.

Lord Derby to Sir George Younger

Confidential — 2 November 1922

. . . I am glad Bonar is going to put a little ginger into his speeches. They want it as there is no doubt whatever at the present moment people think he is too much on the defensive. At the same time I do hope neither you nor he will countenance more than you can possibly help attacks on seats where the sitting member is a Liberal Coalitionist who will promise to give general support to the Government. In this part of the world there is still a very strong feeling towards the Coalition, and it would be a great pity to excite animosity amongst the Liberal Coalitionists who on the whole I think are helping us.

Did you see F. E.'s attack on me? I am writing an answer to him which I hope will be an effective one. He has deliberately accused me of appealing to Liberal Coalitionists to assist Unionists in order to put myself in and keep L. G. out, whereas it is exactly the contrary. My appeal was made to Conservatives to help Liberal Coalitionists, and I am going to repeat this appeal in a speech I have to make at Bolton on Saturday.

F. E. has done more harm in his speeches towards co-operation between the two sections than any other man, and when we remember some of the things that happened in the past with regard to him he is, to say the least of it, a bold man to make some of the statements he has made.

Salvidge is putting his back into it here all right. Of course up to now he has been engaged entirely in Municipal Elections where we have gained a great success. I was over in Ormskirk yesterday. I think we shall win that seat from Labour. . . .

Sir George Younger to Lord Derby

3 November 1922 Unionist Central Office

F. E. has done his party no good by the attitude he has taken in his speeches. He is as sick as a dog in contemplating the wreck he has caused by his stupid attitude, and I think that makes him bitter. I hope you will give it him in the neck when you answer the attack he made upon yourself.

I am delighted to hear about Salvidge. I thought that when the time came for the fight he would not fail, and I expect he already sees what a mess F. E. has made of the whole business.

On Saturday, November 4, Derby spoke at the Central Conservative Club in Bolton, and hit back at Birkenhead:

An attack has been made on me by Lord Birkenhead. He accuses me of inviting Lloyd George Liberals in Lancashire to co-operate in order to put me in and keep their leader out. That means, first, that I am working for my own personal ends; and, secondly, that I am doing what I could to secure that cooperation which I have always advocated between the two branches of the late Coalition government. It is the first time I have ever been accused of trying to get something for my own personal ends, and the last man who ought to make that statement is Lord Birkenhead. He knows perfectly that what he says is not true. It was with the greatest reluctance that I accepted office, and only on condition that when a reconciliation of the party comes about my post should be absolutely at the disposal of anyone who will strengthen the Government. Lord Birkenhead has deliberately misrepresented the facts. I have made only two speeches on the subject, one being at Bolton and one in Manchester. These were addressed in each case to Unionists and to no one else, and it was to Unionists I made an appeal to support Coalition Liberals where they were adopted by a constituency, and not the other way about, as Lord Birkenhead stated. I say 'deliberately', because his attention has been called to his misstatement. When a gentleman makes a misstatement unintentionally, he withdraws it, and apologises. Lord Birkenhead has done neither. ('Shame.')

But I am going to give him my answer in my own way. I have come here today because you have come to an arrangement by which you shall run and support one Coalition Liberal and one Conservative and Unionist candidate, and I ask all you workers here to put as much back into returning the Coalition Liberal as you do to returning your own candidate. (Cheers.)

That is one of my ways of answering Lord Birkenhead. There is another. In another city in Lancashire exactly the same position has arisen, and at the request of both Liberal-Coalition and Unionist candidates I am going to speak on the platform of both of them. And so I give the lie direct to what Lord Birkenhead said.

This quarrel between old political and personal friends was certainly most distasteful to Derby. Salvidge and the Liverpool Tories were outraged at Birkenhead's attack. His years of service as member for Walton and his vast popularity with the Tory democracy on Merseyside counted for nothing in the balance against Derby's position. Later in the election Derby permitted himself the devastating thrust that he was supporting Sir Harold Smith 'despite the fact that he is the brother of Lord Birkenhead'. In an interview published in the *Morning Post* of November 7, Lord Birkenhead returned to the attack: 'Lord Derby is an educated man, and he certainly knows that the verb "co-operate" means "to work with".

Even Lord Derby, brilliant as the consequences might be, cannot co-operate with himself.'

Lord Derby to Sir George Younger

Confidential 7 November 1922

F. E. has I see again returned to the charge but his attacks make him very vulnerable. He cannot deny that he entirely misrepresented what I said and at the very same time that he quibbles about the word 'Co-operate'. He appeals to the women in Liverpool only to vote for those candidates who will co-operate with Lloyd George after the Election. I am going to say just a few words about him tonight but it is best to really leave him alone. He has done himself a lot of harm in this part of the world and Salvidge told me last night that he was coming to speak here but they are doing everything they can to prevent him coming to speak as he would have a very hostile meeting . . .

In the course of his interview in the *Morning Post* of November 7, Birkenhead said that he did not intend to 'bandy abuse' in the country. Instead he challenged Derby to repeat what he had said in the House of Lords, adding that Lord Derby had 'always preferred the incense of the platform to the atmosphere of Parliamentary debate'. He guaranteed that then he would undertake to 'deal faithfully and thoroughly with him'. This prompted a letter in the *Morning Post* of November 8:

SIR,

Lord Derby's spoken charge is: that Lord Birkenhead is (1) one whose statements demand the lie direct, and (2) one who acts unlike a gentleman. Lord Birkenhead is contented to reply: 'If he repeats the words inside the House of Lords I will deal with him faithfully and thoroughly.' Lord Birkenhead has wholly inverted the usual process, which usual process is, for a member who is defamed by another inside Parliament to challenge him to repeat the words outside, where no privilege would protect him in an action for slander. But Lord Derby has openly spoken the charges outside, with no shelter of privilege, and he is asked to repeat it inside. Never before has such a course been taken by any defamed public man.

Or is Lord Birkenhead's reply merely one of those brilliant sparks of a 'first-class brain', so dazzling that it might obscure the vision of 'second-class brains'? Anyway, there is one retort left for Lord Birkenhead, as and when needed. If Lord Derby makes the charge again in the House of Lords, Lord Birkenhead can reply: Repeat those words outside the House and I will deal with you thoroughly.

Yours, etc.
CECIL HAYES.

The *Liverpool Post* of November 14 reported a further salvo from Derby:

Replying to Lord Birkenhead's criticism of his action Lord Derby declared:

In a speech I made before the present Government was formed and indeed when the crisis was at its height, I made an appeal that even if there was not to be a Coalition there should be co-operation, and asked my Unionist friends to support National Liberals in those places where the Unionist party agreed to such candidates. Lord Birkenhead has fallen foul of me in this matter. Any teacher in an infant elementary school will be able to explain to him that appealing to Conservatives to support National Liberals who are supporters of Mr. Lloyd George is not the same thing as asking National Liberals to support Conservatives in order that these might support Lord Derby. With all his intelligence I think he might still learn something from an elementary school teacher.

In the course of the election, Birkenhead attacked Younger for the excessive authority which he sought to exercise over the Party. 'I have never been among the number of those', he told a meeting, 'who when the storm rages high and the captain would naturally be at his post on the bridge, would offer any special inducement to the cabin-boy to seize the helm.' The phrase stuck. Derby hastened to console his fellow-victim:

Lord Derby to Sir George Younger

Confidential 13 November 1922

I congratulate you on F. E. attacking you. It will probably have the same result that it had here when he attacked me which is that he has not been allowed to speak in a single Lancashire Constituency, and even in those places where he was booked to appear they have asked him to cancel the engagement.

I have been going about a good bit and on the whole am fairly satisfied, though I cannot help thinking too much hope rests on the result of the Municipal Elections. People forget that many of the young men who have no votes in Municipal Elections have got them at the Parliamentary Elections and that is the Class that the Labour candidate is getting rather a hold on. . . .

Writing to Fraser, the chief Tory agent, two days later, Derby offered an estimate of the Party's prospects in Lancashire:

Lord Derby to Sir Malcolm Fraser

Private 15 November 1922

. . . I have been to a good many meetings, some big, some small, and have been very attentively listened to, but I am not quite happy about the state of affairs in Lancashire, and I think myself that the Wee Frees [the Asquith Liberals] have done us a lot of harm. I expect we shall lose Leslie Scott's seat in Liverpool. He might just scrape in, but it is doubtful. We shall lose two in Manchester. I am doubtful about Oldham and Bolton, though it is just possible at both places we might scrape in; but in both these places the Wee Frees have done us a lot of harm. We shall, I think, lose Accrington, Darwen and Rossendale. Royton, they seem to think, is safe, and they have some hopes of winning Leigh and Clitheroe; I do not myself think we shall do so. On the other hand, I think we shall certainly win Ormskirk, and they have very strong hopes of being able to beat Henderson in Widnes, and Clynes. Personally, however, I think that Labour will come back with about 7 seats stronger in Lancashire than they were. I am foolish to prophesy because by the time you get this you will know whether I am right or wrong, but I thought you would be interested to know what my opinion was.

* * *

In the course of the election, Derby had some correspondence with Lord Beaverbrook about the form in which his speeches were being reported in the Beaverbrook Press:

Lord Derby to Lord Beaverbrook

1 November 1922

I thought you were quite right that something ought to be said about Turkey at the earliest possible moment and I have arranged to speak at the Bolton Central Conservative Club. It will only of course be a small meeting but still for press purposes it will be all right. It is on Saturday next the 4th at 1.15. You were good enough to say you would arrange for me to be reported in the Sunday papers.

Do you mind my again referring to the article about Salvidge? He really has done so splendidly in the Municipal Elections and is working so thoroughly loyally for Bonar Law that I do wish you could see your way to putting something in the *Express* that is nice about him. The article in the *Daily Express* was printed and circulated as a leaflet in the Municipal Election and there is no doubt it did him a certain amount of harm and I am so afraid of its being repeated again at the Election. We are having a hardish fight here but I think things are going well and even Liberals are talking of a Conservative majority over all others combined.

In the course of his Bolton speech on November 4, Derby carried out his undertaking to Beaverbrook to speak about Turkey. *The Times* reported him as follows:

Explaining why he found himself opposed to the Coalition government, Lord Derby said that for a long time he had had divergent views from them and these came to a head by their conduct of their Near Eastern policy. He was not going to quarrel with what they did when they were on the edge of the precipice, but with what they did in bringing the country to this dangerous point. They might claim credit for what they did in this last moment, but they were entitled to no credit for the policy they adopted before we were brought to the edge of the precipice. We were on the brink of war, and, while he wished to see our colonies going with us, he desired to see them in agreement with our policy and not brought in by an appeal at the last moment. He read that appeal to the colonies as little less than a declaration of war on Turkey, a war in which they would have had none of the support of the country which they thought they would get.

The policy of the late Government with regard to Turkey had been tragic from the beginning. Lord Kitchener once told him that it was his wish to be a Peace Commissioner at the end of the war, his reason being that there should be no more cases like that of Alsace-Lorraine because to tear from a country provinces that that country believed to be her own was the way to sow seeds for future warfare. Surely in the Treaty of Sèvres were the seeds of future warfare.

He deprecated Mr. Lloyd George's speech at Manchester. The ex-Premier was like the Irishman in a quarrel who punched the heads of friend and foe alike. Mr. Lloyd George was hitting heads all round, and one of these was Turkey's. It was like shaking hands with a person with your right hand and boxing him over the ears with your left. This was not the way to ensure confidence and impartiality in the treatment of outstanding questions. 'This was the final blow', said Lord Derby. 'I could see that there could be no possible confidence between the Turkish Government, with whom we have to make peace and us. Peace terms have to be laid down and adhered to, but they will be discussed by Turkey with a Government in whose integrity they can thoroughly rely.

Meanwhile Beaverbrook hastened to exploit the doubts which Derby had expressed at Bolton about the Near Eastern policy of the Coalition Government. A day ahead of *The Times*, Beaverbrook's infant *Sunday Express*, under the headlines:

THE WHOLE TRUTH. LORD DERBY'S GRAVE CHARGE. CABINET THAT LOADED THE DICE. SECRETS OF THE WAR CLOUD REVEALED. PUBLISH THE FACTS!

interpreted the speech as Lord Derby's indictment of Mr. Lloyd George and his Government as 'war-makers'. Evidently the epithet 'war-monger' was not yet in current parlance. Derby was greatly angered that while the *Sunday Express* reported only a few selective lines of his speech they had put misleading headlines to the story. He complained to Beaverbrook who replied obliquely on November 6, complimenting Derby on his speech and adding:

You have done more for the campaign than anyone else. I note what you say about Salvidge. I am not concerned with him, but I feel that I ought to do everything I can to co-operate with you in your fine work for the Conservative Party. I do hope you will let me know when you are going to speak again so that I can arrange for the *Express* to deal with your utterances properly.

This General Election was one of the most bitter ever fought in Britain. Many wartime friendships were ruptured and the animosities inevitably engendered when old political associations are sundered were sharpened by Beaverbrook's personal tactics. Informal arrangements had been made between the chief agent of the Unionist Central Office, Sir Malcolm Fraser, and Mr. Cope, the organiser of the Lloyd George Liberals, to avoid wherever possible running candidates against each other's leading figures. In a letter already quoted Younger explained this:

Sir George Younger to Lord Derby

3 November 1922 Unionist Central Office

. . . We have countenanced no attacks whatever upon Liberal Coalition seats. We were, of course, obliged and indeed had no other alternative in the circumstances but to leave the constituencies perfect freedom to put up a candidate where they were determined to do so, but we have influenced a very large number of withdrawals, and we are supporting officially quite the majority of independent Liberals. If their threat to fight in many of our seats matures to any serious extent, they will run the very great risk of having the whole of our organisations withdraw their assistance and support from the candidates whom they have up till now accepted. I have warned the new Organiser, Mr. Cope, this morning that anything of that kind would be quite fatal to their chances. In many of those cases our people would probably switch on to the Wee Free and in others abstain altogether, so that I think we have stopped effectually any very serious inroad upon our own seats. I have used my own personal influence in a considerable number of cases, one being that of Lloyd George's own son . . .

Beaverbrook attacked these arrangements violently in the *Sunday Express*. Moreover he personally financed a number of independent Tory candidates against leading Liberal Coalitionists, or 'Coalies' as Asquith and the Wee Free Liberals called them. In East Dorset the Beaverbrook nominee, Mr. Hall Caine, son of the famous Manx novelist, was actually elected and the National Liberal Chief Whip,

Captain F. E. Guest, was defeated. Elsewhere these Beaverbrook candidates were less successful but in a number of seats they succeeded in splitting the anti-Socialist vote, notably in Dundee, where Mr. Winston Churchill went down to defeat. These tactics employed by the new Conservative leader's closest friend were naturally regarded by the Lloyd George Liberals as a breach of faith and the Unionist Central Office was greatly embarrassed by the whole affair.

Sir George Younger to Lord Derby

6 November 1922 Unionist Central Office

. . . Things are promising very well, and if you happened to see yesterday's *Sunday Express* with its poisonous leading article, do not be at all disturbed. As a matter of fact, this Office has done extraordinarily well, and instead of having showered upon us a considerable number of N.L. candidates at the last moment, I was able to put a revolver at Mr. Cope's head, and they were compelled to withdraw a considerable number who had already been put up against some of the new Ministers. To save their faces Fraser said nothing about half a dozen whom they put up in a few places, where we had really no chance of winning the seat. I am sorry for Fraser as he is the person pointed out in the letter, and solely because the other day he most properly told Beaverbrook he would stand no interference from him, and would take no instructions or orders from him. This is his retaliation. Just the kind of thing you would have expected him to do, and I do not doubt that Fraser will be even with him in the end, and that when all this electioneering is over he will probably get it in the neck.

Beaverbrook's compliments and assurances do not seem to have proved an effective emollient to Derby's irritation.

Lord Derby to Sir George Younger

Confidential 7 November 1922

. . . Beaverbrook is going to be a great trouble. I had spoken about the Turkish matter which I feel strongly about, but he leaves out my speech in the *Sunday Express* and only puts in abominable headlines. If Bonar Law is not careful Beaverbrook will pull him down. He is calling for papers which if they are produced will only show what I said in my speech that when the crisis arrived the late Government acted well. What I complain of is their policy during the last two years and that I think is quite a subject for attack. . . .

It appears that on reflection Derby thought that more was to be gained by taking advantage of Beaverbrook's offer of more accurate reports of his future speeches than by pursuing his grievance about the bad reporting of his previous one; for he replied to Beaverbrook:

Lord Derby to Lord Beaverbrook

9 November 1922

Thanks for your letter. You ask when I speak again. Apart from to-night, when I speak at the Mansion House on behalf of the Army, and where I strike a note of warning against too great a reduction in the Army until things are more settled, I have many speeches to make, but only one, I think, which I would call an important speech which is at Accrington tomorrow. I am not quite sure what subject I am going to deal with, but it may be I shall deal with the relationship with France; a note about Reparations and a warning to the French to behave loyally to us. They have been pretty highly tried, but at the same time they have not behaved quite straight over this eastern question.

Lord Derby and his son Lord Stanley both relied on a more effective form of political propaganda than attacks upon the record of the Coalition Government. There was racing at Liverpool during the election, and both father and son tipped their horses wherever they spoke.

As a rule [commented the *Liverpool Courier* on November 11] it is a bad policy for any one to give a public tip, and when Torlonia and Indelible failed on Wednesday it looked as though Lord Derby had raised a hornets' nest around him. However, the success of two of his runners on Thursday did much good, while another double yesterday sent all away smiling.

The winners on the Thursday were Burnt Sienna (8–1) and High-brow (9–4). On the Friday the Stanley House winners were Sierra

Leone (3–1) and Selene which, after a false start, won the Liverpool Cup by two lengths at 9–2. The Stanley horses were in great form at this time, and a week later, by which time Mr. Bonar Law had been returned with a comfortable majority, Lord Derby had another double event at Hurst Park when Selene (5–4) won the Hampton Court Stakes and Pharos (11–4) won the Hurst Park Great Two-year-old Stakes.

Polling took place on November 15 and the following day it was clear that Bonar Law had secured a working majority for his Government. Three hundred and forty-six Conservatives were returned in all; and of Bonar Law's Cabinet only Griffith-Boscawen was defeated. The Labour Party returned 138 members as compared with 59 in the 1918 election. Mr. Asquith's Liberals improved their position winning 60 seats as compared with 26 in 1918; while the strength of Lloyd George's National Liberals fell from 136 to 57. Of those who lost their seats, Mr. Winston Churchill was the most prominent.

An interesting aspect of the campaign had been the ambivalent attitude of Mr. Asquith's Liberals towards Mr. Bonar Law. Although traditionally hostile to the Conservative Party they, nevertheless, welcomed its action in breaking up the Coalition and ending Mr. Lloyd George's tenure of power. Their bitterness towards the National Liberals is well illustrated in two letters which Mrs. Asquith wrote to Bonar Law shortly after the Carlton Club meeting, and which are quoted in Mr. Blake's *Unknown Prime Minister*.

> Sir George Younger deserves every word of praise, and this from *every one* of us, from the lowest to the highest. . . .
>
> You will find no lack of generosity in my husband if and when he has to criticise and *all* of us wish you God speed.

And again:

> Don't believe a word about Reunion. Never was a greater lie. We would rather be out for *ever*. Smashing the sham of the Coalition was the right thing to do. Be firm and poke fun at these warriors.

And after the results were known Asquith according to 'H. H. A.' (*Letters from Lord Oxford to a Friend*) wrote:

Mr. Asquith to a Friend

17 November 1922

The general result does not greatly surprise me. The suicide of the Coalition before the election took much of the punch out of the fight, and left the country divided between Tranquillity and Socialism. It will be interesting to see how the thing develops. For the moment the thing that gives me the most satisfaction is to gloat over the corpses which have been left on the battlefield, Winston, Hamar Greenwood, Freddie Guest, Montagu, Kellaway—all of them renegades—and among the lesser fry Harry McLaren. I am terribly disappointed at the loss of Donald Maclean and Geoffrey Howard. They are both most difficult to replace.

Making all allowances for Asquith's bitterness, the word renegade was somewhat inapposite to apply, at least in the case of Churchill. Asquith, perhaps willynilly, had dismissed him from the Admiralty. Churchill had played no part in the Lloyd George-Beaverbrook-Carson plot to pull Asquith down; and it was not until 1917 that he entered the Lloyd George Government. However, these extracts from the letters of Mr. and Mrs. Asquith seem worth recording since they express in large measure the corroding hatreds which suffused and gnawed at the Liberal Party even in the case of the high-minded Asquiths, and which were responsible more than anything else for the decay of that Party as an instrument of Government or even of useful political activity.

Derby summed up the election results in a letter to Salvidge:

Lord Derby to Sir Archibald Salvidge

17 November 1922

I must write you one line to supplement my telegram of congratulation. The result in Liverpool is perfectly splendid, as indeed the result generally in Lancashire. Of course I am terribly upset at my brother being beaten at Preston, but apparently the Liberal went on the platform on the last night, threw over Asquith and stood as a second Labour candidate. The consequence is he got all the Liberal plus the Labour votes. It was a dirty trick to do, but still I suppose in an election one must expect such a thing. Bootle was a tremendous surprise to me. Did you ever know the seat was in danger? I never knew for one moment there was any doubt about it. I wish you would let me know if you have heard anything about the cause of the defeat. Also what sort of man it is who has got in. He was a Territorial Officer and I have a sort of idea I have heard he is a very good fellow.

The whole result is certainly very satisfactory. Bonar Law has got a working majority in addition to which you may be perfectly certain that the National Liberals and the other Liberals will never vote in the same lobby so they will either vote with us or abstain, so really the majority is bigger than it looks and I hope we shall be able to do something.

I am sorry in some ways that Winston was beaten. He is a plucky fighter and he was fighting under great disabilities.

Lloyd George certainly played the game and there was a significant absence of Limehouse, which indeed seems to have been reserved for Birkenhead. Everybody agrees that he has done for himself. Of course with so clever a man as he is 'never' is a long word, but I do not believe the Conservatives will ever really trust him again. . . .

The next day Derby reported to the King:

Memorandum from Lord Derby to the King[1]

18 November 1922

. . . On the whole we had a very successful Election in Lancashire, although I personally am very much upset by my brother's defeat in Preston. That came about in an extraordinary way. The Liberal, Hodge, after he had actually had Asquith down to speak for him, on the Saturday night went on the Labour Candidate's platform, threw over Asquith and said that he had definitely joined the Labour Party and would support the entire Labour programme. That, of course, sealed my brother's fate, as he got all the Liberal votes as well as the second vote of Labour. It is a seat that would be won back at a By-Election, but I feel confident would never be held at a General Election. . . .

[1] Royal Archives.

I was more than satisfied with Manchester, where I had expected to lose two seats, but I had to rather take the bull by the horns and declare myself, as I have always been, a Free Trader. If by any chance there is ever a Tariff Reform programme put forward, Labour or a Free Trade party would sweep Lancashire. It is essentially a Free Trade County.

I had appealed before the Election to Conservatives to vote for National Liberals. For making this appeal I was the subject of a gratuitous attack by Birkenhead. Why, Heaven only knows. He chose to think that, as he put it himself, although I was appealing to the Unionists to support National Liberals what I really meant was that I was appealing to National Liberals to support Conservatives and get Lloyd George out. As a matter of fact his attack did me personally a tremendous lot of good. His own brother was not adopted for Liverpool until he had publicly disassociated himself from Birkenhead's statement.

Birkenhead's engagements to speak in Lancashire were cancelled. We did not run a single Unionist against a National Liberal. I went on the Platform in both cases where Conservatives and National Liberals were standing together and that my advice was taken in Lancashire is proved by the fact that every single National Liberal who was standing got in. . . .

Birkenhead was plainly disturbed at the consequences of his unprovoked and thoughtless attack on Derby. He sent emissaries to seek an accommodation.

Diary

Tuesday 21 November 1922

When I got home in the evening I found a message from Chilcott asking me if I could see him. He came and was evidently the bearer of a message from F. E. though he did not give it direct. He said F. E. admitted that he was entirely wrong in what he said. He had been told so by everybody including Lloyd George and he was very anxious to make peace. I told him I was quite ready to meet him and would withdraw what I said of him if he made the first step and apologised for what he had said. He seemed to think it was perfectly possible that this could be done. He then told me that F. E. had no idea of what the feeling was against him in Lancashire but that Salvidge had been to see him and also his brother Harold and Chilcott himself and it was a fearful blow to him to find out what the feeling was. Apparently

Salvidge had told him his portrait which was being painted for the Conservative Club at Liverpool would certainly not be hung in that Club. I also received a message from Winston saying he would like to see me. I presume on the same subject as I had had a talk to him about it.

Wednesday 22 November 1922

Went to see Winston who is trying to arrange an exchange of letters between me and Birkenhead to terminate our quarrel, but I do not know whether he will succeed as I certainly will not be the first to apologise. I think we may be able to do it by means of a letter from me to Winston in the first instance.

On November 23 Austen Chamberlain came to luncheon at Derby House:

Thursday 23 November 1922

. . . We then talked first of all of the quarrel with Birkenhead in which he said he entirely agreed with me that Birkenhead made a blunder in the first instance. He thought that I had been perhaps rather harder in what I said than he would have been but he quite agreed that the circumstances I told him about justified me being very angry. He said he thought there was no doubt the matter would be decided in a friendly way.

The *Manchester Guardian* of 3 March 1923, under the headlines:

LORD DERBY AND LORD BIRKENHEAD
The hatchet publicly buried.
Mutual friend as Mediator,

recorded:

Lord Derby, Secretary for War, presiding tonight over a Conservative meeting in the St. George's Hall, referred to the 'tremendous Conservative victory at the general election'. There was one particular incident arising out of it, he went on to say, which he was glad to think could now be forgotten. He and Lord Birkenhead at that time had a rather sharp and acrimonious controversy. 'I want to tell you', Lord Derby went on, 'on this, the first occasion where, addressing a political audience, I should wish to say it, that, thanks to the mediation of a friend, he and I have shaken hands.'

The friend was Mr. Winston Churchill.

Mr. Winston Churchill to Lord Derby

Private 29 November 1922

MY DEAR EDDIE,

F. E. added himself the last sentence in order to make his answer more cordial. I hope now we may take this matter as settled and that you and he will resume your old relations without delay.

All good wishes.

Yours very sincerely,
WINSTON.

Lord Birkenhead to Lord Derby

26 November 1922

MY DEAR DERBY,

I had no intention whatever of imputing personal bad faith to you but only of pointing out the unfair position in which National Liberals were being placed. I can quite see, however, on re-reading my remarks that you might easily have thought that the argument was intended to apply in a personal and invidious sense to yourself, which you naturally resented. I did not receive any message from you through any channel before you made your speech, otherwise I would have hastened to reassure you in this sense and make immediate public reference to the matter.

I trust that with this letter you will consider closed an incident which I am sure we both regret, interfering as it has done with a friendship which has lasted for twenty-five years and which I have greatly valued.

Yours sincerely,
BIRKENHEAD.

This adroitly ungenerous communication, which can hardly be called an apology or even a withdrawal, sufficed to end this unfortunate dispute in which Derby was certainly the injured though victorious party.

XXII

Back at the War Office

THOUGH, as we have seen, Derby would have preferred some office without portfolio, such as Lord President of the Council or Lord Privy Seal, he was genuinely glad to be back at the War Office, where he had served as Financial Secretary at the end of the Boer War and also as Under Secretary and Secretary of State during the Great War. His appointment was in a sense a vindication of his earlier term of office. His seals had been snatched peremptorily from him by Lloyd George in March 1918, and though any mortification he might have felt was assuaged by his appointment to the Paris Embassy, he was sufficiently shrewd to know that at any rate in Lloyd George's eyes he had been found wanting. That Bonar Law, who had had ample opportunity during the war of judging the quality and character of Derby's work at the War Office, should now wish to restore him to his former post must have been to him a matter of considerable satisfaction. As he had judged, it was thought unsuitable that his brother George should remain as his Financial Secretary. He was found a satisfactory billet at the Home Office.

Derby had for many years been one of King George's most intimate friends. Now that he was once more a Minister, he resumed his habit of keeping the King informed about the work of the War Office, knowing as he did the keen interest the King took in the armed forces. Within a few days of returning to the War Office, he reported his first impressions:

Lord Derby to the King[1]

28 October 1922

I came here on Thursday to find myself working with many of the old civilians with whom I have been here not only in 1916–1918 but also some who were with me when I was Financial Secretary in 1900,[2] and of course amongst the heads of the Military department there is not one that I do not know intimately. Fatty Cavan is my oldest friend. We joined the same Battalion within a few weeks of each other. It is therefore very pleasant indeed to resume relations with them. ... I think, however, it is quite possible that, in safeguarding the natural interests of those who are already in the Army, there may be and should be some reduction in the amount of pay given to new entrants, both officers and men. The present scale was rather hurriedly determined on at a moment when it was difficult to get men at all and when the price of living was very high. All other salaries are coming down as the price of living comes down, and I really see no reason why the Army, and of course the Navy, should not do the same. At the present moment a Corporal gets with meal and malt more pay than I did when I joined as a Subaltern, which I admit is now many years ago. . . .

* * *

At the height of the election campaign Derby found time to reply to a letter of congratulation from Lord Midleton who, as St. John Brodrick, had been his chief at the War Office during the first three years of the century:

Lord Derby to Lord Midleton

Private 3 November 1922

I know you will forgive me sending you a dictated letter in answer to your very kind one. What with preparing speeches and making them one's time is very fully occupied. It was very nice of my old chief to write me the letter he has done and I am very much touched by it. Going back to the old Office reconciles me to a great extent for that loss of independence which one enjoyed outside a Government, and when I went there the other day, I really felt—seeing all the old

[1] Royal Archives.

[2] Notably Sir Herbert Creedy, who joined the War Office in 1901.

faces with whom I worked so much during the war—as if I had only just come back from a long leave. . . .

The first matter which awaited Derby's attention at the War Office and which called for immediate action arose from the failure, a few days before, of McGrigor & Co., a small firm of army agents which afforded banking and other facilities to the Army. Many Army officers, both serving and retired, received their pay and allowances through McGrigor's. Though the Government had no legal liability in the matter, it was obvious that some action was necessary to avoid widespread hardship. Derby acted with his usual energy and promptness, and took an early opportunity of informing the King of the situation:

Lord Derby to the King[1]

28 October 1922

The failure of McGrigor's Bank has quite naturally caused much distress amongst those officers and retired officers and pensioners who kept their money there. Morally I feel the Government is responsible, but I don't want this responsibility to go too far, and I do not think it should be extended to the accounts of those who neither have been serving soldiers or in receipt of either pensions or retired pay, but who chose to continue their banking account there. For the moment, at all events, it is impossible to make any definite proposals, but I arranged at once that both retired pay and pensions should be put on the same footing as the ordinary pay of the serving soldier, and that a month's pay should be advanced. That should enable us to help those in the greatest distress and give us time to investigate individual accounts. I am afraid that the Bank will not be able to pay more than 5/– in the pound. I have had a talk on the subject with both Mr. Bonar Law and the Chancellor of the Exchequer, and I am glad to say they are both extremely sympathetic in the matter.

The King commented in the margin—'Some help ought to be given'. Three weeks later Derby had settled this business and he wrote to the King:

[1] Royal Archives.

Lord Derby to the King[1]

8 November 1922

I had an interview with certain representatives of the sufferers. I had expected rather a nasty one, but on the contrary they acknowledged one had been very sympathetic and had done one's best and were very grateful. . . .

We accept no legal responsibility whatsoever, and only a moral responsibility with regard to those cases where it can be shown that the account at McGrigor's was opened owing to Army payments. We exclude altogether any idea of assistance to civilians who banked at McGrigor's. . . . It is hoped that the assets of the Bank will amount to certainly 5/– and probably 6/– in the Pound. We have divided all the depositors into categories, i.e., Serving Soldiers, Retired Pay, Widows with Pensions, etc. To all of these we shall be able to make an addition of 10/– in the Pound. There is one class in which it is said that there is some sort of connection, without being a very definite one, between the Depositor and the Army, and we are asking the Chancellor to let us set up a small Committee to deal with hard cases under this Category. The amount we have asked for and which the Chancellor is prepared to give is £290,000 for the 10/– rate that I mentioned above, and £30,000 to deal with the hard cases. The result probably will be that those people for whom we can be said to have had a moral responsibility will get 16/– in the Pound, and gathering from what the deputation said the other day to me, they really were not prepared for greater assistance from the Government than 5/– in the Pound which with the 6/– would only have made eleven. I hope, therefore, that we shall get the credit of having very generously assisted the sufferers. . . .

* * *

British Sovereigns are the fountain of honour, and they have always concerned themselves with everything affecting decorations and awards. King George V maintained a particular punctilio in such matters as can be seen from the letter which Stamfordham wrote to Derby at this time:

[1] Royal Archives.

Lord Stamfordham to Lord Derby[1]

31 October 1922

. . . There is a question which I know is coming to you from the Foreign Office and that is about a British Decoration for the Belgian 'Unknown Warrior' who is to be buried in Brussels on Armistice Day. The King is strongly opposed to the Victoria Cross being given: unfortunately a precedent was created by the V.C. being conferred, much against His Majesty's wishes, on the American 'Unknown Warrior', but on the other hand no similar favour was granted, or indeed asked for, by the French. The Military Cross would be quite sufficient for the Belgians. I talked to Curzon last evening about it and he quite agreed with the King.

* * *

No one among the Tory leaders was more distressed than Derby at the disagreeable quarrel which had opened between the leaders of the Tory Party, so many of whom were his friends. Chamberlain and Birkenhead had been his friends and associates for many years and within a week of the results of the Election being known we find Derby exploring the possibilities of reconciliation:

Diary

Thursday 23 November 1922

Austen Chamberlain came to luncheon. Had a long talk with him upon all matters connected with the present split. He was delightfully frank and transparently honest. . . . He told me something which was quite new to me of course and which very much explains his attitude. He knew that if Bonar Law came to the Carlton Meeting it was to oppose him, and therefore he was perfectly determined to make a speech which would bring the matter to a direct vote which should be decisive either one way or the other. He therefore refused to wait for the National Union Meeting because he felt then if such a meeting were held there would have to be a discussion and a fight between the members of the Conservative Party and whichever was the beaten party would secede from the Conservative Party and the result would be a complete break up whereas in the Carlton it was quite possible to

[1] Royal Archives.

have an adverse vote and still for all to remain friends. I told him that I did not quite agree with him, but I did see the point he made that it would be very undignified to have had a fight between members of the same Cabinet and who were still members of the same Cabinet.

We then talked about his coming back into office. I think he is perfectly prepared for Worthington-Evans and others to return, but as far as he himself is concerned there is a feeling that Bonar Law behaved badly to him and that he could not serve under him. He put it to me in this way: 'First of all I helped to make him Leader of our Party. When the fight came between me and Walter Long I do not know which would have won—I think I should have done, but it was obviously to the disadvantage of the Party that there should be any fight. I therefore suggested through a third person Crawford, or Balcarres as he was then, that if Walter [Long] would propose Bonar I would second him and we should get a unanimous vote. This was agreed to with the result that is known. To have then Bonar come out against me made me feel bitter and, moreover, I realised that if his health had not prevented him from staying in office, and he had been where I was he would have taken precisely the same course that I did.'

I must say I feel there is a great deal in what he says. We then proceeded to talk about Curzon and there is where the whole bitterness lies. There is no doubt Curzon did promise to go with them. Curzon had some legitimate grievances with regard to Lloyd George, but he never would bring them to a head in the Cabinet when Austen and others would have supported him. There is no doubt that he promised at a dinner at Winston Churchill's to go with them and it was only at the last moment that he turned. He never had a real Foreign Policy. He used to put forward suggestions tentatively and then if overridden by L. G. he used to give way.

The conclusion I came to after our talk, which was most friendly in every way, was:

(1) As far as I personally was concerned he thought I should have been wrong after what I had said to him and others not to have joined the Government. That I had made my position perfectly clear and that he had not a word to say against me.

(2) That he wants to see a reconciliation between the two wings of the Conservative Party and as far as possible with some of the Lloyd George Liberals. He told me incidentally that quite apart from Winston whom I knew was much more to the right than to the left, that that

opinion was shared by both Macnamara and Kellaway, but that Mond whom I also thought leaned that way was very much to the contrary and had been trying to make Lloyd George bitter.

(3) That he would not serve under Bonar Law but that in the event of B. L. retiring he would be perfectly ready to come back, even if not as P.M. at all events into the Cabinet.

The most clamant of the matters awaiting the attention of the new Administration was the passage into law of the Irish Free State Bill. Under the terms of the Irish Treaty the Bill had to be put on the Statute Book by December 6, which was exactly three weeks after Polling Day. Derby's task was to organise the evacuation of British troops and supplies from the newly created Free State. A solution had to be found to the problem of what to do with those Irish soldiers who had now become under the treaty citizens of the Free State and who were serving prison sentences for offences during the troubles. A particular problem arose over those who had been sentenced to long terms of imprisonment for mutiny. In reply to a letter of good wishes which Derby had written to his old friend, Tim Healy, the newly appointed Governor General of the Irish Free State, came a whimsical communication suggesting a solution to this problem:

Mr. Tim Healy to Lord Derby

22 December 1922 — Vice-Regal Lodge, Dublin

How handsomely those who are native and to the manner born can write! If I could catch that accent, there should be penned a sweet reply. Still you will take in no bad part even uncouth words suddenly springing up at an unexpected stroke of friendliness. For Heaven knows you have had enough to engage you since your return from France, without thinking of me. Well you have so thought, and in such wise that I am greatly moved, nor am I ashamed to avow it. I wish you, too, peace in your great office. I felt the Turkish cloud hang very heavily. I rejoiced that you were able to strengthen your Forces by men from here, and that they left with such acclaim, that not an Irregular dared to fire a popgun to disturb the send-off. The Station Master at Warrington told me on Tuesday of the delight of the Lancashire lads, home on leave, at Dublin's demonstration of affection. If General Macready could seize the occasion to plead for the release of the few English soldiers still held for Irish offences, and of the Connaught Rangers, what a happy Xmas he would bring to many homes, were clemency accorded. What is wanted here now is more diplomatic than anything else. A few wildcats must be caged, but the soldiers about me treat with contempt their expiring scratches. It is painful to punish one's own, for political misdeeds, but I seem to sense more jealousy than principle in their affected fanaticism. A happy Xmas.

Derby was quick to profit by this suggestion, and just before Christmas wrote to the King recommending that he should exercise his prerogative of mercy:

Lord Derby to the King[1]

24 December 1922

. . . There is one other very serious difficulty—the bill for the indemnity for soldiers for any action they may have taken in the past trouble is coming before the Free State Parliament. Mr. Cosgrave is thus honouring the undertaking which was given by Michael Collins. He has written to the Prime Minister to say that though he hoped it would have been non-controversial he is afraid there will be a good bit of trouble over the prisoners of the Connaught Rangers, who, His Majesty will remember, were sentenced to long terms of imprisonment for mutiny, and he asked the Prime Minister to liberate them. I had a long talk with the Prime Minister on the subject. It is a very difficult matter as there is no doubt political expediency clashes with military discipline. As regards the military expediency there is this to be said: the Connaught Rangers no longer exist. The men now under sentence are undoubtedly citizens of the Free State Government, and if one takes as a precedent the similar trouble that occurred at Calais when the men from the Canadian troops were sentenced to long terms of imprisonment, but who on the conclusion of the war were handed back to the Canadian Government to deal with and were immediately released, the balance appears to be in favour of releasing these men, as an act of grace and an instance of His Majesty's clemency. The members of the Army Council are undoubtedly against such a proceeding, but taking upon myself full responsibility I have overridden them, and informed

[1] Royal Archives.

Mr. Bonar Law that if he thinks it absolutely necessary to release these men I should be prepared to agree. I admit I hate doing so, but still I feel that under the circumstances—thank goodness we do not have an Irish Free State created every day—it is right we should do so. I have therefore made it quite clear to the Military members that if these men are released it would be said to be done by His Majesty as an act of clemency on the advice of the Government, and that they will be absolved from all responsibility I being prepared to accept that and to bear it upon my own shoulders. Though I feel His Majesty will dislike the decision as much as I do I hope that under the circumstances His Majesty will approve of my action.

In April of the new year Derby paid a visit to Ulster to inspect the Police Forces, and the success of his visit clearly gave heart to the new Ulster Government and a sense of solidarity with the rest of the United Kingdom:

Sir James Craig to Lord Derby

Prime Minister's Residence.
12 April 1923 Belfast

I cannot call to mind any visit to Ulster by a British Statesman that has given such general satisfaction as your tour round the Border, and I tender on behalf of this Government and of the People, our grateful thanks for your sacrifice in coming over and for your kindness and encouragement while here.

You have, at a stroke, greatly strengthened the ties with and the confidence in the British Government which it is my constant endeavour to foster: and further you have established a firm bond between Ulster and Lancashire and that may have far reaching and satisfactory consequences.

Thank you again and again for a bold stroke.

Unlike the generality of Cabinet Ministers during the last twenty years, Derby did not in any way restrict his field of interest and responsibility to his own department. He rightly felt that as a member of the Cabinet he was responsible to Crown and Parliament for all the decisions of the Government, and when he was disturbed about any issue he seldom hesitated to say so. His successful Embassy in Paris had given him a special interest in Anglo-French relations, and though he was sometimes irritated by some aspects of French policy, he always strove to maintain the *entente* and, as we have seen, to transform it into an alliance. There were two vexatious problems which threatened to disturb Anglo-French relations at this time. First, making peace in the Near East between Greece and Turkey, and second, the dispute between Germany and the Allies about the payment of reparations as laid down in the Treaty of Versailles.

The Foreign Secretary, Lord Curzon, had left London two days after the General Election for Lausanne, to attend a conference of the Allied Powers to settle the terms of peace with Turkey. The terms hammered out at Lausanne were subsequently incorporated in the Treaty of Sèvres. Not only did Derby have his old-fashioned view about the responsibility of Cabinet Ministers for the whole policy of the Government, he had an independent view of his own about foreign policy both in regard to France and in regard to the Near East. He was also quite ready to fall foul of Curzon for whom, partly despite and, perhaps, partly because of his glittering intellectual equipment, he had a profound contempt.

Little direct evidence is available as to Curzon's true feelings about Derby. It seems that jealousy was the main ingredient. How could a man of such inferior parts have become almost his equal in the Cabinet? And by what authority did he presume to call in question the conduct of the Foreign Secretary? The Curzons had been longer established at Kedleston than the Stanleys had been at Knowsley or even Lathom. It was not for nothing that one of Curzon's sisters, when showing a visitor round the tiny church at Kedleston where some twenty generations of Curzons lie buried had declared: 'No Tom, Dick or Harry is buried here—all Curzons.'

Somehow every achievement which came with such pain and difficulty to Curzon seemed to come so easily to Derby. Curzon had been to Eton and Balliol, and except for a First had won all the prizes. Derby had been to Wellington and Sandhurst, at which the standards of scholarship were a good deal less exacting. Derby of course left without a prize. Yet Derby was everyone's best friend, while people only poked fun at Curzon. Is it presumptuous to suggest that sometimes in a mood of self-pity Curzon quoted to himself the words of the ancient prophet—'They hated me without a cause'?

Derby was everything that Curzon wished to be—not merely the bearer of an ancient and illustrious name but a man of great possessions which had come to him by right of birth; in addition a man whose geniality was the cause of geniality, not of ridicule, in others. Curzon could boast a lineage which outranged the Stanleys. His houses surpassed, if not in magnificence, at least in elegance, the houses of his rival. Against Knowsley, Crag, Stanley House, Derby House and Coworth he could set Kedleston, Hackwood, Montacute and Bodiam. But to acquire all save the first, he had twice had to marry for money as well as for love. Derby and Curzon were both magnificoes, but Derby was a genuine, sterling, copper-bottomed magnifico. And there was a slight kick in Curzon's gallop. Both men knew this.

On December 6 Curzon was stung into complaining to the Prime Minister about Derby's 'interference' in matters of foreign policy:

> The quasi-political activities of the W.O. are a perfect curse. You will remember that before I went to Paris, Derby, without ever telling the F.O., had sent over Burnett-Stuart to Paris, and he had shown a W.O. memo on the whole question of Peace with Turkey to Foch—many of the proposals being in violent disagreement with my policy. . . .
>
> Derby is particularly bad in this respect, for he fancies that he is the only man who has any influence with the French and that his mission in life is to vary attendance at Parisian race meetings with attempts to correct the blunders of the British Ambassador and Foreign Secretary.[1]

* * *

The opening of the year 1923 brought a situation which very nearly led to the fall of the Government. The Chancellor of the Exchequer, Mr. Baldwin, had gone to Washington to negotiate a settlement of Britain's war debt to the United States. On his return

[1] *The Unknown Prime Minister* by Robert Blake.

at the end of January, he announced at Southampton the terms which the Americans had proposed and added that in his opinion they were the best that could be got. This he did without any prior consultation with his colleagues. However, even those members of the Cabinet who thought that Baldwin had been out-manœuvred felt that they could not stomach the idea of the Government repudiating the word of its accredited spokesman. The Prime Minister, certainly animated from outside the Government by his friend Lord Beaverbrook, was almost alone in favour of repudiating the terms. Derby's diary tells the story as he saw it at the time:

Diary

Monday 29 January 1923

Went to see Bonar Law with reference to the Edgehill seat. After discussing the question he suddenly said he would like to talk over the American Debt question with me. I had been with him when Baldwin's first telegram came from America, and I had been in favour, on the spur of the moment, of accepting the American proposal. He, on the contrary, had been very much opposed to it. He told me that the more he thought of the matter the more he felt what an iniquitous proposal it was and it was quite impossible for us to agree. I asked him quite plainly whether he did not consider that his proposal was more or less a repudiation of the debt, and he agreed that it was but also said that there were worse things than repudiation, and that this was not an ordinary debt—in which I quite agree with him—and therefore he did not look upon repudiation of such a debt as being so iniquitous as I apparently did. He said he had really made up his mind and that he could not take the responsibility of signing. I asked him whether he would wait and hear what the Cabinet said, and he said Yes, he would, but he did not think they would shake him.

Tuesday 30 January 1923

At the Cabinet, Baldwin stated his case for acceptance of the American terms very clearly, very concisely and with a very strong recommendation that we should accept. Bonar Law then did an extraordinary thing. Instead of asking for expression by each of us of our opinions he produced the same arguments as he had used to me the day before, said his mind was quite made up and that nothing would induce him to remain the head of a Government which consented to sign. We were all aghast at this, and the Lord Chancellor [Cave] really voiced our opinions when he made in a very tactful way a remonstrance against a pistol being put to our heads. Bonar agreed that he had done this and thought it best to let us know his views, but he then proceeded to ask each one of us what we thought. With the exception of Lloyd-Greame we were absolutely unanimous in saying that we ought to accept the terms, and it looked at the moment as if there would be a break of the Government there and then, but luckily somebody—I cannot remember who—suggested that we might adjourn and meet again the next day.

Cave came to me afterwards and asked me whether I would go with one or two others to his room at the House of Lords at 12 o'c. the next day in order to discuss our position.

In the evening . . . met Victor Devonshire and we had a little talk. He was more indignant about the matter than I am, and said that he thought we had all been put in an extremely false position and it practically meant that there was not a Cabinet but a Dictator, the one thing we had complained of with regard to the last Government. I asked him what he meant to do about resigning, and he said he was very divided in his mind, and it would depend very much on what Baldwin himself did. If Baldwin stayed, he thought it might be essential for us to stay to help him, though even under these circumstances he was doubtful if he would remain and his present inclination was most certainly to resign. I told him that was very much my feeling too, and I did not see how I could remain a member of a Government which repudiated a debt. We both agreed that Bonar's attitude was most unreasonable, especially in view of the alternative that he himself put forward. The amount that we should have to pay to America under Baldwin's arrangement would be roughly £32,000,000 a year, but I asked Bonar myself what did he propose to do towards payment. His answer was that he meant to pay the £32,000,000 a year but with no definite funding. We pointed out to him that what that meant was that under the present obligation we have got to pay 5% on all borrowed money. This is to be brought down to 4% which includes a Sinking Fund, which will clear the debt in 62 years. To pay such a sum would require exactly the amount that he proposed to pay but that under his arrangement the Americans would hold us to the 5%. The consequence was that whilst under the two schemes we should pay exactly the same amount, under Baldwin's scheme we should have a debt which ended in 62 years. Under Bonar's scheme we should have a debt that would ever go on increasing, as the difference between the $3\frac{1}{2}\%$ and the 5% would simply be added to the Capital charge. Bonar's answer to that was 'a great deal may turn up in 62 years. America may see that it is to her advantage to make less Shylock terms, but if we sign this we are bound for 62 years.'

Victor Devonshire asked me whether I had noticed something which I confess I had not, and that was a letter in *The Times* signed 'Colonial', which embodied word for word and almost phrase for phrase as Victor put it, the arguments that Bonar had used at the Cabinet, and he said he had an uncomfortable feeling that Bonar might have instigated Beaverbrook to write that letter, or even perhaps have sent it himself. I can hardly credit that when I remember that it was only at the last Cabinet that Bonar put an obligation on all of us not to write letters or articles to the press.[1]

Wednesday 31 January 1923

Met in Cave's room. All the Cabinet present except the Prime Minister. Cave started giving his views which were absolutely and entirely my own, but ended up by saying that he thought it would be so fatal for Bonar to go that if we could not persuade him to the contrary he would stay on. Victor Devonshire and I took a different line, saying that if we believed it was wrong for the Country and wrong as a question of principle of National integrity we neither of us could stay in the Cabinet. It was agreed after a long discussion, in which Peel was very discursive and bored us all, that Cave, Baldwin and Victor Devonshire should see the Prime Minister. Tell him the views of the meeting which was unanimous, with the exception of Novar and Philip Lloyd-Greame—the former entirely in Bonar's favour and the latter sitting on the fence—and see if they could get him to change his mind before the Cabinet.

[1] Sir Evelyn Wrench's recently published life of Mr. Geoffrey Dawson, at this time editor of *The Times*, reveals that it was Bonar Law himself and not Beaverbrook who wrote under the pseudonym 'Colonial'. Doubtless the Prime Minister felt that the obligation which he had laid upon his colleagues did not apply to him as the King's first minister. Alternatively he may have felt that as he was using a pseudonym his lapse would not become known. There is incidentally no reference in Mr. Blake's *Unknown Prime Minister* to this curious, anonymous and propagandist activity of the Prime Minister in defiance of his own ruling.

Cabinet at 4 o'c. All over by 4.5. Bonar said he had slept on it and had come to the conclusion he was asking his colleagues to make too great a sacrifice, and although he still held the same opinion he gave way and agreed to the American proposal. A great relief to all of us.

During these first four months of Conservative Government the most vexed problem was the inability of Germany to fulfil her obligations to pay the reparations imposed under the Peace Treaty. M. Poincaré's Government insisted on its full rights, and threatened if Germany defaulted to occupy the Ruhr. A conference was held in London in December at which the Germans put forward a new offer; it was rejected by the French Prime Minister. A further conference of the Allied Prime Ministers was held in Paris early in the New Year, but no agreement was reached. On January 11 the French marched into the Ruhr. The British attitude in this dispute was one of mediation. France was our ally, and we understood her feelings. Yet our policy towards Germany was one of reconciliation; and, further, it seemed to the Government that in the long run more reparations would be secured from Germany if she were allowed to suspend payment until she had recovered more of her economic strength. The Government, therefore, had to walk on a tight-rope. No one was better fitted to lead the way than Derby. There was no firmer friend of France, nor one more trusted and admired by Frenchmen.

The British zone of occupation in the Rhineland separated the French zone from the Ruhr. Although we allowed French troop-trains to cross our zone, it was inevitable that delicate situations would arise from time to time. One such is heralded in a letter which the Prime Minister asked Derby to write to the British Ambassador in Paris, Lord Crewe:

Lord Derby to Lord Crewe

Strictly Confidential 22 January 1923

I am very much disturbed about the position at Cologne and have discussed the matter with the Prime Minister this morning. He has sent you a telegram, but it is not possible to put into such a short space some of the features of the situation as they occurred to both of us. If the French persist in taking action against German Officials and requiring their arrest in the area occupied by us, there is no doubt that a movement already growing in this country for the withdrawal of our troops will be very much strengthened and when Parliament meets, if any incident has occurred in our area which can in any way endanger the lives or, by the withdrawal of Civil authorities, the health of our men, the pressure to withdraw altogether would become, as the Prime Minister has told you in his telegram, 'almost irresistible'.

It was impossible to add in that telegram a personal feature of the case and that is that Lloyd George is almost certain to identify himself with this movement. It would be, as I say, popular with a large number of people, and he would derive support not only from his own Party but also undoubtedly from Conservatives, Liberals and the whole of the Labour Party. That would mean that we might have to withdraw our troops and at the instance of Lloyd George, thus securing a great triumph for him.

Now this I am certain is the last thing that the French Government would wish. They know that under considerable difficulties we are endeavouring to be as loyal to them as we possibly can and to do nothing to hinder what we believe to be an ill-judged venture on their part and the best way we can show our appreciation of their difficulties and our desire to help them is by maintaining our troops. To take them away and at the instance of Lloyd George, would be to make an irreparable break in the Entente. The amount of good that they can get out of the arrest of German officials in our very small area must be infinitesimal, and surely it would be possible to confine themselves to the collection of Customs on the frontier and not in any way interfering with the administration of our particular area. If they do persist in doing this, then I foretell that at no very distant date we shall be forced to take the extreme action I have mentioned.

Please forgive me for troubling you, but the Prime Minister thought it would be advisable for me to write to you privately as he naturally did not wish to put the part with regard to his predecessor into a telegram.

A few weeks later Derby was in Paris and immediately on his return he reported to the Prime Minister:

Lord Derby to Mr. Bonar Law

12 March 1923

I got back all right this afternoon from Paris having had as usual a delightful time. Saw no official people but met a Deputy or two at Dinner, but in Paris everybody is political and of course all conversation turns invariably on the Ruhr. You may remember when I was there in December I wrote to you when I got back and said I was perfectly certain that although they talked of going into the Ruhr to obtain Reparations they were really going in with the idea that it would give them safety. Now what I said then has been entirely justified. They all admit that as far as reparations are concerned they will probably get very little but they are still hoping that the possession of the Ruhr will give them safety though none of them can quite explain how that is to arise unless they remain there indefinitely and this is what a certain section are apparently clamouring for. They are quite convinced that they are very anxious that we should remain at Cologne. They feel that as long as we are there the Entente lasts and if their entry into the Ruhr is a failure that we shall be able in some way to extricate them from their difficulties. . . .

The extent to which Derby was walking a diplomatic tight-rope can be seen from a speech which he made in Liverpool on March 2:

. . . We must not wholly condemn France. The Frenchmen recalled that they have waited four years and received no reparations. They have made concession after concession, and they say England does not quite understand the psychology of the German. The longer you give him to pay the longer he will take. I will not be one of those to say to France 'You have done wrong from a moral point of view', but perhaps they have done wrong from a practical point of view of getting money, and I entirely approve of the Government's attitude of not going into the Ruhr with the French. My heart goes with the French. My head remains on the other side of the Rhine.

Before further moves towards the settlement of this dispute could be made, the fortunes of the Conservative Party, the Government and the country were all to be given a new twist.

XXIII

The Advent of Mr. Baldwin

ON 27 April 1923, the King received the Prime Minister in audience. Bonar Law told him that his health made a sea voyage imperative. He advised the King that during his absence Lord Curzon should act as deputy Prime Minister, and that Mr. Baldwin, Chancellor of the Exchequer, should lead the House of Commons.

Diary

Tuesday 1 May 1923

Dined with Locker Lampson at a Dinner given by the Empire Review. Found myself sitting next to Birkenhead who was really very nice indeed. Proposed my health. Nothing could have been more friendly. We had a long talk at Dinner and discussed future relationships. Very bitter against Curzon repeating word for word to me what Chamberlain had told me on Saturday and adding that Curzon had told him that he would be at the Carlton Meeting and fight the battle alongside him. The next thing he heard from him was the letter in which Curzon said it was wrong for a Peer to attend at all. He said he did not mean to attack the Government or any individual except Curzon but he did mean to attack him.

I then spoke to him about his article in the *Sunday Times*. He said if he was attacked he could not help hitting back and then I told him perfectly frankly that I thought he was making a great mistake, not only on his own account but also on behalf of the Party. . . . He told me Austen Chamberlain had said exactly the same thing as I was saying and that he did not mean to make any further attack at all. That he was only too anxious to see the joining up of the Party though for pecuniary reasons he was better off now with literary work, etc., than he was when Lord Chancellor. He was very bitter against Beaverbrook who he says is a real schemer and much more intimate with Bonar than we have any idea of. He says Beaverbrook has dined with him certainly twice a week and for the last 6 Saturdays to Monday Bonar has been down to stay with him. I do not myself think this is accurate as I certainly know one Saturday to Monday about 3 weeks ago when Bonar was in London—at all events on Saturday afternoon.

I asked him about serving with people in the present Cabinet. He told me he could not serve under Bonar Law nor if Bonar Law went under Stanley Baldwin, and that under no circumstances would he sit in the same Cabinet with Curzon. Except with regard to the latter there was none of the bitterness which appeared in his article.

Any possibility of Birkenhead serving under Bonar Law was soon to vanish. For, on his return from his cruise, it was found that Bonar Law was suffering from cancer of the throat and on May 20 he resigned. He was so stricken that he sent his resignation in writing. Six months later he was dead. Going away from his funeral, Asquith is said to have passed the mordant comment: 'How appropriate that we should have buried the unknown Prime Minister next to the unknown warrior.' The full irony of Asquith's epitaph was to be found in the fact that Bonar Law was to be succeeded as Prime Minister by someone even less known to the public than himself.

Bonar Law had felt so ill on his return to England that he sent word to the King through his son-in-law, Sir Frederick Sykes, who brought his letter of resignation, that he did not wish to be consulted as to his successor. The King was placed in a position of considerable constitutional difficulty, and as Bonar Law's resignation took place at the time of the Whitsun holidays, there were several days during which speculation and intrigue could sprout. Not for the first time there were many who thought that Derby might be a suitable stop-gap selection for Prime Minister. As before Derby felt little confidence in the motives and credentials of those who approached him. It seems likely also that he lacked the ambition to strike out for power, and also doubted his own ability to maintain himself happily in the first position, even if it could be obtained.

Diary

Sunday 20 May–Tuesday 22 May 1923

Philip Sassoon came to see me bringing messages from Austen Chamberlain and also from Beaverbrook, who said that he was speaking not only in his own name but in Rothermere's. This apparently was a fact, as Rothermere telegraphed to Beaverbrook to say that he was ill but that he would follow whatever Beaverbrook suggested. The purport of it was that the Austen Chamberlainites would serve under nobody except me. That if I came forward they would at once put themselves unreservedly in my hands. I told Philip that he was trying to take me into a line of country which I did not like. That while I felt myself quite unfitted for the post, I did see the great necessity of getting the Austen Chamberlainites back into the fold. That I was not prepared to serve under Curzon as I thought, brilliant as he was, he must have a restraining hand over him, but that I was prepared to serve under Stanley Baldwin. He pressed me a great deal to say that I would not do this or at all events to say that I would not serve unless Austen Chamberlain also agreed to serve. After he had gone I thought I had better write him a letter, of which unfortunately I have not kept a copy, but it was to reiterate my opinion that it was my duty to serve under Stanley Baldwin, but that I would do my very best to secure his asking Austen and Horne to serve.

Further communications passed. Locker Lampson asked to see me. I refused to see him. F. E. telegraphed to me to say that I alone could unite the Party and wished to see me. I again refused and telephoned to Stanley Jackson and got him to come and see me this morning (Tuesday), having also arranged to see Beaverbrook later.

I explained my views very fully to Jackson who was in entire agreement with me. He says that there are other members of the Cabinet, Bridgeman and Amery, who are of exactly the same way of thinking as myself. He says that he is sure at the present moment it would be a bad thing to have Curzon as Prime Minister and would split the Party and that the only Peer who would be possible would be myself, but he entirely held my view that Baldwin would be the right man.

It was agreed that if he saw Baldwin, Bridgeman and Amery he should tell them my views without saying anything with regard to the overtures from the Chamberlainites. I to do my best if the occasion arose to induce Austen and Horne to come in, and if necessary to speak at the Party Meeting and say publicly what I had said to him. . . .

He was going to see some other people today and then would communicate again with me but he fears from what he hears that the King may send for Curzon and that Curzon may promptly try and form a Government and that a lot of people who do not agree with Curzon being Prime Minister would accept.

A week later when the crisis had been resolved, more or less to the satisfaction of everyone, except Curzon, Derby met the King at dinner with Lord Farquhar.

Diary

Tuesday 29 May 1923

Dined with Horace Farquhar. After dinner the King said he wished to speak to me and told me all the circumstances with regard to the election of Baldwin as Prime Minister. He said that it had been a very trying time for him, as when Sykes came down with Bonar Law's resignation he expressly told him that Bonar was not in a condition of health to be able to give him any advice and begged that he should not be asked for it. The King therefore sent Stamfordham up to London to see anybody he could but as it was Whitsunday naturally nobody was in London and the only person he managed to see was Salisbury. Salisbury told him that the only acceptable Prime Minister to him would be Curzon and that he would strongly recommend his being sent for. Stamfordham afterwards received a message from Bridgeman who came to see him with Amery and they were both very insistent that it should be Baldwin. Stamfordham telephoned to the King at Aldershot and strongly recommended Curzon being sent for. Meanwhile the King said he had made up his mind that it must be Baldwin, so he telephoned to Stamfordham to take no further action till he got to London but to get Baldwin and Curzon to come to London. On arrival at Buckingham Palace he sent for Baldwin to see him, and sent Stamfordham to see Curzon and tell him that it was impossible for the King to send for him. I believe there was the most awful scene. Curzon took it very badly saying that under no circumstances would he consent to go on with the Government, etc.

I ought to mention that A. J. B. was also sent for to see the King and though the King did not tell me this, except that he had seen one other person of authority, A. J. B. was most emphatic in recommending that Baldwin should be sent for. This as I have since heard has come to Curzon's ear and has made him very bitter against A. J. B.

The selection of a Prime Minister is the only important part of the Royal Prerogative which a modern constitutional monarch can exercise without the advice of Ministers. This is inevitable since a vacancy in the office can only arise through death or resignation. In either case, the Sovereign at the moment of choice has no Prime Minister to give advice. Sir Harold Nicolson in his life of *King George V* writes a little misleadingly on this point: 'Moreover, the retiring Prime Minister will usually himself indicate to the King the name of his successor.' This implies that an outgoing Prime Minister has the right to tender advice as to his successor. In a footnote he adds: 'The closest analogy is the situation that arose in 1894. On the resignation of Mr. Gladstone, Queen Victoria had herself to decide between the rival claims of Lord Rosebery and Sir William Harcourt.' This again is misleading. The Queen could with perfect ease and propriety have consulted her outgoing Prime Minister, who was more than ready to offer his advice. She did not choose to do so; instead she sent for Lord Rosebery. Mr. Gladstone had been much exercised before his resignation as to whether or not the Queen would seek his guidance. He had determined, if asked, to recommend Earl Spencer.[1] It is possible that the Queen knew this, and that Mr. Gladstone was not consulted for that very reason.

The two situations, so far from being a close analogy were opposed in two important essentials. King George V had an outgoing Prime Minister whom he wished to consult but who did not wish to be consulted. Queen Victoria had an outgoing Prime Minister who was eager to give advice which she did not wish to receive. It is strange that Sir Harold should have misunderstood this situation because in his next chapter, describing the accession to office of Mr. Ramsay MacDonald and the first Labour Government, he quotes the King as saying: 'I never consulted Mr. Baldwin in any way when he came to resign, nor asked his advice as to whom to send for.'

[1] *Life of Gladstone* by Morley.

And, of course, Mr. Baldwin, like Mr. Gladstone before him, would not have thought of offering advice unless he had been asked. Other instances could be cited. When Mr. Chamberlain resigned in May 1940, King George VI sought no advice from him. He sent for Mr. Churchill on his own initiative. There is no evidence as to what happened in 1922 when Lloyd George resigned and the King sent for Bonar Law, but it seems likely that if the King had consulted Lloyd George he would have noted it in his diary. This he did not do. In a more recent instance, that of the resignation of Sir Winston Churchill and his replacement by Sir Anthony Eden, although there was a minimum of doubt as to the succession, exceptional pains were taken to underline the continuing integrity of the Royal Prerogative. Though Sir Winston resigned at 4.30 p.m. on 6 April 1955 it was not till the following morning that Sir Anthony received his summons to the Palace. This delay, which surprised many people and might have found its reflection in the newspapers had it not been for the fact that they were all strike-bound, was no accident. It was intended to mark in an emphatic way the true constitutional position. The absolute quality of the Royal Prerogative in this matter was further illustrated at the time of the resignation of Sir Anthony Eden. The Queen did not consult Sir Anthony as to his successor, nor, naturally, did he presume to volunteer advice. Instead, the Queen consulted Sir Winston Churchill and Lord Salisbury, the latter of whom had already sounded the opinions of all his available Cabinet colleagues before recommending that the Queen should entrust the formation of a new Government to Mr. Harold Macmillan.[1] Sir Winston's advice coincided with that of Lord Salisbury and, despite an ill-informed newspaper campaign in favour of Mr. R. A. Butler, Her Majesty summoned Mr. Macmillan to the Palace.

A Prime Minister who resigns is in a sense admitting the abandonment of the task with which the Sovereign has entrusted him. It would be presumption for him to volunteer advice as to his suc-

[1] Of the fifteen members of the Cabinet whom Lord Salisbury saw, only one, Mr. Patrick Buchan-Hepburn, was in favour of Mr. Butler. He was not included in the new administration but was elevated to the peerage as Lord Hailes and sent out to govern the new Federation in the Caribbean.

cessor, and he might easily lay himself open to a just rebuke if he had the hardihood to give advice at the moment he had ceased to be a Minister. At the same time it would be altogether natural for a Sovereign who felt in any doubt as to who could most readily secure a majority in the House of Commons and thus carry on the Government, to turn amongst others to the outgoing Prime Minister who, though *functus officio*, would normally be among the most eminent and experienced of those elder statesmen from whom counsel might be sought.

It will be noted that there is scarcely any discrepancy between the account of this transaction as recorded by Derby from the King's lips in 1923 and that which Sir Harold Nicolson defined thirty years later. If discrepancy there be, it is only in emphasis as to how significant was the part played by Balfour. However, Mr. Robert Blake has recently discovered among the Royal Archives and published in *The Unknown Prime Minister* a memorandum which Colonel Ronald Waterhouse, Bonar Law's private secretary, handed either to the King or to Stamfordham at Aldershot on May 20 when, accompanied at the family's suggestion by Bonar Law's son-in-law, Sir Frederick Sykes, he delivered the Prime Minister's letter of resignation. Waterhouse claimed that this document 'practically expressed' Bonar Law's real attitude in the matter. The document urged that Baldwin should be preferred to Curzon because the latter was a member of the House of Lords and also because he was 'regarded in the public eye as representing that section of privileged Conservatism which has its value but which in this democratic age cannot be too assiduously exploited'. Mr. Blake reveals that this memorandum, which was concealed by Waterhouse from Sykes, had been penned by Mr. J. C. C. Davidson after discussion with Mr. Baldwin. It seems plain that Waterhouse engaged in an intrigue which seriously misrepresented the views of the outgoing and dying Prime Minister. Sir Harold Nicolson, writing without knowledge of the Davidson memorandum, took the view that Balfour's was the decisive voice in barring Curzon from 10 Downing Street. He records that in the Royal Archives at Windsor there is a memorandum in which the King's Secretary, Lord Stamfordham, noted:

> Lord Balfour said he was speaking regardless of the individuals in question, for whereas, on one side, his opinion of Lord Curzon is based upon an intimate, life-long friendship, and the recognition of his exceptional qualifications; on the other, his knowledge of Mr. Baldwin is slight and, so far, his public career has been more or less uneventful and without any signs of special gifts or exceptional ability.

Having prefaced what he had come to say with this impeccable summary, Balfour proceeded to damage Curzon's prospects to the utmost by limiting his advice to the single point that the Prime Minister ought to be in the House of Commons.

Balfour, though suffering from phlebitis, had travelled to London from Sheringham on the Monday in order to acquaint the King with this view. On his return the next day, a friend inquired: 'Will dear George be Prime Minister?' 'No,' he replied with that bland other-worldliness of which he was such an adept, 'dear George will not be Prime Minister.' Nearly twenty years had passed since Curzon's long-drawn and pedantic dispute with Lord Kitchener, the Commander-in-Chief in India, had led to his resignation of the Viceroyalty. Balfour was at that time Prime Minister. He was an intimate friend of Curzon's; yet in the Cabinet he had taken the side of Kitchener.

High-minded, aloof, feline, crafty and ostensibly disinterested, Balfour yet had some human characteristics. He could easily have forgiven an injury that Curzon had done to him; but it was impossible to forgive or to repair the injury which he himself had inflicted upon his fellow 'Soul'. It was inevitable that he should inflict another.

When he turned his thumbs down on Curzon's claim to be Prime Minister and used the argument that the office could not be filled by a peer, in a sense he did a constitutional disservice to the country, since what was then decided might well be held in entirely different circumstances to be a precedent which could never be disregarded.[1]

[1] Indeed, less than nine months later when, after Mr. Baldwin's defeat in the Tariff Election, many Conservatives were casting around for some form of stop-gap Government, and Derby wrote to Stamfordham on December 7: 'I cannot help thinking, myself, that if Baldwin resigned there is only one man who can keep His Majesty's Government going and that is Arthur Balfour' either Stamfordham

In default of any further information becoming available it is difficult to pronounce whether it was Lord Balfour's advice or the Davidson-Waterhouse memorandum which provided the decisive influence on the King's mind.

Both candidates for the job of being the King's First Minister had powerful advocates at Court. Salisbury and possibly Stamfordham were for Curzon, and the latter's opinion certainly carried exceptional weight with his Royal master. Baldwin's candidature had the backing of Balfour, Bridgeman and Amery and the Davidson-Waterhouse Memorandum which was either falsely or dishonourably represented by Waterhouse to Stamfordham to represent the views of Bonar Law.[1] It is profitless to argue which of all this advice, interested and disinterested, was decisive in the Sovereign's mind, but from what we know of the sturdy character and clear-cut opinions of the late King George V it seems reasonable to conclude that he had from the start a clear view of his own for which he found ample fortification both in the cogent terms of the Davidson memorandum and in the suave and *rusé* advice of Balfour. The exact part played by Waterhouse in the matter will probably never be

---

or the King underlined the name and wrote in the margin 'a peer'. Balfour, of course, was not anxious to form a Government, but Stamfordham, recording a conversation with Balfour on December 8 wrote: 'Without actually putting a direct question as to whether he would . . . undertake to form a Government, I hinted at such a possible contingency arising and he did not give an absolute refusal.' (Royal Archives.)

[1] Falsely, if we accept the view that Bonar Law declined to express any opinion, dishonourably, if we are to believe Lady Waterhouse in her account *Private and Official*. In her reminiscences she recalls that Waterhouse had breakfast with Bonar Law on Sunday morning before leaving for Aldershot and pressed him for his opinion as to his successor. She records the following conversation:

'Ronald: . . . You *must* tell me what your answer would be if you had to give it.
B.L.: But I would not and I will not.
Ronald: If I give you my word of honour to preserve your confidence?
B.L.: In that case . . . I am afraid . . . I should have to say—Baldwin.'

Lady Waterhouse proceeds to record how her husband's mind worked during the journey with Sir Frederick Sykes to Aldershot:

'He found himself being driven fatefully to an immediate choice between unqualified service to the State and the silence imposed by his word of honour given that morning to Bonar. The two were diametrically opposed but the former prevailed. . . .'

known. It may be less than most writers have supposed. The author is indebted to Lord Davidson for the following account:

'... When I dictated on to the typewriter that memorandum which came to light in Harold Nicolson's *Life of George V*, I had no time to read it through but took it from Miss Watson, folded it and gave it back to her to put in an envelope which I saw addressed to Lord Stamfordham and sealed. I then handed it to Waterhouse to deliver personally to Lord Stamfordham at Aldershot when he arrived, and Waterhouse, unless—which is inconceivable—he broke the seals, certainly did not read it nor did he know its contents, unless Stamfordham gave it to him to read after he had read it himself. . . .

'I am perfectly certain also that the account of the breakfast conversation alleged to have taken place between Waterhouse and Mr. Bonar Law on the Sunday morning was not true. Mr. Bonar Law had made up his mind not to make any recommendation to the King with regard to his successor and he refused to discuss it even with me, who was a much older and more trusted friend and confidant than Waterhouse. It therefore would be completely wrong to suggest that Bonar Law ever indicated to anyone whom he would wish his successor to be.'

The new Prime Minister seems to have been in little doubt as to where he thought his obligations lay. He retained the services of Waterhouse as principal private secretary at 10 Downing Street, while Davidson, at the early age of thirty-four and after only three years service in the House of Commons, found himself elevated to the dignified sinecure of Chancellor of the Duchy of Lancaster.

Derby's own summing up of the change of Prime Minister is given in a letter:

Lord Derby to Lord Rawlinson

Private 28 May 1923

Many thanks for your letter just received. Since you wrote it and my receiving it much has happened. Poor Bonar Law suddenly became very much worse and I fear there is something radically wrong with him. Anyhow he has given up and after many alarms and excursions Baldwin has been made Prime Minister. Quite the best choice. It has been a bitter blow to Curzon, but he has taken it extraordinarily well and has made a most generous speech about Baldwin today. I am afraid he himself could never have been Prime Minister. He had a great reception at the Party meeting today because people think he has played the game, but if the King had made him Prime Minister it would have been a very different pair of shoes and I fear his reception would have been almost an hostile one as he is not popular with the Party.

* * *

When Mr. Baldwin became Prime Minister on May 22 he wished to be succeeded at the Treasury by Mr. Reginald McKenna or Sir Robert Horne. Neither wished to leave the City at this time, though McKenna undertook to accept the Treasury in a few months if a seat could be found for him in Parliament without exposing him to the rigours of a contested election. While the possibilities of this situation were being investigated Baldwin decided to remain as Chancellor at least until the Finance Bill had been safely piloted through the House:

Lord Derby to the Prime Minister

Confidential and Personal 31 July 1923

I am very grateful to you for our little talk this morning. I can only repeat what I said to you then, namely that from my point of view Horne as Chancellor of the Exchequer is preferable to McKenna and for these reasons:

(1) It absolutely heals the breach between the two sections of our Party because Austen Chamberlain has put himself out of court by the two speeches he has made and
(2) that you get a Conservative as Chancellor of the Exchequer instead of a Radical who however much he may profess to be a Conservative will as a matter of fact still retain many of his Liberal opinions.

I have always felt that the Imperial Economic Conference in October will present great difficulties to our Party because it must mean some form of Imperial preference unless you send the representatives of the Dominions away empty-handed and therefore disgruntled and McKenna would undoubtedly prove a thorn in your side on any such question as Imperial Preference. . . .

In the event the Tories of the City of London proved unwilling to afford a political haven for McKenna and when in August McKenna wrote asking to be released from his conditional undertaking Mr. Neville Chamberlain, the Minister of Health, was appointed Chancellor of the Exchequer.

* * *

Derby's service at the Paris Embassy had given him a clear and strong view on many aspects of foreign policy. His interest in Franco-German affairs was naturally reinforced by the responsibility which he had as Secretary of State for War for the British Army of the Rhine. He did not allow Lord Curzon's resentment of his interest to discourage him from discharging his responsibilities in this matter. Indeed Curzon's petulant and proprietary attitude in foreign affairs seems only to have acted as a spur:

Lord Derby to the Prime Minister

Confidential — 17 July 1923

I hate asking you to depart from fixed custom but I wonder whether next week it would be possible for you to have the Cabinet on Thursday instead of Wednesday? My reason is this. The Duke and Duchess of York are coming for ceremonies in Liverpool on the Tuesday and the Wednesday. I am their host and I feel I must be there. I cannot possibly get down to London on the Wednesday before 8 o'clock at the very earliest. On the other hand if you cannot change perhaps you would be able to instruct Hankey to put nothing which concerns my Department on the Wednesday agenda.

I am a little disturbed at not having got so far the Draft Note to the Germans and if none of the other members of the Cabinet have got it I do not see how it will be possible to discuss the matter properly tomorrow, and it is such an important matter that really it must have proper consideration before we arrive at any decision.

The more I see of the Paris comments and from what I hear personally, I believe that if we preface our Note to the Germans by an intimation that not only do we consider that they should withdraw the ordinances with regard to passive resistance but that they should cooperate to the full in working the resources of the Ruhr, we should save the faces of the French. It also would enable the Germans to pretend that they are doing under compulsion what they would anyway have to do and then the rest of our proposals would be easy to carry.

Poincaré only represents France when it is a question of *amour propre*. He does not represent France when it comes to a practical policy. Put him in a position of being able to say that they have conquered passive resistance and I believe you will find him much more amenable. You will read between the lines when I say that I feel the Note will have to be tactfully drawn up.[1]

I do not know what your views are with regard to Inter-Allied debts. Personally I have never felt that we should recover them. I should not give up the hold that it gives us but I would willingly support any proposal which, while maintaining the right of exacting the debt, would make its payment dependent on Germany's power to pay after she has satisfied the demands of France for restitution of her devastated area. It would pay us hand over fist to give up any ideas of recovering the debt if only we could get trade going with Germany.

When in January of this year France had occupied the Ruhr, ostensibly to collect reparations but in reality to add to her sense of national security, this event had been greeted with dismay by nearly all sections of British political and public opinion save that Lord Rothermere's *Daily Mail* had characteristically saluted it with the headlines 'HATS OFF TO FRANCE'. In April Curzon in the House of Lords had hinted to the Germans that if they would make some conciliatory gesture to France by indicating a genuine willingness to pay reparations Britain would then support such a *démarche*. The German Government took the hint and in May addressed an identical note to all Allied Governments. The German note offered to abide by the decision of an International Commission; but save for this the proposals were of a vague character and for the payment of sums which even the British Government were to find inadequate. And these German proposals were to be contingent upon international loans being made to Germany. Three days later the French and Belgian Governments sent summary rejections of the German offer, M. Poincaré, the French Premier, stressing that

[1] i.e. not by Curzon.

the German note contained no offer to disavow passive resistance and sabotage as a prerequisite to the French evacuation of the Ruhr.

The British Government was irritated that the French and Belgian Governments did not consult it before making so precipitate an answer, but a week later, on May 13, sent their own reply to the German Government which, though less peremptory in character, found fault with the German note. The British answer did not constitute any breach of Allied solidarity.

Throughout June and July Curzon conducted a long, skilful but increasingly acrimonious correspondence with Poincaré, the object of which was to persuade the French to moderate their demands so that an agreement could be reached.

Meanwhile Lord D'Abernon, the British Ambassador in Berlin, had been seeking to persuade the Germans to adopt a more conciliatory attitude, and on June 7 a second German note was forthcoming. This, though an advance on the previous note, was still unacceptable to the French because there was no guarantee of cessation of passive resistance or sabotage. Curzon bent all his efforts to ensure that this time there should be a joint Allied reply. The month of June was consumed in abortive discussions between the British and French Governments as to its nature. Curzon addressed an elaborate questionnaire to the French Government which Poincaré, under the pretext that Belgium was temporarily without a Government, delayed answering for many weeks. On July 30 the French replied. Their answer was somewhat bleak and it was clear that the British and French positions were still widely divergent. Derby was much concerned at the situation and put his views before the Prime Minister in a letter, part of which has already been quoted on page 510:

Lord Derby to the Prime Minister

31 July 1923

. . . Now just one word about the answer to the French. I agree with Joynson-Hicks, at all events to a large extent, that Poincaré's answer would be subscribed to by a large majority of our Party. In many ways it is an unanswerable document, especially if it was taken by itself and not as being an answer to our covering letter. It therefore will require very careful and very sympathetic consideration at our hands.

My view of the possible answer would be in the first place to say we agree with them that passive resistance must cease and we will inform the Germans accordingly. Notwithstanding D'Abernon's dispatches I am quite convinced from all one hears privately that that resistance is on its last legs and it would not be continued by the people on the spot if they had any intimation from the Government at Berlin that it ought to be dropped.

I should then continue to say that we agree that the Reparations Commission is the right body to deal with the amount to be paid but that you think that a Travelling Committee going throughout Germany to make investigations on the spot and to report to the Reparations Commission would be of material advantage to the latter in deciding what Germany should pay and that it would be for the latter body to make their recommendations to the various Powers. I should endeavour to secure an American representative on such Travelling Committee.

Third and lastly I agree with Poincaré when he says that he does not think that you can now definitely lay down the total amount that Germany can pay. It must depend to a very large extent on the recuperative power of the Nation as a whole and what I should endeavour to secure would be the payment that is to be made say for the next ten years, leaving the total amount to be paid rather in obscurity. . . .

If you had the time I should like to have discussed the matter further with you but I recognise you have not and therefore I have put down in very bald sentences my general opinion and please remember that this is only for your private eye. Under no circumstances do I wish it to be shown to Curzon and here I must raise one personal matter. I rather agree with the Belgian Note that a Conference might be of great advantage but it must be a Conference between you and Poincaré and not between Curzon and Poincaré. That to my mind would be fatal; whereas if in going through to Aix you had a short conversation with Poincaré in Paris you would not come up against that personal antagonism that exists towards Curzon and although I admit Poincaré is very narrow-minded, still I think you would find him more reasonable than George Curzon's opinion of him would make you think.

Early in August Derby went to Evian to take the cure. He stayed at the Royal Hotel:

Diary

August 1923

Went to Evian, the understanding with the Prime Minister being that before the answer to the French Note was actually delivered it should be sent out for Amery and myself to see and for our criticisms, if any, to be considered before the dispatch. The Note was duly sent. Amery came over from Chamonix to see me. We went through it. Found it in our opinion very bad but more especially in the last paragraph which threatened separate action, and as far as we knew no separate action could be taken or had even been considered. We wrote our criticisms. Sent them back by the Messenger the same night and Amery went back to Chamonix the next morning. I was very much surprised to see two days later that the Note had gone in without waiting for our criticisms, and I got a very indignant message from Amery on the subject.

A letter came from Baldwin explaining the reasons which to my mind and also to Amery, gave a very inadequate excuse. The note was bad throughout. It threatened something which we could not enforce. It questioned the legality of the entry into the Ruhr which however right it might have been in January was entirely out of place now, and entered into an acrimonious discussion of what took place in 1871.

I wrote to Baldwin saying I entirely disagreed with the Note. That it was not possible for me to support it or to defend it in the Country and though I would take no immediate action I did not see much good in my remaining a Member of the Government. I arranged by telegraph to see him before he went abroad.

Curzon's activities continued to agitate Derby:

Diary

Thursday 23 August 1923

Saw the Prime Minister. Had a very interesting talk with him and on the whole a satisfactory one. I began the interview by saying that though I accepted his explanation that it was necessary to send in the Note immediately I still was angry as I felt the real truth was that he and the Cabinet had been rushed by Curzon. He admitted this and then made an extraordinary statement which was that in his opinion Curzon's four years as Foreign Minister had been more harmful to this Country than any previous Foreign Secretary. It was thanks to him that foreign nations had not only lost confidence in us but no longer believed in our honesty or truthfulness. He would not disagree with me in any remarks I made about Curzon's administration of his office.

I then went point by point through the Note and he admitted he had nothing to say to any of my criticisms. With regard to separate action he said that there was no doubt they had no thought-out plan when they put that Note in and it was bluff which if the French called it, which luckily they have not, would have exposed us to ridicule.

I asked him what his next move was going to be because if our policy rested on our last Note I should have to ask him to let me resign. He said that he thought the new French Note, although unbending to a large extent, did offer some opening for compromise and certainly did not close the door but he did not mean to send a formal Note until after his holiday in France.

I impressed upon him the great necessity for having a personal interview with Poincaré and this he told me he meant to do.

We then discussed whether it would be possible for Maginot the War Minister and myself to be present. He began by saying that he thought if I could happen to be in Paris at the time it might be a good thing but it was a matter which would have to be carefully considered as some reason would have to be given both for Maginot and myself being there. I suggested that if I were there the way to get over that was that they should come to luncheon to my apartment. He liked the idea but as we both agreed it would be one which would be very much resented by Curzon and therefore nothing was definitely settled.

Lord Derby to the Prime Minister

Strictly Confidential 1 September 1923

I have seen in the papers with the greatest alarm that our friend G.C. has asked for an interview with Poincaré either separately or with you. I hope it is not true, because I am certain such an interview would end in failure, and I do hope you will insist that there should be no such meeting, but that you should see Poincaré first and alone. I see that Henri de Jouvenel wants to have an interview with you. If I may say so I think that it would not be at all a bad thing if you saw him.

He is a very nice fellow indeed and I found him absolutely straight, very reasonable and has a large amount of sense. I forget if he talks English, but he certainly understands it well. . . .

Lord Derby to the Prime Minister

Confidential and Personal 9 October 1923

I was sorry not to get a word with you yesterday as I think it would have interested you to hear some account of what people are saying in Paris. I dare say I shall see you within the course of the next few days and can then tell you about it.

But roughly the position is this. Curzon's speech was very bitterly resented but the order went out, and I think it will be religiously obeyed, that no further notice is to be taken of the speech. He is in fact to be ignored. Various reasons which I will tell you when I see you—they are rather amusing—are given for this order, but the one thing that everybody gave me to understand quite clearly—and I saw a good many people in authority—was that the speech has in no way diminished the good effect of your conversation with Poincaré and which I think is even better than you yourself thought. You may have noticed that in Poincaré's speech he made no allusion whatever to Curzon's.

I had a long talk to Philip Lloyd-Greame last night. He told me of a private letter he had prepared for you and has sent me a copy of it today. I heartily endorse every word of it but if it is to have any effect it ought to go at once. Poincaré held out the right hand to you on Sunday. You have got to grasp it and I should hang this letter on that sentence of his in which he says that he would welcome any further conversations. The time is not yet ripe for you to see Poincaré again but the contact can be kept and I think it is essential it should be kept by sending over these experts to discuss matters. . . .

A few days before, Derby had marshalled his thoughts on the Ruhr in a document which showed remarkable sagacity and prescience:

Memorandum on Ruhr

5 October 1923

In order to appreciate the English and French attitude with regard to the Ruhr it is necessary to go back a year, and to consider the Notes that passed between the two Governments this summer as being non-existent.

Last December the French Government announced that if the Germans defaulted any further they would enter the Ruhr. They asked the British Government to associate themselves with them in this enterprise but they declined. The difference was not one of principle, as both Governments were entirely in accord with each other that it was right that the German Government should not be released from payment of the indemnity. They disagreed as to the best method of securing this payment. There are arguments which can be used on both sides but it would be useless now to recount them; suffice to say that the French occupied the Ruhr without the co-operation of the English and we can now look at what the result is.

Before doing so one must remember that underlying the demand for Reparations there was on the part of the French Government, and even more so on the part of the French people, a desire to do something which might tend to their security and to prevent at all events in the immediate future, any war of revenge for the reconquest of Alsace and Lorraine.

The position now is the French have occupied the Ruhr for nine months. They have not secured in that time one penny of Reparations and the receipt of coal, coke, etc., has fallen very materially. It is therefore essential there should be some consideration of the position and a discussion with the German Government. The French decline to enter into any discussion until passive resistance ceases. Here I think we English who have witnessed passive resistance and hunger-striking, realised much better than the French that this passive resistance although undoubtedly it was subsidised by the German Government originated and is maintained by the people themselves and that our view was correct is proved to my mind by the fact that although the German Government has removed its official sanction for this resistance and withdrawn all subsidies, the resistance still continues and will continue, and as long as it does so there can be no hope of reparations being received by any of the Nations concerned or the material goods being received by France. You can tell a man that he is to work but nobody can make him work if he is determined not to do so, and I believe the German population of the Ruhr is perfectly determined not to work whilst under French domination.

Meanwhile the general state of Germany has gone from bad to

worse. The mark is now of no value whatsoever. Works are closing down. People are starving. One Government succeeds another quite powerless to act and a general break up of the German Federation seems to be imminent. I know that in the minds of a great many French people that is a very desirable object. They think, in my opinion wrongly, the break up of Germany will tend to their safety. I do not believe it will. The break up, if it occurs, will be superficial and sooner or later, having found out their mistake, the various nationalities will come together bound stronger than ever, owing to the fact that they have found out that division means weakness. I cannot therefore look upon this as a great gain to the French nation.

There is one thing however the occupation of the Ruhr has done. It has brought home to the German nation, as a nation, what they did not realise because they had not seen war, that they are a conquered nation. That is to the good but on the other side we see a nation ruined. We see no chance of any reparations because what you might have got from Germany as a whole you certainly won't get from Germany divided into various nationalities. We see from the English point of view markets that used to take many of our goods destroyed, with the result that unemployment is rampant in this country, but we also realise that though Germany is for the moment ruined there will come a moment when having reconstructed, as she has done, her factories, her railways, and wiped out by the deflation of her currency her National Debt, she will be an infinitely more dangerous rival to us in the Commercial world than she ever was in the past; and what France on the other hand has got to realise is this that whereas the feeling for a war of revenge was only existent in the minds of a comparatively small minority when peace was signed, her occupation of the Ruhr has created a hatred in Germany which nothing will ever eradicate and though for the moment, and probably in my lifetime, she has staved off a war of revenge, such a war of revenge is bound to come sooner or later and what can be the result. If France, with a population of forty millions which is decreasing, stands alone face to face with a nation with a population of eighty millions which is ever increasing, there can be but one result.

It may be that the moment has passed when the situation can be made good. I am perfectly certain if M. Poincaré perseveres in his present attitude he will alienate the sympathies of this country. He will find himself involved in enterprises into which French money will have to continue to flow without result and land the country eventually in a war of revenge which can only have one end.

* * *

On October 1 an Imperial Conference attended by all the Dominion Prime Ministers assembled in London. A good deal of the work of the Conference was concerned with the still vexed question of German reparations. On October 11 the Conference was electrified by a speech by President Coolidge, who was thought to be uninterested in Europe, in which he repeated an earlier American offer by Secretary of State Hughes, the previous November, that the United States would join in an inter-Allied conference on debt settlements and reparations, if invited by all the Allied Powers. This offer transformed the character of the previous negotiations and offered real hope that some progress might be made. Curzon's handling of Coolidge's offer afforded Derby another opportunity for finding fault with his old enemy:

Lord Derby to the Prime Minister

Confidential and Personal 22 October 1923

Will you allow me to make a protest with regard to the procedure adopted by the Foreign Secretary having reference to American participation in the Reparations question?

I am not one of those who regularly attend the Imperial Conference and when I read the telegram sent to our Minister in Washington I was under the impression that at all events its substance if not its wording had been considered and approved by the Conference. I confess to some surprise that the Cabinet had not first been consulted but recognised that at an exceptional moment like this a decision arrived at by the Imperial Conference should be accepted without demur. Judge of my surprise when, by a pure accident, I was present at the Conference when the question again arose. I realised that not only was the telegram not authorised by the Imperial Conference but that they resented their name having been taken without any authority from them.

If the matter had stopped there not much harm would have been done as the telegram was only seeking for information, but the Foreign Secretary went far beyond that. Acting on the answer received from the U.S.A. he sent instructions to our Ambassadors in Paris, Brussels and Rome to lay before the respective Governments a definite proposal and again took the name of the Dominion Prime Ministers in vain. When a protest was raised he informed the Conference that the telegram had already been sent. This was not accurate as I find it is coded as having been sent at 1.30 whereas his statement was concluded at 12.15. The Dominion Prime Ministers, as well as the Cabinet, find themselves committed to a proposal which in the language of both Smuts and Bruce is not only futile but harmful. The Prime Ministers will repudiate the proposal and infinite harm will be done, not only to our credit abroad and in this country, but also to the smooth working of the Conference.

If joint Cabinet responsibility is to be maintained and if our foreign policy is to receive the wholehearted support of your colleagues, the Cabinet must be consulted before the Foreign Secretary takes action of so important a character instead of being faced with a *fait accompli*, and I trust that you will give the Foreign Secretary to understand that he has no right to speak either in the name of the Imperial Conference or the Cabinet unless and until he has received definite authority for so doing.

Mr. Baldwin does not appear to have sent any written reply to this complaint.

XXIV

Mr. Baldwin's Tariff Election

IMMEDIATELY after the war there had been a boom in Britain and despite the difficulties of demobilisation and the reabsorption of men into industry, unemployment was no more than 700,000 in December 1920. By the turn of the year, however, signs of a trade recession began to make themselves felt, and by the middle of 1921 unemployment had trebled and stood at 2,100,000. It fell slightly in the next six months, but in December 1921 it still stood at the appalling figure of 1,900,000. Unemployment was particularly acute in iron and steel (36 per cent. of insured workers), shipbuilding (36 per cent.), engineering (27 per cent.) and building (20 per cent.). Some improvement took place during 1922 but throughout the whole of 1922 and 1923 the figure never fell below 1,200,000. In October 1923 the figure had been rising for some months and stood at 1,350,000.

This dead-weight burden of unemployment, which had not been known in England since the 'Hungry Forties', brought with it not only great distress but many social evils. Inevitably the Conservative Party, which since 1906 had fought very shy of the ideas of tariff reform and protection, began to turn once more in this direction. The immense prosperity and economic power of the United States under a protective system dazzled many eyes. The McKenna duties of $33\frac{1}{3}$ per cent. on motor-cars (which had been introduced in 1915 and a third of which had been remitted in 1921 for manufactures from the Empire as a first step in Imperial Preferences) had breached and compromised the iron-clad doctrines and seemingly unalterable shibboleths of Free Trade.

Now in October 1923 there was assembled in London not only

the Imperial Conference but adjoined to it an Imperial Economic Conference. All the nostalgic yearnings of the Tory Party for a return to the doctrines of Joseph Chamberlain were stirred by the needs and the signs of the times. All this was most painful for Derby. He was no doctrinaire in these matters. But his knowledge of Lancashire and Lancashire interests was even more profound and intimate now than it had been in 1912 when he had prevented Bonar Law and Max Aitken from re-saddling the Tory Party with the incubus of food taxes. He was convinced in his bones that protection and, above all, food taxes would be disastrous for the Party. In the middle of October Baldwin cast an oblique fly over Derby in his capacity as Lancashire's principal spokesman. Derby at once gave measured expression to his doubts and fears:

Lord Derby to the Prime Minister

Confidential 22 October 1923

. . . I have never been so blind a Free Trader that I have not recognised that Free Trade within an Empire that can produce all the raw material that we desire, and provide markets for our own manufactured goods, may give us a measure of real Free Trade which we do not possess at this moment. But I see two difficulties before this can be attained, and I put them in the form of questions.

(1) Can it be done without putting a tax on foreign wheat, or other raw material? I understand you are absolutely opposed to any such policy, and there, if I may say so, I cordially agree with you.
(2) Can you give a definition of what is—or is not—a raw material? We deal so much in this country with partially manufactured articles which we complete and then sell that any definition appears to me very difficult. For instance, are dyes raw material? They are not to the dyemaker, but they are to the calico printer. Is steel a manufactured article? It is to the steel producer—it is not to the engineer—it is his raw material.

The old proverb of what is one man's meat is another man's poison seems to me particularly applicable, and my fear is that whilst you will probably be relieving unemployment in one trade you are increasing it in another. You may say to me these are only the old arguments used in the Tariff Reform controversy of the beginning of the century,

> are there no new factors now? I admit at once that the over-population and want of employment in Great Britain, and the increasing demand of our Dominions for British settlers, is not perhaps a new, but still a much more important argument than it was in 1905 and one which cannot be brushed aside when considering this question; and a comprehensive scheme of Empire Settlement on a large scale if coupled with the introduction of a policy of Tariff Reform would eliminate some, if perhaps not all, of my objections to that policy. . . .

Baldwin took little note of this warning. Looking back we can now see that his mind was already made up. Nonetheless he set about achieving his rash and electorally disastrous policy with cautious steps. His first move was the speech he made at Plymouth to the annual meeting of the National Union of the Conservative Party, three days after Derby had written to him. In this famous speech Baldwin, after depicting the country's economic plight in the darkest hues and dwelling with poignant emotion on the evils of unemployment, said, 'I can fight it. I am willing to fight it. I cannot fight it without weapons. . . . I have come to the conclusion myself that the only way of fighting this subject is by protecting the home market.' After reciting the pledge which Bonar Law had given a year before that he would not introduce a protective tariff in the life of the present Parliament, Baldwin went on: 'That pledge binds me, and in this Parliament there will be no fundamental change, and I take those words strictly. I am not a man to play with a pledge. But I cannot see myself that any slight extension or adoption of principles hitherto sanctioned in the Legislature is a breach of that pledge. But at any time that I am challenged I am always willing to take a verdict.'

This meant that Baldwin held himself free to extend the McKenna Duties which had long been justified even by many Liberals on the grounds that they were intended solely for 'revenue purposes' and also to protect some additional specific 'key' industries as authorised by the Safeguarding of Industries Act of 1921. Baldwin was also making it plain that if such extensions of the McKenna Duties and the Safeguarding Act were challenged as a breach of the Bonar Law pledge he would have no hesitation in dissolving Parliament and going to the country. Baldwin's Plymouth speech was only a trial balloon but it created a political sensation. Commentators did not fail to mark that two other comparable balloonlets had been released almost simultaneously. The newly appointed Chancellor of the Exchequer, Mr. Neville Chamberlain, also speaking in Plymouth at an overflow meeting, said that if the Government were to deal adequately with the situation of unemployment next winter they would have to ask to be released from Bonar Law's pledge. Sir Samuel Hoare on the same day spoke at Salisbury in the same sense. It was obvious that Baldwin had consulted at least some of his colleagues and that a concerted plan was afoot.

A week later Baldwin journeyed north to Manchester and in the historic Free Trade Hall made proposals of a far more specific character than he had advanced at Plymouth. He put forward a six-point programme: a tax on foreign manufactured goods with special regard to those imports which caused the greatest amount of unemployment, preference to the Dominions, no tax on wheat or meat, an investigation as to the best way to help agriculture, an improved insurance against old age, ill health and unemployment and the development of our 'own estates, our Empire'.

Derby was in the chair. The embarrassment which Baldwin's declaration had caused to the Party, at least in Lancashire, is well shown by Derby's introductory remarks as reported in the *Morning Post* of November 3: 'We have got to think over it, to see what good and what possible harm might come from it, and then to make the decision we think right in the interests of the country'. In his speech Derby said: 'I have been and still am a Free Trader but at the same time I have never been a bigoted Free Trader'. Speaking of Baldwin's protective policy which would certainly exclude 'a tax on wheat and meat', he added with typical caution: 'It is a policy which I do not hasten to adopt; but it is a policy which I do not exclude as a policy I can support'. He concluded his remarks by assuring the audience that it was not a question of 'an immediate election'.

This was on the Friday. Mr. and Mrs. Baldwin were spending the week-end at Knowsley. On the Sunday Sir Archibald Salvidge received an urgent invitation to have luncheon there. The extent to which Baldwin was concealing his political strategy, even from men like Derby and Salvidge on whom he would have largely to rely in an election, is well illustrated by the account which Salvidge recorded in his diary:

Diary

November 1923

I found Lord Derby very disturbed, and in the short conversation I had with him before we joined his guests he said he really knew no more of the Prime Minister's immediate intentions than what I would have gathered from the Press. Derby had taken the chair at Baldwin's Manchester Free Trade Hall meeting, and the latter had made a strong Protectionist speech. Sir Edwin Stockton had warned Baldwin of the Lancashire dangers of a Tariff election, and Derby had merely rounded off the proceedings by 'thanking the Prime Minister for his honest advice, to which earnest thought would be given in the hope of arriving at a right solution'. Derby believed that after the Manchester speech an early General Election was inevitable.

Yet Baldwin had not made a single inquiry as to whether Derby was willing to shoulder the delicate task of trying to preserve the allegiance of the numerous influential Unionist Free Traders in Lancashire. I hinted to Derby that if he cared to come out publicly and give a strong lead he could, with his great position and popularity, rally Lancashire and the entire country and kill the whole silly business stone dead. But he was not contemplating anything so drastic. Instead he suggested we should both endeavour to gather from Mr. Baldwin some idea of what he actually contemplated doing, and that, if my opinion was invited, I should say how precarious it seemed to us in Lancashire for a Tory Government to give up a comfortable majority in Parliament for the purpose of letting our opponents raise the old 'dear food' cry in the constituencies, and adding that, though I was a Tariff Reformer just as Derby had always been a Free Trader, this was our joint view in the light of our past experience of electioneering in the North. With this good intention we went in to lunch.

During most of the meal Mr. Baldwin talked about how to grow raspberries. He said the raspberry was 'a jolly little fellow' and provided an interesting hobby for anyone who took the trouble to cultivate him. Mrs. Baldwin listened with rapt attention, and from time to time beamed in appreciation of the Prime Minister's remarks.

Later, over coffee in the Library, Lord Derby and I were alone with the P.M. He was fairly definite about his conviction that to fight unemployment properly he must have weapons, and that the only effective weapon was the tariff. But as to whether such a policy would carry the country he asked for no opinion, and never allowed the conversation to get down to practical politics from the point of view of electioneering. There seemed nothing to be gained by prolonging the conversation, and when Derby came out to see me off I told him my impression was that the P.M. hardly contemplated an appeal to the country before next year, thus giving some chance of educating the new electorate, especially the women, on the subject of Protection. As it turned out, I was hopelessly wrong. Nine days from then Parliament reassembled only to learn from Mr. Baldwin that he had advised the King to dissolve, and on opening the morning paper I received my first intimation that a General Election was upon us.

* * *

At the end of the following year Derby had a talk with Sir Auckland Geddes which casts some additional light on the disingenuous treatment of which he and Salvidge were the victims at this time. It makes clear what one had already assumed, that it was with Baldwin's authority that Derby declared at Manchester in Baldwin's presence that there was to be no immediate election:

Diary

Friday 14 November 1924

Auckland Geddes stayed here for the night. Very interesting about his experiences in America. I knew they had been bad but I had no idea that for two years he had practically been a prisoner in the Embassy.

What interested me enormously was the account of a conversation he had had with Baldwin in 1923. He went down to Chequers to stay Saturday to Monday with him before the latter came up to make his speech at Manchester. He told Geddes that he was going to walk about and, so to speak, think aloud and ask him to question him and argue with him. This he did and at the end when he said goodbye he said 'I have quite made up my mind that we shall have to go very slowly with this question of Tariffs and under no circumstances will I be rushed into having an election for another twelve months. We shall then know better how things stand.' He repeated a second time 'Under no circumstances will I have this immediate election'. That of course confirms exactly what he told me when he was here and when he authorised me to say at the meeting that there would be no immediate election.

I asked Geddes what he thought had made him change his mind. Was it Amery? He said he thought Amery might have had something to do with it but the real person was Neville Chamberlain who had made two speeches going far beyond what Baldwin had meant to do, one at Plymouth and one at Preston. He had to make up his mind either to have an immediate election or to disavow Neville Chamberlain and he took the former course. It was a reason I had never heard given before but I feel perfectly certain Geddes is right and that was the reason.

Geddes told me another thing which I had not heard but which I should think is accurate with regard to the present Government and that was that Baldwin meant to leave Curzon altogether out of the present Cabinet but that Curzon had insisted on having something and took the Lord Presidency of the Council which was to have been offered to Victor Devonshire and that is why Victor Devonshire got nothing.

It is now established that what drove Baldwin to make his Plymouth speech was information which he had received that Lloyd George intended to declare for the same policy on his return from his visit to the United States in the autumn of 1923. In a pamphlet published by *The Times* in December 1947,[1] Baldwin is quoted as saying:

On political grounds the tariff issue had been dead for years, and I felt that it was the one issue which would pull the party together, including the Lloyd George malcontents, i.e., Austen Chamberlain, Birkenhead, Horne, Worthington-Evans, etc. Lloyd George was in America. He was on the water[2] when I made the speech and the Liberals did not know what to say. I had information that he was going

[1] *Lord Baldwin, a Memoir*, a pamphlet issued by *The Times* in December 1947; an expansion of *The Times* obituary notice, it is now known to have been written by Dr. Tom Jones.

[2] Mr. Baldwin was inexact. Mr. Lloyd George did not sail from New York until nine days after the Plymouth speech.

protectionist and I had to get in quick. I got the Cabinet into line. But for this move Lloyd George would have got Austen Chamberlain with Birkenhead, and there would have been an end to the Tory Party as we know it. Bonar Law had no programme and the only thing was to bring the tariff issue forward.

Lloyd George had in fact decided on these opportunist tactics before he sailed for the United States at the end of September. Winston Churchill went down to the station to see Lloyd George off. As the train pulled out, Sir Robert Donald, former editor of the Liberal *Daily Chronicle*, told Churchill that he had something important to tell him. They went back to Churchill's home at 2 Sussex Square, where Donald told him that Lloyd George intended to declare for Protection and that all the Tory dissidents, Birkenhead, Austen Chamberlain, Worthington-Evans and Horne, would support him in this step which would be used as a means of re-building the Coalition. Churchill was thoroughly shocked at the proposal which he thought devoid of principle and utterly opportunist and told Donald that he would have nothing whatever to do with it.

Baldwin's Plymouth speech was made on October 25. Lloyd George sailed from New York in the *Mauretania* on November 3. He arrived at Southampton on November 9. Throughout the voyage he had been bombarded with messages from Lord Beaverbrook urging him to outbid Baldwin's Plymouth speech.[1] Churchill sent Sir Archibald Sinclair with a letter for Lloyd George. Sinclair was conjured to make sure that he saw Lloyd George before the Press got at him. This letter informed Lloyd George of the latest developments and urged him on no account to abandon Free Trade which indeed, in the circumstances, he was unlikely to do, now that he had been forestalled by Baldwin. Sinclair fulfilled his mission; and Lloyd George before leaving the ship announced to the Press that he was still an 'unswerving Free Trader'. One of the effects of Baldwin's pronouncement was to drive Churchill, who was feeling his way to rejoin the Tory Party, back into the Liberal Party, both wings of which reunited for the Election.

Derby and Salvidge had perhaps been a little naïve in failing to

[1] *Tempestuous Journey* by Frank Owen.

realise that Baldwin's Manchester speech following upon the one at Plymouth made an early election inevitable. Doubtless, however, Baldwin had his reasons for putting the Lancashire Tories off their guard. If there was to be an immediate election no doubt shock tactics were best. Only four days before Baldwin announced the dissolution of Parliament we find Derby still treating an immediate or even early election as an open question:

Lord Derby to Colonel Stanley Jackson

Personal and Confidential 9 November 1923

I was in Manchester with the Duke and Duchess of York on Tuesday and this week at the races have seen all sorts and conditions of men, but it is very difficult to give you any general idea of how the Prime Minister's proposal has been taken.

Generally I should say that the question of putting on a tariff to prevent dumping is welcomed but to change the whole character of our financial system is looked upon with grave suspicion and I think you must reckon that there will be a great slump in our Party in this county. . . .

There is one thing however on which everybody is united and that is in protesting against an immediate election, or indeed—if it can be avoided—an election even next year. To have one now would be absolutely fatal and I think it is as well to warn you what the sentiment is. . . .

Baldwin continued his instinctively clandestine treatment of the Free Trade wing of his party to the very end. In 1912 it had been a combination of Derby and the Cecils which had successfully resisted Bonar Law's attempt to saddle the Tory Party with food taxes. Now once more the Cecils and Stanleys found themselves together. But this time they were outmanœuvred by the abrupt ruthlessness of their new leader's tactics:

Diary

Monday 12 November 1923

Jim Salisbury asked me to go and see him. Went to his office. Found Bob Cecil there. They both told me that there was no doubt a dissolution was going to be announced at once. We discussed first of all the tactics which we all thought wrong and then our own position, whether we should be justified in remaining in the Government and not being able to defend their tactics with regard to the dissolution even if we approved of the policy. We agreed to meet again, on the whole thinking that probably it would simplify matters if we resigned as soon as the dissolution was announced.

I then went to see the Prime Minister who had asked me to go and see him. He confirmed his intention of asking for a dissolution. I put forward all the arguments I could against it. He answered by stating the impossibility of keeping the House together and he sent for the Chief Whip [Commander Bolton Eyres-Monsell] who was very strong on the subject. He would like to have postponed the Election but he said circumstances have completely taken the possibility of so doing out of our hands and he could not guarantee that we should keep a majority in the House of Commons.

After he [Eyres-Monsell] had gone the Prime Minister told me that he had seen F. E. and Austen and they were both coming into the Cabinet without Portfolio. He asked me what I thought of it. I told him that as far as I was concerned I was delighted. That I had always been doing my best to get a reunion of the Conservative Party and that therefore as far as that was concerned I was entirely on his side but I thought he would have grave opposition from other of his colleagues, and I mentioned Salisbury, Curzon and last but certainly the most important, Bridgeman. I persuaded him, I think rightly, to send for Bridgeman tonight and to tell him exactly what the position was. At the same time I got permission from him to tell Devonshire, but he did not wish me to tell Salisbury and the others that he was bringing these two into the Cabinet. He thought it best that it should come from him later.

* * *

All his life Derby had been a great reconciler of men and opinions. He was ever anxious to appease old enmities and to assuage present differences. It was this genial characteristic of his, carried perhaps to a fault, which had involved him in such humiliating toils in Lloyd George's campaign against Haig and Robertson. Ever since he had joined the Bonar Law Government in 1923 he had made it plain that his place was available at any time if the dissenting Tory leaders, Chamberlain, Birkenhead and Horne could be lured back into the fold. A man who acted on instinct rather than on doctrinaire principle, his attitude towards Baldwin's precipitate action was mollified by the assurance that Chamberlain and Birkenhead were to join the Government forthwith. Derby had been grieved that so many Tory friendships had been ruptured when the Coalition was destroyed. He had been quick himself to make friends with Birkenhead after the 1922 Election and had lost no occasion since the break-up of the Coalition to employ his gift of friendship and his talent for hospitality to reduce animosity and reunite both socially and politically the chieftains of the party he had worked with so long. Prompt to anger, he was always ready to forgive, and we may be sure that the prospect of new-found party unity, on which theme he persisted with obvious satisfaction throughout the campaign, was so gratifying to him that his resentment about the policy into which the Party had been stampeded lost much of its edge.

Derby did his best to adjust himself to the policy, or at least to find a form of words which enabled him to straddle the issue of Protection and Free Trade. He did not disguise the fact either in private or in public that he thought the timing of the Election was a great mistake. As in the General Election of 1922 it fell to him, through the chance of a speaking engagement to which he was already committed, to make one of the opening speeches of the campaign. The dissolution of Parliament was announced on November 13 and Derby was due to speak at Northwich in Cheshire three days later. Before leaving London for his speech at Northwich, he addressed in private a meeting of forty-two Lancashire Conservative Members of Parliament in a committee room at the House of Commons. No statement was issued but according to reports which appeared in the *Daily Express* and the *Manchester Daily Dispatch* Derby declared that the General Election was unnecessary, that he himself was opposed to a general tariff, that he did not himself know what the Prime Minister's views were on this question, and that a few days before he had recommended to the Prime Minister that if an election were to be precipitated Birkenhead and

Austen Chamberlain should be invited into the Government in the interests of Party unity.

At Northwich Derby had to take an equivocal line. This was essential if the traditionally Free Trade Tories of Cheshire and Lancashire were not to be driven away in confusion and despair. The *Manchester Guardian* of November 17 reported him as follows:

> I am sure that my general feeling is in favour of Free Trade. It is perhaps to some extent hereditary. At the same time, looking back on the past and seeing what Free Trade has done for us, I have that gratitude for the policy which makes me reluctant to leave it except on sufficient grounds.
>
> You can sum up in a few words as to why I have changed. I say that abnormal times must require and do require exceptional measures.
>
> The real test question today is unemployment and how to deal with it, and you have got three parties who are all going to take their hand with their various remedies. As a matter of fact, and do not let us disguise it, the real fight is between constitutionalism and Socialism.

Derby had recently had fun poked at him by both the Liberal leaders, Asquith and Lloyd George. He hit back with his customary geniality:

> Mr. Asquith in a speech the other day described me as cross-bred. I know what cross-bred animals are and why you have cross-bred animals. You have them because you hope to get the best from both sire and dam. I therefore appreciate his description, because I hope to get the best from two policies by not being a hard and hide-bound Free-trader and not going to the fullest extreme that some Protectionists would have us go . . .

Lloyd George, doubtless recalling Derby's repeated resignations from the wartime Coalition Government, had gibed that Baldwin's pockets were now bulging with Derby's resignations. Derby retorted:

> I have never resigned, and I don't mean to now. It is untrue that divisions in the Conservative Party are more acute than in any other

party. In the Liberal Party the lion has lain down with the lamb, but I venture to predict that before long the lion will have had a very healthy dinner off a very aged lamb.

Though Baldwin had assured Derby that Birkenhead and Chamberlain would rejoin the Government before the election, and had even obtained the King's assent to their doing so, without Portfolio and without salary, he failed to carry out this undertaking. Writing ten years later to Sir Tresham Lever (Austen Chamberlain's biographer), Derby recalled what happened at this time:

Lord Derby to Sir Tresham Lever, Bt.

Confidential — Knowsley

21 November 1934

. . . When Mr. Baldwin determined in the autumn to appeal to the country and to ask for a dissolution he wanted if possible to bring Lord Birkenhead and Sir Austen Chamberlain into his Cabinet so that they should go to the country as members of the Cabinet.

I must preface what happened by saying that when Mr. Baldwin succeeded Mr. Bonar Law he wanted me to continue in his Cabinet. I told him at the time I was not in the least anxious to remain on in political life and that my resignation was in his hands to be used at any time that he liked if by so doing he could facilitate the two former members I have mentioned returning to the fold and he accepted my offer.

When it was, as I have said before, apparent dissolution was imminent, Mr. Baldwin asked me to come and see him. He told me that he was anxious to get Lord Birkenhead and Sir Austen Chamberlain into the Cabinet and I naturally reminded him of my offer and said he could make use of it at once. His answer was he did not want to do that; he wanted to bring them in as two members without Portfolio, and it would be time enough to accept my resignation if we won the Election and when he re-formed his Government. But he asked me if I should have any objection whatever to their coming into the Cabinet. I told him that I thought he had known the one object I had always had was that they should come back into the Government, and acting on that he said 'Very well then, I will bring them in'. I think they were in the next room at the time and he sent for them to come in. When they came in he said 'Here are your two new colleagues'. What followed is immaterial except this, that Lord Birkenhead and I, who had been rather at loggerheads in the previous election, agreed we would work absolutely together in Lancashire in the forthcoming election, so much so that Lord Birkenhead asked me to go to luncheon with him at the Hyde Park Hotel, where I think he was at the moment staying, to talk over the definite arrangements. This I did. We discussed everything. Settled exactly what meetings we would each take and when I went I said good-bye to him and Sir Austen, who was also there, and said 'We shall meet at the Cabinet tomorrow'.

Judge of my surprise, when the Cabinet met the next day, to find they were not present. I said something to Mr. Baldwin afterwards, 'why were they not there' and his answer was that there were some difficulties. I never went further into the question as I went straight away from the Cabinet to Lancashire. We were in a minority after the Election and I never took any real steps to find out what happened, but my impression is that their absence from the Cabinet meeting was due to the influence of Lord Salisbury and one or two others, and I am bound to say that remembering what one does of Lord Birkenhead's speech with regard to Lord Salisbury, one cannot be surprised at Salisbury's attitude. However afterwards in the shadow Cabinet they were both admitted.

I write you this in case it may be of any interest to show that it was before the Election and not after the Election that Mr. Baldwin was anxious to have them in his Cabinet and if he had had his way they would have been Ministers without Portfolio before that Election.

* * *

Derby campaigned vigorously all over Lancashire, addressing meetings among other places at Fleetwood, Liverpool, Crosby, Rawtenstall, Darwen and Manchester. Half-way through the campaign he reported to Baldwin:

Lord Derby to Mr. Baldwin

Confidential 26 November 1923

You will be rather surprised to have got a telegram from me asking you not to commit yourself not to impose a tax on fish. It is rather a burning question along the Lancashire coast as there are many trawlers and thanks to German competition, not on this coast of course, but on the other, some 25% or more have to be laid up. I do not quite know how you could give any protection except perhaps by a tax on every German boat coming into the port, which could be based on the difference between the rates of wages paid to a German as compared to an English seaman.

Rothermere has out-done himself in an article which I have only just had time to glance through in the *Daily Dispatch* this morning. It is headed 'Give Free Trade another chance'. It begins by saying he is an out and out protectionist! It appeals to the public to give Free Trade another chance and then he proceeds to say what under Free Trade he would do. It includes a general tariff of 10% and other taxes far in excess of what even the most extreme protectionists advocate. I do not think however that much attention need be paid to his papers. They are cutting no ice here at all at the present moment.

There is one thing that is rather important as far as I am concerned. You may remember you told me that you accepted my position as being one where abnormal times required exceptional methods and that you were ready when times became normal again to reconsider the whole position. I have laid that down as my policy. May I say that it has your agreement? I think it would have a very good effect up here.

It is difficult at the present moment to say how things are going. I am afraid we stand to lose several seats in this county. Comyn Platt, Southport, I think is sure to go. He is a bad candidate and having no local associations I feel certain that he will lose. My brother in Blackpool will have a hard fight. At the same time when he went up there on Saturday the enthusiasm for him was so great that I hope he may just keep the seat. My second boy Oliver has a great chance of winning back Edgehill. On the other hand Harmwood-Banner will have a very hard fight of it. I have not heard much about East Lancashire, but I fear we shall lose two seats in Manchester and we may also lose Rossendale and one or two other seats in that area. It will be a hard fight at Bolton. My estimate is that we shall lose on the balance something like 6 or 7 seats. We may win Bootle. . . .

Baldwin seldom answered his colleagues' letters. He usually preferred to wait until he could settle the matter verbally. On this occasion he sent a staccato reply:

The Prime Minister to Lord Derby

27 November 1923 — 10 Downing Street

I found your letter on my arrival from Bristol.

Fish is an open question.

After the L'pool meeting I shall be grateful for a bed at Knowsley.

As to reconsideration of policy if circumstances change, what I have said is that it would be open to Parliament and the country to review the whole situation in the light of new circumstances.

Of course you have full liberty to do that yourself.

I had a great meeting in Bristol.

I agree with you about the Rothermere press.

I am off to Glasgow in the morning.

As the campaign progressed Derby, while maintaining a buoyant air in public, became increasingly despondent in private. On November 26 he had predicted to Baldwin a loss of six or seven seats in Lancashire. Five days later he had doubled this figure:

Lord Derby to Lord Younger

Confidential — 1 December 1923

. . . We may have a regular land-slide like we did in 1906, but I am not pessimistic enough to think that that will happen. I fear however that our losses in seats will be greater than I said to you in my last letter and I should put it that the balance of loss will be about twelve seats.

I must have a talk with you afterwards because I think we really must put our foot down and prevent Elections being sprung upon us without any of those who know about election work being consulted; without a single agent being consulted; with the Chief Agent of the Party a candidate himself and away the whole time; and with a policy which was only disclosed in brief to the Cabinet forty-eight hours before it was launched on the public.

Lloyd George made a considerable tour of Lancashire during the campaign and he and Derby engaged in a good deal of amiable badinage. At Preston Lloyd George revived an old jeer of his about the harpooned walrus in the best Lloyd Georgian manner. The *Southport Guardian* of December 1 reported him thus:

> Last night Lord Derby was giving his nightly exhibition of looping the loop. One moment he is a Free Trader, and the next a Tariff Reformer. One moment he is sitting upright for the principles of Free Trade, and the next he is head down and heels up calling for Protection. He would have fallen out long ago if he had not been strapped in. . . . The question is not so much as to what Lord Derby thinks of me, but it is important what he thinks of Free Trade. Honestly, I cannot find out. He seems to flounder about like a harpooned walrus. . . . Not that he believes in Protection; but he is a Conservative. . . . The Carlton Club has condemned Free Trade to death, and Lord Derby must do his duty as sheriff. The gallows must be trimmed with crêpe, tears will be dropped but Free Trade will be doomed all the same.

According to the *Liverpool Post* of November 27 Mr. J. H. Hayes, the Labour candidate for the Edgehill Division of Liverpool, which was being fought by Derby's second son Oliver, referred to the ground rents drawn from Lancashire by the House of Stanley and said they were a 'toll which is strangling the economic life of our people'. Hayes continued: 'Lord Derby says he is a Free Trader, but he stands for Protection at the same time. When I speak of Lord Derby I am inclined to think of racehorses. I remember a horse called "Tishy". When I think of Lord Derby, I believe he is really a "Tishy" in politics—he has got his ideas mixed and his legs crossed.'

The *Manchester Guardian* of November 29 reported Derby's answer to Hayes:

> I think he got a little mixed in the sex because whatever can be said of me I am not a mare. If Mr. Hayes wants to go further into the resemblance between me and 'Tishy' I would refer him to the racing-books, from which it would appear that 'Tishy' was so ashamed of herself that she won on the next occasion. . . .

Derby also replied to Hayes's attack on his ground rents. The *Liverpool Courier* on November 29 reported:

> 'I find the time is coming when I may have to leave the home [Knowsley] which my ancestors have lived in for so many years', said Lord Derby, referring to the burden of taxation, at a mass meeting in

the Pavilion Theatre, Liverpool, yesterday, in furtherance of the candidature of his son, the Hon. O. Stanley, in the Edgehill division. 'I don't want to press my personal affairs on any audience, but I wish to point out this—that taxation at the present moment is so high that I may call myself a tax collector for the Government. At present I am not living on my income. I am living on my capital.'

Derby's reference to quitting Knowsley caused widespread concern throughout the county. The radical *Manchester Evening News*, stable companion of the *Manchester Guardian*, on November 30 commented:

'Lancashire people who have an admiration for Lord Derby, realising the immense part he plays in the country's affairs, are much perturbed by his hint that owing to the burden of taxation he may have to leave the ancestral home. The Stanleys to leave Knowsley! It is unthinkable to those who have felt a county pride in possessing the greatest host in the north of England. It is to be hoped that the intimation was not an earnest one and it was only voiced by Lord Derby in a controversial moment.'

Others, however, took the threat less seriously. The *Liverpool Post* on November 29 reported one Labour spokesman as saying: 'I am very sorry for Lord Derby, and I hope that when he looks for a new home he will put his name down on the Liverpool Corporation list. I hope he will have to wait his proper turn. He will be about the 15,000th down.' And Mr. Harry Walker, Labour candidate for the Everton division of Liverpool, commented: 'If Knowsley Hall is going to be let, I know a good many people in Everton living in garrets and cellars who would be glad to take rooms in the mansion. We might utilise the back and front gardens to produce food for the people.' However, Mr. Hayes, who started the controversy, evidently was advised that attacks on Derby did not pay, for the same issue of the *Liverpool Post* reported him as saying: 'I believe that Lord Derby took all my remarks the other day in a real sporting spirit. I believe that Lord Derby is as high-minded and honourable as any man in his class.'

* * *

Early results on the night of the Election showed that a major electoral disaster had occurred. However, Derby hastened to congratulate his leader on his personal success at Bewdley.

Lord Derby to the Prime Minister

7 December 1923

I write you one line to congratulate you on your big majority! I am afraid you will have been as disappointed as I am with the result in Lancashire, and although we are holding the County seats fairly well the Boroughs have gone dead against us, entirely on the cry of 1906 'Your food will cost you more'. It is impossible to counteract this, and there is no doubt that where there was a straight fight between a Conservative and Liberal or Labour, that the two latter voted together, and where it was a three-cornered fight the Liberals took away just enough to prevent our winning. It is very disappointing and I am afraid we have got to recognise that you will never get Lancashire as a whole to vote for tariffs.

I shall be in London on Monday if you care to see me about anything.

The full results revealed that Baldwin had thrown away the useful working majority which he had inherited from Bonar Law. These figures tell the story:

November 1922			*December* 1923	
Conservative	346		Conservative	258
Labour	138		Labour	191
Asquith Liberal	60	177	Liberal	159
Lloyd George Liberal	57			
			Independent	7

The Conservatives were still the largest party in the House, but they were in a minority of 99 against all other parties. Derby had from the outset warned of the folly of this rushed election on an issue for which the electorate had been in no way prepared. Now he did not hesitate to show his disgust.

Lord Derby to Lord Birkenhead

Very Confidential 7 December 1923

Our great leader has indeed led us to disaster, and the landslide which I was always a little afraid of but had hoped might be avoided has come. There has been active co-operation here between the Liberal and Labour, and if there is any cheering result it is to show how right all of you were in trying to stick to the Coalition, because Liberals and Conservatives together would very easily have beaten Labour. As it is, quite apart from the political losses I have had personal ones, as have you, and it makes one very bitter, knowing how unnecessary the whole thing was. But it is no use crying over spilt milk and the question is, what are we to do now? Our majority has gone, and it looks almost as if we should not be the biggest party of all, but I still hope we may be that; and then the great question is, which is the second party? If it is Labour, Baldwin after resigning will probably advise the King to send for Ramsay MacDonald, and to my mind, that would be absolutely fatal, as I believe he might be able to get a working agreement with the Liberals, and the Conservative Party would cease to exist. On the other hand, if Baldwin could be persuaded to resign, always supposing we are the largest Party, and ask the King to send for somebody in our Party to see if he could form a Government, why should not you or Austen take it and see if you could not come to an agreement with Lloyd George for a Coalition Government. There would have to be concessions on both sides; but Lloyd George's appreciation of your loyalty to him last year might make him come to an agreement, and I am perfectly certain that you two people are the only two who could arrange this. Don't you think you could get into touch with Lloyd George on Sunday and discuss the situation with him? There would be no fear of any Die-Hards opposing a Coalition now that they see what they have brought us, and there will be no more trouble in that direction.

XXV

Mr. Baldwin Retains the Leadership

THE Election had produced a stalemate: no party could form a Government without the help of another. The Tories, though easily the largest party, had lost more than eighty seats and stood under the rebuke of the nation. Even if they were prepared to abandon their tariff proposals it was very unlikely that they could earn the support of the temporarily reunited Asquithian and Lloyd George Liberals. Many of the Tories might have been prepared to support a Liberal Government under Mr. Asquith, but few would have done so if that Government had included Lloyd George. And that would have been inevitable. Moreover if the Tories were unable to form a Government themselves it would have been thought a constitutional abuse for the Sovereign to have sent for Mr. Asquith, the leader of the smallest party, in preference to Mr. Ramsay MacDonald, the leader of the Labour Party which held 191 seats compared with the 159 held by the Liberals.

It should have been obvious to everyone that no Tory-Liberal compact for carrying on the King's Government was possible. Yet at the outset this simple political truism was only apparent to the King and, it must be added, to Geoffrey Dawson, Editor of *The Times*, which carried an important leading article on Monday, December 10 that helped to destroy many illusions and to crystallise opinion. Most of the Tory Party and many Liberals were genuinely horrified at the idea of a Labour Government. This was understandable. In their long struggle from small beginnings to the seats of power it was Socialist extremists, particularly from the Clyde, whose voices had been heard. They had urged policies of the most radical character, ranging from a capital levy to the 'nationalisation of all the means of production, distribution and exchange' and from free love to the abolition of the monarchy. Anti-Socialist propaganda had naturally fixed on these extremists and it was not to be wondered at that quite sensible people felt genuine alarm. It was hard at this stage to foresee how the trade union organisations would keep control over the Parliamentary party they had created or to estimate the degree of conservatism which was already beginning to bring a sense of national obligation to many of the trade union leaders. Nor was it possible to gauge how men like Ramsay MacDonald and Philip Snowden, J. H. Thomas, George Lansbury and J. R. Clynes would react to the responsibilities of office. Confronted with a novel and alarming situation it is not surprising that the leading Tory politicians behaved in a way which, certainly in retrospect, does little credit either to their nerves, their foresight or their sense of statecraft. This was very far from being the finest hour of Tory leadership, particularly for Birkenhead.

In this atmosphere it was natural that there should be much coming and going, stratagems propounded only to be abandoned as soon as they had been scrutinised and a welter of intrigue around the Palace which might have had disastrous consequences had it not been for the true, clearsighted and instinctive constitutional view of the King and Stamfordham who, while listening at any rate with an air of respect to the torrent of contradictory advice with which they were deluged, stood like rocks.

* * *

Baldwin, unversed in these matters and having no instructed view of the constitution, was in favour of resigning instantly before Parliament met. Some of his colleagues naïvely imagined that he could do so without obliging them to surrender their offices and that Baldwin might simply be replaced by some other Tory who had not been involved in the electoral *débâcle*. This, of course, betrayed remarkable ignorance. The resignation of the Prime Minister always involves the resignation of the whole administration. This is a most important constitutional device since it is the strongest weapon which the Prime Minister holds in reserve to procure the loyalty of his colleagues, just as the Prime Minister's ability in many situations to advise the Sovereign to dissolve Parliament is often his best hold upon his majority in the House of Commons. This is a most absorbing though frenzied period of British politics and we are fortunately well placed to study it from the ringside. Derby kept his diary daily throughout the crisis and he was the repository of many of the stratagems and rumours of stratagems which were agitated around from hour to hour. The author has also had access to the Royal Archives and has been graciously accorded permission to draw upon the diary which Stamfordham kept of these transactions with his usual punctilio. An almost complete account of everyone's conduct in these days is available from these two sources. There is indeed no comparable political crisis in the annals of British politics which is so much documented as that which convulsed the Tory Party in the month of December 1923. And the lessons which can be learnt from this crisis are deeply instructive.

Diary

Monday 10 December 1923

Birkenhead came to luncheon with me. The following is what he told me about the situation: that Baldwin was going to resign. That the King was going to send for Balfour to ask his advice and Balfour was going to advise that Austen Chamberlain should be sent for. That Balfour thought that that was the right course to pursue as it gave the King one other alternative before sending for Ramsay Macdonald. Austen Chamberlain came in afterwards and confirmed this having got his information through Locker-Lampson and moreover added that Asquith had sent him a communication to say that they could not under any circumstances support Baldwin but if there was a combination in which Balfour and Chamberlain were concerned in the Government that he would give a benevolent support to them and prevent Ramsay MacDonald forming a Government. Joynson-Hicks and Worthington-Evans also came in and we agreed that under these circumstances we should try and persuade Baldwin to accept this alternative.

In the evening Charlie Montagu told me that Balfour had sent me a message to say that he thought Baldwin would be right to meet Parliament and he begged I would take no action without seeing him first. This made me suspicious of the afternoon's conversation and I arranged to see Balfour.

Stamfordham's account of the same day's activities makes it plain that he called on Derby that afternoon and it is strange that Derby, while noting his talks with four or five other people, omitted any reference to Stamfordham's call:

Memorandum by Lord Stamfordham[1]

Monday 10 December 1923 Buckingham Palace

This afternoon I saw Lord Derby: and found him, perhaps not unnaturally, very sore at the outcome of the General Election, to which he had been strongly opposed from the very first moment of its suggestion. He recapitulated the facts with regard to the proposal to bring Lord Birkenhead and Mr. Austen Chamberlain into the Cabinet without Portfolio prior to the opening of the Electoral Campaign, in which he felt that neither he nor the two individuals in question had been fairly treated by the Prime Minister.

He deprecated any idea of sending for Mr. Ramsay MacDonald to form a Government: and he was in favour of the Conservatives remaining in office but under a Prime Minister other than Mr. Baldwin, against whom he declared there was a very bitter feeling in the Party. I enquired whether he meant that this bitterness existed among the 235 members of the House of Commons; he seemed to think that certainly this was the case amongst some sections in the House.

He wished me to understand that there was not one word of truth in the press reports that he was a party to a movement to make him Prime Minister: but he did think that Mr. Austen Chamberlain would be an acceptable Prime Minister in place of Mr. Baldwin and he hoped that the King might accept Mr. Baldwin's resignation and send for Mr. Austen Chamberlain. I merely said that I did not think that the King would approve of this course and that His Majesty felt that Mr. Baldwin should stay on and meet Parliament as Prime Minister.

Lord Derby mentioned in referring to Lord Birkenhead that the latter was in the house at that moment.

[1] Royal Archives.

On Monday evening Derby dictated a memorandum of what he proposed to say the next day in Cabinet:

> I felt that the object of this meeting of the Cabinet would be for the Prime Minister to ask his colleagues what they thought the proper course under the present circumstances would be and as I realised the difficulty of giving an answer clearly I have written it out.
>
> There appear to be three courses open.
>
> (1) To go on as a Government and meet Parliament.
> (2) Resign as a Government, the Prime Minister recommending that Mr. Ramsay MacDonald be sent for as leader of the official Opposition: or
> (3) The Government as a whole to resign, the Prime Minister recommending that another Conservative, not within the present Government, be asked to form a new Conservative Government.
>
> With regard to the first I am entirely opposed to any such course. There can be no question of the Prime Minister resigning and the rest of the Government going on. Whether we all liked the policy or not we all accepted it and the responsibility of defeat weighs equally on the shoulders of every one of us.
>
> Look what the result would be. We should say to the public: It is quite true that you defeated our policy at the poll. It has met with an overwhelming disaster but nevertheless we, the very people who recommended this defeated policy, are going to continue to try and keep the reins of Government in our hands and to trust that we may pull through and last six or seven months longer. That to my mind would be simply flouting public opinion and moreover we should not last six months longer. As the authors of the scheme we should be beaten on the Address, probably by some amendment such as this: 'That this Government having recommended to His Majesty an unnecessary election no longer deserves the confidence of the Country'. No Liberal could refuse to vote for that and we should undoubtedly be beaten and we should be beaten on the resolution of Mr. Ramsay MacDonald and the King would be forced to send for him.
>
> There are some people who think it would not be a bad thing that the Labour Government should come into power for a short time and

show how incapable they are of ruling. I believe that if we allowed them to get into power now it is the absolute death warrant of the Conservative Party.

In the King's Speech they would put forward a number of very attractive propositions. No matter whether they could pass them or not the public would see a programme of measures which they would like carried out. Our own people would be in a great hole. They might vote against the Address as a whole but against any one of the individual items they would be very loth to pledge themselves, especially seeing that there was certain to be another election within a very short time. We all know the difficulty that there is at any time in a Government's life to get men to pledge themselves and to vote against various attractive proposals. It would be doubly the case under such circumstances as the present.

You would probably get many if not all of the points of the Speech carried and that would mean that it would not go out simply as the programme of Labour but as a programme endorsed to a large extent by Conservative votes.

This would be followed up by a Budget which would be ruinous. Which would destroy everybody in this country who had got anything to lose. It would probably be defeated but again it would be an attractive programme for those who have nothing.

I repeat therefore that the argument that the Labour Party should have a chance of governing seems to me the maddest idea that ever was put forward.

If you agree with me this disposes of the second proposition namely the proposition that the Government should resign and that the Prime Minister should recommend that Mr. Ramsay Macdonald should be sent for.

I come to the third course, and that is the one that I recommend, namely that we should resign and that the Prime Minister should recommend that Lord Balfour be sent for.

I admit there are many reasons that can be urged against it but there is much that can be urged for it. In the first place he enjoys the respect of every single man in our Party, and what is more enjoys the respect of the Liberals. I think myself that it would be quite possible that if he was Prime Minister they would give him their support as long as he brought in nothing contentious. He was not a member of the Government which led our people into the last election. He therefore has no stigma of that kind hanging over him. He would be able to form a Government and my belief is that if he did so that he would be able to carry on for a year or even longer. A precarious existence but during that time we should be able to recover; to set our house in order and many of those who were defeated in this election but who would very likely regain their seats, would be ready to stand, which I do not believe they would if we had an election again in three months time.

One thing I want however to make perfectly clear. Even if the Liberals would agree there can be no question of a Coalition Government. If any support is to be given by the Liberals to us no bargain can be made except the one that the policy which has been condemned by the country should not be put forward and that as far as possible nothing of a contentious character should be brought forward.

There is one reservation however I would make and that is with regard to the arrangement that was come to with the Colonies about dried fruit and raisins. I think we should have the right to ask Lord Balfour, if he took over the reins of Government, to implement this bargain and I do not believe he would have any difficulty in securing Liberal, if not Labour approval for doing so.

Finally therefore I urge, and I am sure it is the right course to adopt, that we as a Government should resign, but that His Majesty should be urged to try and find another Government within the Conservative Party.

In a letter to Stamfordham the same evening, in which he summarised what he proposed to say in Cabinet if the Prime Minister rejected the view that the Government should resign, Derby wrote: 'I feel that it will be my duty as an individual to resign. I cannot go on as a Member of a Government which has met defeat at the Poll but which if it went on as a Government under the same leadership would carry the implication that it still adhered to the policy which led us to disaster.'[1]

Diary

Tuesday 11 December 1923

Went to see Balfour. I found that the information given me the day before as to Balfour's intentions was absolutely inaccurate. That he

[1] Royal Archives.

was strongly of opinion that although there were precedents for another course, constitutionally the right procedure was for the P.M. to meet Parliament and to abide by the decision of a vote of confidence, and he strongly advised me to support that point of view.

I had telephoned to Worthington-Evans and Joynson-Hicks to meet me at the War Office. The latter came in a great state of indignation as after our conversation of yesterday which was supposed to have been private, Birkenhead had gone down to the Carlton Club and detailed the whole of it. I told them what Balfour had said and we all three agreed that we had been absolutely misled and that although if it had been possible the other alternative was better, namely that Balfour should form a Government, in view of his statement it was quite impossible for us to suggest or support any such course. We agreed therefore to put our views before the Cabinet but to agree to the proposal which was quite unanimously accepted by the Cabinet, namely that Baldwin should meet Parliament.

Thus by the time that the Cabinet met Derby no longer felt it right or expedient to do more than make a formal expression of his earlier convictions. This was partly due to what Stamfordham had said to him on the Monday and also to what he had heard from Balfour before attending the Cabinet. Balfour had himself up to the previous Saturday toyed with the idea of a stop-gap Government of which he himself might have been the head. But it seems clear that his reflections over the week-end disabused him of such ideas and put him in a position by the Tuesday to give Derby such sensible advice.

Memorandum by Lord Stamfordham[1]

Saturday 8 December 1923 Buckingham Palace

Later in the morning, after seeing Sir George Murray, I saw Lord Balfour and with him talked over the situation. His present view is, that, as the Conservatives had the largest representation in the House of Commons, in the event of Mr. Baldwin's resignation, the King would naturally turn to someone else in the Party to form a new Administration: but no lasting Government could be formed without Coalition. He reminded me that he had always been in favour of the

[1] Royal Archives.

late Coalition under Mr. Lloyd George and strongly regretted the course taken by the Conservatives which resulted in its downfall.

I referred to a proposal in *The Times* of this morning that a Government might be formed with him as Prime Minister, but we both recognised that the reasons for the King's decision, come to in May last, not to appoint a Peer as Prime Minister, because it was, in His Majesty's opinion, essential that the Prime Minister should be in the House of Commons, were even more urgent today than at that time—though, on the other hand, it might possibly be argued the reasons in favour of a Peer Prime Minister might now be stronger than they were then.

Without actually putting a direct question as to whether he would, on the grounds of public urgency, undertake to form a Government, I hinted at such a possible contingency arising and he did not give an absolute refusal: but said that, according to present arrangements, he was leaving for Scotland next week and he hoped circumstances would not compel an alteration in his plans, but, in case the King should later on require to see him, he would prefer to remain in London than be obliged to come back from Scotland. I promised to let him know and, later in the day after seeing the King, wrote and asked him to defer his departure, as the King would be glad of his counsel and advice during this anxious situation.

In the afternoon Geoffrey Dawson called on Stamfordham who, according to Dawson, 'was also revolving possible Prime Ministers in his mind (with an obvious preference for coalition under an elder statesman such as Balfour, Asquith, Derby or Grey)'.[1] This diary entry of Dawson's indicates that at the outset of the crisis even Stamfordham did not have a clear view of the ultimate and inevitable solution that Labour must be given its chance. It thus becomes almost certain that it was the King himself who first realised this political truth and that it was he who in the course of the week-end persuaded Stamfordham of its justice and inevitability.

Meanwhile Baldwin, who had spent the week-end at Chequers, where, according to Geoffrey Dawson, he had had the advantage of the company of Mr. Neville Chamberlain and Mr. J. C. C. Davidson, had himself swung round in his opinion. The develop-

[1]*Geoffrey Dawson and Our Times* by Sir Evelyn Wrench.

ment in his thought between the Saturday when he saw Stamfordham and the Monday when he saw the King is admirably illustrated in the Royal Archives:

Memorandum by Lord Stamfordham[1]

Saturday 8 December 1923 Buckingham Palace

I saw the Prime Minister at 10 a.m.

He asked that the King would postpone seeing him until Monday next, the 10th instant; he had only returned last night, had so far only seen a few of his colleagues and therefore had come to no decision as to his action. But his present view was, not to meet Parliament but to resign. He had asked the country for a mandate for Tariff Reform, this had been refused and the honourable thing would be for him to resign at once.

He then touched upon the question of his successor; and, though he was aware that the choice of the Prime Minister was entirely the prerogative of the Sovereign, if the King should seek his advice it seemed to him that there were only two alternatives:

(1) A Liberal-Conservative Government; or
(2) A Liberal-Labour Government.

The latter seemed to him almost impossible, as the Labour policy was primarily based upon the two principles of a Levy on Capital and Nationalisation. Also, he did not believe that Labour would coalesce with a Government of which Mr. Lloyd George was a member. But he thought that Mr. Asquith might form a Coalition with the Conservatives, although there again Mr. Lloyd George might be a difficulty.

I asked him if it would not be possible for someone else to form a Coalition and I mentioned Mr. Austen Chamberlain, but this did not seem to appeal to him much.

Anyhow he considered his first duty was to ensure that the King had a Ministry to carry on the Government of the country. He talked for some time about the extraordinary and unexpected result of the Election, which had upset every calculation made by the experts both on the Conservative and Liberal sides.

[1] Royal Archives.

Memorandum by Lord Stamfordham[1]

Monday 10 December 1923 Buckingham Palace

The King saw the Prime Minister at 12 noon: and began asking what his views were as to his course of action and His Majesty was glad to find that, on the whole, they coincided with his own.

After the result of the Election, Mr. Baldwin's first thought was to resign immediately: but he found on reflection that he should meet Parliament and that former precedent did not apply in this instance, in which the question at issue was one concerning not two but three Parties, and that the House of Commons was the proper place for the choice of the electorate to be made known. The Prime Minister was not quite certain whether his resignation necessitated that of his Cabinet, but the King held that the one involved the other.

His Majesty gave his reasons for holding that the Prime Minister and his Government should meet the House of Commons and added that, so far as His Majesty could ascertain, it looked as if neither of the Parties in Opposition were anxious to assume office. The King also put forward that it had been suggested as a dangerous possibility that, in the event of his sending for Mr. Ramsay MacDonald, the latter might introduce a Budget including a Levy on Capital, increased income and super-tax and death duties and, on its being thrown out, go to the country with the cry that this splendid and tempting proposal had been turned down, which would probably result in an overwhelming Labour victory throughout the country.

The Prime Minister expressed himself as absolutely opposed to any Coalition: he had killed one and would never join another.[2] The King suggested that, if Mr. Baldwin continued in office, he might be able to approach Mr. Asquith with a view to ascertaining what, if any, cooperation the Government might receive from the Liberals. Possibly the latter might be glad to make some working arrangement to maintain the Conservatives in power for the present. The Prime Minister, whom the King found most pleasant and amenable, said he would lay the whole matter before his colleagues at a Cabinet Meeting tomorrow, and express to them the King's views in which His Majesty hoped his Government would concur.

Meanwhile, those who operated on the fringes of politics were

[1] Royal Archives.

[2] He was to do so in 1931.

unrelenting in their activities and Stamfordham records a visit on the Monday from Commander Oliver Locker-Lampson, one of Birkenhead's most loyal henchmen:

Memorandum by Lord Stamfordham[1]

Monday 10 December 1923 Buckingham Palace

This morning, Commander Locker-Lampson came to see me, speaking on behalf of Lord Birkenhead, Mr. Austen Chamberlain and, he added, but rather parenthetically, Lord Balfour. Lord Birkenhead had wished to come and see me yesterday but, I gathered, he had been restrained from doing so chiefly by Commander Locker-Lampson, who now found that the situation, as Lord Birkenhead saw it yesterday, had today changed. What Lord Birkenhead understood yesterday was —that Mr. Baldwin had decided to advise the King to send for Mr Ramsay MacDonald. Here I interposed to remind Commander Locker-Lampson, and also Lord Birkenhead, that it was not the province of the outgoing Prime Minister to advise the King what he was to do, unless that advice was sought for by His Majesty, with which Locker-Lampson concurred.

He then proceeded to explain that Lord Birkenhead foresaw a very dangerous possibility in entrusting Mr. Ramsay MacDonald to form an Administration: as he might do so and then postpone the meeting of Parliament say until March, having only time to bring in a Budget, which might include a Levy on Capital, increase of Death Duties, and Super-Tax. This would, naturally, be defeated in Parliament and then Mr. Ramsay MacDonald would go to the country with what would be regarded by the mass of the electorate as the most popular Budget that had ever been produced. The Labour Party would sweep the country and be in office for the next five years.

Locker-Lampson apologised for troubling me on this matter: but I begged him to say that, of course, I should have been delighted to see Lord Birkenhead and that I was very much obliged for and interested to hear his views but that evidently, as Lord Birkenhead would now see, this situation is not likely to arise.

Commander Locker-Lampson then went on to say that the Conservatives ought to carry on with someone at their head who was not identified with the policy which had brought about this disaster and

[1] Royal Archives.

talked of either Austen Chamberlain, Balfour or Birkenhead: but I was silent on this point.

Stamfordham showed his usual insight in putting parentheses round Balfour. That morning Balfour had written to Birkenhead and had later sent a copy to Stamfordham:

Lord Balfour to Lord Birkenhead[1]

Private

4 Carlton Gardens
11 December 1923

Your letter reached me just after Derby's departure; so that it had no effect upon our conversation. Let me, however, hastily summarise the situation as it appears to me.

I assume, for the sake of argument, that it would be a national disaster if Labour came in now, even for a brief period. It would give, so the City firmly believe, a shock to our tottering credit, and might have serious electoral consequences.

It is, of course, evident, not as a problem of high politics, but as a question of simple arithmetic, that if Labour is to be kept out, it can only be kept out by the joint action of the two other Parties in the State. Joint action then in some shape is an absolute necessity. For reasons which we need not go into, joint action cannot take the form as yet of Coalition. It must be either something less than Coalition, or Coalition called by some other name. An arrangement between the two parties it must be—or the general feeling of insecurity will be intolerable.

To make such an arrangement must require a little time, a good deal of patience, and the cooling of some personal animosities. I therefore am in favour of not hastening a crisis; and this can best be accomplished (as it seems to me) by the Government following the very sound constitutional practice of waiting for the decision of Parliament.

Now those who would assent to this general reasoning tell us that it cannot be applied to the present case if Baldwin remains Prime Minister. The Leaders of the Liberal Party, it is said, will never consent to give even an unofficial support to so unsuccessful a politician; and the suggestion is made therefore that by some means or other Baldwin should be excluded and Austen put in his place.

[1] Royal Archives.

If it were left to me to settle who should be the Unionists' Leader, I should not hesitate for a moment. In personal claims, in political experience, in debating power, Austen seems to me incomparably the superior. But I hope his friends will hesitate before they attempt to change horses while crossing the particular stream which threatens to overwhelm us. I have very imperfect sources of information; but nothing has reached me which suggests that the Party as a whole, however bitter its feelings may be about recent events, at the moment desires the change. And if it does not, it would, I am sure, be a great mistake to force the change upon it by transactions which could be misrepresented as having in them something in the nature of 'intrigue'. Our Party has been reduced by the unhappy folly of the late Election to miserable proportions; it is already torn by personal divisions; and I feel that it would be still further weakened by the course which I am deprecating—even though that course were followed with the sole object of substituting the more efficient and the more experienced man, for the less efficient and the less experienced.

But it is said (I gather) that Asquith has declared that nothing would induce him to lift a finger to keep in Office any man so stupid as Baldwin. I cannot, however, believe that this represents a settled policy in the face of a grave national danger. The Unionist Prime Minister, whoever he may be, is not going to be asked to fight difficult Bills, or to make great departures in domestic legislation; and I imagine that, so far as the House of Commons is concerned, Baldwin, if supported by the Liberals, would get on without much difficulty.

Nothing can be more unsatisfactory, I admit, than the prospect of a session carried on under the conditions that I have sketched. But can anybody improve upon them? Of course, it would be much better that the Liberals should be 'in' with Unionist support, than that the Unionists should be 'in' with Liberal Support. But I see no possible way of securing the first of these arrangements, while the second may perhaps be within our reach. . . .

Thus by the time the Cabinet met many rash and ill-considered projects had foundered and with very little discussion a unanimous decision was reached that Baldwin should meet Parliament and take his defeat there. Derby hastened to report the situation and his own conduct to Birkenhead and Stamfordham:

Lord Derby to Lord Birkenhead

Confidential 11 December 1923

I went to see Balfour this morning and had a long talk with him. His advice was very definite. He thought that the Prime Minister ought to meet Parliament and he strongly advised me, and told me I might give the same advice to his friends, that under no circumstances should we resign in order to force the Prime Minister to make an alternative Government. I got hold as you know of Worthington-Evans and Joynson-Hicks. I told them what he said and we unanimously agreed that in face of such a recommendation it was our duty to support the Prime Minister in his decision to meet Parliament. I feel we had no other alternative. We all three put the alternative case before the Cabinet but the decision in the end was perfectly unanimous. I am sure you will agree with this decision especially as, if Balfour were asked, it would have been the advice he would have given to the King.

As I told you yesterday after my interview with Stamfordham I was quite convinced that the story you had heard that the King would not ask Baldwin's advice but would send for Arthur Balfour who would advise his Majesty to send for Austen was incorrect. There was evidently no such intention in the King's mind and if Baldwin had resigned I think there is little doubt but that he would have sent for Ramsay MacDonald.

We can only hope for the best. I think however it would be as well for you to enquire as to the truth of the information that if Balfour or Curzon took office they would receive a benevolent support from Asquith because Balfour evidently knew nothing of that and disbelieved its accuracy.

Lord Derby to Lord Stamfordham

Confidential 11 December 1923

I think it only right to tell you that after I had seen you I had a long talk with Arthur Balfour and took his advice which was that the Prime Minister should meet Parliament and that I should take no action whatever to prevent his doing so. Under these circumstances while putting forward the alternative policy as having something to recommend it I agreed with the rest of the Cabinet that the proper course was for Parliament to be met.

I shall be in London this week and will come down if I may and have a talk with you. I could tell you more in conversation than I can possibly put down in a letter.

Lord Stamfordham to Lord Derby

11 December 1923 Buckingham Palace

Many thanks for your letter which is a relief to me but, what is far more important, I know it will be a relief to the King, who was not a little disturbed by what you wrote last night forecasting your possible resignation.

I do firmly believe that the really constitutional course is to wait until the decision of the electorate is made known through its *representatives in the House of Commons.* And I may mention that this was the King's own view as made known to Baldwin.

I understand your feelings: but I venture to think you have done the loyal and disinterested thing. I should much like to have another talk.

With the Cabinet decision to meet Parliament and to take its defeat there, the Governmental crisis ended. Some observers had supported the idea of Baldwin's immediate resignation on the grounds that to prolong the life of the Government until Parliament met on January 8, more than a month after the General Election, would merely give time for intrigue. At this time Esher, in a letter to Stamfordham, quoted Geoffrey Dawson, editor of *The Times*, as having said to him: 'The argument that a month's delay would give time for intrigue is manifestly grotesque. One day is obviously time enough in view of what is going on.'[1] Intrigue, of course, continued to flourish but the main essentials were now settled. Baldwin would meet the new Parliament and there would be a speech from the throne outlining in necessarily academic circumstances the policy of the Government. On the motion for a loyal address the Labour Party would put down an amendment which would be couched in such terms as to bring the vast majority of the Liberals into the opposition lobby. The Government would fall and the King's duty would be plainly marked out; he would send for Mr. Ramsay MacDonald. The Liberals having participated in the downfall of the

[1] Royal Archives.

Conservative Government would have an obligation to give general support to the new Government so long as nothing of an extreme or predatory character was undertaken. Nonetheless considerable political activity continued inside the Conservative Party between the settling of the crisis on December 11 and the meeting of Parliament in the New Year. This, however, no longer concerned itself with means of blocking the advent to office of a Labour Government. It was concerned with the various projects for getting rid of Baldwin from the leadership of the Party.

Diary

Monday 17 December 1923

Philip Lloyd-Greame telephoned to say that he would like to see me and also Sam Hoare. The former came in the afternoon and we discussed what we thought should be in the King's Speech over which I think there is going to be a great deal of difficulty as there is no doubt many of the members of the Cabinet would like to stick unreservedly to our policy put forward at the last Election—or would like in other words to brazen out defeat. I consider this would be fatal, as anything we put in the King's Speech is really the text of our policy at the next Election. Philip Lloyd-Greame saw that but at the same time he would go a good bit further than I would in the way of sticking to our programme.

Afterwards went down to see Sam Hoare who was not well. He and I are much more in agreement as to what should be in and he is drawing up a form of words which would meet our views. We afterwards had a heart to heart talk about the Prime Minister. He thinks it is quite impossible for him to go on as our leader in which I cordially agree, but at the same time he says, and with perfect truth, as long as he does not resign himself it is impossible for him (Sam Hoare) to do anything disloyal to him as he was his leader in the House of Commons as well as leader in the Party. I think he is right but I do not think any such obligation falls upon me though naturally until we are defeated in opposition I should take no step against him.

We agreed that the only alternative was Horne and that Austen Chamberlain was quite impossible. The Party would not look at him. Hoare told me that he found talking to fellows in the Carlton that they were very bitter against Baldwin but at the same time for sentimental reasons they do not like throwing him over and still less were they inclined to do so after Beaverbrook and Rothermere had told the public that they ought to throw him over. That had caused a complete revulsion in his favour. . . .

Dining in the evening with the Shaftesburys I met George Younger and the stories he told me fitted in very much with everything else I had heard. There was no doubt that on the Sunday the Prime Minister had determined to resign and to advise the King to send for Ramsay Macdonald at once and it was with the greatest difficulty that Younger prevented him doing this. Younger was of the opinion that Baldwin should give up the leadership of the Party. He never will again have their confidence. He did not know what I did that Horne would be prepared to take on the leadership, provided it meant the reversion of Prime Minister, and of course it would be much easier for him to do this in opposition when he could still hold his directorships than it would be if he was in office. Austen he said the Party would never look at and although there was a good bit of feeling against Birkenhead there was even more against Austen. He quoted the precedent of the 1906 Election when Arthur Balfour was the leader of the Party. There was just the same feeling against him then as leader and at the Party meeting a lot of people were prepared to insist on his going but when the meeting came, his great reputation and personality and the wonderful speech he made silenced for the moment the opposition. It broke out again of course in renewed force later and Arthur Balfour went. Younger did not think that if there was the same amount of opposition to Baldwin that there was against Balfour that Baldwin would be able to withstand it, or indeed would even try to do so, but would resign. At the present moment however nobody knew that Horne would take on the job and therefore people were not prepared to cut off Baldwin's head and make Austen Chamberlain king.

I think there are two fatal objections to Younger's idea. In the first place I do not believe that the King will refuse to give Ramsay MacDonald a dissolution. It would put him in the position (and I pointed this out to Younger) of resisting the first Labour Government ever created in this country and would no doubt mean that the Labour Party as a whole would turn against the King personally. Younger saw the force of this but still thought that he would not give a dissolution and he told me what I did not know that he had refused at first to give Baldwin one in November 1923. It was only after tremendous pressure that he did so and that he registered a formal protest against Baldwin's action.

The second objection that I had, and with this Younger agreed, was that Asquith is so bitter against the Conservative Party partly because we had the Election before he was prepared and more so because a Conservative was run against him, and even more personally bitter against Baldwin, that I did not believe he would come to our Party and ask us for help. It is possible he might have some communication with Austen Chamberlain and others and hope that they would be able to give him sufficient support to enable him to carry on, but I do not believe that Austen would carry enough men with him to be of any avail. Asquith would want a promise of at least 100 men and I am quite sure Austen could not give any such pledge.

Lord Derby to Sir Archibald Salvidge

23 December 1923

I am afraid I cannot come in and see you on Monday, but really what I have got to talk to you about will wait. I could not manage it this afternoon as I am in great trouble here. We have got foot and mouth disease at the Home Farm and I have got to destroy the whole of the herd. I had to wait and see the Board of Agriculture Inspector. An awful bore, as apart from the loss we are not allowed to shoot or do anything.

Really what I wanted to talk to you about is what line we ought to take in the future with regard both to the leadership and the policy of our Party. I am thinking of calling a meeting of the Lancashire Branch of the National Union towards the end of January, and I think we shall probably exclude the press and just have a heart to heart talk. If things are to be done again as they were done last time it is goodbye to our Party for ever. It will be hard work enough now to get it straight again, and I am not going to attempt that if we are again going to have a Tariff Reform election sprung upon us; nor if the dissolution comes from either of the other Parties am I going to support such a policy. It will be rather difficult to frame a resolution, and I am afraid whatever happens we shall have rather a split in our camp, but still it is much better to see how we stand, and if I find I am in the minority, well and good—I can then resign.

I go to London Thursday and to Cannes on Friday till about the 8th or 9th; then remain in London till after we are beaten, which I suppose will be the 18th, and probably come up here then for a few days when we might have a talk.

Sir Archibald Salvidge to Lord Derby[1]

18 January 1924 Constitutional Association
Liverpool

I will not say I was alarmed but I was concerned to read, amongst the strictures upon myself to be found in today's *Morning Post*, the paragraph implying (I do not know on what authority) that you are unlikely to allow at the forthcoming Manchester meeting any debate or resolutions bearing on party policy.

To me it seems ridiculous to rule out criticism of tactics when, to quote the notice convening the meeting, we are being called together 'to consider the recent political events and the future of the Unionist Party'. This surely must allow of some opportunity of protesting against the way the country and our party have been plunged into the present sorry mess, and I do hope that so far as you are concerned there has been no change from the position you outlined to me at our interview at the Liverpool Town Hall last Saturday.

Believing the time for straight speaking has arrived, I have, since seeing you, made the public statement to which the *Morning Post* takes such violent exception. I know that you are in agreement with me as to the main points I raise: (1) that the Conservative Central Office took no effective steps to ascertain the feeling in the large centres of organisation before rushing the Tariff Reform issue upon the country; (2) that under modern conditions, with three parties in the State, we have to realise how much more easy it has become to move the present vastly increased electorate from allegiance to any one party; (3) that it is bad psychology to expect the new women electors to vote for something which, though we claim it as a cure for unemployment, leaves itself open to misrepresentation on the score of being likely to increase the price of foodstuffs, and (4) that today Protection versus Free Trade is practically the only question which can divide the anti-Socialist vote, and therefore the raising of this issue in existing circumstances is a menace to national stability.

I do not wish you to gather from the tone of my letter that I con-

[1] *Salvidge of Liverpool* by Stanley Salvidge.

sider you are weakening in the position you took up in your last interview with me. Nothing is further from my mind.

However, this being so I do not see how you are to avoid resolutions at Manchester. I have heard that Col. Buckley has already given notice of a motion requesting that Protection be definitely abandoned as part of the party's policy. That, I think, is going a little too far, and after much thought I have drafted and intend to move the enclosed resolution.

Whatever the pressure from London, I do most earnestly appeal to you not to let the Manchester meeting be abortive. I am confident that if you take a strong line the bulk of the party will be behind you, nor would I be dissuaded from adopting the position you sketched out to me, since when I have been tilling the ground and sowing the seed.

In his reply Lord Derby reaffirmed the attitude agreed upon, but deprecated the passing of a definite resolution that could be construed into an attempt to prejudge events before Baldwin had addressed the Party meeting which it had now been decided to hold in London after the Lancashire Unionists had met.

It is interesting to notice in Derby's correspondence, and in that of other leading Tories of the time, how for the first two or three weeks after the Party's defeat in the Election there was an unchallenged assumption that Baldwin could not survive the catastrophe. It seemed simply a matter of choosing his successor. The trouble was that so many names were suggested and that nothing like unanimity could be procured for any of them. There were a number of times in his life when Derby might have achieved the leadership of the Tory Party and have become in due course the Prime Minister. This was perhaps his best opportunity. The Party, if it was to return to power, plainly had to give guarantees against continuing the policies of protection into which Baldwin had led it. The easiest way to have done this was for Derby, who was not only a Free Trader, but the man who had most strongly opposed the timing of the Election, to have laid claims to the leadership. With skilful management by others and a strong thrust by Derby such a claim might well have prevailed. But so many names were being produced that the multiple complaints and recriminations against Baldwin cancelled each other out; and Derby seems to have had no desire to assert any claim for himself to primacy. Indeed from his last letter to Salvidge it is quite plain that he had, on his way through London from Cannes, abandoned belief in the necessity, which he had outlined in his letter of December 23, of deciding 'what line we ought to take for the future with regard to the leadership and the policy of our party'. So far as ousting Baldwin was concerned Derby had thrown up the sponge.

Diary

23 January 1924

. . . On the Friday before (Jan. 18) Birkenhead came to see me at the War Office to talk to me about what I was going to say at the National Union Meeting in Lancashire. I told him, and he quite agreed, with the general line that I was taking. He then authorised me to tell Jackson that if Stanley Baldwin was proposed again as Leader of the party he and Austen were both prepared to get up and support him. Indeed Austen would be ready to propose him. I said I was rather surprised at this after all he had said about Baldwin and I tried to get at what was behind it all. He gave nothing away except that he did not think Horne would take it but from further conversation I am quite certain that what he has in his mind is the return of Winston Churchill to the Conservative Party and his becoming our Leader. I agree with him as to Winston's great capabilities and think that he would be a most valuable addition to our fighting strength, but I think F. E. and those who may think with him, entirely underrate the feeling that there is against Winston, not only in the House of Commons, but in the Country.

I have just returned from Buckingham Palace after giving up the seals. I had no talk with the King and he has asked me to go down there tomorrow at 11 o'clock, but he seemed in very good spirits. The whole of the Ministers were there, Cabinet and others. All apparently in very good spirits with the exception of Amery who seemed very gloomy. Baldwin himself was not there having said good-bye to the King yesterday.

We had a Cabinet yesterday morning which was really due to me as Baldwin had not meant to have one but I begged him to do so just so that we should meet again for the last time and as a body pass a vote of thanks to Hankey who well deserves our thanks. Nothing but desultory conversation with regard to procedure. Afterwards I had a short talk with Curzon who wants to have a meeting of his colleagues in the House of Lords, just before the meeting of Parliament, to consider our position with regard to the Party Meeting.

The Chief Whip sat next to me during the meeting and I had a talk with him about who should come to the Party Meeting. I told him I thought it would be entirely wrong to do what the papers suggest is intended, namely only to ask Conservative Members of the existing House of Commons and Peers who were in the Government. I thought he ought to extend the invitation to all candidates who were defeated at the last election and who had sat in the late House of Commons, and also all Peers who took the Government Whips. He told me he thought he would act on this advice and the meeting would be held soon after Parliament reassembles on February 12.

It is very difficult to find out what Baldwin's attitude is. I have never known a man so secretive and what I gather is this. He means to tender his resignation. A vote of confidence in him will be proposed and he will be asked to reconsider his decision. This he will do and will accept the Leadership but with the full intention if anybody comes forward, of resigning in their favour. The question is who is the alternative. I can only think of Horne but there is another aspirant in the field—Joynson-Hicks, who asked to see me after the Cabinet and came to the War Office. He is an able fellow who has done very well since he has been in the Government. Increased his reputation enormously both by his administrative work and by the speech he made the other night, but his self-confidence is something beyond belief. He said to me that he had been thinking over what I had said about his being a possible leader when I was at Cannes. I had no recollection of ever saying anything of the kind, but let that be as it may, he evidently thinks that he is the right man for the mantle to fall upon. He told me Sir Martin Conway had been to see him and had been touting amongst Members of Parliament to see what they felt about it and to use his own words 'Sir Martin said I am tired of going on with this. I have spoken to 60 Members of Parliament. They are quite unanimous and enthusiastic over it.' He also pointed to the paragraph which certainly was very complimentary, in the *Daily Mail* leading article. I told him that I did not think the latter counted for very much. Indeed at the present moment with the majority of our party against the Rothermere group it might even go against him. That he would have to now show what he could do in opposition and I was quite certain that he would realise it meant very hard and continuous work. He was quite ready to give this and again his self-confidence came out when he said that he knew he would succeed and that his chief duty would be to sit by Baldwin and get him out of the mess which he would get into by every speech he made.

Thursday 7 February 1924

Meeting of the Shadow Cabinet. All the members of the ex-cabinet, with the exception of Bob Cecil were there, and in addition Balfour, Birkenhead, Austen Chamberlain and Crawford.

Austen Chamberlain was splendid. He took complete charge of the meeting. He started off by laying down a policy which was almost word for word the same as a speech that I had already prepared for the meeting at Manchester next Saturday. He was supported by Curzon who amplified his remarks to a certain extent, and the meeting was unanimous with the exception of Amery who still wished to stick to Tariff Reform unadulterated and with food taxes. Bridgeman in a half hearted way supported him. However, luckily the opinion was so overwhelming against them that there was no question of any vote. Baldwin took practically no part whatever in the discussion and I am bound to say that if any outsider had been in the room he would have thought that it was Austen Chamberlain and not Baldwin who was leader of the Party.

At luncheon I met Rothermere. Very difficult. His policy and mine are identical but he has got a personal hatred of Baldwin that he allows to overrule anything and he told me that as long as Baldwin led the Party he meant to oppose it even to the extent of supporting Henderson for Burnley. One feels that he is quite impossible and it is no use arguing with him. He is terrified of the Socialist Party but at the same time cannot help letting his personal animosity against Baldwin override anything else.

The true extent of Derby's opportunities can only be a matter of surmise. When all the bitterness and recriminations had passed away there was Baldwin, who had sat tight and not said a word, firmly in possession of the reins of party power. Nonetheless Baldwin's reputation had suffered among those whose opinion carried weight in the Tory Party. He was also under fire from the Rothermere and

Beaverbrook Press. It was thought expedient to adopt the course of having a Party meeting where any malcontents could be faced and Baldwin's authority plainly re-established. This was announced for February 11. Two days before the meeting of the Lancashire division of the National Union was held. Derby presided. Salvidge moved a resolution of which he had given notice and it was carried almost unanimously. This resolution proclaimed that it was undesirable that protection should be included in the Conservative Party's programme, protested against the rushing of an election and urged that a more satisfactory method of liaison be established between the leader of the Party, the Central Office and the local organisation. In the interests of party unity Derby sought to make out that this was not a vote of censure upon the leadership of the Party. But this was playing with words.

Two days later, when Baldwin addressed a meeting of Conservative Members, Peers and defeated candidates at the Hotel Cecil in London, he said:

> I do not feel justified in advising the party again to submit the proposal for a general tariff to the country, except on the clear evidence that on this matter public opinion is disposed to reconsider its judgment of two months ago.[1]

Without further ado Balfour proposed and Austen Chamberlain seconded 'that this meeting, having heard the statement of the leader of the Party, desires to express its agreement with the policy he has outlined'. This was carried by acclamation. Baldwin had capitulated over tariffs and it was to be many years before his leadership was to be challenged again. But the glory of the Tory leader's unconditional surrender to the Lancashire interest must be attributed on this occasion to Salvidge and not to Derby.

[1] *Morning Post*, 12 February 1924.

XXVI

King of Lancashire

BRITAIN'S first Labour Government, though its life was destined to be short, did better than many people had expected. Being in a minority and dependent on the Liberal Party for its day-to-day existence it was not able to embark on any far-reaching legislation. The Prime Minister, Mr. Ramsay MacDonald, was his own Foreign Secretary and the Government's most important action in the field of foreign affairs was to enter into diplomatic relations with the Soviet Union. The Tory Party being now in opposition, Derby played little part in politics. Though he had not yet taken the decision to quit national affairs, office no longer tied him to London and he was able to resume his life and work in Lancashire. He had been succeeded at the War Office by Mr. Stephen Walsh, who had represented the Ince Division of Lancashire since 1906:

Lord Derby to Lord Rawlinson

Private 19 February 1924

. . . You will probably have heard from the War Office their opinion of my successor Stephen Walsh. He is a very honest straightforward little miner whom I have known all my life, and I am certain will work most harmoniously with the soldiers . . .

Walsh certainly fulfilled Derby's expectation. It is said that when on his first day at the War Office the C.I.G.S., Field Marshal the Earl of Cavan, came into his room to pay his respects Walsh was so impressed by this military potentate that he rose from his chair, bowed and said: 'My lord, this is an honour'.

'None of that, Secretary of State,' replied Cavan. 'You see that bell on your desk? When you want me you just ring it.' This was an admirable example of the way in which the British military hierarchy have usually submitted themselves with a good grace to civilian authority.

Early in the new year Derby paid a visit to Paris, where he saw a number of his French friends and had an interesting talk with Marshal Foch:

Diary

30 January to 5 February 1924

. . . He went back to the old theory that the Rhine ought to be the frontier of France, but he took quite a new line about the dangers of the future. He said that the great danger is Russia and China. That Russia before was a buffer to Asia encroaching on Europe. Now she really is a conductor. Nobody knows what is going on in China. The only thing that is known is that the population is increasing enormously and that they are getting poorer and poorer every day. That there is no order or law at all and sooner or later they are bound to break out. That Russia realises this and will combine sooner or later with China. Overrun the whole of Asia Minor and encroach into Europe . . .

* * *

As we have seen, Derby had resumed after his return from Paris his practice of giving an annual house party at Knowsley for the Grand National. The 1924 party afforded him special pleasure:

Lord Derby to Hon. H. C. Wallace

2 April 1924 Knowsley

. . . Our party was I think a very successful one and for the first time in our history we had the owner[1] of the Grand National winner staying in our house. I have never seen a man so excited as he was and it really was a bit of luck for him to have a horse that he bought for £250 and which has now won him close on £10,000. Of course he is half shares in it with a certain Captain Green. Lady Airlie unfortunately was not able to come as the week before her children developed measles and as she had been with them we could not risk her carrying infection, especially with the King there.

[1] The 11th Earl of Airlie.

I have never seen the latter in such form and I think he really enjoyed himself, in addition to which he backed Master Robert though it was only for £1. Still he got 25 to 1 . . .

Derby's pleasure in his new-found freedom from office was soon marred by an attack of erysipelas, a painful skin disease which owing to the violent inflammation which it produces is sometimes known as St. Anthony's Fire:

Lord Derby to Lord Durham

5 May 1924 Coworth Park

. . . I wish I could have been with you but it is not possible as, though I am going on very well, it is a slow job getting back one's strength, in addition to which this beastly disease got into my mouth and I am just going across to the dentist to have 3 or 4 teeth out. I never knew what pain was till I had this erysipelas. It is the most dreadful thing though luckily I was so ill that I did not really realise how much I was suffering, but I was stone blind for 3 days and even now my eyes are very bad.

He appears to have made a fairly rapid recovery from this affliction and to have suffered no lasting ill-effects.

In 1924 Derby fulfilled his long-nurtured ambition of winning the Derby. His colt Sansovino, with Tommy Weston up, started favourite at 9 to 2 and won in a canter by six lengths from Lord Astor's St. Germans. The correspondent of the *Sportsman* wrote as follows:

After an interval of 137 years the head of the House of Stanley has won the Derby. It was in 1787 that Sir Peter Teazle [owned by the 12th Earl of Derby] secured the prize, the eighth time it was run for, and since then, although various holders of the title have tried again and again to repeat the victory, it has been left to the present Earl of Derby to accomplish the feat, and to no more worthy member of the family which gave the race its name could the honour have fallen. Sansovino's success yesterday was the most popular seen at Epsom since the late King Edward won the Derby with Minoru in 1909, and apart from the fact that the horse's position as favourite necessarily caused the victory to be hailed with acclamation, the cheering was a sincere recognition of Lord Derby's sporting efforts to breed a winner of the Blue Riband of the Turf. The British public, particularly the racing section of it, dearly loves a good sportsman, and is never slow to appreciate grit and determination such as Lord Derby has shown in spite of so many disappointments; yet it is questionable whether there was not a deeper feeling at work, amounting almost to personal affection for the winning owner.

Three times have horses belonging to Lord Derby run second for the coveted prize,[1] and only last year he experienced a serious blow when Pharos, after looking all over a winner, succumbed to Papyrus, All is well now, and a great ambition has been satisfied, and no one was more pleased than Lord Derby that the public shared in the success of his good horse. Nor must we forget in our congratulations the trainer of the horse, whose anxiety to bring his charge fit and well to the post must have been well rewarded when Lord Derby, after the race, greeted him with the words, 'I am so delighted for your sake.' Now that the Epsom spell of ill-luck has been broken it is not too much to expect that the magnificent stud got together by the Hon. George Lambton for Lord Derby will produce more winners of the Blue Riband, but no future victory will efface the memory of the Derby of 1924, nor will the cheering outvie the applause which burst forth when Sansovino, through the mud and rain, came striding along from Tattenham Corner, a gallant and easy winner . . .

. . . After a breakaway, a fair start was effected, and Dawson City quickly took the lead, while St. Germans, Corolet, and Salmon Trout, who began slowly, were noticeable in the rear. Sansovino, too, did not get well away, but he quickly improved his position, and a mile from home he was 'there' with Dawson City, Polyphontes, and Defiance. Making the bend at Tattenham Corner, Sansovino held a clear lead, while St. Germans had sufficiently improved his position to lie handy with Polyphontes, and it was soon apparent that the only danger to Sansovino was Lord Astor's colt, but gamely as the latter struggled he could make little impression on the leader, whom Weston kept going to the end, a winner by six lengths, while Hurstwood, running on, finished within a neck of his stable companion St. Germans. Needless to say, the victory was received with all the cheering that it deserved, and, indeed, no success could have been more popular. At the same time it was a delight to see Lord Astor taking his defeat like a true sportsman, and smiling at so many narrow-margin reverses in recent years. For-

[1] 1911—Stedfast; 1920—Archaic; 1923—Pharos.

Derby leading in his first Derby winner, Sansovino, at Epsom, 1924.

Derby's Hyperion, winner of the 1933 Derby, with Tommy Weston up and his trainer, Mr. George Lambton, at Stanley House, Newmarket.

tunately, our owners know how to accept defeat quite as well as victory, and so long as such a spirit reigns the prestige of the English Turf must remain supreme.

Derby gave 5 per cent. of his winnings to the British Legion and more than £10,000 to the Hon. George Lambton, Sansovino's trainer. Derby told the *Daily Mail*:

> The only thing I can say to you about the race is that I am damned glad, damned glad. I am very proud that I am the first Derby to win the Derby since 1787. I have tried hard for a very long time, and now my luck seems to have changed. It is very fine. Everybody has been pleased, and I thank everyone for all their kind congratulations. I am a proud man.

Early in 1926 Derby bought a villa at Cannes, in which he was to spend a few weeks each year between Christmas and Easter during the next thirteen years, until the outbreak of war made travel impossible. In honour of his great colt he called the villa Sansovino.

* * *

Otherwise the year 1924 passed uneventfully and Derby contented himself with the role of observer. Like Baldwin and unlike the great majority of the Tory Party at that time, Derby was disposed to view benevolently the first attempt of the Labour Party to govern; if he expected the worst he did not hope for it. We have seen in a letter already quoted that he held a most favourable opinion of his successor at the War Office; he did not approve so warmly of the Government as a whole, but was eminently prepared to give them a chance:

Lord Derby to Sir William Birdwood[1]

Confidential — 1 April 1924

. . . The present Government undoubtedly has done well up to the present moment but you must not forget that the one argument they have been able to use all through up to the present time is that they are

[1] At that time Commander-in-Chief, Northern Command, India. Later Field-Marshal Lord Birdwood.

only carrying on their predecessor's policy. It is when they begin to launch out on schemes of their own I think they are certain to fall and the Miners' Minimum Wage Bill, which it is well known they do not want to bring in but which they have been forced to do, may well prove their downfall. The Labour Party as a Party is even more divided than our own Party. We can come together again. I doubt whether they can and the Liberal Party has practically ceased to exist. I only hope that there will not be an Election in the immediate future. If there is Heaven only knows what might happen. If we are able to wait for another year, or even till November or December, I think you would see a great revulsion of opinion. The Labour Party made too many promises. They have realised what we always told them when we were in office. They could not do some of the things they promised and they will have a difficult task in persuading their followers that the promises of a new Heaven and a new Earth are incapable of fulfilment. . . .

By August Derby's view of the Government's prospects was distinctly less optimistic. In their conduct of foreign affairs he found much to criticise and regarded their handling of Middle Eastern problems as especially unsatisfactory. There was trouble both in Egypt and in Trans-Jordania and Derby commented, perhaps not unjustly: 'It is rather amusing to think that these people who prophesied that when they came in there would be universal peace are already having to prepare for two small wars'.

In the same letter he predicted that the Irish question, that chronic affliction of British Governments, would be the immediate cause of the Government's collapse:

Lord Derby to Lord Rawlinson

Private 15 August 1924

Things are in a very queer state politically here and I have not the least idea what will happen. Personally I do not think there is any chance of the Government being able to get a settlement by agreement between the North and South of Ireland with reference to the Boundary Commission. They will therefore have to call Parliament together on September 30: introduce their Bill which will pass the House of Commons but will I think most certainly be thrown out by

> the House of Lords in which case I think Ramsay MacDonald will ask for a dissolution and will be rather glad to get it as he is in a peck of troubles . . .

The accuracy of Derby's prognostications about the difficulties that the Government might encounter over Ireland must remain a matter of surmise. For this important issue was anticipated by a minor matter, though one involving important principles, which precipitated the Government's defeat in August. As the result of a raid which took place on 5 August 1924 on the offices of the Communist paper *The Workers' Weekly* it was proposed to prosecute the acting editor, Mr. J. R. Campbell, under the Incitement to Mutiny Act. The Attorney-General, Sir Patrick Hastings, in answer to questions in Parliament, said that the Government intended to press the charges. This course of action was unpopular with many Labour members and on August 13 the Cabinet overruled the Attorney-General and the case against Campbell was dropped. The Government's weakness in the face of clamour from its own backbenchers caused a scandal and a motion of censure was tabled by the Conservatives. The Liberals proposed an amendment calling for a select committee of enquiry and the Government decided to treat both motions as matters of confidence. There was a debate on October 8, in the course of which Mr. Baldwin announced that the Conservative Party would support the Liberal amendment. The amendment was carried by a large majority and Mr. MacDonald accordingly asked for a dissolution, which the King, not without reluctance, granted.

Sir Patrick Hastings was judged to have acted with ineptitude in allowing himself to be overruled by the Cabinet. Not for the first or the last time it was found that an able lawyer introduced in middle age into the political world may lack the political talent and experience necessary for the effective discharge of his functions. Even lawyers who enter Parliament early in life do not always make a success of this alternative profession. Their fellow-members tend to distrust the facile way in which they can speak to any brief and to regard them all too often as mere legal hacks and mouthpieces who with their showy gifts take the bread out of the mouths of the professional politicians.

When one reflects on the number of lawyers who, particularly in recent years, have come flooding into the House of Commons, it is remarkable how few of them have made any serious contribution to the political life of our country. One can think of many who have climbed their way into high political office, such as the late Sir Stafford Cripps, the late Lord Simon, Lord Monckton and Mr. Selwyn Lloyd, but in the first half of this century, with the exceptions of Haldane, Asquith, Birkenhead, Hailsham[1] and Attlee, no names readily occur to one of barristers whom any reflecting person would dignify with the name of statesman.

* * *

There followed a General Election in which the Conservatives were returned to power with a huge majority, the distribution of seats being as follows:

Conservatives	415
Labour	152
Liberal	42

With this unequivocal mandate from the electorate Baldwin proceeded to govern the country for five years until the resounding defeat of the Conservatives in the General Election of 1929.

An interesting document has survived from the General Election of 1924 which shows the extent of Derby's contribution to the success of his Party:

Lord Derby to Lord Clarendon

Private and Confidential 28 October 1924

No I am afraid I cannot assist the Unionist Election Fund. I am paying the expenses of 3 candidates and also subscribing largely in 5 other seats and I cannot do more than that.

But Derby in fact did more than he had disclosed to Lord Clarendon. The Conservative candidate for Oldham was Mr. Alfred Duff Cooper, later first Viscount Norwich. In his delightful memoirs,

[1] First Viscount, 1872-1950.

Old Men Forget, Lord Norwich recounted a story which illustrates Derby's habitual generosity:

October 10th. I went down to the Central Office in the morning in order to get them to give me one of the leaders to come and speak for me. All was pandemonium there but very exciting. I only succeeded in getting my name put on a list which already seemed pretty long I walked back to White's and taking my courage in my hands wrote to Lord Derby asking him to come and help me. I caught the five o'clock train to Wilton, where I found a telegram from Lord Derby saying he would come any day I liked, except one.

I shall never forget Lord Derby's kindness on this occasion. My only claim to his acquaintance was the hospitality he had already shown me at the Embassy in Paris. After this prompt reply it was arranged that he should speak at an afternoon meeting. There was no ex-Cabinet Minister in England whom the people of Oldham would have been more pleased to see. He told me to arrange a luncheon party at the Midland Hotel before the meeting and to invite my principal supporters. When the election was over I gladly paid my three-weeks' hotel bill without examining the details. Some time later I had a letter from Lord Derby saying he had been 'horrified' to discover that I had paid for this luncheon; he had found out from the hotel what it had cost and enclosed a cheque for the amount. It was a shining example of how a great patrician can behave to somebody of no importance, and show not only generosity but thoughtfulness.[1]

In Baldwin's new Cabinet no place was offered to Derby. That this decision was by no means unwelcome to him is clear from a letter which he wrote at the time to Lord Beaverbrook:

Lord Derby to Lord Beaverbrook

Confidential — Knowsley

5 November 1924

Thanks for your letter. As I shall not be in London for some time I write to you as a personal friend in confidence to tell you what the position is. Baldwin has apparently made up his mind as to who is to be in his Government and as he has said nothing to me I naturally con-

[1] *Old Men Forget* by Duff Cooper.

clude I am not one of those and I think personally he is quite right to make changes. Of all those he may leave out I think I can safely say the one who will be best pleased will be myself. Do not think it is sour grapes when I tell you that I had made up my mind definitely that, even if offered, I would not take any post in the Government and for reasons which are sufficient to my mind to justify my decision, and I think will be sufficient to yours.

In the first place if I have any standing in Lancashire it is from the fact that I have always done many things which might almost come under the head of 'the daily round, the trivial task'. It has brought me into contact with all sorts and conditions of men of every shade of politics and I have not only got to know people but also to form a fairly accurate judgment of what the feeling of the country is. During my absence in Paris and then in the Government, I lost this touch. I have regained it a little during the past year but I think it is a thing that I must keep up for the future and I feel it can be of considerable use to the leaders of our Party if I let them know from time to time whether I find that their policy is not meeting with approval.

Secondly I feel that one has more power outside than inside a Cabinet. If you are inside and you disapprove of a policy you have either got to do one of two things, resign or loyally accept it. Now to resign, especially if it is a one man resignation, is really of very little use and is sometimes ridiculous. On the other hand I feel it is quite possible that the present Government may institute legislation which I should only half-heartedly approve of and yet by remaining in the Cabinet should have to loyally support.

At about the same time Baldwin explained in a frank letter his reason for excluding Derby and indicated, perhaps with a view to consoling him, that he would find jobs for Derby's brother George and for his elder son Lord Stanley:

Mr. Stanley Baldwin to Lord Derby

Private

Palace Chambers,
Westminster

You have told me more than once that you would be content to stand out for a time if it would help me, and I have taken you at your word though with real reluctance.

With the object of strengthening the government in the Commons and having so many to fit in, I have had to part with some most valued friends.

I may tell you in confidence that I shall give George a job which I hope will be to his taste and I am trying to arrange for Edward to be taken into the Whips' room for a start if he cares for it.

If we should be colleagues again in the future, I should be delighted: and I believe that a rest will be of real benefit to you for as I told you, an operation such as you have had demands a year's respite from arduous work.

Lord Derby to Mr. Baldwin

Strictly Confidential — 8 November 1924

. . . As you have been frank with me I will be equally frank with you with regard to the proposed post for my brother George and your suggestion that my elder son should go into the Whips' Room. I cannot help being a little disappointed that my brother should have been preferred to my son. The former has now left Lancashire and sits for a London seat and cannot be said in any way to represent this County, whereas my son is I am glad to say taking many things off my hands and is intimately connected with the political life of Lancashire.

Baldwin, however, was unmoved by these considerations and proceeded to make Sir George Stanley Parliamentary Secretary to the Ministry of Pensions, while Edward had for the time being to content himself with the post of a junior Lord of the Treasury:

Lord Stanley to Lord Derby

12 November 1924 — 3 Portman Square, W.1

After all that I have said, I have taken an unpaid Whip's job!! I had a long interview with Baldwin this afternoon who told me that the question of salary did not affect my status in any way. He said several other things (which you can guess) which made my acceptance inevitable. I went to Downing Street meaning to refuse but I should have been mad if I had done so—after our conversation.

Further confirmation of the sincerity of Derby's wish to retire is afforded by a letter he wrote shortly afterwards to his American friend Wallace:

Lord Derby to Hon. H. C. Wallace

8 December 1924.

. . . As you know, I have not joined the Government. I told Baldwin beforehand that I did not want him to offer me anything, and I should certainly have refused. I have got so many other things to do, and I like being my own master. If I am tied to an Office in London it prevents my doing many things that I ought to do up here, and many things I want to do, like racing and France.

This correspondence marks, with one exception, Derby's final retirement from national politics. Although in the remaining twenty-five years of his life he continued to play a considerable role behind the scenes, above all in Lancashire, where his influence continued to wax, he never again sought or held office. Henceforth the House of Stanley was to be represented in government by Derby's two sons Edward and Oliver. We have already seen that Derby was a man of very strong family affections and ambition who took an almost patriarchal interest and pride in the doings of his children and of all his other relations. He liked to be surrounded by as many members of his family as possible and when they were not together he would send, and expect to receive, frequent and detailed letters. But this minute and lively interest never seems to have degenerated into mere possessiveness; and Derby deserved and won, by his affection and generosity, the deep love of those who were nearest to him.

* * *

In 1927 Derby suffered a cruel loss by the death in the hunting-field of his only daughter, Lady Victoria Bullock, to whom he had an exceptional devotion. Lady Victoria had been spending some weeks that winter with Lord and Lady Blandford (now the Duke and Duchess of Marlborough) at Lowesby Hall in Leicestershire. She kept her horses there and had planned to hunt regularly with the Quorn from the Blandfords' home. At the time of the accident Derby was on his way to the South of France. He had not planned to stop in Paris but intended to stay in the train while it went round the *ceinture*, the loop line which connects the Gare du Nord with the

Derby at Ascot c. 1926 with (left to right) Major Milner, Lord Stanley and Lady Stanley; behind Major Milner, in white, is Derby's daughter, Lady Victoria Bullock.

Gare de Lyon. However, shortly before the train arrived at the Gare du Nord, he told his manservant to pack up his things, adding: 'We will get off at the Gare du Nord and go to the Embassy. I have a feeling that something terrible has happened to Lady Victoria.' His premonition proved all too true. He was met at the Gare du Nord by a member of the British Embassy staff who gave him the news. Derby returned to England by the next train; but Lady Victoria died shortly after his return, without recovering consciousness.

The intensity of Derby's grief appears from a letter which he wrote a month later to his son-in-law:

Lord Derby to Captain Malcolm Bullock

31 December 1927 Sansovino,
Cannes

I send you a photograph of our darling. It is not really good, but she liked it. I can't talk or write to you about her—I am too great a coward, but I loved her, as no man has ever loved his daughter, and with her has gone all joy from my life.

I want you to think that I am to you all that I tried to be to her—that you have in me a friend to whom you can always turn, and who would always try to the best of his ability to help you.

I won't do more than send you every good wish for 1928. I know that for you, as for me, no year can in future be a happy one—except the one in which I rejoin her.

* * *

Early in May 1929 Baldwin recommended the dissolution of Parliament; polling day was on May 30. The Conservative Government had been in office for more than four and a half years and their statutory five-year period of office would have made an election in November inevitable in any case. In retrospect Baldwin and his colleagues seem to have governed well, if unimaginatively. They had to contend with the exceptional difficulties of the general strike of 1926 and their term of office was further scarred by the seven-month coal stoppage which caused damage to British coal exports that proved largely irreparable. At the time of the Election unemployment was about one million and the Government was inevitably blamed for this. Despite its considerable social legislation, the Government was plainly not popular with the country. People felt in the mood for a change. The Tory majority of about 200 was swept away overnight and Ramsay MacDonald was called upon to form his second minority Labour Government. The figures for the new Parliament were:

Labour	287
Conservatives	261
Liberal	59

Derby, who had been appointed Lord Lieutenant of Lancashire in 1928, for the first time took no outward part in the election; but the aftermath of the Conservative defeat was soon to involve him once more in discussions about the leadership of the Party.

Baldwin's electoral reverse under the slogan of 'Safety First', incited a variety of agitations against him in the Tory Party. Beaverbrook in particular saw the opportunity to impose upon the Party now that it was in opposition the tariff policy which he had never managed to impose while it was in power. Sensing Baldwin's vulnerability he had proclaimed his crusade for Empire Free Trade in July 1929 immediately after the general election. He ran candidates, initially with some success, at by-elections, and the principle for which he stood made a considerable appeal to a large section of the Tory Party. Moreover many Tories who did not love Beaverbrook or his policies did not love Baldwin either. What they wanted at all costs was unity in the Party so that the Socialist Government could be turned out as soon as possible. Thus Baldwin to survive in the Party leadership was compelled, however distasteful it may have been to him, to enter into negotiations with Beaverbrook. Rothermere, proprietor of the *Daily Mail*, *Sunday Dispatch*, *Daily Mirror*, *Sunday Pictorial* and *Evening News*, had joined Beaverbrook in his campaign and they had jointly formed a United Empire Party. The newspapers of both Press magnates sought to stir up public opinion with a Press campaign which greatly exceeded anything that has ever been seen outside election time in this country.

So great was the pressure on Baldwin that early in March he

abandoned his previous policy, which was limited to safeguards on key industries, coupled with Imperial Preference, and which specifically excluded any tax on food. Instead, after a series of complicated negotiations with Beaverbrook, he announced that if and when the Tories should obtain a majority in Parliament there would be a nationwide referendum on food taxes. Beaverbrook eagerly grasped this solution. For a man of his political sagacity it was a strange mistake. There has never been a referendum in this country, and he himself first entered English political life at a time when the pledge of a similar referendum on the same issue was in process of being abandoned. For a few weeks there was peace so far as Beaverbrook was concerned, though Rothermere continued his attacks. In an endeavour to reassure his supporters that a serious attempt was being made to reorganise the Party, Baldwin early in June persuaded Mr. Neville Chamberlain, the most influential of his colleagues, to accept the chairmanship. This involved throwing to the wolves his closest political friend, Mr. J. C. C. Davidson, who had been partly responsible for making Baldwin Prime Minister in 1922. Davidson was subsequently solaced for this indignity by being made Chancellor of the Duchy of Lancaster without a seat in the Cabinet in the first National Government of 1931.

Traditionally the chairman of the Tory Party, who is the appointee of the leader, has never been a man of the first political rank[1] and this exceptional appointment caused surprise. It did not, however, prevent further attacks on Baldwin's leadership. Indeed Beaverbrook, noticing that the Party, despite its commitment to the referendum on food taxes, was still conducting its propaganda in the country solely on the policy of the safeguarding of key industries with Imperial Preference, soon joined forces once more with Rothermere and denounced the concordat into which he himself had entered with Baldwin.

In an attempt to quell the attacks upon his leadership Baldwin was driven to the unusual expedient of calling a Party meeting to sustain him. Rothermere, whose political ineptitude was of a unique

[1] The appointments of Lord Woolton and Lord Hailsham in recent years show that this tradition has been abandoned.

character, played into his hands by writing him a letter on the eve of this meeting in which he sought, as his elder brother Lord Northcliffe had done some years before, to obtain guarantees about the appointment of particular ministers. Baldwin was able to turn so gross an intrusion upon the whole spirit of the constitution to admirable account and obtained an effective vote of confidence:

Lord Derby to Hon. Oliver Stanley

Private 26 June 1930

Certainly the accounts of the meeting read like a personal triumph for Baldwin. He seems to have made a very good speech and to have hit out in a way I never expected of him. I think you are probably right that Beaverbrook thought that he would be able to get the leadership of the Party. Of course that is knocked on the head but I am afraid his intriguing will do us harm at the General Election. Of course to my mind the man at the bottom of the whole thing is a man I have always disliked and distrusted—Amery. I must say I wish this trouble had never come about and if Beaverbrook had been more reasonable it need never have done because really he and Baldwin have got the same object at heart. It is only that their methods of dealing with the matter are different and I think Baldwin's is the best.

I was up at Liverpool yesterday and although there is not the slightest doubt that a tremendous change-over in favour of safeguarding has taken place, there is equally no doubt that they will look very askance at any question of tax on food, until they know exactly what they will get in return for it. Give them a sort of balance sheet and I believe people would accept it—not otherwise.

Neville Chamberlain's first step as Chairman of the Party was to try and negotiate a settlement with Beaverbrook and Rothermere. To this end he laboured unsuccessfully all through July. The Press campaign was intensified and in October, Vice-Admiral E. A. Taylor was put up as Empire Free Trade candidate in the South Paddington by-election against the official Conservative candidate. Beaverbrook made such a lively showing in the campaign that Baldwin thought it necessary in the middle of it to write him a conciliatory letter in which he asked him to re-affirm his support of his policy which, while it did not commit the Party to food taxes, at the same time refrained from closing the door on this device. In effect Baldwin was asking Beaverbrook, no less than the country, to give him a free hand. Speaking next day at South Paddington Beaverbrook peremptorily rejected Baldwin's proposal and stated that his crusade would go forward. A few days later Derby, who was at Knowsley, received a telegram from Lord Salisbury asking him to come to London urgently as Baldwin wished to see him. On his return to Knowsley Derby wrote a letter which happily preserves the main outline of what must have been a most embarrassing meeting:

Lord Derby to Mr. Stanley Baldwin

Confidential 28 October 1930

I shall never look back to any interview with more pain and regret than the one I had with you yesterday. Believe me there is nobody in political life for whose high motives I have ever had so high an opinion as I have had of yours. There is nobody—with the possible exception of Arthur Balfour. Therefore it was with the greatest reluctance that when you asked me definitely, 'Do you think I ought to resign?' I answered 'Yes'. I felt then and I feel now, to have given that very definite answer without some explanation may have hurt your feelings and believe me that is the last thing I would wish to do. I would ask therefore that I might just tell you what my reasons are.

There is no question of it being a sin on your part either of omission or commission, but I find there is that general want of confidence not in you personally so much, as in your surroundings as to make a victory at the next Election very problematical.

May I first look back to the past? You had four years of Office with a large majority. People looked to you then for economy and for reestablishing the financial position of England. What was the result? As far as one can see there was practically no economy and instead of husbanding our resources money was spent with a lavish hand in an attempt to outbid the Socialists, a task which is not congenial to the Conservative Party and at which they are certain to be outbid.

Then came the Women's Vote. It is quite true if we had not given it the next Party that came in would have done so. Let them have done that. Our doing it did us nothing but harm and it has flooded the electorate with a vast number of electors, outweighing the vote of the men and for the most part composed of girls who take not the slightest interest in politics.

When therefore at the end of your time of office not only did we see no changes whatever made in the personnel of your Government, but more than that Austen Chamberlain announced that you had invited him to stay on in his then position as Secretary of State for Foreign Affairs in your new Administration, the first thing everybody said was 'the old gang and the old policy' and that lost us thousands of votes.

Still going back to the past. What attempt was there made in your time to find out—not in open session but privately as it might well have been done—what the Colonies were prepared to do for us and what they were prepared to ask. You would then have been in the position of knowing exactly how you stood and have been prepared at the last election to put forward a genuine Imperial Policy.

Now as to the present. I will pass over the incidents at the beginning of the year when I told you that your speech was not understood by the mass of the people—at all events in my part of the world—and ask you whether I was right in a statement I wished to make to the Press in our part of the world and to our National Union, as to what I thought your intentions were. Your answer was to refer me back to the speech which I told you was not understood and since then I have taken practically no interest whatever in politics, especially because I know that if you had permitted the publication of that letter it would have secured harmony between the warring elements of our Party.

And now we come to your present policy of the Quota. It may be perfectly right and I am sure that if you vouch for it that it can be easily worked, we can accept that, but nobody understands in the least what the Quota system means and it will require a lot of explanation to make people understand. The consequence is many of them have at the back of their minds an impression that the tax on wheat is going to be very much higher than they would be willing to agree to. Why not have said straight out, as you have to say in the end, that if, as you believe, the offer now made by Mr. Bennett is of the greatest value to this country, that then you are prepared to accept it and to give the quid pro quo, even if that necessitates a tax on wheat. You would have been in no worse a position as regards the cry of a tax on food than you are at the present moment and people would have understood exactly where they were and I believe you would have carried it. You will now, in my opinion have to drop the Quota system and make some such bald statement as I have just adumbrated.

But all these changes can only do harm and can only destroy confidence in a leader. They give the impression that he won't go forward until he is driven. That he has a fence in front of him which he hesitates to take although he knows to get to the winning post he must get over it. Therefore when you asked me whether I thought you ought to resign I said, Yes, because I do not feel that under your leadership there will be that confidence which is absolutely essential to ensure success.

I shall not come to the meeting on Thursday. It is I regret to say impossible for me to speak in the way that you wish me to do and I certainly am not going to speak against you. Moreover I promise you this that if the Party keep you as their Leader, although I shall take no particular interest in politics, you can rest assured I would do nothing to undermine your influence.

Derby's meeting with Baldwin coupled with this perhaps over-candid letter constituted one of the most incisive and unequivocal actions in his political career. It is of additional interest since it shows a recession on Derby's part from his lifelong opposition to food taxes. It seems likely that he had been much influenced by Beaverbrook's opinion. Derby was doubtless sent for by Baldwin because of his well-known opposition to tariffs in general and food taxes in particular. Baldwin plainly hoped that Derby would come to the Party meeting planned for October 30 at Caxton Hall and swing Lancashire opinion behind him. This letter is thirdly of interest since it shows how near Baldwin was to throwing in his hand. Baldwin's canvassing of Derby's opinion on this question was a tremendous sign of weakness. And what we know of Derby must incline us to the opinion that he would scarcely have given the advice he did unless he had thought that it was likely to be accepted, or that coming events would make Baldwin's resignation inevitable.

It was Beaverbrook's rejection of Baldwin's proposal on October 22 which led Baldwin to announce a Party meeting for October 30. The date was significant. It was polling day in South Paddington. When Baldwin, together with Bonar Law and Beaverbrook, torpedoed Lloyd George at the Carlton Club meeting in 1922, the

Tory leaders who were faithful to Lloyd George had carefully timed the meeting so that the result of the by-election at Newport would be in. It was hoped that the Government candidate would defeat the Independent candidate and that this would sway the meeting. In the event, however, the election went strongly against the Government and only served to encourage its critics. Baldwin may very well have had this in mind when he fixed the date of the Caxton Hall meeting. He evidently had no faith in his candidate's fortunes in Paddington and when the result was announced the next day he was vindicated in his judgment, if not in his policy. The Beaverbrook candidate was narrowly returned for this strongly Conservative seat. Meanwhile the Tory Party at their meeting the day before had rejected a resolution calling for a change of leadership by 462 to 116. Many members who were dissatisfied with Baldwin's leadership and preferred Beaverbrook's policy voted to sustain Baldwin. If Baldwin was to be pole-axed the Party did not mean it to be done by the Press lords.

Baldwin had won for the moment; but in retrospect he must have resented the distasteful advice which Derby had given him, and for some time there seems to have been little contact or correspondence between them. Meanwhile Beaverbrook maintained his onslaught and continued to put candidates in the field against official Tory candidates. Speaking at Islington on 30 January 1931, he said: 'It is my purpose to break up the Conservative Party if the Conservative Party does not adopt the policy [of Empire Free Trade]'. Though Beaverbrook had been repulsed Baldwin was far from secure in the leadership. Indeed at the end of February the death of Sir Laming Worthington-Evans, the member for St. George's, Westminster, opened the safest Tory seat in the country, and Rothermere's candidate, Sir Ernest Petter, was put in the field. It seemed for some days impossible for the official organisation to find a candidate to oppose him. Baldwin decided to resign. *The Times* had prepared a leading article headed 'Mr. Baldwin withdraws' and it was only the last-minute intervention of Mr. Bridgeman, later Viscount Bridgeman, a senior Party stalwart, which persuaded Baldwin to go on. In the end a strong official candidate was found in Mr. Alfred Duff

Cooper, later Viscount Norwich, and he was elected by a majority in excess of 5,000.

A few days later an exchange of letters was published between Neville Chamberlain and Beaverbrook in which Beaverbrook stated his policy in much more moderate terms, and Chamberlain wrote that he was authorised by Baldwin to say that this was a correct statement of the Party's policy on agriculture. Though Beaverbrook's face was saved, most people thought the victory lay with Baldwin:

Mr. Neville Chamberlain to Lord Derby

Private
10 April 1931

Cairnton,
Banchory, N.B.

The pact with Max was a real victory though as you say one does not want to be sounding any note of triumph publicly. But he had had a severe disappointment in East Islington and a worse one in St. George's and it seemed to me that the psychological moment had arrived when he would be glad to find some way out.

You are of course perfectly right in saying that Baldwin has given up nothing. It is Max who has now accepted our policy. The danger is that neither he nor Rothermere understand what is meant by playing the game and the result will probably be to give us a good deal of trouble. Still it is difficult to see how Max can go back on his bargain and there is no doubt that his and Rothermere's support will be very valuable to us at an Election. R. [Rothermere] is in the deal, by the way, although this did not appear in the published correspondence.

If the Election is not too long delayed I think S.B. will carry on all right. Some of us had some plain words with him as the result of which he suddenly hit Ramsay most viciously in the House next day. Ramsay's astonishment and alarm were comic.

* * *

Early in 1931 there was a large-scale stoppage of work in the Lancashire textile industry. The employers wished to introduce the 'more-looms-to-a-weaver' system, which had been used successfully in the Burnley district for some time, and which allotted eight looms instead of four to the care of each weaver. The weavers, fearing that the adoption of this system would mean a reduction in their wages, refused to conform to it. The President of the Board of Trade, Mr. William Graham, was unsuccessful in his attempts at conciliation; and on January 17 the employers declared a lock-out of some 200,000 weavers. The resultant stoppage of work lasted for nearly four weeks, both sides proving obstinate. Finally it was the employers who surrendered: and this was largely due to Derby's influence.

Since the beginning of the year Derby had been enjoying the sunshine at his villa, Sansovino, in Cannes. From there he viewed the continuance of the lock-out with concern. The British Cotton Textile Trades Exhibition of which he was president was due to open on February 16; its purpose would be frustrated if a continued stoppage were to incapacitate the industry from meeting the orders which the Exhibition was designed to procure. In these circumstances it occurred to Derby that his special position in Lancashire might make an appeal from him effective where negotiation had failed.

He sent to Mr. (now Sir) John Grey, acting president of the Master Cotton Spinners' and Manufacturers' Association, a telegram, described by the latter as eloquent, urging the employers to end the lockout. By this time the employers may well have felt disinclined to hold out. The dispute was estimated to have cost the industry between three and four million pounds; and the intransigence of the weavers, who had actually forbidden their leaders to negotiate further, made an early victory for the employers appear improbable. Derby's telegram, which arrived on February 13, was decisive on the employers; and the same evening Grey announced that the weavers were to be allowed to return to work on the old basis of four looms to a man. Derby was widely praised for his intervention which meant, as he told the *Daily Sketch*, that foreign buyers at the Exhibition who visited Lancashire would see the mills in full working order instead of standing idle. The settlement was, however, received with mixed feelings on the Manchester Royal Exchange; a manufacturer from the Nelson district described it as 'a victory for Moscow'.

Derby's appeal was made at the instance of a group of influential people connected with the Exhibition; but meanwhile Lord Stamfordham, the King's Private Secretary, had arrived independently at the conclusion that Derby's voice was the one most likely to be heeded in the dispute, the more so if he intervened at the King's request. He therefore drafted the following letter which was never sent but has been preserved in the Royal Archives:

Draft of proposed letter from H.M. the King to Lord Derby

Buckingham Palace

The industrial position in Lancashire causes me grave anxiety: and especially the apparent failure of the Government to arrive at any settlement of the weavers' difficulty. The continuance of the existing state of things would seem to threaten ruin to employers and untold misery to the workers.

Recognising as I do your position in the County, and the mutual regard between you and its people, do you think they would listen to an earnest appeal from me: that in this time of national anxiety all hearts should join in sinking individual interest and unite in a spirit of true patriotism and self-sacrifice to face and solve the formidable question which confronts us, not only in Lancashire, but throughout the whole industrial community?

I would like to think that the Heads of all the Churches would combine in calling for general intercession that these ends, so devoutly longed for, may be attained.

The King rightly felt that it would be unconstitutional for him to send such a letter except on the advice of his Prime Minister, and the matter was shelved until Stamfordham should have obtained the latter's consent. Before any decision had been taken Derby sent his telegram and the dispute was over:

Lord Derby to Lord Stamfordham[1]

Confidential — Derby House

15 February 1931

. . . I am glad to think that I to a certain extent anticipated what His Majesty might have wished and intervened in the Cotton Dispute.

[1] Royal Archives.

> You might like to know what happened. I got a telegram from responsible people connected with the Exhibition suggesting that I should send a telegram from me to Mr. Grey, the Employers' Chairman, begging him to realise that if the strike went on whilst the Exhibition was open all our efforts of propaganda for cotton goods would be nullified. I immediately telegraphed on these lines and I am glad to say that I had a telegram, and found letters from Mr. Grey, to say that it helped him very materially to secure the abandonment of the lock-out. So my friends were evidently justified in saying that intervention on my part would not be resented . . .

MacDonald's second Labour Government, which had boasted that it could solve the problem of unemployment, found itself impotent and hamstrung. In retrospect, of course, the Labour Party claimed that their failure was due to the lack of a majority; they had enjoyed office but not power. These explanations were delusive. If the Labour Government had produced any coherent plan for grappling with the urgent problem of the hour they would have had the support of all parties in the House. The only plan that was forthcoming was that of the Chancellor of the Duchy of Lancaster, Sir Oswald Mosley, who with Mr. J. H. Thomas was specifically charged to cope with unemployment. His plan was overruled and nothing was substituted in its place. Unemployment in fact nearly trebled under the MacDonald administration, but it was as silly to blame them for this fact as it was for them to pretend that if they had had more power they could have solved the problem. The 1929 crash on Wall Street had dislocated the whole economy of the world and catastrophies erupted overnight for which no one had a solution.

An Economy Committee was set up in March under the chairmanship of Sir George (later first Lord) May, the distinguished economist, to inquire into national expenditure. Its report was published at the end of July just after Parliament had risen. By this time the unemployment figure stood at over two and three-quarter millions, while the Bank of England was losing gold at the rate of £2,500,000 a day. The Committee recommended various economies and a general reduction in public expenditure. MacDonald appointed another committee, under Snowden's chairmanship, to study the

May Report; and, apparently considering that no further action was required, went on holiday. Almost immediately he was recalled to London by an urgent message from the Bank of England. A panic flight from sterling had started and it appeared that the pound could only be saved by the adoption of far more stringent economies than those hitherto contemplated. Mr. Baldwin pledged the support of the Conservative Party for any efforts the Government might make to overcome the crisis. A new set of proposals was prepared by the Economy Committee and placed before the Cabinet on August 19. These proposals, formulated on the principle of 'equality of sacrifice', involved considerable departures from socialist doctrine, including the curtailment of unemployment benefits. It soon became clear that the trades unions would bitterly resist such a measure; and opinion in the Cabinet itself was sharply divided. Meanwhile the crisis grew graver and the Directors of the Bank of England stated that they would be unable to secure the American credit which was desperately needed unless the May proposals were adopted in full.

In these circumstances the 'National Government' was born. After a series of consultations with the leaders of the opposition parties, MacDonald decided to offer the resignation of the Labour Cabinet to the King and at the same time to accept His Majesty's commission to form a new, 'National' Government. The change of Government took place on August 24. Baldwin became Lord President of the Council in the new Cabinet and the acting leader of the Liberals, Sir Herbert Samuel, went to the Home Office. Snowden (who remained Chancellor of the Exchequer), Lord Sankey and Mr. J. H. Thomas were the only three Labour members who followed MacDonald into his new Cabinet. Neither Mr. Lloyd George (who was undergoing an operation) nor Mr. Churchill was invited to join the Government.

Though the leaders of the 'National' Government had loudly asseverated that the Coalition had only been formed to deal with the emergency, and that it would be dissolved as soon as the remedial measures had been taken, few were deceived by this and it came as no surprise to the country when the Government decided in October to dissolve Parliament and have a General Election. There is nothing dearer to the heart of the average Englishman than a first-class catastrophe. Assured by distinguished leaders of all parties that the country was on the rocks, that the pound was down the drain, and that if the Socialists were to be elected they would steal all the money in the Post Office Savings Bank, the electorate had no doubt where its duties and its interests lay.

The result of the 1931 Election was a landslide for the Conservatives: they lost no seats and won over two hundred. Labour, on the other hand, won no seats and lost over two hundred. The National Government as a whole was returned with the enormous majority of 502. Derby wrote to congratulate the leader whom a year before he had advised to retire. Baldwin replied:

Mr. Stanley Baldwin to Lord Derby

31 October 1931 — Trent, New Barnet

Thank you so much for your generous letter.

What a responsibility for us! The country has sent out an S.O.S. to the Government and now we have to rise to it.

By gad but we will do our best.

* * *

In 1933 Hyperion won the Derby by four lengths from the tobacco magnate Sir Hugo Cunliffe-Owen's King Salmon. This was the second time that George Lambton had trained a Derby winner for Stanley House; and once more Tommy Weston was the jockey. The race, unlike Sansovino's in 1924, was run in perfect weather conditions; there was almost a record crowd and the King and Queen were present. Lambton achieved the remarkable distinction of being the trainer of three horses out of the first five: for besides Hyperion, he had trained Scarlet Tiger, which came fourth, and Thrapston, which came fifth, and, like the winner, belonged to Derby. Hyperion, a chestnut colt by Gainsborough out of Selene, stood just over fifteen hands high, and if he had been only an inch smaller would have been eligible for pony racing. Moreover he had four white socks, a peculiarity which is traditionally regarded as a sign of weak legs. However, his general appearance was superb and he started favourite at 6 to 1. Nor did he disappoint his backers, for he won without difficulty in what was then the record time of two minutes thirty four seconds.[1] Many competent observers thought at the time that Hyperion had won by far more than the four lengths of the official verdict. *The Times*' racing correspondent wrote: 'Never in my time has a Derby been won more easily. There was no doubt about the result half a mile from the finish.'

* * *

Since he had left the War Office in 1923 Derby had taken very little part in national politics. But when in 1933 the Government set up a Joint Select Committee of both Houses of Parliament to consider its Indian policy which had been earlier embodied in a White Paper Derby agreed to serve as a member. He was invited so that Lancashire interests might be represented and since it was an issue affecting the welfare of the county, Derby naturally agreed. The protracted investigations and discussions of the Select Committee, which was presided over by Lord Linlithgow, were interrupted by an unusual incident. Mr. Winston Churchill, who had been a strong opponent of the Government's Indian policy, alleged that two members of the Committee had been guilty of breach of privilege. The two members were the Secretary of State for India, Sir Samuel Hoare, and Derby. Since the author was to some extent involved in the raising of the complaint and since his sympathies were opposed to Derby and Hoare in this matter, it has been thought right to print the admirably lucid and impartial account of these events published shortly afterwards in the *Annual Register* of 1934:

> . . . The Speaker, after hearing Mr. Churchill, ruled that he had made out a prima facie case for a breach of privilege, and allowed him formally to move that the alleged action of Sir S. Hoare and Lord Derby should be forthwith referred to the Committee of Privileges. Sir S. Hoare then made a statement in which he exonerated himself

[1] This record was beaten in the following year by Mr. Tom Wall's Windsor Lad.

from Mr. Churchill's charges, and declared himself delighted with the prospect of being able to prove that his critic had found another mare's nest. The motion was accepted by the Government, and being supported by both the Opposition leaders was agreed to without a division.

. . . The Committee of Privileges which had been appointed by the House of Commons to examine the charges brought by Mr. Churchill against Sir Samuel Hoare and Lord Derby issued its report on June 8. It came to the unanimous conclusion that no breach of privilege had been committed. It was not disputed that the facts were as Mr. Churchill had stated; the first draft of evidence submitted by the Manchester Chamber of Commerce had been criticised by the Secretary for India and Lord Derby as unsuitable, and a very different statement had eventually been laid by the Chamber before the Joint Committee. Contrary, however, to Mr. Churchill's contention, it was held that the Joint Committee was not a judicial body and therefore there was nothing improper in the representations made by Sir Samuel Hoare and Lord Derby to members of the Manchester Chamber of Commerce, and in any case the change in the views of the Chamber had been brought about not by these representations but by those of the delegation which went out from Lancashire to India in the autumn, and which came to the conclusion that more was to be gained from Indian goodwill than from tying the hands of the future Indian Government.

On June 13 the Prime Minister submitted the report to the House of Commons for its approval. He asked it, in fairness to the two members charged, to give a clear-cut decision without any qualification or addendum, which might be taken as evidence of doubt on their part. He also asked the House to agree that the documents presented to the Committee should not be produced. Mr. Churchill followed with a long speech in which he tried to show that the report did nothing to invalidate the charges which he had brought when he first raised the question. He still maintained that the two members concerned had exercised a pressure which was equivalent to 'tampering' and that the Joint Committee was or ought to be a judicial body. The net effect of his speech was to confirm a suspicion which had already been generally held, that his object in raising the question had been not so much to defend the privileges of the House as to put a spoke in the wheel of the Joint Committee. Lord Hugh Cecil pointed out the absurdity of treating select Committees of Parliament as judicial bodies, and Mr. Amery asked Mr. Churchill why he had not first brought the matter to the attention of the members concerned, who were his old friends, or of the Chamber of Commerce, while Sir John Simon made a merciless exposure of his case. The report was ultimately adopted with acclamation.

Mr. Churchill's action in raising this matter was to rankle with Derby for many months. He was particularly nettled that his conduct in giving a dinner party at Derby House, at which Hoare had sought to persuade members of the Manchester Chamber of Commerce to alter their evidence, should have been publicised and called in question. However at the time he affected indifference:

Lord Derby to Lord Stanley

24 April 1934

. . . I suppose I ought to be extremely annoyed with Winston but I really am not because I think it is impossible to conceive anything more gratifying than the general tribute of confidence I am getting from Lancashire and which more than makes up for all the annoyance. Of course I do not know exactly what points he is going to bring forward but I think I have got a complete answer for every one and I only hope everything will be published as I think it will show up what a petty, mean action Winston's is. There is not a single person who dined with me that night who is not just as angry as I am about it.

The Committee of Privileges reported on 8 June 1934. Its findings were open to a charge of lack of objectivity in that it was exclusively composed of members nominated by the Party Whips of all three Parties who were committed to support the Government's policy on India. Nonetheless the report was unanimously accepted by the House, Mr. Churchill and his supporters not caring to challenge the unanimous report of the Committee of Privileges in the lobby. Derby and Hoare, though they could claim a victory in the matter, had had a disagreeable time and Mr. Baldwin hastened to send his good wishes:

Mr. Stanley Baldwin to Lord Derby

Private — 11 Downing Street
8 June 1934

I want to be among the first to wring your hand. These last weeks must have been hard for you to bear but it must be some satisfaction to you to know that after the most critical examination of the facts and circumstances ever made by an investigation committee, no shadow of doubt remains with any member but that our decision is right and justified up to the hilt . . .

That Derby despite his vindication was still nettled is shown by a letter he wrote to Mr. Baldwin at the end of the month asking whether he thought it would be advisable at a meeting he was shortly to address in Lancashire to 'tell them a thing or two about him [Churchill] and his methods and to refer to the report of the Committee of Privileges'. Derby indicated that he would like to read a letter which he had written and which was put before the Committee of Privileges and went on: 'I should not hesitate to do so if it were not for the fact that if it became known that I had written such a letter there might be a demand for the whole of the correspondence to be produced, and as that has been refused I do not want to give Churchill any handle for renewing the request'.

Mr. Stanley Baldwin to Lord Derby

Private — House of Commons
3 July 1934

I have considered your letter very carefully.

I think it would be unwise to read the letter.

We are in a very strong position now vis-à-vis our enemies and we must not risk weakening it by a false step.

You can paraphrase the letter and say those are the principles which guided you in all your dealings with the Chamber [of Commerce] and you can say with confidence that your attitude was understood by all.

I have not consulted any member of the Committee and this opinion, for what it is worth, is my own.

Lord Derby to Mr. Stanley Baldwin

Private 4 July 1934

Thanks very much for your letter. I think your advice is right. I should like to have read the letter because I think it would be a knock-out blow for Winston, who I am sorry to say has still got a big following in Lancashire. I do not think it will last, but at the same time it is for the moment doing mischief. However I think I can get round it.

When the report of the Joint Select Committee was about to be published Austen Chamberlain and Derby were concerned to see that it got a good Press. Lord Beaverbrook and his newspapers had not taken a decisive part in the controversy and it was felt that early action might procure his support:

Lord Derby to Sir Austen Chamberlain

Private 22 October 1934

. . . It will be up to you to let me know when you would like me to go with you to see Max.

. . . I am quite sure if we do not get at him to keep him on the right path Winston will and therefore I think it is very imperative we should make a move. I do not know that he will ever pay much attention to me but he certainly will to you. The more I think of it the more I hope that moderate people will come round to our view and I believe we have found the happy medium which will enable all those members of our Party who are not extremists to unite to support the views we have put forward . . .

Sir Austen Chamberlain to Lord Derby

24 October 1934 58 Rutland Gate, S.W.7

. . . I do not think that we can usefully see Max until a few days before the Report will appear which I now understand will be on the 22nd November, but I am not very happy about the idea of going down to his house to see him. It would make our visit very formal and put us too much in the position of suitors for his favour; do you think you might ask him to lunch in a private room at the Savoy or some similar place? . . .

Lord Derby to Sir Austen Chamberlain

Private 25 October 1934

. . . Yes, I think perhaps you are right about Max. I would certainly ask him to luncheon in a private room at the Savoy but I do not quite like doing that, and I will make arrangements to give a luncheon just to you and him—I am sure you won't mind it being a small one—at Derby House . . .

Sir Austen Chamberlain to Lord Derby

1 November 1934 58 Rutland Gate, S.W.7

Beaverbrook will be glad to lunch with you on November 20. Will you therefore now write to him yourself?

It was more than a year before the breach between Derby and Churchill was healed. Sir Abe Bailey, a South African magnate who spent three or four months each year in England and who was acquainted with all the leading English political personalities, was responsible for bringing this about:

Sir Abe Bailey to Lord Derby

Private 38 Bryanston Square, W.1
8 September 1935

I am giving a dinner to Neville Chamberlain on November 9th. I have invited Winston.

I am writing you this to ask you to come and make it up. This country will not be flowing with milk and honey unless we all work together. I do hope you will be one of the party. It is a wonderful list—all bankers, economists and heads of big firms, no doubt you know many. Sir Robert Horne is the only politician.

Lord Derby to Sir Abe Bailey

Confidential 12 September 1935

Many thanks for your kind invitation which under ordinary circumstances I should have been delighted to accept. But I have to hesitate when you tell me that I shall meet Churchill. I quite agree with you that nothing should be left undone to secure complete unity in our party before the next election, but I could not accept reconciliation with Churchill in the way you suggest, kindly though I know your intention to be. To meet casually under your roof would from my point of view be impossible. Churchill had always been looked upon by me as a great personal friend; without a moment's warning he tried to stab me in the back with baseless accusations. His charges have been proved to be without any foundation. The unanimous report of the Select Committee was accepted by the whole House of Commons with the single exception of Churchill, and he has not in any way since shown that he equally has accepted the verdict as completely exonerating me personally. Until he does so reconciliation is impossible. The initiative for reconciliation must come from him. You may rest assured that if it did so come I should meet, and gladly meet, any such action half way, and would completely forget and ignore the past. I am sure that if you were in my shoes you would feel as I do.

Sir Abe Bailey to Lord Derby

21 September 1935 — 38 Bryanston Square, W.1

Many thanks for your letter. I do hope you can come 9th 8 o'clock Winston is coming. That must not prevent your coming—do come.

He is I know anxious to 'make it up'. England requires you all—with guts. The air force and navy must be gingered up.

Mr. Winston Churchill to Lord Derby

Private — Chartwell

27 September 1935

Abe Bailey has told me about his correspondence with you.

I have on several occasions testified in Parliament that you acted throughout from the highest sense of public duty, and your good faith and honour were never impugned in any way by me. I hope you will not deny me similar claims. We were opponents in an historic controversy which has now been settled. I was deeply grieved that the course I thought it my duty to take caused you pain, and severed those cordial relations which had subsisted between us for so many years. It would be a great pleasure to me if you felt that bygones could be bygones.

Lord Derby to Mr. Winston Churchill

Private Knowsley

29 September 1935

I only arrived here late last night to find your letter for which I thank you. I was very pleased to get it and gladly welcome the opportunity thus afforded me of letting bygones be bygones and resuming a friendship which was so agreeable to me for many years. I shall hope to see you at Abe Bailey's dinner and in burying the hatchet I mean that no resentment whatever on my part shall remain.

Lord Derby to Sir Abe Bailey

Private 29 September 1935

I only got here late last night, too late to telegraph, but I have done so this morning to say I should like to come to your dinner. I have received a letter from Winston Churchill which I can quite accept as healing the breach between us and allowing bygones to be bygones. I have written to him to that effect . . .

Lord Derby to Lord Beaverbrook

Confidential Coworth Park

6 October 1935

I want to tell you, as an old friend, that there is peace between Winston and myself. He wrote me a very nice letter offering the olive branch—and I at once accepted it as such. I am very glad, as at my age I dislike the breaking of old friendships. We—he and I—shall meet at Abe's on Wednesday, and am glad to think I may also see you.

* * *

On 4 April 1935 Derby celebrated his seventieth birthday. On this occasion the deep affection which he had inspired in the hearts of the people of Lancashire evoked a remarkable and touching manifestation. At a gathering of nearly five thousand people in Preston Public Hall he and Lady Derby received presents towards which more than eighty thousand Lancastrians had each contributed a shilling. For Lady Derby there was a jewel, and for Derby himself a rose water dish of gold plate. The dish was not yet wrought, so a copy of the design was handed to Derby in its stead.

But the principal token of Lancashire's esteem was more memorable. It consisted of a cabinet containing twenty-two thick volumes, bound in red morocco and stamped with the Stanley arms in gold. The volumes contained the signatures—more than eighty-three thousand—of all the subscribers to the presentation; and in each volume there appeared the following words:

> We, men and women of Lancashire, whose signatures are appended in the accompanying volumes, desire to offer to your Lordship on your 70th birthday a message of affectionate greeting. We recall with gratitude the part which you have taken over many years in every phase of the public and charitable activity of the County Palatine, the largeness of sympathy and the generosity of spirit which have informed all your actions and have made your Lordship welcome in every assembly, and endeared you to the hearts of Lancashire people. We ask you to accept this tribute of friendship to a gracious neighbour, and with it a piece of gold plate, in token of our admiration and regard and of our earnest wish for the long and happy continuance of your presence among us.

Derby was deeply moved and spoke with more emotion than was his custom. The *Preston Guardian* of 6 April 1935 records:

> Lord Derby spoke with great emotion, and there were tears in his eyes. Thanking the subscribers, he said:
>
> 'The English language provides three words in which to express the gratitude I feel to-day. "I thank you," and if you will take that, as I know you will, as coming from the bottom of my heart, it is all I can say to you in return for your kindness, but you will know at the same time that it means all the gratitude I can possibly convey to you for such kindness.
>
> 'It is a unique position certainly for me, and I don't think anybody else has had the same thing, to stand in the midst of some thousands of his fellow-countrymen and receive from them a welcome such as you have given me, and are giving me at the same time such wonderful proofs of the affection of so many other thousands.'
>
> A voice: 'You deserve it'.

'It is wonderful for me to think that these have been given to me from every town and every district in the county in proof of their affection and friendship. There is nowhere I could go, I feel, in the whole of the county where I should not find at least one friend.

'I am not a great Shakespearean scholar,' continued Lord Derby, 'but I saw in the paper the other day a sentence quoted from a speech put into the mouth of one of my ancestors by Shakespeare when speaking to the King, "My friends," he said, "are in the North".

'It is nice to think,' said Lord Derby, 'that after a lapse of many generations the present titular head of the family can say with the same truth as his ancestor did, "My friends are in the North".

'I have looked back on what those who have gone before me have done, and hoped that in my time I should not let them down. There are many things of which one can be proud, but for my part the one thing I am proud of is that through successive generations each Lord Derby in his day has done his best to play his part in his county and his country. I have only to look back for that force of example which, if you have a pride of family, will keep you in the straight path.'

He next referred to his ancestors. He described his father as one of the most lovable and courteous men who ever stepped the earth.

'Then I come to my uncle, a man who, to my mind, was very much misunderstood, and whose life, if it were written down, would show that a great many people greatly loved him. He was a naturally shy and retiring man. He was not known as some of the others have been known.'

'. . . I have entered into the seventies,' he went on, 'on the last lap of a life which may be long or may be short. I really ought to look backwards, but I want to look forward.

'People ask one, "Would you have changed your life?" I always think it is a very silly question to ask, for, of course, there is not a man or woman living who, if they had the chance to change something in their lives for the better would not willingly have changed. But there is one thing in my life that I can look back on that I would never change, and that is the day on which I married Lady Derby.

'She has always done her best to help me with advice and she has always taken her part in those works in the county that a woman can do so much better than a man. Apart from my love for her, I will always be grateful to her for the help she has given to me and for the children which she has also given me.

'I have sons and I know that in the future they will carry on the work probably better than I have done. But certainly with no more love of the county. (Hear, hear.) They have some of the same pride that I have of being one of the county and not an absentee.

'It is the last lap, but I feel full of running. . . .'

* * *

In October 1938 Derby's life was clouded by the death of his elder son and heir, Lord Stanley. Like his younger brother, Oliver, Edward had served in the 1914 war and followed a Parliamentary career. He was elected Member for the Abercromby division of Liverpool in 1917 and became the youngest Member of the House of Commons. Like his father he first served in the Whips Office in 1924 as a junior Lord of the Treasury and between 1927 and 1938 he filled a variety of Parliamentary Under-Secretaryships in successive governments. Oliver, the more brilliant of the two, had attained Cabinet rank on being appointed Minister of Labour in June 1934 but it was not until May 1938—only six months before his death—that Edward entered the Cabinet as Secretary of State for the Dominions.

It was a great satisfaction to Derby to have two sons in the Cabinet simultaneously. Since his detachment from national politics in 1924 he had sought no office or advancement for himself and had concentrated almost entirely on his Lancashire duties. He obtained a vicarious but deep enjoyment from his sons' growing success in the national arena. He was much closer to Edward than to Oliver. Edward took after him while Oliver's principal characteristics were derived in the main from Lady Derby. Edward moreover was his heir and shared to the full his interests in blood stock and racing. Derby placed a great reliance on his judgment and always consulted him on major decisions. Edward had married in 1917 Sibyl Cadogan, eldest daughter of Viscount Chelsea, son and heir of the fifth Earl Cadogan. She and her three sisters, Mary, who married the future Duke of Marlborough, Cynthia, who married Sir Humphrey de Trafford, and Edith, who married the third Lord Hillingdon, were inevitably known as Cadogan Square. Derby, who was so fortunate in every other aspect of his life, had the misfortune that two of his three children died in his lifetime while Oliver only survived him by two years. He was especially vulnerable in such matters as he had few intimate friends outside the family circle in which his whole life was bound up. He lived to know part of the truth of Bacon's grim apophthegm 'He that hath wife and children hath given hostages to fortune'.

Edward died after a long and painful illness shortly after the signing of the Munich Agreement. Derby wrote to congratulate Chamberlain on what he judged his success at Munich and received the following answer:

Mr. Neville Chamberlain to Lord Derby

12 October 1938 — 10 Downing Street,
Whitehall

I was very much touched by your kind and generous letter. I feel that I have been terribly over praised for having done no more than was my clear and obvious duty, but all the same letters like yours are a great encouragement in these very anxious and difficult times. I am glad indeed to think that Edward was pleased by my visit. He seemed better than I expected, but of course I realise that he is very seriously ill and I do sympathise very deeply with you and the rest of his family in your anxiety.

After Edward's death Derby's old friend Lord Beaverbrook wrote:

Lord Beaverbrook to Lord Derby

22 October 1938 — Cherkley,
Leatherhead

MY DEAR EDDY,

I will be at your call at any time—night or day.

I have been nursing a cold for several days. But this day I am better.

My dear friend. The leaders of our newspapers would give you a testimonial of affection and devotion now—if I would encourage them. You hold the love of the people. And they mourn with you.

Take up the task of Edward and carry it, along with your own duty. That is the way you have always walked.

I send you my devotion.

Yours affectionately,

MAX.

* * *

It was in these years between the two wars that Derby built for himself a position of influence and authority which was not only unique in Lancashire but unrivalled by any territorial magnate in any other English county in the nineteenth and twentieth centuries. Knowsley became the focus for the whole life of the county and there was no Lancashire activity too large or too small to lay claim to his interest, encouragement and support. Many landed proprietors out of tradition and a sense of duty play an active role in county life, but Derby's success was a thing apart. It was not merely that he was more assiduous than others in a like situation; he genuinely enjoyed local functions, particularly when they were small. No bazaar or fête was too remote for him to attend, no foundation stone too small for him to lay; no swimming pool too unimportant for him to open. He often used to remark that he preferred small gatherings as these really gave him an opportunity to get to know the people concerned. He loved Lancashire folk and they loved him in return. His racing activities not only endeared him to Lancashire but made him a national figure.

Lancashire felt that in him the County Palatine had a man who could effectively plead its interest at Westminster, Whitehall, Downing Street and Buckingham Palace. Though Lancashire people may have overestimated the weight he carried in the councils of the nation they never turned to him in vain. His friendship with the Royal Family, and above all with King George V, inevitably magnified his stature, and through this friendship Lancashire certainly secured more than its full share of Royal visits. The magnificence of his life, the geniality of his person, his unstinted support of and interest in all Lancashire activities, combined to give him a pre-eminence among his fellow Lancastrians which, though it naturally pleased his vanity, he never exploited for personal advantage. He was so grand and rich and beloved that he had no ambitions for himself except to do his duty in the spacious world into which he had been born. Not even the first Lord Derby, who crowned Henry VII on Bosworth Field in 1485, or the seventh who was executed by the Parliamentarians at Bolton for his support of Charles II in 1651, or the fourteenth who was three times Prime Minister, ever enjoyed such extensive popularity.

His mind and character were not sufficiently decided to fit him for supreme success in the world of politics. He had, however, in the highest degree all the gifts and characteristics that would make a perfect constitutional monarch. And it was as a king that he came to be regarded in Lancashire. The due deference he always showed to his sovereign only increased the respect in which he himself was held. Yet it can be said without any *lèse-majesté* that he was more popular than the King himself in a county which has always been distinguished for its loyalty to the throne.

Derby talking to the late Mr. J. A. Dewar outside the weighing-in room at Newmarket, May 1939.

XXVII

Last Years

WHEN Britain declared war on Germany on 3 September 1939, Derby was in his seventy-fifth year. The war years were to be especially distressing for him. He was too old to play an effective part and within a year or so he experienced a series of minor but crippling maladies which eventually made it hard, especially for a man of his bulk, to get about. He felt cut off and isolated and had very little to do except to worry. He never doubted Britain's ability to survive the war, but he felt lonely and out of touch, and his correspondence reflects this in a rather pathetic way. After the first year he could not go to London; few people came to Knowsley; he felt frustrated that for the first time in his life he was not well informed of what was going on and that he was too old to help.

Like the overwhelming majority of Englishmen of all classes and parties, he had welcomed the Munich Agreement. But in common with nearly all those who had mistakenly thought that Munich promised a lasting peace, he quite soon readjusted his view and realised that the policy of appeasement had failed and should certainly not be extended:

Lord Derby to Captain Malcolm Bullock

Private

Coldstones
17 August 1939

. . . I am always as you know a pessimist, but I think I have every reason to be now. I have never thought a war could be altogether avoided. I am quite sure it cannot be now—and I think the blow will come soon and very suddenly. The Germans have got two million men under arms. They are to be sent back—the reservists—by the middle of September. I am convinced that Hitler will have a settlement by then either by war or by our giving way. The latter alternative is out of the question.

Though Derby accepted the fact that war was inevitable, like many other Englishmen he was in some perplexity as to our true war aims:

Lord Derby to Lord Beaverbrook

Personal Knowsley

24 September 1939

... I wish I knew what we are fighting for—if to beat Hitler to a pulp, I understand and strongly sympathise, but if it is to reconstitute Poland, I am not so enthusiastic. If it had not been for the League of Nations, which I abominate—or for Locarno, which I always thought a very much overrated treaty—we should not be fighting now for Poland—and if it is to reconstitute Poland, when we have beaten Hitler we shall have to fight and beat Russia, a tough proposition.

Altogether, things are *hell*.

* * *

Like other British subjects who owned property abroad Derby was concerned about his villa in the South of France:

Lord Derby to Mr. J. G. Taylor

16 November 1939

... You will have heard of the death of my brother-in-law Lord Charles Montagu. He was devoted to Cannes and more especially to Sansovino and, as you know, I built a special room for him there and I do not think he was ever so happy as when he came to us. That makes another link gone and I do not think I shall ever come back to Cannes. If, therefore, you do hear of a likely purchaser of Sansovino please let me know. I know I shall have to sell at a big loss but I should be willing to do that.

Mr. J. G. Taylor to Lord Derby

2 December 1939

... I think we shall have some kind of a season and in fact as far as my own business is concerned up to the present we have done as much business as we did for the corresponding period last year. I cannot however expect to go on at that rhythm unless something is done to allow people to bring money to France to spend on the Riviera.

I know that many people are working in England in that direction and more especially the Directors of the Hôtels Réunis who own the Carlton Hotel in Cannes and who have interests in the hotels in Monte-Carlo.

The Monte-Carlo gambling-rooms have opened and I am told that the authorities expected something like 50 or 60 people, whereas 700 turned up and insisted on gambling until two o'clock in the morning. I cannot imagine who the people are but I intend to go over one day and have a look for myself.

There is much activity in Cannes owing to all sorts of charities, but this activity, unfortunately, is marred, so I am told, by a great deal of squabbling, and in fact real quarrelling.

One lady is reputed to have thrown a plate of sandwiches at the head of another lady at the Cantine in the Cannes Station.

When, following upon the Anglo-American landings in North Africa in November 1942, German troops crossed the armistice line in France and occupied all the territory which had previously been administered by Vichy, new problems arose:

Lord Beaverbrook to Lord Derby

8 January 1943 Cherkley

This is a brief note, as usual, asking for information. I appear to spend much of my life seeking out things.

On the borders of Monte Carlo on the French side I have a house called 'La Capponcina'. I am paying £400 a year through the firm of John Taylor for the purpose of discharging rates, taxes and caretaking.

Now the question arises, with the invasion of the Riviera by the enemy, if the payment should be continued or dropped altogether.

Would it be asking too much for you to let me know what you decide to do in your own case . . .

Lord Derby to Lord Beaverbrook

Confidential 11 January 1943

Thanks very much for your letter. I had exactly the same difficulties with regard to sending money for the maintenance of my villa at Cannes as you have about yours. One has got to be extremely careful what one does so as not to in any way go contrary to the regulations with regard to sending money that might be helpful to the Boche.

I am sure the best, indeed the only way of being able to send any help to one's dependents in the south of France is through Messrs. John Taylor & Son of Cannes, whose address is Cooks Building, 10 Mayfair Place, W.1 (Tel.: Grosvenor 4000, Extension 477).

Now what has happened with regard to myself is this. I wrote to them on the matter in December and the answer I have received from Mr. J. Taylor, whom I find most reliable, is to the effect that they are quite prepared to continue to make remittances to the south of France as in the past. It will be the Swiss authorities who will do the work in place of the Americans. The Foreign Office sound rather confident that the usual channels of communications which they employ will be kept open and would prove effective. Under those circumstances although they say that communications may take longer than they did in the past I have sent them a cheque to continue payments to my servants at Sansovino and they have agreed that if the money is not paid over to their firm in Cannes it will be reimbursed.

I cannot feel that that is entirely satisfactory but at the same time I think it is satisfactory enough for me to send through Taylor in London more money for the payment of wages and expenses so as not to give the Boche or anybody else any excuse for seizing the property.

I send you all the information I have and if anything occurs afterwards, which I think may be of use to you, I will see that it is sent on to you at once. But of course the whole question is very problematical as to whether the money does in the end get to the right people but I hope and believe that it may do. All I can say is that I have always found John Taylor & Son absolutely trustworthy.

* * *

For Derby it was to be a long and lonely war. At first he threw himself with a will into the sort of minor but far from unimportant activities which, since his retirement from national politics, had been his delight and his greatest merit. He presided over several war charities and undertook important work for the welfare of the troops at home:

Lord Derby to Lord Beaverbrook

9 December 1939 Knowsley

. . . Things seem to be going all right. I feel Hitler is realising what a tiger—in Russia—he released from its cage and how difficult it will be to put the tiger back in the cage.

The two things here we have to contend with. *First*. These frequent speeches saying we are not fighting Germany, but Hitler, and pretending they are essentially different. The wish is father to the thought—I feel certain the mass of the German people are still behind Hitler, and all this hope of internal dissensions in Germany is a very false one: Write me again and tell me when you think you will come back. There are lots of things I should like to talk over with you, and I am afraid there is no chance of my coming to the S. of France much as I should like to. Then I have taken on this 'Welfare of the troops' work for the N. Western Command—a big job as the area is from the North of Cumberland to the South of Wales—but it is very important work, as our people are suffering from many hours of blackout—and boredom! a very insidious disease. I am very rheumatic, as I am afraid my writing shows!

Do write again. Tell me what you think of the feeling in France. I know there is a lot of propaganda, by people who should know better, to the effect that England has drawn France into a war. Write again.

* * *

The surrender by King Leopold of the Belgian Army in May 1940 came as a tremendous shock to Derby as it did to many other Englishmen and Frenchmen. In the confusion and excitement of the moment many people in the countries allied to Belgium formed hasty and unjust opinions of the conduct of the King which they were subsequently to regret, few more than Derby:

Lord Derby Calls Leopold

'MASTER MIND OF PERFIDY AND TREACHERY'

Lord Derby, at meeting of Liverpool Chamber of Commerce to-day, said: 'We had many difficulties to face before the catastrophe of the desertion of the King of the Belgians.

'I say advisedly the King of the Belgians, because I do not think the country as a whole sympathise with him in what he has done.

'I think we can still rely on very active support from the Belgian people.

KING LEOPOLD'S COWARDICE—THE SON OF A BRAVE FATHER—HIS UTTER DISREGARD FOR THE WELFARE OF HIS OWN COUNTRY AND FOR THE SAFETY OF THE ALLIES, WHICH HE HIMSELF CALLED IN TO HELP HIM, SHOWS HIM TO BE A MASTER MIND OF PERFIDY AND TREACHERY.

'I wish I had stronger words to say what I think, notwithstanding that his country will to a very large extent rally still to us and the Allies, and in the end we shall be able to carry through, as right always does carry through, to triumph.

'This is very strong language, but I feel at the present moment that through the treachery of one man the lives of many who are very dear to us are in danger.

'In these circumstances I feel that I am justified in saying what I have said.'[1]

Lord Hardinge of Penshurst to Lord Derby

22 April 1941 Oakfield
Penshurst Kent

. . . There is a matter upon which I have hesitated to write to you as it is no business of mine and you can burn this letter when read—It is this:

I met the Belgian Ambassador a few days ago, Baron Cartier [de Marchienne] whom you must know. He said this to me: You are a K.G., Lord Derby is a K.G. and King Leopold is a K.G. and Lord Derby made a speech in Manchester [*sic*] the other day in which he made a statement about King Leopold and the surrender of the Army which shows that he was misinformed. He asked me to send you the accompanying papers. When he tried to discuss with me the question I declined to do so, saying that I did not know what you had said, that it was no concern of mine, and that I did not know enough of what had happened to express an opinion. I did not even say that I would send you the papers. You are therefore quite free to do as you like and to ignore the whole question.

I thought however that I ought to tell you in case he should be a friend of yours, and in case you might wish to smooth his ruffled feathers. That is all.

Lord Derby to Lord Hardinge of Penshurst

24 April 1941

. . . I am both glad and sorry that you should have drawn my attention to my remarks with regard to the King of the Belgians, because it enables me to correct a misunderstanding. When the Belgian Ambassador speaks of my having condemned his King quite recently he is wrong. When I spoke it was in May last year and let me admit at once

[1] *Lancashire Daily Post*, 29 May 1940.

that I spoke hurriedly and without really knowing what the position was. I regret more than I can say now that I did not wait until I was better informed but I confess at that moment I was very upset by the action of King Leopold and I think I can rightly say I was not the only person who was so upset. No explanation was ever given at the time of why the King and his country had, as I thought, deserted this country. I realise now that the information that I had and which the general public had was not sufficient to justify the very scathing comments that I made at the time and I further feel that if only I had waited till I had real information rather than rumour to go on I should not have made the speech I did.

I am bound to point out that that speech was not made a short time ago in Manchester. It was made a year ago and I think His Excellency will admit that the incident could only come as a great shock to the people of this country.

I now see that the King had much to justify the course that he took and I would ask you to beg his Excellency to think of that speech as not having been made and to offer my personal apology to His Majesty. When I said what I did I was certainly misinformed and I repeat if I had known then what I know now I should not have made it.

I shall make no public withdrawal unless his Excellency would like me to do so. I feel it would only perhaps emphasise the feeling that undoubtedly existed at the moment when I made my speech and which was, I can say without fear of contradiction, very much against the King. If, however, his Excellency would like me to say anything I shall be very happy at the earliest possible opportunity to try and clear away the effect of what I then said.

I do not like writing to his Excellency direct but perhaps you would do so and assure him of my sincere regret that I should have done anything that was hurtful to him, as I look upon him as an old friend of mine, or to his King and his Country.

For Hardinge's eyes alone Derby wrote in a slightly different vein:

Lord Derby to Lord Hardinge of Penshurst

Confidential 24 April 1941

Thanks very much indeed for your letter. I have written you a letter which I should be very much obliged if you would give to the Belgian Ambassador. Let me say at once that I am afraid it is rather a humbugging one as at the moment when I made my speech, which was in May last, I did feel very bitter towards the Belgian King, as I think everybody else in this country did. Still after looking through the accounts that you have been good enough to send me I do quite realise what difficulties he had and that there was at all events a great deal of justification for the action the King took.

Of course at the moment one did not realise, and I am not quite sure that I quite do even now, that he had taken our Government into his confidence as to what he intended to do, but looking back at what happened one can safely say that more than half our present trouble came from the action that King Leopold took a year ago.

If you would not mind sending him on the letter, if you approve of it, I should be very grateful. I don't like, so to speak, to enter into a wordy correspondence with the Ambassador for whom I have got the greatest respect but I am certain that what I said at the time I spoke not only represented my own feeling but represented the feeling of 99 people out of every 100 in this country . . .

* * *

In the second half of 1940 a motor accident left Derby partly crippled. He did not at first realise the full gravity of his injuries, for these were not spectacular and he was soon out of bed. But he was an old man of seventy-five whose bulk and rheumatism already made it difficult for him to get about. After his accident he was largely incapacitated; his right hand especially would not get better and for a long time he could hardly even sign his dictated letters.

So he was tied to Knowsley, almost his only excursions being his annual visits as Lord Lieutenant to the mayors of Lancashire, a ceremony in which he always took the keenest pleasure. On these occasions it was impossible for him to enter or leave his car unaided. At Knowsley he lived in what must have seemed the bleakest solitude to such a gregarious man. Only Lady Derby and their granddaughter Priscilla were with him constantly; and soon Priscilla was called up:

Lord Derby to Captain Malcolm Bullock

Private Knowsley

2 April 1941

I wish I could have seen you the other day. I should like to have talked over things with regard to Priscilla's calling up notice but I am sure you will do everything that is necessary with regard to that.

I hope they won't take her away from here as she is such a stand-by to Alice but of course if she has got to go she has to, but I daresay you could put in the necessary plea to allow her to remain here. It would be very lonely for us here without her and more especially perhaps for me as Alice now generally goes to bed before Dinner and Priscilla does so much for me in many ways and keeps me in touch with the outside world. I shall do nothing, but if there is anything you want me to do you have only got to let me know.

I cannot help thinking that doing her farm work in the morning; driving her library in the afternoons and in addition doing the stamp work—I do not quite know what it is but apparently it takes up a good bit of time several days in the week—would justify the authorities in allowing her to remain here. There is something too which we cannot put forward but it is this. I am continually being asked to entertain various people here—the King and Queen: the Duke of Kent: and now the Duchess of Kent is coming: other people like Willkie. If Priscilla goes I certainly won't do it any longer as Alice is not up to doing this entertaining and Priscilla is therefore my only stand-by.

Fortunately it proved possible to arrange a compromise: Priscilla joined the W.R.N.S. and worked in Liverpool until the end of the war. She lived in a hostel there but spent her free time at Knowsley.

Wendel Willkie had visited Knowsley earlier in the year and had made a favourable impression on Derby, who reported to the Minister of Aircraft Production:

Lord Derby to Lord Beaverbrook

4 February 1941 Knowsley

One line of a private character to tell you about Willkie's visit here which you may care to hear about. I must tell you at once that you are the blue eyed boy and he is very impressed by you. In fact he looks upon the Prime Minister and yourself as being the working machinery of the Government and I can say that I entirely agree with him.

You can tell me whether Willkie was impressed with his visit here. I hear he is going from Manchester to Ireland instead of returning to London. I liked him very much indeed. I was rather predisposed to think he advertised himself too much but I must say I found him anything but that. It is quite true he likes popularity and why should he not; but, to my mind, there was equally no doubt that he was thoroughly in earnest in trying to find out in what ways he could help us.

Personally I think it is a mistake showing him too much the effects of bombing and when he went to Manchester for a luncheon I gave there I tried to impress upon people who were going to talk to him that what he should see was not the amount of damage that was done but the amount of work that people were doing *notwithstanding* the damage done and though I did not know it at the time I realised afterwards that what he had seen at our Cathedral here, where the work is being carried on irrespective of the War, had really impressed him very much indeed. He is a good fellow and if and when you see him you could tell him how really and sincerely I enjoyed his visit you would be doing me a great service because it is very difficult to make a guest understand that his host is really honest in what he says to him.

And now to tell you my own impressions. People are standing up to all this bombing very well indeed. Willkie wondered how long they would stand up to it if it was continuous. I am not a bit afraid. For what it is worth my own feeling is this: the more they are bombed, however much at the moment it may upset them, the more determined they are to beat the bomber . . .

Lord Beaverbrook to Lord Derby

7 February 1941 — 56 Farringdon Street,
London, E.C.4

I am most interested to hear from you about Willkie's visit. He is a fine chap and I am sure that his desire to help us was strengthened and fortified by his stay with you in the North.

He came back immensely pleased with it. I can assure you that Manchester people are no more delighted with Willkie than Willkie is with you. And, if I may be allowed to say so, you performed a most splendid service to the country at this time by taking care of him as you did.

* * *

During the war all the classics were run at Newmarket for considerably reduced stakes. Here in 1942, Derby, for the third time, succeeded in winning the race which bore his name. His colt, Watling Street, trained by Frank Butters, and ridden by Harry Wragg, beat Lord Rosebery's Hyperides by a neck. Mr. A. E. Allnatt's Ujiji was two lengths behind third and Shahpoor was fourth. There were thirteen runners and Watling Street's time was 2 minutes 29$\frac{3}{5}$ secs. The King's horse Big Game which was ridden by Gordon Richards and started favourite at 6 to 4 on took the lead towards the end of the race but was unplaced in the dramatic finish. Wragg rode a carefully judged waiting race and came through from behind at the last moment. He said afterwards to Mr. J. H. Park ('Ajax' of the *Evening Standard*): 'It was more or less what I had planned to do and it all came off as I anticipated'.

Derby was not there to see his horse win and in his absence Watling Street was led in by Lady Derby. Among many telegrams of congratulation which came to Knowsley, there was one from the Prime Minister:

Lord Derby to the Prime Minister

Confidential

15 June 1942

It is really only today that I have discovered your most kind telegram of congratulations to me on winning the Derby. I did send you a brief answer, but I want now to thank you very much indeed for having thought of me. It is especially good of you at such a time as this when you must be overwhelmed with work and worry.

I did not go to the races myself. It would amuse you to hear that I was engaged to open a big Gymkhana in North Lancashire, and as I had promised I would go I did not like to chuck, and so went and sat through a somewhat melancholy performance as it was pouring with rain. Anyhow I am glad that I kept my engagement.

Watling Street's race was not the last classic success to fall to Derby for in the following year his filly Herringbone won both the One Thousand Guineas and the St. Leger. In 1944 he won the Two Thousand Guineas with Garden Path (the first filly to win since 1902); and in 1945 both the One Thousand Guineas and the Oaks fell to Sun Stream. But the Derby of 1942 was the last of the three occasions on which he achieved one of his great ambitions; and so it seems a fitting moment to take leave of him. There is no need to chronicle in detail the remaining five years of Derby's life during which his physical suffering grew ever greater while the war and its aftermath imposed their privations on him as on everyone else.

He died on 4 February 1948 at Knowsley and was buried in Knowsley churchyard. He was eighty-three. His widow survived him for another nine years and died on 24 July 1957.

Despite the difficulties of his last years he had led a happy and useful life. Since the rise of the Tudors no territorial magnate had exercised a wider influence than he; certainly not in so benevolent a fashion. And it seems improbable in the extreme that anyone of his sort will ever exercise such influence again. Kindly, generous and public-spirited, he represented the genial sunset of an age which has now departed and which all civilised Englishmen, save those who with self-deception call themselves 'progressives', may mourn. There are those today who like to deride privilege in an age when it is only enjoyed by upstarts, and who, in their ignorance, fail to recognise that such privileges as a man like Derby enjoyed only arose from the instinctive acceptance of the responsibilities and duties which he had inherited.

It must be gratifying to all those who are not animated by spite and greed to reflect that in the face of the pressure of modern taxation his grandson John, eighteenth Earl of Derby, still lives at Knowsley where he upholds the standards of hospitality and public service inculcated in him by the example of his forebears. He never had the opportunity of serving in the House of Commons, though his younger brother Richard worthily maintains the family's Parliamentary tradition, having represented the North Fylde Division of Lancashire since 1950. Both John and Richard Stanley served in the war in the Grenadier Guards: the former was awarded the Military Cross for gallantry on the bloodstained beaches of Anzio in 1944.

* * *

Lancashire and England and the Stanleys have travelled far from Bosworth and Flodden to Anzio. And it must have been a high and rich consolation to Derby in his decrepitude that with victory now in sight the name of Stanley was still honoured on the battlefield. 'On, Stanley, on!'

Index

Where the name Derby *occurs under main entries it is the Seventeenth Earl who is referred to*

Abercromby (Liverpool constituency), 1917 by-election, 274–8
Abram (Lancs.), 395
Accrington (Lancs.), 471
Acts of Parliament
  Government of Ireland Act (1920), 402; National Registration Act (1915), 190; Parliament Act (1911), 118, 123, 126–7; Wireless Telegraph Act (1904), 83
Addison, Rt. Hon. Joseph, M.P. (1869–1951) (First Baron Addison), 356
Aftermath, The (Churchill) *quoted*, 435
Airlie, Eleventh Earl of (1856–1900), 568
Aisne, river, 267
Aitken, Sir Max *see* Beaverbrook, Lord
Alexander, King, of the Hellenes, 434
Alexandra, Queen (1844–1925), 76
Allan, Maud, 374–5
Allenby, Field Marshal (1861–1936) (First Viscount Allenby), 297, 299
Alten, Countess von (*later* Duchess of Manchester, *later* Duchess of Devonshire), 26–7, 353
Alycidon, 49, 51
American Debt crisis (1923), 493–7
Amery, Rt. Hon. Leopold, M.P. (1873–1955)
  and food taxes, 181, 182; recommends Baldwin as P.M., 503, 508; Derby's dislike of, 582
  mentioned, 62, 502, 513, 563, 565
Anchora, 52, 53
Armagh, 409
Army recruiting (in First World War)
  early difficulties, 184–7; Derby appointed Director-General of Recruiting, 187; in Lancashire, 187–9; Kitchener and conscription, 189–90, 191–2, 210; Derby Plan, 194, 195, 201; Asquith's pledge on call-up of married men, 194, 195, 196–8; result of Derby Plan, 201–2; conscription of unmarried men, 202; demands for universal conscription, 202–5; Bill introduced, 206; Derby answers critics of his recruiting policy, 206–8; exemptions and re-examination, 269–71, 277
Army reforms, 70–2
Arras, battle of, 267
Arthur, Sir George, 186, 189
Asquith, Rt. Hon. H. H. (1852–1928) (First Earl of Oxford and Asquith)
  and Parliament Act, 118; and mass creation of peers, 118, 123, 126–7; and conscription, 192, 194; pledge on call-up of married men, 194, 195, 196–8; and National Register, 201; criticism of his attitude to conscription, 205–6; Kitchener's admiration of, 210; and appointment of S. of S. for War (1916), 211, 213–14; and Derby, 212; Ll. George demands small War Committee, 228, 229; agrees, 230; announces reconstruction of Govt., 230–1; events leading to his resignation, 232–9; attitude of his Liberals to Conservative Party (1922), 477; on election result, 478; on B. Law, 501; and Dec. 1923 crisis, 544, 552, 555, 560
  mentioned, 37, 38, 116, 186, 187, 240, 282, 344, 533, 542
Asquith, Margot (1864–1945) (Countess of Oxford and Asquith), 213, 477
Ashton-under-Lyne (Lancs.), 395
Aston-in-Makerfield (Lancs.), 395
Astor, Astor of Hever, First Baron (*b.* 1886), 222
Ataturk, Mustapha Kemal *see* Kemal, Mustapha
Atherton (Lancs.), 395
Atholl, James, Second Duke of, 6
Attested Married Men's Union, 203–4
Audley, Adam de (*d. c.* 1203), 2
Audley, Henry de (*d.* 1246), 2
Audley, Liulf de (*c.* 1150), 2

Baden-Powell, Robert (1857–1941) (First Baron Baden-Powell), 65
Bailey, Sir Abe, Bt. (1864–1940)
and reconciliation between Derby and W. Churchill, 598–600
Balcarres, Twenty-seventh Earl of Crawford and (1871–1940)
and Balfour's resignation from Party leadership, 148, 149, 153
mentioned, 107, 173, 174, 175, 177, 180, 565
Baldwin, Lord: A Memoir (Jones)
quoted, 528–9
Baldwin, Stanley (1867–1947) (First Earl Baldwin of Bewdley)
President of Board of Trade, 391; 'Idiot Boy', 459; and American Debt crisis, 493–7; proposed as Leader of Commons, 500; account of his being asked to form Govt. (1923), 502–9; and appointment of Chancellor of Exchequer, 510–11; and Anglo-French relations over Germany, 513–17; advocates protectionist policy, 524–7, 528–9; and raspberry growing, 526; decides on dissolution, 527–8, 530–2; and promise to bring A. Chamberlain and Birkenhead into Cabinet, 531, 532, 534–5; 1923 election result, 540; considers resigning, 543; and Dec. 1923 crisis, 544–57 *passim*; wish to remove him from Party leadership, 558–62; promised support by Birkenhead and A. Chamberlain, 563; Leader still, 564, 565, 566; returned to power, 574; does not ask Derby to join Govt., 576–7; posts for Derby's brother and son, 577; asks for dissolution, 579; Govt. defeated, 580; promises referendum on food taxes, 581; and reorganization of Party, 581; strengthened by Rothermere's threats, 581–2; writes conciliatory letter to Beaverbrook, 582–3; Derby advises him to resign, 583; record and present policy, 583–5; his efforts to maintain the Leadership, 585–6; prepares to resign, 586; and sterling crisis (1931), 591; replies to Derby's congratulations, 592; congratulates Derby on success in Privilege case, 596
mentioned, 373, 459, 461, 523
Balfour, Rt. Hon. Arthur J. (1848–1930) (First Earl of Balfour)
relieves Buller of his command, 61; and Committee of Imperial Defence, 71–2; and Tariff Reform resignations (1903), 79–81, 82; resigns (1905), 86; writes to Derby on loss of seat, 91; and Asquith and 'guarantees' crisis, 119–20; writes to Derby concerning B. Law's seat, 121; Tory criticism of, 146, 147; his resignation from Party leadership, 148–52; and food tax referendum pledge, 160, 161; tries to dissuade Derby from public opposition to food taxes, 169–70; Derby replies, 172–3; and Ll. George's new Govt. (1916), 239–40; and War Cabinet, 257; in favour of keeping Robertson as C.I.G.S., 322, 323; and Robertson's objections to Versailles Agt., 325–6; withdraws support for Robertson, 326; Derby writes to him on Paris post, 338–9; at Peace Conference, 376; Ll. George persuades him to support pro-Greek policy, 426; pressed to accept peerage, 429; and Conservative decision to leave Coalition, 449–50; advises George V to send for Baldwin, 503–4, 507–8; and Dec. 1923 crisis, 544–60 *passim*
mentioned, 77, 125, 155, 158, 212, 228, 238, 349, 354, 367, 371, 372, 403, 442, 457, 459, 565
Balfour, Lord, of Burleigh (1849–1921), 79
Banks, Cyril, 88
Banner, Harwood, 536
Barnes, Rt. Hon. G. N. (1859–1940)
against retaining Robertson as C.I.G.S., 322, 325
Beach, Sir Michael Hicks *see* Hicks Beach, Sir Michael
Beaconsfield, First Earl of (1804–81), 10, 44, 58, 152, 153
Beaumont, Etienne de, 353
Beaverbrook, First Baron (*b.* 1879) (*formerly* Sir Max Aitken)
and Tariff Reform, 78, 164; and B. Law's election to Party leadership, 152–4; and food taxes, 181, 182; and Ll. George's demand for small War Committee, 228, 230; and fall of Asquith, 231, 232–4; created a Baron, 244; and Conservative decision to leave Coalition, 450, 452–3; attack on Salvidge, 463–4, 473; and Derby, 473–4; attacks Tory agreement with Ll. George Liberals, 474–5; and

American Debt, 494; and B. Law, 501; and Empire Free Trade, 580; promised referendum on food taxes, 581; seeking Leadership? 582; Baldwin's conciliatory letter, 582–3; continues his protectionist campaign, 585–6; plans to break up Conservative Party unless it accepts Empire Free Trade, 586; comes to agreement with Baldwin, 587; and Report on Indian policy, 597–8; and death of Ld. Stanley, 604–5; asks Derby about payments to Riviera, 609
mentioned, 213, 221, 243, 412, 439, 459, 476, 559, 575, 608, 610, 615
Bell, Moberly (1847–1911), 62
Bentinck, Lady Anne, 101
Bertie, Lord (1844–1919)
his illness, 354; Esher's criticism of, 358; and Leroy Lewis, 360
mentioned, 337, 338, 339, 349, 351
Bevin, Rt. Hon. Ernest, (1881–1951) 243
Bibesco, Princess Antoine, 150
Bickerstaffe, 95
Billing, Noel Pemberton, and the Black Book, 374–5
Birdwood, Field Marshal (1865–1951) (First Baron Birdwood), 571
Birkenhead, First Earl of (1872–1930) (*formerly* F. E. Smith)
and Tariff Reform, 160–1, 164; tries to dissuade Derby from public opposition to food taxes, 165, 168–9; writes to Derby on food taxes, 178; and conscription, 192; and Conservative decision to leave Coalition, 450; attack on Derby, 465, 467, 468–9, 480; Derby replies, 467–8, 470; quarrel with Derby patched up, 480–2; and reconciliation with Coalition Conservatives, 487–9; and Curzon, 500, 501; dislike of Curzon and Beaverbrook, 500–1; to join Cabinet, 531, 532, 534–5; Derby writes on election result, 541; and Dec. 1923 crisis, 544–57 *passim*; offers support for Baldwin, 563
mentioned, 82, 113, 133, 148, 276, 277, 356, 439, 459, 464, 466, 475, 502, 528, 529, 543, 565
Bispham, 96
Black and Tans, 402
Black Book, the, 374–5
Blackpool (Lancs.), 395, 536
Blackrod (Lancs.), 87
Blessed Girl, A (Lutyens)
quoted, 39, 40–3
Bloemfontein, 64
Boer War *see* South African War
Bolton (Lancs.), 395, 467, 468, 471, 536
Bolton Evening News
quoted, 87–8
Bonham Carter, Lady Violet, 213 *n.*
Bootle (Lancs.), 110, 111–12, 155, 395, 396, 479, 536
Bootle, Sir Thomas, 16
Borden, Sir Robert, 162
Bouillon, Franklin, 356, 358
Bourne, Cardinal, 405, 406
Breightmet, 98
Briand, Aristide (1862–1932)
discusses Nivelle Plan, 247; Ld. Esher's opinion of, 356
Bridgeman, W. C. (1864–1935) (First Viscount Bridgeman of Leigh)
recommends Baldwin as P.M., 503, 508; prevents Baldwin's resignation, 586
mentioned, 502, 531, 565
British Cotton Growing Association, 130, 399
British Political Parties (McKenzie), 153
Broad Corrie, 51
Brodrick, St. John (*later* First Earl Midleton) *see* Midleton, First Earl
Brusiloff, A. A., 216
Buller, Sir Redvers, Bt. (1839–1908)
and South African War, 60; relieved of command, 61
Bullock, Sir Malcolm, Bt. (*b.* 1890), 108, 109, 371, 392, 393, 579, 607, 614
Bullock, Lady Victoria, *see* Stanley, Lady Victoria
Bunbury, E. J., 46
Bunbury, Sir Thomas, 46
Burgoyne, General (1732–92), 47–8
Burscough, 96
Bury (Lancs.), 395
and Derby's property, 98

Cachin, M., 356
Cadogan, Lady Cynthia, 603
Cadogan, Lady Edith, 603
Cadogan, Lady Mary, 603
Cadogan, Lady Sybil, *see* Stanley, Lady Sybil
Cadorna, General, 289

Caine, Hall, 474
Calais Conference (1917), 247–9, 250–2, 253, 254, 255
Cambon, Jules, 356
Cambrai (battle), 295–6, 298, 301
Cambridge, George, Second Duke of (1819–1904), 70
Campbell, J. R., 573
Campbell-Bannerman, Sir Henry, Bt. (1836–1908)
forms Govts. of 1905–6, 86, 116
Canterbury Pilgrim, 49, 50, 51, 52
Cape Colony, 56–7, 58, 59
see also South African War
Cape Town, 56–7
Caporetto, 289
Carlton Club
meetings at: A. Chamberlain elected Leader, 390; Party to withdraw from Coalition, 447–51
Carson, Sir Edward (1854–1935) (Baron Carson of Duncairn [life])
and B. Law's and Ld. Lansdowne's threats to resign, 181; and Ll. George's demand for small War Committee, 229; and fall of Asquith, 231, 232, 233, 237; 1st Ld. of Admiralty, 242–3; and War Cabinet, 257; defends Army and Navy against Ll. George's attack, 290
mentioned, 112, 114, 148, 169, 164, 178, 186, 205, 207, 211, 240, 281, 293
Cavan, Field Marshal (1865–1946) (Tenth Earl of Cavan), 567–8
Cave, First Viscount (1856–1928)
and American Debt crisis, 495, 496
mentioned, 359, 460
Cecil, Lord Hugh (1869–1956) (First Baron Quickswood)
on food taxes and Derby, 165–6, 179
mentioned, 82, 394
Cecil, Lord Robert (1864–1958) (First Viscount Cecil of Chelwood)
and fall of Asquith, 229, 231; 'a shifty person', 430; and Baldwin's decision to hold election, 530–1
Censorship in South African War, 61–4
Chaloner, Col., 274
Chamberlain, Rt. Hon. Sir Austen, K.G. (1863–1937)
Chancellor of Exchequer, 83; commiserates with Derby on loss of his seat, 90; and Tariff Reform, 147; denounces food tax referendum pledge, 160, 161; and conscription, 192, 193; and Ll. George's demand for small War Committee, 229; offered S. of S. for War, 331; Leader of Commons, 390, 391; congratulated by Derby, 392; tries to persuade Derby to accept India Office, 428–9; Derby writes to him on state of Govt., 440–2; replies, 443; and possibility of election (Oct. 1922), 446; and Conservative decision to leave Coalition, 447, 448, 451, 452; and Derby's quarrel with Birkenhead, 481; and reconciliation with Anti-Coalition Conservatives, 487–9; followers want Derby as P.M., 502; and Imperial Preference, 525, 528, 529; to join Cabinet, 531, 532, 534–5; and Dec. 1923 crisis, 544–60 *passim*; and Beaverbrook and Report on Indian policy, 597–8
mentioned, 84, 148, 151, 152, 164, 169, 178, 181, 404, 423, 445, 459, 463, 500, 503, 510, 541, 558, 565, 585
Chamberlain, Rt. Hon. Joseph (1836–1914)
and Tariff Reform, 77–8; resigns from Govt. (1903), 79, 80, 81, 82
mentioned, 37
Chamberlain, Rt. Hon. Neville (1869–1940)
Chancellor of Exchequer, 511; and Imperial Preference, 525, 528; and Dec. 1923 crisis, 550; made Party Chairman, 581; and agreement with Beaverbrook, 587
Chanak, 436, 443, 444–5
Charteris, Brigadier-General John (1877–1946)
his dismissal sought, 296–7, 299–300
Chavasse, Dr., 137
Chevigné, Mme. de, 353
Chipping (Lancs.), 96
Chorley (Lancs.), 395
Christ Church (Oxford), 157
Christ Church Miscellany (Hiscock), 7
Churchill, Lord Randolph (1849–95), 37, 43, 44
Churchill, Sir Winston, K.G. (*b.* 1874)
in South Africa, 60, 64–5; and Tariff Reform resignations (1903), 79–81; and 1906 election, 87; advocates conscription, 192, 193; Ll. George wishes to include him in Govt., 278–9; Derby's op-

position, 279–80, 280–2, 283–5; Minister of Munitions, 280–1; and Ll. George's wish for C.I.G S. to resign, 288; and Spears as Military Attaché in Paris, 366–7, 368; and Spears and Derby, 368–9; suggests compromise, 369; Derby rejects it, 370; and Chanak, 435–6; upset at Conservative withdrawal from Coalition, 457–8; loses seat in '22 election, 475, 477, 478, 479; mediates between Derby and Birkenhead, 481–2; his resignation as P.M. (1955), 505; and Ll. George and protection, 529; considered as possible Conservative Leader (Dec. 1923), 563; accuses Derby and Hoare of breach of privilege, 593–6; reconciled with Derby, 598–600
mentioned, 116, 165, 271, 303, 359, 427, 439, 488, 591
Chief of the Imperial General Staff
powers, 218; revised under Versailles Agt., 315–16, 319; Sir W. Robertson on duties of, 317–18
see also Robertson, Field Marshal Sir William *and* Wilson, Field Marshal Sir Henry
Clarence, H.R.H. Duke of (1864–1892), 33
Clarendon, George, Fourth Earl of (1800–70), 1, 14
Clarke, Sir Edward (1841–1931), 112, 113, 114
Clemenceau, Georges (1841–1929)
Lord Esher's opinion of, 356; Derby's friendship with, 357; and Henderson as Military Attaché, 366
mentioned, 291, 306, 351, 355, 364, 368, 376
Clery, Sir Francis (1838–1926), 61
Clevelys (Lancs.), 395
Clitheroe (Lancs.), 471
Clynes, Rt. Hon. J. R., 471, 543
Cocteau, Jean, 353
Cohn, Jefferson, 358
Colenso (South Africa), 60, 61
Collins, Campbell, 138
Colne and Derby's property, 98
Complete Peerage, The
quoted, 2, 3, 5
Connaught Rangers, 490
Conscription *see* Army recruiting
Conservative and Unionist Party
and the working-class, 44; and Tariff Reform, 77–9; defeat in 1906 election, 86; and 1909 Budget, 117; and Tariff Reform, 146–8, 159–83; election methods, 139, 278; and possible fusion with Liberals, 386–7, 424; and talks with Sinn Fein leaders, 421–2; selfish element in, 438–9; decision to withdraw from Coalition, 447; in 1922, 460; Derby's desire to unify, 531–2; policy after 1923 election, 558–66 *passim*; reorganisation, 581
see also Tariff Reform, *and under names of Conservative politicians*
Constantine, King, of the Hellenes, 434
Conway, Sir Martin, M.P. (1856–1937) (First Baron Conway), 564
Coolidge, President Calvin, 520
Cooper, Alfred Duff (1890–1954) (First Viscount Norwich)
on Derby's generosity, 574–5; wins seat at Westminster, 586–7
Corkhill, Percy, 136
Cotton growing, 399, 400
Cowan, Col., 67
Cowdray, First Viscount (1856–1927), 279
Coworth Park, 98, 104
Crag estate, 96
Craig, Sir James (1871–1940) (First Viscount Craigavon), 421, 491
Crawford and Balcarres, Twenty-seventh Earl of, *see under* Balcarres
Creedy, Sir Herbert (*b.* 1878)
Derby writes to him about Leroy Lewis, 363
mentioned, 280, 484 *n.*
Creevey Papers
quoted, 102
Crewe, First Marquess of (1895–1945), 127, 333, 497
Cronje, Piet (1835–1911), 65
Crosby (Lancs.), 535
Crowe, Sir Eyre (1864–1925)
at Peace Conference, 378–9
Cunliffe, F., 203
Cunliffe-Owen, Sir Hugo, 592
Curzon, First Marquess, of Kedleston (1859–1925)
opposes food taxes, 162; and conscription, 192, 193; and Ll. George's demand for small War Committee, 228, 229; and fall of Asquith, 231; member of War

Cabinet, 242, 243; Derby's dislike of, 259–60, 371–2; Derby complains of his private use of Govt. car, 260–3; his reply, 263; Derby acknowledges, 264; in favour of keeping Robertson as C.I.G.S., 322, 323; withdraws support for Robertson, 326; and non-acceptance of Derby's resignation, 333; his banquet (June 1918), 372–3; Derby's opinion of, 373; official relations with Derby, 379; Ll. George persuades him to support pro-Greek policy, 426; and foreign affairs, 427, 428; objects to Derby speaking on foreign affairs, 432–3; and Conservative decision to leave Coalition, 449; lectures Derby, 458; his patriotism triumphs over his pledges, 459; and A. Chamberlain, 488; relations with Derby, 492–3; proposed as Deputy P.M., 500; and Birkenhead, 500, 501; almost becomes P.M., 502–10; and Anglo-French relations and Germany, 513–17; Derby complains, 520–1; Ld. President of the Council, 528
mentioned, 123, 151, 207, 240, 253, 429, 456, 457, 459, 460, 461, 511, 564, 565

Curzon, Grace Marchioness (*formerly* Mrs. Alfred Duggan)
her appearance, 372–3
mentioned, 260, 262, 263

Cust, Mrs. Harry, 260

D'Abernon, First Viscount (1857–1941), 512, 514

Daily Chronicle, 232, 529

Daily Dispatch, 536

Daily Express
attack on Salvidge, 463–4, 472
quoted, 111, 416–17, 463–4
mentioned, 221, 232

Daily Herald
quoted, 184–5, 461–2

Daily Mail, 571
mentioned, 167, 512, 564, 580

Daily Mirror, 580

Daily Sketch, 588

Darling, Mr. Justice (1849–1936) (First Baronet), 113, 114, 374, 375

Darwen (Lancs.), 471, 535

Davidson, First Viscount (*b.* 1889)
and B. Law and Derby, 431–2; and Baldwin being asked to form Govt., 506, 508, 509; and Dec. 1923 crisis, 550; abandoned by Baldwin, 581

Dawson, Geoffrey (1874–1944) (*formerly* Geoffrey Robinson)
and fall of Asquith, 232, 238; and dismissal of Repington, 312, 313; and result of 1923 election, 542; and Dec. 1923 crisis, 550, 557
mentioned, 311, 496

Dawson, Geoffrey, and our Times (Wrench), 496 *n.*, 550

'Derby Ground', 19

Derby House, 15, 98–101

Derby House, Old, (Chester), 96

Derby Stakes
origin, 46; Derby wins with Sansovino, 50, 569–71; wins with Hyperion, 50, 592–3; wins with Watling Street, 50, 616

Derby, Thomas, First Earl of (*c.* 1435–1504), 2, 3, 4, 606

Derby, Thomas, Second Earl of (*d.* 1521), 96

Derby, Edward, Third Earl of (1508–72), 4–5, 96

Derby, James, Seventh Earl of (1607–51), 5, 6, 96, 109, 606

Derby, Charles, Eighth Earl of (1628–72), 5

Derby, William, Ninth Earl of (*c.* 1655–1702), 5, 7

Derby, James, Tenth Earl of (1664–1736), 6, 101

Derby, Edward, Eleventh Earl of (1689–1776), 6, 7, 47

Derby, Twelfth Earl of (1752–1834), 45, 47, 48, 89, 101, 102

Derby, Thirteenth Earl of (1775–1851), 7, 89–90

Derby, Edward, Fourteenth Earl of (1799–1869)
1; life and political career, 6–9; Derby's god-parent, 14; and Wellington College, 18; proclaims Natal a Colony, 57; electoral defeat (1830), 89; and cotton trade, 129
mentioned, 57, 606

Derby, Edward, Fifteenth Earl of (1826–93)
marriage, 1; political career, 9–11; offered Greek throne, 11; obituary notice, 11–12; congratulated by Queen Victoria on Derby's birth, 12, 13; on Derby's recovery from illness, 14;

approves Derby's fiancée, 27; congratulates Derby on speech, 34; some estates bought by, 98; bequest to servants, 104–5; chairman of Lancs. Quarter Sessions, 129
mentioned, 23, 29, 32, 41
Derby, Frederick, Sixteenth Earl of (1841–1908)
Prince of Wales congratulates him on Derby's birth, 12, 14–15; and money, 17–18; created Baron Stanley of Preston, 27; Governor-Gen. of Canada, 27, 30; advises Derby on his election prospects, 34; and racing, 49, 50; career and death, 92; opinions of Edward VII and Prince of Wales on, 92–3; and Newmarket estate, 98; Ld. Mayor of Liverpool, 129
mentioned, 1, 23
DERBY, EDWARD, SEVENTEENTH EARL OF (1865–1948)
AND HIS ESTATES
succeeds to the Earldom, 94; extent of, and income from, property, 95–8; on Derby House, 99–100; and Knowsley, 101–3; style of living, 103–4; attacked by Ll. George for 'slum' property, 109–10; replies to de Forest's attack, 110–11; offers to sell him his property, 111–12; buys villa in Cannes, 571; wishes to sell, 608; payments for upkeep, 609–10
AND THE TURF
persuades Lambton to train family horses, 48–9; as breeder, 50–1; successes, 51–5; wins Derby with Sansovino, 569–71; wins again with Hyperion, 592–3; and Watling Street, 616; W. Churchill congratulates him, 617
PRIVATE LIFE
birth, 1, 12; schooling, 2; christening, 14; illness at 1 yr. old, 14; anecdotes of early childhood, 15–16; goes to Perceval House school, 16–17; at Wellington College, 18–22; his physique, 22; gazetted as Lieutenant, 23; early interest in politics, 23; joins Grenadier Guards, 23–4; to Ireland with Guards, 24–5; travels round world, 25–6; becomes engaged, 26–7; wedding, 27–9; to Canada, 30; at Sandringham, 30–1; financial troubles, 31–2; first child born, 33; King's condolences on father's death, 92; Prince of Wales', 93; replies to Prince, 94; his style of living, 103–4; appearance, 131; T. P. O'Connor's opinion of, 143–4; discusses education of Prince of Wales with George V, 156–8; and George V's relations with his children, 159; and engagement of eldest son, 272; death of Neil Primrose (son-in-law), 293; illness, 378; Grand National party, 392–5; entertains Prince of Wales, 395–6; and mother's death, 401; illness, 569; death of his daughter Victoria, 578–9; his 70th birthday, 600–3; death of his eldest son, 603–5; further illness, 607; partly crippled by motor accident, 614; his death, 618
PUBLIC LIFE
1891–1913
'nurses' Westhoughton constituency, 33–4; elected, 37; in Commons, 37–8, 39; and Salvidge, 44; becomes a Whip, 45; S. African War: goes to S.A., becomes Chief Press Censor, 59–60, 63; chance of office after Khaki Election, 65–6; returned as M.P. with increased majority, 66; offered post at War Office, 67; returns to England, 67–8; his work at War Office, 69–70, 72; and Army expenditure and contracts, 72–3, 74–5; and Tariff Reform resignations (1903), 79–81; Postmaster-General, 83–4; his 'bloodsucker' speech on Post Office pay, 84–6; loses seat in 1906 election, 87–8, 90–1; attacked by Ll. George for 'slum' property, 109–10; replies, 110; replies to de Forest's attack, 110–11; offers to sell him his property, 111–12; testifies in de Forest's slander action, 112, 113; influence in Lancs. and London, 115; Ld. Mayor of Liverpool, 115, 131–2, 133–9; and B. Law and N. W. Manchester seat, 120–3; mass creation of peers: first a 'ditcher' then a 'hedger', 123–6; records George V's account of his 'guarantee', 126–7; 'uncrowned King of Lancashire', 129; his work in Lancs., 130–1; gives coronation ball, 141–3; T. P. O'Connor's opinion of, 143–4; and food taxes, 146–8; on Balfour's leadership, 147; tries to prevent Balfour's resignation of Party leadership, 148–52; congratulates B. Law on becoming Leader, 154; opinion

of B. Law, 155–6; and education of Prince of Wales, 156–8; and George V's relations with his children, 159; views on food taxes to B. Law, 162; protests to Balcarres, 163; intends to speak against food taxes at Conservative Assn. meeting, 165; F. E. Smith tries to dissuade him, 165; so does Ld. Hugh Cecil, 165–6; and H. A. Gwynne, 167–8; and F. E. Smith again, 169; finally, Balfour, 169–70; question adjourned at Assn. meeting, 170; reports to B. Law, 171; replies to Balfour, 172–3; B. Law warns of possible Party split, 173, 174; circulates questionnaire on food taxes, 174–6; writes to Long on food taxes, 176–7; suggests meeting of Lancashire Conservatives and B. Law, 177; writes to E. Hulton on Tariff Reform, 178–9; Gwynne tells him of defeat of food taxes, 181–2; adjourned Assn. meeting held, 183

1914—APRIL 1918

recruiting speeches, 184–5; recruiting difficulties, 185–7; appointed Director-General of Recruiting, 187; *Manchester Guardian* on his recruiting work, 187–9; account of his accepting Director-General post, 191–3; Derby Plan, 194; discusses recruiting with Ld. Riddell, 195; and Asquith's pledge, 195, 196–8; his attack on Ld. St. Davids and Ld. Ribblesdale, 198–201; result of Derby Plan, 201–2; demands for universal conscription, 202–5; answers critics of his recruiting policy, 206–8; and Kitchener's opinions, 209–10; wish to become S. of S. for War, 212; appointed Under-S. of S. for War, 214–15, 219; and Ll. George and Haig, 222–4; Robertson's proposed visit to Russia, 223–4, 226–7; supports Ll. George's demand for small War Committee, 228–9; and fall of Asquith, 235–6, 236–9; becomes S. of S. for War, 240–1; congratulated by Haig, 244; and Nivelle Plan, 247; and unified command under the French, 247, 248–9; not informed by Ll. George of intention to unify command under the French, 247, 248, 250–4; tells Haig of Cabinet's confidence in him, 249–50; requests Ll. George that he should attend certain War Cabinets, 255–6; protests to Ll. George that promise not kept, 256; Ll. George replies, 256–9; dislike of Curzon, 259–60; and Curzon's use of Govt. car, 260–4; conference to discuss joint command, 264–5; writes to Haig on Anglo-French relations, 265–6; congratulates Haig on success at Arras, 268–9; Ll. George writes re call-up exemptions, 269–70; writes to Ll. George on Army manpower shortage, 270–1, 272, 274; writes to Haig on manpower shortage, 273; and adoption of eldest son as parliamentary candidate, 274–7; writes to Haig on Churchill being brought into Govt., 279; to Ll. George, 279–80; threatens resignation when Churchill made Minister of Munitions, 280–1; offers to recommend Haig for peerage, 285; Haig writes on his lack of confidence in Govt., 286; expresses confidence in Haig, 288, 291; and Wilson's and Robertson's positions on Supreme War Council, 291–2; on Ll. George, 293; urges Haig to dismiss Charteris, 296–7, 299–300; on proposed dismissal of Haig and Robertson, 297–9; Cabinet decides to dismiss Robertson, Derby threatens to resign, 301–2; and the control of Inter-Allied Reserve, 307–8; and Robertson's dismissal, 309–11; not associated with Repington's article, 314; and Ll. George's plan for working of Versailles Agt., 314–16; Robertson offers resignation, 317–18; tries to dissuade him, 318–20; suggests alternative to Ll. George, 321–2; and George V and Robertson's dismissal, 323–6, 327–8; accepts Robertson's resignation, 326–7; considers resigning himself, 329–30, 343; sees Ll. George and Haig, 330, 331; resigns and withdraws resignation, 331, 332, 333; defends Govt's. and his own position in Lords, 333–4; Ll. George's criticism of his conduct, 335–6; Ll. George's desire to remove him from War Office and send him to Paris, 336–7, 341–2, 343, 349–50; asks Haig's advice, 339; his support for Haig, 344, 346, 347; blamed by Col. Repington for not supporting generals' demands, 345–6; Haig's attitude to, 347, 348–9; official appointment as Ambassador, 350–2

APRIL 1918—NOVEMBER 1920

his success as Ambassador, 353; first report to Ll. George, 354–5; Esher's advice, 355–6, 358–9; his friendship with Clemenceau, 357; his changeable opinions, 359; on Leroy Lewis, 359, 361, 363; on Spears, 364; and Spears' wish to be made Military Attaché, 365–8; relations with Spears, 368–9; W. Churchill suggests compromise, 369; rejects it, 370; difficult relations with Curzon, 371–2; opinion of Curzon after he died, 373; and the 'Black Book' case, 374, 375; resists Sir E. Crowe being made an Ambassador to Peace Conference, 378–9; official relations with Curzon, 379; congratulated by the Govt., 379–80; Ll. George's opinion of, as Ambassador, 336

NOVEMBER 1920—MARCH 1922
relations with Lancashire since 1912, 383; offered Colonial Office, 383; refuses, 383–4; advocates an alliance between Britain and France, 384–5, 396–8; on possible fusion of Conservative and Liberal Parties, 386–7; writes to B. Law on Lancs. loyalty to Coalition, 387; and to Sir P. Sassoon, 387–8; on suggestion that he wanted to form a new party, 388–9; explains his Lancs. activities to B. Law, 389–90; writes to Ll. George on B. Law's resignation, 391; congratulates A. Chamberlain on becoming Leader, 392; and Ireland (1921), 404–5; suggested that he meets Sinn Fein leaders, 405–6; meeting arranged, conditions, 407–9; meets de Valera, 409–10; reports to Ll. George, 410; sends message to de Valera for Ll. George, 410; de Valera's reply, 411, 412, 413, 414; acknowledges reply to de Valera, 415; complains of Fr. Hughes' behaviour, 415–16, 418; newspaper comment on his visit, 416–17; Fr. Hughes replies to his criticism, 418–19; he acknowledges and outlines his own position, 420; value of his meeting with de Valera, 420–1; and Party Conference and anti-Irish diehards, 422, 423–4

MARCH 1922—DECEMBER 1923
Northcliffe offers support if he accepts India Office, 428; discusses offer with A. Chamberlain and Balfour, 428–9; refuses it, 429–30; proposed as Party leader in Lords, 431–2; advocates Anglo-French Alliance, 432; Curzon objects to his speaking on foreign affairs, 432–3; his reply, 433–4; thinks Coalition cannot last, 440–1; disapproves Govt. foreign policy, 441–2; his criticism, 442–3; fears war with Turkey, 444–5; writes to B. Law over Chanak crisis, 444–5; tries to dissuade A. Chamberlain from early election, 446; Salvidge tries to dissuade him from anti-Govt. action, 446–7; and Conservative decision to leave Coalition, 450; discusses offices he might have with B. Law, 453–5; and Tariff Reform, 455; offered and accepts War Office if Conservatives returned, 456; and Pig for Hogg, 461; *Herald* on, 461–2; appeals for moderation, 462; attacked by Birkenhead, 465, 467, 468–9; replies, 467–8, 470; and Birkenhead's attack on Younger, 470–1; estimates Party's chances in Lancs., 471; writes to Beaverbrook about attack on Salvidge, 472; speech on Turkey, 472–3; complains about Beaverbrook, 475–6; plans for speeches, 476; on election result, 478–80; quarrel with Birhead patched up, 480–2; at the War Office, 483; reports to George V, 483–4; replies to Ld. Midleton's congratulations, 484–5; and McGrigor's Bank, 485–6; and reconciliation between two wings of Conservative Party, 487–9; and Irish Free State Bill, 489–91; visits Ulster, 491; relations with Curzon, 492–3; and American Debt crisis, 493–7; and German reparation payments, 497–9; friendly talk with Birkenhead, 500–1; suggested as P.M., 501–2; on Baldwin becoming P.M., 509–10; Anglo-French relations over Germany, 511–12, 513–20; complains to Baldwin about Curzon, 520–1; on Imperial Preference and Baldwin, 523–4, 525–7, 530; equivocates on Free Trade, 525, 533–6; and Baldwin's decision to hold election, 527–8, 530–1, 532–3; desire to unify Party, 531–2; and Baldwin's promise to bring A. Chamberlain and Birkenhead into Cabinet, 531, 534–5; writes to Baldwin on election situation, 535–6; Baldwin's reply, 537; Ll. George calls him 'a harpooned walrus', 537–8; and taxation, 538–9; on result of 1923 election, 540–1; suggests coalition with Ll. George, 541; and Dec.

1923 crisis, 544, 545, 548–57 *passim*; his view of crisis, 546–8; no coalition with Liberals (expect on dried fruit and raisins), 548; and removal of Baldwin from Leadership and policy, 558–62; realises that Baldwin must remain as Leader, 562–4; and Joynson-Hicks, 564–5; and Party policy, 565

DECEMBER 1923—APRIL 1941

to Paris, 568; opinion of first Labour Govt., 571–2; and its probable collapse, 572–3; financial support of candidates, 574; generosity to Duff Cooper, 575; glad not to be offered post in Baldwin's Govt. (1924), 575–6, 578; and Baldwin and posts for brother and son, 577; Ld. Lieut. of Lancashire, 580; and Baldwin's continued leadership, 582; advises Baldwin to resign, 583; outlines to Baldwin his record and present policy, 583–5; ends lock-out of weavers, 587–8; George V's wish that he should intervene, 589–90; congratulates Baldwin on election victory, 591; member of Jt. Select Cmtee. on Indian policy, 593; W. Churchill accuses him of breach of privilege, 593–5; vindicated by Committee of Privileges, 595–6; and Beaverbrook and Report on Indian policy, 597–8; reconciled with Churchill, 598–600; congratulates N. Chamberlain over Munich, 604; on likelihood of war (1939), 607–8; on the reasons for war, 608; war-time activities, 610–11; opinion of King Leopold's conduct, 611–14

Derby, John, Eighteenth Earl of, 24, 400, 618

Derby, Lady [Charlotte] (wife of Seventh Earl), 5

Derby, Lady [Mary] (wife of Fifteenth Earl)
writes to Derby approving his fiancée, 27
mentioned, 1, 29, 42

Derby, Lady [Alice] (*Derby's wife*)
becomes engaged, 26–27; wedding, 27–9; to Canada, 30; writes to Prince George, 30–1; writes to her husband about money, 32; helps Derby in obtaining office after Khaki Election, 65–6, 67; at Balmoral, 76–7; advises Derby to accept Paris post, 338; her cultural interests in Paris, 353–4; leaves Paris, 380–1, 382; Derby's 70th birthday, 600, 603
mentioned, 91, 156, 278, 401, 457, 614, 617

Derby, Lady [Constance] (*Derby's mother*)
1; Derby's birth, 12; Derby's illness, 14; birth of twins, 15; anecdotes of Derby's babyhood, 15–16; and money, 17–18; writes to Derby from Canada, 32–3; her death, 400–1; writes to Derby on her 50th wedding anniversary, 401
mentioned, 19, 20, 21, 24, 25, 40

Derby Plan *see* Army recruiting

Desborough, Lady
tells Derby of Curzon's banquet, 372–3

Devonshire, Eighth Duke of (1833–1908) (*formerly* Lord Hartington)
27; and Govt. post for Derby, 65, 66; and Army reform, 71; and Tariff Reform resignations (1903), 80–1
mentioned, 126

Devonshire, Ninth Duke of (1869–1938)
refuses India Office, 430; Colonial Secretary, 460; and Sir Douglas Hogg, 460–1; and American Debt crisis, 495, 496; why no Govt. post, 528
mentioned, 457, 461, 531

Devonshire House, 460

Diaz, General, 289

Dilke, Sir Charles (1845–1911), 457

Disraeli, Benjamin, *see* Beaconsfield, First Earl of

'Ditchers', 123–6

Dockers' Battalion, 188

Donald, Sir Robert, 529

Douglas, Lord Alfred, 375

Douglas, Sir Charles, 217

Duggan, 'Countess', *see* Curzon, Grace Marchioness

'Earl of Derby's Gift', 18

Eccles (Lancs.), 395

Echo de Paris
tribute to Derby, 381

Eclipse Stakes, 52

Eden, Rt. Hon. Sir Anthony, K.G. (*b.* 1897), 505

Edward VII, King (1841–1910)
congratulates 16th Earl on Derby's birth, 12; condolences to Derby on his father's death, 92–3

mentioned, 28, 76, 84, 119
Edward VIII, King (*b.* 1894)
education, 156–8; at Knowsley, 394; Lancashire tour, 395–6
Elgin, Lord (1849–1917), 71, 72
Elwin, Rev. Whitwell, 39; letters to, from Lady E. Lytton, 40–3
Empire Cotton Corporation, 399–400
Empire in the Air (Templewood) *quoted*, 436 *n.*
Errington, Lord (1877–1953) (*later* Second Earl of Cromer), 236
Esher, Second Viscount (1852–1930)
71; his book on Kitchener, 191; his talents, 355; opinion of French politicians and Embassy staff, 356; more advice to Derby on French politics, 358–9; opinion of Leroy Lewis, 360
mentioned, 293
Eton College, 9, 18
Evening News, 580
Evening Standard, 463
Everton (Lancs.), 539
Eyres-Monsell, Cmdr. Bolton, 531

Fairhill House Estate, 98
Falkenhayn, Eric von (1861–1928), 217
Farquhar, Sir Horace, 503
Farran, Elizabeth, 48
Fayolle, General, 289
FitzAlan of Derwent, First Viscount (1855–1947), 391
Fitzgerald, Lt.-Col. Oswald, 360
Fleetwood (Lancs.), 395, 535
Foch, Marshal Ferdinand (1851–1929)
asked opinion of British generals by Ll. George, 222; member of Supreme War Council, 289, 295, 316; in charge of Inter-Allied Reserve, 307; Lord Esher's opinion of, 356; and Derby's departure from Paris, 382; on Yellow Peril, 368
mentioned, 324, 358, 380, 493
Food Taxes
see Tariff Reform
and Imperial Preference
Ford, Patrick, 124
Forest, Baron de (*now* Baron de Bendern)
attack on Derby, 110; Derby offers to sell him his property, 111–12; sues Lady Gerard and Major Milner, 112–13
Formby (Lancs.), 395
Franco-German relations
reparation payments, 497–9; French occupation of Ruhr and its aftermath, 511–20
Fraser, Sir Malcolm, 471, 474, 475
Free Trade, 77, 522, 523
see also Tariff Reform
and Imperial Preference
French, Sir John (1852–1925) (First Earl of Ypres)
and Kitchener, 217; adviser to Cabinet, 288; and Spears, 367–8
mentioned, 227, 311, 391
Furse, Maj.-Gen. Sir Ralph (*b.* 1887), 283
Fylde, the, 96

Gatacre, Maj.-Gen. Sir William (1843–1906), 60
Geddes, Sir Auckland (1879–1954) (First Baron Geddes), 527
Geddes, Sir Eric (1875–1937)
Derby uses him in his campaign against W. Churchill, 282–5
mentioned, 281
George V, King (1865–1936)
and Princess May, 33; and Asquith and mass creation of peers, 118–19; account of his 'guarantee', 126–8; coronation, 140–1; Derby gives him opinion of Bonar Law, 155–6; on choice of university college for Prince of Wales, 156–8; relations with children, 159; congratulates Derby on being made Under-S. of S. for War, 214–15; and Ll. George and Haig, 222–4; and crisis over Sir W. Robertson's dismissal, 323–6, 327–8, 329–30; advises Derby to resign, 329–30; on Ll. George taking over War Office, 343; on Derby's appointment to Paris, 350–2; at Knowsley, 392, 394, 395; and McGrigor's Bank, 485; 'Military Cross sufficient for the Belgians', 487; Derby suggests Royal clemency for Irish prisoners, 490–1; and B. Law's resignation, 501; his account of Baldwin becoming P.M., 503–4, 506–9; and his constitutional position, 504, 506; and Dec. 1923 crisis, 544–57 *passim*; grants dissolution to MacDonald, 573; and Derby's intervention in weavers' lock-out, 589–90
mentioned, 30, 140, 211, 479, 483, 605

George V, Life of King (Nicolson), 119, 506, 509
quoted, 504
George, Prince
(*later* King George V)
see George V
George, David Lloyd (1864–1945) (First Earl Lloyd George)
attacks Derby for owning 'slum' property, 109–10; and 1909 Budget, 117; his near-pacifism, 193; Derby's opinion of, 195; Kitchener's dislike of, 210; wishes to become S. of S. for War, 211; appointed, 213–14; and Sir W. Robertson, 218–19; and the generals, 219–20; and the press, 220–1; alleged criticism of generals, 222–4; demands small War Committee, 228–30; and fall of Asquith, 231–9; forms new Govt., 239–41; sets up War Cabinet, 242–3; tries to get unified Allied Command, 245, 246; impressed by Nivelle Plan, 246–7; manoeuvres Haig and Robertson into accepting unified command under the French, 247–8, 250–2, 252–3; Derby requests permission to attend certain War Cabinets, 255–6; Derby protests promise not kept, 256; on difficulties of Derby's attendance at, and function of, War Cabinet, 256–9; calls conference to discuss joint command, 264–5; on call-up of agricultural workers, 269–70; Derby writes to him on manpower shortage, 270–1, 272, 273; his attitude to shortage, 272, 273; Derby writes on bringing Churchill into Govt., 279–80; makes Churchill Minister of Munitions, 280–1; and Derby and Churchill, 284; support for Haig, 287–8; appalled by casualties, 288; Rapallo Conference, 289–90; Derby's opinion of, 293; seeks dismissal of Haig and Robertson, 295, 297, 298–9, 341; Cabinet decides on Robertson's dismissal, Derby threatens to resign, 301–2; refuses reinforcements for Haig, 303, 304, 343; considers German offensive unlikely, 303, 305; 'opposes' idea of a Generalissimo, 305–6; conference on control of Allied Reserve, 306–8; assures Derby of support for Haig, 308–9; and Robertson's dismissal, 310–11, 314, 321–2, 323–5, 327–8, 330–1, 341; plan for working of Versailles Agt., 314–16; and Robertson, 317; criticises Derby's conduct, 335–6; and Derby's appointment to Paris, 336–7, 340, 341, 342, 350–1; considers taking over War Office, 343; and Spears as Military Attaché, 367, 368; his appearance, 373; at Peace Conference, 376, 379; accuses Sir E. Crowe of being anti-German, 379; offers Colonial Office to Derby, 383–4; popularity in Lancs., 387; on possible alliance with France, 398; and Ireland, 402; and Derby's meeting with de Valera, 410; sends message to de Valera, 410; de Valera's reply, Derby passes it on, 411, 415; and talks with Sinn Fein leaders, 421, 422; Derby tells him of feeling against Coalition, 424; and Venizelos, 425; pro-Greek policy, 426; offers India Office to Derby, 427; refused, 429–30; refused by Duke of Devonshire, 430; accepted by Ld. Peel, 430; and Chanak, 435; his Govt. near downfall, 438, 439, 440–1; Derby's criticisms of his foreign policy, 441–2, 443, 444, 473; and Conservative decision to leave Coalition, 447, 448, 449, 452, 455; and German reparations, 498; and Imperial Preference, 528–9; on Derby, 537–8; Derby suggests coalition with, 541
mentioned, 111, 116, 133, 187, 191, 205, 206, 215, 344, 372, 389, 446, 466, 483, 591
Gerard, Lady, 112
German reparations payments (1923)
497–9; and French occupation of Ruhr and events following, 511–20
Gisborough, First Baron (1856–1938), 274
Gladstone, W. E. (1809–1908), 8, 10, 11, 37, 38, 39, 58, 504
Gladstone, Life of (Morley), 504
Globe, 314
Gondolette, 52, 53
Goschen, First Viscount (1831–1907), 82
Goulding, Edmund (1862–1936) (First Baron Wargrave), 121, 122
Government of Ireland Act (1920), 402
Graham, William, 588
Grahame, Rt. Hon. Sir George (1873–1940)
Lord Esher's opinion of, 356; complains of L. Lewis' conduct, 361–2, 362–3

Grand National party at Knowsley (1921), 392–5
Great Crosby (Lancs.), 395
Great Trek (of the Boers), 57
Greenall, Thomas, 188
Greenwood, Sir Harmar, 408, 478
Gretton, Col. John (1867–1947) (First Baron Stapleford), 421, 422, 423, 463
Greville Memoirs
  quoted, 8
Grey, Rt. Hon. Sir Edward, Bt. (1862–1933) (First Viscount Grey of Falloden)
  on Govt.'s action over Chanak, 411
  mentioned, 58, 116, 227, 231
Grey, Sir John, 588, 590
Griffith-Boscawen, Rt. Hon. Sir Arthur (1865–1954), 459, 477
Griffith, Arthur (1872–1922), 414, 418
Grove, the, 29
Guest, Capt, the Rt. Hon. F. E. (1875–1937), 282, 475, 478
Guineas, One Thousand, 50, 52, 53, 617
Guineas, Two Thousand, 50, 52, 617
Gwynne, H. A. (1865–1950)
  tries to dissuade Derby from public opposition to food taxes, 167–8; writes to Derby re defeat of food taxes, 181–2
  mentioned, 63, 313, 314, 359

Hackwood, 260, 263
Haig, Field Marshal (1861–1928) (First Earl Haig)
  Ll. George's lack of faith in, 222–4; congratulates Derby, 244–5; and unified command under the French, 247–8; assured of Cabinet's confidence in him, 249–50; opinion of Nivelle Plan, 250; tells Derby he has no ill-will against Ll. George, 255; and Nivelle, 259; at conference on unified command, 264, 265; Derby writes on Anglo-French relations, 265–6; Derby congratulates him on success at Arras, 268–9; Derby writes on manpower shortage, 273; refuses Derby's offer to recommend him for peerage, 285; lack of confidence in Govt., 286; plan for attack, 286–7; Passchendaele, 287; Derby expresses confidence in, 288; Ll. George's attack on, 290, 291; and Cambrai, 296; urged to dismiss Charteris, 296, 299–300, 301; refuses, 296–7; Ll. George considers dismissing, 297–9, 341–2; Derby tells him about Robertson's proposed dismissal, 302–3; considers German offensive likely, 303–4, 305; is refused reinforcements, 304, 343; and control of Inter-Allied Reserve, 308–9, 310; and Robertson's dismissal, 310; agrees to Ll. George plan of working of Versailles Agreement, 314–15, 325, 326; and Robertson's dismissal, 328, 329, 330, 331, 335; and Derby's resignation, 332; Derby asks his advice on Paris post, 339; agrees to Foch's command of British armies, 342; Derby's support of, 344, 346, 347; attitude to Derby, 347, 348–9
  mentioned, 216, 218, 229, 247, 272, 290, 295, 311, 320, 338, 343
Haig (Duff Cooper), 335–6
  quoted, 268, 290, 303–4, 327, 347
Haig, The Private Papers of Douglas (Blake)
  quoted, 250–2, 254–5, 302–3, 305, 348
Hailsham, First Viscount (*formerly* Sir Douglas Hogg)
  see Hogg, Sir Douglas
Hale (Lancs.), 395
Halecote, 15, 17, 23
Halsbury, First Earl of (1823–1921)
  leader of 'ditchers', 123, 124
Hamilton, Sir Edward (1847–1908), 85
Hamilton, Lord George (1845–1927), 79
Hamilton, Gen. Sir Ian (1853–1947), 64, 67, 75
Hampshire, H.M.S., 209
Hanbury-Williams, Maj.-Gen. Sir John (1859–1946), 224
Hansell, Henry, C.V.O. (1863–1935), 156, 157, 158
Harcourt, First Viscount (1863–1922) (son of Sir William Harcourt *q.v.*), 231
Harcourt, Rt. Hon. Sir William (1827–1904), 214, 504
Hardinge of Penshurst, First Baron (1858–1944)
  writes to Derby about Leroy Lewis, 361–2; Derby replies, 362–3; at Peace Conference, 376–8; Ambassador to France, 380; and Derby's remarks about King Leopold, 612–14
Harford, Austin, 144

Harington, Gen. Sir Charles (1872–1940), 435–6
Hartington, Marquess of
see Devonshire, Eighth Duke of
Hastings, Sir Patrick, K.C. (1880–1952), 573
Hayes, J. H., 538
Healy, Sir Tim (1855–1931), 489–90
'Hedgers', 123–6
Henderson, Rt. Hon. Arthur (1863–1935)
member of War Cabinet, 242, 243
mentioned, 190, 471
Henderson, Lt.-Gen. Sir David (1862–1921), 364–5, 366
Hennessy, Mme.
Derby's friendship with, 357–8
Henry VII, King, 4
Hettie Sorel, 49, 51
Hewins, W. A. S. (1865–1931), 148
Hicks Beach, Sir Michael (1837–1916), 69, 75, 82
Hillingdon, Third Baron (1887–1952), 603
Hindley (Lancs.), 395
Hoare, Sir Samuel (1880–1959) (First Viscount Templewood)
and Chanak, 436; and Imperial Preference, 525; accused of breach of privilege, 593–5
mentioned, 558
Hogg, Sir Douglas (1872–1950) (First Viscount Hailsham)
mistaken for Pig, 461
Hogge, J. M., 276
Hollins, Capt., 186
Holwood, 29, 98
Home Rule, 38, 117–18, 156, 159, 161
Horne, Sir Robert (1871–1940) (First Viscount Horne)
Chancellor of the Exchequer, 390; possibility of becoming Chancellor again, 510; and Dec. 1923 crisis, 559, 564
mentioned, 459, 502, 503, 528, 598
Horrocks, John, 89
Hughes, F. B., 277
Hughes, Father
visits Ireland on behalf of Derby, 406–7, 409–14; arranges conditions of Derby's meeting with de Valera, 407–9; Derby's annoyance with, 415–16, 418; replies, 418–19; Derby's reply, 419–20
Hulton, Sir Edward, Bt. (1869–1925)
Derby writes to, on Tariff Reform, 178–9; on his support of Haig and Robertson, 346–7
Hume-Williams, Rt. Hon. Sir Ellis, K.C. 1863–1947), 374–5
Hyperion, 49, 50, 54, 592–3

Imperial Defence, Committee of, 71–2
Imperial Economic Conference (1923), 510, 520–1, 523
Imperial Preference
B. Law on, 455; Derby on, 523–4; Empire Free Trade, 580; Baldwin promises referendum on food taxes, 581
mentioned, 510
see also Tariff Reform
Inter-Allied Reserve, control of
see Versailles Agreement
Ireland
condition of (1920–1), 402–3; Derby and Wickham Steed on, 404–5; Derby's meeting with de Valera, 405–10; Ll. George's message, 410; de Valera's reply, 411; London talks (1921) and Conservative Conference, 421–3; talks end, 424; Irish Free State Bill, 489–91
Irish Republican Army, 402
Irish Republican Brotherhood, 402
Irlam (Lancs.), 395
Isabel of Lathom (*c.* 1380), 3, 101

Jackson, Rt. Hon. Sir Stanley (1870–1947), 502, 530, 563
Jameson Raid, 59
Jellicoe, First Earl (1859–1935)
and U-boat menace, 268
mentioned, 238, 290
Joffre, Marshal (1852–1931)
Lord Esher's opinion of, 356
mentioned, 245, 247, 267, 268
Johannesburg, 58
Johnson, Pte. S. A., 262–3
Jouvenal, Henri de, 516–17
Joynson-Hicks, Sir William (1865–1932) (First Viscount Brentford)
and Dec. 1923 crisis, 544, 549, 556; proposes himself as possible Leader of Party, 564–5
mentioned, 513

Kemal, Mustapha (1880–1938), 425, 426, 435, 441, 442, 443

Kiggell, Lt.-Gen. Sir Launcelot, 226, 265
Kimberley, 60, 62, 65
Kipling, Rudyard, his 'Gehazi', 225–6
mentioned, 60, 63
Kirkdale, 139
Kirkham (Lancs.), 395
Kitchener, Life of Lord (Arthur)
quoted, 190
Kitchener, First Earl (1850–1916)
and Winston Churchill, 64; Derby writes to him about recruiting, 185–6; and conscription, 187, 189–90, 191–2, 194, 202, 210; his death, 209; his wishes for the future, 210; opinion of Ll. George and Asquith, 210; administration of War Office, 217–18
mentioned, 56, 65, 66, 69, 158, 186, 195, 208, 345, 473, 507
Knollys, First Viscount (1837–1924), 119
Knowsley
life at, in nineties, 40–3; described, 95, 101–3; style of living at, 103; and servants, 103–5; lack of art treasures, 107; poaching at, 140; Grand National Party at (1921), 392–5; 45½ acres presented to Liverpool Corporation, 398–9
Komati Poort, 65
Kruger, President (1825–1904)
and the Uitlanders, 58–9; flees, 65
Kyffin-Taylor, Col., 137

Labour Party
first straight fight against a Unionist, 139; pledges support for War Minister, 190; and support for Ll. George's Govt., 258; possibility of Labour Govt. (1923), 542–3, 551; and consequent ruin of country, 546–7, 552, 553, 554; first Labour Govt., 567
mentioned, 293
Ladysmith, 60, 61, 65
Laing's Neck, 58
Lambton, Hon. George, 49, 52, 570, 571
Lancashire
Derby's work and position in, 115, 129–31, 383, 605–6
Lancashire Conservative Association
and Tariff Reform, 162–83 *passim*; loyalty to Coalition, 387
mentioned, 206, 390, 445, 462, 560, 566
Lancashire Daily Post
quoted, 611–12
Lancashire Territorial Association, West, 187, 188
Lansbury, Rt. Hon. George (1859–1940), 543
Lansdowne, Fifth Marquess of (1845–1927)
67; leader of 'hedgers', 123, 124; Bonar Law writes on food taxes, 175; meets Lancs. members, 180; threat to resign, 181; averted, 182; and conscription, 192
mentioned, 125, 151, 167, 170, 178, 229, 429
Lathom, First Earl of, 16
Lathom, Lady [Alice] (wife of First Earl), 16
Lathom, Isobel, 3, 16
Law, Rt. Hon. Bonar (1858–1923)
loses seat in 1910 election, 120; stands for N.W. Manchester, 121–2; loses, 122–3; election to Party leadership, 152–4; congratulated by Derby, 154; Derby's opinion of, 155–6; and Tariff Reform, 161; in favour of retaining food taxes in Party platform, 162, 163–4; writes to Derby on possible Party split, 173, 174; on Derby's T.R. questionnaire, 174–6; meets Lancs. members, 180; threat to resign, 181; averted, 182; backs Ll. George for S. of S. for War, 213; and Ll. George's demand for small War Committee, 228, 229, 230; and fall of Asquith, 231, 233, 236, 237, 238; asked to form Govt., 239; member of War Cabinet, 242, 243–4, 257; against retaining Robertson as C.I.G.S., 322; and Derby's resignation, 331, 332, 333; at Peace Conference, 376; Derby tells him of Lancs. loyalty to Coalition, 387; his popularity, 387–8; Derby explains his Lancs. activities, 389–90; resigns from Govt. (1921), 390; health improves, 391; proposed as P.M., 431–2; criticises Govt., 439–40; and Chanak crisis, 444–5; supports withdrawal from Coalition, 447–51, 452–3, 487; discusses possible offices with Derby, 453–4, 456–7; Rothermere asks for an Earldom, 457; composition of his Govt., 459–61; his election speeches, 466; returned to power, 477; A. Chamberlain's support for, 488; and American

Debt crisis, 494–7; his illness, 500; resignation and death, 501; Asquith on, 501; alleged recommendation of Baldwin as successor, 506, 508 *n*, 509
mentioned, 158, 167, 168, 169, 170, 172, 178, 179, 211, 240, 243, 259, 260, 284, 330, 331, 384, 392, 431, 464, 479, 483, 485, 499
Lawrence, General Sir Herbert, 301
Lawyers in politics
author's poor opinion of, 573–4
Leigh (Lancs.), 471
Leopold, King of the Belgians
Derby's remarks on, 611–14
Leslie, Sir John, 99
Leslie, Sir Shane, Bt., (*b.* 1885), 99
Letters from Lord Oxford to a Friend
quoted, 478
Lever, Sir Tresham, Bt. (*b.* 1900), 534
Lewis, Col. Leroy
Lord Esher's opinion of, 356, 360, 361; Derby's opinion of, 359, 361, 363; and Ld. Bertie, 360; Sir G. Grahame complains of his conduct, 361–2; and his C.M.G., 363
mentioned, 364, 367
Leygues, M., 380
Leyland (Lancs.), 395
Liberal Party
and Home Rule, 39, 161; victory in 1906 election, 86; and Land Tax, 109; and social reform, 116–17; and support for Ll. George's Govt., 258; and possible fusion with Conservatives, 386–7, 424; arrangement with Tories for 1922 election, 474, 475, 477
Linlithgow, Second Marquess of (1887–1952), 593
Litherland (Lancs.), 395
Liverpool
Derby elected Ld. Mayor, 115; Derby President of Chamber of Commerce, 130; politics in, 133; Irish in, 133, 405; Derby's duties as Ld. Mayor, 133–9, 144; recruiting in, 188; Prince of Wales' visit to, 395, 396; Derby presents land for reservoir, 398–9
mentioned, 535
Liverpool Conservative Club, 386
Liverpool Conservative Working Men's Association, 43, 44, 81, 82, 110, 133
Liverpool Courier
quoted, 135, 135–6, 386, 417, 466, 476, 538–9
Liverpool Cup, 50
Liverpool Post
quoted, 538, 539
Liverpool Trade Review
quoted, 130
Lloyd George *see* George, David Lloyd
Lloyd-Greame, Philip (*b.* 1884) (*Now* First Earl of Swinton *formerly* Sir Philip Cunliffe-Lister)
and Dec. 1923 crisis, 558
mentioned, 495, 496, 517
Lloyd, Rt. Hon. Selwyn (*b.* 1904), 574
Locker-Lampson, Cmdr. Oliver
and Dec. 1923 crisis, 544, 553
mentioned, 500, 502
Logue, Cardinal
and Derby's proposed meeting with Sinn Fein leaders, 405, 406; agrees to help, 407, 408, 409
Londonderry, Sixth Marquess of (1852–1915)
opposes food taxes, 162
Long, Walter (1854–1924) (First Viscount Long)
Derby writes to him on food taxes, 147–8, 176–7; on possibility of Ll. George becoming S. of S. for War, 211; and B. Law's election as Leader, 488
mentioned, 151, 152, 164, 169, 178, 211, 229, 274
Longridge, 96
Lord Riddell's War Diary
quoted, 195
Lutyens, Lady Emily
at Knowsley, 39–43
Lyautey, General
discusses Nivelle Plan, 247, 264
mentioned, 251
Lytham (Lancs.), 395
Lytton, Second Earl of (1876–1947), 11
Lytton, Countess of (wife of Second Earl), 40, 42
Lytton, Lady Constance, 40

MacDonald, Rt. Hon. Ramsay (1866–1937)
and result of 1923 election, 541, 542; and Dec. 1923 crisis, 544–60 *passim*; Prime Minister, 567; asks for dissolution, 573; asked to form new Govt., 580; and

second Labour Govt., 590–1; and birth of National Govt., 591
mentioned, 504, 543, 587
McGrigor & Co. (bankers)
failure of, 485–6
McGuigan, John, 53
McGurk, John, 188
McKenna Duties, 522, 524
McKenna, Rt. Hon. Reginald (1863–1943)
B. Law asks him to become Chancellor of Exchequer, 454; offered Chancellorship by Baldwin, 510
mentioned, 228, 231, 459
Mackensen, August von (1849–1945), 217
Macmillan, Rt. Hon. Harold (*b.* 1894), 505
McNeill, Prof., 414
Macpherson, Sir Ian (1880–1937) (First Baron Strathcarron), 277, 278, 310, 331, 333
Macready, Gen. the Rt. Hon. Sir Nevil (1862–1946), 226
Mafeking, 65
Magdalen College (Oxford), 157
Magersfontein, 60
Majuba, 58
Malcolm, Sir Ian, 377
Manchester
and Derby's property, 98
mentioned, 395, 468, 525, 535
Manchester Chamber of Commerce, 384
Manchester Constitutional Club, 388
Manchester, North-west (constituency), 121–3
Manchester Daily Dispatch, 532
quoted, 203–4
Manchester Evening News
quoted, 539
Manchester Guardian
quoted, 187–9, 203, 204, 388–9, 481, 533–4, 538
Marchienne, Baron Cartier de, 612, 613
Marlborough, Ninth Duke of (1871–1934), 64–5, 66, 603
Marsh, Sir Edward (1872–1953), 117 *n.*
Mary, Queen, 33; at Knowsley, 392, 394, 395
Mary, Princess (daughter of George V), 394, 395
Master Cotton Spinners and Manufacturers Association, 588
Maurice, Maj.-Gen. Sir Frederick (1871–1951), 358
Maxse, L. J. (1864–1932)
and Derby becoming a 'hedger', 123–6
May, Princess (*later* Queen Mary) *see* Mary, Queen
May, Sir George (1871–1946) (First Baron May), 590
Messines Ridge, 287
Methuen (Third Baron) (1845–1932), 60
Michael, H.R.H. Grand Duke, 66
Middleton (Lancs.), 395
Midleton, First Earl (1856–1942) (*formerly* St. John Brodrick)
Secretary of State for War, 67; writes to Derby about his work, 69–70; and Army reforms, 70–2; and Army expenditure and contracts, 72–3, 54–5; on Derby's refusal of India Office, 431; congratulates Derby, 484
Millerand, M., 380
Milner, First Viscount (1854–1925)
and Kruger, 59; member of War Cabinet, 242; and Supreme War Council, 289; Derby's opinion of, 293; against retaining Sir W. Robertson as C.I.G.S., 322, 326; appointed S. of S. for War, 343; at Peace Conference, 376
mentioned, 69, 207, 211, 219, 254, 307, 308, 310, 341, 383
Milner, Major Marcus Harvey ('Trepoff'), 22, 112, 113, 393 *n*, 394; and the censored duck's egg, 395
Monckton, First Viscount (*b.* 1891), 574
Monro, Gen. Sir Charles (1860–1929), 198, 200, 298
Montacute, 262, 263
Montagu, Lady Alice
see Derby, Lady [Alice]
Montagu, Lord Charles, 80, 212, 544, 608
Montagu, Rt. Hon. Edwin (1879–1924)
pro-Turk policy, 426; dismissed from India Office, 427
mentioned, 228, 230, 231, 478
Monteagle, Baron, 4
Montrose, Duchess of (widow of Fifth Duke; *m.* Milner, Major Marcus Harvey *q.v.*), 49, 50
Morning Post
and South African War, 60, 64; and control of Allied Reserve, 311; editor fined, 311 *n.*
quoted, 311, 345–6, 469–70, 525, 566

mentioned, 167, 222, 223, 224, 313, 359, 423, 468, 469, 561
Morris, Frank, 88
Mosley, Sir Oswald, Bt.
and unemployment, 590
Mowbreck (Lancs.), 395
Munitions, Ministry of, 218
Murat, Princesse Lucien, 353
Murray, Gen. Sir Archibald (1860–1945), 217
Murray, Sir George (1849–1936) (ret'd Civil Servant), 549
Murray, Prof. Gilbert (1866–1957), 7 *n.*
My Political Life (Amery)
quoted, 62, 205

Natal, 59, 60
National (Wholesale) Manufacturers Association, 138
National Liberals
arrangement with Tories for 1922 election, 474, 475; Asquith on, 475
see also Liberal Party *and* George, David Lloyd
National Register, 194, 201
National Registration Act (1915), 190
National Review, 123
Newburgh, 95
New College (Oxford), 157
Newmarket
and Derby's property, 98; Stanley House, 104
Newport (Mon.), 452
Nicholson, Field Marshal (First Baron Roundhay), 64
Nicolson, Hon. Sir Harold (*b.* 1886), 119, 159
Nivelle, General (1856–1924)
impresses Ll. George and Cabinet, 246–7; Nivelle Plan, 246–7, 247–8, 250; and Haig, 259, 264, 265, 287; launches offensive, 267; fails, 267–8, 269; dismissed, 268
mentioned, 249, 251, 253, 254, 286
Noblesse Oblige (ed. Mitford)
quoted, 108
Northcliffe, First Viscount (1865–1922)
and food taxes, 167, 175; offers Derby support if he accepts India Office, 428
mentioned, 231, 235, 312, 332, 404
Northern Daily Mail
quoted, 184
Northumberland, Eighth Duke of, 423
Norwich, First Viscount, *see* Cooper, Alfred Duff
Novar, First Viscount (1860–1934), 460, 461

Oaks Stakes, 47, 48, 50, 51, 52
O'Connor, Rt. Hon. T. P. (1848–1929)
on Derby, 45, 143–4
mentioned, 87, 137
Oise, river, 342
Old Men Forget (Cooper), 575
Oldham (Lancs.), 395, 471, 574, 575
Oliver, E. L., 168
O'Mara, James, 409
Orange Free State
founded, 57; annexed by British, 57; annexation annulled, 58
Ormskirk, 96, 275, 395, 467, 471
Our Old Nobility (Evans)
quoted, 4
Oxford and Asquith, First Earl of, *see* Asquith, Rt. Hon. H. H.

Paardeberg, 65
Painlevé, Paul (1863–1933)
meeting with Ll. George on unity of command, 295, 306; Ld. Esher's opinion of, 256; and Spears, 367
mentioned, 360
Pall Mall Magazine
quoted, 45, 143–4
Palmerston, Third Viscount, 9
Pams, M., 356
Parliament Act (1911), 117; and royal guarantee of creation of peers, 118, 123, 126–7
Passchendaele, 285, 287
Paul, Prince, of the Hellenes, 434
Peace Conference (1919), 376–80
Peake, Col. Malcolm, 187
Peel, First Earl (1867–1937)
Secretary of State for India, 430
mentioned, 459, 460, 461
Pétain, Marshal (1856–1951)
succeeds Nivelle, 268; 286; and German offensive (March, 1917), 342; Ld. Esher's opinion of, 356
mentioned, 269
Petter, Sir Ernest, 586

Phipps, Rt. Hon. Sir Eric (1875–1949), 356
Pichon, M., 356, 357, 376
Platt, Comyn, 536
Plumer, Field Marshal (1857–1932) (First Viscount Plumer)
offered post of C.I.G.S., 326, 337; and working of Versailles Agt., 329, 330
mentioned, 289, 298
Plymouth, 524, 528
Poincaré, Raymond (1860–1934)
and German reparations, 497, 512, 513, 514, 516, 519
Politicians and the War (Beaverbrook)
quoted, 211, 213, 235–6, 239
Post Office, Derby and the
made Postmaster-General, 83–4; his 'bloodsucker' speech on pay, 84–6; P.O.'s revenge, 91
Prescot (Lancs.), 395
Press
power of, 220–2; campaign for Empire Free Trade, 580
see also Rothermere, First Viscount; Beaverbrook, First Baron; *and names of newspapers*
Preston, 89–90, 395, 528, 600, 601
Preston Guardian
quoted, 601–3
Pretoria, 65, 96
Prime Ministers and the Sovereign, 504–6
Primrose, Hon. Neil, P.C. (1882–1917)
marriage and death, 293; and the Black Book, 374–5
mentioned, 258, 371
Private and Official (Waterhouse)
quoted, 508 *n.*

Ralph, Julian, 63
Ranaï, 52, 53–4
Rapallo Conference, 289, 291
Rawlinson, First Baron (1864–1925)
and Calais Conference, 252
mentioned, 67, 298, 334, 356, 567, 572
Rawtenstall (Lancs.), 535
Reading, First Marquess of (1860–1935)
Kipling's lampoon of, 225–6; suggests amendments to Treaty of Sèvres, 426
mentioned, 223, 231, 336, 350, 354
Recruiting in First World War
see Army Recruiting
Redmond, John, 118
mentioned, 124
Reparations, German, 497–9, 511–21 *passim*
Repington, Col. Charles (1858–1925)
and control of Allied Reserve, 311, 313–14; dismissed from *Times*, 312–13; on Derby going to Paris, 340–1; on Derby's administration of War Office, 344–6
Reynolds, Sir James
and proposed mission to Ireland, 405–7
Reynolds News, 229, 232, 233
Rhodes, Cecil (1852–1902), 59
Rhondda, First Viscount (1856–1918), 340
Ribblesdale, Fourth Baron (1854–1925), 198, 199, 200–1
Ribot, M., 356
Riddell, First Baron (1865–1934), 194
Ritchie, First Baron (1838–1906)
67; resigns over Tariff Reform (1903), 79, 80–1
Roberts, Field Marshal (1832–1914) (First Earl Roberts)
to South Africa, 61; and Winston Churchill, 64–5; military successes, 65; returns home, 66; appointed C.-in-C., 70; and Army reform, 72; and conscription, 189
mentioned, 62, 63, 187
Roberts, Major, 362, 365
Robertson, Field Marshal Sir William, Bt. (1860–1933)
writes to Haig re casualties, 216; appointed C.I.G.S. with increased powers, 217–18; and Ll. George, 218–19; proposed visit to Russia, 223–4, 226–7; not informed by Ll. George of intention to unify command under the French, 247–8, 250, 251, 252; its effect on him, 254; opinion of Nivelle, 259; at conference on unified command, 264; and W. Churchill, 283, 284; confidence in Haig, 288; and Supreme War Council and H. Wilson, 291–2, 294; Ll. George considers dismissing, 297, 298, 299; Cabinet decides he must be replaced, 301; Derby's reaction, 301–2; and Haig's request for reinforcements, 304; on control of the Inter-Allied Reserve, 306–7; Ll. George determined to dismiss, 309, 310, 341; enlists help of Press, 311; and working of Versailles Agt., 315–16; to

be Military Representative at Versailles, 316; refuses and offers resignation, 316–18; Derby tries to dissuade him, 318–20; alternative suggested by Derby, 321–2; rejects it, 322–3; George V's views on his dismissal, 323–6, 327–8; Derby accepts his resignation, 326–7; Haig, Ll. George, Derby, discuss position, 330–1; appointed to Eastern Command, 332; Derby defends Govt.'s action, 333–4; advice to Derby on Paris post, 339–40; Derby's support of, 344, 345, 346
mentioned, 211, 215, 227, 247, 253, 255, 268, 273, 290, 295, 297, 300–1, 338, 343, 356
Robinson, Geoffrey (*later* Geoffrey Dawson) *see* Dawson, Geoffrey
Rosebery, Fifth Earl of (1847–1929), 38–9, 44, 504
Rossendale (Lancs.), 471, 536
Rothermere, First Viscount (1868–1940)
asks B. Law for Earldom in exchange for his support, 457; and protection, 536; dislike of Baldwin, 565; United Empire Party, 580; his political ineptitude, 581–2; serves to strengthen Baldwin, 582; comes to an agreement with Baldwin, 587
mentioned, 502, 512, 559, 581, 582
Rothschild, Evelyn de, 375
Roumania, 217
Royal Prerogative of choosing a Prime Minister, 504–6
Royton (Lancs.), 471
Ruhr *see* Franco-German relations

Sackville-West, Maj.-Gen. C. J.
Military Attaché to Paris Embassy, 368, 369, 370
mentioned, 354
St. Annes-on-Sea (Lancs.), 395
St. Davids, First Viscount (1860–1938), 198, 199, 200
St. Helens (Lancs.), 395
St. Leger, 50, 53
Salford (Lancs.), 395
Salisbury, Third Marquess of (1830–1903), 37, 42, 61, 69, 153
Salisbury, Fourth Marquess of (1861–1947)
and new party, 440; and Chanak, 444; Lord Pres. of the Council, 459–60; 461; recommends Curzon as P.M., 503, 508; and Baldwin's decision to hold election, 530–1
mentioned, 535
Salome (Wilde), 374, 375
Salvidge, Sir Archibald (1863–1928)
career, 43–4; and Tariff Reform, 81–2, 164; and Liverpool politics, 132–3; and election of Derby's son (Ld. Edward), 275, 276–8; and Derby's proposed meeting with Sinn Fein leaders, 406, 407; and Party Conference and Anti-Irish diehards, 422, 423; tries to dissuade Derby from anti-Govt. action, 446–7; and decision of Party to withdraw from Coalition, 448–9; and attack by *D. Express*, 463–4, 472, 473; and Birkenhead's attack on Derby, 465, 468; and Baldwin's protectionist policy, 526–7; and Dec. 1923 crisis, 560–2
mentioned, 131, 137, 139, 144, 151, 177, 183, 388, 466, 467, 469, 478, 566
Salvidge of Liverpool (Salvidge)
quoted, 82, 561–2
Samuel, Sir Herbert (*b.* 1870) (First Viscount Samuel), 591
Sandars, J. S., 119, 150, 151, 160
Sandringham 30–1
Sankey, First Viscount (1866–1948), 591
Sansovino, 50, 54, 569–70, 571
Sassoon, Rt. Hon. Sir Philip, Bt. (1880–1939)
Derby writes on reconstruction of Govt. (1917), 281–2
mentioned, 250, 269, 330, 387, 502
Saunderson, Edward
writes to Derby on Irish affairs, 403–4; reply, 404
Sclater, Gen. Sir Henry (1855–1923)
Derby writes to him about recruiting, 186–7
mentioned, 186
Scott, C. P., 203
Seddon, J. A., 188
Selborne, Second Earl of (1859–1942)
and conscription, 193
mentioned, 67, 151
Sembach, M., 356
Sensee, river, 342
Sèvres, Treaty of, 425, 426, 473, 492
Sexton, Sir James, 139–40, 188, 396

Shute, Col. John
and Derby's proposed visit to Ireland, 405; and Fr. Hughes and Derby, 415–16
Simon, Sir John (1873–1954) (First Viscount Simon), 202, 574, 595
Sinclair, Sir Archibald, Bt. (*b.* 1890) (First Viscount Thurso), 529
Sinn Fein, 402, 405
Sir James Sexton, Agitator (Sexton)
quoted, 140, 396
Skelmersdale, Second Baron, *see* Lathom, First Earl of
Smith, F. E. *see* Birkenhead, First Earl of
Smith, Sir Harold (brother of Ld. Birkenhead), 465–6, 480
Smith, Sir Harry, 57
Smuts, Field Marshal (1870–1950)
opinion of Sir W. Robertson, 328
mentioned, 293
Snowden, Rt. Hon. Philip (First Viscount), 543, 590
Soldiers and Statesmen (Robertson)
quoted, 216
South African War (1899–1902)
causes, 56–9; Boers invade Cape Colony and Transvaal, 59; defeats for British, 60; Buller replaced by Ld. Roberts, 61; censorship during, 61–4, British successes, 65; peace, 67; peace talks, 75
Southport (Lancs.), 395, 536
Southport Guardian
quoted, 537–8
Spears, Brig.-Gen., M.P. (*b.* 1886)
Ld. Esher's opinion of, 360, 361; career, 364; Derby's opinion of, 364; wants to be made Military Attaché, 365–6, 366–8; his relation to Embassy, 368–71
Spectator
quoted, 204
Spiers, Brig.-Gen. E. L.
see Spears, Brig.-Gen., M.P.
Sportsman
quoted, 569–71
Stamfordham, First Baron (1849–1931)
writes to Derby on decisions of Calais Conference (1917), 253–4; account of crisis over Robertson's dismissal, 323–6; and Derby's resignation, 329–30, 322; on Ll. George taking over War Office, 343; on Derby's appointment to Paris, 350–2; Military Cross for the Belgians, 487; recommends Curzon for P.M., 503, 508; and Dec. 1923 crisis, 545–57 *passim*
mentioned, 195, 211, 236, 252, 340, 378, 506, 589
Stanley, Adam de (*c.* 1150), 2
Stanley, Sir Albert, 244
Stanley, Hon. Algernon (*b.* 1874) (*Derby's brother*)
17, 25; career, 35
Stanley, Hon Arthur (1869–1947) (*Derby's brother*)
20; career, 35
mentioned, 122, 177, 180, 275, 451
Stanley, Hon. Charles (*brother to Fourteenth Earl of Derby*), 23–4
Stanley, Lady [Constance] (*Derby's mother*) *see* Derby, Lady [Constance]
Stanley, Sir Edward (*later* Eleventh Earl of Derby) *see* Derby, Edward, Eleventh Earl
Stanley, Edward (*c.* 1513), 4
Stanley, Lord Edward (1884–1938) (*Derby's eldest son*)
adopted as parliamentary candidate, 274–6; wins seat, 277–8; Whip in1 924 Govt., 577; career and death, 603–5
mentioned, 24, 156, 272, 451, 476
Stanley, Hon. Ferdinand (1871–1935) (*Derby's brother*)
17; career, 35
mentioned, 215
Stanley, Hon. Frederick Arthur (*later* Sixteenth Earl of Derby)
see Derby, Frederick, Sixteenth Earl of
Stanley, Frederick (1878–1942) (*Derby's brother*), 36, 215
Stanley, George (1872–1938) (*Derby's brother*)
17, 25; career, 35; writes to Derby re meeting of Lancs. members on food taxes, 180; loses seat, 478, 479; Under-Secretary of State for Home Affairs, 483; post in 1924 Govt., 577
mentioned, 154, 155, 177, 215, 451, 454
Stanley, Lady Isobel (*b.* 1875) (*Derby's sister*), 36
Stanley, Sir James (*brother of Second Earl of Derby*), 6
Stanley, Sir John de (*d. c.* 1413), 3, 16, 101
Stanley, Col. Oliver (1896–1950) (*Derby's son*)
98, 278; and Tariff election, 536, 538; career, 603

mentioned, 582
Stanley, Hon. Richard (*brother of Eighteenth Earl of Derby*), 618
Stanley, Lady Sybil [Portia] (*Derby's daughter-in-law*), 272, 603
mentioned, 275, 278
Stanley, Sir Thomas (*son of Third Earl of Derby*), 129
Stanley, Lord Thomas (*later* First Earl of Derby)
see Derby, Thomas, First Earl of
Stanley, Hon. Victor (1876–1934) (*Derby's brother*)
describes Derby's wedding, 27–9; career, 35
mentioned, 16, 18, 19
Stanley, Lady Victoria (1892–1927) (*Derby's daughter*)
born, 33; in Paris, 354; death, 578–9
mentioned, 53, 278, 293, 371, 375, 392, 393
Stanley, Walter de (*d. c.* 1285), 2
Stanley, Sir William (*c.* 1480), 3–4
Stanley, William de (*c.* 1180), 2
Stanley family, ancestry of, 1–12
Stanleys of Knowsley, The (Pollard)
quoted, 89
Stanley House, Newmarket, 104
Steed, Wickham (1871–1956)
and Col. Repington, 312; on Ireland, 404–5; offers support for B. Law in ending Coalition, 450–1
Steel-Maitland, Rt. Hon. Sir Arthur, Bt. (1876–1935), 165, 169, 174; 'a shifty person', 430
Stockton, Sir Edwin, 526
Stormberg, 60
Strachie, First Baron (1858–1936) (*formerly* Sir Edward Strachey), 201
Strand Magazine, 79
Strange Case of Andrew Bonar Law (Taylor)
quoted, 163–4, 449
Stuart, Eileen Villiers, 375
Sunday Dispatch, 580
Sunday Express, 473, 474, 475
Sunday Pictorial, 580
Supreme War Council, 289–90, 295, 315–34 *passim*
see also Versailles Agreement *and* Robertson, Field Marshal Sir William
Sykes, Sir Frederick, 501, 503, 506
Talbot, Lord Edmund *see* FitzAlan of Derwent, First Viscount
Tariff Reform
outlined, 77–9; food taxes and Conservative Party, 146–8; and Party after 1910 election, 159–60; Derby's opposition to, 160–1, 162; food taxes to remain in Conservative platform, 162–3; Derby protests, 163; opposes policy, 164; colleagues try to dissuade him from public speech against, 165–70; question adjourned at Assn. meeting, 170; Derby writes to B. Law and Balfour on, 171–3; likely to split Party, 173–4; Derby's questionnaire on, 174–6; Derby writes to Long on, 176–7; Derby suggests Lancs. Conservatives and B. Law should discuss, 177; F. E. Smith to speak at adjourned meeting, 178; Derby writes to Ld. Hugh Cecil and E. Hulton, 179; defeat of food taxers, 181–3
mentioned, 523
Taylor, Vice-Admiral Sir Ernest Augustus (*b.* 1876), 582
Taylor, J. G., 608, 610
Taylor, John, & Son, 609, 610
Teck, Princess Mary of *see* Mary, Queen
Tempestuous Journey (Owen), 529 *n.*
Templewood, First Viscount *see* Hoare, Sir Samuel
Thomas, A., 356
Thomas, Rt. Hon. J. H., 543, 590, 591
Thornley, 96
Thrush, H.M.S., 30
Tillett, Ben, 243
Times, History of The
quoted, 238, 312–13, 404–5, 450–1
Times, The
and L. Amery, 62; and fall of Asquith, 231–2, 233, 234; Col. Repington: his resignation and Dawson's 'frequent and drastic revision' and 'judicious deletions', 312–13; on Derby as Ambassador, 381
quoted, 198–201, 206–8, 381, 385–6, 430, 472–3, 593
mentioned, 63, 167, 311, 416, 439, 444, 462, 496, 586
Tinker, Joe, 189
Tory Party *see* Conservative and Unionist Party
Trafford, Sir Humphrey de, Bt. (*b.* 1891), 603

Transvaal
founded, 57; annexed, 58; gold discovered, 58; and Jameson Raid, 59
Trevelyan, Rev. C. W., 22

Uitlanders, 59
Unemployment
in 1920–3, 522; remedies for, 533; in 1929, 579
Unionist Party *see* Conservative and Unionist Party
United Empire Party, 580
United States of America
declares war, 267; and manpower, 272, 273; and German reparations, 520–1
Unknown Prime Minister, The (Blake), 153, 213 *n.*, 496 *n.*, 506
quoted, 190, 211, 233, 431–2, 440 *n.*, 477, 493

Valera, Eamon de (*b.* 1882)
Derby's proposed meeting with, 405, 407–9; meets Derby, 409–10; and possible meeting with Ll. George, 410, 411; and Fr. Hughes, 411, 412, 414; his reply to Ll. George's question, 411, 413; on value of Derby's visit, 420–1; London talks (1921), 421, 424
Venizelos, M., 125, 131
Versailles, Treaty of, (1919), signed, 376
Versailles Agreement on control of Inter-Allied Reserve
306–8, 318–19; Ll. George's plan for working of, 314–16; Sir W. Robertson's objections, 317–18, 320–1; in favour of it, 318–20, 329, 333–4
see also Robertson, Field Marshal Sir William *and* George, David Lloyd
Victoria, Princess, 30
Victoria, Queen
10, 11; congratulates 14th Earl on Derby's birth, 12, 13; on Derby's recovery from illness, 14
mentioned, 504
Vigilante, The, 374
Villiers, Lady Alice, *see* Lathom, Lady Alice
Villiers, Lady Constance, *see* Derby, Lady Constance
Vimy Ridge, 267, 287
Viviana, M., 356

Wales, Prince of (*later* King George V), *see* George V
Wales, Prince of (*later* King Edward VII), *see* Edward VII
Wales, Prince of (*later* King Edward VIII), *see* Edward VIII
Walker, Harry, 539
Wallace, Hon. H. C., 392, 393, 394, 577–8
Walsh, Arthur, 189
Walsh, Rt. Hon. Stephen (1859–1929)
S. of S. for War, 567–8
mentioned, 188, 207
War Cabinet
set up by Ll. George, 242–3; Ll. George on functions and membership, 256–9
War Memoirs (Ll. George)
quoted, 228–9, 308, 310–11, 314, 329, 331, 335–6
Waterhouse, Lieut.-Col. Sir Ronald (1878–1942), 506, 508, 509
Waterloo (Lancs.), 395
Watling Street, 50, 617
Waugh, Evelyn (*b.* 1903), 108
Wedgwood, First Baron (1872–1943), 241
Wee Frees (Asquith Liberals), 471, 474
Wellington College, 18–22
Westhoughton, 33–4, 37, 66, 87
Weston, Tommy, 569, 570, 592
Weygand, General, 307
White, Sir George, 61
White, Field Marshal Sir Thomas (1835–1912), 278
Whiteside, Dr., 137
Widnes (Lancs.), 471
Wigan (Lancs.), 395
Wilbraham-Bootle, Richard, 16
Willkie, Wendel, 615, 616
William of Wied, Prince, 374
Wilson, Field Marshal Sir Henry, Bt. (1864–1922)
head of mission to French H.Q., 264; and Haig, 265; relegated to Eastern Command, 286; adviser to Cabinet, 288; and Supreme War Council, 289, 291, 292, 294, 295; proposed as C.I.G.S., 310; appointed 316, 317, 329, 330, 334; proposed as Deputy C.I.G.S., 321; George V's attitude to appointment as C.I.G.S., 323; Derby's opinion of, 349; Derby writes to him about Spears, 365–6, 367–8, 368–9; his (reported) opinion of Spears, 370

mentioned, 219, 222, 255, 303, 310, 316, 322, 328, 332, 358, 365
Wilson, Leslie, 453, 457
Wilson, W. T., 87, 88
Wilson, President Woodrow
at Peace Conference, 376
Wireless Telegraph Act (1904), 83
Wise, Rev. George, 144
Witherslack, 15, 17, 23, 98
Witley Park Estate, 98
Witwatersrand, 58
Wolfe-Murray, Lieut.-Gen. Sir James (1853–1919), 217
Wolseley, Sir Garnet (1833–1913) (First Viscount Wolseley), 70
Wolverton, Lady, 73, 76
Workers' Weekly, The, 573
World Crisis (Churchill)
quoted, 288
Worthington-Evans, Rt. Hon. Sir Laming, Bt. (1868–1931)
and Dec. 1923 crisis, 544, 549, 556; dies, 586
mentioned, 423, 459, 488, 528
Wragg, Harry, 616
Wyllie, Wallace, 53

Younger, Sir George, Bt. (1851–1929) (First Viscount Younger)
and possible fusion of Conservative and Liberal Parties, 385–6; Derby writes to him on the Party and Ireland, 422; corresponds with Derby on Birkenhead and B. Law, 466–7; attacked by Birkenhead, 470–1; and Liberal candidates, 474, 475; and Dec. 1923 crisis, 559
mentioned, 451, 453, 463, 537
Ypres, First Earl of, *see* French, Sir John